MEDIEVAL ENGLISH SONGS

MEDIEVAL ENGLISH SONGS

E. J. DOBSON
and
F. Ll. HARRISON

Cambridge University Press
New York

Published in the U.S.A. and Canada
by the Syndics of the Cambridge University Press
32 East 57th Street,
New York, NY 10022, U.S.A.

Cambridge University Press ISBN
0 521 22912 X

Library of Congress catalog card number: 79-51498

Printed in Great Britain

CONTENTS

TABLE OF SONGS

Left column page references – Text and Textual Commentary
Right column page references – Music / Musical Commentary

PREFACE

This book contains the words and music of all songs with English text up to about 1400 which are known to have survived with their music, together with certain songs with Latin (and in one case French) text which are relevant to the English songs. Two English songs are also included for which music is not recorded in the manuscripts because they can be fitted to the music of others and it seems possible that they may have been intended to be so fitted. We have supplied Introductions to the texts and the music, Commentaries on and critical apparatus for both, notes on pronunciation and performance.

The guiding purpose of the enterprise was originally an essentially practical one, for the collaboration of which it is the result began in making a sound-recording with the title *Medieval English Lyrics*. This involved decisions not only about the content and interpretation of sources, but also about such practical matters as the pronunciation of the words and the character of linguistic and non-linguistic sounds. The much larger collection of songs in this book has been edited with a similarly practical object, that of making them available to singers in a form which is usable and which also takes account of available historical knowledge. Accordingly, the supplementary material includes a guide to the pronunciation of the texts, translations into current English, and suggestions about performance; and many of the notes on both text and music are intended to assist singers who may not be familiar with medieval English or with medieval music.

Nevertheless it became apparent, during the detailed work of preparing the songs for publication, that theoretical as well as practical questions concerning the editing of medieval texts were involved, and that these were made more complex by the existence of a music text which was itself an important part of the evidence. We hope that our discussion of these problems, and the texts that we have formed, will be of interest to medieval scholars; for we have aimed, not merely to improvise a text that can be sung, but to recover the true text, as far as the evidence and our knowledge permit. We have therefore not printed, with minimal changes, the words as they are given by the manuscript that happens to record the music, but have taken into account all other available manuscripts in which the words occur, and we have given reconstituted texts, in the appropriate linguistic forms, that will satisfy the requirements of the metrical and musical patterns. Above all we have made it our principle, on theoretical as well as practical grounds, that words and music must fit; and we have held ourselves free to emend the transmitted text of the words and, less often, of the music when it seemed to be defective.

The book has also been planned with the needs of teachers and students in mind. The Introductions are intended as general accounts of the historical and practical questions which arise in making editions whose aim it is to be both scholarly and performable. The Commentaries on each song provide detailed information about sources and discussion of their interpretation, while the Notes are concerned with the explanation of the meaning, grammar, and scansion of the texts. We have not given a glossary, believing that the purposes of this book were better served by the explanations of words and longer phrases in the notes and the full translations in the supplementary material.

Our thanks are due to the authorities of the libraries in whose possession are the manuscripts from which the songs of this collection are taken. In particular we are indebted, for the supply of photographs of manuscripts in their keeping, to the librarians of the Cambridge University Library and of Corpus Christi and St. John's Colleges, Cambridge; of Trinity College, Dublin, the Guildhall Library, London, and the Maidstone Museum; of the Bibliothèque Nationale, Bibliothèque Mazarine, and Bibliothèque de l'Arsenal, Paris; and of the Bibliothèques Municipales of Évreux and Rouen. We are also indebted to Miss Pamela Stewart, Assistant Archivist of the diocese of Salisbury, and to the librarian of the Bibliothèque Municipale, Metz, for their answers to our enquiries. Finally we acknowledge with gratitude the help and encouragement we have received from friends and colleagues: Professor Norman Davis, Dr. A. B. Emden, Dr. Pamela Gradon, Mr. Douglas Gray, Mr. John Lyerle, Dr. George Rigg, Miss Celia Sisam, and especially Miss Joan Rimmer, who has been associated with the making of this book since its inception.

We have worked in close collaboration, not without

vigorous argument, and we have learned much from each other; but in the last resort each remains responsible for his own parts of the work. To this there is one over-riding exception: the fitting of the words to the music has at all stages been our joint responsibility.

E.J.D.
F.Ll.H.
Jesus College, Oxford
Universiteit van Amsterdam

NOTE ON ABBREVIATIONS

The abbreviations used in the textual sections are those customary in editing and commenting on Middle English texts. Thus there are: (1) Abbreviations for frequently cited works, such as *OED* for the *Oxford English Dictionary* (*A New English Dictionary,* edited by J. A. H. Murray, H. Bradley, W. A. Craigie, and C. T. Onions), *MED* for the *Middle English Dictionary* (in progress), edited by H. Kurath and S. M. Kuhn, and Bosworth-Toller for *An Anglo-Saxon Dictionary* edited by J. Bosworth and T. N. Toller; (2) Abbreviations for the names of languages, thus OE for Old English (Anglo-Saxon), ME for Middle English, OF for Old French, ON for Old Norse; (3) Abbreviations for grammatical terms, thus sg. and pl. for singular and plural; nom., accus., gen., and dat. for nominative, accusative, genitive, and dative; indic., imper., and subj. for indicative, imperative, and subjunctive; pres. t. and p.t. for present tense and past tense; pres. p. and p.p. for present participle and past participle; adv., adj., sb., and vb. for adverb, adjective, substantive, and verb.

INTRODUCTION TO THE TEXTS

E. J. DOBSON

INTRODUCTION TO THE TEXTS

This edition of Middle English songs is by design restricted to those of which the music is preserved; for it is a work of collaboration between a musicologist and a philologist, each aiming to use his specialized knowledge towards the one end of producing texts of music and words which shall fit each other and be singable as, to the best of our belief, the original authors and composers intended them to be sung. It differs, therefore, from the collections of medieval English lyrics, which include literary lyrics never intended for singing, as well as numerous pieces known or presumed to have been songs of which the music has not been preserved (though in some cases settings have been provided in modern times). But the music of our songs is not always of English origin; in some instances it is that of Latin songs, in at least one case certainly of French origin, for which English words were written as substitutes for the Latin, and in such cases we have edited the Latin texts as well. In one case (no. 4) there are parallel French and English texts, written for an adaptation of a Latin *planctus;* in another (no. 9) it is doubtful whether the Latin or the English text is to be given priority, though the music was certainly composed in England; in yet another (no. 16b) the Latin words are known to have been written as a substitute for the English. Although, therefore, the nucleus of our collection is English poems set to music that has been preserved along with the words, it includes Latin and French poems as well, of which we also give musical settings; in the case of no. 11, for which only part of the music is preserved in MSS which give the English text, we have had to complete the music from a MS which gives it for the Latin text. To our general principle of admitting only English songs of which the music is preserved in the same MSS as the words we have allowed two exceptions. In the Cotton and Jesus MSS (closely descended from a common original), no. 6b follows immediately no. 6a, for which music is preserved in the Maidstone MS; and as 6b proves to fit this music, though in a slightly different way, I assume that it was written to do so and that the juxtaposition of the two pieces in the Cotton-Jesus collection was because its compiler knew that 6b went to the same music as 6a. *Maid in the moor lay* (no. 16b (i)) is known to have been a song, for Richard de Ledrede, Bishop of Ossory, wrote *Peperit virgo* to go to its music; and though the music is not preserved with either the English or the Latin text, they prove to fit the music which by a lucky chance is recorded for no.16a, *Brid one breere.* Indeed, it seems possible that *Maid in the moor lay,* and not *Brid one breere,* was the poem for which this music was originally composed.[1] We have had to supply an ending for our no. 23, which breaks off at the foot of a leaf in the MS, a little short of its close; and I assume that no. 26 must originally have had a second stanza, which I have ventured to supply. On the other hand I have rejected the last three stanzas of no. 13 as unoriginal, and given them only in an appendix to the notes on this piece; and we give only sixteen of the thirty-seven stanzas recorded in the Advocates' MS for no. 20, holding that the last twenty-one stanzas are probably an addition and that in any case enough is enough (a view shared by the scribes of the other MSS, who give fewer stanzas than we do).

The present volume contains songs written between, perhaps, the mid-twelfth century (those of St. Godric, who died in 1170) and about 1400, and aims at completeness within this period. It is of course possible that MSS dated to the fifteenth century may contain songs (especially perhaps carols) written before 1400, but on grounds of musical style and language it is in most cases unlikely. The pieces in this book are those which there is good reason to believe belong before 1400, though it is possible, without being probable, that the latest of them (some of those in Group V) may belong to the first decade or so of the fifteenth century. They divide naturally into two main groups, those written before 1300 and those written after 1350; for it is a curious fact that only one or two English songs which are probably to be dated between 1300 and 1350 are recorded with music. The reason is perhaps the growing divergence, in the fourteenth century, between the

---

[1] For the detailed discussion, see the commentary on no. 16b below (p. 189). The literary editor must take responsibility for inducing his colleague, in both these cases, to include pieces for which music is not preserved in the MSS, and to provide them with settings derived from the music preserved for other pieces. To do so is to go beyond the documentary evidence; but I argued that as the metrical forms were by no means commonplace, but indeed unusual, it was unlikely to be accident that the words could in fact be fitted to the music.

literary lyric and the song, and the fact that the main MS collections were concerned more with the literary lyric; but beyond that there is mere chance. Before 1400 not many songs are recorded with music in any case. Of the pieces we print, Richard de Ledrede's *Peperit virgo* was written after 1316, when he became bishop of Ossory, but its English original *Maid in the moor lay* is likely to belong before 1300, especially if the music recorded for *Brid one breere* belonged in the first instance to *Maid in the moor lay*. *Brid one breere* itself was recorded in the early fourteenth century, but there can be no real doubt that it was written before 1300; and the same is true of *Worldes blisse, have good day* (no. 17). *Lou, lou, lou! wer he goth* (no. 19) is the likeliest of the pieces recorded in the early fourteenth century to have been written in that period. Of the pieces in Group V, the earliest is the carol (no. 20), of which the words are recorded in a MS dated 1372; and as the text of this MS is already corrupt and evidently separated by several removes from the original, it is possible that the carol (or at least its words) was written before 1350, though hardly much before. In general, however, it is true that by some accident of transmission we have songs written before 1300, and songs written after 1350; I proceed, in what immediately follows, to discuss them in turn.

THE SONGS BEFORE 1300

The only songs in our collection that date from the twelfth century are St. Godric's, which had probably been written by the middle of the century, as Godric was a very old man when he died in 1170 and was probably born between 1070 and 1080. That there should be no English songs recorded with music that were written in the latter half of the twelfth century is not surprising, for English literature was then in a depressed state, and original work of merit was exceptional. The native aristocracy had been dispossessed and destroyed after the Norman Conquest, the native upper class replaced by foreigners, and the administration gradually transformed; and in consequence the vigorous Old English literary tradition had died away by about 1150, except to some degree in the West Midlands. Godric's use of English for his songs must be reckoned one of the survivals of the old tradition rather than as the start of something new. But it is evident that only his unusual personal history really accounts for them. He was of English stock, born within a generation of the Conquest, and had lived as a merchant, seaman, and (it seems) privateer before adopting the religious life. If he had been an ordinary religious, with a normal clerical training, any religious songs that he wrote would have been in Latin; it was because he was essentially untrained, and probably very imperfectly literate, that he wrote these English pieces in a curious blend of the general stanza-shape of Ambrosian hymns and native metrical rhythms. It is also clear that we owe the preservation of his songs only to the veneration in which the monks of Durham held this unusual hermit and to the reported circumstances of the origin of the songs. Few will be so credulous nowadays as to believe that they were taught to Godric by the Virgin, by the soul of his sister, or by St. Nicholas, appearing to him in visions; but it was not only in the Middle Ages that men found it difficult to distinguish the processes of poetic composition from divine inspiration. Especially is this so when verses 'come to' a man who lacks, or appears to lack, literary and musical knowledge. One must no doubt allow something for Bede's account, which the Durham monks might be expected to know, of another and more famous instance — the 'Hymn of Creation' dictated in sleep to the cowherd Cædmon.

But in spite of the monks' veneration for Godric, they give unequal treatment to his songs. Eight MSS give the English text of the first stanza of no. 1, only four that of the second; it is possible that it was a later addition, especially as there exists a version of the music written for a one-stanza text.[2] Three give the English text of no. 2, and only one — an inserted leaf in the Royal MS — gives no. 3. But only three MSS give music for the first stanza of no. 1, and for the rest of the music we are dependent on the inserted leaf of the Royal MS. The biographers of Godric, and their successors the St. Albans chroniclers, were concerned with the events of Godric's life, and not to give the complete text of the songs; hence they may give a Latin translation instead of the English original. It is really only the inserted leaf of the Royal MS which testifies that a collection of Godric's small corpus of songs had been made and preserved at Durham; on this the biographers were evidently drawing, and the inserted leaf is a copy of the collection. Whether or not the music was changed in transmission, there is no reason to doubt the authenticity of the word-texts; the

[2] The alternative explanation would be that the two-stanza version was original, and the biographers Reginald and Geoffrey chose only to quote the first stanza; and that the scribe of the Cambridge MS or some predecessor, not knowing that this was not the complete song, altered the music of the last line of stanza 1 so as to produce an ending that was musically satisfactory.

As Godric's hymns must have been complete by the time Reginald wrote, even though he began to write before Godric's death, and as Geoffrey certainly wrote after his death, neither of them is likely to have been merely ignorant of the existence of the second stanza, unless it was an addition made after their biographies were written. But they may have known that the song originally had only the one stanza. The second adds little to the sense of the first.

MS tradition begins early, and the songs are such as one would expect to be written by a man born when and where Godric was, and with his history.

Of the thirteenth-century English songs, ten are religious (nos. 6a, 6b, 7, 10(ii), 11-14, 15(ii) and 17). With these should probably be listed no. 4, for though it deals with the secular theme of unjust imprisonment it is a prayer for deliverance to Christ and Mary; it is at least ambivalent.[3] Only four pieces before 1300 are wholly secular (nos. 5, 8, 16a, and 16b (i)); to these is to be added no.19 in the early fourteenth century. The English text of no. 9 (*Sumer is icumen in*) is secular, the Latin text religious. This marked predominance of religious pieces is characteristic of the recorded literature of the period. For until the later fourteenth century it was unusual for a layman to be literate; literature was largely composed, and was certainly preserved, by the clergy. It is true that the clergy often differed little from the laity in their interests and tastes, though they normally differed in their education. They certainly wrote and enjoyed worldly literature. But their own love-songs and other lyrics, their parodies and satires, were usually written in Latin, the international language of their class; they would be most likely to use the vernacular when they were writing for lay patrons. In England, until the later fourteenth century, the position was further complicated by the fact that there were two vernaculars in use, French and English, and that of the two French, though its position during the thirteenth century was undoubtedly being continuously weakened, continued to enjoy the greater social and cultural prestige. Until the time of Chaucer courtly literature, the literature of kings and nobles and great merchants, was in French; and the musicians who entertained them would normally have sung French songs. Even in the fifteenth century, after English had reasserted itself as a literary language, French songs occur beside English in musical MSS. Moreover MSS were preserved very largely by the religious houses and cathedral libraries, especially in the earlier period. The odds were heavily weighted in favour of religious against secular literature, of Latin against the vernacular, of French against English.

In some songs in this collection the English words are substitutes for Latin or French words and are intended to be sung to the same music, or to an adaptation of the original music. Poems written to go to the music of a pre-existent song, and therefore to reproduce its metre and stanzaic form, are known as *contrafacta*; they may or may not be translations of the original. The English text of no. 4, *Ar ne kuth ich sorghe non*, is a *contrafactum* of the French text, *Eyns ne soy ke pleynte fu,* and is also a translation, sometimes close, sometimes free. The two texts were almost certainly written by the same man, for though the French has obvious priority, it must have been written by an Englishman, and the English text shows independent knowledge of the metre of the original. For both English and French texts are in turn written to fit a selection from and arrangement of the music of a well-known Latin song of the late twelfth century, Godefroy of St. Victor's *Planctus ante nescia*, which we give as an addendum to no. 4. As the relation of the French and English texts to Godefroy's *planctus* shows, a *contrafactum* need not be a translation, or even deal with the same theme as its original; and the extent to which its metre can vary from that of the original depends on the nature of the music.[4] On the other hand a translation need not be a *contrafactum*; an English verse translation of (say) a Latin song, even when on a superficial view it appears to be in the same sort of verse or stanza-form, may on a closer inspection prove to vary so much from the metre of its original that it could not possibly be fitted to the same music, any more than a prose translation could. Most Middle English verse translations of Latin hymns and sequences, though they are sometimes assumed, by literary critics who do not bother really to analyse the metre or to consider the nature of the music, to be meant for singing to the original tunes, are in truth only 'literary' versions, meant to be read or recited as poems, not sung to music.[5] We have not searched among Middle English verse translations of hymns,

---

[3] It is unlikely that the poem is in any way autobiographical; the situation is probably an imagined one. But on the other hand I do not think that the 'imprisonment' is intended as a mere allegory for the situation of the Christian in this world. It is rather a dramatic lyric, of the sort predicated for the Celtic lyric lay.

[4] See further below. In this case the musical notation is non-mensural; it was therefore possible for the author of the French and English songs to vary from the metrical rhythms of the corresponding stanzas of Godefroy's Latin, and even to use different rhythms in his French and English texts (the English being sometimes closer to the Latin). If the music is mensural, the author of a *contrafactum* is much more strictly obliged to follow the metre of his original, both in syllable-count and in rhythm. Apparent cases of discrepancy between original and *contrafactum* are often due to failure to scan one or other correctly, and in particular to neglect of the evidence of the music in determining the true scansion. Latin texts are often scanned wrongly owing to the automatic and unjustified assumption that the words were intended to have their Classical stressing.

[5] These mistaken judgements are sometimes due to ignorance of medieval music, and to the belief that it was infinitely adaptable; more rarely, to a forcing of the English words to the music, regardless of their probable scansion and of clashes between musical rhythm and the stressing of the words. Sometimes they are due to a failure to make any detailed metrical analysis — as when the 'accentual' rhythms of Theodulph of Orlean's *Gloria, laus, et honor* (which in fact is written in quantitative elegiacs) are thought to have influenced those of William Herebert's rendering in rough accentual

sequences, and other religious songs, to find any that are sufficiently close in metre to their originals to justify a presumption that they were meant for singing to the original music; we give only those that are actually recorded with music in at least one MS. Their texts, even as mis-spelt and corrupted in individual MSS, show a much greater conformity to the original metres than is normal in ME verse translations; and when properly critical texts are made, they vary only slightly from the original metrical forms. It is evident that when these medieval English poets set out to write a *contrafactum* they knew very well what was required of them, and that their verse-technique was fully equal to the task. On the evidence of these pieces, known to have been intended for singing, a Middle English verse translation can be accepted as meant to go to the original tune only if it is capable of being so edited, by credible emendations, as to conform quite closely to the metrical form of its original, at least in syllable-count and, if the music is mensural, in stress-patterns also.

The variety of method that might be employed in *contrafacta* can well be studied in our texts. As the writer's task is difficult, he has to have regard to the essentials, which are imposed by the rhythmic character of the music. If it is of the plainsong type and non-mensural, it is not essential for him to preserve a regular accentual rhythm, and he may not do so even when it is present in his original; so in nos. 4(i) and 4(ii), as contrasted with the corresponding stanzas of *Planctus ante nescia,* and again in the English sequences (nos. 10(ii), 11, and 12) derived from the Latin *Stabat juxta Christi crucem* (no. 10(i)), which is a 'regular' sequence with identical stanzas written to a single syllabic and accentual pattern. Again, though syllabic regularity is usually aimed at, it is possible to fit in an extra syllable or two easily enough without serious modification of the music, e.g. by the repetition of notes; and a *contrafactum* may vary from its original by slight increases in the length of lines. The French and English texts of no. 4 thus increase the line-lengths, as compared with those of *Planctus ante nescia,* by one syllable in every line but the first of stanza 1, in all but the first, fourth, seventh, and tenth lines of stanza 3, and in the first and second lines of stanza 5; in stanza 4

the length of every line is increased by two. In no. 10(ii) the English author freely adds an extra unstressed syllable at the beginning of the line, and twice adds two unstressed syllables, one at the beginning and the other at the end of the line; and in no. 11 the lines are more often than not lengthened by the addition of one unstressed syllable, at the beginning of the line.[6] But it is to be noted that in no. 11 the first and fourth lines of the stanzas are never lengthened, and therefore always assert the basic pattern, and that the final stanza completely conforms to the pattern of the Latin original. No. 12, the most skilful of the *contrafacta* of *Stabat juxta Christi crucem,* does not vary from the Latin at all in its syllable-count; and in no. 4 the English version never varies from the syllable-count of the French, even when the French is varying from the Latin.

All these pieces are in sequence-form, of which it was a basic principle that each stanza divided into two halves which were sung to a repetition of the same music and therefore were required, normally, to match each other exactly; and though it was permissible to introduce slight variations in the music, and therefore in the metre, of one or other half-stanza, in fact neither *Planctus ante nescia* nor *Stabat juxta Christi crucem* does so. The authors of the *contrafacta* of the two pieces seem to have paid special regard to this technical requirement. In no. 4, there are four instances in which a line of the first half-stanza is a syllable shorter or longer than the corresponding line of the second half-stanza, but even where these irregularities occur the English version carefully follows the French. In no.10(ii), the musician, by ignoring the possibility of elisions in the penultimate line, has deliberately extended it for the sake of emphasis; the poet may have intended regularity. In nos. 11 and 12 the two halves of the stanza were evidently intended always to match.[7]

These examples show a high regard for the technical requirements of the music, intelligent awareness of the variations that are possible, and skill in conforming to the necessary metrical patterns. But in such conditions it is not surprising that translation is usually free, and aims rather to reproduce the general sense of the original than to follow closely its wording. The English text of no. 4 is

---

septenarii, or the rhythm and stanza-form of the English *Glad and blithe mote ye be* are taken to approximate 'quite closely' to those of its Latin original, the sequence *Lætabundus,* in spite of the considerable disparity of the line-lengths (e.g. four syllables with two stresses in the first and fourth lines of the Latin; seven in the first English line, eight in the fourth, both with four stresses). *Glad and blithe* is set to music, but it is unrelated rhythmically to the original music; Herebert's are literary translations.

[6] In no case in our collection is the increase greater than two syllables.

[7] These statements are of course based on the *edited* texts, not on those given by the MSS, which often show other irregularities. Except for no. 11, there is only a single MS in each case, and the text can therefore be corrected only by conjectural emendation (though in the case of no. 4 the existence of two parallel vernacular texts provides some basis for emendation, since each is a check on the other). In the cases of nos. 10(ii) and 12, the balance of the two halves of the stanzas is sometimes produced by emendation. The test must be whether regularity can be attained by simple changes that are credible for the text in question. Sometimes there are other reasons for suspecting the MS text, beside the irregular metre.

the most successful in reproducing the sense, as well as the syllable-count, of its French counterpart — perhaps because, as I have suggested, it is by the same author. Of the three *contrafacta* of *Stabat juxta Christi crucem*, no. 10(ii), in the stanzas that survive, follows with reasonable fidelity the general sense, though not the exact wording, of the corresponding Latin stanzas. No. 11, *Stond wel, moder, under roode*, being cast in dialogue form, is virtually a new poem which owes only general suggestions to no. 10(i), though it does not lose sight of the Latin original and makes use at various points of its material; but, like no. 10(ii), it is set to the music of the Latin, with only such modifications as were made necessary by the variations from the Latin metre. No. 12, *Jesu Cristes milde moder,* is a free translation of the Latin but generally follows its gist stanza by stanza (except that it has nothing to correspond to stanza 8 of the Latin, and expands the material of the Latin stanza 9 in its stanzas 8 and 9). It is written by the most skilful versifier of the three, and is by far the most successful in reproducing the form of the Latin; in syllable-count, though not always in accentual rhythm,[8] it is, like the Latin, a 'regular' sequence and could be sung to the original music, without change. But surprisingly it is the only one of the three English versions which is not set in its MS to the music of the Latin; it has its own two-part setting.

The most skilful and successful of our English *contrafacta* is undoubtedly *Gabriel fram heven-king* (no. 15(ii)), which occurs in the same Arundel MS as no. 12, is in the same dialect, and is almost certainly by the same author. The technical problem in this case was even greater, for the music of the original, *Angelus ad virginem*, was probably mensural and has, as transcribed, its own strongly metrical rhythm; it was therefore necessary for the translator to keep strict metre which should exactly match, in stress-pattern as well as in syllable-count, the complex stanza-structure of his original, and he has made his task even more difficult by preserving (as the music, of course, did not oblige him to) the fairly intricate rhyme-scheme, in which one of the rhymes is used four times. Though the degree of his success is somewhat disguised in the Arundel MS by the scribe's use of linguistic forms which are plainly not those intended by the author, he has triumphantly solved his technical problem, with no more recourse to artificial stressings than is normal in ME rhyming verse and with only a single use of assonance in place of rhyme; but it

must be allowed that he has taken much advantage of the variation in the pronunciation of final -*e* which was evidently a feature of his dialect. He so exactly matches the verse of his original that his English words can be sung to the music of the Latin without need of adaptation; and he has given a rendering of the Latin which, though free, conveys its general sense and has both fluency and life. It is a remarkable technical achievement.

The areas in which the songs (or rather their words) were composed are to be deduced chiefly by the analysis of the linguistic forms, and more especially the forms shown to be original by metre and above all by rhyme. Such an analysis shows a remarkable concentration of the songs in the east of the country.[9] To the London area, or the South-east Midlands, there belong nos. 4, 6b, 7, the first five stanzas of 13, and 14; and no. 16a also appears to belong to the East Midlands, perhaps towards the south of the area, though it has at least passed through the hands of a Norfolk scribe. No. 19, probably recorded in Cambridge, may have been written in Essex or Suffolk. From further north in the East Midlands, perhaps within a radius of some 20-25 miles from Peterborough, come nos. 5 (possibly Thorney Abbey in north Cambridgeshire), 11, and 17; no. 8 is probably from this general area, with East Anglia perhaps the likeliest location; nos. 12 and 15 are East Anglian, probably from Norfolk. For the rest, no. 6a is undoubtedly Kentish, perhaps from Canterbury itself; no. 9 is from Reading Abbey; the continuation of no. 13 (stanzas 6-8) is from Llanthony Priory, near Gloucester; no. 16b(i) is either from the North-west Midlands or from Ireland; no.10(ii) is Northern (perhaps from Lancashire, though York would seem a more likely place for such a piece to be written); and St. Godric was an East Anglian by birth who lived most of his long life near Durham and there wrote his songs (nos. 1-3). This distribution of the songs is somewhat surprising, for it does not correspond to the general distribution of the Middle English lyric, much of which was written in the West and North-west Midlands, represented in our collection possibly by one song (no. 16b(i), recorded without its music) and by a continuation (ill-suited to the music) of another (no. 13); but it does correspond to the main centres of wealth and power, and above all to those areas of England most affected by French cultural influences.[10]

It must, however, be added that the evidence of the MSS is that these songs, and especially their words,

---

[8] But in its sixty-six lines there are only ten that diverge, wholly or in part, from the regular trochaic rhythm of the Latin.

[9] For the detailed analysis, see the introductory notes to the individual songs.

[10] But the number of songs that survive with music is small, and their distribution may not be fully representative of what was written.

circulated more widely. Some are preserved in MSS written, as far as we know or can judge from the spellings used by the scribes, either where the songs were composed or not far away. St. Godric's songs were recorded by the monks of Durham, but the circulation of copies of their lives of the saint brought the knowledge of the first song to the St. Albans chroniclers Roger of Wendover and Matthew Paris. No. 4(ii) (and presumably therefore no. 4(i)) must have been written in the London area and copied by a London scribe. No. 5 was written in the East Midlands, and the volume in which it is preserved may come from Thorney Abbey; no. 8 is perhaps from East Anglia, and copied by a scribe whose linguistic forms (as far as one can judge in so short a piece) did not diverge from the author's. No. 9 was written and copied in Reading Abbey. No. 17, written in the East Midlands, is preserved in a copy written by a South-eastern (probably Essex) scribe. None of these may have had a wide circulation. The same is perhaps true of three of the pieces preserved in MS Arundel 248, whose earliest known owner lived in Chrishall in the extreme northwest of Essex and which probably came from Cambridgeshire or Suffolk; of its English songs, no. 14 seems to have been written in the London area, nos. 12 and 15(ii) are from East Anglia (probably Norfolk), so that all three are, in general terms, Eastern songs preserved in an Eastern MS, and may not have been very widely known. But the fourth of its songs, no. 7, probably written in the London area, also occurs in two West Midland MSS, Digby 86 and Rawlinson G.18, of which the former gives the music, the latter only the words. No. 13, also probably written in the London area, is preserved only in a MS from Llanthony Priory, near Gloucester, where the additional stanzas were added. No. 10(ii), written in the North, is preserved in a MS believed to have been written in Chester. No. 16a was composed in the East Midlands and its spellings show that it has passed through the hands of a Norfolk scribe (unless indeed it was composed in Norfolk, though I think this unlikely), but it is preserved on the back of a document that belonged, until the fifteenth century, to the priory of St. James by Exeter. If no. 16b(i) was composed in the North-west Midlands, it is preserved in a copy whose spellings are those of a Southern scribe, and it was made the basis of a pious Latin *contrafactum* by the bishop (himself an Englishman, surnamed from Leatherhead in Surrey) of the Irish diocese of Ossory, whose clergy had apparently been in the habit of singing this among other worldly songs. The situation is still more complex with some of the songs extant in a plurality of MSS. No. 6a was certainly written in Kent, and there are incomplete Kentish texts. But complete texts

of its words are given in the Cotton and Jesus MSS (West and South-west Midlands); music and words are given by the Maidstone MS, a copy now preserved in Kent of a song composed in Kent but believed to have been made in Northampton. No. 6b was composed in the South-east Midlands, but all the extant MSS appear to derive from a West Midland copy; three of these (including Cotton and Jesus) are themselves from the West or South-west Midlands, but the fourth seems to have been written in the North Midlands. No. 11 is the most complex of all, but perhaps only because it has most copies. It was composed in the East Midlands, and the best copy (the Royal MS) is itself from the East Midlands. But the famous Harley 2253 is a Herefordshire MS, and Digby 86 is from Worcestershire; the St. John's College, Cambridge, MS was written by a South-eastern (probably Kentish) scribe, and the Trinity College, Dublin, MS by a Midland scribe, but both of them derive from a lost copy by a Northern scribe. This English sequence at least was widely known throughout England, no doubt in recognition of its merit.

The surviving English songs composed by 1300 or shortly after are not preserved in special musical MSS. The words of some are indeed given in famous collections of Middle English verse — MS Digby 86; MSS Cotton Caligula A.ix and Jesus College, Oxford, 29, two closely related copies of an anthology of English and Anglo-Norman poems; MS Harley 2253, the most valuable of all collections of Middle English verse (as well as of French and Latin items, in verse and prose). But these give only the words, with the exception that Digby 86 also gives the music of no. 7. Only MS Arundel 248 has a collection of songs — four of our English pieces (nos. 7, 12, 14 and 15(ii)) and others in French and Latin — but it is not in any sense a musical MS; it is a miscellaneous collection, in which the songs are a comparatively minor part. Even in this case, use has been made of conveniently blank pages in what was evidently being used as a commonplace book; and this is how most of the songs have been recorded. But in some instances the leaves on which the words and music are given were not originally part of the volumes in which they are bound, but apparently loose leaves. The inserted leaf in the Royal MS of Geoffrey's life of St. Godric may be of this nature, or a copy of such a sheet of words and music. No. 4 is preserved on leaves inserted at the end of a volume containing a chronicle, and had been written before the leaves were inserted. No. 5 is preserved, with two French songs, on a sheet of parchment used as the fly-leaf of MS Rawlinson G.22, a copy of a Latin psalter and other devotional material; and it is possible that there was originally at least one other companion leaf on which the

English song was continued. No. 10 (ii) is preserved on a leaf which was certainly the companion of another, since lost, on which were written the words and music of the first four stanzas; and as these would not have occupied a full page, they may have been preceded by other music. The leaf in the St. John's College MS which gives the words and music of the first twenty-seven lines of nos. 10 (i) and 11 must originally have been followed by another which gave the rest. The leaves of MS Douce 381, discussed below, which give the only texts of nos. 21-24 and one of the two texts of no. 27, are a further example of survivors of a larger number (for the last of the songs in the MS, no. 23, breaks off incomplete) that may originally not have been properly bound. No. 19 was jotted down on a blank space of a leaf in a university text-book. But the oddest place of all for a text with music, and that a love-song, is the only surviving copy of no. 16a, written on the back of a duplicate of a papal bull, preserved as an important muniment of the Cluniac priory of St. James by Exeter and later, when the deeds of the priory passed with its lands to King's College, Cambridge, among the muniment rolls of the college. Presumably whoever wrote the song there had a chance to take a copy — for it is obviously copied from a written exemplar, not noted down from an oral performance — and this was the only piece of parchment that was conveniently to hand. By this strange means were preserved not only the words and music of no. 16a itself, but also, as I suggest, the tune of no. 16b, which otherwise would be unknown.

THE SONGS AFTER 1350

All our fourteenth-century pieces are contained in two MSS of the beginning of the fifteenth century, Cambridge University Library MS Additional 5943 and Bodleian MS Douce 381. There is however this qualification to be made, that though we are dependent on Additional 5943 for the music that it gives for the carol *Lullay, lullay: Als I lay on Yoolis night* (no. 20), its words are in other MSS, one of which is dated 1372, and it is possible, as has already been pointed out, that the words of the carol may have been written before 1350. The rest of the pieces in Douce 381 and Additional 5943 were, to judge from their language, probably written during the last quarter of the century. No. 21 (*Ye have so longe keepyt o*) is perhaps the earliest and may have been

written about 1375, and the final group (nos. 27-33) is likely to belong to the last decade of the fourteenth century; for Southern poems, as they are, their language is very advanced in its forms (especially the loss of *-e*).

It is characteristic of the songs in the Additional and Douce collections that they are all short (less than twenty lines). The only exception is the narrative carol (no. 20), which by contrast is long — very long indeed in the Advocates' MS; the other MSS abbreviate it, and Additional 5943, which alone gives music, has only the first stanza of the words. But it is, in a sense, an intruder into the collection, a song quite different in type from the rest. Most of the other pieces[11] are variations on a single musical and therefore stanzaic formula which may be described as the ABB pattern. There is a first stanza sung to one tune, followed by two stanzas or half-stanzas sung to a second tune which is repeated (though with a variation at the close). The first stanza may have its own shape, and if it falls into two halves they need not balance each other; but the second and third stanzas (or the two halves of the second stanza), being sung to a repetition of the same music, must match in syllable-count and in accentual rhythm. But two of the Douce collection (nos. 23 and 24) are refrain songs, and my reconstruction of no. 26, from Additional 5943, assumes that it was also. The refrain lyric was a well-known fourteenth-century type, very fully exemplified in the literary lyrics of the Vernon MS; the refrain might be invariable, but commonly it was varied so as to fit the sense of the preceding lines. Both nos. 23 and 24 are of two stanzas only, each of four lines followed by a single refrain-line; in no. 24 the two stanzas are set to the same music, with a variation at the close, and necessarily follow the same metrical pattern,[12] but in no. 23 each has its own music and the second diverges in metre and rhyme-scheme from the first. In no. 24, though the scribe gives only a single form of the refrain-line, it must in fact have varied in one word; in no. 23 there can have been no occasion for variation.[13] For no. 26 the MS (Additional 5943) gives a plainly defective text, but there are clear signs that this too was a song with a variable refrain; probably again there were two stanzas originally, as in nos. 23 and 24, and in this case the music shows that if there were indeed more stanzas than one (as the indications of a variable refrain imply there must have been), they were sung to a repetition of the same

---

[11] Nos. 22, 25, 27, 28 (with a variation at the end of the basic pattern of an ABB song), and 29-33. The recorded word-text of no. 21 (which is very corrupt) is also in ABB form, but the music given for the first stanza has both an *ouvert* and a *clos*, as has that given for stanzas 2 and 3; the music-text, as it stands in the MS, implies a structure AABB. See further p. 206 below.

[12] Except for the first word of stanza 2, which fits into the music at the end of stanza 1.

[13] Unfortunately the end of no. 23 is missing and has to be supplied; but there can be little doubt about the way the word-text ended.

music and must therefore have been identical in metrical pattern. The fifth line links with the stanza and forms a bridge between it and the final refrain-couplet; and the scribe of the MS so marks the music as to show that he took this fifth line with the stanza, and regarded only the final couplet as a distinct unit in the form.[14] No. 26, as I reconstruct it, was, like no. 23, sung to a repeated tune, but with the difference that the refrain was sung twice after each stanza, with a variation at the close; in metrical structure (as distinct from method of performance) it differed from no. 23 chiefly in the elaboration of its refrain. It has indeed the same general metrical pattern as Amiens's song *Under the greenwood tree* in *As You Like It* — two four-line stanzas followed by a refrain of three (counting the bridge-line with the refrain) or, in Shakespeare's case, four lines — with the difference that the refrain in the early song was evidently meant to be variable, in Shakespeare's is invariable. In general it is true of the texts of the songs of these two MSS that analogues are to be sought not only in fourteenth-, but also in fifteenth- and sixteenth-century literature; in literary form and style, and in content and feeling, they look forward as well as back, and their language, for the time at which they were written, is often remarkably modern in tone.[15]

MS Douce 381 is a composite, in which a number of diverse items have been gathered together and mounted on modern sheets of paper. The part that concerns us is item H, four leaves of parchment numbered ff. 20-23[16] which give the music and texts of English and French songs. They were dated 'late 14th cent.?' by Madan, and 'about 1425' by Nicholson and Maunde Thompson; the latter may be a bit late, and it would probably be safer to say 'first quarter of the fifteenth century'.[17] The four leaves are obviously survivors of a larger number, for *With ryght al my hert* (our no. 23) breaks off incomplete at the foot of a leaf, and must have been completed on the recto of a leaf that has since been lost. The parch-ment is rather coarse and discoloured by the foolish use of a reagent since the leaves were mounted, and two of the leaves are creased;[18] especially at these creases the surface is badly rubbed and some letters and words are illegible or else to be read only with difficulty and uncertainty. Four of the five English songs in the surviving leaves are, on linguistic grounds, to be ascribed to the North Midlands, though almost certainly not to the same part of the area; no. 21 is the most northerly in its forms and may even have been written in the southern part of the North itself (e.g. in southern Yorkshire), nos. 22 and 23 are probably from the North-east Midlands, and no. 24 is perhaps from the North-west Midlands — though the evidence is slight, for the songs are short and the original forms have been overlaid by those of a Southern scribe. To these North Midland songs has been added one from the South of England, shared with MS Additional 5943, our no. 27.

MS Additional 5943 is miscellaneous in its contents; it consists chiefly of religious works and other pieces that would be of interest to a priest.[19] But it contains, on ff. 161[r]-169[r], a collection of English, French, and Latin songs with music, and ff. 169[v]-172[v] had been ruled for music at the same time, as if the scribe had expected to write more songs, or at least to need more space. These twelve leaves ruled for music constitute a separate quire, bound into a composite MS. On various pages, both earlier and later, the MS gives texts, without music, of other English carols, songs, and verses, both secular — indeed in two cases erotic — and sacred; four of these pieces[20] were written on ff. 170[r]-171[r], i.e. on pages of the quire that had been ruled for music. But whereas the hand that writes the words of the songs with music is to be dated about 1400, the carols and lyrics without music are written by a much later hand or hands, and have evidently been added at various times, on leaves that were conveniently blank, in what was being used as a commonplace book.

---

[14] But he was undoubtedly confused; he clearly thought that he was copying a song of the ABB pattern, to which the words certainly do not conform as he has given them. That what the scribe takes as a 'secundus versus' is a final refrain-couplet seems probable; and his own text is most explicable on the assumption that he has muddled together the form of the refrain required after the second stanza with that required after the first. See further the introduction and notes to no. 26, pp. 212-4 below.

[15] Though I hope that this is not especially true of the second stanza that I have written for no. 26.

[16] So on the paper mounts; on the parchment itself, ff. 21-24.

[17] For a description of this item of Douce 381, see F. Madan, *Summary Catalogue of the Western MSS in the Bodleian Library*, iv. 614 (no. 21956) and E. W. B. Nicholson in *Early Bodleian Music*, i. xix.

[18] F. 21 was folded vertically about half an inch in from the right margin; f. 22 horizontally, about one inch down from the top margin.

[19] The MS is described by R. L. Greene, *The Early English Carols*, pp. 341-2, and also in his *A Selection of English Carols*, pp. 180-1. But much of his account is inaccurate; the MS is not from Somerset, he seriously misrepresents the note on the penultimate flyleaf concerning the ownership of the book, and his distinction of the hands of the MS requires modification. In his *Selection*, p. 181, *haroer* is a printer's error for *harper*.

[20] Those printed by Robbins, *Secular Lyrics of the XIVth and XVth Centuries*, nos. 30, 31 and 62, and in his notes on p. 245.

The history of this MS, which is of considerable interest and importance, is to be discovered from various entries on its leaves from f. 179^r onwards. On the recto of its penultimate fly-leaf (which would have been f. 184 if the numbering had been continued to the fly-leaves) are three entries relating to ownership. At the top of the page, in faint and difficult writing, is the note:

Memorandum quod ⟨istum librum⟩ donauit magister Thomas Turk quondam vicarius de Biere monachus. (Note that this book was the gift of Master Thomas Turk, formerly vicar of Bere, monk.)

Below this, in a large clear hand, is inscribed:

Wm. Hennynges
Harper

Still lower, in a different hand from the last, though superficially similar, are a series of entries:

Wymundus permissione diuina
Wy. Wymundus
bonum
Wymundus permis.

These last are evidently attempts at Latinizing the name *Wymund Godlef* or *Godelef*, which, though distinctive and interesting, I have been unable to identify.[21] On the verso of the same fly-leaf, at the top, is a longer note about the ownership of the MS, perhaps in the same hand as that at the top of the recto:

Iste liber constat / constat [*struck through*] magistro Johanni [M . . . Joc]ulator emptor erat sibi a magistro Thoma Turke quondam vicario perpetuo de Biere nunc autem apud Henton in domo Cartusiensi monachus. ¶ et dedit mihi vt supra se [*struck through*] decimo die mensis decembris anno domini millesimo ccccxviij Dominus secum Amen

(This book belongs to Master John [Morton. A *joc]ulator* [entertainer] bought it for himself from Master Thomas Turke formerly perpetual vicar of Bere [Regis] but now a monk of the Charterhouse at Hinton. And he [the *joculator*] gave it to me, as above-named, on 10 December 1418. The Lord be with him, Amen.)[22]

Apart from these notes of ownership, blank leaves in the MS were also used for financial and other memoranda, in which a good many place-names are mentioned. Greene identified some of these with places in Somerset, but he is certainly mistaken.[23] These memoranda, which I arrange as far as possible in chronological order, are in the hand of John ——, who acquired the MS on 10 December 1418. On f. 179^v are a series of entries relating to the sale of tithes. The first records that of what John Appleby owes, half is to be paid on the feast of the Purification of the B.V.M., [14]18, i.e. on 2 February 1419 by our reckoning; this entry must have been made soon after John —— obtained the book. Other entries on ff. 179^v-180^r, obviously made about the same time (i.e. December 1418 – January 1419), refer to a part of the parish of 'Hynton' called 'Uppenton', to a William Aleyn of Holt, to the corner of 'Enwode' by the road leading to 'Wymborne' as far as the field of 'Stanbrigg' next to the wood, and to 'Woodcotes' and 'Northfeld'. The places mentioned are Hinton Martell, Dorset, north of Wimborne Minster,

---

[21] E. Ekwall, *Early London Personal Names* (1947), p. 67, says of an early fourteenth-century instance of the name *Wimund* (< OE *Wigmund* or Norman *Wimund*) that it is 'a late instance'; but ours is fifteenth-century (probably mid-fifteenth century). Reaney, *A Dictionary of English Surnames* (1958), p. 141, s.n. *Goodliff*, says that it is from the OE personal name *Godlēof* (or feminine *Godlēofu*) 'good *or* god dear', which was 'long used in Kent'; and he gives, as a late example of its use as a feminine personal name, *Godelef* 1508. As examples of its use as a surname he cites *John Godelef* 1296 (Sussex) and *William Godeloues* 1327 (Worcs.). The attempted Latinization shows confusion between *leef* < OE *lēof* 'dear' and *leve* < OE *lēafa* 'permission', probably because of shortening to -*liff*, -*live*.

[22] For *constare* in the sense 'belong' see R. E. Latham, *Revised Medieval Latin Word-List*, s.v. *constamen*, 1. The surname of the owner is erased and mostly illegible, but the first letter was almost certainly *M* and traces of the last three survive. For the name supplied in the translation, see below. The first three letters of the following word are also affected, but the remaining traces are consistent with *Joc*; the following *ul* is expressed by the abbreviation *l'*, which is clear. *Joculator* is really the only possible word. The grammar of the second sentence is irregular. As *monachus* is in the nominative, it ought strictly to be construed with *joculator*, which would give the meaning that the entertainer is now a monk. But probability, and the run of the sentence, are strongly in favour of the assumption that it is Thomas Turk, formerly vicar of Bere, who has now become a monk, in spite of the lack of concord between the ablative *vicario* and the nominative *monachus*. That this is the correct interpretation is confirmed by my reading *mō* (for *monachus*) of the faint and difficult final word of the memorandum at the top of the recto of the fly-leaf.

Greene says that it is John — who is now (10 December 1418) a Carthusian monk at Hinton, but the note cannot possibly mean this; it is against both grammar and word-order. He also says that Thomas Turk gave the MS to John —, but this is a misunderstanding. Even if one does not read the damaged word in the first line as *Joculator,* the note plainly says that someone bought the MS from Thomas Turk; and if Turk had sold (or given away, as the note on the recto says) his MS to a third person he could not give it to John —. The unexpressed subject of *dedit mihi* must be this third person. The note is concerned to state the chain of ownership and to establish the right of the intermediary to give the MS to John —.

[23] He was misled by the reference to the Charterhouse at Hinton, which was of course in Somerset, SSE of Bath. He went on to identify the *Biere* where Turk was vicar with Beer in Somerset, and was then predisposed to identify other place-names mentioned with places in Somerset. But it is a matter of record that Turk was vicar of Bere Regis, in Dorset. Greene also held the view that the memoranda were made 'apparently by an archdeacon'. But the holders of the archdeaconries of the diocese of Bath and Wells at this time are known, and none of them will fit; the only one whose Christian name was John was John Ikelyngton (archdeacon of Wells 1398-1419), who died too early (before 13 April 1419) to make most of the entries in the MS and whose surname is too long for the gap in the inscription of ownership.

the village of Holt, two miles SE of Hinton, and Stanbridge, one and a half miles S of Hinton on the road to Wimborne. An entry at the foot of the page refers to a Dom. Richard Skyloc, who has sold hay and straw, and who reappears in entries on later pages. On f. 181ᵛ there are entries recording the payment by Skyloc of sums due from him (including altarage) for the period between 24 June and 8 August 1418, and a payment to him on account of salary; evidently he was a paid vicar. Another entry on this page is of a payment to 'William my kinsman at Shaftesbury, for Ralph's table' between Michaelmas 1417 and 15 August 1418. All these entries must be records of payments in arrear, if John —— did not get the book until December 1418; but this is probable, for the next entry on this page records an arrangement to send his horse to graze in the park at Sherborne in May, 1419. On the verso of the penultimate fly-leaf, under the inscription of ownership, is an entry recording that Richard Skyloc, now 'vicar of Horton', has paid 26s. 8d. for the fruits for the year 1420 of the same vicarage, sold 'to him by me', in part payment of the larger sum, as in the bond of 11 April 1421; this must be Horton in Dorset, one and a half miles NE of Hinton Martell. Beneath this are undated memoranda recording the receipt of payments from the rector of 'Staunton Quinton' (Stanton St. Quintin, Wiltshire, N of Chippenham), from the vicar of 'Hyworth' (Highworth, Wiltshire, NNE of Swindon) for a letter of compulsion, and from the vicar of 'Schapewyke' (probably Shapwick, Dorset, WNW of Wimborne Minster, and not Shapwick, Somerset, W of Glastonbury) for procuration; these (or at least the last two) are evidently fees received for legal work, perhaps at the bishop of Salisbury's court, since the places are all within the diocese of Salisbury. Finally, at the foot of the page, is a note that the vicar of Hungerford 'keeps Joan Broune in incontinence'; this is likely to be Hungerford, Hampshire, SE of Fordingbridge, which is only nine miles ENE of Hinton, Dorset, and not Hungerford, Berkshire, W of Newbury, still less Farleigh Hungerford, Somerset, SE of Bath. On f. 180ᵛ there is an entry recording the oblations received in the year 1425 from 'Brydemer'. This connects with a series of memoranda on a fly-leaf at the beginning of the book (f iiiʳ) recording agreements made 'by me the rector' with tradesmen for the repair of the chapel at 'Bridmere'. The stonemason John Gefferey is *inter alia* to make a window like that in the church of 'Berwyke' and the carpenter is William Hogges of Iwerne. The

combination of names leaves no doubt that 'Brydemer' or 'Bridmere' is the village of Bridmore in the parish of Berwick St. John, in southern Wiltshire five miles E of Shaftesbury; Iwerne is about the same distance S of Shaftesbury. Finally, on f. 179ʳ there are entries in a different hand, of which the first records moneys received from John Geffray of 'Berewyke'[24] on behalf of William Norton of Shaftesbury; this must again be Berwick St. John, five miles E of Shaftesbury. The payments are for corn, as are others recorded on this page from various men. At the foot of the page is a memorandum that on 16 July [14]44 the rector of Newton received 40s. from Walter Hyne in part payment for the tithe lambs of 'Crokeyston'; the places are to be identified with Maiden Newton, Dorset, and Cruxton (pronounced [krɔkstən] and formerly spelt *Crokeston*) in the same parish.

John ——, the owner of the MS, is to be identified with John Morton, B.C.L. and Lic.C.L. of Oxford. He became rector of Hinton Martell, Dorset, in 1417, but exchanged the living in December 1418; this would account for the sale of the tithes, recorded in the MS, at that date. He then became rector of Stoke Abbot, Dorset, where he was admitted on 21 December 1418; Stoke Abbot is fourteen miles SW of Sherborne, whither John —— sent his horse to graze in May 1419. Morton vacated this living in April 1420 to become vicar of Horton, Dorset, where he was admitted on 19 April 1420 but vacated the living by October 1420. The MS records that John —— received the fruits of the vicarage of Horton for 1420 from the man to whom he had sold it, and who had apparently been his paid vicar at the neighbouring parish of Hinton Martell in 1418. Morton then became rector of Berwick St. John, where he was admitted on 22 October 1420; it is not known when he vacated the living, but his successor Robert Mere had probably been recently appointed in November 1427, when he was granted a licence of non-residence by bishop Neville of Salisbury. John —— was at Berwick St. John in 1425. In 1420 John Morton also became rector of Maiden Newton, Dorset, and held this living till his death; and on 22 October 1420 he was admitted rector of the free chapel of Witherstone, Dorset. His high legal training seems to have brought him appointments other than his livings. During the vacancy of the see of Salisbury before bishop Chaundler's appointment in 1417 he was appointed by archbishop Chichele to act as his commissary in the diocese.[25] Bishop Chaundler's

[24] Apparently the stonemason mentioned in the memorandum on f. iiiʳ. The place-name has been read as 'Besewyke', but there is no Beeswick or Beswick in the South of England.

[25] *Reg. Chichele*, i. 36-38. I owe this reference to Dr. Emden.

Register (1417-26) shows that in 1419 he was appointed one of the proctors for the clergy; in 1421 he issued a certificate of an inquisition taken concerning the 'ordination' of the vicarage of Worth; and in 1425, described as the Bishop's Commissary and Sequestrator General in the archdeaconries of Dorset and Sarum, he issued a certificate about illegal altars set up in Melcombe Regis.[26] Unfortunately the records of the Consistory Court for this period do not survive, but it is at least clear that Morton exercised the sort of functions in the diocese that would account for his receipt of fees from his fellow-clergy, as recorded on the verso of the penultimate fly-leaf. But it is really sufficient that the list of his livings fully accounts for the dates and place-names mentioned in the memoranda written in the MS; and his surname will fit the space in the inscription of ownership and is consistent with the traces of the letters that remain. The identification appears to be confirmed by an inscription on f. 173[r] which reads *Vnguentum effusum nomen tuum J° Morton*. Morton had died by January 1441; and his MS evidently passed into the possession of his successor in the living of Maiden Newton, John Paslewe, who must have made the entries in the different hand, and showing the date 1444, on f. 179[r].[27]

John Morton got the MS as a gift from a *joculator*, who was doubtless the harper William Hennynges whose name is written on the recto of the penultimate fly-leaf, and whose interest in the MS must have been for the songs which it contained. But it is likely that the harper had owned it only for a short while, perhaps a matter of months. For Thomas Turk is described in both the memoranda on the fly-leaf as 'formerly vicar of Bere' and as 'monk'. But until 1410 he was vicar of Downton, Wiltshire, and is first recorded as vicar of Bere Regis in 1411. On ff. 176[v]-178[r] there are predictions of eclipses of the sun and moon, with diagrams, which were probably written by (or for) Turk, and would certainly not be written by or for a harper; those for the sun are from January 1415 (presumably 1416 in our reckoning), those for the moon from January 1414 (1415), and it is likely that the entry was made in later 1414, before the date of the first of the predictions. Probably Turk

parted with the MS only after he had decided to become a Carthusian monk. Unfortunately we do not know when he entered religion, but if he was the Thomas Turk who was rector of Warpsgrove, Oxfordshire (as A. B. Emden supposes he may possibly have been), he resigned the rectorship in January 1418. The note on the verso of the fly-leaf, which says of him '*nunc* autem . . . *monachus*', may mean that in December 1418 he had quite recently become a monk. The harper's only real importance in the story is that he was the means of bringing Turk's MS to Morton, but I doubt whether he had to bring it back from Hinton Charterhouse in Somerset; as Bere Regis is only thirteen miles SW of Hinton Martell, the odds are that the harper got it from Turk before he left Dorset and carried it some time later to Morton as he was preparing, in December 1418, to leave Hinton Martell for his new living at Stoke Abbot.

Thomas Turk is the important figure in the history of the MS.[28] He came from Swindon, Wiltshire, and was a fellow of Exeter College, Oxford, from 1384 to 1399, and chaplain from 1395 to 1397. He was one of the first fellows of Winchester College, from 1395, and was subwarden from 1395 to 1397. From 1399 to 1400 he was principal of Hart Hall, Oxford, but returned to Winchester, being re-admitted fellow in April 1400. In 1401 he finally left Winchester on being presented by the College to the vicarage of Downton, Wiltshire, to which he was admitted on 10 December 1401; he vacated it in 1410. By 1411 he was vicar of Bere Regis, Dorset; in May 1411 he was cited by the bishop of Salisbury on a charge of heresy. He is, Emden suggests, possibly the same as magister Thomas Turk, rector of Warpsgrove, Oxfordshire, who had resigned by January 1418. We can now add to Emden's account that some time before December 1418 he became a Carthusian monk at Hinton Charterhouse, Somerset.

Turk supplies the necessary link between this supposedly 'Somerset' MS and Winchester College. For there can be no doubt that the songs of ff. 161[r]-169[r], the pieces for which music is given, are a collection made in Winchester College for use there at the Christmas feasts. William of Wykeham in his statutes had provided that when on feast-days in winter-time a fire was lit in hall for

---

[26] I am indebted for this information to Miss Pamela Stewart, Assistant Archivist at the Diocesan Record Office, Salisbury.

[27] For John Morton's career, see A. B. Emden, *Biographical Register of the University of Oxford to A.D. 1500*, ii. 1317. Dr. Emden drew my attention to a list of the rectors of Berwick St. John in Sir Thomas Phillipps's *Institutiones Clericorum in comitatu Wiltoniae;* the succession is continuous except for the doubt about when Morton's tenure ended and that of Robert Mere began. For the latter, see *B.R.U.O.*, ii. 1263. It must seem, from the evidence of the MS, that Morton held the living throughout 1425, and probably until Mere's appointment in 1427, and that in Phillipps's list no name has been omitted between them. I also owe to Dr. Emden the information that Morton's successor at Maiden Newton was John Paslewe, B.Cn. and C.L. (Hutchins, *History of Dorset*, ii. 690); he held the living until his death, and his successor, instituted on 21 March 1457, was another John Morton, the future archbishop of Canterbury, of dubious memory. I am greatly indebted to Dr. Emden for his help and advice.

[28] The details of his career are taken from Emden, *B.R.U.O.*, iii. 1917.

the fellows and scholars, then the scholars and fellows might after the meal, for the sake of recreation, pass the time by songs and other decent entertainments and occupy themselves more seriously with poems, chronicles of kings, and the marvels of this world, and with other things which were suited to the clerical state.[29] The connection of the songs of the MS with Christmas and New Year is shown by *Thys Yool* (no. 28) and by the choice of a Christmas carol (*Als I lay on Yoolis night,* no. 20). The connection with Winchester is shown by the song in praise of the city (*Me lykyth ever the lenger the bet,* no. 30). And the connection with Winchester College is shown by the note in the MS, below the main part of *Thys Yool,* 'quod Edmund'; for the records of the college give Edmund as the name of a clerk of the chapel in 1396-7 who may also have been the *informator choristarum.*[30] It would appear, then, that the quire containing the 'Winchester College' group of songs must have been added to Thomas Turk's MS during one or other of the periods of his Winchester fellowship, i.e. between 1395 and 1398 or between 1400 and 1401, of which the earlier is perhaps the more likely, as it includes the period when Edmund is recorded as a clerk of the chapel; and this is consistent with the dating of the handwriting of the songs to 'about 1400'.

Not all the English songs of the group are of Winchester origin. The carol (no. 20) was certainly written in the North-east Midlands and its words are recorded in other MSS. Nos. 25 and 26 are courtly love-songs; their language is that of the South-east Midlands, without Southernisms, and their form and style differ from those of the rest of the English songs of the group. But the others are closely linked. Most are written to the ABB formula, usually in a fairly simple version of it, at least from the metrical point of view; they all contain Southernisms either of grammar or of spelling;[31] and though they show some metrical accomplishment, they are mostly flat, prosaic, and clumsy in literary style. The worst is perhaps the Winchester poem (no. 30), the best *Thys Yool* (no. 28); indeed the latter is distinguishable from the rest, for it is metrically more varied and elabo-

rate, it is livelier in style, and its last stanza, somewhat surprisingly in view of what goes before, is in the terms of courtly love. It may be that 'Edmund' wrote only this one piece. But it is linked to no. 27 by similarities of thought and phrasing (cf. especially ll. 7-8 of no. 28, ll. 2-4 of no. 27), though this could mean no more than that the author of the one song knew the other. With the possible exception of no. 28, the only piece attributed in the MS to Edmund, nos. 27-33 give an impression of common authorship. But their word-text is poor, and it is most unlikely that Turk's copy was made directly from the author's original. One possible explanation might be that copies had been made for the use of choristers in performance, and that in these the words had been less carefully copied than the music, perhaps because the words had been memorized or could be taught or corrected by word of mouth; and that the quire bound into Turk's MS was such a performing copy.[32]

Greene[33] distinguishes five hands (B-F) which write the carols and songs in the MS (omitting the mutilated poem on the last fly-leaf), and in addition hand G (that of John [Morton]) and a hand H which writes the building accounts on f. iii[r]. But some of these distinctions lack validity. The building accounts relating to Bridmore were plainly made by the same man as recorded oblations from Bridmore, i.e. hands G and H are both Morton's. I can see no difference, other than what might be produced by the use of a different pen, between hand E, to which Greene attributes the carol with music (our no. 20) on f. 169[r], and hand D, to which he attributes the other songs with music, including no. 33 on f. 168[v], the facing page of the same opening. With the other hands of the MS we are not concerned; one of them must be Turk's (probably that which writes, among other things, the predictions of the eclipses). As already noted, the carols and lyrics without music are written in a later hand or hands, and must have been added to the MS while it was in Morton's possession, or even that of his successor John Paslewe.[34]

It is probable that there is some connection between the songs of Douce 381 and those of Additional 5943.

[29] Kirby, *Annals of Winchester College,* p. 489.

[30] F. Ll. Harrison, *Music in Medieval Britain* (2nd ed., 1961), p. 32.

[31] It is noteworthy that no. 27, which occurs in both Additional 5943 and Douce 381, has different Southernisms in the two MSS. Their common original may have been more markedly Southern than either of the copies.

[32] One can imagine that the boys themselves might be set to make copies, and that they would do so carelessly.

[33] *E.E.C.,* p. 341. Greene seems to assume that each hand works systematically for a few pages and then gives place to another. I do not think that this is what happened at all. Originally blank pages of the MS were used unsystematically by the various owners, as convenience or whim directed.

[34] The linguistic forms and spellings of these pieces have common features, some of them distinctive; certain of these features are also found in the songs with music. As the scribe who wrote the words of the songs was different from the scribe or scribes who wrote the other pieces, these linguistic resemblances must be due to the region within which the scribes lived.

Their musical texts are similar in general appearance. Both contain songs in the ABB form, both have French as well as English pieces, and both include *I rede that thou* (no. 27). Comparison of a facsimile of the Cambridge text of the song with the original of the Bodleian text shows that the hands, though similar, are distinguishable, but suggests that the two scribes are following, with individual modifications and errors of copying, the lay-out of a common original. The two MSS also have in common that the word-texts of the songs are exceptionally unreliable, and may omit not only individual words, but whole half-lines. Unfortunately nothing seems to be known of the provenance of the leaves in Douce 381, but it seems likely that both its songs and those in Additional 5943 are independent selections from a larger collection, assembled in some place where there were singers of part-music.[35]

EDITORIAL PRINCIPLES AND METHODS (ENGLISH TEXTS)

The texts given in this book do not profess to follow the manuscripts uncritically. They are edited texts, designed to remove scribal corruptions of sense, grammar or word-form, and metre, and to produce a good fit of words to music. Where the words of songs exist in more MSS than one, the traditional methods of textual criticism have been applied, to the extent that the case allows; the versions given in the different MSS have been fully collated, a *stemma codicum* has been worked out on the basis of agreements in error, and the archetype has been reconstructed, as far as possible, by recension. Where there is only a single MS which critical inspection shows to be corrupt, or where the archetype[36] to which the extant MSS point itself proves to be unsatisfactory, the text can be restored only by emendation, necessarily 'conjectural' though not mere uncontrolled guessing (since it is based on, and seeks to explain, the evidence of the transmitted text(s)); such emendation is an essential part of the textual critic's work, and it has been used, in the formation of my texts, to whatever extent has seemed necessary. It has not been

my object to reproduce the texts given by the scribes, but to recover as far as might be the text written by the original author; and I would rather go wrong in the attempt than fail to make it. Nor is the spelling in all respects that of the scribes; it has been deliberately modified, for the reasons given and in the ways described below in a special section of this introduction.[37]

So to treat the text of medieval English lyrics is contrary to the established practice of the chief collections. In these, the texts of the MSS, as read by the editors, are mostly printed without even the most obviously necessary changes: abnormal spellings, false forms, bad rhyme and worse metre, irregular or impossible accidence and syntax, and even sheer nonsense are left uncorrected. Sometimes even the reporting of the MSS is unreliable. When there are more MSS than one, their variant texts are either printed one after the other, or else one is chosen for printing and variant readings (generally incomplete) are given from the others; no attempt is made to form a critical text. One reason is that the collectors, though industrious and highly talented in the discovery of lyrics in medieval MSS and enthusiastic and thorough in recording and reporting them, often lacked the knowledge necessary to produce proper texts; their glossaries and notes, as Middle English scholars know, are witnesses to the extent of their failure to understand their texts and even to identify the words in them. Moreover to edit poems in any true sense, rather than merely to print them, is a very time-consuming and anxious business. But a more fundamental reason for the failure to form proper texts was a tradition of scholarship. In reaction against the eclectic and arbitrary texts of the traditional ballads made by eighteenth- and early nineteenth-century editors, Child in his great work of collecting the ballads established a doctrine that each version, each text, had its own validity and was to be recorded separately and exactly; and editors of ballads became very reluctant to produce conflated versions, and banned emendation as if it were an unnatural vice.[38] And the same methods and doctrines have been applied to the medieval English lyrics and carols, without real enquiry whether the conditions are the same. The result of this 'scientific' and 'scholarly' procedure is that we are

---

[35] The initials 'E.H.' written on the last page of the musical section of Douce 381 do not help; they appear to be much later in date than the leaves themselves.

[36] In the terminology of textual criticism, 'archetype' does not mean the original as written by the author; it means that MS (normally lost) from which all the extant MSS descend. The archetype may itself be removed from the original by intervening copies (sometimes many, sometimes few) and by the lapse of time, and may well be — indeed normally is — itself already corrupt, though less corrupt than its individual descendants.

[37] See pp. 44-7 below.

[38] 'No passage, no phrase even, will be found in any of the selections, which is not taken word for word from a recognized text of the ballad in question' (preface to Francis B. Gummere's *Old English Ballads*).

given to read texts which no sane and competent poet, speaking and writing a real language, can ever have intended to write. Of recent years there have been protests from scholars well qualified to protest, but there has hitherto been little change in the practice.

Among medievalists, as commonly also among amateurs of literature, an almost superstitious regard is often paid to the texts given by the MSS. They are held to be 'real' texts, written in the Middle Ages themselves by medieval scribes and intended to be read, or sung, by medieval people. That the copy may have been made a hundred or more years after the date of composition is set on one side as irrelevant; and indeed medieval English lyrics are commonly dated as if they were composed contemporaneously with the MSS in which they are preserved, whatever other evidence there may be. By contrast a modern editor's text, produced by the use of the techniques and tools of scholarship, is 'artificial', a theoretical reconstruction by a modern of an original often denigrated as 'hypothetical' — as if the existence of a copy did not of itself prove that there must have been an original. Now it is true, and every sensible scholar recognizes, that a man who lived in, say, the fourteenth century would have had a much livelier and more extensive knowledge of *his own* dialect than any modern scholar can have, and that he may often have recognized as possible and natural words and meanings and forms and idioms that seem improbable to us; the history of Middle English scholarship provides ample evidence of readings once rejected as corrupt that are now accepted as correct. But it is obvious that almost all medieval scribes possessed far worse knowledge of dialects other than their own, or of earlier stages of the language, than a well-trained modern scholar does; once they started to copy a text written in another dialect, or in an older form of the language, they were beyond the safe limits of their understanding and liable to error. Nor does it follow that the scribe himself thought the text satisfactory merely because he copied it. Even if he was intelligent and critical and conscientious, there was little he could do if he were given a text to copy which he recognized was faulty. He could perhaps try to get another exemplar, and if he did he might conflate the two, usually arbitrarily and unsatisfactorily because he was not trained for such work; he could try to improve his text by guess-work, sometimes successfully but more often badly, again because he lacked the techniques and the resources for successful emendation; or he could resign himself to copying faithfully a text which he knew was bad, because it was that or nothing. But most

medieval scribes were not especially careful and conscientious, and as time passed they seem to have got worse. No one who has closely studied the texts of Middle English poems, and especially perhaps of the lyrics, which were so often hastily jotted down on whatever was available, is prepared to allow much credence to the scribes and their work; a few were good, many were downright bad, and none is to be blindly trusted.

It is not only modern scholars who condemn the inaccuracy of the transmitters of medieval texts; scholars and poets in the Middle Ages were equally aware of their faults. The universities made elaborate arrangements to try to ensure the accuracy of copies of text-books. Sisam[39] cites Robert Mannyng of Brunne (Bourn in Lincolnshire), who in his *Chronicle* (completed in 1338) says of the tales

> of Erceldoun and of Kendale,
> non þam says as þai þam wroght,
> and in þer sayng it semes noght.
> Þat may þou here in *Sir Tristrem* —
> over gesstes it has þe steem,
> over alle þat is or was,
> if men it sayd as made Thomas:
> but I here it no man so say
> þat of som copple som is away.

Mannyng is here discussing texts recited by entertainers, and therefore probably transmitted orally; but, as Sisam goes on to observe, he blames their vanity more than their memories. But though texts transmitted in writing were liable to less rapid corruption, they too were not safe. Chaucer could not trust Adam 'his owne scriveyn', who would have had a perfect or near-perfect exemplar to work from and was no doubt specially instructed; he threatens him with a broken head

> but after my makyng thou wryte more trewe;
> so ofte a-daye I mot thy werk renewe,
> it to correcte and eek to rubbe and scrape;
> and al is thorugh thy negligence and rape.

'Negligence and rape' are terms quite as strong as any employed by modern critics of scribes and their work. Still earlier, in the closing stanzas of *Troilus and Criseyde*, Chaucer had written:

> And for ther is so gret diversite
> in Englissh and in writyng of our tonge,
> so preye I God that non myswrite the,
> ne the mysmetre for defaute of tonge.
> And red wherso thow be, or elles songe,
> that thow be undersonde, God I biseche.
>
> (V. 1793-8)

[39] *Fourteenth Century Verse and Prose*, ed. K. Sisam, p. xxxiii.

These lines are commonly cited in discussions of the general history of the English language, to which indeed they are relevant; but they more directly concern the point with which Chaucer is actually dealing, the transmission of a poetical text. What he is saying is that, failing divine intervention, scribes are apt to miscopy ('myswrite') texts and in particular to spoil their metre ('mysmetre' them) because of linguistic errors ('defaute of tonge'), and he attributes this specifically to the diversity of English and especially of its spelling ('writyng'). And there cannot be any doubt that he has correctly picked out the greatest single cause of the corruption of Middle English texts — the almost universal tendency of scribes to substitute for the forms used in their exemplars those of their own dialects, and the spellings which they had been trained or were accustomed to use in place of those intended by the author. The immediate victim is the metre, as Chaucer clearly saw, for no verse can scan if forms different from those intended are substituted; but rhyme and grammar and even sense suffer, for the scribes, in their self-imposed work of 'translation' and modernization, did not stop merely at altering spellings and grammatical forms, but also substituted what they took to be synonyms for words and phrases that they did not like or understand.

It is obvious that lyrics and songs are a form of literature which may well be transmitted orally; but proof of the oral transmission of a text is very difficult unless there is external evidence of it — best of all a record that the text has been taken down from oral performance. There is no external evidence of the oral transmission of the texts of the songs in this collection; Robbins's statement[40] that Richard de Ledrede wrote his pious *contrafacta* to replace worldly songs that his clergy had 'picked up from contact with the local people' is without warrant in the *Red Book of Ossory*.[41] There is no conclusive means of proving from internal evidence that a text has been transmitted orally. All textual critics would be prepared to make a list of the types of corruption to which oral transmission exposes a text, and which, if they occur, may suggest that the text under consideration has been so transmitted; but there is none of them that cannot also occur in a written transmission. The surest

sign is very wide divergences between versions, produced in a relatively short period of transmission, but to demonstrate this several extant versions are required, and preferably a relatively long text. On the other hand there are types of corruption that are distinctive of, and prove, a written transmission: errors due to confusion between similarly shaped letters or between words that are alike in their written rather than in their spoken forms, those due to misunderstanding of archaic and obsolescent letter-forms (such as ð in Middle English), or those due to a scribe's eye coming back to his exemplar at a wrong point (e.g. omissions due to homeoteleuton or homeoarchy). The mixture in one text of inconsistent orthographic systems is another sign of a written transmission, for a scribe writing down a text from dictation would consistently use his own orthography. More generally, if collation is able to demonstrate clearly the affiliations of MSS by shared distinctive features of detail, it is highly probable that the tradition is written, for oral tradition is unlikely to leave detailed signs of the descent of the versions. On such grounds it is clear that the proximate descent of the texts of all those of the songs included in this volume which exist in more than one MS is in every case a written descent; and it is probable, or virtually certain, that the same is true of most of the songs that exist only in a single MS.[42] This conclusion holds good even in instances where there occurs one of the types of corruption which are accepted as possible signs of oral transmission. Thus consideration of the detailed textual variations in no. 6b shows clearly that its tradition was written; and the derangement of the order of stanzas, which is frequent in oral transmission (owing to failure of a reciter's memory), is in this case due to a deliberate and mistaken alteration by the scribe of a lost intermediate MS which produced a result so unsatisfactory that further changes were forced on his successors. The signs of written transmission in no. 11 are manifold; the revisions which occur at various points are plainly not enforced substitutions made by singers for lines which they had forgotten, but deliberate re-writing which took place at various stages of the descent of a written text.

To say that the *proximate* descent of the extant texts of

---

[40] *Secular Lyrics of the XIVth and XVth Centuries*, p. xxxv.

[41] The note in the Red Book reads as follows. 'Nota: Attende, lector, quod Episcopus Ossoriensis fecit istas cantilenas pro Vicariis ecclesie Cathedralis, sacerdotibus et clericis suis, ad cantandum in magnis festis et solatiis ne guttura eorum et ora Deo sanctificata polluantur cantilenis teatralibus turpibus et secularibus, et cum sint cantatores provideant sibi de notis convenientibus secundum quod dictamina requirunt' (J. T. Gilbert in *Historical Manuscripts Commission, Report X, Appendix, Part V*, p. 242).

[42] Thus no. 16a, though recorded in a Devon MS, has characteristic Norfolk spellings; and no. 16b(i), written by a Southern scribe, has a characteristic North-west Midland 'reverse' spelling (*ng* for *nk*); no. 17, though its normal spellings are those of the East Midlands, has an inconsistent Essex spelling evidently due to the scribe; and so on. No. 21 has an omission of half a line evidently due to homeoteleuton, and an error *sa* for *wo* probably due (whichever of two possible explanations is accepted) to misreading of copy; no. 22 has in the last line an omission due to the occurence of the abbreviation *þᵗ* for *þat* immediately after *yt*; and so on.

our songs was in writing is not to deny that at an earlier stage there may have been a period of oral transmission, though I can see no real need to assume it. It would be a possible explanation of the gross derangement of the word-order, involving sometimes even the rhyme-words, which occurs in some texts (especially in nos. 17, 21 and 32); but it is not a necessary explanation. It must be remembered that when songs are set out under a musical stave, they are not usually written in verse-lines but as prose; there is nothing to show where one line ends and another begins, and the stanzaic structure and therefore the rhyme-scheme are not apparent to the eye. To pick out the rhymes and to work out the stanza-form often requires careful attention. It is obvious in many cases that the scribes cannot have been fully aware what the rhyme-scheme was or which were the rhyming words, and they probably sometimes thought a line was not rhymed when in fact it was; and they therefore sometimes substituted a normalized 'prose' word-order (which was also usually a modernized word-order) that displaced the rhyme-word from its intended position or altered the intended verse-rhythm. Indeed, if one considers, such errors may well be more readily committed by a copyist, following words on a page with his eye, than by a singer or reciter who might be expected to have the spoken words, and therefore the stanza-form and the rhyme-scheme, more clearly in his mind.

It seems to me that the commonly held view that the transmission of the Middle English lyric was such as to make the traditional processes of textual criticism inapplicable requires some revision, and that in many cases a close inspection of the texts would reveal evidence of a written transmission, similar to that found in the texts of our songs. But even when a text has probably or possibly descended orally, and when the versions differ radically, it is not true that nothing can be done effectively to edit it. At the very worst the editor can choose what seems to him the best, or the best-authenticated, version and edit that as if it were a text preserved in a single MS. But generally he can in fact get a good deal of help from the other versions. It is often the case that though some stanzas may differ widely (as in our no. 11), others run close together; and the affiliations of the texts can sometimes be worked out from the stanzas that they have in common and may throw light on the processes of revision in the stanzas that differ.

Even when the affiliations cannot be worked out, the readings of the 'discarded' versions may be of great help in revealing, and in helping to cure, corruptions in the 'selected' version. The traditional textual criticism still has a valid part to play, even though some of its processes may be inapplicable; most Old English poetry exists only in single MSS, but it is not left lame and deformed as Middle English poetry so often is. Emendation and conflation are legitimate parts of the editorial process; the doctrine that each version must be left in sterile isolation is an absurd pedantry.

It should not be necessary to defend emendation of sense and grammar, or of rhyme if the intention to rhyme is clear and no harm is done to the sense.[43] Emendation on metrical grounds is commonly thought to be more dubious. I do not defend my practice of it merely because in this volume the words are being edited so as to be set to music, and without regularity of metre, in many cases, no proper fitting of words to notes is possible. If the evidence is that the words as originally written were irregular in metre, either in syllable-count or in accentual rhythm, or that there was from the first a discrepancy (whether due to poet or composer) between the metrical and musical rhythm, it is an editor's duty to say so; and we do occasionally say so, though in our judgement the case does not often arise in these songs. There cannot properly be two texts of a song, one edited for singing to produce regularity even against the evidence or against probability, another more conservatively edited for reading. The function of every editor is to recover, as far as he can, the text written by the original author.[44] If the evidence is that the words were not perfectly regular in metre, an editor, even if his task is to produce texts for musical performance, must stop short of a spurious and imposed regularity; but equally an editor producing texts for reading who fails to take into account, in editing the words of a song, the technical requirements of the music and the actual evidence of the recorded musical text is leaving out of account an important part of the evidence. But this in fact is what has hitherto been done; though collections of Middle English lyrics, and of carols treated as literary texts, are normally meticulous in recording the fact that the words are accompanied in the MSS by music, I do not recall ever seeing emendations proposed on the ground that the music proves that the word-text has been corrupted;

---

[43] Often an emendation proposed in the first place to restore exact rhyming proves actually to benefit sense. Allowance of course must be made for various Middle English licences of rhyming — assonances and inexact rhymes of other sorts — and for what, in the editor's judgement, is the degree of skill in rhyming shown by the author concerned. What in one poet would be highly suspicious is in another an unremarkable instance of his carelessness or incompetence.

[44] Or, in appropriate cases, by the redactor of a distinct version.

and occasionally emendations have been made that destroy the fit of words and music.[45]

It is sometimes argued, against metrical emendation, that even when it is clear what the metre should be there may be more ways than one of achieving the desired result. But this is likely to be true of all types of emendation; the editor, after considering all the possibilities that may occur to him or have been suggested by others, must exercise his judgement and choose the emendation that seems best, that in his view most convincingly both cures the fault and accounts for the actual reading(s) of the transmitted text(s). Others again hold that only the most essential changes should be admitted to the actual text, and that other emendations — including, commonly, purely metrical changes — should be proposed only in notes or in a section of the introduction which, in discussing metre, may point out that the transmitted text misrepresents the author and that apparent irregularities may be cured in such-and-such a way. Their reason is that if a text is extensively altered in the process of editing, it may soon be superseded and discarded if the editor's judgement proves to have been faulty or if advances of scholarship invalidate his premises — as has indeed happened in some cases; but if his text is conservatively edited, it may remain serviceable even if his editorial apparatus becomes outmoded. This is an expedient, not to say worldly-wise, doctrine likely to commend itself to a publisher. But it is of no assistance to us, who must put into our texts the words which we believe that a singer should use, and cannot bury them in a textual commentary; and it may be doubted whether it is ever desirable. An editor should not leave in his text a reading which he is convinced is wrong unless he is unable to think of a satisfactory alternative; the proper place for wrong readings — which can only mean those which the editor *judges* to be wrong — is in the *apparatus criticus,* not the text. Generations of students have been left to believe that some of the most admired Middle English poems were written in rough and incompetent metre because their editors have declined to make even the most obvious corrections of the words and forms used by the scribes.[46]

But the commonest objection to emendation of Middle English texts on metrical grounds is that it is too

uncertain, that we do not know enough of Middle English metre. It is true that no contemporary English *Ars Metrica* survives, and that the practice of Middle English poets has not been subjected to an analysis so thorough, a codification so seemingly strict, as that achieved for Old English verse by Sievers and others. Some carry agnosticism so far as to write as if the principles of Middle English verse were as yet quite uncertain, and would deny the right of an editor, not only to emend, but even to choose between variant readings on metrical grounds. But there is in fact no mystery about Middle English rhyming metre; modern English metre is its direct descendant, and any native speaker of English who understands the one can understand the other. The difficulty is to determine, in individual cases, whether a rare or irregular rhythm was in fact intended by the author. Much depends on the ease with which an irregularity can be removed; if all that is necessary is the substitution of a variant form of the same word, current in the author's known or probable dialect, there is little or no reason to refrain from the change, and similarly if all that is needed is a change of word-order, for there is ample evidence that scribes were careless of word-order. Much also depends on a general judgement of the reliability of the transmitted text; the more frequently there is need for change the more reason there is to emend, for the MS is shown to be suspect, but if the great majority of the lines are obviously acceptable as the scribe writes them, he may be given the more credence when he writes an irregular line, especially if there is no easy way of regularizing it. No one would wish to, or could, impose on the great bulk of Middle English verse the sort of metronomic regularity that Orm practised. Middle English metre was not ordinarily syllabic, nor did it aim at uniformity of accentual rhythm. It could vary the normal length of line by the addition of unstressed syllables, most commonly at the beginning or end of the line or before the mid-line caesura, but also at other points; it could omit an unstressed syllable that would be present in the basic pattern, either at the beginning of the line (to produce a 'headless' line) or at the caesura (to produce 'clashing stresses' on either side of the caesura) or more rarely at other points. It could vary the normal accentual rhythm, e.g. by substituting, in a normally iambic metre,

---

[45] The reason of course is that literary scholars who are trained in philology and textual criticism are not usually trained in medieval music, and require the help of a musicologist if they are to make use of the evidence of the music. But a transcription of the music independently made by a musicologist, though it may be of great assistance to the textual editor, is by no means a perfect guide, for if the music is in non-mensural notation fundamental decisions about rhythm may have been made on the basis of a corrupted word-text.

[46] Kenneth Sisam, in editing *Sir Orfeo,* contents himself with a remark, in his notes on its inflexions, that 'the original text preserved final *-e* better than the extant MSS' (*Fourteenth Century Verse and Prose,* p. 208), but does not restore it even in the lines that he cites as examples; and A. J. Bliss, in his widely used and scholarly edition of the poem, nowhere discusses its metre or even points out (as Sisam does) the evident failure of the Auchinleck MS to preserve the original inflexional forms (his discussion on pp. xxiii-xxxiv being limited to the forms actually written by the scribe).

trochaic feet, especially at the beginning of the line or after the caesura. Nevertheless there are some rhythms that are so clumsy as to be highly suspect, and others that are plainly impossible. When in a poem written in four-stress couplets we meet the line

Al þe utmast wal

we know it must be wrong; no one can get four stresses out of five syllables, and no competent poet is going to interpolate a three-stress line in a poem written regularly in another metre. It is one thing to recognize the variability of Middle English metre; it is another to tolerate the chaos and disorder produced by bad transmission of the texts.

But our concern is not with narrative or expository verse, or even with the 'literary' lyric, in all of which metrical variation was freely practised, but with songs; and in a song the technical requirements of the music control the versification of the poet. The music, depending on its type and its details, may require perfect or near-perfect metrical regularity, in syllable-count and in rhythm. Once an editor of a lyric has reason to believe that it is the words of a song, he is really confronted with a different editorial problem; he must ask himself what sort of a song it is likely to have been, and whether he should not so edit the text as to produce regularity of metre if he credibly can. If no music is recorded, the most certain proof that the lyric is a song is some external evidence of its having been sung, or a note by a scribe that states or implies that it had music. Of internal evidence, the most important is the conformity of the lyric's structure to some known song-type (e.g. the carol); others are an indefinable but nevertheless important 'singable' quality, the use of devices (e.g. repetitions of words or phrases) effective in a song but less justifiable in verse intended merely for reading, the approach of the verse, even as recorded in the MS, to the regularity needed in a song, and the evident possibility of increasing this regu-

larity by easy emendation. I should also allow some weight to the use, in a lyric, of the formulae 'my song' and 'I sing'. It is true that in Old and Middle English, as in other languages, 'song' is often used to mean no more than 'metrical composition', and the verb 'to sing' to mean no more than 'to declaim, to recite'; Chaucer, when he wrote of *Troilus and Criseyde*

and red wherso thow be, or elles songe,

obviously did not mean singing in any strict sense of the word,[47] and even in lyrics the use of these formulae might be merely conventional. But if they are allied with a form potentially suitable for singing, they may be significant.

A simple example of a lyric which must in fact have been the words of a song, though recorded without music, is *I sing of a maiden,* which has indeed been given musical settings in modern times. It has, to my mind, not been edited as a song should be, if indeed it has been edited at all and not merely printed. I give below, in parallel, the text of MS Sloane 2593 as printed by Carleton Brown[48] and a text edited as a song. I assume that it was meant to be sung 'hymn-fashion' to mensural music, so that each stanza had to have the same basic metrical structure; that this was, in terms of syllable-count, 6566, the first three lines being normally trochaic and the fourth normally iambic; and that the rhyme-scheme was *abcb.*[49]

I syng of a myden	I sing of a maiden
þat is makeles,	þat is makëles,
kyng of alle kynges	king of allë kinges
to here sone che ches.	to hirë sun heo ches.
he cam also stylle	He cam also stillë
þer his moder was	þer his moder was
as dew in aprylle,	asë deaw in April
þat fallyt on þe gras.	þat falleþ on þe gras.

---

[47] In this case it is plain that *or elles songe* is a line-filler, used for the sake of rhyme. If any distinction was intended between 'read' and 'sung', the former must mean reading silently or aloud from a book, the latter recitation or declamation from memory.

[48] *Religious Lyrics of the XVth Century*, no. 81. But Brown prints the text in long lines with a mid-line gap, where I for convenience print it in short lines.

[49] A variant form of stanzas 1 and 5 is given in ll.3-4 and 19-20 of a poem (probably also a song) preserved in the thirteenth-century MS Trinity College, Cambridge, 323 (no. 31 in Carleton Brown's *English Lyrics of the XIIIth Century*), and it is certain that *I sing of a maiden* was itself written long before the date of the Sloane MS, though Carleton Brown, in his notes to the poem of the Trinity MS, speaks of its being 'quoted verbally [which is an over-statement] in a song of the beginning of the fifteenth century' (op. cit., p. 192). This is to date songs by the extant MSS. I think it unlikely that there is any great gap in date; *I sing of a maiden* could easily belong to the thirteenth century, and it is not beyond doubt which of the poems is 'quoting' the other. Certainly *I sing of a maiden* must belong before 1400; final -*e* is preserved except when elided.

The elision of the -*e* of *sone* (so MS) in l.4 of stanza 1 implies that the feminine third personal pronoun had one of the forms beginning with *h*; the thirteenth-century Trinity MS has both *heo* and *he*, and I choose the former, for the poem of the Sloane MS probably originated in the West or South-west Midlands, though that of the Trinity MS is probably an East Midland poem in a Western or South-western copy. In stanzas 2-4, *stille* in the first line does not rhyme with *Aprille* in the third; the latter is an unphonetic fifteenth-century spelling of a word of which the true form was disyllabic, *April*, and in this poem was stressed on the first. Cf. the first line of the *Canterbury Tales* and Robinson's note to it in his second edition (which follows Dorothy Everett in *Medium Aevum* i (1932), p. 46). My reconstruction of the first two lines of the last stanza follows the text of l. 19 of the poem in the Trinity MS. I modify the spellings in the direction of those of the thirteenth-century text.

he cam also stylle
to his modres bowr
as dew in aprille,
þat fallyt on þe flour.

he cam also stylle
þer his moder lay
as dew in aprille,
þat fallyt on þe spray.

moder & mayden
was neuer non but che;
wel may swych a lady
godes moder be.

He cam also stillë
to his modres bur
asë deaw in April
þat falleþ on þe flur.

He cam also stillë
þer his moder lay
asë deaw in April
þat falleþ on þe spray.

Maid and moder was never
[wimon] non but heo;
wel may swich a levëdi
Godes moder beo.

But even so simple a case, where the MS text is relatively good, illustrates the difficulties that may confront an editor if the music is not preserved. For the last stanza, as edited, shows two variations from the preceding four. The last line, as given in the Sloane MS, has only five syllables instead of the normal six; it lacks the initial unstressed syllable. The explanation assumed in the edited text is that this syllable has been moved back to the end of the preceding line (for what I print as two short lines may as well be regarded as one long line); by reading trisyllabic *levëdi* for MS *lady* at the end of the third line it is possible to make the third and fourth lines, taken together, of identical length and rhythm in all stanzas. There is little reason to doubt that the music, if recorded, would show that the composer had treated the two short lines as a unit; only if the music had a rest at the end of the third line would this moving back of the unstressed syllable be precluded. In the songs which we edit in this volume (e.g. in nos. 16a and 20) there are examples of this technique of shifting the point of division between verse-lines, or the two halves of a long line. The other difficulty in the last stanza is that the first two lines have obviously been corrupted in the Sloane MS at least by an omission, for though, taken together, they have the right number of syllables (eleven), they have only five stresses instead of six; and comparison with the version of the Trinity MS suggests that there has been a reversal of word-order as well. Yet the reconstruction to which the Trinity version points gives the first line seven syllables instead of the normal six.[50] It seems likely that the music of the first line would have been such as to allow of a dactyl instead of a trochee in the second foot (e.g. it may have had at this point a 'spare note'); but without the music we cannot be sure.

The aid that the music can give in settling details of the text may also be illustrated from our no. 16a, *Brid one breere*. Here the words as written in the MS provide no clear guide to the rhythm, for necessary repetitions are omitted; but the musical text itself, in the opinion of the editor of the music, was in need of emendation. A word-text was provided, edited to produce complete metrical regularity; but at two points this metrical uniformity had been achieved only at the cost of unconvincing alterations of the MS text. When the music was emended in the light of this draft text, it appeared that at both these points it was such as to permit of the metrical variations shown by the transmitted text, and the latter was restored.

But the music does not merely enable the textual editor to settle details; it may be essential evidence of the metrical form itself. The editor, working from irregular MS texts, has to decide by analysis of their readings what the original metrical scheme was; but the literary evidence may be conflicting. It may not be apparent whether what was aimed at was regularity of accentual rhythm, or merely uniformity in the number of syllables to a line; for the latter would be sufficient for music that did not have its own metrical rhythm. Or it may not be clear what was the metrical pattern for individual lines. Thus in the Sloane text of *I sing of a maiden*, stanzas 1-4 suggest that the third and fourth lines both had six syllables, the third being trochaic and the fourth iambic. But stanza 5, as the text is given in the MS, has the expected trochaic line of six syllables for the third line, but for the fourth a trochaic catalectic line of five syllables. Which is the right pattern? The balance of evidence and considerations of style are strongly in favour of the first pattern, i.e. that the two lines together should have twelve syllables (as assumed in the text given above), but a doubt remains, for it would be possible to reduce the final line, in stanzas 1-4, to five syllables by reading *hir* for *hirë, falþ* for *falleþ*. The music, if it survived, would be decisive, for it would show whether one or two unstressed syllables had been provided for between the last stress of the third line and the first stress of the fourth. It so happened that I made a first draft of the texts of our nos. 6a and 6b in complete ignorance of the music given by the Maidstone MS for 6a, or even of its type; it seemed to me that as the texts of both poems were given in four MSS (not to mention the fragmentary texts of no. 6a), it should be possible by collation and recension to form satisfactory texts without the music.

[50] The Trinity MS has *maiden and moder nas never,* but its own metre presupposes, instead of *maiden,* the reduced form *maid* (produced by loss of *-n* and then elision of the exposed *-e*). If we kept the word-order of the Sloane MS, *moder and maiden was never,* the line would have two extra syllables, which it is possible (but less likely) that the lost music could have accommodated. It seems better to follow the word-order of the Trinity MS, which permits one of the extra syllables to be got rid of by substitution of a variant linguistic form.

But in fact it was not; one could get so far, but not to the end. Though the evidence was strong that both poems were written to syllabically regular schemes, the reconstructed archetypes of both had some lines which, though syllabically regular, were rhythmically irregular; and I guessed that the music must be of the type that does not require rhythmical regularity. In fact the notation is non-mensural, but seems to be suited by transcription in three-four time; and when I knew this I had to look again at lines which I had taken to be legitimate variations on the normal rhythm. Again, at certain points the evidence of the MSS left even the length of individual lines uncertain. In no. 6b, the MSS make it very clear that in their archetype the first lines of stanzas 1, 3, and 5 were of eight syllables with iambic rhythm; thus the opening line in the archetype was

On hir is al mi lif ilong.

But the first lines of stanzas 2 and 4 had seven syllables and were trochaic catalectic lines; thus stanza 2 began

Al þis world hit shal ago.

Which was the original pattern, or were both intended as variants? The music[51] leaves no doubt that the shorter line is right, but the balance of the literary evidence seems in favour of the longer line. The longer lines can all be easily emended to conform in length and rhythm to the shorter; the shorter lines can be extended to agree in length with the longer but cannot possibly be made to conform to a regular iambic rhythm. If one knows only that the music is better suited by regular rhythm it is possible to decide that the shorter form, though given by the MSS in fewer stanzas, is preferable; but without this knowledge the question is open, with the evidence pointing slightly the wrong way.

Mensural music, which has its own regular rhythm, gives most guidance to the textual editor, for unless the original poet or musician has been unskilful (as sometimes happens) the poetic and musical rhythms usually should not clash; stressed syllables were normally set to accented notes.[52] Such music can give clear guidance to the scansion, and can be decisive between textual variants or in revealing corruptions; it can, for example, make it certain that a line must begin with a stressed

syllable though the MS text may begin with an unstressed syllable. Non-mensural music can give less help. But in plainsong there is a tendency for the more prominent of contiguous syllables to be set to higher notes, and occasionally this can aid the textual editor in deciding between variants that differ in stressing, or may tip the balance in favour of an emendation intended to alter the metrical rhythm.

Sometimes technical considerations of performance have to be taken into account. I give two examples from fifteenth-century carols not included in this volume. The first is in the carol *Now make we merthe: Now God Almighty*.[53] The final line of the burden reads in the MS

þat makyth good chere,

but the Southern plural *makyth* is not very consistent with the language of the carol[54] and a four-syllable line

þat mak*e* good cheer

would be more consistent with the normal line of the burden. But so altered the line creates difficulties for a singer, for it brings a *k* before a *g* at a point where there are quick notes to be sung; and a highly skilled professional singer himself asked that the text should be made into *makë* (with pronounced -*e*) to separate the consonants and give an additional light syllable to go to two short notes in his part. Offered a return to the MS text, he declined it because *makyth* itself ended in a consonant and involved a difficulty similar to, though less than, the one he was seeking to avoid; the shortest possible syllable was what he wanted, and one that would separate the consonants. As in the first line of the burden the subjunctive *make* is undoubtedly a monosyllable and a monosyllable would give more regular metre in the last line, it is possible (since the MS gives a disyllabic form, though one that is both linguistically and technically less suitable than *makë*) that it was the composer, rather than the poet, who introduced a metrical variation by using *makë* and that his purpose was to avoid the collocation of *k* and *g* to which the modern professional singer objected.

The other example is in the St. Stephen carol *Pray for us: In this valey*.[55] In the third line of the stanza the third syllable from the end of the line is set to two and one-

---

[51] That is, the music recorded for no. 6a, which I assume was also the music of no. 6b.

[52] But the reverse does not necessarily hold; unstressed syllables need not be set to unaccented notes.

[53] No. 22 in Greene, *Early English Carols*.

[54] The forms are mostly those of the East Midlands and the characteristic Norfolk *xul* plural of *xal* 'shall' occurs in the preceding line of the burden. But *icom* occurs for the p.p. of 'come', where metre requires *cum* without prefix; it looks as though there may have been some influence from a Southern copyist.

[55] No. 99 in Greene, *E.E.C.* In the first line of stanza 1, *valey* (stressed on the second) must be read for MS *vale* for scansion and to fit the music. The MS text is not at all good in detail.

third bars of music,[56] and though the composer provides no rest, it is essential, even for skilled singers, that they should be able to snatch a breath before the second-last syllable, which is itself set to an even longer musical phrase (two and two-thirds bars), followed of course by the last syllable before there is a rest. It follows that, as these two syllables (the third-last and second-last) must be separated by a brief pause for breath, they must not belong to the same word. This condition is fulfilled by the MS text for the third lines of stanzas 1 and 3, but not in stanzas 2 and 4, where the lines are given (in Greene's transcription of the MS) as

> prechyng the pepill of Godes myghth

and

> but rathere to dye for Godes sake.

Both lines are unsatisfactory in other ways, for they are irregular in metre, and in addition *of Godes myghth* in stanza 2 is unduly repetitive of the phrase *as Godys knight* that ends the previous line. The solution that we have finally adopted is to emend the lines to read

> preching the peepil of His might

and

> but rather dyën for God sak*e*

which are regular in metre and idiomatic for the period, and though there is no sense-pause (just as there is no musical rest) permit a brief snatch of breath before the second-last syllable without splitting a word into two.

The music can therefore be of great help to the textual critic and is often decisive; but it should not be allowed to fetter his judgement. Thus there may be a 'spare note' at a point where a metrical variation occurs because an additional syllable was present from the beginning and the composer allowed for it; but the extra note does not *prove* that an extra-metrical syllable was intended. A single syllable is often set to two or more notes; it follows that if a textual corruption introduces a spurious additional syllable, there is a good chance that it will occur at a point where there are notes enough in the music to permit of it. The textual editor must in such a case be guided primarily by considerations proper to the word-text; if metrical regularity can be restored by an easy and credible emendation which satisfactorily explains the transmitted text and does not harm it in other ways, and which fits the music equally well and in a way more consistent with what is done in other stanzas, then in a song he should emend, for the presumption of metrical

regularity is strong. Only if he cannot think of a convincing emendation, or if any metrical emendation he can think of is plainly inferior to the transmitted text in sense or style (or, more rarely, for such technical reasons of performance as those illustrated above) — in short, only if, after testing the possibilities, he is convinced of the essential rightness of the transmitted text — should he rely on the fact that the music can accommodate the metrical variation. An isolated irregularity in a normally regular word-text is more suspect than a number of similar variations all occurring at the same or similar points and always where the music will permit them. But an irregularity should not be defended on the mere ground that it can be accommodated by the music.

In any event the musical text is itself not sacrosanct; it can be corrupted in transmission, and it can be deliberately altered to fit corrupted words. Sometimes, when corruption of the words caused them no longer to fit the metrical scheme or the music, medieval scribes attempted to emend them. This can be demonstrated only when there are sufficient MSS to enable the descent and the successive alterations of the words to be traced with some accuracy, but it undoubtedly occurred; there are examples in the texts of our no. 11 (*Stond wel, moder*). But more usually, in the songs with which we are dealing here, the scribes adapted the music to the corrupted text: if it had lost a syllable, they could set two notes, originally intended for separate syllables, to the same syllable; if it had gained one or more syllables, they could redistribute the notes if there were any to spare, or more simply and more commonly provide additional notes by repeating a previous note or anticipating a following note. There were two main reasons why the scribes should thus alter the music to fit the corrupted words instead of attempting to emend the words. The first was that it was much easier, especially when the method was the purely mechanical doubling of a note. The second was their method of working. Normally in a medieval MS the words were written first, and the musical notation added later. This is shown often by the spacing of the notes at irregular intervals as the lengths of the words dictate. In MS Paris Bibliothèque Nationale f.l. 15163 of *Planctus ante nescia* the scribe evidently began with the expectation that the music was to be copied as well as the words; he ruled a four-line stave for the first two stanzas on f. 229ᵛ, and for the rest of that page and the next left enough space between his lines of text for a stave to be inserted later; but on the third page he began to write his lines closer and closer together, till no room for a stave was left. He had evidently given up

---

[56] That is, in the modern transcription.

his intention of copying the music even before he had completed the copying of the words; but it is clear that his practice was to write the words first. Often a different scribe put in the musical notation. But if the words were written first, it was natural to fit the notes to them; and this seems all too often to have been done in a very mechanical way. It is remarkable how little regard the scribes pay to the scansion; obvious cases of the syncope of medial unstressed vowels (e.g. *heuene* written where *hevnë* is required) or of elision of final -*e* are overlooked time and again. The latter is especially surprising, for it was not the normal practice in English poetical MSS to indicate elision by omitting the -*e* in spelling; thus in the excellent MSS of Gower's *Confessio Amantis,* written in a consistent and intelligent orthography which does not normally employ forms contrary to those required by metre, final -*e* is nevertheless written even when it is obviously to be elided before a vowel or *h*. The normal full form of the word was used in spelling, and the reader was left to realize that elision would occur in speech and was assumed by the metre; and this must imply that trained and intelligent readers could safely be left to make the elisions. But the scribes of the MSS of our English songs for the most part, or at least very commonly, fail to recognize elisions. They normally treat every *e* that is present in the spelling as pronounced. This has relevance to the controversy that took place some years ago on the pronunciation of final -*e*, in which it was argued (partly on the basis of an ill-judged pronouncement by C. S. Lewis on Chaucer's metre) that final -*e* was not sounded nearly so regularly, at least in the fourteenth century, as the traditional philology and metrics assumed. But these scribes of thirteenth- and early fourteenth-century English musical MSS, so far from treating -*e* as something that was often silent, assume that it was pronounced even when it is obvious that the poet could not have intended it to be, and even though the assumption drove them to alterations of the musical notation. The reason was doubtless partly the nature of their work, which would encourage them to consider the text word by word rather than line by line, still less stanza by stanza, and which would give primacy to the written word; it is obvious that they were often not thinking of how the text would sound if read aloud. Beyond this one must allow for the fact that some of these copies may have been made by scribes whose normal experience would be in copying music written for Latin texts. In medieval Latin verse syncope and elision, though they occur, are comparatively rare, partly because many poets deliberately avoided the bringing of vowels into hiatus;[57] a scribe used to copying the music of Latin songs and liturgical texts would be habituated to expect that every written vowel or diphthong would mark a separate syllable and have at least one musical note, and vowel-letters unaccompanied by notes would be outside his experience. If an English word *could* be pronounced with as many syllables as it had written vowels, he would assume that it *should* be so pronounced, and would provide each written vowel with a note.

Generally this situation is easy to deal with. The textual editor must simply say what the scansion should be, and what forms of the words it requires; and if his regularized text can be fitted to the music by a mere redistribution of the notes (reversing a presumed scribal redistribution) or by the excision of doubled notes, it should be. Only if it does not fit the recorded music, or if a metrical irregularity is accompanied in the MS by a deliberate variation of the music (as in 1. 65 of our no. 10(ii)), should he refrain from restoring a regular scansion. It is true, of course, that a trained musical copyist might write in a good musical variation to accommodate a corrupted text, but the odds are against it; the usual practice was more mechanical alteration. A deliberate musical variation is likely to show that there was a metrical variation at the start; at the least the benefit of the doubt is to be given to such a text.

Not all medieval musical MSS were written in the way described above — words copied first, and then music written in later. In the two latest of our MSS, Douce 381 and Additional 5943, the reverse seems to have applied; the musical notes are more evenly spaced and the words were fitted beneath them, often crowded or abbreviated and sometimes ill-aligned. There is even an instance where a word is written twice, once at the wrong place to which an omission had brought it and again at the right place. As was remarked above, the words in these two MSS are especially carelessly copied; priority was clearly given to the music. It seems likely that the two MSS derive from copies made primarily to give choristers copies of the musical texts; certainly the interest was in the music rather than in the words.

The ways in which the technical requirements of the music affect the word-text vary with the nature of the music and the type of song, as described in the Musical Commentary. Though the metre of songs set to non-mensural music may be perfectly regular, such music does not of its nature require strict regularity of accentual rhythm or even of syllable-count. Thus in our no. 4, the French and English versions often differ in rhythm even though they agree in syllable-count, and one or

---

[57] Cf. Dag Norberg, *Introduction à l'étude de la versification latine médiévale,* pp. 31, 32-37.

both may differ from the regular rhythms of *Planctus ante nescia*. Similarly the three English versions (nos. 10(ii), 11, and 12) of *Stabat juxta Christi crucem* (no. 10(i)) allow themselves variations of accentual rhythm where the Latin author evidently intended regular trochaic verse. In this respect the English authors seem less advanced technically than their Latin contemporaries and predecessors, though allowance should no doubt be made for the somewhat greater difficulty of writing a *contrafactum* than an original poem. But they also took some advantage of possibilities of variation in the number of syllables to the line, as we have seen; again no. 4 provides clear examples. Mensural music, on the other hand, may require strict regularity of accentual rhythm, and may preclude metrical devices, such as the substitution of a trochaic for an iambic foot, which in 'literary' verse would be unexceptionable.

In songs sung 'hymn-fashion', with each successive stanza set to a single repeated tune, it is necessary, if there is to be no variation of the music or of the method of distributing the notes over the syllables, that each stanza should be written to the same metrical pattern, without variation in syllable-count or (if the music is mensural) in accentual rhythm. In practice some variations may occur, as in our no. 14, which freely adds an unstressed syllable at the beginning of the lines, though otherwise it keeps regular rhythm; or, as we have seen, an additional unstressed syllable may occur at other points where there is a 'spare' note, or may be accommodated by the 'splitting' of a note; or when successive verse-lines are treated as a single phrasal unit a syllable may be shifted from the end of one line to the beginning of the next (or *vice versa*). But all such variations in metre between one stanza and another call for careful scrutiny, and may require emendation if credible emendation is possible; there is a presumption, in songs performed in this way, that the stanzas will be uniform, though it may be displaced by clear evidence of a metrical variation.

In a sequence, on the other hand, owing to the different method of performance (each stanza sung to its own music), it was possible for the stanzas to vary in metrical pattern, though in the 'regular' sequence as practised by Adam of St. Victor and other writers the stanzas were in fact made uniform, not only in syllable-count, but normally also in accentual rhythms. Though they are not themselves sequences, but songs of different type

written in accordance with similar metrical principles, *Planctus ante nescia* and the French and English *lais* (nos. 4(i) and 4(ii)) are excellent examples of the variability of stanza permissible in the early sequence. But *Stabat juxta Christi crucem* (no. 10(i)) is a regular sequence, and so is *Jesu Cristes milde moder* (no. 12) as far as syllable-count is concerned, though it allows of a few variations of rhythm. But nos. 10(ii) and 11, though they preserve the general stanzaic structure and rhyme-scheme of their model, no. 10(i), allow the lengths of the lines to vary from stanza to stanza, so that each piece is written in a number of metrical variations on the basic stanza-form. To this degree they follow the earlier type of 'irregular' sequence; and once again the metrical technique is less advanced than in their Latin original. The stanza of a sequence divides into two halves, sung to a repetition of the same music;[58] it follows, if a variation of the music is to be avoided, that the two halves of each stanza must be written to the same metrical pattern, though their identity of verse-structure may extend only to the syllable-count. Occasionally a line in one half-stanza may be extended or reduced in length, apparently for special effect; this seems to have been the intention of the musician, though perhaps not of the poet, in l. 65 of our no. 10(ii), and there are a number of instances in no. 4 in which the lines of one or other half-stanza are a syllable shorter or longer than the norm. But the expectation in a sequence is that the two halves of the stanza will match, and apparent failure to do so may be a sign of scribal corruption of the text.

Our collection in this volume contains only one carol. The distinguishing feature of a carol was that it had a 'burden' sung before the first stanza and repeated after every stanza; this burden usually had a tune distinct from that of the stanzas and therefore could be different in metrical structure from the stanzas. But the latter were sung 'hymn-fashion' to a single repeated tune, and therefore should, as in a hymn, follow a single metrical pattern, in syllable-count and in rhythm (for the music is usually in a regular rhythm, as is to be expected in a type of song originally intended to accompany dancing). The writers of carols, however, were evidently not always strict in their technique; though most irregularities of metre in carols are plainly due to faulty transmission of the texts, some remain that are attributable, it seems, to the authors. Our sole example, no. 20, is in any case somewhat abnormal in form, as it uses the popular

---

[58] Except that a sequence may begin or end (or both) with a stanza, normally short, which does not so divide and is sung to music which is not repeated; so the final stanza of *Planctus ante nescia*.

What are here referred to as 'half-stanzas' are often, for convenience, written and printed as separate stanzas; in that case what is said here of 'stanzas' applies to the successive *pairs* of stanzas. When a regular sequence is so printed, with the half-stanzas made into separate stanzas, the formal distinction between the word-text of a sequence and that of a religious song intended for singing 'hymn-fashion' may be obliterated, which is probably why literary scholars sometimes describe as 'sequences' songs which their music shows were not.

ballad-metre; and the evidence is that the author allowed himself to vary the beginning of his stanzas by introducing or omitting an unstressed syllable before the first stress, though this requires a modification of the music. Fifteenth-century carols sometimes show a variation of the metre by the introduction at other points of an additional unstressed syllable that appears to be due to the author, not to corruption by copyists, and there are some which, by practising the normal freedom of Middle English verse to substitute a trochee for an iamb at the beginning of the line, produce clashes between metrical and musical rhythm. Nevertheless the musical requirement is for regularity of stanza-form, and irregularities are always to be regarded with suspicion and emended wherever it is reasonably possible. In the published texts of carols, even those published with their music, this has seldom been done; the versions of the MSS have been printed with only the most essential corrections for sense or word-form, though their metre is often suspiciously irregular.

The other forms used in our songs require no special description here. The 'ABB' songs of Douce 381 and Additional 5943 and the refrain-songs (nos. 23, 24 and 26) have been discussed above (pp. 21-2). No. 17 is a motet. From the point of view of the textual critic, all of these, and the burden of a carol, have in common that at least part of the text is set to its own special music that is not used again for other words, so that the metrical pattern may be unique and not repeated elsewhere in the song; and if there is only one MS this may well create difficulties in deciding what was the metre intended by the original author. If a metrical pattern is repeated because the music requires it to be, even if it is repeated only once, it is possible to compare the two (or more) stanzas, to analyse the pattern, and to isolate the irregularities; and there is a presumption that the irregularities would not have been intended by the author. But if a verse-passage is set to its own music and can have its own individual metrical rhythm, there is no real possibility of comparison. It may be obvious that in the passage the author is predominantly using one type of line (say, in a carol burden, an iambic line of six syllables) and that an individual line diverges from the scheme (say in having seven syllables). If an obvious way of emending it to produce regularity is available, there may still be some presumption that regularity was intended, but it is not nearly so strong as when, on comparing a parallel passage, one finds regularity at the point in question. The music alone can give help; but it may be the case that both the regularized and the irregular line can be fitted to the notes, with little or nothing to choose between them. When this is so, the balance of advantage between retaining the transmitted text with its irregular metre and substituting a regularized text can be very fine, and may depend on whether or not there are other defensible irregularities in the transmitted text which can also be fitted satisfactorily to the music.

As two very different disciplines are involved, the editing of songs in a medieval vernacular will probably always require collaboration between a textual critic with philological training and a musicologist. It may be of some value to record how we have worked. Often the textual editor had available to him from the start a modern transcription of the music and a draft setting of the words made by his colleague, but even when he did, his practice was to edit the words from the literary evidence alone, analysing the transmitted text or texts to discover as best he could the intended metrical scheme, and consulting the music, as far as his ability permitted, only on doubtful points or often only after he had completed a first draft. On other occasions he worked entirely without a musical transcription, either because one had not yet been made or because it was physically in his colleague's keeping. When he had made his provisional text he sent it, with his explanations and draft notes, to his colleague, with a list of his doubts and difficulties. The musical editor then tried the draft word-text to see how it fitted the music, and made his own list of comments and questions. Then we would meet to discuss our texts and resolve our doubts. I fear that this was often not the end of the matter; even when it was clear what was required in the word-text there were alternative ways, in many cases, of achieving it, or I would think only later, sometimes much later, of a better way than I had first proposed. It would seem essential, from our experience, that both parties to this sort of collaboration should be vigilant to preserve the integrity of their own points of view and their own disciplines, and should not accept or be content with what is not fully satisfactory; a text is not correctly edited merely because it fits the music, nor is the music correctly edited merely because it can be made to carry the words. Every editor knows the nagging doubt, often not at all explicit, which it is dangerous to ignore or to argue away, however tempting it may be to do so; it is the warning that one's own mind is not really satisfied with what seems a convenient and even an attractive solution. It would be foolish of us to suppose that our texts are perfect; there may well be better ways than we have thought of to achieve the same ends. But we have, as we believe, given texts edited in accordance with scholarly method that are really singable, as the first authors and composers meant them to be, and have tried as far as possible to recover, if perhaps not always the original words, then the sort of words that were intended, freed of the deformities and gaps produced by 'negligence and rape', by human frailty or misunderstanding, or by physical damage, over long centuries, to perishable books.

MIDDLE ENGLISH PRONUNCIATION AND METRE

As the scansion of any verse depends on the pronunciations used by the authors, an understanding of Middle English metre depends on a knowledge of Middle English pronunciation. Two features are particularly involved: (i) the placing of the stress, and (ii) the number of syllables in the words, which in turn depends on whether certain unstressed vowels are or are not present in the spoken forms, to which the written forms may give imperfect guidance.

The stressing of words in Middle English was by no means freely variable; most syllables were either necessarily stressed, or necessarily unstressed. As English stressing in native words (i.e. words of Anglo-Saxon origin, with which in practice may be grouped words derived from Old Norse or, much more rarely, from other Germanic languages) has been very stable, a speaker of modern English should rarely have any difficulty in telling which syllable of a native word bore the stress in Middle English. But even in native words there were some possibilities of variation.

(1) Compound adverbs and conjunctions, such as *thereby, whereby, therefore, wherefore, forthy* 'therefore', etc., might be stressed on either element, as still often in modern English; this reflects the varying degrees of stress, relative to each other, which would be received in a sentence by the adverbs, prepositions, and pronouns of which these compounds are formed.

(2) But other compounds (nouns, adjectives, and verbs) normally had, in ordinary speech, a fixed stress. Compound verbs (such as *forbid, understand*) were stressed on the stem and the prefix was unstressed.[59] But occasionally a verb might be influenced by the stressing of a related noun, and some compound verbs were originally derived from nouns and so followed their stress; in Middle English the verb *an(d)sweren* 'answer' may be stressed on the first syllable (the original stressing), like the noun from which it is derived, or on the second, following the analogy of the normal compound verb. Compound nouns and adjectives, in contrast to

verbs, were properly stressed on their first elements, even if this were only a prefix. But already in Old English the prefix *ge-* (from which comes the Middle English prefix *y-*) had become unstressed; in Middle English the *y-* can never be stressed, whatever part of speech it is prefixed to. By late Old English and in Middle English certain other prefixes of nouns and adjectives had also become unstressed (e.g. *eþ-* in the adjective *eþ-seene* 'evident' in no. 13, l. 5). Generally modern English is a good guide to the stressing of the prefixes of native nouns and adjectives, but it should be remembered that in Middle English they may sometimes still be stressed even where they are unstressed in Modern English; in particular the prefix *un-* is often stressed, as late as the seventeenth century.

(3) Very occasionally the stress shifted from the first to the second element of nouns and adjectives when the first was not a prefix. In Old English the word *mancynn* 'mankind' was stressed, in accordance with rule, on the first element, in modern English *mankind* in the sense 'the human race' is stressed on the second; in Middle English *mankin* and *mankind* seem to have had variable stress. But this, I think, is the only instance of this sort of shifting stress in our songs.

(4) The cases so far discussed are types of varying stress that occurred in the developing spoken language, i.e. they were not poetic licences, but variations of actual pronunciation. But in many words, though the main stress was on the first syllable, there was a strong secondary stress on the second syllable, either because it was the second element of a compound (e.g. *wimman* 'woman' < OE *wīfmann*) or because it was an identifiable suffix (or part of one) and a long syllable (i.e. contained a long vowel or ended with two consonants or a double consonant): the most important suffixes to notice are *-hood* (< OE *-hād*), *-head* (ME *-hēde* < OE *-hǣde*), *-ing*, and *-ness(e)* in nouns, *-full, -lich* or *-ly (ME -lī* < OE *-līc*), and *-y (ME -ī* < OE *-ig*) in adjectives, and *-liche* or *-ly(e)* (ME *-lī(e)* < OE *-līce*) in adverbs. Such elements, though secondarily stressed, were properly subordinate to the first elements, which bore the main or primary stress; but in Middle English verse there is very often an inversion of the stress, the stem-syllable (or in a compound the first element) being made metrically unstressed and the suffix (or the second element) being made metrically stressed: thus *wimmán, quedhéde, tidíng, gladnésse, blisfúll, heȝlích, lightlí*. This seems without doubt to have been an artificial stressing, a poetic licence; it occurs especially at the end of lines, for

---

[59] In Old English there was a type of semi-compound verb, e.g. *ūtgān* 'to go out', which was stressed on the prefixed adverb. But in Middle English such verbs either fell out of use or came to be stressed like the full compounds, i.e. on the stem (though nouns and adjectives derived from them, e.g. *income, outgoing*, retained the stress on the prefixed adverb).

rhyming convenience, but is not altogether confined to this position. It was practised within strict limits; it was very rare for short syllables, which were more weakly stressed, to receive artificial stress in this way, though there seems to have been some extension of the licence in the later fifteenth and early sixteenth centuries. It should not be assumed unless the evidence is very clear (a sound text and undoubted scansion), except in the circumstances defined above; and even in them it is hardly to be assumed if another scansion is possible, for though it was common enough it is a freedom which an accomplished metrist would not employ too often. The historical reason for it is doubtful. It was entirely foreign to Old English metrical practice, which paid scrupulous regard to the natural stressing of words; it entered English with and was used in rhyming verse. The obvious analogy is the variable stressing in English of words adopted from French (see below), especially as end-stressed forms of the latter were also used mostly at the ends of lines; but this is not a completely satisfactory explanation, for though the words from French really did vary in stress in English pronunciation, the native words can hardly have done (since there is no evidence of the shifted stresses outside verse). The original model may rather have been the variation of stress in medieval Latin verse, which would have seemed to offer a respectable literary precedent, and one independent of so local a factor as the English uncertainty in the stressing of French words. The licence is found very early (there is an instance in the first of St. Godric's songs) and is freely practised by Orm, whose metrical models were Latin; but once established, it continued in use throughout Middle English poetry.

The commonest variation in stressing, in Middle English verse generally, is in words adopted from French. In Old French the main stress was placed on the final syllable of a word, unless it consisted of or contained the weak vowel known as 'feminine e', in which case the stress fell on the preceding syllable. But this end-stressing was alien to native English speech-habits (with the exceptions indicated above, notably verbs formed with a prefix), and quite soon English stress-patterns began to be applied to words from French; they were assimilated to such native analogues as were available. Verbs were to some degree exempt, but normally the main stress was shifted towards the beginning of the word, either by one syllable (if there was only one before the syllable that bore the French stress) or by two. In the latter, which was the normal case, the metrical value was not at first affected; in a word like *emperour* it does not matter to scansion whether the first or the third syllable has the main stress, so long as both have some

degree of stress and serve as metrical 'lifts'. But in words in which the stress shifted by only one syllable (*vértu* against *vertú, ríchesse* against *richésse, cíte* 'city' against *cité*) the metrical value was of course completely different. Both modes of stressing, the original French and the altered English accentuation, were current in Middle English and indeed often much later, but the English mode must rapidly have become the more usual in most words. Poets took advantage of the fluctuation to scan variable words as suited their convenience, but there was a marked tendency to use the end-stressed French forms at the ends of lines, where they were convenient for rhyme, and the English stressings elsewhere (though French stressings were not limited to the line-ends); in our no. 30, *cite* 'city' is stressed on the second at the end of l. 2, on the first early in l. 6. But this variation affects our songs less than might have been expected; the French vocabulary is not at all large, and in almost all cases the word either is one in which the stress did not shift (or shifted without affecting the metrical value), or already has its English stressing and presents no difficulty. Oddly enough it is in the Anglo-Norman song, no. 4(i), that most account has to be taken of differences between the French and English stress-systems.

Metre is of course also affected by the stressing of words within sentences, according to the meaning or the particular emphasis given; and it not infrequently happens, in Middle English verse, that strict metre requires one stressing, sense apparently another. Such divergences, which may set up a tension between the metrical and rhetorical patterns, are not necessarily faults; but there are instances in our songs where the metre requires a word to be stressed which one would have thought it was more natural to leave unstressed. Where it seems useful we indicate the stressing by an acute accent over the vowel of the metrically stressed word or syllable.

Apart from stress, the most important linguistic feature for the scansion of Middle English verse is the pronunciation of unstressed *e*. Readers untrained in Middle English grammar and linguistic history often seem to think that this *e* was used in an entirely arbitrary manner: that *e* could be inserted into the middle of a word, or *-e* (and even *-en*) added at the end of a word, entirely at will and to suit rhythmic convenience. It could not; its incidence was determined by etymology, or by the development of pronunciation, or by grammar. But many words varied in form, grammar was changing, and so was pronunciation. Where there was variation, a poet might take advantage of it, and poets did, very freely; but they were only choosing between real variants in actual speech. Even in the fifteenth century, when the pronunciation of final *-e* was largely an archaism, and probably almost entirely restricted to verse, it is rare to find that metre appears to require a spoken -e in a position in which it lacks historical or grammatical justification; there was obviously a survival of an accurate tradition. What is not rare in later Middle English, and especially in the fifteenth century, is to find e being added *in writing* without historical or grammatical justification,[60] and it is this arbitrary, or sometimes orthographic, use of written -e by the scribes that gives the impression that such a writer as Chaucer is suiting himself which -e's he pronounces, which he does not. It is dangerous to attempt to determine, from an ill-spelt text written by a later scribe, which e's were intended to be pronounced unless one has some knowledge of the linguistic and grammatical principles involved. In this book, as far as possible, we omit unpronounced e's;[61] if one has to be kept for some orthographic reason, it is italicized to show it is silent; and in addition we print *ë* to indicate a pronounced unstressed e, regularly at the ends of words and often also in other positions. But these markings are not used in the performing texts, where the laying-out of the syllables beneath the notes shows whether or not an e is to be separately pronounced.

It is not the function of such an introduction as this to give a detailed survey of the incidence of unstressed e in Middle English; individual points are discussed in the notes to the texts, as they arise, and general discussions are to be found in the historical grammars. Unstressed e in medial position (*loverd* 'lord', *woreld* 'world', *levedi* 'lady', *hevenes* 'heavens', *evere* 'ever' etc.) sometimes represents an unstressed vowel already present in early Old English, more usually a glide-vowel developed later; and there were often variant forms from which, by one process or another, it had been lost or in which it had not developed. Such variations are well illustrated by the forms cited, between about 1200 and 1400, by the historical dictionaries, the *Oxford English Dictionary* and the *Middle English Dictionary,* and are systematically classified and explained in the text-books of historical phonology.[62] Unstressed e followed by a consonant or consonants in word-endings (chiefly inflexions) such as -el, -ed, -est, -eth was normally kept in Middle English in words of two syllables (including forms in which an inflexion is added to a monosyllabic

stem), and for this reason, in our texts, we do not specially mark the e of such endings as pronounced; it may be assumed to be sounded. But in longer words (three or more syllables) it was normally lost by phonetic process in the course of Middle English, though it might be restored by the analogy of the shorter words which preserved the full forms of the inflexions. In the disyllabic forms its loss was a very protracted process which did not have much effect, especially in the South, until after 1400 and was never extended to all the possible cases;[63] but even in these forms the e was sometimes lost before 1400, and there are examples in our songs.

From the point of view of metre, the most important of the endings was -en, chiefly used as an inflexion (in verbs especially) but also occurring as the ending of uninflected words (e.g. *maiden*). For n differed from the other consonants that ended words by being unstable; if the word or syllable that it ended was unstressed, it could be lost. The phonetic principle seems in general to have been that it was lost before consonants, kept before vowels (as in the indefinite article in modern English), but in most cases the double forms, with and without n, that had arisen came sooner or later to be used without regard to the following sound. In some general cases, or in individual words, one of the two forms might drive out or predominate over the other: thus in Northern dialects the full -en was regular in the strong past participle, though Southern dialects preferred -e in this function and Midland dialects varied. But variation between forms with -en and forms with -e was the common result, and a poet might choose which he preferred, for convenience of rhyme or of metre. The importance of the loss of -n was that it left forms with final -e, which itself might be elided in connected speech or be lost by a further phonetic change, so that the variation between -en and -e might become a variation between a form with an additional syllable -en and an endingless form; and these ultimate variants had of course different metrical values. One of the commonest ways in which scribes 'mismetre' poems (including Chaucer's) is by using the wrong form of this ending, generally the full -en when it was not intended, though sometimes the reverse; by so doing they often prevent, or bring about, an elision against the poet's intention, or spoil a rhyme.

---

[60] Or often the use of a scribal abbreviation which originally had implied an -e but which in many cases evidently came to be used thoughtlessly, as a mere flourish; the -e's of printed texts are often equally automatic and uncritical expansions of these dubious MS abbreviations.

[61] We do this even when an -e that would normally end a word is lost by reason of elision. In so omitting elided -e we go against the normal practice of Middle English scribes, as remarked above; but it seemed better to indicate clearly the forms presupposed by the metre.

[62] Notably by Luick in his *Historische Grammatik der englischen Sprache,* especially §§ 451-9, 469-76.

[63] Thus modern English still retains a pronounced e in some past participles used as adjectives (e.g. *learned*) and in all superlatives (e.g. *highest, dearest*).

The most significant difference, again from the point of view of metre, between Middle English pronunciation and that of modern English is that in the former a great many words ended in a pronounced final -*e*, i.e. in an unstressed *e* (pronounced like the *a* of modern English *idea*) that came at the very end of a word, with no consonant after it. The nearest parallels are the -*e* of French, which continued to be pronounced until a much later date than in English and is still sounded in poetry (except comparatively recent poetry) and occasionally in declamation, and the surviving -*e* of modern German. As in these instances, Middle English -*e* was sometimes part of the stem of the word, and due to the word's etymology and history, sometimes a grammatical inflexion. In most cases, so long as final -*e* continued to be pronounced, there was no choice whether or not it should be used; it was a necessary part of the word or a necessary inflexion. But there were many circumstances in which variation did occur. Occasionally a word might have two sources, of different form (thus ME *will* is from OE *will*, ME *wille* from OE *willa*, two different formations on the same root). More often there was grammatical variation; in the process of simplifying grammar, one grammatical form might begin to displace another. Thus in nouns that had originally been 'strong' masculines and neuters the form of the nominative and accusative singular, which in most such words was endingless, increasingly replaced in use the dative, which added -*e*; it was not that the dative lost its -*e*, or that there was a choice whether or not to inflect the dative, but there was in practice a choice, in certain syntactic contexts, whether to use what was historically the dative or what was historically the accusative. By the later fourteenth century the dative had virtually disappeared, except in fossilized expressions, but in early Middle English it was still often used, and in the same literary work there may be variation between dative and accusative forms in the same context. Nouns that had been feminine in early Middle English, while grammatical gender was still preserved, commonly ended in -*e*, whether they were native or adopted from French; but many Old English feminine nouns had been endingless in the nominative singular though they added -*e* in the oblique cases of the singular (including often the accusative). In early Middle English there was a strong tendency to generalize the oblique form with -*e* in this type of noun and to use it also in the nominative (and accusative), thus making almost all feminine nouns end in -*e* throughout the singular; and some grammars of Middle English state this as if it were an invariable rule. But in fact the endingless nominative singular often remained and might be extended to other cases of the singular. Originally feminine nouns of this type may therefore be variable, in the singular, between forms with and without -*e*. In yet other cases differences in inflexion between one word and another used in the same grammatical function are because they belong, or originally belonged, to distinct declensions or conjugations that had not yet been assimilated to each other: thus in some types of verb the imperative singular was endingless, in others it ended in -*e*.[64]

A different type of grammatical variation, and one that was very common, occurred in adjectives. All plurals of adjectives ended in -*e*, unless it had been lost by phonetic process. But in the singular there were two forms, the relics of two different types of declension in Old English. The ordinary singular adjective (the 'strong' adjective as it is called in the merely arbitrary terminology adopted from German grammar) was endingless. But there was also a 'defining' form of the adjective (the so-called 'weak' adjective) used in special syntactic combinations in which there was some limitation or restriction of the sense: after the definite article or a demonstrative pronoun or a possessive, in combination with proper names or some nouns (e.g. *God*) used as names, or in address where Latin used the vocative. This 'weak' form of the adjective added -*e*. Thus one said *a good man* but *the* (*that*) *goodë man*. Some adjectives, however, always ended in -*e* because it was part of their stem, not an inflexion (so *deerë* 'dear', *sweetë*, *sheenë* 'beautiful', *triwë* 'true', etc.); and positive adverbs were formed from adjectives by adding -*e* (in this case a suffix).

All these are examples of variation in the use of -*e* determined by methods of word-formation or inflexion or grammatical usage. But final -*e* might also be lost by phonetic process, since it was completely unstressed. (1) If the word which it ended was itself weakly stressed in the sentence, the -*e* was lost early; and words that were often weakly stressed (conjunctions, pronouns, auxiliary verbs, etc.) developed two forms, a strong (stressed) form that kept -*e* and a weak form without it. But after they had become well-established, the two forms might achieve independent existence apart from the degree of stress they received; in particular the shorter forms developed under weak stress in time came to be used even in stressed position (e.g. *hir* 'her' < *hirë*, *wer* < *werë*, etc.). (2) In words originally of three syllables in

---

[64] 'Strong' verbs, and some verbs of the first OE first 'weak' conjugation, were endingless in the imperative singular; the rest (including some 'strong' verbs that had 'weak' present tenses) ended in -*e*.

which the first was long and stressed and the second had secondary stress,[65] unstressed *e* in the third syllable was lost very early in Middle English. A particular result of this phonetic process was that an adjective such as 'holy', of which the Old English plural was *hālige* and which, but for this process, would have had the plural **holïë* in Middle English, in fact has an uninflected plural *holi*, whereas 'merry', from Old English *mȳrige,* has the Middle English form *mirië* because the first syllable is short. But the distinctions of inflexion produced by the operation of this phonetic process were often obliterated in later usage by analogy; the *-e* might be restored to the words from which it had been lost. (3) Gradually, in the course of Middle English, final *-e* was lost not by particular processes, but by a general disuse; its articulation was so weakened that it disappeared. The loss began in the North, probably towards the middle of the thirteenth century (indeed there are already signs of it in MSS of St Godric's hymns[66]), and was virtually complete there by 1300. It also began early (before 1300) in the North-east and East Midlands; but in the South, including London, it is later and was not completed until the early fifteenth century. By its nature it must have been a change that occurred first in quick and less careful speech, and then probably first in phrasal groups that had the stress-patterns that encouraged loss of unstressed *e* in words of three or four syllables; in more careful speech, especially in declamation, it would have been kept longer, perhaps much longer.[67] In all dialects it is probable that for several generations forms with and without *-e* coexisted and were used according to the style of speech. Moreover dialects in which the *-e* was fairly generally lost could be influenced by more conservative dialects in which it was kept, especially as these included the language of London. Poets normally based their metre on the more formal modes of speech in which the *-e* was

maintained, but it would be surprising if they consistently did so in a time of fluctuating usage, and there is ample evidence that they did not.[68] After the *-e* had begun to be lost in the dialect concerned, a poet deliberately writing in a lighter style or aiming at a more colloquial effect might drop the *-e* when in a more formal style it would be kept. But to a large extent poets were guided by metrical convenience; at an earlier period they mostly kept the *-e* but dropped it occasionally, at a later they mostly dropped it but used it when it suited. There seem to have been some differences in the rate of loss between the various parts of speech, perhaps because they were apt to enter into different types of phrasal groups, some of which encouraged the loss of *-e,* others its retention; in late use it is particularly found in adjectives,[69] at an earlier date it seems especially likely to be lost in verbs, as in our no. 11. It is probably not merely poetic convenience that makes it more likely to be kept before stressed syllables and to be lost before unstressed; but if this reflects a real linguistic tendency, it was one very useful to poets writing in iambic or trochaic metre.

These are all processes of loss of final *-e* that are independent of the nature of the following sound. But throughout Middle English it could be lost before a somewhat more strongly stressed word beginning with a vowel or *h* by the process known as elision.[70] This, though mostly (but by no means entirely) evidenced by metre, was not a poetic licence, but a reflection of something that naturally occurred in connected speech; it was simply a running-together of the words, in which the very weakly stressed final *-e* disappeared before another vowel. Elision of *-e* before a word beginning with a vowel seldom fails to occur in Middle English verse, unless a pause intervenes to separate the words. Most poets treat the line-end as constituting a pause sufficient

---

[65] Secondary stress was not maintained on the second syllable when the first was short.

[66] Notably in *rych* for OE *rīce* 'kingdom' in MS Harley 322, which Zupitza dated probably to the late twelfth century. But this spelling *rych,* it must be said, does not look like a late twelfth-century form.

[67] Cf. the position in French, in which *-e* was lost towards 1600, but was long maintained in oratory and declamation and in verse.

[68] Thus in Chaucer, *-e* is sometimes certainly silent in words which historically should have it; and there are many lines which would be more regular in metre if the *-e* were treated as silent. Yet there can be no doubt that in Chaucer's speech the *-e* was still normally pronounced; this follows from technical arguments about the processes by which vowels lengthened in open syllables became phonemically distinct, and their bearing on Chaucer's rhyming. But it is significant that his rhyming, in the features concerned, is not fully consistent; he is relying on two modes of speech, in one of which the *-e* was preserved and the lengthening of the vowels was not phonemic, in the other of which the *-e* had been lost and the lengthening had become phonemic. Of these two modes, the former was evidently his own, or was normally his own.

[69] There are signs of this in our last group of songs, in which the pronunciation of *-e* is irregular.

[70] The accounts of Middle English elision are not very satisfactory. Either they are imprecise and fail to distinguish elision clearly from other sorts of loss of *-e* (as in Schipper, *History of English Versification,* Book I, ch. vii), or they deal with the practice of individual authors, or, though precisely expressed, they are too summary and general (e.g. Luick, *Historische Grammatik,* §§ 451-2). Luick in particular seems to rely especially on the evidence of Orm, obviously because his syllable-counting verse leaves no doubt when elision occurs. But Orm, who deliberately aimed at linguistic consistency, can hardly be taken as characteristic of Middle English poetry, even at his own time. Luick's object of course was merely to define the circumstances in which elision occurs, not to describe the varying practice of poets; but his definition is itself too restrictive.

in itself to prevent elision, even when the sense runs on; but a musician setting two consecutive verse-lines as a single unit to a continuous musical phrase may well ignore the end of the verse-line and practise elision over the line-division, as occurs in our no. 13, though this was certainly against the intention of the author of the words.[71] Similarly elision often fails at the mid-line caesura, and more rarely at other points of the line if there is a sense-pause. But sometimes poets elide -*e* even when one would have thought that a pause should naturally be interposed between the words. Probably, as they became consciously aware (as obviously they did) that forms or words without -*e* had developed by elision, they began to extend their use a little and to employ them, when it was convenient, even before a pause if the next word began with a vowel or *h*[72]—just as forms without -*e* that had developed under weak stress were generalized and used in stressed position. The converse is the use of the full forms with -*e* before a vowel in cases in which there is no possibility of a sense-pause (e.g. *miȝtë ich* 'if I could'). Elision before a vowel is so common in Middle English that one is apt to assume that it would always occur; but there is really no good reason why it should. The full forms of words were preserved before consonants and before pauses (i.e. in the great majority of cases), and could perfectly well be restored before vowels in precise and careful speech in which the words were deliberately distinguished; and the general practice of keeping the full forms in writing even when elision was intended must indicate that, in theory at least, they could always be used, if desired, before a vowel.[73] And if elision could thus be avoided in careful speech, it could equally be avoided in poetry. Medieval Latin verse, which must often have served as a model, permits both elision and hiatus, sometimes in the same poem.[74] In Middle English verse failure of elision before a vowel is not lightly to be assumed, but there seems no reason to doubt that it could exceptionally occur.

Elision before a word beginning with *h* differs chiefly in that it is less regular. It is sometimes said[75] that it occurs only before weak-stressed words, but though it is most common in this case it can also occur before stressed words — usually, it is true, words which are commonly weak-stressed though they happen to be used in metrically stressed position. It is clear that elision before *h* depends on weak aspiration (if not on complete loss of *h*), which is most likely when the word is unstressed; and that it will fail if the word is stressed and the aspiration strong. But loss of *h* from stressed words is found in many English dialects from early in the fifteenth century, and an *h* that is between vowels has always been specially vulnerable; it is hardly surprising, therefore, that elision before the *h* of stressed words should occasionally be found in the late thirteenth and fourteenth centuries, even though this may well imply weakening or complete loss of the *h*.

Elision does not affect only the -*e* of words of two or more syllables; it can also affect the vowels of weak-stressed monosyllables,[76] so that we get such forms as *þoþre* < *þe oþre* 'the others', *tabiden* < *to abiden* 'to abide', *softe* < *so ofte* (in our no. 7, 1. 33), *þoli* < *þe holi* 'the holy' (in our no. 13, 1. 28 and no. 15, 1. 18). The last of these clearly demonstrates the possibility of elision involving the *h* of a stressed word. By the same or similar phonetic processes certain negative forms of verbs, such as *nis* < *ne is* 'is not', *nabben* < OE *nabban* < *ne habban* 'have not', and *not* < OE *nāt* < *ne wāt* 'know not', had already developed in Old English and remain very common in Middle English. Other elisions of the negative particle *ne* are more familiar because they survive in modern English (e.g. *never, nought*).

THE SPELLING OF THE ENGLISH TEXTS

Middle English spelling was very variable. Its conventions differed from district to district and from time to time, and their application depended to some degree on

---

[71] For details, see the commentary on no. 13 (p. 168).

[72] In effect, this amounts to an over-simplified rule of usage: 'forms without -*e* are used before a word beginning with a vowel or *h*', the qualifying clause 'if no sense-pause intervenes' being dropped. Such over-simplifications are often made when men begin to rationalize linguistic usage. In Old French, the forms of certain words without -*e* that were produced by elision were completely generalized and might be used even before consonants. This can hardly be demonstrated for Middle English; the general loss of -*e* occurred so much earlier than in French that when forms without -*e* are found that are not due to some recognized special cause (e.g. weak stress) it is natural to explain them as early examples of the general loss of -*e*. But the widespread existence of doublets without -*e* produced by elision may have played a part in easing the way for the general loss of -*e*.

[73] Cf. the common practice of the copyists of the music, who often ignore elision even when it is obviously necessary.

[74] Norberg, *Introduction*, pp. 33-37.

[75] As by Luick, § 452, who is perhaps partly influenced by a desire to rationalize the process, but more by the usage of Orm. It is also true of Gower that he allows elision before *h* only when the words which it begins are weak-stressed (Macaulay, *Works of John Gower*, ii. cxxv).

[76] Luick, § 451.

the judgement of the individual scribe. Moreover the spoken forms that were being represented by the spelling themselves varied according to dialect and date. Much uncertainty was occasioned by the clash, or rather mingling, of native and French traditions of orthography; and some particular aberrations of spelling, in individual MSS, were caused by the attempts of Anglo-Norman scribes to spell a language whose pronunciation. they imperfectly understood. Recent important work has shown that there was much more order in the apparent disorder than was previously supposed; nevertheless it remains true that to anyone who is not a professional philologist the variations, inconsistencies, and ambiguities of Middle English spelling can be very daunting.The situation is made worse by the fact that most scribes, when copying a text, tried to alter its spellings to the system to which they were themselves accustomed; but as they seldom, if ever, were able to free themselves entirely from the influence of the spellings present in their exemplars, the common result was an inconsistent mixture of forms. Nevertheless the alteration of the original spellings, even if imperfectly carried out, meant in many cases that the dialectal forms intended by the original author were replaced by others that might be very different; and in the case of verse texts the linguistic basis of the metre and rhyming might be destroyed.

It is, however, the normal practice of editors of Middle English texts to preserve the spellings used by the final copyist; if there are more MSS than one, they usually choose one of them as a 'base' MS and follow its spellings except when they are patently erroneous (and sometimes even then). There are good reasons for the practice, especially from the point of view of the philologist; and it provides an editor with a simple and straightforward rule of working. It would be very arbitrary to impose a normalized orthography on a language which lacked one, and no one system of spelling could be devised which would suit all dialects and all periods. There have not been many attempts even to restore the original forms of texts known, or generally thought, to survive in dialects different from those in which they were written;[77] most medievalists regard such reconstructions as too hypothetical and uncertain, and they certainly involve much more work. Even more moderate alterations of the MS spellings, as in Skeat's edition of *Havelok,* are regarded as somewhat dubious departures from correct method. But what is easy and

safe for the editor, and useful for the philologist, is difficult for the literary student, who is not only given the task of recognizing aberrant or strange spellings but may also be presented with a text which its own author might barely acknowledge, and which may seriously misrepresent the forms that he intended.

To follow the normal practice in this book has seemed impossible. If the words are to be fitted to the music, the forms required by metre must be restored; and it is a natural extension to use spellings that indicate as accurately as possible the spoken forms on which the metre and rhyming rest. It is for this reason, as explained above, that I have as far as possible eliminated all unpronounced *e*'s from the spellings. In cases in which it seemed expedient to keep an *e* that is not pronounced, it has been italicized in the 'literary' texts of Part I as a warning that it is silent; and in addition a final *e* that is pronounced (and in many cases a medial *e* also) is printed as *ë*. In general, spellings inconsistent with metre or rhyme, or with what appears, from the evidence, to have been the original dialect, have been replaced. In two instances (nos. 6a and 10(ii)), in which the extant versions are in dialects markedly different from the original, an attempt has been made to restore a more consistent text, in the one case Kentish, in the other Northern, following the hints of the MSS. But I have not attempted to impose any form of normalized orthography; in every case I have worked from the spellings of the extant MS or MSS, though I have held myself free to alter them as seemed necessary. I was the more willing to do this because texts giving the unaltered spellings of the MSS are in almost all cases readily available in print, and are accessible to those who require them.

In addition to replacing spellings inconsistent with the verse-technique, it also seemed desirable, in such a book as this, to do away with those that might cause special difficulty to readers who were not professional students of Middle English. Thus to spell such a word as 'right' as *rith* or *ryth* is common enough in certain Middle English dialects, but it can be very confusing, and may sometimes cause even a trained philologist to check. I have replaced such forms by others more easily recognizable. 'Inverted' or 'reverse' spellings (those that are the opposite of phonetic) may give valuable evidence of the falling-together of sounds previously distinct, but to interpret them requires special knowledge, and I have removed them from our texts.[78] Or to take another case, the use of *ch* to represent the palatal spirants in such

---

[77] The most notable is C. T. Onions's restored text — by far the most readable — of parts of *The Owl and the Nightingale* ('An Experiment in Textual Reconstruction', *Essays and Studies* xxii. 86-102); but it is praised rather than emulated.

[78] Thus in no. 13 the scribe uses ʒ as an 'inverted' spelling for original *w* in *deuʒ* 'dew', &c.; I restore *w*.

words as *nicht* 'night' and *þocht* 'thought' is common enough in Middle English and is paralleled in Welsh, Gaelic, and German orthography, but it is ambiguous; in Middle English the more frequent use of *ch* was as in modern English, as in *rich* or *choose*. A reader who is not a philologist cannot possibly tell that *sichen* 'to sigh' has *ch* pronounced as in *rich*, but *loch* 'laughed' has *ch* pronounced as in Gaelic *loch* or in German *doch*. Where I could, I have tried to replace ambiguous as well as abnormal spellings.

I have also been influenced by the desire to make the spelling as indicative as possible of the pronunciation; for there can be no doubt that medieval poems, and especially perhaps songs, sound better if they are read or sung in the original pronunciation, and experience shows that professional singers prefer to sing them in as close as possible an approximation to the original pronunciation, rather than in some modified form of modern pronunciation. It is for this reason that notes on pronunciation are appended to the texts, on pp. 317-21 below. But it is very difficult to give instructions for the pronunciation of Middle English that are based on its spelling, because it was imperfectly phonetic. If one is to have any chance, it is necessary to do what little is possible to make it more phonetic without altering it radically and without introducing conventions which, though they might have some justification in Middle English practice, would be of doubtful assistance to a modern reader. I have not made many changes, but even so it may well be thought that I have gone too far, for I have certainly introduced conventions unknown in the period itself.

(1) I have distinguished *u* from *v*, and *i* from *j*, as vowel and consonant respectively, though this is a convention unknown to scribes before 1400 and not adopted by English printers until the seventeenth century.

(2) Except in certain early texts, Middle English spelling failed to distinguish between two pairs of vowels: 'long close *e*' (denoted by philologists ME *ẹ̄*) and 'long open *e*' (denoted ME *ę̄*) were both spelt *e* (or *ee*), and similarly 'long close *o*' (denoted ME *ọ̄*) and 'long open *o*' (denoted ME *ǭ*) were both spelt *o* (or *oo*). But though they were spelt alike (owing to an unfortunate influence from Old French spelling), the distinction between the sounds was significant for meaning, and in poetry for rhyme, and it is desirable that a singer or reciter should be able to distinguish between them. In order, therefore, to give some indication of which should be used, I have adopted the device of spelling the two

close vowels as *ee* and *oo*, though this is a convention that was not established in English spelling until the sixteenth century, and then only imperfectly. But I have made some exceptions: I have refrained from doubling the *e* in the pronouns *me, we, he, she* (though I use *þee* for 'thee', in distinction from *þe* for the definite article) and in the verb *be*, though all these have the close vowel (ME *ẹ̄*), and similarly I have not doubled the *o* in *do, doth, to, moder* 'mother', *oþer* 'other', *broþer* 'brother', though again all these have the close vowel (ME *ọ̄*). My reason for making these exceptions has been to avoid spellings which, though they are to be found in medieval texts and indeed later, might seem too strange to a modern reader in such common words. Apart from these cases, single *e* and *o* are used to represent the open vowels (and also, of necessity, the short vowels *ĕ* and *ŏ*, which had the same quality as the long open vowels). It should be noted that as some words varied in pronunciation, according to dialect, between close ME *ẹ̄* and open ME *ę̄*, the same word will sometimes be found differently spelt in the various texts, according to my judgement of the form appropriate to the dialect concerned.

(3) Middle English also had two distinct diphthongs which in most texts were not distinguished in spelling but were both written *eu* (or *ew*). The less common of the two had an open first element and is denoted by philologists ME *ęu*. In the few cases in which it occurs in our songs I write it *eaw*, a spelling found in some Middle English MSS.[79]

(4) In Middle English spelling, especially after about 1250, an unphonetic *o* was often substituted for *u* (mostly when it represented a short vowel) in the neighbourhood of similarly-formed letters (e.g. *n, m, w*) to avoid difficulties in reading the script. I have often replaced this *o* by the original and phonetic spelling *u*. I have done this regularly in the earliest texts (those written by about the middle of the thirteenth century, i.e. nos. 1-11) and also in some cases in later texts, especially if the scribe himself varied between *o* and *u* (as in the Advocates' MS of no. 19). But in the later texts, if the scribe was consistent in his use of *o*, I have kept it in words in which it still remains in modern English (e.g. *love, come, sone* 'son', *company*) and in which no one can doubt that it really stands for *ŭ*; but even in the later texts I have replaced it by *u* in words in which it seemed desirable not to use a spelling which might give a false impression of the pronunciation.

These modifications of course do not remove all the ambiguities of Middle English spelling or make it fully phonetic. Particular problems are discussed in the

---

[79] But in no. 13, in which ME *ęu* is rhymed with ME *ęu*, I use *ew* for both sounds.

introductions or notes to the individual texts. In each case I have tried to produce a text spelt with reasonable consistency, starting from the forms used in the MS or MSS that give the song. But I have not tried to impose a single uniform system, and there are certainly inconsistencies between one piece and another — some of them no doubt of my own making.

The special Middle English letters *ȝ*, *þ*, and (in tests before 1300) *ð* are retained in the 'literary' texts of Part I; indeed in some cases they have been introduced by emendation. They are easy to learn; those who can learn, for example, the Greek alphabet need not be troubled by these three special English letters. But the native (originally runic) letter for *w*, named *wynn*, which is used, for example, in the Corpus MS of no. 13, has been replaced by *w*, as is the common practice. In the 'performing' texts in Part III, *þ* and *ð* are replaced by *th*, and *ȝ* by *y*, *gh*, or *w*, as the case may require. But it is to be observed that when early thirteenth-century forms such as *laȝe*, *sorȝe*, and *dreȝen* are replaced by *lawe* 'law', *sorwe* 'sorrow', and *dreyen* 'endure', there is involved a modernization not only of the spelling, but also of the pronunciation; for in such words (though not in most) the *ȝ* of forms earlier than about 1250 (and in some conservative dialects still later) represented a distinct sound, unknown in modern English, which in later Middle English changed in some cases to *w*, and in others (as a first stage) to the consonant *y* (i.e. [j], to use the phonetic symbol).[80] But apart from this replacement of the special letters *þ*, *ð*, and *ȝ*, it has been our object to use the same spellings in the 'performing' as in the 'literary' texts, and we have made only one or two minor exceptions in special cases. My modifications of the MS spellings have in part been occasioned by this desire to use in the 'literary' texts spellings that could also be used without change (other than the modernization of the letters and purely typographical changes) in the 'performing' texts.

In listing the variant readings of the MSS I do not necessarily record mere variations of spelling, though I have often recorded them if they seemed of possible significance (e.g. for the dating of the MS, or in showing the affiliations of the MSS, or in explaining corruptions). It has been my purpose to record all spelling-variants that reflect real variations of word-form (i.e. variations in the spoken word), though in some cases in which MSS varied consistently in a linguistic feature I have recorded the variation only once (with a note 'and so throughout'), and of course all variations of substance.

THE LATIN TEXTS AND THEIR SCANSION

Of the Latin texts in our collection, *Perspice, Christicola* (no. 9) and *Peperit virgo* (no. 16b(ii)) are each extant only in a single MS. The other three — *Planctus ante nescia* (addendum to no. 4), *Stabat juxta Christi crucem* (no. 10(i)), and *Angelus ad virginem* (no. 15(i)) — have been re-edited, and in each case I have consulted more MSS than were used by Dreves for his texts in *Analecta Hymnica Medii Aevi,* though it is possible, and indeed probable, that there exist other early MSS than those which I have found listed. I have attempted to apply a stricter editorial method than Dreves seems to have done; and it is hoped that our texts will be found better. The spelling has been normalized by the substitution of *æ* and *oe*, as required, for the medieval spelling *e*, and I have distinguished *i* and *j*, *u* and *v*, as vowel and consonant respectively. I have also followed Dreves in substituting *t* for *c* in appropriate cases in *Planctus ante nescia* and in *Stabat juxta Christi crucem*; in the former text in particular, the MSS themselves vary between *c* and *t* in the words concerned. But in the other three pieces I have followed the MSS (in the case of no. 15(i), the Arundel MS, which I took as a base) in using *c*. In the lists of variants given for the three songs that are extant in more MSS than one, I do not record mere variations of spelling.

Perspice, Christicola was written in England, presumably at Reading Abbey; *Peperit virgo* by the Englishman Richard de Ledrede (Leatherhead) in his Irish diocese of Ossory. *Planctus ante nescia* is undoubtedly of French authorship, and the attribution to Godefroy of St. Victor can hardly be questioned. *Stabat juxta Christi crucem* and *Angelus ad virginem* are anonymous; they may be of French origin, but both were known early in England and English authorship is possible (and indeed, in the case of the former, probable).

The extent to which the parallel English and Latin texts agree, or diverge, in metre can only be judged if the

---

[80] There is no automatic way of modernizing *ȝ*, and specialist advice is necessary. Mr. R. T. Davies produces some extraordinary forms in his text of *Edi be thu* (*Medieval English Lyrics*, pp. 64-66) by substituting *s* for *ȝ*, apparently on a false analogy from certain fourteenth-century texts in which *ȝ* has been printed where *z* should be because the scribes of the MSS made no distinction between the forms of *z* and *ȝ* (just as they often make no distinction between the forms of *y* and *þ*). It may be pointed out that, except in a few anomalous texts unlikely to come the way of a musicologist, *ȝ* was not used for, and cannot be replaced by, *g*. Thus *ȝiue* should be modernized as *yive*, not as *give*, unless one is aiming to alter the forms of the words as well as to replace obsolete letters; *yive* is one of the native forms of the word, *give* a form adopted from Danish which eventually drove out the native forms. In the Middle English alphabet both *ȝ* and *g* were used, and had distinct phonetic values; the whole point of having the two letters was to distinguish their uses, and misuse of the one for the other was rare.

Latin as well as the English texts are not only accurate, but are correctly scanned. There is no reason to doubt the text of *Perspice, Christicola.* That of *Peperit virgo* might be thought to be guaranteed by its being an official copy in the Red Book of Ossory; but in fact the Red Book's text has, in my view, an error in the lay-out of the first stanza. No single MS of the other three Latin songs is fully reliable; apart from mechanical miscopyings, the commonest errors are alterations of word-order, the substitution of synonyms, and attempts of various other sorts to improve on the original. Where necessary, notes are given to the texts to explain the readings adopted.

Wilhelm Meyer, in what has generally been accepted as the standard treatment of the metre of medieval Latin accentual verse,[81] assumed that the accentuation of Latin words was essentially the same at all periods, apart from minor details; and in consequence he was obliged to assume that in the rhythmical verse, 'the word accent and the verse ictus may conflict except at the end of the verse or half-verse, where they must coincide; it is this *close* that determines the rhythm of the verse.'[82] The concept of a 'verse ictus' existing independently of, and in conflict with, the stressing of the words that make up the verse is hardly a happy one; what in effect is meant is that in individual lines there may be variations from the basic metrical pattern, and that these variations may occur anywhere in the line (or half-line) except at the close, where for obvious reasons (especially rhyme) the basic rhythm must be preserved. Such a doctrine is reasonable in itself, and is in conformity with the variation in metrical rhythm that was obviously allowed in vernacular accentual verse, and notably in English verse. Nevertheless Meyer's views are unsatisfactory, as has been shown by Professor Norberg of Stockholm in an admirable discussion.[83] The basic assumption, that the Classical system of stressing was preserved in all essentials, is itself unsound. It is not true, on this assumption, that at the close of the line the 'word-accent' always coincides with the 'metrical ictus'; there are cases in which a false rhythm would be produced even at the end of the line, where it is plainly impossible. Indeed, the study of the rhymes in medieval Latin accentual verse is sufficient to demonstrate that they do not regularly depend on Classical stressings, just as they do not regu-

larly depend on Classical quantities. There are other cases in which the rhythms produced in the line as a whole would not be acceptable as metrical variations. And what particularly concerns us is that, in accentual Latin verse written for mensural music, the assumption that the words always had their Classical stressings time and again produces unacceptable clashes between the rhythm of the words and the rhythm of the music;[84] for what matters in this case is plainly not an abstract 'metrical ictus' but the actual rhythm of the syllables that have to be sung to the notes. In many cases the music presupposes perfect metrical regularity, and even in other cases in which the music would allow of metrical variation it is clear enough that the poet was in fact writing to a fixed accentual scheme (as in the balanced half-stanzas of *Planctus ante nescia,* or the 'regular' sequence *Stabat juxta Christi crucem*); but if so, then the words cannot have their Classical stressings, and the notion of a 'word-accent' that can differ from the 'metrical ictus' must have been unknown to the song-writers.

It is a remarkable fact that in the otherwise very useful handbooks of medieval Latin, practically no attention is given to changes in pronunciation, other than the few that affected spelling, no doubt because Latinists are accustomed to deal with a written language, not a spoken one. A clear account of the varying pronunciation of medieval Latin is much to be desired. A great deal is in fact known, but it is to be found in the writings of philologists dealing with the Romance languages and with English, who cannot ignore the changes in spoken Latin, since they determine the forms and the pronunciation of Romance and English words derived or adopted from Latin. As far as word-stress is concerned, there are important classes of words in which the stress shifted in later Latin, as the forms taken by the words in the Romance languages show; and though medieval Latin accentual verse normally relies on the Classical stressings, which were known from the rules of the grammarians, it quite often takes advantage of altered stressings, some of them in general use throughout Western Europe, others more localized in occurrence.[85] Instances that occur in our songs are discussed in the notes to the individual texts. One of the more common is the shift of stress on to the penultimate

[81] W. Meyer, *Gesammelte Abhandlungen zur mittellateinischen Rythmik* (Berlin, 1905, 1936).

[82] C. H. Beeson, *A Primer of Medieval Latin,* p. 27, summarizing Meyer's doctrine (cf. p. 5, where he states that for the metric he has 'depended largely on Wilhelm Meyer').

[83] Dag Norberg, *Introduction à l'Étude de la Versification Latine Médiévale* (Stockholm, 1958); see especially chapter i.

[84] So in *Perspice, Christicola* in ll. 6, 7, and 11, and in *Angelus ad virginem* in ll. 6, 24, 30, &c.

[85] Norberg, pp. 10-28, gives an important discussion of many of the cases.

syllable of words ending in *-ia*. Norberg[86] treats such stressings as *sophía, melodía* (with a long stressed *i*) as a particular case of the influence of Greek accentuation on medieval Latin stressing, and *María* as an instance of the arbitrary stressing of proper names of non-Latin origin. But the same stressing can affect native Latin words such as *gratía*, which on Norberg's view would have to be explained by analogy, as would the rarer shift of stress to an *i* in hiatus before *-um*, as in *mensíum, mortalíum*.[87] But it is doubtful whether Norberg's explanation is correct. The shift of stress is rather a tendency proper to medieval Latin pronunciation itself, and to be explained from the phonetic structure of the Romance languages, especially French (or its antecedent, Gallo-Roman). It is associated with the deliberate restoration, in a 'reformed' learned pronunciation of Latin (based largely on the spelling), of the unstressed ('atonic') vowels of penultimate syllables; these vowels, in late Latin or Gallo-Roman, had either become consonants or had been lost altogether by syncope.[88] The consequence of these changes in popular speech was the virtual disappearance of words stressed on the third-last syllable ('proparoxytones'), since the second-last syllable had been cut out; by Old French all words were stressed either on the last syllable ('oxytones') or on the second-last ('paroxytones'). It can only have been by a deliberate and conscious effort that men who were native speakers of Gallo-Roman or, later, of Old French were able to maintain proparoxytones in the 'learned' pronunciation of Latin; the slightest 'popularization' of pronunciation would lead either to the renewed syncope or consonantalization of the unstressed vowel of the second-last syllable, or to a stress-shift designed, however unconsciously, to move the stress to the second-last or the last syllable, on which they were accustomed to put it in the vernacular language. Such stress-shift is a

characteristic and distinguishing feature of Old French 'learned' words directly adopted from literary Latin,[89] and it undoubtedly also occurred in the French pronunciation of Latin itself. A shift of stress to the second-last syllable would be most likely in words ending in Latin *-a*, since it alone remained regularly as a final unstressed vowel (Old French *-e*) with separate syllabic value in Gallo-Roman and Old French,[90] but it might occasionally occur before other endings, including *-um*, since in certain circumstances these could survive to give, also, Old French unstressed final *-e*.[91] A further example of such stress-shift to a deliberately retained or restored penultimate vowel is *dextéra* (in rhyme with *fera*) in *Planctus ante nescia*, l. 42; it is explicable only as a stressing unconsciously modelled on such French feminine nouns and adjectives as *man(i)ere* and *legiere* (modern French *manière* and *légère*).

But even in the case of words with the Latin feminine ending *-a*, which was so easily identifiable with the French feminine *-e*, the 'popularization' of stressing did not always operate to produce paroxytones. The normal effect of stress-shift in the medieval French pronunciation of Latin was to produce oxytones, i.e. words stressed on the final syllable; and this is especially relevant to the scansion of our songs, since they are of French or English provenance. In Old French the stressing of the last full syllable (i.e. the last syllable whose vowel was not the obscure *e*) had become so regular and so much an inevitable feature of French speech-habits that it was carried over into Latin, and despite attempts at reform remained characteristic of the French pronunciation of Latin into modern times.[92] Its most important effect, from the point of view of metre, was on words of two syllables, which in Classical Latin, with rare exceptions, were stressed on the first, but in this French pronunciation of Latin on the second.[93] But other words

---

[86] Op. cit., pp. 18-19.

[87] See the note to *Angelus ad virginem* (no. 15(i)), l. 42. In this song the irregular stressing could be avoided by reading *mensium novem* for *novem mensium*, but the MSS agree on the latter word-order; in other instances, such as that cited in the note referred to, the text cannot be altered.

[88] Vowels in hiatus were consonantalized in late Latin; in particular *i* in hiatus became [j] (M. K. Pope, *From Latin to Modern French*, § 220). All vowels that had not been consonantalized were effaced in the unstressed penultimate syllable in the course of Gallo-Roman, though some earlier than others (Pope, §§ 250, 261-4).

[89] Cf., for example, the French stressing of *Proserpíne*, in contrast to Latin *Prosérpina*. The modern French stressing of such words as *philosophie, melodie*, &c. testifies to the shift of the stress to the *i*; and so (allowing for the later operation of English stress-shift) do the modern English stressings, which presuppose in Old French the same stressings as in Modern French.

[90] Pope, § 251.

[91] Pope, § 259. Cf. the French stress-shift in adjectives in *-ide* < Latin *-ĭdum*, e.g. *solíde* < *sólidum* and *liquíde* < *líquĭdum*, both of them adoptions from Latin into Old French.

[92] Pope, § 648.

[93] Norberg, rather surprisingly, does not explicitly recognize this characteristic French stress-shift. On pp. 25-27 he cites examples of disyllables stressed on the second, but explains them as due to sentence-phonetics, the coalescence of two successive words into a phrasal unit (which he calls a 'metrical word') with the stressing /x\ (or more rarely x/x\); and in particular he sets up a principle that after a stressed monosyllable a disyllable may take metrical stress on the second syllable. This is certainly the commonest case, doubtless because, in iambic or trochaic verse, the end-stressed

properly stressed on the penult, such as *lavábo* or *catérva*, could also undergo a shift of stress to the final syllable, thus *lavabó* and *catervá* (with, in consequence, a secondary stress on the first, so that the words might scan \x/ instead of x/x). Words properly stressed on the antepenult, like *cánticum*, had always been capable of taking a light secondary stress on the final syllable, thus /x\; the effect of the French end-stressing was merely to reverse the importance of the two stresses, \x/, leaving the metrical value, in the ordinary case, unaffected.

The medieval English pronunciation of Latin was undoubtedly based on the French.[94] As a result of the Norman Conquest, English cathedral and monastic schools came under the control of French-speaking clerics, and their influence was reinforced by the international dominance of the great French centres of learning, especially the University of Paris. French was the language of instruction in English schools; the chronicler Ralph Higden, in his *Polychronicon* (c. 1352), tells us that English children, 'contrary to the usage of all other nations', had to construe Latin into French, not their own language, and his translator John of Trevisa adds that this custom had continued until the Plague of 1349, but had since been somewhat changed, so that by 1385, when he was writing, the use of French was being replaced by English in 'all the grammar-schools of England'. It is not surprising, therefore, in view of this long French dominance, that the medieval English pronunciation of Latin should have been, to begin with, essentially the same as the French. Its features are well-known both from the pronunciation of Latin words adopted into English, and from the traditional English pronunciation of Latin,[95] which, allowing for the results of English sound-changes since 1400 (which affected the English pronunciation of Latin as well as English itself) and for certain reforms, mostly minor, introduced in the

sixteenth and seventeenth centuries, is the direct descendant of the medieval English pronunciation. But even in medieval times there were, or there developed, differences between the French and English pronunciations of Latin which reflected the different phonetic systems of French and English themselves. The most important concerns vowel-quantity: whereas the French pronunciation of Latin almost certainly failed to make significant distinctions of vowel-length, the English did—not, however, in accordance with the Classical quantities, but with purely native tendencies which in part represented a survival of those of the Anglo-Saxon school-pronunciation of Latin.[96] Again, the English pronunciation seems for the most part to have preserved Latin *qu* as [kw], though it was apparently sometimes influenced by the French pronunciation [k]. As for the French end-stressing of Latin words, its effects on the English pronunciation of Latin must have been in most cases very temporary, for it was counteracted by the English tendency to shift the stress towards the beginning of the word, which affects English words adopted from Latin much as it does those adopted from French and undoubtedly also influenced the English pronunciation of Latin itself. In words of two syllables, the English stress-shift, operating on French end-stressed forms, would automatically restore the Classical Latin stressing on the first syllable. Similarly, in words properly stressed on the antepenult, the English stress-shift would reverse the French tendency to move the main stress to the final syllable; but in some cases relics of the end-stressing can be detected in later English pronunciation.[97] But in words properly stressed on the penult, such as *caterva*, the results were more complex: for if the English stress-shift operated on a French end-stressed pronunciation *catervá*, the result was *cáterva*, and indeed in an early seventeenth-century phonetic transcription of the

---

forms of disyllables were most useful after monosyllables. But they did not occur only in this case, as Norberg himself shows (p. 27). He has, as I think, missed the real reason for the shift of stress in disyllables; it is significant that the named authors from whom he cites examples are French.

[94] The Anglo-Saxon pronunciation of Latin is not here in question. It was probably more correct than the contemporary Gallic pronunciation; the first of the attempts to reform continental Latin usage, including pronunciation, was carried out under the aegis of Charlemagne by the Englishman Alcuin (Pope, §§ 21, 646).

[95] By this, it is nowadays necessary to explain, is not meant the pronunciation now almost universal in the schools of the English-speaking countries, which is a 'reformed' or 'new' pronunciation introduced in the later nineteenth century and gradually extended in use during this century, but the 'old' pronunciation which it has displaced, and which is now used mostly by older men, especially in England itself.

[96] Cf. Luick, §§ 423-5, especially § 425. The consequence was that for many centuries English schoolmasters and schoolboys taught and learnt that vowels were long which in practice they pronounced short, and that vowels were short which in practice they pronounced long (or as diphthongs). Whereas in France they learnt that some vowels were short, and others long, when in practice they made no significant distinction at all.

[97] Words ending in *-ia* had a secondary stress on the *a*, which was long (the reflex of ME *ā*) as late as the seventeenth century, and indeed is still so pronounced in some American dialects (cf. Dobson, *English Pronunciation 1500-1700*, ii. §§ 1, 271), and other final vowels were sometimes long, against Classical quantities, in the early seventeenth-century English pronunciation of Latin (Dobson, *The Phonetic Writings of Robert Robinson*, p. xx). The lengthenings are most likely to have occurred under full final stress, though they could perhaps have occurred under secondary stress.

English pronunciation of Latin the word is given with an unstressed second syllable.[98] In such words the preservation or restoration of the correct Classical stressings must have been due to a deliberate rejection of the French stressings or to a later reform by the sixteenth-century humanists. It is probable that in the medieval English pronunciation there was a good deal of uncertainty in the stressing of Latin owing to the interplay of knowledge of the Classical rules, of French end-stressed forms, and of native speech-habits.

Other features of the medieval French and English pronunciations of Latin affect rhyming. Latin *c* before *e, i,* and *æ* had become first [ts] and then [s], and Latin *t* before unstressed *i* in hiatus, as in *gratia,* also passed through [ts] to [s], so that, for example, *-cia* and *-tia* could rhyme together. Latin *æ* became an open vowel [ɛ], and so was identified, and could rhyme, with Latin *ĕ,* which had also become an open vowel.[99] Latin *oe* became a close vowel [e], identified and capable of rhyming with Latin *ē* (as in the rhyme *lēnis : poenis* in *Planctus ante nescia,* ll. 44-45). Latin *ē* itself had become a close vowel in Romance and was so pronounced in the earlier medieval French pronunciation of Latin, but later it was identified with the Old French open vowel *ę.* In the English pronunciation of Latin there was a corresponding fluctuation, Latin *ē* (when kept as a long vowel)

being sometimes identified with Middle English *ę̄* (the long close vowel), sometimes with Middle English *ę̄* (the long open vowel); the latter was regarded as the more correct pronunciation in the sixteenth and seventeenth centuries, but the former evidently persisted. In later Middle English, when Latin words are rhymed with English in macaronic verse, Latin *ē* sometimes rhymes with Middle English *ę̄* (thus *Stephanē : be*), sometimes with Middle English *ē* (thus *Johannēs : pes* 'peace'). Latin *ō* was regularly made an open vowel in the French and English pronunciation of Latin; in the English, if it was kept as a long vowel, it was identified with Middle English *ǭ* (the long open vowel). Latin *u* was regularly made [y] (the vowel of French *du*) in the French pronunciation of Latin; in the English, this was replaced by *ŭ* (originally as in *pull*) when the vowel was followed by a consonant belonging to the same syllable, and ang-licized by the substitution of the diphthong [iu], at least in the dialects of the East Midlands, when the Latin *u* ended a syllable. Vowels followed by a consonant in unstressed final syllables seem commonly to have been made short even when they were long in Classical Latin; the rhyme of *grăvĭs* with *clāvīs* in *Planctus ante nescia,* ll. 18-19, well illustrates the loss of the Classical distinctions of quantity.

---

[98] Dobson, *Robinson,* p. xix, n.1; p. 27, l. 5.

[99] In the seventeenth century Latin *æ* and *oe* were both, by a rule of the schoolmasters, made regularly 'long', i.e. were identified with Latin *ē* (then pronounced with the reflex of ME *ę̄* in the more 'correct' mode of the English pronunciation of Latin), but this was a deliberate reform, intended no doubt to remove a discrepancy between the pronunciation and the quantities taught for the writing of verse. The development of Latin *æ* in late Latin had been to identify with *ĕ,* not *ē.*

INTRODUCTION TO THE MUSIC

F. Ll. HARRISON

INTRODUCTION TO THE MUSIC

(References to pitch in this Introduction and in the Musical Commentary are made in small italics. These may be grouped to indicate the grouping in the original notation, e.g. *f gfg a*. Where it is desirable to show the octave of the pitch, the following system is used: for notes within the bass clef the letters *c* to *b*; for notes in the octave from middle *c* upwards the letters *c'* to *b'*; for notes in the second octave above middle *c* the letters *c''*, etc.)

SOURCES AND TRANSMISSION

As in all European countries, the amount of notated music of any kind which survives is minute compared with that of written words. Further, the relatively small number of English vernacular songs surviving from the twelfth century to the beginning of the fifteenth is in marked contrast to the hundreds of songs, both monophonic (tune only) and polyphonic (in part music), with French or Italian texts and to the considerable number with Spanish or German texts which survive from these centuries. The reasons for the relative scarcity of English songs seem to lie not only in the wastage or deliberate destruction of written sources and in the fortuitousness of preservation in general, but also, and perhaps more importantly, in differences in the sources, uses and methods of transmission of vernacular song in an insular situation.

The paucity of surviving songs corresponding in genre to those of the troubadours and trouvères, for example, makes us wonder to what extent these songs, or others modelled after them, were used in the British Isles during those centuries when French was to some extent a vernacular language. There exists in England a small number of monophonic secular songs with French texts of which at least one seems to have been derived from an original in France.[1] Two thirteenth-century songs in this volume (*Eyns ne soy ke pleynte fu / Ar ne kuth ich sorghe non*, no. 4, and *Miri it is*, no. 5) have clear connections with French practice, one in genre and the other in both genre and kind of source. But the known English sources of secular songs of trouvère type in both vernaculars, with the exception of no. 5, suggest that usually only one or a few songs were noted down at any one time, often in non-musical or only partly musical manuscripts, and that vernacular songs were rarely gathered into formal written collections like the contemporary French chansonniers. Similarly, the almost complete absence of motets with English words seems to show that members of upper ecclesiastical and lay society in England, unlike their counterparts in France, were not generally accustomed to being entertained on occasions of festivity and relaxation with quantities of music in this sophisticated genre.

CLERICAL REPERTORY IN THE THIRTEENTH AND FOURTEENTH CENTURIES

Johannes de Grocheo, who lived in Paris in the late thirteenth century, wrote of the motet, 'This sort of song should not be performed before ordinary people because they do not notice its fine points, nor enjoy listening to it, but before learned people and those on the lookout for subtleties in the arts.'[2] A motet could not be fully appreciated without an understanding of its special structure, which involved the composition over a pre-existing tune (*cantus prius factus*) of one or more upper voices, each with a different text. In France, as elsewhere, the musical material of the tenor, which was a motet's lowest and primary structural part (*cantus firmus*), was most often a relatively short phrase (*neuma*) from a liturgical chant, usually stated more than once. The text of this tenor, generally only a few words such as *domino, in saeculum* or *in omnem terram exivit sonus eorum*, was not underlaid; it was either

---

[1] *Bien deust chanter,* in British Library, MS Arundel 248, f. 155 (facsimile in H. E. Wooldridge, *Early English Harmony,* London, 1897, pl. 36) is a version of Blondel's *Bien doit chanter.* I owe this information to the kindness of Mr. J. E. Maddrell.

[2] For Latin text see E. Rohloff, *Die Quellenhandschriften zum Musiktraktat des Johannes de Grocheio* [sic], Leipzig, 1967, p. 144.

omitted or written under the beginning of the tenor's notes without regard to the original syllable distribution. Some French motets were composed over a vernacular secular song or song refrain. As with plainsong tenors, the complete text was rarely given. There is little direct evidence about the medium of performing motet tenors. A great deal of circumstantial evidence suggests that generally they were either vocalized on a vowel or vowels, or played on organ, harp or large fiddle as appropriate, though in some instances they may have been sung to their original words.[3] The simultaneously sung texts of the upper voices of a motet in more than two parts could be in the same or in different languages and either or both could be sacred or secular. Latin texts were not always sacred nor vernacular texts secular.[4] While sacred poems were rarely set over a secular tenor (two exceptions are of English provenance), secular poems or occasionally a secular and a sacred poem together were commonly set over a tenor from church plainsong. At times this conjunction of secular upper-voice poems and sacred tenor seems to have involved an element which many present-day church people would find sacrilegious. The Good Friday neuma *dolor meus* was used to construct a pair of motets whose upper voices sing about the sorrows of love-sickness; the words *Tristis est anima mea* spoken by Christ in the garden of Gethsemane underpinned settings of poems about the pains and death-wishes of unrequited passion.[5]

The motet *Worldes blisse, have good day* on the tenor *Benedicamus domino* (no. 17) was transcribed and discussed by Manfred Bukofzer in a paper published in 1936 entitled 'The first motet with English words'.[6] It still remains not only the earliest known but also the only surviving motet with an English text in the upper voice. The only other known motet in which an English text was used has Latin words, formerly thought only partly legible, in the upper voice, and the tenor *Dou way Robin, the child wile wepe, dou way Robin* (see no. 18). The words of the tenor are absent in one manuscript; the fact that they are written in red in the other manuscript suggests, on the analogy of this usage with e.g. *Benedicamus* identifications in liturgical manuscripts,

that they were not used in performance. The tenor's tune,[7] which is probably the refrain of an otherwise lost song, shares in a simple form a characteristic of some other medieval tunes: it revolves around two notes, in this case *g* and *f*.

The poem of *Worldes blisse, have good day,* while in the vernacular, is not secular but moralizing, like those of *Man mai longe lives weene* (no. 6a) and *Worldes blis ne last no throwe* (no. 7). Its creator was capable of using a relatively sophisticated motet-technique, but since he used a vernacular text he presumably intended this item to be sung outside the church's ritual, where Latin and a minute amount of Greek were the only languages normally allowed.

Preceding *Worldes blisse, have good day* and on the same double leaf there survives the conclusion of an apparently secular song for two voices (Ex. 1). The text

in lyde joye and blisce bringet me to bride[8]

is written under the lower of the two parts, which are notated on parallel staves, unlike motet parts which were notated in separate units. The music that survives

Ex.1

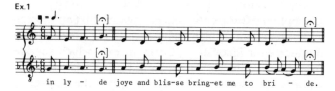

in ly - de joye and blis-se bring-et me to bri - de.

with these few words is uncomplicated; it is written by the same or as competent a scribe as wrote down the motet which follows it. The other contents of this fragment of manuscript are an item with a secular French text, two with Latin text and a page of music which is textless except for the cues *fecit do* (three times) and *suavitatis.* These last may be parts of *clausulae,* the textless predecessors of the motet. The double leaf containing this material came from a large book, for the four pages have original page numbers in the five-hundreds. The nature of the texts, the musical techniques and the writing suggest that the manuscript belonged to a clerical community and contained polyphonic music for church

[3] See F. Ll. Harrison, 'Tradition and innovation in instrumental usage 1150-1400', *Aspects of Medieval and Renaissance Music,* New York, 1966, pp. 319-35.

[4] For examples see L. Schrade, ed., 'The Roman de Fauvel' and F. Ll. Harrison, ed., 'Motets of French Provenance', *Polyphonic Music of the Fourteenth Century,* vols. I and V, Monaco, 1956, 1968.

[5] Ibid, vol. V, p. 80.

[6] *Music and Letters,* xviii (1936), pp. 225-33.

[7] For source and further discussion, see p. 307.

[8] *Lyde* means the month of March.

use as well as music for recreational occasions in the community's common hall.

The contents of medieval music-books were not necessarily homogenous in the present-day sense. Their contents were determined by the overall needs of their user or users rather than by a single genre or particular kind of occasion. This usage may help to explain not only the existence of motets whose texts and tenor-sources show what might now be considered anomalous mixtures of the devotional and amatory, but also their co-existence, particularly in French motet collections, with strictly sacred items such as Alleluias and responds, which belonged to the ritual cycle. The reason seems to be that there was a distinct category of consumers, mainly the communities of clerics and professional singers attached to secular cathedrals, of all these technically sophisticated kinds of music. They presumably sang music with sacred texts either in church or hall; in hall they also sang some secular songs deemed by their superiors to be appropriate to their station and others whose subject matter was decidedly unclerical. Judging by its few remaining contents, the book which contained *Worldes blisse, have good day* probably belonged to a community of this kind.

The incomplete piece with secular French text which is on the other side of the double leaf from *Worldes blisse* is anomalous in having only one text, though it has three voices in addition to a tenor. This makes it an unusual motet — if that is indeed how it should be classified — since motets typically had a different text in each voice over the tenor. It may possibly be an indigenous item; as survivals go, it is a rare one.

Such evidence as there is about British cathedrals after the Norman Conquest suggests that although their personnel-structure closely resembled that of French cathedrals,[9] their hall-repertories were in some respects dissimilar. Musical and archival evidence shows that some English ecclesiastical institutions used liturgical music, including sacred motets, of French origin;[10] there is little evidence, however, that French secular motets were written down or emulated to any extent. Apart from one thirteenth-century instance of this,[11] the only notable cases are in the surviving part of a collection from the Benedictine cathedral of Durham, whose monks had in the fourteenth century copies of at least four motets of French origin with amatory texts, three in French, and one, Philippe de Vitry's *Vos quid admiramini*, in Latin. These secular items were contained in a manuscript which also had sacred Latin motets of both English and French provenance. About the same time the Benedictines of the Abbey of Bury St. Edmunds added some French items to their repertory, among them a motet with amatory French words. The music was evidently used for church purposes, for they went to the trouble of composing sacred Latin words to fit it.[12] In one of the two texted voices the adapter achieved a regular metre which was not identical with that of the French original; the lines of the other texted voice have an irregularly varying number of syllables.[13]

Although amatory words in the upper and therefore more obvious parts of a motet presumably disbarred it from normal church use, even when it had a sacred tenor, the reverse was apparently not true. There exist a few motets of English provenance which were probably sung in church, though their tenors are secular French tunes. A motet in honour of St. Lawrence, for example, has as tenor a song *Trop est fol ky me bayle*; a virelai entitled *Mariounette douche* (with no further text) was used as the tenor of a motet on the mission of St. Augustine and the founding of Canterbury, and also as an upper voice of another motet in the same manuscript with a Latin *contrafactum* beginning *Virgo mater et filia*.[14] A Durham motet, certainly indigenous, has Latin texts beginning *Herodis in pretorio* and *Herodis in atrio* over a tenor with the text:

Hey, hure, lure, hey horpendoy!
mettez moy iuse accolez moy.
(Hey, hure, lure, hey horpendoy! come and embrace me.)

---

[9] See F. Ll. Harrison, *Music in Medieval Britain,* London, 1963, pp. 2-17, 46-57.

[10] For some thirteenth-century evidence, including the 'St. Andrews' manuscript, now Wolfenbüttel 677, see *Music in Medieval Britain,* pp. 129-33; on some fourteenth-century French motets in English manuscripts see F. Ll. Harrison in *New Oxford History of Music,* ii, 1960, pp. 94-95, and 'Ars Nova in England: a new source', *Musica Disciplina,* xxi (1967), p. 67; for examples see *Polyphonic Music of the Fourteenth Century,* V, nos. 4, 15, 16a, 19, 21.

[11] A motet in Bodleian Library, MS Douce 139, f. 179v, of English provenance and dated c. 1270 (facsimile in J., J.F.R. and C. Stainer, *Early Bodleian Music,* i, London, 1901, pl. viii) is a version of one in the Montpellier MS (ed. Y. Rokseth, *Polyphonies du treizième siècle,* iii, Paris, 1936, no. 260) and in two other non-insular sources.

[12] Both forms are transcribed in F. Ll. Harrison, *Motets of French Provenance,* nos. 16, 16a.

[13] Ibid., *Supplement,* pp. 12-13, 27.

[14] See F. Ll. Harrison in *New Oxford History of Music,* iii, 1960, pp. 83-86.

The tune seems to be that of a pastoral song whose *hure lure* syllables probably imitated the sounds of a shepherd's pipe. They have persisted as refrain syllables right to the present day. The layout of this tenor in the Durham manuscript is unusual in that the text is clearly underlaid to the music.[15] It seems that in some instances a secular vernacular text may have been sung in a liturgical situation when it formed part of a musical and textual complex which included one or more sacred texts.[16]

'COURTLY' SONG

The indigenous and non-indigenous elements in English motet-writing — and this includes the unique vernacular survival *Worldes blisse, have good day* — may best be identified in the light of present-day knowledge of motet-practice elsewhere, especially within the extensive sphere of French influence and interchange. The apparent scarcity of secular vernacular polyphony in England in the centuries under discussion should be considered with both the history of French secular polyphony and the particular English situation in mind. The earliest surviving written-down examples of what is generally called 'courtly' polyphonic song in France are by Adam de la Halle in the thirteenth century.[17] There is a large number of fourteenth-century French polyphonic *chansons* by named and anonymous practitioners, of whom the most celebrated is the poet-composer-ecclesiastic Guillaume de Machaut. In England, however, no trace survives of anything musically resembling French courtly polyphony before the late fourteenth-century songs which are nos. 21-24 and 26-33 in this volume. While French secular polyphony seems to have been used mainly in the social context of lay and ecclesiastical aristocracy, most of the group comprising the eleven oldest known English songs with relatively sophisticated part-music can be associated, as Professor Dobson's investigation has confirmed, with the school and university circle of William of Wykeham's colleges of St. Mary at Winchester and at Oxford (the latter now called New College). The question arises whether this apparent lateness of artful secular part-music is merely the result of the hazards of survival, or whether the kinds of entertainment music cultivated in English court, aristocratic and high ecclesiastical circles differed considerably during most of the time under discussion from those current in equivalent circles in France.

There is some evidence to confirm the latter view. Whatever indigenous and regional musics the English kings and church and lay aristocracy patronized in their households during most of the thirteenth and fourteenth centuries, they do not appear to have cultivated courtly music after the French fashion. Richard Coeur-de-Lion is said to have been musically talented, and one song credited to him, though perhaps only written in his person, survives. This is the ballade *Ja nuns hons pris,* in which the writer complained of being a captive of Leopold of Austria without one among his friends coming forward with ransom money.[18] An inventory of Edward I's chapel in 1299-1300 contains two books of polyphonic music (*de cantu organi*), one of which began with *Viderunt,* almost certainly the first word of the Christmas gradual *Viderunt omnes fines terrae.* Settings of this appear at or near the beginning of some of the chief surviving manuscripts of the French thirteenth-century liturgical repertory, including one used in the Augustinian priory of St. Andrews in Scotland throughout the Middle Ages.[19] Edward I's book, when complete, may have contained mainly items of the French repertory; in the case of some French manuscripts, these included both sacred and secular music.

From about the middle of the fourteenth century some names of writers and performers of polyphonic church music in the Royal Household Chapel and in the royal foundations of St. Stephen's, Westminster (1348) and St. George's, Windsor (1352) have been preserved. The main sources of information about the chapel personnel are the Wardrobe Books of the household and a motet written by Canon John Aleyn of Windsor (d. 1373) on the tenor *In omnem terram exivit sonus eorum,* whose upper-voice texts begin:

---

[15] This is also the case in *Doucement mi reconforte,* the tenor of *Deus Creator/Rex genitor* in Bodleian Library, MS E. Mus. 7, from Bury St. Edmunds; see *Early Bodleian Music,* i, pl. xiii.

[16] The *Deo gratias* motet which concludes the *Messe de Tournai* has a sacred Latin and an amatory French text (ed. L. Schrade, *Polyphonic Music of the Fourteenth Century,* I, p. 129).

[17] See N. Wilkins, ed., *The Lyric Works of Adam de la Halle,* American Institute of Musicology, 1967, pp. 49-59.

[18] Facsimile in J. Beck, *Le Chansonnier Cangé,* i, Philadelphia & Paris, 1927, f. 62v; transcriptions, differing in rhythm, in ibid., ii, p. 144 and in A. T. Davison and W. Apel, *Historical Anthology of Music,* i, Cambridge, Mass., no. 19a.

[19] Facsimile in *An Old St. Andrews Music Book,* ed. J. H. Baxter, St. Andrews, 1931.

Sub arcturo plebs vallata
plaudat melos; laus ornata
psallatur altissimo

(Let the people encamped beneath Arcturus [the brightest star of Boötes, a constellation in the northern hemisphere, or the whole constellation] sing joyfully: let ornate praise be sung to the Highest)

and

Fons citharizantium
ac organizantium
Tubal praedicatur.[20]

(Tubal is said to be the father of all who play the harp and organ.)

One of these texts is in honour of the traditional sequence of famous theorists, from Tubal and Pythagoras to Franco of Cologne; it ends, with due modesty, with the name of the composer, John Aleyn himself. The other text provides fifteen musicians, most of whose names also appear in the archives as members of one or more of the royal institutions.[21]

The personnel lists in the Royal Wardrobe books differentiate clearly between the chaplains and singing clerks in the royal chapel on the one hand and the minstrels attached to the royal household on the other. Until about 1400 there was a relatively small number of chaplains and clerks — fewer than the eleven listed in Richard II's Wardrobe Account of 1393 and never as many as the statutory seventeen plus six boys maintained by both St. Stephen's and St. George's. While John Aleyn's motet and other late fourteenth-century items inform us about some of the sacred music sung by the chapel staff, not one of the many names of minstrels listed or referred to in household accounts and archives throughout the fourteenth and fifteenth centuries has been found in association with any surviving written music, nor has the name of any clerk of the chapel been associated in writing with non-sacred music.

It is striking that fourteenth-century items of English vernacular song are relatively even rarer than those of the thirteenth century, apart from the fourteen homogenous items which form the last group in this volume. This seems to suggest two hypotheses: (1) that the musical activities of the royal chapel's practitioners of polyphonic music did not generally include much esoteric secular polyphony of the kind cultivated in France; and (2) that the instrumental skills and ceremonial and entertainment duties of the royal household's minstrels (rarely specified in writing at that time) were largely concerned with bodies of material, whether written, partly written or unwritten, which were exclusively professionally circulated and whose transmission was effected, as far as we can tell, by individual enterprise or within the circle of guild training. The interrelations of written and unwritten musical practices and repertories is a neglected part of medieval musical study, though one most relevant to the fourteenth and fifteenth centuries.

It is known that Richard II was interested in literature, both French and English, and that Gower and Chaucer received his encouragement. It was also said of him that he made 'balades et chançons, rondeaulx et lais très bien et bel — si n'étoit il que homs lais'.[22] If these terms are accurately intended, Richard II wrote in the French *formes fixes* of the fourteenth century, and it is possible, though not explicitly stated here, that he or a professionally-trained member of his household composed polyphonic music for his poems. However, neither verse nor music has survived. Chaucer knew the French *chanson* forms and used them for poems in English, but there is likewise no evidence that any of these were ever set to music. He wrote of the roundel, *Now welcom, somer, with thy sonne softe,* which occurs in the *Parlement of Foules*:[23]

The note, I trowe, maked was in Fraunce.

The form of this roundel is precisely equivalent to that of the French *rondeau,* and music written for it would have been constructed accordingly; that is, it would have consisted of two strains so devised that the first strain had a satisfactory intermediate musical ending and could be repeated or not. This feature was needed to accommodate the part-refrain which was characteristic of the *rondeau* form, and whose relation to its musical setting may be diagrammed thus, A and B representing the two strains of music:

---

[20] *Polyphonic Music of the Fourteenth Century,* V, no. 31; the reading *arcturo* in place of the hitherto accepted *Arturo* was kindly suggested by C. A. Robson.

[21] See B. Trowell, 'A fourteenth-century ceremonial motet and its composer', *Acta Musicologica,* xxix (1957), p. 65.

[22] G. Hayes, *King's Music,* London, 1927, p. 34.

[23] Line 677.

Text	Music
Complete refrain	A+B
New text of the same length as the first part of the refrain	A
First part of the refrain	A
New text of the same length as the complete refrain	A+B
Complete refrain	A+B

Chaucer's roundel form has been described as having 'the rhyme scheme abbabababbbab and a system of repetition whereby the first two lines act as the refrain for the second stanza and the whole first stanza is the refrain of the third'.[24] This description has the disadvantage of using the word 'stanza' for the text-units of different lengths — in Chaucer's case a first 'stanza' of three lines, a second 'stanza' of four and a third 'stanza' of six. The text-music relationship of a roundel is not stanzaic; the term is more appropriately used of a song with stanzas of identical metrical design all set to the same music. This could not be true of Chaucer's roundel, a hypothetical musical setting of which would be related to the text in the following way:

Unit of text	Rhyme-scheme	Music
1. Now welcom, somer, with thy sonne softe,	a	A
That hast this wintres wedres overshake,	b	
2. And driven away the longe nightes blake!	b	B
3. Seynt Valentyn, that art ful hy on-lofte,	a	A
Thus syngen smale foules for thy sake:	b	
4. Now welcom, somer, with thy sonne softe,	a	A
That hast this wintres wedres overshake!	b	
5. Wel han they cause for to gladen ofte,	a	A
Sith ech of hem recovered hath hys make;	b	
6. Ful blissful mowe they syngen when they wake:	b	B
7. Now welcom, somer, with thy sonne softe,	a	A
That hast this wintres wedres overshake,	b	
8. And driven away the longe nightes blake!	b	B

Editors of French *rondeaux* with music have been accustomed to describe their design as refrain-form with two complete refrains which frame an incomplete stanza, a correspondingly incomplete refrain, and a complete stanza. In laying out editions, they have usually shown this plan as a relation of eight units of text to two strains of music, the order of performance being indicated by numbering below the music the corresponding units of text:

Music	A	B
Text Units	1.4.7	2.8
	3	6
	5	

These numbers indicate neither lines nor stanzas, but only units of text whose metrical design may or may not be the same under B (the second strain) as under A (the first strain). Chaucer's five-stress lines occur relatively infrequently in French polyphonic *rondeaux*. Only one surviving *rondeau* with music by Machaut — *Dame, se vous n'avez aperceu*[25] — has a five-stress line. Some of Machaut's varied metrical designs have refrains of two lines, one to each strain of music. Here, music-design and rhyme-scheme correspond and the total rhyme-scheme is *ab*aa*ab*, the italicized letters indicating refrain lines. A similar correspondence occurs in a *rondeau* with three four-syllable lines rhyming aab to each strain. When there is a three-line refrain, which is rare in Machaut, the rhyme-scheme is abb and the total rhyme-scheme is therefore *abb*ab*ab*b*abb*ab, which Chaucer used with five-stress lines. With this plan Machaut set two lines to the first strain of music and one to the second.

The line 'Qui bien aime a tard oublie', which appears in some versions of *The Parlement of Foules* in connection with the roundel 'Now welcom, somer', is also the first line of a *lai* by Machaut.[26] However, its occurrence in connection with a roundel/*rondeau* is surely either a coincidence — the reference being to an unknown *rondeau* tune identified by these words — or a mistake, since there is no possibility that the music of a *lai,* whose text and music were designed in metrically identical half-stanzas, often varying in design from one stanza to another, could have served also for a *rondeau.* The line 'Qui bien aime a tard oublie' has eight syllables and four stresses. This is an additional reason why music to which it could have been sung would not have served for the five-stress lines of 'Now welcom, somer'.

Chaucer probably wrote a triple roundel with the title *Merciles Beaute.* This consists of three five-line roundels with rhyme-scheme abbab. The lines are of eleven syllables, apart from the a-lines in the first and second roundels, which are of ten syllables. The idea of a triple poem may have a musical implication since a triple *chanson* in the French context would probably have been a song for three voices singing simultaneously different though related poems. While Machaut is not known to have written a triple *rondeau,* he wrote two triple *ballades* with music, one of which is a three-part canon. In both cases the three simultaneously sung texts have the same final refrain line. Chaucer's balades agree

[24] C. C. Olson, 'Chaucer and the music of the fourteenth century', *Speculum,* xvi (1941), p. 84.

[25] Ed. L. Schrade, *Polyphonic Music of the Fourteenth Century,* iii, Monaco, 1956, p. 156.

[26] Ibid, ii, Monaco, 1956, p. 90; I am grateful to Professor Barnes of Pomona College, California, for communicating this identity.

with those of Machaut in having three stanzas with identical rhymes and the same final line as refrain. Poems like the *ballade, To Rosamounde,* and the moral balade, *Gentilesse,* would presumably have been set, if music were made for them, in the same way as a *ballade* was in France — in two strains, the first of which was repeated, generally with different first and second endings. The first two units of the poem, which had an identical rhyme-scheme, were sung to this repeated strain and the succeeding units to the second strain, the music of whose ending often referred back to the ending of the first strain. The musical design of the stanza of a *ballade* may be diagrammed thus:

A (ending x) A (ending x^1) B (ending x)

In Machaut's *ballades* with music the unit of text set to the first strain may be two, three or four lines, with various metrical patterns; the line-number and metre-pattern of the words sung to the second strain are similarly varied. While Machaut did not write an *envoi* to any of his surviving *ballades* with music, Chaucer sometimes wrote an envoy whose line-length was not always that of the stanza. If a *ballade* with such an envoy were set to music, the envoy could not be sung to the same music as the stanza.

According to one of the surviving texts Chaucer introduced the balade 'Hyd, Absalom, thy gilte tresses clere' in *The Legend of Good Women* with these lines:[27]

> And after that they wenten in compas,
> Daunsynge aboute this flour an esy pas,
> And songen, as it were in carole-wyse,
> This balade, which that I shal you devyse.

The term 'carole-wyse' means in the manner of a sung round-dance. Though the *formes fixes* had doubtless been danced songs at an earlier time, French fourteenth-century polyphonic *chansons* were highly-wrought chamber pieces; those in the mannerist style of the last decades of the century were rhythmically sophisticated and complex to a degree which has not been matched in Western music until the present century. With the possible exception of some *virelais* (notably Machaut's neo-rustic monophonic tunes), most French fourteenth-century *chansons* could not have been danced.

In *The Legend of Good Women* Chaucer says of himself that he wrote 'balades, roundels, virelais', that is, the three main *formes fixes* practised in France. In the *Franklin's Tale* he wrote of the squire Aurelius that he loved in silence,

> Save in his songes somwhat wold he wreye
> His wo, as in a general compleynyng;
> He seyde he lovede, and was biloved no thyng.
> Of swich matere made he manye layes,
> Songes, compleintes, roundels, virelayes.[28]

It might be suspected that the poet here used 'layes' as a convenient rhyme with 'virelayes', and that the term need not therefore be taken too literally. The 'lay, or maner song' beginning 'I have of sorwe so gret woon', which was 'sayde . . . withoute note, withoute song' by the black knight in *The Book of the Duchess* is there also called a *compleynte*. Its single stanza has twelve lines rhyming aabbaaccdedc. For comparison Machaut's only surviving *complainte — Tels rit au main* in the *Remède de Fortune*[29] — while corresponding in theme to Aurelius's *compleynte*, was set in stanzaic musical form, with the same monophonic tune for all its thirty-six sixteen-line stanzas. The music has two strains, each repeated, making a AABB design, with eight lines (rhyming bbba bbba) to the repeated second strain. Chaucer's other *compleyntes* have varying numbers of stanzas; the *Complaint of Venus* consists, like its known French original, of three three-stanza *ballades*, each however with a different final refrain-line, plus an envoy. Though the *ballades* could have been sung simultaneously, the envoy could not have been sung to their music since it has ten lines to the *ballade* stanzas' eight.

In France Machaut was the latest practitioner, as far as surviving written examples with music are concerned, of the medieval musico-poetic form called *lai*. His *lais*,[30] most of which are monophonic, are extended pieces usually of twelve stanzas, written and set in paired half-stanzas of varying metrical design, and their subjects are mostly elaborations of static love-concepts (one, *Le Lay de Notre Dame,* is sacred), not knightly adventures. In both respects they are clearly in the tradition of such thirteenth-century *lais et descorts* as those of Gautier de Dargies and Thomas Herier.[31]

While it seems clear that Richard II and some of the court and literary circles of his reign were familiar with

---

[27] *The Legend of Good Women,* Prol. A, 199-202.

[28] *The Franklin's Tale,* 944-8.

[29] Ed. L. Schrade, *Polyphonic Music of the Fourteenth Century,* ii, 1956, p. 106, with the first and last stanzas of the text.

[30] Ed. L. Schrade in ibid., pp. 1-105.

[31] See A. Jeanroy, L. Brandin and P. Aubry, *Lais et descorts français du XIIIe siècle,* Paris, 1901.

the main poetic conventions of the French *formes fixes,* the surviving poems suggest that these conventions were used in England in a more stereotyped way than in France. Interest in the French forms may not have extended far outside these circles, for the only fourteenth-century occurrences of the terms *balade, roundel* and *virelai* cited in the *Oxford English Dictionary* are from Chaucer and Gower. It is reasonable to suppose that some of the royal musicians may have been acquainted to a certain degree with the secular musical styles current in France; archival evidence for this seems lacking, however, and no English music in these styles is known to survive from the relevant time. With this situation in mind, the group of songs given as nos. 21-24 and 26-33 in this volume may be seen as part of an indigenous repertory of vernacular polyphonic song whose musical techniques were somewhat affected by French or Italian usages or both. Though influenced musically by French *chanson* practice, if not also by the polyphonic *ballate* and *madrigale* of northern Italy, their formal designs do not correspond exactly to any of these,[32] nor did their text-writers use a courtly vocabulary. They seem to be what earlier musical terminology would have called provincial, but which may more appropriately be termed hybrid, since continental influences in the British Isles operated then, as always, on existing practices.

THE WINCHESTER SONGS

Among the aims of William of Wykeham's foundations of Winchester and New College, Oxford, which he stated in the preamble to the statutes dated 1400, when the colleges had been open for about ten years, were 'the advancing of the divine ritual and the increase of the liberal arts, sciences and faculties'. The former of these objects in particular was in opposition to the anti-ritualistic campaigning of John Wyclif, who lampooned as 'veyn japis' such current techniques of polyphonic church music as

> deschaunt, countre note and orgon and smale bre-kynge, that stirith veyn men to daunsynge more than to mornynge, and here-fore ben many proude

and lecherous lorelis founden and dowid with temperal and worldly lordischipis and gret cost.[33]

Elsewhere he abused

> knackynge of newe song as orgen or deschant and motetis of holouris.[34]

'Brekynge' and 'knackynge' both refer to rapid notes, whether written or added by singers as extemporized ornament. In both words short notes are thought of as longer notes broken up. 'Brekynge' was used in this sense in the rule of the Briggitine nuns of Syon, Middlesex, founded in 1414. They were told that their singing of the offices should be 'sadde sober and symple withe out brekyng of notes and gay releysing withe alle mekenes and devocion'.[35] Though the word 'brokkynge' which Chaucer used of Absalon's courting of the carpenter's wife in *The Miller's Tale:*[36]

> He syngeth, brokkynge as a nyghtyngale

is of dubious etymology, it may be from the same root as 'break'. 'Brokkynge', in the sense of using quick notes, would be appropriate to a comparison with a nightingale's song. 'Lorelis' means rascals and 'holouris' means whoremongers. So scabrous a description of motets suggests that Wyclif may have heard motets which either incorporated secular love-texts or had tenors which were commonly associated with them.

To ensure the continued cultivation of church ritual and its music, Wykeham established chapel staffs of chaplains skilled in plainsong, three at Winchester and ten at New College, with three singing clerks and sixteen boys in each college who were trained in polyphonic music by their *informator choristarum.* In 1396-7 this post at Winchester was filled by 'Edmund, a clerk of the chapel', who may have been the composer of no. 28 in this volume. A Winchester statute which was copied later by other colleges but seems to have originated there provided for a fire in hall after supper on important church festivals and college occasions, when the members might sing songs and entertain one another with 'poems, chronicles of kings, wonders of the world and other recreations appropriate to the clerical state'.[37]

The songs contained in the manuscript which was

[32] For a discussion of their forms see pp. 21-22.

[33] 'Of feigned contemplative life', *The English Works of Wyclif,* ed. F. D. Matthews, Early English Text Society, London, 1880, p. 191.

[34] 'Of prelates', ibid., p. 91.

[35] G. J. Aungier, *The History and Antiquities of Syon Monastery,* London, 1840, p. 319.

[36] See C. C. Olsen, 'Chaucer and the music of the fourteenth century', *Speculum,* xvi (1941), p. 77, fn. 6.

[37] F. Ll. Harrison, *Music in Medieval Britain,* pp. 31-2, 419.

early associated with Winchester College consist of ten items with English texts (nos. 20 and 25-33), four with French texts and four with Latin texts. Presumably these were used both for post-supper recreations and as teaching material for the boy choristers. Their subjects include the Christmas festivity of the Yule-log, moral sentiments, decorous devotion to womanhood and didactic commentaries on *Pater noster, Credo in Deum* and *Ave Maria*. Chaucer's little clergeon in *The Prioress's Tale* was learning from his 'prymer' (the lay person's book of hours in the vernacular, which included English versions of these texts) when he heard the older boys singing from the antiphoner:[38]

> As he sat in the scole at his prymer,
> He *Alma Redemptoris* herde singe,
> As children learned hir antiphoner.

That the Latin texts of the Lord's Prayer, the Apostles' Creed and Gabriel's Salutation were a usual part of a choir-boy's training in religion and grammar is shown by Bishop John Grandisson's instructions for the education of the choristers of St. Mary Ottery in Devon, which he refounded as a collegiate church in 1337. Grandisson ordered that the boys should be able to construe and understand the Latin texts of the Lord's Prayer (*Oratio Dominica*), *Ave Maria (Salutatio Angelica),* the Creed *(Symbolum)* and the Matins and Hours of the Virgin Mary, before having their first tonsure and before going on to other book-studies (*alii libri magistrales et poetici aut metrici*).[39] The three songs which are nos. 31-33 seem well suited to remind boy-singers of some of the meanings of these Latin texts, simultaneously giving them practice in mensural notation. The items in the Douce fragments in the Bodleian Library, which have one concordance (no. 27) with the Winchester songs and may be assumed to have belonged to a similar repertory, consist of five songs with English texts (nos. 21-24 and 27), two with French and one with Latin text. While the songs with French texts in both sources are on non-religious subjects, all but one of the Latin items are settings of liturgical texts familiar to any medieval choir-

singer. *Felix namque* was the Offertory at the Lady-Mass during most of the year;[40] *Pange lingua* was the Corpus Christi hymn; *Benedicamus Domino* was sung, usually by two boys, at the end of the main offices, and *Gloria in excelsis Deo* (the text is identical with that of the Mass *Gloria,* ending with the word *voluntatis*) was the verse of the Christmas respond *Hodie nobis caelorum rex* which was sung by five boys representing the angelic host.[41] The secular Latin item is a setting in the form of a round of a text beginning *Si quis amat.*

FOURTEENTH-CENTURY TERMINOLOGY

From the late fourteenth and early fifteenth century there survive a number of short treatises in English on methods of teaching beginners the elements of part-music.[42] One of the purposes of these little manuals was 'to enforme a childe in his counterpoint', as it was put by the composer Leonel Power (d. 1445), who may have taught the choirboys of Canterbury.[43] Their main topic was the process of teaching a beginner to extemporize a tune, called a descant, as a second voice to a given tune or tune-formula. The acquiring of this technique was facilitated, or thought to be facilitated, by complicated routines of pitch-transposition called 'sights'. The given tune was called the tenor, in conformity with long-established terminology, while the term for the extemporized tune and by extension for its maker (descanter) depended on its pitch-range relation to the tenor. A descant below the tenor was called a counter. One in the same range was called counter-tenor; its technical function and therefore name seem not to have been current in England much before 1400. A descant with a range about five notes higher than the tenor was called a mean; one around an octave higher was a treble. The term quatreble for a part around a twelfth (octave plus fifth) higher than the tenor does not appear in these treatises and seems not to have been current until the second half of the fifteenth century. All these terms were drawn from numerology.

---

[38] Lines 1707-9.

[39] Ed. J. M. Dalton, *The Collegiate Church of Ottery St. Mary, being the Ordinances and Statutes 1338-9,* London, 1917, p. 108.

[40] This has been regarded as possibly an organ item; see p. 311.

[41] This was the procedure in the Use of Salisbury, which was followed at Winchester and New College. At Exeter the boys mimed the text; see *Music in Medieval Britain,* p. 107.

[42] Some were printed by S. B. Meech in *Speculum,* x (1935), p. 235. They were discussed in two printed dissertations: M. F. Bukofzer, *Geschichte des englischen Diskants und des Fauxbourdons,* Strasbourg, 1936, and T. Georgiades, *Englische Diskanttraktate aus der ersten Hälfte des 15. Jahrhunderts,* Munich, 1937.

[43] *Music in Medieval Britain,* p. 42.

The descant-manuals were meant chiefly for the education in polyphonic music of boys up to young adulthood but could be set to suit any pair of voices. Although the manuals dealt only with training a single singer to descant above or below a given tenor, their terminology was affected by that of medieval composition techniques for more than two voices. Polyphonic music was most often composed by means of the technique already described, that is by adding one or more complete parts successively to a primary structural part (tenor) which might or might not be the composer's original creation. The terms used for the voices of a motet were, progressing upwards, tenor, *duplum* or *motetus*, *triplum* and *quadruplum*. Some four-part motets were constructed with a tenor, a textless voice operating in the same general pitch-range as the tenor and complementing it structurally, and two texted voices. In England a textless voice of this kind was sometimes indicated as *quartus cantus*; elsewhere it was usually called *contratenor*. The criss-cross of these two terminologies has caused some confusion in later attempts to define English vernacular musical terms of the fourteenth, fifteenth and sixteenth centuries.

The Latin motet terms — *duplum, triplum, quadruplum* and *quartus cantus* — denoted the order of successive addition of voices to a tenor. The terminology of the descant treatises used two similar words — treble and quatreble — in a series which indicated pitch-range relationships with the tenor; treble was not the exact equivalent of *triplum* nor quatreble of *quadruplum*. In English polyphonic practice from about 1450 onwards the vernacular terms and their largely newly-fabricated Latin equivalents (*medius* = mean, *triplex* = treble and *quatruplex* = quatreble) conveyed both an order of successive composition, and a general though not hard and fast pitch-range relation to a tenor. The definition of *mean* in this musical sense given in the *Oxford English Dictionary* as 'a middle part in any composition or performance, esp. the tenor and alto' is therefore not applicable to the use of the term in the fourteenth century when the tenor was the first structural voice and the term *alto* had not acquired its later musical connotation. For a similar reason the nineteenth-century explanation of *quinible* by William Chappell as 'to descant by fourths' is incorrect. In the *OED*'s definition of this term as 'a

note higher than the treble being an octave higher than the mean', the word 'note' should read 'voice-part a fifth'. The observation also quoted in the *OED* that 'the quatreble began and ended a twelfth above [the plainsong] and the quinible a fifteenth' might seem a valid extension of the principles given in the descant manuals but for the facts that a sustained quinible range would be vocally almost impossible, and the word itself does not occur in any musical source. Pre-determined beginning and ending intervals were not, in any case, applied in actual composition.[44] Besides a numerical use of *quinible* dated about 1398, *OED* gives two instances of musical application, one from Chaucer, concerning the clerk Absalon in *The Miller's Tale,* who could

> pleyen songes on a smal rubible;
> Thereto he song som tyme a loud quynyble[45]

and one from Skelton about 1550. Chaucer may have quizzically applied this further numerical term to describe the clerk's absurdly high-pitched voice and also perhaps to provide a rhyme for 'rubible'.

The basic techniques and at least some of the terms used in the vernacular manuals had been current earlier in the fourteenth century. Robert Mannyng wrote, about 1330, of 'clerkes that best couthe synge, wyth treble, mene and burdoun'. It is extremely difficult to establish retrospectively a primary meaning for the term *burdoun* (French *bourdon*). Clearly Robert Mannyng used it in the sense of *tenor* — the lowest of three voice-parts. Chaucer used it in a similar sense when, in the Prologue to the *Canterbury Tales,* the Pardoner sang *Come hither love to me* and the Somonour 'bar to hym a stif burdoun', or lower part, and also satirically of the miller's wife in *The Reeve's Tale,* who snored louder and deeper than her husband and 'bar him a burdon, a ful strong'.[46] It was used in French from the twelfth century, as it still is, for the sustained note or notes of bagpipes with drones.

It is convenient to use the term *shifting drone* for an auxiliary part which employs only two adjacent notes. A number of medieval tunes seem to have been made on the basis of a two-note nub of this kind, whether explicit as in *Sumer is icumen in* (no. 9), or implied as in *Dou way Robin* (see no. 18). An auxiliary voice-part or accompanying instrumental part or parts using forms and

---

[44] A nomenclature of *c.* 1510 for the voices of a nine-part composition is given at the opening of a *Salve regina* by Robert Wylkynson, *informator chori* at Eton. The highest voice is called *quatruplex,* i.e. quatreble. Facsimile in *The Eton Choirbook,* ed. F. Ll. Harrison, i, 1956, p. xxvi.

[45] Lines 3331-2.

[46] For line references see C. C. Olsen's article already referred to. His comment that Chaucer's 'stif bourdoun' of the Somonour and snoring 'burdon' of the miller's wife refer 'evidently to fauxbourdon, a method of accompanying songs much used in church music' is invalid on two counts: (1) the earliest occurrence of the term *fauxbourdon* so far known is *c.* 1430; and (2) a connection, if one existed, between the musical terms *bourdon* and *fauxbourdon* has not been conclusively established.

extensions of shifting-drone technique have been added to some of the songs in this volume. The tune of *Miri it is while sumer ilast* (no. 5) seems suited by the two-note form; it is here elaborated into tune and accompaniment for harp and a variation for harp and specially-tuned viola (substituting for large thirteenth-century fiddle). A similar part for unison voices has been added to the stanza tune of *Lullay, lullay: Als I lay on Yoolis night* (no. 20). The two surviving monophonic versions of *Angelus ad virginem / Gabriel fram heven-king* (no. 15 (ii), first and second versions) have been given an editorial accompaniment which uses the shifting drone on two pitch levels, *c′ d′* and *f g*.

PART-MUSIC TECHNIQUES

The part-writing techniques used in the polyphonic songs in this volume, apart from editorial additions and excluding *Jesu Cristes milde moder* (no. 12) and *Sumer is icumen in* (no. 9), which will be discussed in other contexts, may conveniently be grouped under seven headings, as shown in the following table:

TABLE 1

Technique	Item
Motet	17
Bourdon	9, 13
Two-part descant	8, 15 (ii) third version, 19
Three-part descant	15 (ii) fourth and fifth versions
Gymel	25
Two-part French *chanson*/Italian *canzona*	21, 22, 24, 26-28, 30-33
Three-part *chanson*	29

The techniques of the motet and bourdon items have been discussed. The three items of two-part descant employ in closely similar ways the basic resources of this technique, which was used in both sacred and secular music: stepwise parallel motion, chiefly in sixths (especially in no. 19) which may be interspersed with octaves (noticeably in the third version of no. 15 (ii)), and stepwise contrary motion, often starting on and returning to an octave (as in no. 19). Oblique motion, in which one voice stands or repeats while the other moves, is less characteristic of two-part descant. It occurs relatively often in no. 8, whose primary tune may possibly be the lower, not the upper voice.[47] The upper part of no. 19 seems to be the primary one, while that of the third version of no. 15 (ii) is known to be so from other sources.

The three-part settings of *Angelus ad virginem* given here with the English text *Gabriel fram heven-king* as no. 15 (ii), fourth and fifth versions, are orthodox workings of two slightly varying forms of the tune. Their part-writing technique is similar to that of many sacred compositions of the second half of the fourteenth century; the tune — the tenor in the structural sense — is in the middle voice of the texture, a counter is below it and a part which is a mean in the structural sense but would often have been called a treble — being the third voice of the texture — is above it. Stepwise parallel motion with the tenor a third and the treble a sixth above the counter is common, especially approaching cadences (fourth version bars 3-4, 7-8, 10, 15-end; fifth version bars 3-4, 15-16, 19-end). Successive parallel octave-fifth formations, which were implicitly disallowed in later descant-teaching and expressly banned in Leonel Power's treatise written probably *c.* 1400, occur in both settings, as in the fourth version at bar 13 and in the fifth version at bars 6-7. This ambivalence between third-sixth and octave-fifth interval formations and successions is also characteristic of contemporary English sacred music in descant technique.

The term *gymel* (Latin *cantus gemellus*) is not known to occur in a musical context earlier than the second half of the fifteenth century. It was used then of two voice-parts, whether alone or in a fuller texture, whose pitch-ranges were identical and whose tune-contours consequently crossed and re-crossed. It may also be used validly to describe retrospectively earlier instances of this technique. Some musical historians, following Manfred Bukofzer, have used it inappropriately for a two-part structure-outline of treble and tenor whose pitch-relation is not truly twin. *Jesus Cristes milde moder* (no. 12) is a thirteenth-century example of gymel, and written twelfth-century instances are extant. While *Trew, on wam ys al my tryst* (no. 25) occurs in a group of late fourteenth-century songs which we have described as hybrids of English and Franco-Italian practice, its indigenous characteristics are more marked than those of the other songs in this group. The voices are gymel-related, are rhythmically homogenous and are apparently both intended to be sung. Two elements in this song, however, are probably non-insular in origin. One is the cadence-formula which falls one note and rises two (commonly though unjustifiably called a 'Landini cadence'); it is used, among other places, in bars 3-4 and 18-19 of the first tenor part. The other is the rhythmic idiom in the eighth bar, which involves simultaneous groupings of twice three and thrice two (in present-day usage notated in simultaneous 6/8 and 3/4 time signatures).

The effect of non-insular usages on the part-writing techniques of the songs in the sixth group in Table 1 (p. 65) are observable in the rhythmic differentiation of the parts and in the use of a texted *cantus* (the term most appropriate to a higher part in this style) above the textless tenor.[48] The preponderance of duple rhythm with triple subdivision, which is used in all but one item in this group, probably results from contact with secular songwriting usage in France rather than Italy, where the rhythmic frameworks of polyphonic song were more varied. The falling-one-note rising-two cadential formula usually appears over a one-step down cadence in slower rhythm in the tenor, as was common in continental usage. Both voices of *Thys Yool* (no. 28), whose composer Edmund was probably the music-teacher of the Winchester College choristers, have syncopations which produce three-against-two rhythms — at this time an unequivocal sign of French influence. This technique is used more fully in the last three songs in this group (nos. 31-33), whose rhythm and tune features are the most nearly related to those of the contemporary French *chanson* of all the songs in this hybrid group.

The three-part song *Wel wer hym that wyst* (no. 29), though less Frenchified in these respects, shows that its composer was conversant with a French method of three-part composition of which there is little evidence among surviving English church music of that time. Its structural basis, consisting of texted cantus and untexted tenor, has the same interval and rhythm techniques as the two-part songs. The third voice, textless, is a true countertenor in the French manner; it is written in the same pitch range as the tenor (unlike the middle voice in typical English descant) and is consequently below as often as above the tenor in pitch. Its technical function is to complement the structural parts (cantus and tenor) in both interval-content and rhythmic flow. The use and name of the countertenor voice in three-part song had been current in France by the mid-fourteenth century. *Wel wer hym that wyst* is one of the earliest surviving instances of an English use of countertenor technique and of its designation 'Contra Tenor' in an English manuscript.

TUNE CHARACTERISTICS

Tune characteristics and the techniques of tune construction have been largely neglected by modern Western musical historians in favour of counterpoint and harmony, whose origins and development have been their chief preoccupation since Charles Burney's *General History of Music* (1776-89).[49] Four primary features of tune-structure — mode, contour, overall unit-design and rhythm — are in practice totally interrelated. Written medieval discussions were concerned almost entirely with mode and contour, and with those only in a certain part of the plainsong repertory, chiefly antiphons and psalms. While a Tonale, the book which contained this information, had both practical and pedagogical aims, the concept of mode on which it was based was primarily functional. Though the tune-material of Mode I, for example, was usually defined in the abstract terms of its basic compass d - d' and its final d, examples were invariably given of the many tunes which in practice exceeded this compass. The main object of a Tonale was to catalogue antiphons according to their final (that of Modes I and II was d; of III and IV e; of V and VI f and of VII and VIII g), their compass (basically within the octave above the final in odd-numbered modes and within the octave surrounding the final in even-numbered modes), and their initial tune-formula (*variatio*). The initial formulae of each mode were grouped according to the ending (*differentia*) of the psalm-formula with which modal propriety decreed a particular antiphon should be sung.

A Tonale was mainly a chant reference-book, to be used as a check on musical choirbooks. It was also a repertory catalogue and as such was included in most manuals concerned with the training of church musicians. Since a Tonale's approach to the relevant characteristics of the tune-repertory was almost entirely formulaic, mode and contour — at least the contour of the *variatio* — tended to merge into one concept. In addition to this, the formula-vocabulary of a Tonale's repertory of tunes was strictly confined to idioms which had been sanctioned at an earlier time; it deliberately excluded many formulae associated with the music of non-Christian religious rituals and social customs. The earliest surviving Tonales are from the early ninth century. When reduced at this time to systematic form, the modal theory of Christian ritual chant dealt only with the canonic four finals and their eight compasses, and implicitly confined discussion of tune-formulae and contours to those of the established ritual chant.

Theory and practice allowed for both b flat and b natural (not in immediate succession) but no other inflected notes, not even e flat or f sharp. This built-in

---

[48] See p. 311 for references to contemporary French and Italian examples.

[49] See F. Ll. Harrison, C. Palisca and M. Hood, *Musicology*, Englewood Cliffs, 1963, p. 16.

restraint of tune and contour virtually excluded movement by an interval of more than a fifth in either direction, and in general confined overall contours within a standard pattern of rising beginning and falling end, however few or numerous the intervening contour-curves might be.

Medieval tune-styles outside this highly conservative ritual context have been little investigated by musical historians. Scant attention has yet been given to those of secular song, both monophonic and polyphonic, or of non-plainsong voices in sacred polyphony. The number of songs in this volume which appear not to be directly derived from or modelled on plainsong is so small that they cannot be looked on as typical in any real sense. They may, nevertheless, exhibit at least some of the tune-styles current in medieval England outside the context of ritual chant. St. Godric's songs (nos. 1-3) and the lay *Ar ne kuth ich sorghe non* have special features which will be discussed later, and the songs with strong continental flavour will be considered as a separate group. Table 2 gives the finals and compasses and also indicates the general type of contour of the items whose numbers are shown in the first column.

TABLE 2

Item	Final	Compass	Notes in Compass	Contour Type
5	g	*f-f'*	8	I
6	c	*c-d'*	9	III
8 (upper voice)	*f'* with *b* flat	*d-b* flat	6	IV
8 (lower voice)	*f* with *b* flat	*d-d'*	8	I
9 (rota)	*f* with *b* flat	*e-f'*	9	I
13 (upper voice)	*f* with *b* flat	*d-d'*	8	III
15	g	*f-g'*	9	I
16	c	*a-g'*	7	II
17 (upper voice)	*f* with *b* flat	*e-a'*	11	I
19 (upper voice)	*g'*	*e'-d'*	7	II
20	*d'* with *b* flat	*c-b* flat	7	II

Four of these songs have *f* as final (each with *b* flat as the signature, which the Tonales recognized as orthodox with this final), three have *g*, two have *c* and one has *d* (in this mode also *b* flat was a recognized variant). Compasses in most cases are a seventh, an octave or a ninth; the upper part of no. 8 covers only a sixth (both parts are included in this tabulation for reasons already explained) and no. 17, a motet-duplum which therefore has special structural requirements, has an eleventh. The contour-indication in the table, although of the most general kind, is reasonably serviceable for the present

purpose. As already observed, a descending beginning was unorthodox in plainsong; a rising opening, however, does not necessarily show plainsong influence though this is likely if a recognised *variatio* is used.

Contour-types I and II have a falling opening. Type I tunes have a compass of an octave or more, Type II of less than an octave; it is obvious that compass, contour-type and contour-direction are to some extent interconnected. In Types III and IV there is a rising opening, with compasses corresponding to those of Types I and II respectively. This rough tabulation shows that *Miri it is while sumer ilast* (no. 5), the lower part of *Fuweles in the frith* (no. 8), *Sumer is icumen in* (no. 9), *Gabriel fram heven-king* (no. 15) and *Worldes blisse, have good day* (no. 17) are Type I; *Brid on breere* (no. 16) and *Lou, lou, wer he goth* (no. 19) and *Lullay, lullay: Als I lay on Yoolis night* (no. 20) are Type II: *Man mai longe lives weene* (no. 6) and *Edi be thu, heven-queene* (no. 13) are Type III and the upper part of *Fuweles in the frith* (no. 8) is Type IV.

Detailed analysis of contour cannot be made here. It can, however, be quickly observed that whatever the total compass of a tune may be, one whose contour contains gradients which are steep in relation to that compass has a recognizably different musical character from one with a smoother contour. The contours of six of these songs — nos. 5, 6, 13, 15, 16 and 20 — show a number of steep gradients resulting from ascending and descending interval-leaps of fourths, fifths and sixths, both within and, less significantly, between musical units. A few examples are the falling fifth at the beginning of no. 5, falling sixth in bars 25-26 of no. 6, rising and falling fifths in the first phrase of no. 13, rising and falling sixths in bars 4-5 and 12-13 of no. 16, and rising fourths at the beginning of verse and burden of no. 20. These songs have in common tune elements which are not those of ritual plainsong; for this and for other features which are discussed in connection with unit-design and rhythm, they form a coherent musical group within the corpus of surviving medieval song in English.

RHYTHM AND UNIT-DESIGN

As explained in the notes on the music of the individual songs, not all are unequivocally in constantly and equally measured rhythm. Of the ten songs listed in Table 2 on this page, those whose rhythmic notation is equivocal are transcribed here in measured rhythm, with the exception of no. 8, which is transcribed in flexibly measured, equal-note rhythm. In the others, whether or not they are derived from a rhythmically unambiguous original, account is taken of the fact that duple measure with duple subdivision is extremely rare in written medieval music. Most measured music written down before about 1450 is in duple rhythm with triple subdivision (6/8 in modern notation) or triple rhythm with duple subdivision (3/4). All the measured songs in this group are transcribed in one or other of these rhythms. (This does not imply that medieval song was monotonous to the ear; a further complex of factors, of which tempo and timbre are extremely important, is involved in any execution of music.)

The chief elements in the unit-design of tunes are progression, repetition and recurrence, the last two either with or without significant change. In songs where the relation of syllable to note is relatively straightforward, one line of verse and one unit of music generally coincide. The exceptions here are nos. 16 and 19. The composer of no. 16 matched the characteristic breaks in the text of the first, third and fourth lines in each verse with a unit-separation in the music. He did this in the first line with a unit-repeat, in the third with a falling cadence on d' (bars 10-11), and in the fourth with a rising cadence to c' (bars 15-16) in which to some extent he anticipated the final cadence. The second unit of the music for the fourth line is a recurrence, with the last note changed, of the second unit for the third line. Song no. 19 has a four-bar textless final unit of music, whose technical name is *cauda*. There are many analogous cases of such vocalized units or sections in the sacred music of the thirteenth and fourteenth centuries.

Where music was made for a pre-existing poem, it might be expected that the rhyme-scheme of the poem — obviously a significant element in its structure and sound, whether read silently, spoken aloud or sung — would have some influence on the unit-design of the music. This rarely took the form of identity of pattern, since the functions of unit-repetition and recurrence in music and of terminal sound-repetition and recurrence in verse are not truly analogous. Also, identical music can be used only for lines of identical lengths, which is not necessarily the case with rhymed lines. Rhyme linking successive lines, or a rhyme-scheme which is immediately repeated may, however, often be set to a repeated musical unit or units, provided the number of stresses allows this. Tabulation of the unit-designs and rhyme-schemes of these songs, in the second and fourth columns of Table 3 (p. 69), shows that in no case are these completely identical. They are close to identity in *Edi be thu* (no. 13), where both repetition and recurrence are employed in a simple design of four units. Verse and music elements are consummately matched, in a much more complicated relationship, in *Gabriel fram heven-king* (no. 15(ii)). This has only one small asymmetry, occurring in the first stanza of the English text where the rhyme dd is not exact. (The third of the five versions printed in this volume is used as the basis for discussion.) In the relation of unit-design to rhyme-scheme in no. 15(ii), slight divergence appears at the ninth line in each stanza, shown in the table as e. This three-syllable line with only one stress is set to an extension added to the musical unit D. This lengthened form of D, shown in the table as D + x, is appropriately used again for the penultimate verse-line which rhymes with the ninth line.

The author or authors of the Latin and English poems of *Perspice Christicola / Sumer is icumen in* (no. 9) did not make their rhyme-schemes correspond as closely as did the writer or writers of the two texts of *Angelus ad virginem / Gabriel fram heven-king* (no. 15). Each rhyme-pair of the opening pattern abab of the Latin text of no. 9 is set to a seven-stress unit of music. The rhyme-music relation in this part of the English text is less usual: the verse-segment with rhyme a goes to the first seven-stress unit of music, that with the rhymes bba goes to the second seven-stress unit. There is then close agreement until the final nine-stress unit of music, where the rhyme-pattern of the Latin text has a new element d, giving the pattern ddb, while the English poem has only the original a rhyme — the predominant '-u' ending.

The rota-tune of *Sumer is icumen in* was made in conformity with both the repeated *rondellus*-formula which lies below it and also with the musical requirements of an exact canon. In the former respect it resembles a motet, whose tune(s) and text(s) not only have a unit-rhyme relation but are written, in most cases without doubt jointly, over a pre-existing tenor. Consequently, motet-tunes characteristically have asymmetrical stress-lengths and no unit-repetition or unit-recurrence, and motet-texts are only exceptionally stanzaic and metrically regular, at least in the thirteenth century. The unit-design and rhyme-scheme of *Worldes blisse, have good day* (no. 17) are very typical in these respects. The absence of repetition or recurrence of musical units does not imply lack of coherence in the tune-material; this is provided chiefly by the recurrence of shorter tune- and rhythm-elements, conventionally though not very appropriately called motives. The progressively changing and rarely recurring rhymes of *Worldes blisse, have good day* are a characteristic feature of motet texts. The fact that this feature is also more apparent in *Perspice Christicola* than in *Sumer is icumen in* is probably relevant to the question of text-priority in the Summer Canon. It strengthens the possibility that the Latin text was first and that the writer of the English text, whether or not he was the same person, wrote a *contrafactum* whose musical unit / rhyme-scheme relation is more symmetrical and therefore less motet-like.

Besides the matching of verse-line and music-unit in this kind of song, there is also the internal rhythm-relation of relative stress between syllables and notes. Present-day musical notation, formulated to represent post-seventeenth-century rhythmic idioms, is an imperfect medium for notating medieval rhythmic idioms. One of the uses of bar-lines drawn through a musical staff is to indicate a continuous musical metre, i.e. a theoretically constant stress-pattern. In the case of 3/4 time this is basically:

| Undivided beats | // | X | X |
| Subdivided beats | /x | /x | /x |

In 6/8 time it is:

| Undivided beats | // | X |
| Subdivided beats | /xx | /xx |

//=stressed beat; X=unstressed beat; /=secondarily stressed beat-division; x=unstressed beat-division.

Bar-lines in this sense were not used before the seventeenth century. It was not long after their introduction that Milton wrote that Henry Lawes was the first English musician to set English poetry with 'just note and accent'. This sweeping tribute and its reflection on all previous setters of vernacular texts — including Milton's father, whose music did not have the 'benefit' of bar-lines — are both undeserved. As far as stress and non-stress are concerned, bar-lines do no more than diagram visually their recurrence-pattern. In practice the relative degree of stress and non-stress depends on a complex of many factors, written and unwriteable, and this is equally true whether the music is a text-setting or not.

With few exceptions, bar-lines appear to be inevitable in music published for present-day use. Editors of pre-seventeenth-century music must therefore supply them, though they do not appear in the original notation, and also take account of their stress-implications for a performer of today. The element of stress in the performance of measured music (*musica mensurata*) was not directly discussed by medieval theorists, though word-stress in the performance of plainsong (*cantus planus*) was a concern of ritualists and was explained in the book called an *Accentuarius*. The *figurae* used in written measured music expressed proportionate lengths which, in the performance of group music, were regulated by the beater of the *tactus*. His stroke indicated the tempo of the basic time-value and apparently had no implication of stress or of metrical grouping. Stress-patterns were

undoubtedly implied, but their realization was a matter for the individual performers. In rhythmically complicated part-music an elaborate criss-cross of rhythmic tensions resulted from these constantly shifting stress-patterns, all proportionately related to the *tactus*. Ensemble music with homogeneous rhythm — which did not need a *tactus*-beater — and solo song on a straightforward rhythmic basis automatically set up their appropriate stress-patterns. Since the discussion of rhythm which follows takes the transcriptions in the volume as the point of reference, it necessarily involves presuppositions about stress connected with the present-day use of bar-lines. It is assumed that reader or performer will bear in mind the essentially relative stress function of bar-lines and the *rationale* of their absence in written-down medieval music. Examination of rhythmic matters will inevitably show the nature of some of the rhythmic problems which occasioned long and often passionate discussion between the editors of the volume. Many of the ultimate decisions involved editorial emendation of text or music or both; all of these are recorded in the notes on the texts and music.

TABLE 3

Item	Music-units and Stresses	Rhyme-segment Stresses	Rhyme-scheme
5	A⁴B²/A⁴B²/C⁴/C⁴/D³	42/42/4/4/3	ab/ab/b/b/a
6	A⁴B⁴A⁴B⁴C⁴ D⁴E⁴F⁴G⁴H²	4444444442	ababbaabbb
8	ABCDD (un-measured)	33333	abbab
9	A⁷/B⁷/C²/D⁷/E⁷/F⁹	Latin: 43/43/2/7/223/233 English: 7/223/2/7/223/233	ab/ab/b/b/ccb/ddb a/bba/a/a/cca/aaa
13	A⁴B⁴/A⁴B⁴/C⁴C⁴A⁴B⁴	44444444	ababababab
15	A⁴B³A⁴B³C⁴ C⁴A²(D+x)³ E³(D+x)³E³	434344221333	ababccddecec
16	A²A²B⁴C³D²E³D²	4555	abab
17	A⁴B⁴C⁴D⁴ E⁴/F⁴G⁴H³/ J³/K⁴L⁴M⁴/N⁴O⁴P²/ Q⁴R⁵/S³/T³U⁴V⁵	44444/443/4/ 444/442/442/3/ 344	aabbc/cdd/e/eff/ ggh/hhj/j/jcc
19	A³B²C⁴D²E⁴ (text-less)	4442	aabc
20	Burden: A⁴B⁴ Stanza: A⁴C³D⁴E³	44 4343	aa bcbc

Table 3 above gives the following information about the items indicated — either the complete item or, in the case of stanzaic pieces, one stanza: in the second column the number of stresses in each unit of tune, in the third column the number of stresses in each segment of text which has rhyme, and in the fourth column the rhyme-scheme concerned. A stroke between letter-symbols in the second column indicates a rest in the music. Though the presence of a rest enforces a break, a break is frequently understood without specific indication being given. To facilitate comparison strokes have also been drawn between the figures and letters in the third and fourth columns at the points corresponding to rests written in the music.

Edi be thu, heven-queene (no. 13) is uncomplicated in the relation of the elements shown in Table 3, and *Miri it is while sumer ilast* (no. 5) is only a little less so. The first music-unit of *Man mai longe lives weene* (no. 6) is a four-stress unit five bars in length. The musician set the last word of the line to two bars, though previously each pair of syllables takes one bar. In such a case the first beats of two successive bars (here bars 4 and 5) assume the duple rhythm /X. In a similar way the 4343 stress-pattern stanzas of *Lullay, lullay: Als I lay on Yoolis night* (no. 20) are set to eight bars of music by the device of changing in bars 3 and 11 from the theoretical /x/x in each bar to a whole-bar stress-pattern /X. Temporary changes of this kind to a single-stress bar occur also in *Perspice, Christicola / Sumer is icumen in* (no. 9). In bars 13-14 the relation of half-bar to stress and unstress which obtains in the first two music-units is changed to that of one bar to stress and unstress, on the words 'filio / sing cuccu'. The four syllables 'vitae donat / cuccu, cuccu' are set in this way in bars 23-24. Since this is also the rhythm of the two-part *rondellus*, these two stress-patterns are in fact present continuously throughout the song.

The character of the verse and of the duplum-tune of *Worldes blisse, have good day* (no. 17) are directly connected with the rhythmic structure given to the pre-existing tenor, which was unmeasured in its plainsong matrix. Its length of eighty-four bars contains three statements of the *Benedicamus Domino* tune disposed in twelve statements of the seven-bar rhythm devised for it. A large part of the craft of motet-writing lay in devising an upper voice or voices conforming to the tenor as to intervals, while concealing its repetitive and symmetrical rhythm- and unit-structure. The writer of *Worldes blisse, have good day* fitted seven four-stress units to the first twenty-eight-bar statement of the tenor, which is disposed in four seven-bar rhythmic units. Over the second tenor-statement, beginning at bar 29, he made two three-stress units followed by one two-stress unit whose second stress coincides with the first note of the third tenor-statement. The duplum above that statement has units respectively of four, five, three, three, four and five stresses. While every four-stress unit goes to a four-stress line of the poem, not all other units have the same number of stresses as the line with which they are matched. There is agreement in the three-stress units in bars 29-31, 68-71 and 72-75 (the last two lines have rhyme) and in the two-stress unit in bars 56-57. The three-stress unit in bars 32-34, however, goes with a four-stress line by giving an unexpected and perhaps intentionally arresting twist to its accentuation. The five-stress unit in bars 62-67 accommodates a four-stress and a two-stress line, by setting justifiably the words 'be my sheeld' to an anapaestic rhythm. The final five-bar unit provides an appropriate stretching of the last three words of a four-stress line to three bars with the stress pattern /x/. These comparisons show the special kind of interdependence between tenor, upper-voice tune(s) and poem(s) which is characteristic of a motet; none of these elements can be discussed realistically in isolation.

The part-writing techniques used in the group of songs we have called hybrid (nos. 21-33) have already been noticed. The compasses of these tunes, given in Table 4 below, are not markedly different from those of the ten songs just discussed; their modes, however, are. Though it would be unwise to base trend-deductions on such small samplings, the differences are worth noting: five songs with final *d* as against one, four with *c* as against two, one with *a* as against none, none with *f* compared with four. Three songs in each group have *g* as final.

The greatest differences in tune-style between the two groups of songs are in their contours and unit-designs. In the second group, contour-changes are, in general, more graduated. Tunes are almost completely consistent in the occurrence of interval-leaps of fourths and fifths, while steep gradients are virtually absent. Leaps of both a sixth and a seventh occur only in *Trew, on wam ys al my tryst* (no. 25), some of whose other characteristics have

TABLE 4

Item	Final	Compass of Tune	Notes in Compass
21	c	g-a'	9
22	c	a-a'	8
23	(d) (incomplete)		
24	d	b-a'	
25	g	Tenor I d-d', Tenor II d-e'	8, 9
26	d	g-a'	9
27	d	b-a'	7
28	c	g-g'	8
29	c	g-b'	10
30	d	c'-b'	7
31	g	e-f'	9
32	a	c'-d'	9
33	g	c'-f"	11

been noted earlier as more probably indigenous than foreign-influenced. *Thys Yool, thys Yool* (no. 28) has the only case of an octave-leap, in bar 8; this, however, comes at a point where there is an implied break between units. The consistency of contour in most of these songs is connected with the frequent use of a motive which begins with or includes a descending fourth. *My cares comen ever anew* (no. 22), for example, has eight instances. Descending fifths and rising fourths or fifths are less frequent. The tunes of the last three songs of this group are more complicated than the others in contour and rhythm, and their consistency results from a different set of motives. Some of these are used with slight variations: *Pater noster, most of myght* (no. 31) has five forms of a cadence-motive which includes *b*-flat and ends on *g* (in bars 5, 22, 31, 54 and 56). Some of these are also used in the two remaining songs.

The musical units of these songs are more variable in length and also less closely related to their poem-structures than those of the former group. A complete section of music is now the operative unit in a largely conventionalized set of poetic-musical designs. Unit-repetition (as distinct from section-repetition) does not occur and unit-recurrence is infrequent. The units which make up each section form a tune-continuum whose musical coherence depends largely on repeated or recurring motives, sometimes varied. These may be short, like the eighth bar of *Ye have so longe keepyt o* (no. 21) or occasionally unit-length, like the varied recurrence of bars 12-15 of *I have set my hert so hy* (no. 24) in bars 28-31.

The relations of poetic line to music-unit and of syllable to note are more varied in these songs than in the earlier group. At times, particularly in the last three songs, the division of units within sections tends to overlap and obscure the division of lines; here, the tune-continuum seems to take precedence over the poem-structure. The most obvious design feature is the definition and repetition of sections, which do not, however, have a constant relation to the stanzas and lines of the poetry, unlike the *formes fixes* of the French *ballade*, *rondeau* and *virelai*. The section-definition of these songs and its relation to the stanza- and line-structure of the poem in each case are shown in Table 5.

The layout of the preponderant musical form AB^1B^2, which is that of nine of the twelve songs analysed here (no. 23, whose ending is lost, is disregarded), resembles superficially that of a French *virelai* / Italian *ballata* in showing no repeat of the first section and having an *ouvert* and *clos* repeat of the second section. Unlike the *virelai* and *ballata*, these songs do not have a return (*volta*) to a refrain line (*ripresa*) common to all stanzas.

TABLE 5

Item	Section-design	No. of Stanzas	No. of Lines in each Stanza	No. of Lines to each Music-section
21	A^1A^2(same text) B^1B^2	3	6 5 5	6 6 (same text) 5 5
22	AB^1B^2	2	4 4	4 2 2
24	A^1A^2	2	5 5	5 5
25	$A^1A^2B^1B^2$	1	8	2 2 2 2
26	AB^1B^2	2	7 7	5 1 1
27	AB^1B^2	2	5 4	5 2 2
28	AB^1B^2	3	9 4 4	9 4 4
29	AB^1B^2	2	6 6	6 3 3
30	AB^1B^2	2	4 4	4 2 2
31	AB^1B^2	2	4 6	4 3 3
32	AB^1B^2	2	4 4	4 2 2
33	AB^1B^2	2	8 6	8 3 3

[1] indicates *ouvert* (first ending), numeral [2] indicates *clos* (second).
In nos. 26, 27, 29 and 30 the B section is indicated in the manuscript as 'secundus versus'.
In no. 31 the tenor of the *clos* ending of B is missing.

Neither did the poets of these English songs write a consistent length of stanza (theirs vary from four lines to nine) or number of stanzas (there are one, two or three). Consequently the relation of music to text is not the same in all nine songs with the same musical form. In eight of these the poem has two stanzas; the first is set to the first section of music and the second to the second section of music used twice. The scribe of the Cambridge manuscript indicated the beginning of the second section of music in four cases (*Danger me hath, unskylfuly*, no. 26; *I rede that thou be joly and glad*, no. 27; *Wel wer hym that wyst*, no. 29; and *Me lykyth ever the lenger the bet*, no. 30) with the words *secundus versus*. In the case of no. 26 this is ambiguous because of missing text (see pp. 212-3); the beginning of the second section of music seems to come at mid-stanza, not at the second stanza, and the musical form seems to require that the last two lines of each stanza be sung twice. (For an alternative reconstruction of this song, see note on p. 223.) The other song in this form (no. 28) has three stanzas, the second and third of which are set to the second section of music.

The two other musical designs in this group of songs are A^1A^2 and $A^1A^2B^1B^2$. The poem of *I have set my hert so hy* (no. 24) has a final refrain-line, as did a *ballade*, but with one word-change (as edited). The musical form, however, is not identical with that of a *ballade*. *Ye have so longe keepyt o* (no. 21) has three stanzas, with *ouvert* and *clos* endings for the six lines of the first stanza; each of the second and third stanzas is sung to the second section of music. The manuscript did not provide text for the repeat of the first section of music — that with the *clos* ending. In the transcription the text of the music section with the *ouvert* ending is used again. Though immediate repetition of a section of the text of a solo song was uncommon in the Middle Ages, it seems called for in this song and in no. 26.

The preponderance in these songs of duple rhythm with triple subdivision — the only exception is *I rede that thou be joly and glad* (no. 27) — and the occurrence simultaneously of duple and triple subdivision have been noticed earlier. The example of duple-triple subdivision cited then was in the eighth bar of *Trew, on wam ys al my tryst* (no. 25), where its use involves subdivisions of half a bar in 6/8 time, as it does also in the ninth bar of *Wel wer hym that wyst* (no. 29). It occurs as an idiom covering a whole bar in Edmund's song *Thys Yool, thys Yool* (no. 28) and in the last three songs in this group. Its various guises are pervasive enough in these three songs to act as an integrating rhythmic motive. In this respect, these songs show an early instance of a rhythmic idiom which is one of the most characteristic features of the written music of the first half of the fifteenth century.

PLAINSONG AND ITS NOTATION

The music of songs nos. 21-33 is distinguishable from that of the ten songs listed in Table 2 (p. 67) chiefly by features of demonstrable continental origin. Both of these groups differ from the other songs in this volume (nos. 1-4, 7, 10-12 and 14) by showing little or no evidence of plainsong influence or derivation. It is on the whole true that pre-sixteenth-century plainsong was a supranational music, joined to the supranational ritual language (Latin) of Western Christianity. Its tunes show relatively little variance in different times and places; once established, they were deliberately preserved and defended from the usual processes of musical interaction and change.

This was also true, within narrower time-boundaries, of the public ceremonial music of aristocracy and of signal music for this and less exalted uses. Other kinds of music, as far as we can know them from written records, often show both contemporary regional differences in idiom and technique and considerable changes over periods of time; some of these may validly be described as differences of music-dialect within the total music-language of Western Europe. Truly international tunes seem to have been exceptional in the written music of the Middle Ages outside the sphere of Christian ritual chant. Moreover, the surviving evidence shows that tunes which were used away from their place of origin were generally changed to some extent in the processes of transmission and notation (no. 4 is a good example).[50]

The contrast between the relatively unvarying, unchanging ritual music of the West and its constantly varying and continually changing non-ritual and secular music, while broadly true, is not absolute. Gregorian chant (so-called from St. Gregory's reorganization of the Roman *scholae cantorum* and codification of their repertory) became the common stock, almost totally ousting the other ethnic liturgies — Ambrosian, Gallican, Mozarabic and Celtic; nevertheless, its repertory and tunes were never totally uniform. Secular churches had diocesan and local peculiarities, while the chants of some monastic orders were deliberately 'reformed'.[51] Many differences in liturgical repertory were connected with local devotion to a particular saint or to other idiosyncratic usage, while a few tune-variants were instances of music-dialect. One example of this is the beginning of the angel's *Kyrieleison* in St. Godric's *Crist and Sainte Marie* (no. 2). Its first-mode *variatio*:

was written in north-central European plainsong books in the variant form:

which has a markedly steeper contour and also a suggestion of gapped mode.[52] Similarly, the opening of the Palm Sunday processional hymn *Gloria, laus et honor,* usually:[53]

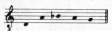

appears thus in a Leipzig Gradual:[54]

---

[50] See also F. Gennrich, 'Internationale mittelalterliche Melodien', *Zeitschrift für Musikwissenschaft,* xi (1928-9).

[51] See, for example, S. R. Marosszecki, *Les origines du chant cistercien,* Analecta Sacri Ordinis Cisterciensis, viii, Rome, 1952.

[52] See Dom J. Gatard, 'Les récitatives modales des 3ᵉ et 4ᵉ modes et les manuscrits bénéventains et aquitains', *Études Grégoriennes,* i (1954), p. 9 for discussion of this and other instances.

[53] As in *Graduale Sarisburiense,* ed. W. H. Frere, London, 1894, pl. 83.

[54] Leipzig, Musikbibliothek, MS 385, f. cxlviii verso.

For some time after its apparently sixth/seventh-century origins, the notation of Western music was merely mnemonic, using accent-symbols called neumes to indicate tune-contour and note-grouping. Following Guido of Arezzo's extension, about 1050, of the principle of using horizontal lines to indicate the exact pitch of neumes, pitch could be defined by setting square-shaped symbols, still assembled in neume-groupings, on a staff of four or five lines. It does not seem likely that a comparably precise and standardized rhythmic measurement was also implied by this kind of notation before the late twelfth century. If it was, this must have been through then-current associations about which we now have no certain knowledge. Though an identifiable system of rhythmic modes came into use for certain kinds of music in the late twelfth century, plainsong was probably still sung in asymmetrically-measured, flexibly-related notes.[55] Whether non-plainsong notation after about 1175 carried the same rhythmic implications for monophonic music as it did for polyphonic music is as yet uncertain. It may have done so in songs whose text was syllabically or nearly syllabically set, but a regular and symmetrically-measured rhythm seems often inappropriate and is sometimes extremely cumbersome in songs with a less simple text-music relationship. In these, a rhythm analogous to that of plainsong seems more probable. It is possible that a twelfth- or thirteenth-century singer of monophonic song selected the rhythmic manner of his performance on then familiar but now lost criteria.

It is true that musical notation has at no time or place in its history given complete specifications for performance. As Charles Seeger has written:

> It cannot be too strongly emphasized that what is sung and the singing of it are not, musically speaking, two things, but one. Abstraction of the song from its singing is a necessary procedure in talking about music that makes two things out of the original one. This is especially evident when the song is envisaged as printed words and notes. A singing of the song in a singing style other than that of its own tradition is likely to be a distortion comparable to the translation of the words into a foreign language.

According to this view a song, properly considered as the singing of a song, is likely to be changed by mere removal from its original performance-context, even though its written form may remain identical. The factors involved in 'the variance and non-variance of the six essential functions or resources of the singing voice' are tabulated by Seeger[56] as two primary tonal functions of pitch and loudness, two primary rhythmic functions of tempo and proportion, together with the tonal function of timbre and the rhythmic function of accent (stress). Each of the last two is a compound of simple functions; timbre is a compound of pitches (upper partials) with varying degrees of loudness, accent is a compound of relative loudness, pitch and duration. Notators of Western song at various epochs and in various places have tried to indicate more or less precisely some of these functions in given songs, but a notation does not yet exist for all of them and is probably impractical as a performance-prescription, though possible in retrospect as a performance-record.

SINGING TIMBRES

While direct knowledge of the timbre of medieval singing, in England or elsewhere, is not possible, some of the factors which certainly bore upon it are known. The European Renaissance of the sixteenth century seems to have been a watershed in singing timbres as in many other musical practices. The style of singing called *bel canto* was developed in the seventeenth century, mainly in Italian opera, which by the eighteenth century had become an international genre. *Bel canto* has been defined as 'Italian vocal technique of the eighteenth century with its emphasis on beauty of sound and brilliance of performance, rather than dramatic expression or Romantic emotion'.[57] The contrast that this definition points between eighteenth-century and later opera-singing was probably less marked than were the differences between *bel canto* and pre-*bel canto*. The kind of difference which may be involved here is suggested by Charles Seeger's observation of the timbres of current conservatory-trained singers and those in oral traditions:

> The singers trained in the *bel canto* of Italian opera or in the tradition of the German *lied* tend to produce a desired quality in the stream of sound rather than in

[55] 'Item cum longas et breves nominentur non sic tenentur in plana musica sicut et in organo [i.e., in polyphonic music]; sed omnes note preter pausaciones strenuant et melos equaliter cantetur'. Rome, Vatican Library, MS Reg. lat. 1146, f. 68v.

[56] C. Seeger, 'Versions and variants of the tunes of *Barbara Allen*', *Selected Reports of the Institute of Ethnomusicology of the University of California at Los Angeles,* i, Los Angeles (1960), p. 120.

[57] W. Apel, *Harvard Dictionary of Music,* London, 1970, s.v. 'Bel canto'.

each separate note (barring, of course, exceptional notes to which they wish to give special effect). The British-American folk-singer, on the other hand, seems to give no special thought to quality of sound, but sings in as 'natural' a voice as that in which he talks. Consequently, the singing voice varies greatly according to sex, age and an infinite number of psychological and physiological factors. The lack of any preoccupation of what it ought to be gives, however, to the quality of the traditional singer's singing a clearly recognizable character that can be instantly recognised by other carriers and by connoisseurs of the tradition.

One of the few surviving sources of information about medieval singing deals with ensemble unisonous, not with solo performance. Rules for psalm-singing in choir emphasize conformity in sound and unanimity in ensemble:

> Psalmodia semper pari voce, aequa lance non nimis protrahatur, sed mediocri voce, non nimis velociter sed rotunde, virili, viva et succincta voce psallatur; syllabas, verba, metrum in medio et in finem versus, id est initium, medium et finem, simul incipiamus et pariter dimittamus.[58]
>
> (Let psalmody be sung with an always even voice, on an equal level, not dragged out too much, but moderately, not too quickly, but in a round, manly, lively and succinct voice; let us begin and end the syllables, the words, the half-verse division and the end of the lines, that is, the beginning, middle and end, together.)

The adjectives which qualify the word *voce* suggest a clear, forward timbre and a brisk delivery. Evidence of this kind suggests that Chaucer may have been poking fun at an individual characteristic of the Prioress who

> . . . soong the service dyvyne
> Entuned in hir nose ful semely[59]

and not describing a widespread way of singing plainsong, as has sometimes been suggested. The evidence of many current non-*bel canto* singing timbres is, if used with due discretion, relevant to pre-*bel canto* practices. It might, for example, suggest models for an attempt to recreate the 'high and clear' voice of the Breton *lai*-

singer (one performance-routine is described in *Horn et Rimenhild*)[60] or for the timbre of a medieval friar's voice in *Stond wel, moder, under roode* (no. 11).

The recording of some of the songs in this volume and others from medieval English repertory[61] has underlined the intimate relation between singing-timbre and text-pronunciation which has been little explored until recently. The vowel pronunciation of most singers trained in Western musical institutions is based ultimately on the sung vowels of Italian or on some notion of them. Similarly, the present-day official pronunciation of liturgical Latin is that of modern Italian, which is clearly invalid for medieval plainsong. Professor Dobson's notes on English pronunciation are aimed not only at text-veracity but also at some degree of historical validity in singing-timbre, as far as this can be achieved. Text-pronunciation can be coded to a certain extent by the phonetic alphabet. There are no symbols to indicate singing-timbre — only roughly descriptive words and indications of technical means. More specific comment on this will be found in Notes on Performance in Appendix 3.

ASYMMETRICAL RHYTHM

Assuming the asymmetrical theory of plainsong rhythm to be valid at least for the Middle Ages, Seeger's compound rhythmic function of stress in performance has to be determined chiefly by the text, since there are no unequivocally regular stress-points in the music. The 'law of accent' in Western plainsong has been enunciated thus: 'Gregorian melody, if its architectonic contour be considered, is bound to the grammatical accents of the liturgical text';[62] that is, by the characteristics of Latin stress at the time the tunes were compiled — mainly in the fifth and sixth centuries. It has been estimated that eighty per cent of the chants which formed the Gregorian corpus show close coincidence between the high points of the tune-contour and the tonic accents of the text. The chief exceptions occur in simpler chants such as psalm-tones, in tunes adapted to new texts, and in hymns, which have the same tune for every stanza. Apart from these cases the rising-followed-by-falling contour of most design units in plainsong also sometimes

[58] S. J. P. van Dijk, 'Saint Bernard and the *Instituta Patrum* of Saint Gall', *Musica Disciplina,* iv (1950), p. 105.

[59] General Prologue, A 122-3.

[60] See p. 87.

[61] *Medieval English Lyrics,* Argo record ZRG 5443 and *Now Make we Merthe,* Argo record ZRG 526.

[62] Dom P. Ferretti, *Esthétique Grégorienne,* Paris, 1938, Chapters II-IV.

goes against this 'accent-law' (in fact a retrospective deduction, not a law) in less ornate chants which have fewer small contours within their overall contour than do the more elaborate chants.

The same analysis has shown that there is no constant relation between accent and quantity, however simple or ornate a chant may be.

> In all styles [of chant], the tonic accent is sometimes short, sometimes long; and when it is long, either it is longer than the syllables that precede and follow it, or it is less long than they. Moreover, the syllables of a word can be all short or all long, and the length varies from syllable to syllable. Finally, in ornate chants, it is sometimes the accent which carries a *vocalise,* at other times this *vocalise* is found on the following syllable or on some other syllable which precedes it. Observe also the frequent case where, in *Alleluias,* it is the second syllable which is given the most ample melodic development. From this ensemble of facts one conclusion is inescapable: that in Gregorian chant, not only the accent, but all the syllables of a word, are neutral as to quantity or duration, in the sense that the accented syllable and all other syllables are as susceptible of shortness as of length and of varied length.[63]

A recurrent feature of chants with prose texts is the setting of a final (or less often, penultimate) unaccented syllable to more notes than a preceding accented syllable. This feature has been related to an observation of the Roman grammarian Varro (116-27 B.C.), who cited musical usage to show that high sounds tend to be short and thin and low (final) sounds to be long and full.[64] A similar principle seems to operate in cases where the music for the last unit of a sectional design such as the Mass *Kyrie* which has nine sections, or the Mass *Alleluia*-cum-sequence which has five, is considerably longer than any of the other sections.

SAINT GODRIC'S SONGS

Considered from these rhythmic aspects, the relation of text and music in St. Godric's three songs (nos. 1-3) is similar to that in Gregorian chant. Occurrences agreeing with the so-called 'law of accent' are statistically higher in *Sainte Marie viergene* and *Crist and Sainte Marie* than in *Sainte Nicholas, Godes druth,* which has one note to a syllable virtually throughout (the two notes on the second syllable of *faire* are one plicated note in the

manuscript). As in plainsong, stress and quantity, measured by the number of notes to a syllable, rarely coincide; the length of a syllable seems related to its position in the music-continuum, which in prose-setting plainsong tends to have in the same chant both monotone and monotone-like reciting passages and ornate vocalizing passages. This apparent incongruity of word-setting seems to be characteristic of some formulaic music when used for prose-texts with their varying sentence-lengths and stress-patterns. Many passages of St. Godric's songs show the characteristic plainsong juxtaposition of single-note recitation and more or less brief *vocalise.*

Godric's possible tune-sources and contexts — leaving aside their alleged supernatural origin — are difficult to specify, since there is nothing contemporary except plainsong to use for comparison. The angels' invocations in *Crist and Sainte Marie* use recognizable plainsong tune-formulae though Burgwen's song does not. That the two sections are not at the same pitch of the mode, although they are said to have alternated in St. Godric's vision, accentuates this difference between the angelic ritual music and language and the singing of a human soul, albeit in paradise. The music of the second stanza of *Sainte Marie viergene* also has plainsong tune-elements and contour. Its outline resembles an elaboration of the psalm-tone of the second mode — white note indicates reciting note:

The other sections of St. Godric's songs have the common feature of seeming to be based on gapped scales, and may (again leaving the vision story out of account) be from secular, or at least non-Gregorian sources. The musical framework of the first stanza of *Sainte Marie viergene* is the following gapped scale (additional *b* flat is structural in the Harley manuscript variant):

Its dramatically rising contour on separate syllables at the words *onfoo, schild, help* is not a common idiom in plainsong. The tune of Burgwen's song has as main notes:

and its first two units have essentially the same framework:

---

[63] Ibid., p. 345.

[64] 'Acuta exilior est et brevior et omni modo minor est quam gravis, ut est facile ex musica cognoscere, cuius imago prosodia'. Quoted ibid., p. 8.

This contour is the same, at a lower pitch, as that on *onfoo, schild, help* in the first song. *Sainte Nicholas, Godes druth* has a tune in the first mode, whose sixth degree is not expressly notated, though it may be implied for singing the plicated note on the second syllable of *faire*. The prominence of intervals of the third and fourth is characteristic of tunes formed on a gapped scale. The pentatonic (with five sounds in the octave) is the commonest gapped scale in Western music, and the tunes of the first and third lines of *Sainte Nicholas, Godes druth* are pentatonic.

The fact that tune-idioms and contours found in Godric's songs also occur among oral-tradition tunes still current in northern England and Scotland lends weight to the supposition of their non-church origin. For example, the contour, intervals and mode of *Sainte Nicholas* and also of *Sainte Marie viergene* as far as the caesura in the second line are strikingly similar to the third and fourth units of the version of the ballad *Inverey* (or *The Baron of Braikley*) as sung by Owen Hand (see Ex. 2). The events narrated in this ballad text are mid-seventeenth-century but the tune elements may well be many centuries older.

Ex. 2

Scale

STANZAIC SONGS
IN ASYMMETRICAL RHYTHM

The music of *Worldes blis ne last no throwe* (no. 7) and of *The milde Lomb, isprad o roode* (no. 14) is stanzaic in form and plainsong-oriented in tune. Both belong to the category of hymn, using the term in the strict Western Christian sense of a metrical poem sung during one of the daily offices (Matins, Lauds, etc.). Though hymns, beginning with eight or so which may have been written by St. Ambrose (*c.* 340-97) [65] or originated not long after his time, are essentially syllabic settings, many

post-Ambrosian tunes and some later forms of fourth/fifth-century tunes do in fact contain single syllables sung across several notes. Ambrose's hymns were meant initially for singing by a church congregation [66] and their tunes probably embodied some secular elements. Their simple and regular form — all have eight four-line stanzas in iambic dimeters throughout — may have been sung to symmetrically measured musical rhythm, with two beats to a long syllable and one to a short syllable. This could not have been done, however, with their later, somewhat ornate forms, which were sung in choir and not by congregations. As in Gregorian chant generally, the groups of two or more notes in the elaborated forms of Ambrosian hymn tunes, and in those composed throughout the Middle Ages, occurred on long and short syllables indifferently. [67] There is no regular relation between stress and quantity, as represented by musical length. It seems certain, therefore, on these rhythmic grounds alone, that the medieval hymns, although their poems were written in regularly stressed metres, were sung flexibly. Metrical regularity in Ambrosian and other hymn-metres did not preclude an occasional 'extra' syllable, which was usually accommodated by a note-repeat.

Hymns were nevertheless written down with the tune over the first stanza only; this procedure was followed in the writing of all the hymn-form songs in this volume (nos. 6, 7, 13, 14 and 16). In *Worldes blis ne last no throwe* (no. 7) there are no 'extra' syllables in this sense; all seven of its ten-line stanzas have the same syllable-count — 8898 9998 88. However, a mensural interpretation of the tune (which survives in two forms with differing degrees of ornateness is excluded not only by the stress-patterns, which vary in stanzas 4-7 from those established in stanzas 1-3, but also by the elaborateness of the tune. It has been observed that the music of this song 'is remarkable for its adherence to movement by step' (see p. 299). It seems very probable, however, that this characteristic, which is apparent in both surviving forms, is the product of singers' elaborations of a simpler, structural contour. A hypothetical reconstruction of a notional — though unverifiable — original (see Ex. 3) shows the unit-design ABCB/DEC^{1}F/E^{1}B; the rhyme-scheme is abab/cccb/cb. The dividing strokes inserted here in both designs indicate a grouping of units into sections which agree with an obvious grouping of the unit note-endings, which are *g g*

[65] See U. Sesini, *Poesia e musica nella latinitá cristiana dall III al X secolo,* Turin, 1949, pp. 60-97.

[66] G. Reese, *Music in the Middle Ages,* New York, 1940, p. 104.

[67] For examples of this and of local variants in hymn-tunes see P. Wagner, *Gregorianische Formenlehre,* Hildesheim, 1962 (reprint), pp. 462-79.

f g / g f d a / f g. This skeletal outline also reveals two recurring note-patterns. That marked x is the first five notes of B, also the last five notes of C¹; that marked y is the last five notes of C, also of E and E¹.

Ex. 3

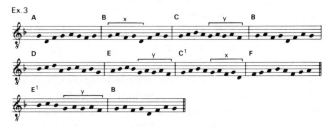

The four-line tune of *The milde Lomb, isprad o roode* (no. 14) is no less ornate than the Arundel manuscript version of *Worldes blis ne last no throwe* and its notation as recorded also has plicated notes, which *Worldes blis* has not. The plica's exact significance in medieval notation, where it was shown by an attached vertical stroke, is unclear. At times it appears to have meant an additional note, at times a lengthening. Some evidence suggests that it denoted a particular manner of sound-production, or that it was used when sounding certain consonants; this last obviously cannot apply in a stanzaic song. None of these usages seems to have been the invariable one. Plicated note-forms in the original notation of this song have been interpreted in the transcription as connecting or anticipating sounds. As in *Worldes blis ne last no throwe* and in plainsong generally, there is no regular relation between syllable-stress and syllable-extension. In *The milde Lomb isprad o roode,* unlike *Worldes blis,* there is considerable variation in syllable-count to a line — though the basic count is 8887 to the half-stanza — with consequent variation in stress-pattern. Separate notes must in some stanzas be sung to a single syllable. Mensural rhythm is ruled out by stress-variation and by ornateness, whose extent may again be suggested by reduction to a hypothetical unadorned form (see Ex. 4). The rhyme-scheme of the complete stanza is aaab cccb, the unit-design of the tune is ABCD and its unit-ending notes are *f a c f.*

Ex. 4

SEQUENCES: THEIR CONTEXT AND DESIGN

While there may well be secular elements in what we have postulated as the 'basic' tunes of *Worldes blis* and *The milde Lomb* and in the kind of elaboration given to them, and also in the earliest hymns of the Western liturgy, there seems little evidence in either case except for the internal evidence of the tunes. The possibility has been put forward that poetic and musical influences from outside the church's repertory were operative on the origins of the sequence, the genre to which belong the English-language laments of the Virgin Mary at the crucifixion of Christ (nos. 10(ii)-12). Besides the apparently non-churchy nature and names of some of the tunes, there are contemporary musical happenings and musical references in the texts of sequences, and there are (though three centuries later) secular and sacred *lais* such as *Ar ne kuth ich sorghe non* (no. 4) in sequence-form and with some sequence tune-characteristics, all of which tend to support the possibility of usages of secular origin in the sequence. The best known document in the early history of the sequence is the dedicatory preface of *c.* 884, by Notker the Stammerer of St. Gall (840-912), to his collection of sequences. Notker said that he was introduced to *versus ad sequentias* (i.e. sections of text set to formerly vocalized tunes) by a refugee monk from the monastery of Jumièges,[68] which was several times sacked by Vikings; one such attack was in 862. Notker showed two sequence-poems of his own to Yso, a native of Thorgau who was teacher of the novices. Yso's advice that each syllable should have only one note[69] was followed by Notker in further sequence-poems, which were so approved by the learned Irish monk Moengal (Marcellus), head of the novices' school, that Moengal had them and other sequences written on rolls, presumably with neume notation, for use by boy-pupils and others.[70]

Notker's account shows that his sequences were based on north-French usage. He used already existing French tunes though none in exactly the current form.[71] Sequence-tunes, changed in detail through adaptation to various texts, nevertheless kept their identities as particular aggregations of a relatively limited stock of formulae. While ninth- and tenth-century sequence-tunes had sacred names derived from a sequence-text or an Alleluia-verse, and the names of others seem to charac-

---

[68] In the Antiphonal brought by the monk 'aliqui versus ad sequentias erant modulati'. W. von der Steinen, *Notkeri Poetae Balbuli Liber Hymnorum,* Bern, 1960, p. 6.

[69] 'Singulae motus cantilenae singulas syllabas debent habere'.

[70] 'In rotulas eos congessit et pueris cantandas, aliis alios, insinuavit'.

[71] See N. de Goede, *The Utrecht Prosarium,* Amsterdam, 1965, p. cxix.

terize the tune or denote its supposed place of origin (*preciosa, nobilissima, Metensis, Bauueristica*), a certain number of names definitely suggest non-church origins: *puella turbata, planctus sterilis, cignea, Berta vetula*. This last category of titles also includes some technical musical terms and names of instruments: *cithara* (lyre or harp), *fidicula* (fiddle), *fistula* (whistle-flute), *tuba* (trumpet), *lyra* (lyre), *organa* (organ), *symphonia* (literally 'sounding together'), *tractus iocularis* (jester's tune), *tympanum* (tabor or lyre).

Some tunes were known by different names in different places. The tune indicated *cithara* and *citharis organisque, Deum modulemur ovantes* in the Winchester Tropers of *c*. 1000,[72] for example, was designated *occidentana* in St. Gall and Limoges. In Winchester this tune was used for the Ascension sequence *Rex omnipotens* and also for *Celsa pueri* on Holy Innocents and *Sancti merita Benedicti* on St. Benedict's day. Notker set to it his sequence *Sancti Spiritus*, which has a Beneventan text beginning *Pange nunc lingua,* and at least two later texts are associated with the tune.[73] As written in neumes in the Winchester troper[74] with the heading SQ CITHARA, it has the word Alleluia followed by eleven sections of varying lengths, each with the letter d (for *denus, duplex* or *dis,* equivalent to a repeat sign), and a short final section without repeat sign. This kind of tune-design, with varying degrees of regularity[75] and varying numbers and lengths of sections, was the primary characteristic of sequences, whose text-music relationship diverged only occasionally from Yso's syllabic rule. Since sequence-texts were created for repeated music-sections, their pairs of verses were isosyllabic. The secular names of some of the tunes and the apparent absence from Western liturgical chant before the sequence of the musical device of progressive repetition both tend to support the opinion, based mainly on textual evidence, that 'the beginnings of the sequence lie in the domain of secular as well as of sacred song, in the vernacular as well as in Latin'.[76]

Though St. Godric's songs (nos. 1-3) are the earliest English vernacular poems with surviving music, they are many centuries later than the earliest surviving vernacular texts which are known to have been sung. One of these, beginning *Fore thaem nedfere*, is said to have been sung by the Venerable Bede (*c*. 673-735), who was skilled in vernacular song, in the last weeks of his life.[77] Bede told the story of Caedmon's gift of song, which, like Godric's, was alleged to have come in a vision. Caedmon, a layman who is said to have known nothing about songmaking or singing (*in habitu saeculari . . . constitutus nil carminum aliquando didicerat*), often left the table on convivial occasions where it was the custom for everyone in turn to sing a song, at the moment when he saw that the *cithara* was about to be passed to him (*ille ubi adpropinquare sibi citharam cernebat, surgebat a media caena*). On one such occasion he went to the cattle-barn to sleep and there was commanded in a vision to sing about the creation of the world. Caedmon's reputed first song (he is said by Bede to have made subsequently many songs on Old and New Testaments subjects) consists of nine lines, with the caesura-division of half-lines and the parallelism of sense-elements characteristic of Old English poetry.[78] What its tune-formulae may have been we can only speculate, though within certain limits of probability. More concrete observations may perhaps be made about its unit-design, which is unlikely to have run counter to the poem's verse-structure, and possibly also about its rhythm and that of other Old English poems which may be thought to have been sung.

Though harps and lyres had existed in western Asia for several millennia, and in the Mediterranean and north-western Europe for many centuries, present-day knowledge of their use has hitherto been derived largely from iconography and from a few written references. Few practical speculations on the way they were used in Anglo-Saxon times were made until Professor John Pope put forward a theory of word-rhythm which

---

[72] For evidence for dating the two Winchester tropers (Oxford, Bodleian Library, MS Bodley 775 and Cambridge, Corpus Christi College, MS 473) see A. Holschneider, *Die Organa von Winchester*, Hildesheim, 1968, pp. 19, 24.

[73] See W. H. Frere, *The Winchester Troper*, London, 1894, pp. 229, 235; N. de Goede, *The Utrecht Prosarium*, Amsterdam, 1965, pp. cviii-cx.

[74] Facsimile in Frere, op. cit., pl. 5, with transcription opposite (p. 5a).

[75] Some early sequences were aparallel; see R. Crocker, 'Some ninth-century sequences', *Journal of the American Musicological Society*, xx (1967), p. 372. It has been calculated that 69% of the Winchester sequences, 45% of the St. Gall sequences and the same percentage of the St. Martial sequences have complete parallelism; see H. Husmann, 'Alleluia, Vers und Sequenz', *Annales Musicologiques*, iv (1956), pp. 40-41.

[76] P. Dronke, 'The beginnings of the sequence', *Beiträge zur Geschichte der deutschen Sprache und Literatur*, 87 (1965), p. 69.

[77] The monk Cuthbert's letter *De obitu Bedae*: '. . . quicquid reliquum fuit diei in psalmorum cantu prout potuit se occupabat . . . In nostra quoque lingua, ut erat doctus in nostris carminibus, dicens de terribili exitu animarum e corpore: Fore thaem nedfere' (etc.); *Bede's Ecclesiastical History*, ed. Bertram Colgrave and R.A.B. Mynors, Oxford, 1969, pp. 580-2.

[78] Printed with translation in S. B. Greenfield, *A Critical History of Old English Literature*, London, 1966, p. 170.

involved the suggestion, among others, that the instrument called *cithara* by Bede and *hearpe* in Old English poetry was used to mark 'initial rests' in a line which began with unstressed extra-metrical syllables.[79] In a musician's view, Pope's closely reasoned and generously exemplified theory suffers from reliance on anachronistic musical concepts and terminology. A few points only can be suggested here. For example, the kind of isochronous delivery implied by the use of present-day Western time-signatures is not necessarily appropriate,[80] neither is a voice-lyre relationship based on post-Renaissance musical criteria.

Attention to the identity of the instrument called *hearpe* and *cithara* was focused by the discovery, in 1939, of the remains of an instrument in the Sutton Hoo burial mound. These were assumed at the time to be the remains of a quadrangular harp but have since been recognized as the remains of a Germanic lyre.[81] The question whether an instrument of this kind is likely to have been used as a 'time-keeper' in the delivery of Old English poetry is not answerable in specific terms. It seems unlikely, however, that Greenfield's belief that 'the harp [*read* lyre] was a formal accompaniment to the recitation of the oldest English verse'[82] could apply to all verse-with-music, of whatever kind, length or subject. Closer identification of the styles and techniques of presentation of Old English verse-with-music must await more precise description than has hitherto been available of the ritual and social functions of formal music and/or speech and of the variety of forms which are known historically and currently. On the musical side, the performing difference between long and short poems (in so far as music was involved) may well have been largely in the character and complexity of the musical formulae, both vocal and instrumental, and in the style and scale of projection. Evidence of narrative performance from the Balkans, for example, is of several different practices. One is of formulaic singing with a *gusle* (bowed stringed instrument), or a *tambura* (plucked stringed instrument) playing integrally throughout; another is of unaccompanied singing, and a third, now defunct, is of unaccompanied recitation.[83]

Though retrospective assessment of a musical instrument's physical capacity is a complex and somewhat speculative matter, on present evidence no form of six-stringed lyre is a rudimentary sound-maker. Research on lyre techniques, with their subtle compound of striking and damping, and on lyre-voice relationships in song (these survive in some regions of western Asia and the northern half of Africa) suggests that the musical resources of Germanic and Anglo-Saxon lyres should not be underestimated, neither should the music played on them be conceived in post-frame-harp terms.

The terminology of plucked instruments gives little help in elucidating the early history of the fully-framed triangular harp in the West, where the earliest depictions known at present are from the ninth century. Then, and for several centuries thereafter, the words *cithara*, *lira* and *hearpe* could apparently be used of a lyre or harp. The instruments depicted with David as poet-musician-psalmist include 'absurd and pseudo-antique conceptions of classical lyres, round Teutonic lyres, sometimes bowed, Western Asiatic psalteries and symbolic ten-stringed psalteries, harps and misconceptions of harps'.[84] The centuries when depictions of this kind were most frequent, that is from about the mid-ninth to about the mid-twelfth, were also those of the first written records of the early development of the sequence, of the organ and of polyphonic music. The interconnection of sequences, organs and polyphony has been observed in a general way by musical historians though many practical questions are still unanswered. Very little is known, however, and little speculation has yet been made about the possible connection between these developments and contemporary Western secular music and secular instrumental usages, among them the appearance of the frame harp and the adoption of the bow in the West.

Interconnections between non-liturgical usage and the sequence have already been suggested in connection with the names of certain sequence-tunes. In addition, the texts of many sequences in England and France alluded to musical instruments, though Notker's sequence-texts did not. The following examples from the texts of some Winchester Troper sequences show all the secular instruments which occur there:

1. Vos per aethera, nos per rura dena/Pars electa, harmoniae vota Damus *hyperlirica cithara*.[85]

[79] J. C. Pope, *The Rhythm of Beowulf*, New Haven, 1942; revised ed., 1965.

[80] Professor Pope's readings on the record *Old English Poems* (Lexington LE 7645) are not symmetrically measured, and are done without a musical instrument.

[81] R. Bruce-Mitford, 'The Sutton Hoo Lyre', *Antiquity*, XLIV, 1970, pp. 7-13.   [82] S. B. Greenfield, op. cit., p. 72.

[83] B. Bartók and A. B. Lord, *Serbo-Croatian Folk Songs*, New York, 1951, pp. 247-9.

[84] J. Rimmer, *The Irish Harp*, Cork, 1969, p. 13.   [85] From *Ad celebres, rex celice*.

2. Divina robusto *tetrachorda plectro* docta manus perite feriat./Resultet virtutum pia *lyra* Deo sonans nunc dramata dulcisona./Est harmonia haec divina sonore virtutum liquidissima./Mixta castitas est quas intra in sede locata *mixtolydica*.[86]

3. Laudes cantica jubilans persolvat, dulcia cordis feriens *tympana*.[87]

4. Canant ac *cymbala* nunc nostra tinnula modulamina/Clementiam salvatricem eiusdem divae sophiae almificam.[88]

5. Sit laus vernans tibi, Christe, semper decus atque rutilans/Luciferi ante ortum, *canna* canit ut Davidica.[89]

6. Nostra quae *tibia* intima et modica musica cantat modulamina iam canora.[90]

1. You in the heavens, we on earth the elect tenth, sing praise to the hyperlyric *cithara*.

2. Let the trained hand strike the divine tetrachord expertly with the robust plectrum: let the sacred *lyra* resound to the God of virtues, sounding now sweet stories. This divine harmony of virtues is most liquid in sound; and among them is intermingled Chastity, placed in the mixolydian position.

3. Let him sing cheerful songs of praise, striking the soft *tympana* of the heart.

4. Let our *cymbala* now also sing tinkling songs, the saving mercy of the same divine wisdom.

5. Praise be to Thee, O Christ, breaking forth ever bright and shining before the morning star rose; the reed-instrument sings like that of David.

6. Our music which the modest and humble *tibia* sings, melodious songs.

At this date a distinction may have been intended between *lyra* meaning a lyre and *cithara* (which is elsewhere in these sequences called *cithara organica*[91] or *cithara Threicia*[92]) meaning a harp; this is at present uncertain. Both words had been used by Bishop Aldhelm of Malmesbury and Sherborne (c. 640-709). *Tetracorda* means four adjacent notes which define a mode, while *mixtolydica* (usually *mixolydica*) is the seventh mode — the g-mode of a large proportion of surviving sequence-tunes. *Tympanum* may have meant tambour, though other meanings may also have been current. *Cymbala* were small tuned bells, both those used ritually in choir and those used for demonstrating a scale or establishing pitch (the Latin word for a tower-bell was *campanum*). The passage in which *canna*, literally a reed, figures in the context of apposition between David and Lucifer, may have a parallel in the musicians depicted on the tenth-century stone cross of Muiredeach at Monasterboice in Ireland. There, the music of the blessed is played on an oblique lyre, the music of the damned on triple reed-pipes. Reed-pipes in this context mean the ancient wind instrument sounded with a single or double reed of cane, palm or other vibrant material, whose body was not necessarily also of reed or cane. The *tibia* (this Roman word for the double-reed instrument whose body was generally made of bone, is often, like the Greek *aulos*, mistranslated as flute) in the sixth quotation seems, however, to have been a proper instrument to play in praise of Christ.

The musical similes used by sequence-text writers to praise Christ and his mother and to memorialize the 'sounding strings of virtues'[93] show a degree of familiarity with instrumental practice which could not have been acquired from ritual music. Christian fathers from the third century onwards had warned Christians against playing musical instruments associated with non-Christian rituals, theatre and banqueting. While these musical sanctions were not observed outside a church building, they were unquestioned for the Christian liturgy. This followed the practice of the Jewish synagogue which, unlike the Temple at Jerusalem, had no cult instruments. Beginning in the eighth or ninth century, the sole exception in Western Christian churches was the organ. Its Western history is usually said to have begun with the bringing in 757 of an organ to the Frankish king Pippin from Byzantium, where it was exclusively an imperial ceremonial instrument.

---

[86] From *Claris vocibus*.

[87] From *Psallat ecclesia*, for the feast of St. Swithin, who died in 863 and whose remains were placed in the cathedral in 971.

[88] From *Laudent condita*.   [89] From *Gloria resonante cymbalorum*.   [90] From *Arce summa*.

[91] In *Exsultate Deo*.   [92] In *Organicis canamus modulis*.

[93] 'Nam et ipsis, quasi quibusdam musicis instrumentis, digito proprio fides agitat, fides virtutum sonoras.
    Has numerose percurrens singulas,
    permiscet singulis diatessaron
    mellifluam melodiam
    quam generat virtutum mater illa,
    quae aliis decenter composita,
    reddit suavem symphoniam' (from *Organicis canamus modulis*).

Aldhelm, however, was familiar with it earlier, since he had written a Latin riddle on the organ and had described its sound in the passage on St. Cecilia in the prose form of *De Virginitate*:[94]

. . . quae licet organica bis quinquagenis et ter quinis sonorum vocibus concreparet armonia, acsi letiferos Sirinarum concentus, cum inexpertos quosque ad vitae pericula pellexerint, sub praetexta integritatis surdis auribus auscultabat.

(. . . when the music of the organ of one hundred and fifteen pipes resounded, like the cheerful songs of the Sirens when they decoyed the unwary into mortal danger, she heard with deaf ears under the cloak of integrity.)

Wulfstan, cantor of Winchester, in a metrical account of Bishop Ethelwold's restoration of the cathedral (he was enthroned in 963) described its enormous organ, which he claimed had four hundred pipes and needed two players and seventy blowers. This instrument was apparently built, or perhaps enlarged from an existing one, under Ethelwold's successor Elphege II, between 984 and 994. According to William of Malmesbury, writing about 1120, St. Dunstan (d. 988) gave an organ to Malmesbury; William observed elsewhere:

illud instrumentum quod antiqui barbiton, nos organa dicimus, tota diffudit Anglia.

(that instrument which the ancients called *barbiton*, and we *organa*, is spread all over England.)

The curious equation of organ and barbiton, which in classical Greece was a type of lyre, occurs also in Aldhelm, whose organ riddle is headed 'De barbito sive organo'. There may have been some parallel or supposed parallel in musical use between the two types of instrument.

Later indications that the organ participated in performance confirms the evidence of early sequence-texts. Two thirteenth-century writers, Bartholomaeus Anglicus and Johannes Aegidius of Zamora, explained in very similar words, perhaps derived from a common

source, why the organ was the only instrument used in Christian ritual. Bartholomaeus wrote about the meaning of the word *organum*:[95]

. . . specialiter cum appropriatum est de instrumento ex multis composito fistulis cui folles adhibentur; utitur iam ecclesia in prosis et in sequenciis et hymnis, propter abusum ystrionum reictis aliis fere instrumentis.

([The word] is specially reserved for the instrument made up of many pipes to which bellows are attached; it is used even in church, for proses and sequences and hymns, almost all other instruments having been abandoned because of their abuse by minstrels.)

Two of the occasions on which the organ was played in St. Augustine's, Canterbury, in the thirteenth century, were the sequence on St. Michael's day and on St. Augustine's day.[96] Since a sequence was sung on all major feasts and on Sundays, it seems clear that this was done with organ on some occasions but not on all.

Sequences, the organ and the *cithara* are all associated with the earliest surviving written record of Western part-music. This is the instruction book *Musica Enchiriadis*, which has been dated 859-60 at the latest.[97] One of its examples is the sequence *Rex caeli, domine*, given in a symbol-notation, called daseian, whose pitches are unequivocal.[98] The writer explained, in terms of the Greek-derived musical theory of tetrachords, a procedure based on a conflation of bourdon and parallel techniques, the latter in parallel fourths. There seems no doubt that these, which he called *organum*, were secular practices[99] adapted for use with certain kinds of chant. His examples are from a sequence, the *Te Deum* and a psalm. Further evidence for the association of *organum* with the sequence (the new liturgical genre of these three) is the use of *organum* terminology in sequence-texts, particularly of the word *symphonia* which in the *organum* context means sounding together notes at the fourth, fifth and octave, and *diatessaron*, the interval of a fourth. In the Winchester sequences, part-music implications occur not only in connection with the organ

---

[94] *Aldhelmi Opera*, ed, R. Ehwald, Berlin, 1919, p. 292.

[95] Oxford, Bodleian Library, MS Bodley 749, f. 280v; for the Johannes Aegidius passage see M. Gerbert, *Scriptores*, ii, p. 388.

[96] Extra payments were given to the organ-blowers on other unspecified days when the organ was used three times during the festival; E. M. Thompson, *The Customary of the Benedictine Monasteries of St. Augustine, Canterbury and St. Peter, Westminster*, ii, London, 1904, pp. 293-4.

[97] P. Dronke, 'The beginnings of the sequence', *Beiträge zur Geschichte der deutschen Sprache und Literatur*, 87 (1965), pp. 70-73.

[98] Printed in Gerbert, *Scriptores*, i, pp. 169-70; transcription in *The New Oxford History of Music*, ii, London, 1954, p. 279. The complete text elaborates a parallel between the Christian's use of a *cithara sapientis* in praising God—even in songs of mirth—and David's calming Saul's afflicted spirit with a plucked instrument's sounding strings (*sonoris fidibus*).

[99] He may have intended to hint this in the following passage: 'Superficiis quaedam artis musicae pro ornatu ecclesiasticorum carminum utcumque in his designata sit'; Gerbert, *Scriptores*, ii, p. 171.

but also with the *cithara* which, as already mentioned, is also once called *organica*. This juxtaposition occurs in the passage from *Organicis canamus modulis* quoted earlier and also in the St. Michael sequence *Ad celebres*:

Ad celebres, rex celice, laudes cuncta
Pangat nunc canora caterva symphonia;
(O King of heaven, let all the songful crowd join in chorus with famous praises.)

in which the *hyperlirica cithara* is the common instrument of angels and of men.

The association in the ninth and tenth centuries of *cithara* with organ, sequence and polyphony was apparently connected with the use, in some circles at least, of the term *cithara* to denote a harp rather than a lyre. While the complex organological details cannot be pursued here, it seems possible that the primary characteristics of the frame harp may have been greater sonority than the old lyres and a suitability for part-music. Speculation on the provenance of the European harp's early development is also outside the scope of this introduction, though it may be noticed that its first

known depictions occur in areas of which some were prominent in the early history of the sequence, namely, the British Isles and northern and eastern France.[100] Ethelwold, while Abbot of Abingdon before going to Winchester, is said himself to have made an organ for the Abbey,[101] to have brought monks from Corbie to teach plainsong and to have sent Osgar, later Abbot, to observe the services at Fleury. The chief sources of the ritual and musical side of the monastic 'revival' in which Ethelwold was prominent were Fleury and Ghent.[102]

We have no direct evidence about refectory and recreation music in the 'reformed' Benedictine monasteries. In northern France this may have had elements of repertory and/or practice from Brittany, where in 818 Charlemagne's son Louis the Pious in person persuaded the monks of Landévennec to give up their Celtic customs in favour of the rule of St. Benedict.[103] In England it probably had both Anglo-Saxon and Irish secular music usages in now indeterminable proportions. Much that passes for fact about pre-Norman Irish music is derived from later sources and from unverifiable 'tradition'. There are few certainties beyond a general

TABLE 6
Analysis of Sequence *Rex caeli* (before 850)

	Stanza[1]	Main Syllable Divisions	Music-unit Symbols[2]	Number of Notes[3]	Music Sub-unit Symbols
Cursus I	1	(6+6)×2	A×2	12×2	A=a+b
	2	(1+6+9)×2	B×2	16×2	B=c+d+b
	3	(3+8)×2	C×2	11×2	C=e+b
	4	(4+8)×2	C×2	12×2	
	5	(6+6)×2	A×2	12×2	
	6	(3+5+4+5)×2	C×4	(8+9)×2	
	7	(8+4+12)×2	D×4	(12+12)×2	D=f+½a
	one line 5		E	5	E=g
Cursus II	8	(6+6)×2	A×2	12×2	
	9	(6+9)×2	B×2	15×2	
	10	(3+8)×2	C×2	11×2	(a=6 notes
	11	(4+8)×2	C×2	12×2	b=6 notes
	12	(6+6)×2	A×2	12×2	c=6 notes
	13a	3+5+4+5	C×2	8+9	d=4 notes
	13b	4+5+4+5	C×2	9+9	e=8 notes
	14	(8+4+12)×2	D×4	12×4	f=9 notes
	one line 5		E	5	g=5 notes)[4]
Final stanza	15	(6+6)×2	A×2	12×2	
	one line 4		E	4	

1. Following Dronke, *The beginnings of the sequence*, p. 45.
2. Ignoring compressions.
3. Following B. Stäblein in *Die Musik in Geschichte und Gegenwart*, s.v. 'Sequenz'.
4. Ignoring some repeated notes.

[100] J. Rimmer, *The Irish Harp*, Cork, 1969, p. 23.

[101] 'Organa propriis manibus ipse fecit'; *Rerum Britannicarum Medii Aevi Scriptores*, Rolls Series, 2, 2, London, 1858, p. 278.

[102] *Regularis Concordia*, ed. T. Symons, London, 1953, pp. xxi, xlvii.

[103] N. K. Chadwick, 'The colonization of Brittany from Celtic Britain', *Proceedings of the British Academy*, li (1966), pp. 294, 289.

resemblance of practice to that of other contemporary and partly-Christianized societies. Nevertheless, the functional classification-names for joyful music, lamentation-music and sleep-music have survived from Old Irish.[104]

If there is an element of truth in the hypothesis that the sequence had a secular prototype, this was probably a kind of verse-with-formulaic-music on a scale somewhere between a relatively short song and a relatively lengthy piece of hieratic chanting. On this and other grounds, the most likely prototype was the lay,[105] whose place as a median between song and formally delivered prose is comparable to that of the sequence as a lengthy ritual praise-song, median in scale between the office hymn and the matins *historia* (an alternation of intoned lesson narratives and sung responds). It was added to the Mass between its intoned readings (Epistle and Gospel) as an appendage to its prose-texted responds (Gradual and Alleluia), a position which could be thought of as analogous to that of the lay in a complex of narrative and song. Observations of the type and use of tune-formulae in sequences may therefore give some clues to the music of *lais* anterior to the early thirteenth-century *Eyns ne soy ke pleynte fu / Ar ne kuth ich sorghe non* (no. 4).

The poem of *Rex caeli* (in *Musica Enchiriadis* and therefore probably before 850) has fifteen stanzas: fourteen double stanzas in two almost exactly corresponding *cursus* of seven stanzas each plus one line, and a final double stanza also plus one line. Its music is strikingly economical, probably more so than any Notker or later sequence, using only five units with some compressions (see Table 6).

The five music-units (shown as A-E in the third column) have common motif-material. They appear to be made from seven sub-units (shown as a-g in the last column) from four to eight notes in length, whose deployment was accommodated to the syllable-count of the text-divisions. Further sub-units were made with three successive notes of sub-unit a (shown as ½a) while sub-unit g has the same contour as the last three notes of b. This sequence-tune is therefore a coherent and highly economical assemblage in which six terse tune-formulae, corresponding in size to the shortest metrical unit or occasionally to a single word, suffice for singing a poem of seventy-nine lines. The recurring formulae are

embodied in five stanza-units, some of which also recur during one *cursus*. Procedures of this kind are observable in sequences for many centuries after.

LAI AND PLANCTUS

The types of formulae in sequence-tunes, the majority of which have *d* or *g* as their final,[106] are much fewer than in Gregorian chant. Many sequences in the *g*-mode have a unit-ending formula *f g g*. Though rarely found in *g*-mode Gregorian tunes, whose cadences usually have a falling contour, this is a characteristic feature of both early and late sequence-tunes and also of the *lai*-tunes of the thirteenth century. It occurs at the end of the second stanza and at the end of the first half of the fourth stanza in *Eyns ne soy ke pleynte fu / Ar ne kuth ich sorghe non*, in the units shown as F and N in Table 7.

TABLE 7
Analysis of *Eyns ne soy ke pleynte fu / Ar ne kuth ich sorghe non*

Stanzas	No. of Syllables per Line	Music-units	Recurring Sub-units
1a	7 8 7	A A¹ B	a b a b
1b	8 8 7	A A¹ B	a b a b
2a	7 7 7 7	C D E F	c d e f
2b	8 7 7 7	C D E F	c d e f
3a	3 4 6 3 4 6	G H I J G K	a g b
3b	3 4 6 3 4 6	G H¹ (I¹+J) G H¹ K¹	a g a b
4a	7 7 7 7	L M (I¹+J) N	h h e a g f
4b	7 7 7 7	L¹ M O P	i h e c b
5a	8 8 7 7 7	D¹ D¹ Q D² R	d d i d a e
5b	7 7 7 7 7	D¹ D³ Q D² R	d d i d a e

The tune has eighteen tune-units and nine recurring sub-units shown respectively as A-R and a-i in the table (see Ex. 5, in which some of the tune's repeated notes and immediately repeated sub-units are omitted). This method of embedding recurring sub-units in progressively repeated and partly recurring half-stanza-units is identical with that of the sequence *Rex caeli*, though here done with more ample formulaic material.

Ex. 5

[104] J. Maillard, *Évolution et esthétique du lai lyrique*, Fontainebleau, 1952-61, p. 33.

[105] In the general sense discussed by A. Campbell, 'The Old English Epic Style', *English and Medieval Studies Presented to J.R.R. Tolkien*, London, 1962, p. 24, Appendix II: 'On the term lay'.

[106] The Utrecht sequentiary, none of whose sequences are by or subsequent to Adam of St. Victor (d. 1177 or 1192) has 21 with final *d* (13 by Notker), 17 with final *g* (10 by Notker), 4 with final *e* (1 by Notker), 1 with final *f* and 1 with final *a*. Of sequences by or associated with Adam, 30 are in *g*-mode (of which 4 end on *d*) and 15 are in *d*-mode (of which 6 end on *a*); see E. Misset and P. Aubry, *Les proses d'Adam de Saint Victor*, Paris, 1901.

The music of the lay *Eyns ne soy ke playnte fu / Ar ne kuth ich sorghe non* is clearly the same in substance as that of some stanzas of the *Planctus ante nescia* by Godefroy of St. Victor (fl. 1170-90). This identity, which has not hitherto been noticed (see p.296) implies either that the lay's music was derived from that of the *planctus,* which must be earlier than the lay's only surviving form, or that the music of both was derived from a common source or similar sources. Godefroy's *planctus* survives with staff-notated music in four thirteenth-century French manuscripts and with neume-notated music in a fifth thirteenth-century manuscript best known for its secular poems; this was first published in 1847 under the title *Carmina Burana,* from the monas-

1. The word *lassor* is written above the neumes over *solor*.
2. *Sic.*
3. There is no neume over *tam*.

tery of Benediktbeuern, north of Innsbruck, which was its original home. The version of Godefroy's *planctus* in the Benediktbeuern manuscript[107] has stanzas 1-3 (with three missing lines) and stanzas 6-8 of the fourteen stanzas in the French sources, while the Anglo-Norman lay corresponds musically and metrically to their stanzas 1-3 and 7-8. Though the neumes of the Benediktbeuern manuscript are only very approximately transcribable as to pitch, its syllable-to-note relationship can be discerned with reasonable accuracy. A hypothetical transcription (Ex. 6) shows that its tune has many variants both from the other manuscripts of the *planctus* and from the English song. The nature of the differences between these five versions (the French sources have three significantly varying forms) suggests that we are concerned in the music with an assemblage whose transmission and performance-conventions, unlike those of ritual plainsong, admitted or perhaps even called for considerable idiosyncrasy in execution and consequently in the written forms in which it was recorded. They strongly suggest that music-scribes of this kind of song commonly wrote down the tunes as they recalled them from performance or copied them from written versions so recalled. It would be inappropriate, therefore, to regard any one version of the music as 'definitive'. Each is no less valid than the others; in each the stamp of an individual adapter or performer seems to have been put on material whose tradition was outside

[107] Facsimile in *Carmina Burana,* ed. B Bischoff, New York, 1967, 'Fragmenta Burana', f. 4.

that of Christian ritual plainsong, from whose performance and written transmission personal elements were excluded.

In the French versions of Godefroy's *planctus* more use is made of recurrent music-units than in the shorter tunes of the Benediktbeuern version and the Anglo-Norman lay. The music-units of the French versions of the *planctus* are given in Table 8, whose information may be collated with the analysis of the lay in Table 7.

Assuming the Benediktbeuern version to be a truncated form of Godefroy's song (though it is possibly an earlier form which was afterwards extended), it is by no means certain that the writer of the lay knew either the longer or the shorter forms as we have them. Given the 'communal' nature of much *planctus* and *lai*-tune material, he may have known these formulae in this general order in an anterior song, unwritten or now lost. Some of the differences between his noticeably less ornate versions of the formulae and those of the *planctus* seem attributable to oral rather than written transmission. Unit B in his first stanza, for example, may be an oral adaptation of the ending of unit A^1 in the Évreux manuscripts (shown as E in no. 4, addendum). Similarly, the third and fourth units in the first half of his third stanza (shown as I and J in Table 7) correspond to one unit in the *planctus* (unit I in Table 8), while his sixth unit in that half-stanza (unit K) is the equivalent of two units (H and I^1) of the corresponding music of the *planctus*. In the second half of this stanza, however, his deployment of these formulae is the same as in the *planctus*. In another

case where two parallel units are not identical — the first unit in each half of the fourth stanza — each unit has an exact correspondence in the *planctus*; unit L in the lay to unit L^1 in the *planctus* and the lay's L^1 to L in the *planctus*. The differing fourth unit in the stanza (unit N) has, however, no corresponding unit in the *planctus*. It seems possible that non-correspondences of this kind where correspondence is usual occur through the matching in performance of a particular group of words to a suitable but non-matching sub-unit within an otherwise matching unit of the same length.

There are other twelfth- and thirteenth-century instances of musical relationship, apparent or probable, between a *planctus* and a *lai* and between these and a sequence. Notker's sequence-tune title *planctus sterilis* has already been noted and similar titles, for example *planctus cigni, planctus pueri captivati,* occur in connection with tenth- and eleventh-century sequences.[108] The music of the third of six *planctus* by Peter Abélard (1079-1142) has much material in common with the thirteenth-century *Lai des pucelles,* whose content — a lovers' dialogue — is unconnected with its title. This particular *planctus-lai* connection, which was first observed in the metres of the poems, is also apparent in the music, even though the music of the *planctus* survives only in neume notation.[109] It must be assumed either that this tune-material in the same general arrangement was in existence before Abélard wrote his *Planctus virginum super filia Jephtae Galaaditae* or that his *planctus* music was afterwards adapted to a *lai*. In view of the simple

TABLE 8
Analysis of Godefroy of St. Victor's *Planctus ante nescia*

Stanzas	Music-units	Stanzas in Benediktbeuern	Stanzas Common in Lay	Sub-units
1	A A^1 B	1	1	a
2	C D E F	2	2	c d e f
3	G H I G H I^1	3 (ll. 1-3, 10-12 and 7-9)	3	g a b
4 (=2)	C D E F			c d e f
5 (=3)	G H I G H I^1			g a b
6	J J^1 J^2 K	4		
7	L M I N	5	4	h e a g
8	D^1 D^1 O D^2 P	6	5	d i a e
9	L^1 L^2 Q Q^1 R			h e d
10	C M^1 S P^1			c h a b
11	C L^1 M^2 S^1			c h i e
12	T U V Q^2			h e
13	O D^2 D^3 P			i e a
14	A A^1 W P^2			a c

[108] See B. Stäblein, 'Die Schwanenklage: zum Problem Lai-Planctus-Sequenz', *Festschrift K. G. Fellerer,* Cologne, 1962, pp. 492, 500-501; P. Dronke, 'The beginnings of the sequence', *Beiträge zur Geschichte der deutschen Sprache und Literatur,* 87 (1965), pp. 57-60.

[109] J. Maillard, *Évolution et esthétique du lai lyrique,* Fontainebleau, 1952-61, pp. 261-71.

nature and repetitive use of the tune-formulae concerned, the former alternative seems more probable, in spite of the fact that the surviving form of the *lai*-tune was written down about a century after Abélard wrote his *planctus*. Abélard was doubtless a capable deviser or assembler of tunes, not only for his *planctus* but also for the hymns whose words and tunes Héloïse asked him to provide and for his now-lost love songs. Only one of his *planctus*, the *Planctus David super Saul et Jonathan (Planctus VI, Dolorum solatium)*, has surviving staff-notated music. The suggestion has been put forward that 'since there is a whole series of similarities between Abélard's *Planctus VI* and the sequence *Planctus ante nescia* in construction and in melodic details, we may assume that Abélard's composition provided the starting point, if perhaps only unconsciously [*sic*], for the later composer. Textual identities and similarities reinforce this impression. Gottfried [i.e. Godefroy of St. Victor], therefore, probably knew and utilized Abélard's *Planctus, Dolorum solatium,* when he created his Marian lament.'[110] Comparison of the complete tunes, however, shows that there is no identity of music-units and that the sub-units which are common to the two (shown in the fourth column in Table 9 below) are

Abélard's repetitive but non-recurring use of units to make a tune in which the music of every stanza except the last does double or triple duty. Comparisons of this kind must, nevertheless, be related to the total pattern of sequence-*lai-planctus* history. It seems probable that Abélard's 'influence' on Godefroy, if it existed, was that of a transmitter of a living and largely oral tradition of *lai* and *planctus* from its place of cultivation, presumably Brittany, to monastic and clerical communities elsewhere. His vivid picture in the last stanza of *Dolorum solatium* of the harpist whose hands feel torn with striking the strings

> Laesis pulsu manibus,
>
> raucis planctu vocibus
>
> deficit et spiritus
>
> (My hands torn with playing
>
> and my voice hoarse with lamenting, my spirit fails)

may well be founded on experience (Abélard was born in Brittany and was for some time Abbot of St. Gildas), as well as on the association of David with the instrument.

In discussing the origins of the sequence we advanced

TABLE 9

Analysis of Abélard's *Planctus VI, Dolorum solatium*

Stanzas	Length of Stanza in Syllables per Line	Music-units in each Stanza	Sub-units in Common with Godefroy
1–2	(7 7 7) x 2	(A A B A A B) x 2	A includes f
3–4	(7 7 7 4 7 4) x 2	(C C D E D E) x 2	E = f + b
5–6	(8 8 8 8) x 2	(F F G H F F G H) x 2	F begins with d G and H include e
7–8	(7 7 7 7) x 2	(I J K H^1 I J K H^1) x 2	I includes g K includes i H^1 includes e
9a	(7 7 7 7) x 3	K^1 K^2 K^1 K^2 I I^1 K^3 L I I K^3 L	K^1, K^2 and K^3 include h L includes e
9b	— ditto —	— ditto —	
9c	— ditto —	— ditto —	
10	(7 7 7) x 2	M N O M N O^1	N includes c O includes e and a O^1 includes f

merely formulae which pervade sequence-*lai-planctus* composition in the *g*-mode. Though Godefroy very probably knew Abélard's *planctus*, they were both using forms of tune-formulae common to this type of song. Godefroy's way of deploying his music-units within the total tune-design is noticeably less economical than

the hypothesis that the lay — for which no written music survives from the relevant time — was its secular prototype and that at least some of its musical characteristics were derived from Celtic sources. Twelfth- and thirteenth-century sequence-form *planctus*[111] and lays, a number of which survive with music,[112] seem to have a

---

[110] L. Weinrich, 'Peter Abaelard as musician—II', *The Musical Quarterly*, LV (1969), p. 485.

[111] Most earlier *planctus* were in strophic (i.e. hymn) form; see E. Jammers, in *Die Musik in Geschichte und Gegenwart*, s.v. 'Planctus'.

[112] See the alphabetical list of 'lais et descorts en langues d'oil et d'oc aux xii et xiiiᵉ siècles' in J. Maillard, *Évolution et esthétique du lai lyrique*, pp. 71–83; *Lais et descorts français du XIIIᵉ siècle*, ed. A. Jeanroy, L. Brandin, and P. Aubry, Paris, 1901, has diplomatic copies and discussion of the music.

similar incursion of Celtic, particularly Breton, song-characteristics, this time over a wider area which included Anglo-Norman England. As the English editor of the narrative *lais* of Marie de France pointed out, her poems have no connection with the lyric *lai*, which he defined as 'a lyric poem of sequence type in which the words are written to conform to an already existing melody'.[113] The word 'melody' in this definition might well be expanded to include at least three word-tune situations: first, the use of intrinsically simple common-property tune-formulae; second, settings by named *trouvères* to relatively elaborate forms of the accepted *lai*-vocabulary; and third, *contrafacta* (text-replacements) with more or less change in tune details. Though Ewart considered that 'the view that the music of the lyric *lais* may represent a survival of the musical element of the original Breton *lais* is little more than speculation', this speculation is nevertheless consonant with the musical facts, including the distinctive way of performing *lais* which is attested by some poets' accounts. The harp appears to have been essential in their formal delivery, as when Tristan taught Isolde:[114]

> Bons lais de harpe vus apris,
> lais Bretuns de vostre païs . . .
> (I taught you good *lais* to the harp, Breton *lais* of your country . . .)

Parallels have been drawn between 'the lyrical *lai*, presumably with musical accompaniment, which the Bretons are said to have composed' and the lyrical verse-passages for which the term *laíd* or *loíd* is used in Irish saga, which was otherwise in prose; there are also parallels with certain elements in Welsh story-telling in the ninth and tenth centuries.[115]

While the musical evidence, if any, bearing on the antecedents of the Breton *lais* which may lie in Celtic language sources has yet to be elucidated, references contemporary with the twelfth- and thirteenth-century *lais* seem clearly to connect them with Celtic musical practices and repertories. Some descriptions of Breton minstrels' performance show that a *lai* would have been clearly recognizable by, among other things, its performance routine. The hero Gudmod of the Anglo-Norman romance *Horn et Rimenhild* is related to have ordered his performance of a *lai* in this fashion:

> Lors prent la harpe a sei, qu'il la veut atemprer.
> Deus! ki dunc l'esgardast, cum la sout manier,
> Cum ces cordes touchout, cum les feseit trembler,
> Asquantes feiz chanter, asquantes organer,
> De l'harmonie del ciel li poüst remembrer!
> Sur tuz homes k'i sunt fet cist a merveiller.
> Quant ses notes ot fait, si la prent a munter
> E tut par autres tuns les cordes fait soner:
> Mut se merveillent tuit qu'il la sout si bailler.
> E quant il out issi fait, si cummence a noter
> Le lai dunt or ains dis, de Baltof, haut e cler,
> Si cum sunt cil bretun d'itiel fait costumier.
> Apres en l'estrument fet les cordes suner,
> Tut issi cum en voiz l'aveit dit tut premier:
> Tut le lai lur ad fait, n'i vout rien retailler.
> E deus! cum li oianz li porent dunc amer!

(Then he took the harp to himself to tune it. Heavens! whoever saw him as he handled it, how he touched those strings and made them sound, sometimes in a tune, sometimes together, might remember the harmony of the spheres. He did things to be marvelled at of all men. When he had set his strings, he took up the harp and made the strings sound in other tones. All wondered much that he knew this so well. And when he had done this, he began to sing loud and clear the *lai* which was once told of Baltof that the Bretons are used to tell. Afterwards, he made the strings of the instrument sound as his voice had sung before. He performed for them the whole *lai* and omitted none of it. Heavens! how those that heard could love him!)

A. J. Bliss deduced from this account that 'the *lai* was usually preceded by an instrumental prelude in two keys, and sometimes rounded off with an instrumental postlude as well'. The term 'key' in the sense of tonality, however, is a musical anachronism here and cannot correspond to the poet's meaning. What he seems to describe is a still normal tuning procedure, and then a performance. The player adjusted the pitch of the strings and then sounded them both tune-wise and chord-wise (*Asquantes feiz chanter, asquantes organer*). When he had set his strings (*Quant ses notes ot fait*) he began the prelude to the *lai*, that is, the performance proper as distinct from the tuning flourishes (*E tut par autres tuns les cordes fait soner*). He then sang the *lai* in a high, clear voice and after it played an instrumental form of the

[113] A. Ewart, *Marie de France, Lais,* Oxford, 1944.

[114] Quoted from the Oxford MS (Bodleian Library, Douce D.6) of *La folie Tristan* by J. Maillard, 'Le lai lyrique et la tradition celtique', *Ar Falz,* xviii (1956), p. 58.

[115] R. Bromwich, 'A note on the Breton lays', *Medium Ævum,* xxvi (1957), pp. 36-37.

tune. The instrumental form may have been played after each stanza,[116] a procedure analogous to the contemporary practice in such liturgical forms as troped Kyries and proses, in which the choir vocalized the melody of each verse of a prose after it was sung by a few singers to the troping text.

Besides having a characteristic mode of presentation and apparently also a characteristic pitch and timbre when sung (*haut e cler*), a Breton *lai* was clearly recognizable by its music alone, without the words. In the *Roman de Brut* Wace wrote of *lais* as instrumental pieces which could be played on fiddle or pipe as well as on harp or rote:[117]

> Mult out a la curt jugleürs,
> Chanteürs, estrementeürs;
> Mult peüssiex oir chançuns,
> Rotruenges e novels suns,
> Vieleüres, lais de notes,
> Lais de vieles, lais de rotes,
> Lais de harpes, lais de frestels.

(There were at the court many jongleurs, singers, instrumentalists: you might have heard many songs, rotrouenges and new tunes, fiddle-players, sung *lais*, *lais* on the fiddle, the rote, the harp and the flute.)

This seems comparable with *flamenco* or *cante hondo*, equally unwritten genres whose musical character and manner of delivery make them immediately recognizable, whether sung (also *haut e cler*) with guitar or played on guitar alone. 'Rote' at this time and in this context must certainly mean a kind or size of harp. The troubadour Giraut de Calanson, who flourished *c.* 1200-20 and wrote descorts in Provençal, mentioned the *rota* as one of the many instruments which a *joglar* should be able to play:[118]

> Sotetz nota,
> fai la rota
> ab deszest cordas guarnir.
> Non esturmens,
> si bels aprens,
> ne potz a tos ops retenir.

> Sapchas arpar
> e ben temprar
> la guiga els son esclarzir.

(The rote with seventeen strings makes a subtle sound. No instrument, however well learnt, can serve for all purposes. Know how to play and tune well the *guiga* and make clear sounds on it.)

The seventeen strings here considered an appropriate number could provide a range of two octaves and one note, with both *b* flat and *b* natural in the lower octave, which suits admirably the requirements of the *lai*-tunes which survive. Their lowest written note is B, the highest *b'*; *b* flat is occasionally required though not *b'* flat.

Some *g*-mode *lai* and sequence-tunes were written down in the transposed pitch a fourth higher, using *b* flat and ending in *c*. This is the case with *Magdalenae laudes piae* in the same manuscript as four songs in this volume, [119] and with *Orbis honor caeli scema* in the same manuscript as *Edi be thu, heven-queene* (no. 13). [120] *Orbis honor caeli scema* has *b* flat, *b* natural and *b'* natural but not *b'* flat. The first and ninth of its ten stanzas end with *b* flat *c' c'*, corresponding to *f g g* at the untransposed pitch, and its Amen ends with *e' d' b* flat *d' d' c*. It is possible that this kind of ending-formula, with its prominent *b* flat at the higher pitch or *f* at the lower, is what the Norman-Welsh cleric Giraldus de Barri referred to in his description of Irish harp-playing in the *Topographia Hiberniae:*[121]

> Mirum quod, in tanta tamque praecipiti digitorum rapacitate, musica servatur proportio; et arte per omnia indemni, inter crispatos modulos, organaque multipliciter intricata, tam suavi velocitate, tam dispari paritate, tam discordi concordia, consona redditur et completur melodia. Seu diatesseron seu diapente chordae concrepent, semper tamen a B molli incipiunt, et in idem redeunt, ut cuncta sub jocundae sonoritatis dulcedine compleantur.

(It is remarkable that, with such rapid fingerwork, the musical rhythm is maintained and that, by unfailingly disciplined art, the integrity of the tune is fully pre-

---

[116] Guillaume de Machaut's lai *Nuls ne doit avoir merveille* has been recorded with added harp accompaniment and interludes on Oiseau-Lyre SOL 310. The passage from *Horn* is quoted from *Thomas: the Romance of Horn*, ed. M. K. Pope, Oxford, 1955, ll. 2830–45.

[117] I. Arnold, *Le roman de Brut de Wace*, Société des anciens textes français, 1940, lines 10543 ff.

[118] K. Bartsch, *Denkmäler der provenzalischen Litteratur*, Stuttgart, 1856 (reprint), 1966, p. 94.

[119] Nos. 7, 12, 14 and 15. The manuscript is Arundel 248 in the British Library; facsimile of *Magdalenae laudes piae* in H. E. Wooldridge, *Early English Harmony*, London, 1897, pl. 33.

[120] Oxford, Corpus Christi College, MS 59, f. 113v.

[121] Translation by J. Rimmer in *The Irish Harp*, Cork, 1969, p. 29.

served throughout the ornate rhythms and the profusely intricate polyphony — and with such smooth rapidity, such unequal equality, such discordant concord. Whether the strings strike together a fourth or a fifth, [the players] nevertheless always start from a *b* flat and return to the same, so that everything is rounded off in a pleasant general sonority.)

Giraldus's reference to *b* flat has puzzled many historians. He may have been saying that a cadence rising a whole tone to the final, which he expressed as *b* flat in relation to *c* but which in most written *lais* was *f* in relation to *g*, was a constant Irish idiom. Giraldus made a parallel comment on Welsh music in the *Descriptio Cambriae* (c. 1188). His description of Welsh 'part-singing' practice is difficult to interpret in modern terms. The description of cadence points is exact — that the singers converged into fewer parts for pre-arranged cadential formulae (*consonantiam et organicam melodiam*) and that the tunes, like the Irish, ended with the characteristic sweet *b* flat-*c* (*sub B mollis dulcedine blanda et convenientia*) or its equivalent. (The use of cadential formulae in unwritten polyphonic song is attested by still-current practice in the Caucasus and the Balkans.)

Though the exact relation of the lost *lais* of the Breton harpers to the surviving *planctus* and lyrical *lais* of the twelfth and thirteenth centuries cannot be known now, it seems probable that the take-over involved such elements of musical practice as tune-conventions, tune-idioms, vocal timbre and particular harp techniques and routines. Descriptions of *lai* performance were rarely as specific as that of Gudmod in *Horn et Rimenhild*. For literary reasons they often give an account which in terms of musical practice is foreshortened or fused, or focussed on a visual or other non-musical factor. An example of this is the concentrated run-down of joglars' music at the heroine's wedding feast in the early thirteenth-century Provençal poem *Flamenca*:[122]

L'uns viola lais de Cabrefoil,
E l'autre cel de Tintagoil;
L'us cantet cel dels Fins Amanz,
E l'autre cel que fes Ivans.
L'us menet arpa, l'autre viula;
L'us flaütella, l'autre siula;
L'us mena giga, l'autre rota;
L'us diz los motz e l'autrels nota . . .

(One played the *lai* of Chevrefeuille, and the other that of Tintagel; one sang that of *Les Fins Amants,* and another the one that Ywain made. One played a harp, another a fiddle; one a flute, another a whistle; one a *giga,* another a *rota*; one spoke the words and another sang them.)

However pellmell the poet's presentation of this musical spectacular may seem, it must nevertheless be true that each genre of poetry-and-music had its particular tune-conventions and idioms, its manner of delivery and instrumental participation. The *lai* seems to have been attended by some of the most impressive routines and perhaps some of the most venerable in age and associations of any kind of medieval song.

THE LATIN CRUCIFIXION LAMENTS

It is probable that there was a basic similarity between the way an organ participated in the performance of a sequence on specially festive occasions and the way a harp was used in the performance of a *lai*. Whether or not organ-playing was interposed, a sequence was sung antiphonally — a method more appropriate to its double-stanza structure than to the stanzaically recurrent music of a hymn (which was also sung antiphonally) and one which gave a sequence some of the character of a dialogue. As described in the Ordinal of Bayeux, the sequence there was done by a few singers picked out in advance from each side of the choir by the *rector chori*. They gathered in two groups, one in front of the dean's stall and the other before the precentor's, and sang the sequence alternating in half-stanzas until the last half-stanza, which they all sang as they walked back to their seats.[123] It seems unlikely that the two sequences which begin *Stabat juxta Christi crucem* were treated as festive items with organ participation, if only on account of their subject. The noted Missal, probably from Canterbury, which contains the sequence *Stabat juxta Christi crucem, stabat videns vitae ducem* (no. 10(i)) with its music, also has a large number of other sequences in honour of the Virgin Mary. These have no indication of their liturgical occasion, unlike most sequences, including those for the regular feasts of the Virgin Mary. It seems certain that they and many similar items, both monophonic and polyphonic, which survive in thirteenth- and fourteenth-

---

[122] *The Romance of Flamenca*, ed. M. E. Porter, 1962, lines 600-607.

[123] *Ordinaire et Coutoumier de l'église cathédrale de Bayeux (xiii⁺ siècle),* ed. U. Chevalier, Paris, 1902, p. 58. *The Ordinal of St. Mary's, York* (ed. J.B. Tolhurst, London, i, 1936, p.99) has the following: 'Dum epistola legitur, si sequentia cantari debet illo die, signum faciet juniori omnibus in choro ut troparia sibi ferat. Qui juvenis statim surgens predictos libros ponit ad pedes suos super terram. Et dum versus de Alleluia cantatur, cantor prefatos illos libros singulis quatuor vel quinque distribuens unam sequentiam eis assignat'.

century sources, were sequences for the Votive Mass of the Virgin Mary. This was increasingly cultivated in Britain, where it was commonly called the Lady-Mass from the thirteenth century onwards. It was celebrated with some solemnity each Saturday and in some large churches daily.[124] *Alleluia* and sequence were always sung in this mass, even in Lent, when other masses had neither. The different sequence *Stabat juxta Christi crucem* which continues *videns pati veram lucem* occurs with its tune in a manuscript from St. Patrick's Cathedral, Dublin,[125] in a similar collection of votive Marian sequences. This sequence has a more specific assignment in the York liturgy, where it is prescribed to alternate with the sequence *Virgini Mariae laudes* for the Lady-Mass in Eastertide and to be used in the Lady-Mass on Fridays between Trinity and Advent.[126]

Although the texts of the two sequences *Stabat juxta Christi crucem* differ after the first line and the York sequence has six stanzas while the other has eleven, the music of both draws on the long-existing common stock of sequence-tune formulae in the *d*-mode. The chief musical consequences of Adam of St. Victor's standardizing of sequence-metre into the almost invariable syllable-pattern 8 8 7 to the half-stanza, were unlimited transferability of tunes — at least theoretically — and conformity of music-unit lengths to the two used in the metre. Nevertheless, Adam of St. Victor still drew upon the established vocabulary of tune-formulae, which continued to be used in sequences devised in the thirteenth century and even into the fifteenth. A thirteenth-century sequence for St. Cyprian is recorded with its tune, in *g*-mode with the conventional formulae, set down and divided into units each marked 'd' to indicate its repeat, apparently in preparation for making the text, which is written with the complete music on the next facing page. Though the metre, which was thus predetermined by or conceived simultaneously with the music, is not strictly Victorine, all its half-stanzas are in the Victorine pattern of two equal lines and a shorter line.[127] An early fifteenth-century sequence for St. Hylarion, whose poem has only minor deviations from the strict Victorine metre, has the characteristic *g*-mode sequence cadence-formula *f g g* in seven of its twelve stanzas and also in thirteen sub-units at five different

pitches.[128] These are perhaps examples of an over-emphasis which sometimes accompanies antiquarianism. The metre, music and unit-length of *lais,* unlike those of sequences, were not 'regularized' in the thirteenth and fourteenth centuries. Machaut made his *lai*-poems in paired half-stanzas of widely varying metrical structure; in his tunes, on the other hand, he used up-to-date fourteenth-century idioms, not the *g*- and *d*-mode vocabularies which were entrenched in both *lai*- and sequence-writing before him and were still used in sequence-writing in the fifteenth century.

TABLE 10

Analysis of Sequence *Stabat juxta Christi crucem, stabat videns vitae ducem*

Stanzas	Music-units	Sub-units and their recurrences
1	A B C	a b c d e
2	D E F	f g h b¹ c i
3	G H I	i d² c¹ e¹ b c
4	J K L	c² c e¹ c h¹
5	M M¹ C¹	b² b² b² e² c e
6	D¹ N I¹	g¹ d² i¹ b² c
7	O H¹ P	j c³ k e
8	Q R S	l e² a¹
9	T N¹ I¹	j¹ f h d¹ i¹ b² c
10	D² U P¹	g² j¹ c k e¹
11	V W P¹	k¹ c b² l e¹

TABLE 11

Analysis of Sequence *Stabat juxta Christi crucem, videns pati veram lucem*

Stanzas	Music-units	Recurring Sub-units	Material Common to both Sequences
1	A B C	a	C=other S
2	D E F	b c d c	b=other b
3	G H I	b e ½d a	e includes other c
4	J K L	f	J almost=other D
			f includes other h+d
5	M K¹ F¹	d¹ e f¹ c	
6	N O I	b ½e d e ½d a	½e=other c; ½d=k

The deployment of tune-material in *Stabat juxta Christi crucem, stabat videns vitae ducem* is shown in Table 10 above. This is based on the version in a manuscript, probably from Canterbury, now in the Bibliothèque de l'Arsenal in Paris. The tune is closely knit;

[124] F. Ll. Harrison, *Music in Medieval Britain,* London, 1963, pp. 77-79.

[125] Cambridge University Library, MS Add. 710 (commonly called the 'Dublin Troper'), f. 117.

[126] *Missale ad usum insignis ecclesiae Eboracensis,* ed. Henderson, ii, Surtees Society, 1874, pp. 209-10.

[127] M. Bévenot, 'St. Cyprian and Moissac: a thirteenth-century sequence', *Traditio,* xix (1963), pp. 147-66. The following stanza structures are found: 10 10 7, 10 10 6, 8 8 7, 8 8 6 and 7 7 6.

[128] R. H. Hoppin, '*Exultantes collaudemus:* a sequence for Saint Hylarion', *Aspects of Medieval and Renaissance Music,* New York, 1966, pp. 392-405. The source is a Cyprus manuscript (Torino, Bibl. Naz., J.II.9).

it has the relatively small number of twelve sub-units which recur with or without change (see Ex. 7 below) and there is no unit without some sub-unit recurrence.

Ex.7

Table 11 shows the results of a similar analysis of the music of *Stabat juxta Christi crucem, videns pati veram lucem,* and also, in the fourth column of the table, some of the tune-formulae which the two sequences have in common. Comparison of either tune with other *d*-mode sequences would show a comparable number of formulae in common. The identity of unit Q in *Stabat juxta Christi crucem, stabat videns vitae ducem* with the music of the first line of the famous thirteenth-century sequence *Dies irae,* reputedly by the Franciscan Thomas of Celano, is immediately noticeable. Similarly, unit D, less the last three notes, is the same as the first unit in the third stanza of the twelfth-century sequence *Veni sancte spiritus.*

THE ENGLISH LAMENTS

There are three English-language adaptations (nos. 10(ii)-12) of the sequence *Stabat juxta Christi crucem,*

stabat videns vitae ducem; the music of two of these (nos. 10(ii)-11) is also adapted from the music of the sequence but that of the third is not. Comparison of the music of the Latin sequence with that which survives for the music-related English-language versions[129] shows that the British Library form of *Stond wel, moder, under roode* (no. 11) and the Arsenal manuscript's version of the Latin sequence resemble each other more than either resembles the other versions. The Arsenal manuscript and the British Library manuscript sources have two units[130] identical note-for-note and four others[131] identical but for note repeats which accommodate additional unstressed syllables in the English text. The only notable differences are the second unit of stanza 2 and part of the first unit of stanza 5. Only one unit in the four-and-a-half surviving stanzas in the Cambridge manuscript agrees precisely with the corresponding unit in the Arsenal manuscript (this is the second unit in stanza 3) and none agrees with *Stond wel, moder, under roode.* However, the two English sources are in near-agreement, against the Arsenal version, in the second unit of stanza 2. The Cambridge manuscript, as far as it goes, has some striking note-divergences in units which are basically the same as in the other two sources (there are three other sources for stanza 5). Among these divergences are *g* for *f* in the first unit of stanza 1, the drop from *a* to *d* (not *c*) in the first unit of stanza 4, two divergent forms of the third unit of that stanza and *c* for *b* as the first note of the second unit of stanza 5. The most individual version of the music, however, is that with the incomplete English text with the putative beginning *Stood the moder under roode* (no. 10(ii)). Compared with the corresponding units of the other versions (three versions for stanza 5, two for stanza 6 and the Arsenal manuscript for stanzas 7-11) its units are almost always more elaborate or else markedly divergent. Among the more strikingly divergent forms are the third units of stanza 6 and of stanza 8. In the second half of stanza 11 the words 'sinne' and 'sorwe' each have a repeated note for their two syllables, followed in the manuscript by a vertical line through the staff. This must indicate that the second syllable of these words was pronounced in performance even though elision would have been normal before the following word 'of'; it also suggests that a break was made after both words, presumably for their more effective delivery.

Although the text of *Jesu Cristes milde moder* (no. 12) was also adapted from the sequence *Stabat juxta Christi*

---

[129] For details of the manuscripts, see p. 300.

[130] Those indicated by the letters C and K (second half-stanza of each) in Table 10.

[131] Units I, L, C[1] and N.

TABLE 12
Analysis of Sub-units in Lower-staff Voice of Sequence
Jesu Cristes milde moder

Stanzas	Sub-units
1	ab cd ec
2	ff^1 gd e^{1}e
3	bf hi a^{1}f^2
4	ja^1 kj^1 lm
5	fn gd ee
6	of^1 hi^1 a^{1}f^2
7	pb qr se^1
8	hm hi^2 a^{1}f^2
9	o^{1}e tu af^1
10	vf^1 wi^3 qf^1
11	b^{1}e xj^1 q^{1}f^1
Amen	hi^{2}y

Ex. 8

crucem, stabat videns vitae ducem, its music bears no relation to that of the sequence. Its two voices sing in an almost identical ambitus (*d* to *d'* in one voice, *d* to *c'* in the other) and constantly cross. This is a relatively early written example of 'gymel',[132] the basic part-making technique perhaps derived from secular unlearned practice, which is distinct from the parallel and parallel-cum-bourdon techniques, of which more written examples have survived. Though some of the tune-material is found in the two voices, the tune-material of the voice written on the lower staff is apparently drawn from common *d*-mode sequence formulae transposed up a fourth; this suggests that it may have been the primary voice. Each of its thirty-four music-units, including the Amen, may conveniently be divided for the purpose of analysis into two sub-units, three in the Amen. Some of these are re-used to the extent that twenty-five sub-units and their variants do the work of sixty-nine (see Table 12 and Ex. 8 above; the sub-units are transposed down a fourth to facilitate comparison with *d*-mode for-

TABLE 13
Analysis of Sub-units in Upper-staff Voice of Sequence
Jesu Cristes milde moder

Stanzas	Sub-units
1	k aa i^{4}l f f
2	e bb cc dd f^{3}f
3	t e ee c^1 y^{1}e^2
4	ff y^1 y^{1}gg hh y^1
5	e ii jj l f f
6	kk e^1 ee c^2 y^{1}e^2
7	f aa ll g^1 r^{1}f^3
8	mm k mm c^3 y^{1}e^2
9	nn f b ii k e^1
10	oo e^1 pp c^4 qq f^4
11	rr aa ee ss kk f^4
Amen	ee c^3 tt

mulae). While this makes for coherence, its limitation of range precludes the climactic use of upper tessitire as in monophonic sequences. Analysis along similar lines of the tune-material of the other voice (Table 13 above) shows that twenty sub-units not in the primary voice account for twenty-eight of its sixty-nine sub-units, while the others are in common with the primary voice though they have a few variants not found there. The gymel technique of unit combination requires a deployment of tune-material which will work in enough combinations of sub-units for the extent of the structure

[132] See p. 65.

concerned. The procedure in this case is analysable into twelve combination-groups of formulae and their variants, shown in Ex. 9 below. Naturally, variants are not combined; this would produce heterophony, not polyphony in the conventional western European sense. Neither are all combinations possible in every group used. Exchange of identical sub-units between the two voices occurs in only two groups — sub-unit a¹ with y¹ in group 1, and b with t and e with f in group 6 — and it does not occur in adjacent units. Since adjacent exchange is the technique of *rondellus*,[133] the usage in this piece may perhaps be called non-adjacent *rondellus*.

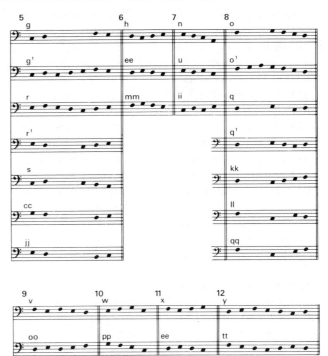

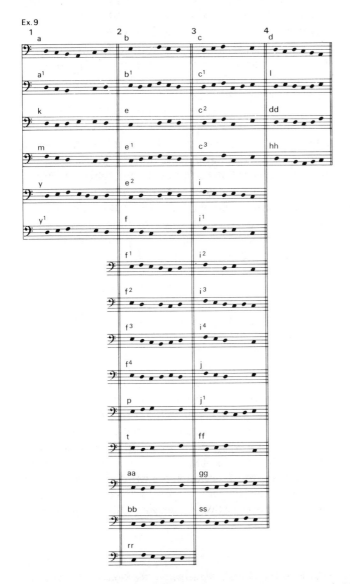

'SUMER IS ICUMEN IN': CONTEXT AND TECHNIQUE

The opinions of competent musical historians up to about 1940 on the music of *Perspice, Christicola/Sumer is icumen in* (no. 9) were summarized by Gustave Reese: 'The skilful construction of *Sumer is icumen in* and the facts that a Latin text appears under the English one and that instructions for its performance are written in Latin, have led some to believe that it is not an example of folk or popular music, as is sometimes supposed, but the work of a trained and expert musician; on the other hand, the presence of the Latin text and directions has led others to the opposite conclusion, for the Latin is obviously not the original text for the music, and the explicit directions for performance might well indicate that they were needed by the learned users of the manuscript, this manner of singing in canon being unfamiliar to them. The origin of the style of composition exhibited in *Sumer is icumen in* thus remains largely an open question'.[134] The evidence for the view, which has been general among musicians, that the Latin text was not the original one is by no means obvious. The opposite view

---

[133] Defined thus by Walter Odington in his *De Speculatione Musicae* (*c.*1300): 'Et si quod unus cantat omnes per ordinem recitent vocatur hic cantus Rondellus, id est, rotabilis vel circumductus'; E. de Coussemaker, *Scriptores de Musica*, i, Paris, 1864, p. 245.

[134] G. Reese, *Music in the Middle Ages*, New York, 1940, p. 397.

has been suggested earlier here,[135] on grounds of the relation between musical units of the *rota* tune and the rhyme-schemes of the Latin and English texts. Among writers on the English text of *Sumer is icumen in,* Carleton Brown thought it easier to believe that it was 'an imitation of a Welsh folk-song [here he had in mind Giraldus de Barri's description of Welsh singing quoted earlier] than that it was the invention of a learned composer'. It was the opinion of Sir Edmund Chambers, however, that it was 'not folk song, but a learned composer's adaptation of a *reverdie* or chant of welcome to the Spring'. Whatever may be the relation between the written form of the Summer Canon and thirteenth-century oral tradition (a term nowadays preferred to 'folk song', many of whose implications can be misleading), there is no doubt that on musical grounds Sir Edmund's opinion is nearer the truth. While canons and rounds may have been a part of unwritten musical practice, though probably in a less complex form than this, there is plenty of surviving written evidence that *rota* (i.e. canon) and *rondellus* were common techniques in English sacred music in the thirteenth century, and that *rondellus* was used at least a century earlier.[136]

Carleton Brown made the point that 'the careful directions in the manuscript for rendering the song suggest that it was of an unfamiliar type'. This does not necessarily follow, however. Directions for performing a part according to a special canon (i.e. rule — in the Middle Ages the word was used in a wider musical sense than the particular one of exact imitation) were sometimes specific, as here; then, as now, some performers might not perceive the technique at first sight, or might not have met it before (even now *Three Blind Mice* is published with directions for performance). Sometimes, however, directions were given in the form of a riddle or cryptic sign — hence Johannes Tinctoris's definition of canon as 'a rule which shows the intention of the composer in an obscure way'.[137] Occasionally a special mode of performance was not indicated in any way, but was left to the ingenuity of the performers to discover.

The technique of *rondellus,* in the form found in the earliest written examples, involves two voices, one of which rises while the other falls through an equal pitch-range; they then exchange parts. Given simple formulae and prearranged exchanges, performances along these lines can be improvised without difficulty. It is possible that the two lower parts of the Summer Canon derive from an oral-tradition practice of this kind. The technique of *rota,* in which one or more singers follow a leader with exactly the same tune, seems more likely to belong to written, contrived musical practice. It may, however, have been derived from extemporaneous singing in three or more parts, combining known tune-formulae and their variants in the manner used for two voices in *Jesu Cristes milde moder.* A further characteristic of the Summer Canon, that its tune-structure and part-structure are superimposed on two alternating notes a whole tone apart, is based on a formula in fairly widespread use in oral tradition. While it is possible, therefore, that there is some substratum of oral-tradition practice in the music of the Summer Canon, this cannot now be exactly determined, and is unlikely, judging from later oral tradition, to have provided more than a point of departure.

The music of the Summer Canon is a four-part *rota* superimposed on a two-part *rondellus,* marked *Pes* in the manuscript. Its composition entailed writing twelve units of tune, no more than four of which are sung together, over the *rondellus* of the two-part *pes.* When the tune is sung in canon by four singers there are nine successive unit-combinations, each of the length of two bars of the transcription, from the time all the singers have entered until they begin to drop out. The first four units must be distinct, though each must be consonant with the *pes,* while the others may be based on new tune-formulae or be variants of previous ones, so long as forms of the same formula do not occur in the same unit. In Ex. 10 below, the two-bar units of the tune are shown in capitals and the nine unit-combinations in numbers.

The Summer Canon seems to be the only surviving six-part piece earlier than *c.* 1400. Besides combining *rota* and *rondellus* in a way that has not survived elsewhere, its composer was obviously aware that his use of a repeating bass was connected with the technique of composing a motet. We have pointed out elsewhere[138] that the five notes *f g f g a* on which the composition was based are the same as the first five notes of the antiphon *Regina caeli,* which contains the words *Resurrexit sicut dixit* and belongs to the season of Easter, as does the Summer Canon's Latin text, whose beginning must have

---

[135] See pp. 68-69.

[136] Some of this evidence is discussed in F. Ll. Harrison, 'Rota and rondellus in English medieval music', *Proceedings of the Royal Musical Association,* 86, London, 1960, p. 98.

[137] 'Canon est regula voluntatem compositoris sub obscuritate quadam ostendens'; E. de Coussemaker, *Scriptores,* iv, 179.

[138] *Music in Medieval Britain,* p. 144.

been suggested by a passage in the Easter Sunday sequence *Fulgens praeclara:*

Perspice Christicolas, qualiter laeti canunt inclyta redemptori carmina.

Whether the identification of the lower part of the *pes* with the opening of *Regina caeli* is valid or not — it has been shown that the same tenor beginning, with a ligature in the same place, occurs in two other thirteenth-century instances[139] — it is nevertheless used here in motet-fashion, and not so used in the two cases cited. In

terms of its special combination of textual and musical elements, therefore, the Summer Canon may be described as a *rota-rondellus*-motet with alternative Latin and English texts on an unidentified *pes duplex* (? *Regina caeli*) with the English text 'Sing, cuccu, nu! Sing, cuccu!'

The editors of the anthology *Early Middle English Verse and Prose*[140] express the opinion that the English words of *Sumer is icumen in* were 'composed to fit the tune (though this was not necessarily a previously existing tune)'. They base this conclusion mainly on the musical setting of the fifth line of the poem, which they interpret as requiring a 'full stress' on each of the three syllables. This, they point out, would be a very unusual occurrence in Middle English verse composed in alternating stressed and unstressed syllables, and would need a special explanation, that is, that the words were 'composed to fit the music'. Apart from the inherent improbability that a tune which was not in the usual sense a previously existing one should be written before the words, the musical stresses of the three notes in line 5 are not equal, though the notes are the same length. The three longs in the original notation do not carry any necessary implication of relative stress apart from that of the poetic metre. In a modern transcription with barlines the stresses of these three notes would be understood as strong, weak and strong respectively.

The editors of the anthology mentioned also dealt with the question of text-priority. Referring to my discovery that the lower part of the *pes* is the same as the beginning of *Regina caeli*, they attributed to me the opinion that the Latin text was written first. My discussion of the point did not, however, include this statement, and was intended to query, mainly on technical musical grounds, the usual assumption that the English text was the original one and the Latin text a later adaptation. (The bearing on this question of the order in which the texts were apparently written down in the manuscript is discussed in the literary commentary, p. 143.) The absence of a Latin text for the *pes,* which the editors of the anthology regarded as telling against the possible priority of the Latin text, is, however, normal in motets, the texts of whose tenors were either not shown or were identified only by an *incipit*-cue. On musical grounds, therefore, the balance of evidence seems slightly in favour of the Latin text's priority. It also seems probable that a single musician-poet devised both texts and their music.

Certain changes in the notes of the *rota* tune which are

Ex.10

[139] E. Sanders, 'Tonal aspects of 13th-century English polyphony', *Acta Musicologica*, xxxvii (1965), p. 21.

[140] Ed. J. A. W. Bennett and G. V. Smithers, Oxford, 1966, p. 108.

apparent in the manuscript, made either by the original scribe or not long after the original writing, have hitherto been discussed mainly in their rhythmic significance. There seems no doubt, however, that the maker of these changes must also have had in mind that some of his alterations affected the order of the occurrence of the tune-formulae of the *rota*. At the words 'murye sing cuccu' / 'a supplicio' the present notes *f e d e f* appear to have been originally *c c d d c*, while the notes *c d c ba* to the immediately following words 'cuccu, cuccu' / 'vitae donat' appear to have been changed from *f d f dc*, or less probably from *f d f d*, as suggested by Manfred Bukofzer.[141] Bukofzer stressed that this latter change eliminated the 'cuckoo call, *f d, f d'* from the tune at the point where the words 'cuccu, cuccu' occur in the English poem. He also commented that with the former change the revised tune 'reverts to its own beginning simply repeating the first five notes'. He went on to say that it is 'an open question whether the melody in a canon should return to its beginning or carry on in a new way'. This question, however, is not answerable in such general terms. It is more pertinent to the scribe's changes to note that while he could have based one or other of the two unit-combinations he was juggling with on the formula *f d f d*, he could not have done so with both, since they would then duplicate each other in three unit-combinations, numbered 7, 8 and 9 in Ex. 10, p. 95. The question that is open, but is at any rate amenable to discussion, is why he decided to change the order of the two tune-units involved, in spite of the resulting loss of the 'cuckoo call' on the English words 'cuccu, cuccu'. Perhaps the most cogent reason is one which would not suggest itself from consideration of the *rota* tune as tune, but which would be immediately apparent in performance. In the amended version the formula *f d f* or a variant of it is present in each of the nine unit-combinations, but is duplicated in none of them. While likewise not duplicated in any combination in the original version, this formula could have been absent from one of the units, numbered 6 in Ex. 10, and its absence could not fail to be noticed and perhaps to be considered a defect. If this reason is valid, the scribe chose to forego the concurrence of the words 'cuccu, cuccu' with the 'cuckoo call' in the music. Since this

would have no relevance to the Latin words, his choice may imply that the English text had for him less importance than the Latin.

The other note-changes which the scribe appears to have made (the second note from *f* to *e*, and a change, perhaps of pitch but perhaps merely of note-shape, on the second syllable of 'cuccu' / third syllable of 'coronat' in lines 11/24) are of minor importance, and do not concern the order of the tune-formulae. He appears also to have added stems to a number of notes, presumably with the object either of changing the basic rhythm from duple to triple, as Bukofzer believed, or alternatively of making explicit the basic triple rhythm which would previously have been read by deduction.

In the monograph referred to above Bukofzer drew the conclusions that the original rhythm had been duple, and that the date of composition must be about 1320, not about 1240, as was previously thought. Neither conclusion was substantiated in the ample discussion that followed.[142] Subsequent research and the wider comparisons made possible by new discoveries have confirmed the original date of *c.* 1240, or at most a decade or two later.

CAROL USAGE AND FORM

Though English vernacular carol-texts, both sacred and secular, survive from the first half of the fourteenth century onwards, no music survives which is demonstrably earlier than that of *Lullay, lullay: Als I lay on Yoolis night* (no. 20). Two carols with surviving music which are probably close to it in date are the two-voice *Lullay, lullow: I saw a sweete seemly sight*[143] and the monophonic *Nova nova: Gabrielle offe hye degre.*[144] Music exists earlier, however, for Latin stanzaic songs with refrain, for example, the twelfth-century *Verbum patris humanatur, O, O* with the refrain *Eya, eya, nova gaudia.*[145] Non-ritual songs of this kind were presumably replacements during the twelve days of Christmas for the usual *Benedicamus Domino: Deo gratias* at the end of Vespers. Bishop John Grandisson's Ordinal for Exeter Cathedral, written in 1337, has this direction on

[141] *'Sumer is icumen in': a Revision,* Berkeley and Los Angeles, 1944, p. 87.

[142] Notably in B. Schofield, 'The provenance and date of "Sumer is icumen in" ', *Music Review,* ix (1948), p. 81, and J. Handschin, 'The Summer Canon and its background', *Musica Disciplina,* iii (1949), p. 55 and v (1951), p. 65.

[143] In British Library, MS Add. 5666, ff. 4v–5; published in *Now Make we Merthe,* ed. F. Ll. Harrison, ii, London, 1968, p. 5 (text ed. E. J. Dobson).

[144] In Glasgow University, Hunterian MS T.3.21, f. 2v; published in *Medieval Carols,* ed. J. Stevens, Musica Britannica, iv, London, 1952, p. 111.

[145] In Cambridge University Library, MS Ff.i.17, f. 299 (facsimile in *Early English Harmony,* pl. 29); published in *Now Make we Merthe,* i, p. 6.

Holy Innocents' Day, when the services were sung by choir-boys:[146]

> Aliquod *Benedicamus* solempniter prout eis placuerit, sed non *Verbum patris*.[147]
> (Any *Benedicamus* setting solemnly [i.e. probably in polyphony] as seems good to them, but not *Verbum patris*.)

They could use any suitable festive song except *Verbum patris hodie*, the *Benedicamus* trope prescribed in the service books for Christmas Day itself.[148] *Verbum patris humanatur, O, O*, which must have been written for this use, has a jovial motoric tune of a kind which otherwise is likely to have been used in a medieval church only during one of the liturgical plays of the same season, such as the Beauvais Daniel play, done by sub-deacons on the feast of the Circumcision on 1st January.[149] It seems clear that there was no objection on these occasions to secular-style tunes either in church or in the clerical common hall provided the words were acceptable. Bishop Richard de Ledrede of Ossory wrote for his clerics sedate poems, for example *Peperit virgo* (no. 16 b, (ii)), in place of song-texts which he denounced as 'lewd, secular and associated with revelry'.[150] At some time, perhaps the early fourteenth century, the song-tunes of round dances (*carole* tunes) were apparently drawn upon for clerical songs for Christmas and other festive seasons[151] and also for love-songs, some of which may have been used in cathedrals and singing-clerks' halls.

The tune for *Lullay, lullay: Als I lay on Yoolis night* is apparently the earliest carol-tune to survive in written form. The unit-lengths both of its burden and stanza seem clearly designed for text lines with four stresses — two lines in the burden and four in the stanza. The poem, however, is written in the common form of ballad-metre, with lines alternately of four stresses and three stresses. The Cambridge manuscript, the only surviving one with music, gives the words of the first stanza only. They are continued for some distance past the music, with no attempt to place them under the notes for which they were intended. The words of the second and fourth lines can be accommodated to four musical stresses by slowing the pace of the last three syllables of each line and stressing them equally. This method, however, cannot be applied in exactly the same way to the second and fourth lines of the other stanzas, which do not appear in the Cambridge manuscript. These can be accommodated to this music only by distributing them so that their stress-pattern is consistently x / / / x / . However, since the tune can conveniently be barred in modern six-eight time, a compound measure in which the first note of the former of two groups of triplets is understood to be more heavily stressed than the first note of the latter group, a present-day singer will understand the stress pattern as / x / x / , while inevitably making the second and third syllables longer than the others.

The need to adjust three-stress text-lines to music which suits four-stress text-lines suggests that if the original writer of these words meant them to go to this tune he was unobservant of this difficulty. Alternatively, the words may have been commonly attached to a different tune with appropriate alternating three- and four-stressed lines, and have been only experimentally fitted to this written tune by the scribe of this item in the Cambridge manuscript. Judging by his notation, he was either an inexpert scribe or was writing hurriedly or casually. An apparently parallel case occurs in a manuscript of the first half of the fifteenth century.[152] Here a carol burden beginning *Lullay, my child and weep no more*, of four lines with alternately four and three stresses, has been written down with a tune which allows for four stresses in each line.[153]

Items like these, which may be mere try-outs, are extreme exemplifications of the general truth that musical notation is not music; it is a coded guide to, or a necessarily inadequate record of, its performance, or something of both. This written recipe-cum-record

---

[146] 'Hac die [i.e., on St. Stephen's day] et in die sancti Johannis et Innocentium fiant quasi omnia ad libitum, quia sunt festa anormala diaconorum, presbiterorum et puerorum'.

[147] *Ordinale Exon*, ed. J. N. Dalton, i, London, 1909, p. 74.

[148] Published in *Now Make we Merthe*, i, p. 8.

[149] *The Play of Daniel*, ed. W. L. Smolden, London, 1960.

[150] See R. L. Greene, *A Selection of English Carols*, Oxford, 1962, p. 42.

[151] There are indications that this was also happening in France; see F. Ll. Harrison, 'Benedicamus, conductus, carol', *Acta Musicologica*, xxxvii (1965), p. 35.

[152] British Library, MS Add. 5666, ff. 2-3.

[153] See the transcription, and also that of *Als I lay on Yoolis night*, in *Medieval Carols*, ed. J. Stevens, Musica Britannica, iv, London, 1952, p. 110.

tends to be particularly summary in a situation like that of pre-Renaissance Europe, where oral transmission of music was overwhelmingly more frequent than its written transmission, and where most written music was ritual or esoteric. The written notation always implied a number of unwritten components — even more than does present-day notation — whose realization was understood, but was neither invariable, nor binding for all occasions. The kinds of evidence from which unspecified or only partly specified elements of a musical performance may be deduced are many and various. For the present study they have included poetry and chronicles, records of Christian liturgy and ritual, writings on musical theory and pedagogy, and remains and depictions of musical instruments. Evidence by analogy from surviving oral traditions and non-Western practices has also been used. Interpretations of such multifarious indications — sometimes mere sidelights — against their own particular musical and historical backgrounds furnish guidelines for the performing material and commentary upon it whose provision is one of the main aims of historical musicology.

CONTEXT AND STRUCTURE

Though the validity of this aim has usually been recognized for post-Renaissance music, most musicologists who have edited pre-seventeenth-century music have presented it as erudite library material, not as material which performers can use. Their commentary upon it has correspondingly lacked any discussion, except in the most general terms, of the music's original use and social context. They have consequently for the most part precluded themselves from consideration of what the music may have meant to those who used it. While the study of music of any time and place necessarily involves close examination of its technical structure, historians of Western music more than two centuries old have rarely gone beyond this, and in any case have often examined structures in terms of anachronistic concepts and vocabulary. In addition, dependence on the idea of autonomous style-periods in the arts of the West has prevented the recognition and analysis of musical processes, such as those of formulaic composition and oral transmission, whose use over-rides conventional style-divisions. Only in the study of music of other cultures than our own, i.e. in ethnomusicology, has analysis in depth of formulaic music-assemblage had any significant place. On this level the analysis of structure, as recorded in the totally specific terms of sound-recording, and the consideration of social use and meaning, are inextricably intertwined. The primary aim of this book is to provide performing material for music and language whose original sound and meaning are separated from us by shifts of usage and wastages of tradition. The endeavour to do this has underlined some inescapable facts and some unfamiliar facets of Western music's nature and use which tend to be obscured or forgotten in too exclusive a preoccupation with the library score.

TEXTS AND TEXTUAL COMMENTARY

E. J. DOBSON

TEXTS AND TEXTUAL COMMENTARY

I. RELIGIOUS SONGS BY SAINT GODRIC

1. Sainte Marie viergene

Saintë Marië   viërgenë,
moder Jésu Cristes   Nazarenë,
onfóo, schild,   help þin Godrich;
onfangë, bring heʒlíchë   wið þee in Godes richë.

5 Saintë Marië,   Cristes bur,
maidenes clenhad,   moderes flur,
dilië min sinnë,   rix in min mood;
bring me to winnë   wið þe selfë God.

2. Crist and Sainte Marie

Angelus a dextris altaris:
     Kyrieleison.
Angelus a sinistris:
     Christe eleison.
Soror:

Crist and Saintë Marië   swa on scamel me ileddë,
þat ich on þis erðë ne sildë   wið minë barë footen itreddë.

3. Sainte Nicholas, Godes druth

Saintë Nicholas,   Godes druð,
tymbre us faiërë   scoonë hus.
At þi burðë,   at þi barë,
Saintë Nicholas,   bring us wel þarë.

COMMENTARY

Source: London, British Museum, MS Royal 5 F. vii, f. 85

St. Godric was born in Norfolk, the eldest child of poor parents of English race. He became a merchant, and in due course half-owner of a trading ship, with an interest in another; finally he was himself captain of a ship. After sixteen years as a trader, he took the Cross and made a pilgrimage, apparently by sea, to Jerusalem; he was probably 'Gudric the pirate from England' who assisted King Baldwin after his defeat at Ramleh in 1102 (see A. L. Poole, *From Domesday Book to Magna Carta* (Oxford, 2nd edition 1955), p. 94). Then he twice visited Rome, the second time in the company of his mother. On his return he spent some time living the life of a hermit, before undertaking a second pilgrimage, overland, to Jerusalem, in the course of which he practised remarkable austerities. Back in England, he lived for a time near Whitby and then as a servant of two churches in succession, at the second of which he learnt to read sufficiently for his purposes. Finally, he withdrew to a hermitage at Finchale on the river Wear, north of Durham; according to his biographer Reginald this was some sixty years before his death, i.e. about 1110. There he built a hut for himself and a wooden chapel dedicated to the Virgin Mary; other buildings were later added, including a church dedicated to John the Baptist. After some twenty years living entirely alone he accepted a servant, and for a time his sister Burgwen lived with him in a hut that he built for her. He placed himself under the protection of the prior of Durham, and monks from Durham came on feast days to say mass for him; in the last eight years of his life, when he was continuously ill, he was tended by monks from Durham. He died on 20 May 1170. If the details of his career are accurately recorded, he cannot have been less than 90, and was probably nearer 100, at the time of his death. Durham Abbey inherited the site of his hermitage and set up a daughter-house there; and Godric's biographies were written before the end of the century by monks of Durham — an extant life by Reginald, who began his work before 1166, during Godric's life; a lost work by Germanus, prior of Durham, who died in 1189; and the life by Geoffrey, in the Acta Sanctorum, which was written by 1196.

At Finchale, Godric inflicted excessive physical hardships on himself, and it is perhaps not surprising that he saw many visions, both of devils and of saints. Two, and perhaps all three, of his songs were associated with visions. One day when he was in prayer in his chapel of St. Mary he saw on either side of the altar two beautiful women in white raiment, who after a while advanced to him. The woman on the right of the altar told him that she was St. Mary the Virgin and her companion was St. Mary Magdalene, and laying her hands on his head she sang to him the words and melody of a new song, which she made him repeat after her until he had learnt it; this was *Sainte Marie viergene* (no. 1 above). The occasion of the second was that after his sister Burgwen's death he was in great sorrow and much troubled about the fate of her soul, and prayed repeatedly to God to reveal to him her fate at the judgement seat. One night in a vision he saw two angels in white, preceded by the Virgin, come into his chapel, bearing between them the soul of his sister, which they placed on the altar. Then his sister's soul, from its position on the altar, sang repeatedly to him the song *Crist and Sainte Marie* (no. 2 above); and each time when she ended her verse the angels on either side of the altar came in with *Kyrieleison, Christe eleison*. The biographer Reginald, who gives these two accounts, does not mention the third song, but he records that once when he was visiting Godric on the eve of Easter, he heard him singing loudly in the night and often calling on St. Nicholas, and when in the morning he asked why, Godric said that angels had descended to Christ's tomb and sung there, and St. Nicholas with them, and that Godric himself, encouraged by St. Nicholas, had joined in their singing. Presumably it was not on this occasion that the song to St. Nicholas was composed, but it may have been during some similar vision of St. Nicholas, since Godric evidently required — or believed that he received — supernatural inspiration for his little verses and their melodies.

Godric's songs are the subject of a meticulously careful study, preceded by a summary account of his life (further summarized above), by J. Zupitza, 'Cantus beati Godrici', *Englische Studien* xi (1887), pp. 401–32. He gives a detailed account of the manuscripts and their readings and affiliations, which we follow below in the discussion of the individual songs, but his text, especially of no. 1, is less satisfactory; it is insufficiently critical, and pays too little regard to rhyme, metre, and grammar. The texts as given in MS Royal 5 F. vii, f. 85^r, are printed by J. Hall, *Early Middle English*, p. 5, without even the most necessary emendations; and Hall's discussion of the metre (ibid., pp. 242-3) is very unsatisfactory.

It is the metre of the songs which presents the most difficult problem. It is rough, but not quite so rough as the transmitted text makes it appear. Godric's melodies are based on plainsong, and it is obvious that in a general way his stanza-forms are modelled on those of Latin hymns of the Ambrosian type. But he was an Anglo-Saxon, born within twenty years at most of the Norman conquest, and his mind must have been full of the rhythms of Anglo-Saxon verse, probably not of the strict literary type but of the more popular sort whose existence is inferred from late OE rhythmical prose, from the surviving fragments of twelfth- and thirteenth-century alliterative verse, and from the verse of the fourteenth-century alliterative revival. For the sake of musicians in particular, and of others who may not be familiar with the metrical analysis of alliterative verse, we describe here, very summarily, its chief principles as they affect these songs.

(1) The verse-line was divided into two halves, separated by a more or less clearly marked caesura, and the metrical unit was the half-line. Each half-line did not have to conform to a single rhythmical pattern, regularly maintained through the poem, but might be any one of a number of accepted patterns; in particular the rhythm of the second half-line did not have to be the same as that of the first. (2) The verse did not depend at all on syllable-counting, but on a regular alteration of metrically stressed and unstressed elements known respectively as 'lifts' and 'dips'. A 'lift' was necessarily a stressed syllable. In classical OE verse it was also normally a long syllable, though there were important qualifications; in ME alliterative verse syllable-length is no longer significant. (Godric's verse conforms in this respect to the ME type; most of the 'lifts' are in fact long syllables, but a considerable minority are short and in breach of the OE metrical rules.) A 'dip' was constituted by one or more unstressed syllables. In theory any number of successive unstressed syllables constituted but a single 'dip', though in practice the number was limited; the normal 'dip' was of one or two unstressed syllables, though 'dips' of three unstressed syllables (as in Godric's no. 1, l. 7a, and no. 2, l. 2b) were not uncommon. But in OE verse a 'dip' at the end of a half-line had to consist of a single unstressed syllable only. If however there were 'resolution' (the counting of two short syllables as the equivalent of a single long stressed syllable), a half-line might in fact end with two unstressed syllables, though in metrical analysis the first of the two belonged to the resolved 'lift' and only the second to the 'dip'; in ME alliterative verse the same rhythmical type continued, though with the loss of the quantitative principle (and therefore of 'resolution') both the unstressed syllables at the end of the half-line now had to be regarded as being in the 'dip'. In Godric's verses, any 'dip' at the end of a half-line consists of a single unstressed syllable except in no. 3, where ll. 1a, 2a, and 4a end in two unstressed syllables. (3) In the normal OE verse, the half-line consisted of two lifts and two dips, and therefore contained a minimum of four syllables. These lifts and dips could be arranged in various patterns: Type A, or falling rhythm (lift-dip, lift-dip); Type B, or rising rhythm (dip-lift, dip-lift); Type C, or clashing rhythm (dip-lift, lift-dip). There were also more complex structures depending on the introduction of secondary stresses; these do not concern us here. In the 'lengthened' or 'extended' verse (which was comparatively rare in classical OE poetry but common in ME, especially in the first half-line) there were three lifts in the half-line, and the patterns were necessarily more numerous and complicated. A common method of analysis is to regard a three-lift half-line as a telescoping of two two-lift half-lines, overlapping at the second lift, e.g. a three-stress half-line which begins rising and ends falling is regarded

as a telescoping of two two-stress half-lines, one rising and the other falling, and is described as Type BA. (4) The two halves of each line were bound together by alliteration of the initial sounds of stressed syllables. The precise rules do not concern us; in ME they were much relaxed. In OE itself alliteration was sometimes supplemented by rhyme as an added ornament; in late OE very occasionally rhyme was substituted for alliteration as the linking principle; and in the 'mixed' verse of early ME the two halves of the line might be linked either by alliteration or by rhyme or by both (or indeed sometimes by neither).

Godric's lines are best regarded as being formed, in this native English way, of two roughly equivalent half-lines which constitute the metrical unit, and it is for this reason that we print them with a mid-line space to mark the caesura. His normal half-line is the short one with two lifts and its normal rhythm is that of the OE A-type (falling) half-line. But the B-type (rising) half-line occurs in l. 8b of no. 1. An innovation not found in strict OE verse is a 'defective' half-line of only three syllables. Such half-lines are not uncommon in ON poetry, and it is significant that Godric, who was born in Norfolk and lived in Durham, spent his life within the area of England that was especially affected by Norse influence. Historically the defective three-syllable half-line developed from the minimal four-syllable half-line of regular verse by the loss, in speech, of one of the unstressed syllables, but it then became, in Norse, a type to be imitated. In Godric's verses the commoner type of 'defective' half-line has the rhythm /x(x)/, which is regarded as an A-type half-line which has lost its second dip; but Godric uses it as the second half of the line after a first half-line that ends with a dip (i.e. he is beginning, under the influence of Latin metre, to treat the full line as the unit, with alternating lifts and dips). Examples are ll. 5b, 6b, and 7b of no. 1 and ll. 1b and 2b of no. 3. In the Royal MS this same 'defective' half-line occurs in the first half of l. 3 of no. 3, but in this case it is probably due to scribal error (or rather alteration of the original) and is emended in our text. A second type of 'defective' half-line is found in l. 3a of no. 1 (onfóo, schíld); this rhythm x// is taken in metrical analysis as a C-type half-line which has lost its second dip, though in this instance it could well be regarded as a B-type half-line in which the second dip is replaced by a sense-pause. Godric also uses the extended half-line of three stresses, which must have been much more common in popular than in strict verse; so in l. 4 of no. 1 and in both verse-lines of no. 2. The rhythm of these extended half-lines is the OE type BA (rising-falling) except in l. 1a of no. 2, where it is type AA (falling throughout). In l. 2 of no. 1 he appears to combine a first half-line of three stresses (type AA) with a second half-line of two, as was common in ME alliterative verse and sometimes occurred in OE; but perhaps the first word *moder* is to be regarded as a two-syllable anacrusis, lacking significant metrical stress.

Alliteration is rare in Godric's verses, but occurs in no. 1, l. 6; no. 2, l. 1; and no. 3, l. 3. Its place has been taken by rhyme, which is used in three ways, all of which can be paralleled in OE verse. (1) Normally it is added at the ends of successive full lines, so that they rhyme together in couplets: so no. 1, ll. 1-2, 5-6; no. 2; and no. 3, ll. 1-2, 3-4. (2) It may be added at the ends of the two halves of a single line, so that there is internal rhyme within the long line (or alternatively the full line breaks into two short lines which constitute a couplet): so no. 1, l. 4 (*heʒ liche* in 4a rhyming with *riche* in 4b). (3) It may be added both at the middles and at the ends of two successive lines, so

that the two long lines break into four short lines rhyming abab: so in no. 1, ll. 7–8 (*sinne* 7a rhyming with *winne* 8a, *mood* (*mod* MSS) 7b rhyming imperfectly with *God* 8b). It is possible that in no. 2 there is meant to be a rudimentary rhyme on final -*e* (such as is found in earlier medieval verse) between *Marie* in l. 1a and *silde* in l. 2a, as well as the obviously intended disyllabic rhyme of *iledde* in l. 1b with *itredde* in l. 2b. In no. 1, the third line is neither alliterated nor rhymed, but there is perhaps an imperfect rhyme intended between the unstressed -*rich* of *Godrich* in l. 3b and *heʒliche* in 4a and *riche* in 4b.

1. Sainte Marie viergene

The, MSS which give texts of this song may be classified as follows. The sigla used are Zupitza's; in his system a capital letter (thus A) denotes an English text, a lower-case letter (which I italicize, thus *b*) a Latin translation.

1(a). Texts in MSS of the life of Godric by Reginald, monk of Durham. Oxford, Bodleian Library, MS Laud 413, f. 39ᵛ (end of 13th century); English text (A). London, British Library, MS Harley 153, f. 26 (beginning of 16th century); English text (B) and Latin translation (*b*). Cambridge, University Library, MS Mm. iv. 28, f. 149 (about 1200); English text (C) with music, with Latin translation (*c*) in a later hand.

1(b). Anonymous redaction of Reginald's work, in London, British Library, MS Harley 322 (probably late 12th century); Latin translation (*d*) on f. 49ᵛ, English text (D) with music on f. 74ᵛ.

2. Life of Godric by Geoffrey, monk of Durham. Zupitza used London, British Library, MS Royal 5 F. vii, which on f. 105ᵛ gives a versified and abbreviated translation (*e*).

3. Inserted leaf, in a different hand of the beginning of the 13th century, in this MS Royal 5 F. vii, f. 85, on which are given the text and music of all three of Godric's songs; English text (F) with music, with a Latin translation (*f*) in a fourteenth-century hand.

4. St. Albans chroniclers. (a) Roger of Wendover, *Flores Historiarum*. Oxford, Bodleian Library, MS Douce 207, f. 125ᵛ (end of 13th century); English text (G) with Latin translation (*g*). London, British Library, MS Cotton Otho B.v, f. 32ᵛ (beginning of 14th century); English text (H) with Latin translation (*h*). (b) Matthew Paris, *Chronica maiora*. Cambridge, Corpus Christi College, MS 26, p. 259 (MS corrected by Matthew himself in many places, and therefore before 1259 at latest); English text (I) with Latin translation (*i*), an abbreviation of Roger's. Two other MSS of Matthew, little later in date (the first also corrected by himself), derive from I and have no independent authority; they are British Library, MS Cotton Nero D.5, f. 150ᵛ, and British Library, MS Harley 1620. The spellings of GHI show the influence of a Southeastern dialect, probably that of St. Albans itself.

5. The Latin translations in John of Tinmouth and John Capgrave (on which see Zupitza, p. 421) derive from the anonymous redaction of Reginald (1(b) above) and have no independent authority.

The affiliations of the MSS are most clearly revealed by the presence or absence of the second stanza. It is lacking in the English texts ABCD and the corresponding translations *bcde*;

it is present in the English texts FGHI and the translations *fghi.* The St. Albans texts are further distinguished by the insertion, in l. 1, of the word *clane (clene)* before *virgine.* The relations of the English texts, as determined by Zupitza, may be expressed as (ABC)D — F[(GH)I]. Music is given by C and D (for the first stanza) and by F (for both stanzas). F is undoubtedly the best witness to the text, though not perfect; in stanza 2 its evidence is to be preferred to that of GHI, when they differ, though at certain points Zupitza, surprisingly, rejects its readings.

Zupitza's stemma, and more clearly his treatment of the text, imply that the archetype of the extant MSS is to be identified with Godric's original text. But this is very unlikely. The words and music must have been written down by someone both literate and musically trained, as Godric was almost certainly not; probably they were taken down, at his dictation, by one of the Durham monks. But the draft made from dictation would have been superseded by a fair copy; the latter (or even some later copy) is likely to have been the archetype of the extant texts. Errors could arise either in the process of taking down the texts or in making the fair copy; in spite, therefore, of the earliness of the textual tradition, emendation, even when it is clear what were the readings of the archetype, is not precluded.

The Latin translations depend on the English text as it was received and understood (or misunderstood) by the authors or revisers of the translations, and have no independent value for the establishment of the English text.

VARIANTS

For further details, see Zupitza, especially p. 423.
1 Sainte] AF Seinte BDGHI Sancte C   viergene] uirgine ABCDF clane uirgine GI clene uirgine H   2 Jesu Cristes] ABCFHI iesus cristes D iesu crist G   3 onfoo] onfo ACFGHI vnfo B onfong D   help] ABCDFGH *om.* I   Godrich] DHI Godric ABCF gorich G   4 onfange] onfang ABCFGHI onfong D   heʒliche] hehliche B hegliche D heʒilich F hehtlic C eʒhtlech A heali GH hæali I   riche] ACFG ric B rich HI rych D   5–8 *om.* ABCD   5 Sainte] F Seinte GHI   6 maidenes] F maidenus G meidenes HI   7 dilie] FHI deliuere G   min] F mine GHI   sinne] F sennen GHI   rix] F rixe HI regne G   in] FG i HI   min] FHI mi G   8 winne] F wunne H pinine I blisse G   wiδ F widh HI wit G   þe] F þi G *om.* HI   selfe] selfd F self GHI

NOTES

1. *Marie* is stressed on the second, as normally in OF and ME; cf. modern French *Marie.*
viergene] All the MSS have *uirgine,* which was obviously the reading of the archetype. But it does not scan, for it leaves the second half-line with only a single stress, and it gives only a rhyme on unstressed final *-e* with *Nazarene* in l. 2. What seems required is the OF and AN variant form *viergene* (four syllables, with a glide *e* before the *r*), which makes an A-type half-line /x/x and gives a disyllabic rhyme with *Nazarene.* The insertion of *clane* 'pure' before *uirgine* in the St. Albans texts is obviously due to an attempt to correct the metre by lengthening the second half-line.

2. On the scansion of the first half-line see the general discussion of Godric's metre above. The line could be reduced to four

stresses by the omission of *Cristes,* but it seems unlikely that the archetype would have inserted a word, and the music provides for the line as given in the MSS. Parallels for the combination of a three-stress first half-line with a two-stress second half-line are to be found in the twelfth-century *Worcester Fragments* of alliterative verse; thus Fragment A, l. 1,

    Sánctus *Bé*da was i*bó*ren   her on *Bré*otene mid ús,
and Fragment C, l. 42,
    fúweles *quá*le hólde   þe þu ic*wé*mdest ǽr,

in both of which the first word (*Sanctus, fuweles*), since it does not alliterate, is obviously subordinated, in the metre, to the second. Similarly in Godric's line the first word *moder* is probably intended to be subordinate to the name *Jesu Cristes,* i.e. the first significant stress of the line falls on the first syllable of *Jesu.*

3. *onfoo* (*onfo* MSS) 'receive', imperative sg. of *onfo(n);* the OE imperative sg. was *onfoh,* but the form has been remodelled on the infinitive. The stress is on the second syllable, as it was always in OE and would be in modern English if the verb survived; Hall's placing of the stress on the prefix in his analysis of the metre, both of this line and the next (*op. cit.,* p. 242), is completely unwarranted.
schild 'shield'.
help belongs in the second half-line, as is suggested by the pointing of A (though the other MSS admittedly point differently). The uninflected form of the possessive adjective *þin* is explicable only if it is unstressed, like *min* (twice) in l. 7; indeed it is possible that we should read *þi* here in l. 3 (cf. *þi* in both instances in l. 3 of no. 3) and *mi* in l. 7. If the possessive were stressed, we should expect *þinne* or *þine,* representing the OE accus. sg. *þinne.* But if *þin* is unstressed, *help* must belong to the second half-line.
Godrich] The name is conventionally spelt *Godric* (the OE spelling, on which is based the Latinized *Godricus*), and so here in most MSS. But the final *c* was, even in later OE, pronounced as *ch,* and we therefore adopt the spelling *Godrich* of the minority of the MSS for use here in the poem, where the pronunciation matters, though otherwise we use the conventional form.

4. As emended, the line means 'received, bring honourably with thee to God's kingdom', i.e. 'when he has been received, bring him honourably . . .'.
The complete agreement of the MSS leaves no doubt that the archetype read *onfang, bring* 'receive, bring', in which *onfang* is a new imper. sg. modelled on the ME infinitive *onfangen* (itself in turn remodelled on the p.p.). The translations correspondingly have *suscipe, porta* (*bcf*) or *suscipe, adduc* (*dgh*). Nevertheless the transmitted text seems unsatisfactory. (1) It makes Godric use two different forms of the imperative, *onfo(o)* and *onfang,* in successive lines, which, though not impossible (Orm in the course of his work uses both *onnfanngenn* and *onnfon* for the infinitive), is improbable, especially as there is no metrical advantage to be gained from the variation. (2) In the MS text, the two imperatives are used without connecting conjunction. It is true that in the preceding line three imperatives are used in parallel without conjunction, but the case is not really the same; indeed the use of the asyndetic construction in l. 3 seems to me a reason why it should not be

repeated in the different circumstances of l. 4a. (3) The MS text of line 4a scans x//x/x, with clashing stresses, which, though easy to parallel in ME verse, is not the same rhythm as that of 4b, which is x/x/x/x; and half-lines linked by internal rhyme tend to have the same rhythm. The second and third objections could be met by emending 4a to *onfang [and] bring heȝliche*, but only the emendation adopted in the text meets all three points. It assumes that the scribe of the archetype has omitted final *-e* from the p.p. *onfange*, as various of the extant MSS do in other cases (including *heȝliche* in this line; see below). If the scribe of the archetype were, as is likely, a Northerner, for whom the strong p.p. would regularly keep its full ending *-en*, he might reasonably regard *onfange* as an improper form, requiring alteration either to *onfangen* p.p. or to *onfang* imper. sg.; and he may simply have made the wrong choice.

The Latin translations, as remarked above, follow the transmitted English text of the song. But Reginald in his life also reports a prayer of Godric's to the Virgin (Laud MS, f. 87ᵛ), which follows the wording of the song but expands it — so obviously indeed that it is at this point that the English text of the song is given in the anonymous redaction (Harley MS, f. 74ᵛ). This prayer has, to correspond to l.4 of the song: 'ac de hoc cenulento ergastulo ("this foul prison") *erutum* tecum hinc perducito et sub umbra tuæ miserationis in cæleste regnum gloriæ perhennis tecum modo hinc *translatum* collocare memento' (Zupitza, pp. 416-17; similarly in the briefer version of the redactor). That is, the prayer has the p.ps. *erutum* and *translatum* (of which the redactor drops the latter) to correspond to the p.p. *onfange* of our emended text of the song, where the transmitted text has an imperative.

heȝliche 'honourably', a new formation on the adj. *heȝ* (or *heh*) < OE *hē(a)h*, in place of OE *hēalice* (which gives the form of GHI). It is correctly translated *gloriose* in *f*, rather less correctly *alte* in *b*; the rest have mistranslations owing to corruption or misunderstanding of the English text. Only B and D preserve the *-e* of the adverbial suffix *-liche* (< OE *-līce*), though it is very unlikely that it would have been lost in the speech of a man born in Norfolk in the eleventh century; moreover it is required by the rhyme with *riche* (< OE *rīce* 'kingdom'), which is thus given by ACFG, though B and D, as well as HI, drop the *-e*. As these two rhyming words show, the preservation of *-e* in the MSS is very erratic. Zupitza accepts the forms *hehlic* and *ric*, because he assumes that an exact rhyme is intended with *Godric* in l. 3; but the latter is stressed on the first, and loss of grammatically or etymologically necessary *-e* is not to be assumed so early in a non-Northern dialect. The MS forms without *-e* must be due to Northern copyists; even so the occurrence of *rych* in D (late 12th century), and of *heȝilich* and *hehtlic* in F (beginning of 13th century) and C (*c.* 1200) respectively, is remarkably early. In *heȝliche* the metrical stress is placed on the suffix. Such a departure from the natural stress is entirely contrary to OE practice, but was very common in ME rhyming verse; it is already a well-established feature in *The Owl and the Nightingale*, which was certainly written before 1200. This is the only instance in Godric's brief verses.

5-8. Though the second stanza is omitted by Reginald and texts derived from him, there is no reason to doubt its authenticity. But as it does not add much to the sense of the first, it may perhaps have been a later addition.

5. *bur* 'bower', 'bed-chamber'.

6. *maidenes clenhad* means literally 'maiden's purity', but the possessive seems here to be used with adjectival force, 'virginal purity'; it is so rendered (*virginalis puritas*) by Roger of Wendover. Owing to the early date, OE *ā* in the suffix *-had* is unchanged; cf. *swa* 'so' in no. 2, l. 1.
moderes flur is translated *matris flos* by Roger of Wendover, but the possessive is I think rather to be taken as a plural, 'flower of mothers'.

7. *dilie* 'blot out, erase'; see *OED*, s.v. *dilghe, dilie*. The word is set as three syllables in the music; but its form is difficult. It is derived from OE *dil(e)gian*, in which the *g* was velar; Orm's *dillȝhenn*, still with velar spirant, is the normal descendant of the OE form, and would later have become **dilwen* and then **dillow* (cf. *hallow* < later ME *halwen* < Orm's *hallȝhenn* < OE *halgian* 'consecrate'). But OE verbs of this type were liable to analogical influences from etymologically related words of which the phonology was different; thus *synegian*, properly with velar *g*, took on palatal *g* from the adjective *synnig*, and similarly OE *dilegian* might be influenced by the noun *diligness* 'destruction' (for which see Bosworth-Toller, Supplement; it is clearly recorded in the Corpus Glossary). The latter would have palatal *g*, and a re-formed verb *dilgian* with palatal *g* would regularly give ME trisyllabic *dilien*; cf. ME *herien* (modern English *harry*) from OE *hergian* 'ravage' (with palatal *g* from Gmc. [j]).

min (both instances) is unstressed and therefore uninflected in F's form, which is obviously correct in this respect, though perhaps the *-n* should be dropped. For the first instance GHI have *mine*, an inflected plural form.
sinne] probably plural, 'sins', < OE *synna* fem. pl. The South-eastern *sennen* of GHI is certainly plural and is so translated by Roger of Wendover (*mea crimina*).
rix 'rule', imper. sg. of OE *rixian*. The OE imper. sg. was *ricsa, rixa*, whence ME *rixe* (given by HI and adopted in Zupitza's text), but the *-e* here elides before *in* and F's spelling *rix* is therefore to be preferred.
mood (*mod* MSS) here means 'spirit'; in form acc. sg., used by syncretism in place of the OE dative.

8. *wiδ þe selfe God* 'with the very God', 'with God himself' (*cum solo deo*, Roger of Wendover). As far as form goes, *wiδ þe selfe* could mean 'with thy self', in which case God would have to be taken as the subject of *bring* ('God bring me to bliss with thy self'), and G actually copies the text as *wit þi self*, but this runs counter to Roger's translation, which the MS itself copies unchanged. Zupitza omits *þe*, following HI against the superior evidence of F (which in effect is supported by G), but the article is essential when the adjective *self* precedes its noun.
selfe] F's *selfd*, though printed without comment by Hall, is an impossible form; the *d* must be due to misreading of an *-e*. Certainly *selfe*, representing the OE weak oblique form *selfan* (or less probably the OE strong dative masc. *selfum*) is what grammar and metre require, though Zupitza adopts the uninflected *self* of GHI (presumably because he does not admit to his text any form or spelling that does not occur in some MS or other, with the exception of his *hehlic* in l. 4, which is a blend of C's *hehtlic* and B's *hehliche*).
God, if Roger's translation of the line is correct, represents the OE accusative, used by grammatical syncretism in place of the dative; similarly in the *Ormulum*.

2. Crist and Sainte Marie

Texts and/or translations of this song are given by Zupitza pp. 425-9 from the following sources.

1 (a) Reginald's Life of Godric. Oxford, Bodleian Library, MS Laud 413, f. 47; English text (A) and Latin prose translation (a). London, British Library, MS Harley 153, f. 31; English text (B) and Latin prose translation (b).

1 (b) Anonymous redaction of Reginald: London, British Library; MS Harley 322, f. 53; Latin translation (d). From this descend, directly or indirectly, the translations in John of Tinmouth and John Capgrave.

2. Life of Godric by Geoffrey, represented by London, British Library, MS Royal 5 F. viii, f. 95^v. The account given is based partly on Reginald's, partly (as Zupitza assumes) on the lost work by Germanus; it gives both a prose translation (e^1) of the second line of Burgwen's couplet, presumed to be derived from Germanus, and a verse translation (e^2) of the whole couplet based on Reginald's prose translation.

3. Inserted leaf, in different hand, in London, British Library, MS Royal 5 F. vii, f. 85; English text (F) with music.
There are thus only three MSS of the English text, A and B, which are related, and F, which is independent; and only F gives the music. My text is based on F, and follows it in giving the angels' *Kyrieleison, Christe eleison* before Burgwen's couplet, though Reginald says that they sang after her. Reginald says that Burgwen sang the words repeatedly, always followed by the angels; and the text in the Royal MS shows at least one repetition, for after Burgwen's couplet, as given in my text above, the MS continues:

> *Item angeli* Kyrieleison. Christeleison. *Item angeli* Kyrieleison. Christeleison. *Soror.* Crist and Sainte Marie. vt supra.

VARIANTS

1 Crist and] FA *om.* B 　　Sainte] F seinte AB 　　swa] FB sio A 　　on scamel] FA *om.* B 　　2 þat] F that B thæt A 　　ich] ic FAB 　　þis] FB this A 　　erðe] F hi erthe AB 　　silde] F sciulde A sulde *altered to* selde B 　　wið] wid F uuit A noth B 　　footen] fote F fot AB 　　itredde] itredie F itreide A hi trede B

NOTES

1. *swa* 'so, thus', i.e. in this way that you (Godric) see. *scamel* 'stool, footstool' and thence 'bench', 'table (especially for the sale of goods)'; but the altar is here apparently meant. The word is from Latin *scamellum*, diminutive of *scamnum* (which Reginald uses in his translation).
　The form used is hardly a mere spelling of the normal ME *s(c)hamel* (modern English *shamble*) < OE *sc(e)amol*, since the scribe of the Royal MS uses *sch* for OE *sc* in *schild* 'shield' in no. 1, l. 3. It is probably an instance, much earlier than those cited by *OED*, of the variant *scamble* sb.[1] < Scandinavian *skamel* (modern Danish *skammel*, ON *skemill*); it could be due to a Northern scribe, but in Godric's own Norfolk speech a form from Scandinavian might well be used in place of the native form.
iledde 'brought, conducted' or perhaps 'bore'; Reginald trans-

lates *Sancta Maria . . . me conduxit,* but John of Tinmouth, evidently with independent reference to the English, has *Christus et sancta Maria me deduxerunt.* The form used is p.t. pl. (with loss of *-n*) of OE *gelǣdan,* not of the simplex *lǣdan,* and the *i-* prefix appears to be established as original by the metre.

2. *ich*] *ic* MSS, the OE spelling; we give the normal ME form. *erðe* 'earth'. The AB reading *hi erthe* is taken by Zupitza as indicating a form *ierthe* with Kentish *ie* for late OE *ēo* by lengthening of *ĕo* before *rð,* but there is no reason why a Kentish form should occur in these MSS. Moreover the *Ayenbite* itself has *yerþe* only once, against common *erþe.*
　It seems more likely that AB's otiose *hi* is due to some oddity in an antecedent copy. It follows a dative *þis,* for which early ME might well use *þisen* even before an OE feminine noun (cf. *þen eorðe* in early thirteenth-century texts); and in a Northern MS, even at this early date, *þisen* might be written *þisin,* with *i* for general ME unstressed *e.* But the inflexion *-in* might be abbreviated *-ī,* with the common mark of abbreviation for *n,* and this in turn might be misread as an ordinary *i* if the abbreviation-mark was mistaken for the accent-stroke commonly placed over the letter *i.* Such a misreading could account for the *hi* in the extant MSS AB; cf. B's *hi* for the prefix *i-* of *itredde* in l. 2.
silde 'should'. The form, which is F's, is usually compared to *scilun* 'we shall' in the Leningrad MS of *Cædmon's Hymn.* If the forms are indeed related, *silde* is likely to be due to a Northern (Durham) scribe rather than to Godric himself. B's original *sulde* is more likely to represent the Norfolk dialect.
mine] so MSS, perhaps because the scribe of the archetype recognized that a plural form was required. But the word is metrically unstressed (the first stress of the half-line being on *bare*), and we should perhaps read *min* or even *mi;* cf. *min* in no. 1, l. 7 (the first instance evidently a plural), *þin* in no. 1, l. 3, and *þi* in no. 3, l. 3 (twice). But the musical setting is for two syllables.
footen] F's *fote,* though translated *nudo pede* by Reginald, is beyond reasonable doubt dative plural from OE *fōtum.* The musical setting is for two syllables, i.e. the *-e* is not elided before the following *i-* prefix (though AB write *fot,* showing elision); and the lack of elision strongly suggests that the original had the fuller form with the inflexion *-en* < OE *-um.* We therefore restore *footen* in our text.
itredde] All three MSS show the *i-* prefix, though this is not the normal ME form, and the musical setting in F requires it; one must therefore assume that it is original. OE *getredan* is very rare; Bosworth-Toller cite only two examples, both from the Lindisfarne Gospels, in which the verb is used transitively, meaning 'to tread down', corresponding to *fortredan* in the WS version. But here its ME descendant is used as an intransitive verb, i.e. as a mere variant on the normal *trede(n).*
　F's form *itredie* also has the suffix *-ie,* and A's *itreide* looks like a miscopying of the same form; the archetype must have read *itredie,* as F. But (*i*)*tredie* is a blend of the ordinary ME *trede(n)* from the OE strong verb *tredan* and the OE (poetic) weak verb *treddian;* cf. Orm's weak p.p. *trededd,* with single intervocalic *d* from the strong verb but the weak inflexion. In a Northern or Eastern dialect of this date the *-ie(n)* ending was obsolescent and is probably a mere literary archaism on the part of the scribe of the archetype; it is ruled out by the rhyme with *iledde.* The form required to make the rhyme perfect is an

East Midland *itredde from an OE *getreddian (i.e. the recorded weak *treddian* plus the *ge-* prefix), and this we adopt in our text. Alternatively one could read *itrede* from OE *getredan* (cf. B's *hi trede*), but in this case there would be an imperfect rhyme of *itrede* with *iledde*, i.e. of single *d* with geminated *dd* (which at this date were still distinguished between vowels).

3. Sainte Nicholas, Godes Druth

The words and music of this song are given only on the inserted leaf in London, British Library, MS Royal 5 F. vii, f. 85; there is no translation.

NOTES

1. *Sainte* is a weak adjective used before a proper name, as often in ME; so probably in the phrase *Sainte Marie* in nos. 1 and 2, though here it might be taken as an OF feminine adjective, taken over into English.

Nicholas] *Nicholaes* MS, which the scribe takes as four syllables and sets to the notes on this assumption. But the three-syllabled form is more usual in English and seems required by the metre; in the last line it goes better with the music.

druð 'darling', an adoption from OF (*drud, drut* < late Latin *drutus* 'friend, beloved', cognate with modern German *traut*). In early OF Latin *d* and *t* between vowels were pronounced as [þ], and early ME adoptions from OF often have this sound; cf. *faith* < OF *feid, feit* < Latin *fidem*. There is an assonance of *druð* with *hus* in place of a true rhyme.

2. *tymbre* 'build' (OE *timbr(i)an*). Orm has *to timmbrenn himm an haliȝ hus.*

faiere] *faire* MS, but the musical setting as copied by the scribe himself is for three syllables. The uninflected OE word was *fæger*, whence early ME *faier*, which became *fair* by early loss of the *e*; but the fuller form was evidently intended here. The inflected *faiere* may, in this context, be either an adverb, in which case it may mean 'beautifully' or 'courteously, kindly' or 'in a suitable way', or a plural adjective; in the latter case it would reduplicate *scoone* in the second half-line. It is perhaps better taken as an adverb.

scoone hus 'beautiful dwellings'. Even if *faiere* is not an adjective qualifying *hus*, the latter is better taken as an uninflected neuter plural (OE *hus*). St Nicholas is being asked to prepare for us beautiful dwellings in heaven, rather than 'a beautiful dwelling'. Hall's emendation to *huð* < OE *hyð* 'harbour' is absurd; in Godric's dialect OE *ȳ* would become ME *ī*, so that the emendation would make the rhyme worse, not better.

scoone (*scone* MS), found otherwise only in the *Ormulum*

(whose spelling is the same as F's), is a variant of the normal ME *s(c)heene* < OE *scēne*; it is probably an adoption from Dutch or Low German (Old Saxon *scōni*, modern Dutch *schoon*), such as might well be current in Eastern England. The vowel must be ME *ǭ*, which we spell as *oo*; neither Orm nor Godric has ME *ǭ* from OE *ā*.

3. Despite Zupitza, a new sentence begins with this line, as Hall recognized. Hall explained *at* as meaning 'by the merits of', with reference to *OED*, sense 11; but the ON use of *at* to mean 'on the ground of, by reason of' is more apposite than the instances cited by *OED*. The line then means 'By the merits of thy birth, by the merits of thy bier'. St. Nicholas displayed miraculous piety in his cradle, observing fasts by abstention from his mother's breast, and performed miracles at his tomb. *At* is metrically stressed in both half-lines.

burthe] *burth* MS, but the normal ME form had *-e*, as the word was originally a feminine, and in any case it is here used in the dative. If we do not emend, the half-line is of the 'defective' type /x/, which Godric undoubtedly uses, but elsewhere only as the second half-line after a first half-line that ends with a dip. If we emend, the half-line becomes the normal A-type /x/x, matching the second half-line. Emendation of the word-text involves emendation also of the music, by the repetition of a note; but this has some advantage, for it makes the musical phrase to which the first half-line is set balance better the musical phrase which the scribe himself gives for the second half-line (since this also ends with a repeated note). We assume that in the transmission of the text, a more Northerly form *burth* has been substituted for original *burthe,* and a note cut out of the music in consequence.

The word is modern English *birth,* and is an adoption of ON *byrð*; but modern English evidence shows that OE and ON *ȳr* could give ME *ŭr* even in Northern and Eastern dialects, and in any case the ON gen. sg. was *burðar,* whence Icelandic formed a new nominative *burðr* masc. (see *OED*).

bare 'bier'. The form is most unlikely to be the 'Essex' development of OE *bǣr* (Anglian *bēr*), and must be from ON *barar* (fem. pl.); in that case the rhyme-word *þare* represents OE *þăra*. The rhyme would admittedly be equally good if we substituted the native form *be(e)re* 'bier' < OE *bǣr* and *þe(e)re* formed on OE *þǣr*, but the scribe's forms may well be Godric's, as Norfolk was an area strongly influenced by Norse.

4. *þare* 'there', i.e. to the fair dwellings in heaven mentioned in l. 2. The word is set in the MS as a monosyllable, in consequence of *Nicholaes* (as the scribe spells it) having been set, earlier in the line, as four syllables; but the rhyme requires that the final *-e* should be pronounced, and so does the etymology if the word used by Godric was from OE *þăra*, as the scribe's own spelling suggests.

II.   SONGS OF THE EARLIER THIRTEENTH CENTURY

4.   (i) Eyns ne soy ke pleynte fu
(ii) Ar ne kuth ich sorghe non

1

Eyns ne soy ke pleyntë fu,
orë, pleyn dangussë, tressu;
   trop ai mal é contreyrë.
Sans decertë, en prisun su;
5   car maydez, trespuis[sant] Jesu,
   duz deus e deboneyrë.

2

Jésu Crist, veirs deu, veirs hum,
   prengë vus de mei pité!
Jetez mei de la prisun
10   u je su a tort jeté.
Jo e mi autrë cumpaignun —
   Deus en set la verité —
tut pur autri mesprisun
   sumes a huntë livré.

3

15   Sirë deus,
ky as morteus
   es de pardun veinë,
sucurez;
deliverez
20   nus de cestë peinë.
Pardonez
et assoylez
   icels, gentil sirë,
sil te plet,
25   par ki forfet
   suffrun tel martirë.

4

Fous est ke sei afië
en cestë morteu vië
ke tant nus cuntralië
30   et u nad fors boydië.
Or est hum en léessë
et or est en tristessë;
or le garist, or blessë
   fortunë kelë guië.

1

Ar ne kuth ich sorghë non,
nu ich moot imanë mi mon;
   karful, wel sor ich sichë.
Geltles, tholich muchel schamë;
help, God, for thi sweetë namë,
   king of hevënë richë.

2

Jesu Crist, sooð God, sooð man,
   loverd, thu rew úpon me!
Of prisún that ich in am
   bring me ut and makë free.
Ich and minë feeren sumë —
   God wot ich ne lyghë noht —
for othrë han misnumë
   been in thys prisun ibroht.

3

Álmihtí,
that wel lihtlí —
   bales hal and bootë,
heven-king —
of this woning
   ut us bringë mootë,
foryef hem,
the wikkë men,
   yef it is thi willë,
for wos gelt
we been ipelt
   in this prisun illë.

4

Hopë non tó this livë —
heer ne mai he bilivë;
heeghë theh he astighë,
   deð him felleð to grundë.
Nu ha ð man wele and blissë,
rath he shal tharof missë;
worldes welë, mid wissë,
   ne lasteð but on stundë.

5

35 Virgine e mere au soverain
ke nus a jeté de la main
al maufé, ki par evain
nus out trestuz en sun ain
a grant dolur e peinë,
40 requerez icel seignur
ké il, par sa grant dulcur,
nus jet de cestë dolur
u nus sumes nuyt e jur
é doint joyë certeinë.

5

Maiden that bar the heven-king,
biseech thi sunë, sweetë thing,
that he habbe of us rewsíng
and us bring of this woníng
for his muchëlë milsë.
He us bring ut of this wo
and us tachë werchen swo
in this lif, go wúsit go,
that we mooten ey and o
habben the eechë blissë.

COMMENTARY

Source: London, Guildhall, Records Office, *Liber de antiquis Legibus,* ff. 160ᵛ-161ᵛ.

The leaves on which this song is written are an insertion at the end of a volume containing a chronicle which covers the years 1178 to 1274. The handwriting of the inserted leaves has been dated to before 1250, and the linguistic forms of the English text are those of the first half of the thirteenth century, perhaps of about 1225. The music to which the two texts, French and English, are set is a selection from that of *Planctus ante nescia,* by Godefroy of St. Victor; we print the Latin text as an addendum, below. More precisely stanzas 1-3 of the French and English texts are set to the music, and reflect the metre, of stanzas 1-3 of the Latin; stanza 4 of the French and English is set to a modification of the music of stanza 7 of the Latin, but differs in metre (having seven syllables to the line where the Latin has five) though not in rhyme-scheme; stanza 5 of the French and English is set to the music, and reflects the metre, of stanza 8 of the Latin. But in all stanzas there are variations in detail from the Latin metre, discussed more fully in the notes to the Latin text, and the French and English poems are quite different in theme, and therefore in phrasing, from the Latin *planctus.*

In the MS the French words are written immediately below the music, carefully aligned with the notes; the English words are below the French, but as the scribe found they needed more space, he did not attempt to align them with the French or with the music. In Carleton Brown, *English Lyrics of the Thirteenth Century,* no. 5, the French and English verses are printed alternately, as if this were a macaronic poem; but as Brown does not punctuate the French and in several places prints nonsense, he would not seem to have made much attempt to understand it. As soon as one translates it, one sees that this is not a macaronic poem at all; the English poem is a *contrafactum* of the French, and a skilful one — a version in a different language intended for singing to the same tune. The French must have been written first; not only is it put above the English in the MS, but also its rhyming is more elaborate and exact, and when the two texts differ in phrasing the French is more natural and pointed, the English apt to be contrived. Moreover in l. 17 of the French text there is a phrase *de pardun veine* which derives from *veniæ vena* in l. 17 of the Latin *planctus,* and the rhyme-word in l. 20 is *peine,* corresponding to *poena* in the Latin. Both these reminiscences of the Latin are lacking in the English text. The Anglo-Norman poem must

therefore be given priority; but its rhythms are deeply influenced by Middle English metrical practice, and the French words often have the stress shifted from the second to the first syllable: so *prisun* l. 4 (contrast l. 9, where it has normal French stressing on the second), *Jesu* l. 7, *pardun* l. 17, *icels* and *gentil* l. 23 (contrast *icel* l. 40), *suffrun* l. 26, *morteu* l. 28 (contrast l. 16), *jeté* p. p. l. 36 (contrast l. 10), and *trestuz* l. 38; cf. also *trespuissant* l. 5, stressed on the second. The poet, in fact, often gave to French words the stressings which they, or words like them, were coming to have in English (cf. *prisun* in the English text, stressed on the second in l. 9 but on the first in ll. 14 and 26), and he had English metrical rhythms in his mind; the probability is that he was natively English-speaking. It is very likely that the Anglo-Norman and English versions were made by the same man; this would account for the detailed understanding shown in matching the one to the other. Where the rhythms of the English diverge from the French, they sometimes follow those of the corresponding line of the Latin *planctus:* so ll. 28, 29 (as emended), 32, and 42, and similarly l. 11 is nearer to the Latin rhythm than is l. 11 of the French. It appears that the English author had independent knowledge of the Latin, and though this might be due merely to a recognition of the fact that the tune to which the French words had been set belonged originally to the Latin, it would be more easily explained if the one man had written both the French and English texts.

The primary object of the English text is to reproduce, line by line, the number of syllables used in the French; this is essential if the two texts are to fit the same music, and places where the texts diverge in syllable-count are undoubtedly corrupt. But sometimes the English text uses 'feminine' rhymes where the French has 'masculine'; in such cases it is self-evident that the author is not trying to match the rhythms of the English to the French, and the English and French lines may differ throughout their length, even (as in l. 13) in the number of metrically stressed syllables they contain. But elsewhere there seems to be a deliberate attempt to make the French and English lines match each other not only in the number of syllables, but also in their accentual rhythms; the English and French lines are to be scanned with an eye to each other, and places where they diverge in scansion are to be looked at critically, though they are not necessarily corrupt. Both texts contain obvious errors, and the surviving MS is plainly a copy; but the errors are not very serious and the copy cannot be remote from the original. There are signs, however, that the scribe has been thinking rather too much about his work; he has occasionally attempted to adapt both the music and the English text to the French text as it came to him, when in fact it was the French that was wrong.

Every stanza is different in rhyme-pattern and structure, and within the stanzas the lines often differ markedly in accentual rhythm. But even on a superficial inspection of the texts as they stand in the MS it is clear that each stanza divides into two halves which closely resemble each other, and the musical setting is one in which the second half of the stanza is sung to a repetition (with possible variations) of the tune of the first half. The song has the same structure as the early sequence, in which the stanza-forms were variable but each stanza divided into two halves exactly matched in the number of syllables in the corresponding lines. Analysis of the two versions shows that the structure implied, in terms of the number of syllables per line, is as follows:

Stanza	1	887 887
,,	2	7777 7777
,,	3	346346 346346
,,	4	7777 7777
,,	5	either 88777 88777 or 77777 77777

Assuming the latter alternative for stanza 5, then of the 44 lines of the poem, 30 conform to the pattern in both French and English versions, if allowance is made for elisions, or else can be made to conform by the simple substitution of an obvious orthographic, phonetic, or grammatical variant. One or other version conforms to the pattern (again allowing for elision) in a further 11 lines (9 in the French, 2 in the English); the other version, in these cases, can be made to conform, but only by emendation which goes beyond the mere substitution of variant forms. Only three lines (1, 11, and 23) certainly diverge from the pattern in both versions, though we should perhaps add l. 35, where the apparent conformity of the French to the pattern seems to be an accident not intended by the scribe himself. There is good reason, then, to suppose that the author intended, in general, to conform to the syllabic regularity demanded by sequence-writing, and the task of an editor is to restore it, emending whichever text diverges from the norm for the line in question. His chief problem is to judge whether the poet intended any variations from the norm, and if so where. After considering the music, the two word-texts, and the possibilities of emendation, we have concluded that he did intend variations in l. 1 (seven syllables instead of eight), l. 11 (eight syllables instead of seven), and in the last stanza, where the first two lines of the first half-stanza were in our judgement intended to have eight syllables, but the first two of the second half-stanza to have only seven. But in l. 23, where both versions have seven syllables, we consider them both to be corrupt; the music provides only for the six syllables that would be normal for this line.

Apart from emendation, the spelling of both the Anglo-Norman and the English has been modified slightly, to indicate more clearly the basis of rhyming and scansion and to remove some inconsistencies. In the French final 'feminine' e is marked ë unless it is elided, when it is italicized; and for further distinction the acute accent is used to mark final 'masculine' e in e.g. pité and jeté p.p. The acute is also used to show that in léesse the first e is separately pronounced, and on é 'and' (ll. 3 and 44) and ké 'that' (l. 41) to show metrical stress and that, in the latter case, the form used is the OF 'strong' variant. The inconsistency in these uses of the acute is shown up in l. 36,

where the p.p. jeté has metrical stress on the first syllable, and less seriously in l. 31, where léessë is stressed (like modern French liesse) on the second.

The spelling of the English text has one or two distinctive features that require explanation. As thirteenth- and early fourteenth-century MSS sometimes do, it replaces the special English letter ð (equivalent to modern English th, and used mostly at the end of words) by d. We restore ð (which in the performing text is replaced by th). The other noteworthy features concern the representation of the English spirantal sounds which in ME orthography were apt to be all written by the special letter ȝ, but in this text are distinguished.

(1) The OE voiceless spirant h is in the MS spelt as c before t: so noct 'nought', ibroct 'brought', almicti 'almighty', lictly 'lightly'. As these spellings would confuse a non-professional reader, we substitute the OE spelling ht (still used in early ME). The same sound is spelt in the MS as gh in thegh 'though' (obviously because thec was objectionable); for the sake of consistency we substitute theh. In all five words the h of our spelling is to be pronounced as German ch in ich, ach.

(2) The OE voiced front spirant (pronounced like the modern consonant y) is spelt yh by the scribe in foryhef 'forgave', yhef 'if'; we normalize by substituting y, thus foryef, yef.

(3) The OE voiced back spirant g is spelt gh in sorghe 'sorrow', lyghe 'tell lies', heeghe 'high' adv. (heghe MS) < late OE hēge, stighe 'rise'. This spelling is retained in our text because it had a distinct phonetic value and is an evidence that the language is that of the earlier part of the thirteenth century. The pronunciation was doubtless still as in OE, the voiced back spirant used in some modern German dialects in sagen; it may be modernized if desired as w in sorghe, as the modern y consonant in the rest.

Both the French and the English texts are given in the original spellings and without emendation by Carleton Brown; but there are three errors in his transcription of the French. Also printed by I. Aspin, Anglo-Norman Political Poems (1953), pp. 6–9, with a much reduced facsimile of ff. 160ᵛ–161.

The language of the English text is that appropriate to a London scribe, but there are signs that he has sometimes replaced the forms of the East or South-east Midlands by those of the South of England. But there is nothing in the language inconsistent with an origin in London or nearby, north of the Thames.

As the English and Anglo-Norman texts are so closely related, they are annotated together; line-references to which a capital A is added (thus 2A) refer to the Anglo-Norman version, those without this addition to the English.

NOTES

1. Ar 'formerly', perhaps but not certainly an Essex form from OE ǣr.
kuth 'knew'; sorghe 'sorrow'.
The English and French lines are both one syllable short of the eight which the stanza-pattern requires, but they match each other perfectly and are supported by the music; and though it would be possible to emend them both, it would be wrong to do so. Both translate the first line of the Latin text.

1A. Eyns 'formerly'; soy 1 sg. perf. of saveir 'know'; fu 'was'.

2. moot originally meant 'may', but here probably 'must'.
imane] imanen MS, but the -n has probably been added by the

scribe; he himself has the infinitive *bringe* before a consonant in l. 20. The word means 'bewail' and is an Essex form of OE *gemǣnan.*

mi] *min* MS, but the scribe has *thi* before a consonant in l. 23. *mon* 'complaint' (OE *mān*, modern *moan*). *To mean one's moan,* a fixed phrase, meant to utter a complaint, to give voice to grief.

2A. 'now, full of anguish, I sweat it out'.

3. *siche* 'sigh' (OE *sīcan*); the *ch* is pronounced as in modern English (e.g. in *riches*) and is not a spelling of *gh*.

3A. *e* (here the second metrical stress of the line, which goes /xx/x/x) is the form of *et* used before consonants. *Contreyre* is a noun, 'adversity'.

4. *Geltles* 'guiltless', a South-eastern form, with *ĕ* < OE *ў*. *tholich*] *ihc tholye* MS, but the inverted form with suffixed pronoun is clearly required for the metre; cf. the first half of the corresponding French line, with its rhythm /x/x. The sense is 'I suffer'.
muchel] *muchele* MS, but the uninflected form of the adj. is obviously what the author intended.
schame] here and in the next line the English has 'feminine' rhymes where the French has 'masculine', and the rhythms of the second halves of the lines consequently differ.

4A. *su*] *sui* MS (modern French *suis*), but the rhyme requires the AN form in which *ui* has become *u*.

5. *thi*] *thin* MS; cf. note to l. 2 above.

5A. *maydez* 'm'aidez'.
trespuissant] *trespuis* MS, but the music and the English line both show that a trisyllabic word is needed, and *trespuis* is nonsense; the scribe has omitted a syllable.

6. *hevene*] *heuene* MS. Though scribes often write this where only the disyllabic *heven* is needed, here the metre shows that three syllables were intended; *hevene* is OE *heofena* gen. pl. used in singular sense.
riche 'kingdom'.

6A. 'sweet God, and gracious'.

7. *sooð* 'true' (*sod* MS, both times).
man] the English has only an assonance (with *am*); so apparently the French (*hum — prisun*), but in the French the final consonant was doubtless lost and the vowel nasalized.

7A. *veirs* 'true'; *hum* (*hom* MS), modern French *homme.*

8. *rew* 'take pity'.

8A. *prenge* 'take'; *mei*, strong form of *me* (modern French *moi*).

9A. *Jetez* 'deliver'; but in the next line *jeté* has the sense 'cast'.

10. *make*] *makye* MS. Metre requires two syllables, and though it is possible that the originally trisyllabic form *makie* had become disyllabic by the change of *i* to *y* consonant (of which the scribe's spelling with *y* is not valid evidence), the simpler solution is to suppose that the author used the East Midland form *make*.

10A. *u* 'where'; *su* is substituted for *sui* MS (cf. note to 4A above); *a tort* 'wrongly' (*atort* MS).

11. The line, in both French and English, has a syllable more than the normal seven, but though the English could be reduced by substitution of the unstressed and uninflected *mi* for *mine,* the French could not be cut down except by the complete omission of the possessive *mi,* which the English supports. The musical phrase is so contrived as to accommodate both the seven syllables of l. 7 (the corresponding line in the first half-stanza) and the eight syllables of l. 11, and we take this to be deliberate. We therefore accept here the MS texts of both French and English.
mine feeren sume 'some of my companions', with the plural adj. *sume* used in direct apposition with the noun, an idiom which continues much later (Shakespeare still has it).

11A. *mi* is the unstressed nom. pl., corresponding to modern French *mes;* and *cumpaignun* (*compaignun* MS) is similarly nom. pl.

13. 'because others have done wrong'.
han misnume] *habbet mis nome* MS. The French line has seven syllables, the English as the scribe gives it has eight; and it is evident that he has substituted the Southern indic. pl. *habbet* (for *habbeth*) for the contracted *han* < *haven,* a new formation used in the East and South-east Midlands. Cf. l. 31, where the scribe himself writes *had* (for *hað,* i.e. *hath*), a contraction of *haveth,* for the 3 sg. pres. indic.; and l. 14, where the scribe has *ben,* the East Midland plural of the verb *be,* not the Southern plural *beeth.*
The English line has only three stresses, x/x/x/x, the French four, /x/x/x/, though in syllable-count they are equal; the divergence is due principally to the use by the English of a feminine rhyme where the French has a masculine. The scribe's substitution of *habbet* may partly have been motivated by a desire to give the English line four stresses, at the expense of the syllable-count.

13A. *autri mesprisun* 'other people's wrong-doing' or 'someone else's wrong-doing'; *autri* is strictly singular, but the English text shows clearly that the reference is to a plurality of persons.

14. *been* 'are'.

14A. *hunte* (so MS) is modern French *honte* 'shame'. For *livré* the MS has the trisyllabic form *liuere,* and the scribe has provided an additional note in the music by repeating the last one of the line. But the metrical scheme and the corresponding English line show that there should be only seven syllables; the French text and the music must be emended.

16A. *morteus*] *mortels* MS, but *morteus* is required for rhyme; the MS itself has *morteu* in l. 28.

17. 'the remedy and cure of evil'. *Hal* (*hale* MS, but the *-e* elides) is an Essex form of OE *hǣl* sb., modern English *heal* sb., 'remedy'.
The MS has for this line *of bale is hale and bote,* which is a syllable too many (cf. the corresponding French line) and in any case destroys the construction of the main sentence; the scribe has evidently not understood his exemplar and has attempted himself to edit it, with the usual ill result. In the text as the scribe writes it, the subject of *is* must be *that* in the previous line, which is therefore made into a pronoun of the 3rd person; and in consequence the verb *moote* in l. 20 (*mote* MS) is left without a subject, for *Almihti* in l. 15 is plainly vocative,

parallel to *Sire deus* in the French. The order and position of *bringe moote* in l. 20 (auxiliary after infinitive at end of clause) are a certain indication that they are the verbs of a subordinate clause (cf. modern German), i.e. their subject must be the relative *that*; and it follows that there is no place in the sentence for the scribe's *is*. It must be rejected, and the choice of reading is then between *of bale hal and boote* and *bales hal and boote*; the latter undoubtedly scans better.

In the text as emended, ll. 17–18 are a parenthesis, and the sentence means: 'Almighty, who very easily (remedy and cure of pain, king of heaven) mayest bring us out of this misery, forgive them . . .'. Cf. also note to l. 20 below.

17A. *veine* 'channel'.

19. *woning* (so MS), here and in l. 38, is shown by the parallel French expressions (*peine* l. 20, *dolur e peine* l. 39) to be the word meaning 'lamentation, grief' (OE *wānung*), but here used to mean 'a cause of grief', hence 'misery'.

20. *moote* (*mote* MS) 'mayest'. The 2 sg. pres. indic. of the OE verb *mōt* 'may' was *mōst,* and this was also the normal ME form. I take *moote* here to be a new 2 sg. pres. indic., modelled on the general analogy of the p.t. of strong verbs, in which the 2 sg. indic. was identical with the subjunctive and ended in *-e*. But it is significant that the sense here is 'may', in which the distinction between indic. and subj. is purely formal and there is no distinction of meaning. As the verb *mot* developed its new sense 'must', there may have been some tendency to use the present subj. in place of the present indic. in the sense 'may'. In Orm's *ȝif þu . . . ȝeornesst tatt tu mote sket Uppcumenn inntill heoffne,* the auxiliary *(tu) mote* is presumably subj. in a clause dependent on a verb of desiring, but it could easily be misunderstood as indic.; and in Langland, *P.P.,* B-text xix. 173,

> Blessed mote thow be   and be shalt for euere,

though *mote thow* in the formula *Blessed mote thow be* was no doubt originally subj., it is evidently taken as an indic., as the coordinate clause shows — indeed Skeat in his glossary marks the form '2 pr. s.' (meaning 2nd sing. present tense) and glosses it 'mayest', i.e. he takes it as an indicative. He does the same for the instance in the B-text, ii. 115, though this could more reasonably be taken as subjunctive. It may be suspected that *OED,* which under *mote* vb. gives only a brief treatment without any detailed illustration of the forms, has been too arbitrary in showing only *most* &c. for the 2 sing. of the present indicative.

23. Both the French and English versions of this line have seven syllables, but the metrical scheme presupposes six and the music provides for six only. The basic fault is probably in the French (see next note); but when, by miscopying, it had been increased to seven syllables, the English must have been deliberately expanded by a copyist by the introduction of *God* before *yef* (so MS). Deletion of *God* not only restores metrical regularity, but much improves the run of the English sentence; it is an unnecessary repetition of *Almihti* in l. 15.

23A. *icels*] *icele* MS. The MS reading not only increases the line to seven syllables, since the *-e* must be pronounced, but also produces an inexplicable divergence in sense between the English and the French; for in the MS text the French means 'absolve that woman . . . by whose fault we suffer this martyrdom' where the English says 'forgive them, the wicked men

. . .', which is consistent with its use of *othre* pl. 'others' in l. 13. Even if the English translator had been a different man from the Anglo-Norman author, he could not possibly have misunderstood *icele*; the text from which he was translating must have had a plural. The assumption that the original was *icels* and that this was simply misread as *icele* solves both difficulties; it reduces the line to the proper six syllables (cf. preceding note) and brings the two versions into agreement in sense.

24. *wos* 'whose', an early instance of the use of the word as a relative pronoun (it was originally interrogative).
gelt (so MS) 'guilt', a South-eastern form.

24A. *plet*] *plest* MS, but the rhyme requires the form without *s*.

25. *been*] *bed* MS, for *beð*, the Southern plural; but in l. 14 the scribe himself uses the Midland inflexion *-n*.
ipelt 'thrust', another South-eastern form with *ĕ* < OE *ў*.

25A. *par ki forfet* 'by whose fault'; *ki* is a form of *cui* from Latin *cui* dat. sg., but was used as a genitive with both singular and plural antecedents.

26. *this*] *thos* MS, probably a spelling for *theos*, representing the OE feminine nom. sg. *þeos,* though it could be a miscopying of *thes.* But in l. 14 above the scribe himself writes *thys prisun,* and I normalize the common form *this.*
ille] *hille* MS, with the otiose initial *h* often used by Anglo-Norman scribes. The word is an adoption from Old Norse, but was current in the London area by this date; it occurs in *The Owl and the Nightingale,* an earlier poem by a Surrey author. The final *-e* is the inflexion of the weak adjective, used because of the preceding demonstrative; it is established by the rhyme.

26A. *suffrun*] *nus suffrun* MS. The French line has a syllable too many, both as compared with the corresponding English line and with the stanza-pattern; the answering line in the first half-stanza is l. 20, with six syllables in both French and English. The music has been adapted to the corrupt French line by the trick of repeating a note, but obviously by the scribe, not the composer. Omission of *nus* not only regularizes the metre, but improves the idiom; for in OF it was more idiomatic to omit a personal pronoun subject than to include it.

27. *Hope*] *Ne hope* MS, but the corresponding line of the French text shows that there is a syllable too many in the English version and that the line should begin with a stressed syllable. The scribe has introduced the negative particle where it is not needed.
this] *his* MS, an obvious error; cf. the French *ceste morteu vie.*
live] dative sg. of *lif* 'life'.

27 A. *sei*] *se* MS, but the word must bear a metrical stress, and I therefore substitute the 'strong' form *sei* (modern French *soi*), even though it was not normally used before a verb. The line in both versions has three stresses, thus /xx/x/x.

28. The English line scans /xx/x/x, i.e. it begins with a dactyl, like the corresponding line of the Latin *planctus,* which scans /xx/x (five syllables). But the French would naturally be scanned x/x/x/x, as would the following line in the French. Here the English text reverts to the rhythms of the Latin (allowing for the greater length of the line in the English and French).
The verb *bilive* (OE *belīfan*) means 'remain'.

29. The English line as given in the MS is a syllable short. Two emendations are possible: (1) to read *an heeghe* 'on high' at the beginning, which would make the rhythm of the English match that of the French; (2) to read *astighe* 'ascend' for MS *stighe*, which gives to this line the same rhythm as the two preceding English lines and makes it agree with the Latin in beginning with a dactyl. I choose the latter alternative.

29A. *cuntralie* (*contralie* MS), a variant of *contrarie* 'opposes'.

30. *deð* 'death' (*ded* MS).

30A. 'and in which there is nothing but deceit'.

31A ff. 'Now man is in joy, and now he is in sadness; fortune now protects, now wounds, him whom she guides.'

31A. *Or*] *ore* MS in both cases, and so in l. 32. The scribe writes the original full form, but metre requires the monosyllabic *or*, developed originally before vowels; contrast l. 2.
est] so MS; misread *eft* by Carleton Brown.
hum] *hoem* MS.
léesse 'joy, revelry' < Latin *laetitia*; rare modern French *liesse*.

32. *rath* 'soon' (*rathe* MS, but the *e* is elided). The line again begins with a dactyl, as in the Latin text; the French does not. Contrast l. 33, where the reverse applies.

33. The metrical scheme presupposes seven syllables in this line, and the music makes provision for only seven. But the English line as written has eight. We must therefore replace *mid iwisse* by the rarer but undoubted variant *mid wisse*, recorded c. 1200 in the *Trinity College Homilies* (see *OED*, s.v. *wis* sb.). As emended, the line scans /x/xx/x. *Mid wisse* means 'assuredly'.

34. *but*] *buten* MS, but the metre requires the form without -*n*, *bute*, of which the final -*e* elides.
on stunde 'an hour, a brief while'.

34A. *kele* is modern French 'qu'elle'. The MS (followed by Carleton Brown) has *ke le*, but perhaps only because the syllables are divided to fit the musical notes; 'que le' is nonsense.

35. *bar*] *bare* MS, apparently an Essex form of OE *bǣre* 2 sg. past indic.; but though this is the historically appropriate form, the line cannot have more than eight syllables. To keep *bare* we should have to elide the definite article before *heven-king*, but this seems less satisfactory than to suppose that the author used the 3 sg. *bar*, not the more conservative 2 sg. *bare* given by the scribe. Apart from the ME tendency to replace the form of the 2 sg. past indic., in strong verbs, by that of the 1 and 3 sg., there is also a marked tendency to use the 3 sg. in relative clauses (cf. the scribe's own *is* in his form of l. 17 above).

35A. *Virgine*] *Virgne* MS, of which the -*e* should elide before *e* 'and' and so reduce the line to the seven syllables which one might expect from the parallel l. 40 below. But the music is for eight syllables, and the scribe himself, apparently ignoring the elision, has set *virgne* to two notes. The probability is that he has simply omitted *i* from the fuller form *virgine*; certainly the author must have intended *virgine* or *virgene*. As emended, the English and French versions of l. 35 match each other and the music exactly.

36. *thi*] *thin* MS.
sweete] *that swete* MS, but this makes the English line one of nine syllables, which is plainly wrong. Evidently the scribe has taken *sweete thing* as being in apposition with *sune* and has supplied *that* to make the point more obvious; but I take *sweete thing* as a vocative, in apposition to *maiden*.

36A. *a jeté*] *jeta* MS. The French line as written has seven syllables, which conforms to the parallel line in the second half-stanza (l. 41). But the English line cannot credibly be reduced below eight syllables, and the music provides for eight. It looks as though the scribe, recognizing the norm of the metre, has substituted *jeta* for *a jeté* by a conscious or half-conscious metrical emendation. The sense of the line is 'who has delivered us from the hand of the evil one'.

37. *habbe*] It is possible that the scribe has substituted the older form *habbe* for *have*, and in l. 44 *habben* for *haven*, just as in l. 13 he substituted *habbet* for *han* (< *haven*); but his forms scan and I therefore retain them.
rewsing 'pity'. The metrical stress is on the suffix; similarly with *woning* 'misery' in the next line.

37A. *par evain* 'by default'. The noun is not recorded in Godefroy, but cf. OF *esvainer* 'fall into default' and medieval Latin *esvanuare* 'declare vacant (or dispossess) on account of non-payment of rent'; the ultimate source is Latin *vanum* 'emptiness'.

38. *us bring*] Here and in l. 40 the MS reads *bring hus*, which in each case would make the line one of three stresses, scanning x/xx/x/. But the corresponding lines of *Planctus ante nescia* scan /x/x/x/, and this also seems to be the intended scansion of the two lines in the French version (with, in l. 38, a stress on the first syllable of *trestuz*). In both cases the rhythm of the English can be brought into conformity with that of the Latin and the French by transposing *us* before *bring* and placing a stress on the first word of the line (*and* in l. 38, *he* in l. 40). For the placing of the pronoun before the verb cf. *us bringe* (so MS) in l. 20, and *us tache* in l. 41.
Bring in both lines is 3 sg. pres. subj., with elision of the final -*e* of the full form *bringe*; the elision is unaffected by the transposition of the word-order.

38A. *out* 'would have had' (so MS, and not *ont* as read by Carleton Brown); *trestuz* 'completely all, every one'; *ain* (*heim* MS), a form of *aim* 'hook' (Latin *hamus*).

39. *muchele milse* 'great mercy'. The rhythm of this line, in both French and English versions, diverges from the regular metre of the corresponding Latin line.

39A. *e*] an ampersand has been erased in the MS, though it is needed for both sense and metre; Carleton Brown omits.

40. See note to l. 38 above.

41. *us tache werchen* 'teach us to work'. *Tache* is an Essex form, with *ā* < *ǣ* in OE *tǣce*.

41A. *ké*] The word bears metrical stress, and is the 'strong' form of the conjunction *ke* (modern French *que*); it has the close vowel [e], not the 'feminine' *e* [ə], and there is therefore no elision.

42. The French and English lines here diverge in metrical rhythm. The English is more regular; it scans /x/x/x/, with the first metrical stress falling on the preposition *in* at the beginning of the line. But the French line has only three stresses, and scans x/x/xx/.

this] *thos* MS. Cf. note to l. 26 above.

lif] *liue* MS, the old dative sg.; but the uninflected *lif* is required, since the line should have seven syllables, not eight.

wusit] *wu sit* MS, a contraction of *wuse it* 'howso it', in which *wu* is 'how' and *se* a common unstressed form of *so*; *go wusit go* is therefore 'let it go however it may go', however things may turn out.

42A. *jet*] *get* MS, 'deliver, save'.

43. *ey and o* 'ever and ever'; *ey* is from ON *ei*, *o* from OE *ā* (ultimately forms of the same word). This use of the Norse-derived *ey*, more clearly than that of *ille* in l. 26, rules out a Southern dialect; but both words might already have been used in London.

43A. *sumes*] *sumus* MS, a Latinism.

44. *eeche* 'eternal'. *blisse*] The rhyme with *milse* in l. 39 is imperfect.

44A. The first metrical stress must fall on the conjunction *e* if the French line is to have the same rhythm as the English. Both diverge from the Latin, which is regular.

doint 'grant'.

Addendum to No. 4

Planctus ante nescia

(Godefroy of St. Victor)

1

Planctus ante nescia,
planctu lassor anxia,
  crucior dolore;
orbat orbem radio,
5 me Judæa filio,
  gaudio, dulcore.

2

Fili, dulcor unice,
  singulare gaudium,
matrem flentem respice
10 conferens solatium.
Pectus, mentem, lumina
  torquent tua vulnera;
quæ matér, quæ femina
  tam felíx, tam misera!

3

15 Flos florum,
 dux morum,
  veniæ vena,
 quam gravis
 in clavis
20 est tibi poena!
Proh dolor!
Hinc color
  effugit oris;
hinc ruit,
25 hinc fluit
  unda cruoris.

4

O quam sero deditus,
  quam citó me deseris!
O quam digne genitus,
30 quam abjecte moreris!
O quis amor corporis
  tibi fecit spolia!
O quam dulcis pignoris
  quam amara præmia!

5

35 O pia
 gratía
  sic morientis!
O zelus,
o scelus
40 invidæ gentis!
O fera
dextéra
  crucifigentis,
o lenis
45 in poenis
  mens patientis!

6

O verúm eloquium
  justi Simeonis!
Quem promisit gladium
50 sentio doloris.
Gemitus, suspiria,
  lacrimæque foris
vulneris indicia
  sunt interioris.

7

55 Parcito proli,
mors, mihi noli;
tunc mihi soli
sola mederis.
Morte, beate,
60 separer á te,
dummodo, nate,
non crucieris.

8

Quod crimén, quæ scelera
gens commisit effera!
65 Vincla, virgas, vulnera,
sputa, spinas, cetera
sine culpa patitur.
Nato, quæso, parcite;
matrem crucifigite
70 aut in crucis stipite
nos simúl affigite —
male solus moritur.

9

Reddite mæstissimæ
corpus vel exanime
75 ut sic minoratus
crescat cruciatus
osculis, amplexibus.
Utinam sic doleam
ut dolore peream,
80 nam plus est dolori
sine morte mori
quam perire citius.

10

Quid stupés, gens misera,
terram se movere,
85 obscurari sidera,
languidos lugere?
Solem privas lumine,
quomodo luceret?
ægrum medicamine,
90 unde convaleret?

11

Homicidam liberas,
Jesum das supplicio;
male pacem toleras —
veniet seditio.
95 Famis, cædis, pestium
scies docta pondere
Jesum tibi mortuum
Barrabamque vivere.

12

Gens cæcá, gens flebilis,
100 age poenitentiam,
dum tibí flexibilis
Jesus est ad veniam.
Quos fecisti, fontium
prosint tibi flumina,
105 sitim sedant omnium,
cuncta lavant crimina.

13

Flete, Sion filiæ,
tantæ gratæ gratiæ
(juvenis angustiæ
110 sibi sunt deliciæ),
pro vestrís offensis.
In amplexus ruite,
dum pendét in stipite,
mutuis amplexibus;
115 se parát amantibus
bracchiis protensis.

14

In hoc solo gaudeo,
quod pro vobis doleo.
Vicem, quæso, reddite:
120 matris dampnum plangite.

COMMENTARY

Sources: see below.

Planctus ante nescia, though it has sometimes been ascribed to St. Bernard, was beyond reasonable doubt written by Godefroy (Godefroid, Godefridus) of St. Victor, for it is included with works undoubtedly by him in two MSS said to be from the Abbey of St. Victor (Paris, Bibliothèque Nationale, fonds lat. 15163 and Paris, Bibliothèque Mazarine, 1002). Little is known of the author other than his literary works, and most of what is professed to be known appears to be mere antiquarian legend, unsupported by any evidence. Thus he is often also referred to as Godefroid of Breteuil because of a false identification made by Brial in his *Histoire littéraire de la France* (Paris, 1820), who appears to have assumed that Godefroy of St. Victor must be the same as Geoffroy de Breteuil, sub-prior of the monastery of Sainte-Barbe en Auge (Normandy), on no better grounds than that they were both authors, both sub-priors, had the same Christian name, and lived about the same time. A curious result is that in J. de Ghellinck's admired *L'Essor de la Littérature Latine au XIIe Siècle* there are separate notices of Godefroid of St. Victor and Godefroid of Breteuil and even separate entries in the index, though both are given the same date of death (itself a scholarly fiction) and credited with the authorship of *Fons Philosophiae* (which was in fact written by Godefroy of St. Victor).

The most recent studies of Godefroid of St. Victor's life and works are in Philippe Delhaye, *Le* Microcosmus *de Godefroy de Saint-Victor: Étude Théologique* (Lille, 1951) and in P. Michaud-Quantin's edition of Godefroy's *Fons Philosophiae* (Namur, 1956); a summary of their accounts is given by Jean Chatillon in *Dictionnaire des Lettres Françaises: Le Moyen Age* (Paris, 1964), p. 324. Delhaye supposes that Godefroy was born about 1125-30 and that he studied in Paris between about 1140 and 1155, and entered the Abbey of St. Victor about 1155-60. He dates the writing of *Fons Philosophiae*, a Latin poem of some length, after 1176; Michaud-Quantin says in 1178, on the authority of a marginal note in the Mazarine MS. Godefroy came into conflict with Gautier, the abbot of St. Victor, and was driven into exile about 1180. The Bibliothèque Nationale MS 15163, in a colophon to the *Canticum beatae Virginis et matris* which immediately precedes *Planctus ante nescia* in that MS, describes him as 'subprior of St. Victor'. Delhaye thinks that he is probably to be identified with a man named Godefroy who was sacrist at St. Victor in 1194; if so, he was able to return to the abbey from his exile. Some scholars (e.g. Dreves in *Analecta Hymnica* xx. 156 and Dreves and Blume in *Ein Jahrtausend* i. 281, and others who plainly derive from Dreves) say that he died in 1196, others (e.g. Raby and de Ghellinck) in 1194; but these dates appear to be taken ultimately from the historians of St. Victor, who, evidently guessing without any evidence, variously fix the date of death at 1192 (so Jean Picard in his early seventeenth-century *Chronicon Ecclesiae Victorianae*), 1194, or even later (cf. Delhaye, op. cit., p. 42). Delhaye himself, followed by Michaud-Quantin and Chatillon, says that the date of death is unknown. It is sufficient for our purposes to note that the period of his literary activity was the last quarter of the twelfth century.

Planctus ante nescia is in form a *planctus* or complaint, and Godefroy works the word into his first line — a feature in which he is followed by the Anglo-Norman author of *Eyns ne soy ke plainte fu*, though not by the English version. The MSS give varying titles for the Latin song: the Mazarine MS has *Planctus beate virginis et matris in passione filii*, MS B.N. 15163 has *Planctus beate Marie virginis in passione domini*, the Bodleian MS has *Dolorosa meditacio matris marie super moriente filio*, and Dreves in *Analecta Hymnica*, presumably following (or abbreviating) the title in the Turin MS, has *Planctus Mariae Virginis*. It is not easy to judge what the title in the archetype may have been, but perhaps it was *Planctus beate Marie virginis et matris in passione filii*.

The Latin *planctus* was an extra-liturgical religious song, the counterpart to the vernacular and secular lyric *lai*, which appears in Old French in the latter part of the twelfth century. It is debated whether there is any connection between the French lyric *lai* and the Celtic lyric *lai*, and as no examples of the latter are known to survive the question can hardly be pursued with much profit. The mere use of the same term *lai* for the French and Celtic lyrics is not conclusive, for the word was also used of narrative poems not intended for singing — originally, in the phrase 'Breton *lai*' (or perhaps 'British *lai*'), to apply to French, and later English, narrative poems by Marie de France and others, which claimed to have Breton (or British) sources (Chaucer's *Franklin's Tale* is a late example); and later, without the prefixed adjective *Breton*, to apply to other narrative poems of the romance type of moderate length and reasonable unity of theme (as, for example, *Sir Gawain and the Green Knight*). The Celtic lyric *lai* is known to have existed from references in Old French romances, of which the most important are cited by A. J. Bliss in his edition of *Sir Orfeo* (Oxford, 2nd edition, 1966), pp. xxxi-xxxii, and from allusions in the French and English narrative 'Breton *lais*'. These all agree that the Celtic *lai* was a song performed to the harp; in *Lai de l'Espine* there is a reference to an Irish harper performing the *lais* of 'Aielis' and of 'Orphei', but more usually the references are to Breton or British harpers (the words Breton and British were not distinguished in OF and ME). The French and English narrative 'Breton *lais*' show a special concern with the titles of the *lais*, and Marie de France in particular sometimes speaks of the *conte* of a *lai* or seems to distinguish between the *conte* and the *lai*. The generally-accepted hypothesis, based on this evidence, is that the Celtic *lai* was a lyric dealing with a named character in a particular story — either a dramatic lyric expressing the emotions of the character at some point of the story, or a lyric in which the poet expressed his meditations on the situation of the character. It was therefore necessary that the name of the character should be known, in order that the *lai* might be understood; and it would also be necessary that the story should be known. It is believed, therefore, that the performance of the song, the *lai* proper, would be preceded by the narration of the story (it is usually held, in prose), and that Marie de France and the other authors of the narrative poems were taking this *conte* and turning it into French (or English) verse, while merely referring to the fact that a *lai* (the song) had been made on the theme by British harpers. But they do not give translations of the *lais* themselves.

Thus we know the titles of many Celtic lyric *lais* (assuming that the French and English narrative poets are to be believed), but not their form. Marie de France, at the end of her narrative poem *Chevrefoil*, tells us that Tristram, who was a good harper, made a new *lai* about the subject which was called *Gotelef* in English and *Chevrefoil* in French; and *Lai de l'Espine*, as remarked above, tells us of an Irish harper's lai of 'Aielis'. Of the surviving Old French lyric *lais*, one is a *Lai du Chievrefeuil*, another a *Lai d'Aelis*; but whether these had anything more than their titles in common with the earlier Celtic *lais* is matter for speculation. It is perhaps not a serious objection that the music of the French *Lai d'Aelis* is different from that given in MS Arundel 248 for a *Cantus de Domina post cantum Aalis*, for (i) there may easily have been more songs than one with the title 'Alice', (ii) there is not the slightest doubt that *Jesu Cristes milde moder* (our no. 12) is written 'after' *Stabat juxta Christi crucem* (our no. 10(i)), and yet the same Arundel MS gives different music for it. If the Arundel MS is giving changed music in the one case, it may be in the other.

What is not speculative, but a matter of observable fact, is that the Old French secular *lai* (i.e., the lyric *lai*, not the narrative poems) and the Latin religious *planctus* have the same musical and poetic form as the early sequence. The metre of *Planctus ante nescia* exactly conforms to the requirements. The stanzas divide into two halves, sung to a repetition of the same music (with the exception of the brief concluding stanza, sung to music which is not repeated, and even this in fact subdivides into two couplets); and the two half-stanzas always match each other exactly. Though the music does not require regularity of accentual rhythm in the words, in fact Godefroy would seem to have intended complete regularity of rhythm; the two halves of each stanza, and also lines which rhyme together, follow the same rhythmical pattern. But we must allow certain variations from Classical stressings, plainly intended by the author. In l. 60 the phrase *a te* (in rhyme with *beate* and *nate*) is treated as a unit with the stress on the preposition (cf. Norberg, *Introduction*, p. 22); in the closely related Évreux MSS, *ate* is written as a single word. In eleven cases the stress is shifted to the second syllable of a disyllable (*mater* l. 13, *felix* l. 14, *cito* l. 28, *verum* l. 47, *crimen* l. 63, *simul* l. 71, *cæca* l. 99, *tibi* l. 101, *vestris* l. 111, *pendet* l. 113, and *parat* l. 115); in each case the preceding word is a monosyllable (cf. the general Introduction, pp. 49–50 above, and footnote 93 there). In two cases (*gratia* l. 36 and *dextera* l. 42) there is a shift of stress to the penult, the final *-a* being identified with OF feminine *-e* and left unstressed (see pp. 48–9 above). Allowing for these stressings, the Latin text preserves complete metrical regularity throughout.

There can be no doubt of its priority over the French and English *lais* (nos. 4(i) and 4(ii)) which take their music from it (or at least have their musical material in common with it). Whenever Godefroy died, *Planctus ante nescia* is likely to belong before 1200; but the French and English *lais* can hardly be dated before 1225. The French *lai* derives l. 17 (and the rhyme-word in l. 20) from the Latin, in spite of the complete difference of theme. Moreover the French and English poems fail to reproduce the metrical regularity of the Latin. Even as their texts are here edited, only stanza 4 is regular in syllable-count, in the sense that the two half-stanzas match and that lines which rhyme together have the same number of syllables. In stanza 3 the two halves match, but the lines which rhyme together in couplets (first and second, fourth and fifth, seventh and eighth, tenth and eleventh) are unequal in length. In stanzas 1, 2, and 5 the two halves do not match, and lines which rhyme together are of unequal length. The disparity in metrical regularity between the Latin on the one hand, and the French and English on the other, is still greater if accentual rhythm is brought into the comparison. In the French and English songs, even allowing (as we should) for variable word-stressings on which the author relied, there is no regularity of rhythm as there is in the Latin. In stanza 3, despite the irregularity of syllable-count (in that rhyming lines differ in length), there is at least rhythmical regularity: the two halves of the stanza balance, and lines of identical length always have the same metrical rhythm. But in the other stanzas there is no regularity; there is not even a matching of the rhythms of the two half-stanzas. In the French text, there is one line in the second half of stanza 1 which does not match the rhythm of the corresponding line in the first half-stanza; there are two such cases in stanza 2, one in stanza 4, and four in stanza 5 — a total of eight instances. In the English, there are three such cases in stanzas 1 and 2 and two in stanzas 4 and 5, a total of ten instances. The author of the French song, in abandoning regularity of syllable-count, still more obviously abandoned rhythmical regularity; and in the English translation, while exactly following the syllable-count of the French, he allowed himself somewhat greater freedom still in metrical rhythm. The order seems clear: the Latin comes first, with its metrical regularity, then the French, and finally the English. But occasionally the

English reverts to the rhythm of the Latin where the French had deserted it, as was remarked in the Introductory note to no. 4 above.

I have found listed eleven MSS of *Planctus ante nescia,* and there are doubtless others. I have myself collated, from photographs or (in the case of B) from the original, the following six early MSS, for which I use the sigla shown:

M Paris, Bibliothèque Mazarine, MS 1002 (formerly 942), ff. 235-7 (with music). Beginning of 13th cent.; from the abbey of St. Victor. The first part of the MS (in which the *Planctus* is the last item) is devoted to the works of Godefroy; there is a picture of the author on f. 144.

N Paris, Bibliothèque Nationale, fonds lat., MS 15163, ff. 229ᵛ-230ᵛ (without music, though a stave is ruled for the first two stanzas, and space for a stave is left for most of the rest of the text). Early 13th cent.; also from the abbey of St. Victor.

R Rouen, Bibliothèque Municipale, MS A 506 (formerly 666), ff. 94ᵛ-96ᵛ (with music). Dated to 12th cent. in the catalogue, but more probably early 13th.

E Évreux, Bibliothèque Municipale, MS 1. 2, ff. 3ᵛ-4ᵛ (with music). Early 13th cent.

F Évreux, Bibliothèque Municipale, MS 39, ff. 1ᵛ-2 (with music). Early 13th cent.; by the same scribe, with corrections by the same corrector, as the preceding. The music is transcribed from this MS by F. Gennrich, *Grundriss einer Formenlehre des mittelalterlichen Liedes* (1932), pp. 143-8, but he takes his word-text from Dreves (with a few variations of spelling and one misprint).

B Oxford, Bodleian Library, MS Additional 44, f. 80ᵛ (without music). Early 13th cent. (*Summary Catalogue*, no. 30151).

I give the readings of the following MSS on the authority of the editors named:

L Paris, Bibliothèque Nationale, fonds lat. MS 4880, f. 83ᵛᵃ⁻ᵛᵇ; 13th cent., from Fleury-sur-Loire: Printed by P. Delhaye, *Le Microcosmus de Godefroy de St.-Victor: Étude Théologique,* pp. 251-5, with some citation of variants from M and from Dreves. But one of the variants cited from M is inaccurately reported.

T Turin, MS E V 20 (12th.-13th. cent.), the sole basis of Dreves's text in *Analecta Hymnica Medii Aevi,* xx. 156-8, which is ill-punctuated and at l. 109 makes no sense; on this is based the text in Dreves and Blume, *Ein Jahrtausend Lateinischer Hymnendichtung,* i. 283, with a still worse reading (apparently a silent emendation) at l. 109. The latter work, on p. 281, refers to N, but it was obviously not collated for the text.

Dreves in *Anal. Hymn.* also gives variants from Prague MS XII D. 8a, an early 14th. cent. MS; but as I am not convinced that his collation was complete, and as the MS is in any case later, I take no account of its readings, which are obviously inferior. If Dreves's collation is in fact complete, the Prague MS must be related to T and is not a fully independent witness, for one would be obliged to assume, from Dreves's silence, that it shared T's error *muneris* at l. 109. I have also not taken into account two other late MSS, namely (i) Rouen, Bibliothèque Municipale, MS 364, f. 16, dated to the 15th. cent. and (ii) Paris, Bibliothèque Nationale, fonds lat., MS 3639, f. 185, dated to the 16th. cent.

The early MSS do not vary greatly, and most errors are confined to a single MS. The crucial variation is at l. 6, where TLR read *gaudio,* MNBEF read *gaudii.* But despite the weight of numbers *gaudio* must be right; both *gaudio* and *dulcore* in l. 6 are in apposition with *filio* in l. 5, as in ll. 7-8 *dulcor* and *gaudium* are in apposition with *fili.* It follows, therefore, that at l. 6 MNBEF are related by agreement in error. Within this group, MNB agree in an error of word-order at l. 12; and MN further agree in errors at ll. 57 and 64 where B is correct. EF were written by the same scribe and corrected by the same corrector, and have many agreements in error, but neither is a copy of the other; they are close copies of a common exemplar. LR are linked by errors of word-order at ll. 32 and 110. The affiliations of T are not clear. On the one hand it avoids the error *gaudii* at l. 6; on the other it agrees with EF in reading *extensis* for *protensis* at l. 116. The probability is that the latter is an independent error, the substitution of a synonym. If so, then T seems to represent an independent line of descent, and the relationships of the early MSS may be expressed as follows:

$$(MN)B(EF) - T - LR$$

But this scheme leaves it to be assumed that the false word-order *est Jesus* shared by B and EF at l. 102 is an independent error, and similarly *pro* MFL (*pro* corrected to *proh* B) for *proh* at l. 21. There may well have been some contamination of the MS tradition. It is to be observed that the two MSS reported to be from the abbey of St. Victor, M and N, though closely allied, do not give perfect texts, though they are good; it would appear that a MS used at St. Victor as the exemplar for these two copies was at least two removes from the archetype. But the archetype seems itself to have been a perfect copy, i.e. presumably it was Godefroy's autograph.

VARIANT READINGS

I do not ordinarily record variations of spelling, including variations of *t* and *c,* which in some of the MSS are not clearly distinguished.

1 Planctus] MNBETLR plantus F   planctu] MNBETLR plantu F   5 Judea] MBEFTLR iudeo *altered to* iudea (*with* iudea *also in margin in different hand*) N   6 gaudio] TLR gaudii MNBEF   8 gaudium] MBEFTLR lilium *altered to* gaudium *by original scribe* N   10 conferens] MNBTLR por-

rige EF   12 torquent tua] EFTLR tua torquent MNB   vulnera] MBEFTL viscera *altered to* vulnera *by original scribe* N   uiscera R   16 dux] MBEFTLR dux *above* mor(?) *struck through* N   20 tibi] MNBEFTR tua L   21 Proh] ETR Pro⟨h⟩ B Proch N Pro MFL   26 unda] MNBEFTR unde L   27 sero] MNBEFTR fero L (*acc. to Delhaye*)   32 tibi fecit] MNBEFT fecit tibi LR   34 amara] MNBEFTR abiecta L   38-39 O zelus o scelus] MNBTLR o scelus o zelus EF   48 Simeonis] BTL Symeonis MNEFR   56 noli] MNBEFTL soli R   57 tunc] BEFTLR tu MN   soli] MNBETLR sola *altered to* soli F   58 sola] MNBETLR *om.* F *but inserted in margin, with appropriate musical notes, by different (?) hand*   59 beate] MNBEFTR bene L   61 nate] MNBFTLR uate E   64 gens commisit] BEFTLR commisit gens MN   effera] MNBEFTR effara L   67 *This line is written after l. 58 in* E; *it runs into the margin, but at the correct place, in* F   69 crucifigite] MNBTLR interficite EF   71 nos simul] MNBETLR simul nos F   73 mæstissimæ] mestissime MNBTLR metissime *altered to* mestissime (*different hand?*) E mefissime F   77 osculis] MNBTLR oculis EF   79 peream] MNBETLR paream *altered to* peream F   84 se] MNBEFLR sic T   85 obscurari] METLR o⟨b⟩scurari B obscura *altered by different hand to* obscurari F obscuravi N   89 medicamine] MNEFTLR medicaine B   92 das] MNBTLR dans EF   93 male] MNBEFTL egre R   toleras] MBEFTR tolleras *altered to* toleras N tollas L   94 veniet] MNBEFTR uenies L   96 scies] MNBTLR scit E *but with* t *underlined, apparently by original scribe;* sci[t?] F *but original scribe writes* es *above last letter, which has also been erased and replaced by* es *in different hand*   pondere] MNBTLR pandere EF   102 Jesus est] MNTL Jesus stat R est Jesus BEF   103 fecisti] MBEFTLR *om.* N *but* fudisti *interlined in different hand and above that* fecisti   104 prosint] MBEFTLR prosunt N   105 sedant] MNBTLR cedat EF   107 Sion] TL Syon MNBEFR   108 tantæ] MNBEFTL tantem R   gratæ] MNBEFTL date R   gratia] MNBEFTL grem R (*but perhaps intended as abbreviation for* gracie)   109 juvenis] MNBEFLR muneris T   110 sibi sunt] MNBEFT sint tibi L sunt sidi R   112 ruite] MNBEFTR rite L   113 pendet] MNBEFTR pendent L   115 se parat] MNEFL separat BR (*but perhaps not intended as single word*) parat se T   116 bracchiis] MNBEFLR manibus T   protensis] MNBLR extensis EFT   119 reddite] MNBEFTL pendite R   120 dampnum] MNBTLR dapnum EF

5. Miri it is while sumer ilast

Miri it is whilë sumer ilast
wið fughëles song;
oc nu neheð windes blast
and weder strong.
5 Ei, ei! what þis niht is long!
And ich, wið wel michel wrong,
sorëgh and murn and [fast].

COMMENTARY

Source: Oxford, Bodleian Library, MS Rawlinson G. 22, f. 1ᵛ.

This piece may be only the first stanza of a longer song, for it comes at the foot of a leaf and there may have been other stanzas on a lost following leaf; but its sense is complete enough in itself. It has been suggested by E. W. B. Nicholson that the main MS may have come from Thorney Abbey in northern Cambridgeshire, and it is possible that the fly-leaf on which this and parts of two French songs are written may have had the same origin. A localization in this area would be consistent with the evidence of the language, though it is necessarily slight. The spellings of *miri* (*mirie* MS) and of *michel*, with *i* for OE ȳ, are East Midland or Northern; those of *song* etc. are probably non-Northern (it is unlikely that they have OE ŏ for WGmc ă plus nasal), and the contracted 3 sg. pres. indic. *ilast*, required for rhyme, is certainly non-Northern. The rhyme of OE ĕ in *fast* vb. (< OE *fǣstan*) with the shortening of OE ǣ¹ in *blast* (< OE *blǣst*) and of OE ǣ² in *ilast* (< OE *gelǣstan*) is a 'Saxon' type of rhyme, but Cambridgeshire, Norfolk, and Suffolk were within the 'Saxon' area in this respect (cf. Jordan, § 49). The contracted 3 sg. pres. indic. *ilast* is normally Southern, but such contracted forms are found in two thirteenth-century Norfolk texts, *The Bestiary* and *Genesis and Exodus*, and also in the *Trinity Homilies*, whose final redaction Jordan assigns to Huntingdonshire; they could obviously also occur in Cambridgeshire. The most unusual feature of the language is the loss of *-e* from the 1 sg. pres. indic. of the supplied rhyme-word *fast* in l. 7; there may possibly be a special explanation (see the note below), but the form would be consistent with the sporadic loss of the *-e* inflexion in the present tense of verbs shown by no. 11 below, which on linguistic grounds I have assigned to very much the same area as that suggested by Nicholson for this MS.

Nicholson's dating *c.* 1225 for the leaf is not inconsistent with the linguistic forms; the retention of *gh*, in place of later *w*, in *fugheles* and *soregh* is in favour of a date before 1250. But the spelling *o* in *song* etc. (assuming that it is ME ǭ < late OE ā by lengthening before *ng*) is against a date much before 1225 in a Midland text, and the loss of *-e* in *fast* is in favour of as late a date as is consistent with the other evidence. A dating between 1230 and 1240 would be rather more comfortable for the linguistic evidence.

NOTES

1. *Miri*] *Mirie* MS, the full form of the ME word (< OE *mўrige*, an old *u*-stem adjective). But here the final *-e* should elide before the following vowel (or unstressed *h* if the author himself had used the full form *hit* instead of *it*); cf. *soregh* (so written by the scribe) and *murn* (written *murne*) in l. 7 below. Moreover, though a sequence of three unstressed syllables is not impossible in ME verse, it is unlikely; elsewhere in this song stresses are separated by either one or two unstressed syllables, and the rhythm of this line seems obviously intended to be dactylic. The author must have intended elision of the *-e*, though the scribe, as was usual, has written the full form. But he has complicated the issue by providing, in the musical setting, a separate note for the final *-e*; it is, however, a mere repetition of the preceding note, and can be omitted.

ilast 'lasts', a contraction of *ilasteð*, 3 sg. pres. indicative of *ilasten* < OE *gelǣstan*.

2. *fugheles*] originally gen. sg. of *fughel* 'bird' < OE *fugol*, but probably here used as a plural. In this word, and in *soregh* in l. 7, the scribe's *gh* is a spelling of a voiced back spirant which later in the thirteenth century changed to *w*; those who wish may modernize the pronunciation a little and make the word *fuwëles*.

song] at this early date the vowel in this word and those which rhyme with it was long ǭ (approximately modern *aw* in *lawn*).

3. *oc* 'but'.

neheð 'draws near'. The MS has *necheð*, and similarly *nicht* in l. 5 where we print *niht*. The scribe is using *ch* as a spelling for the voiceless spirant (as in modern German *ich*), but he also uses it in its ordinary English value (as in *rich*) in the words *ich* 'I' and *michel* 'great' in l. 6. To avoid the ambiguity of his spelling, we use the OE spelling *h* for the spirant; it was still in common use in ME at this date.

4. *weder strong* 'rough weather'. The *d* of *weder* was pronounced as spelt.

5. 'Alas! how long this night is!'

6. *wið wel michel wrong* 'with very great wrong, most unjustly'.

7. *soregh* 'sorrow'. The full form would be *soreghe*, with the *-e* inflexion of the 1 sg. pres. indic., but the inflexion has been elided before *and* and is not written by the scribe himself. The *gh* is again a spelling of the voiced back spirant, which a little later became *w*; it may be replaced by *w* if desired, in which case the *w* should be run on to the following word. The *e* before the *gh* is an unstressed glide-vowel (the OE stem is *sorg-*) but is required by metre and music.

murn] *murne* MS. Here the scribe has written the *-e* inflexion, but it is elided and therefore omitted in our text.

fast] The word is not now visible in the MS; it was supplied by the editors of *Early Bodleian Music*, and is clearly right. But it involves a difficulty of which they may not have been aware, for the proper form of the 1 sg. pres. indic. is *faste,* with pronounced *-e;* at this early date an uninflected form is not to be expected. But it is undoubtedly required by the rhyme, for *ilast* in l. 1 cannot have *-e.* It is probably an early example of the loss of *-e* shown in the present tense in no. 11 below. But it may not be an accident that it occurs in a word whose stem ends in *-st,* for early ME may have had a sporadic tendency to lose *-e* after *st,* even when it was preserved in other circumstances; thus OF *beste* 'animal' turns up in ME as *best* or *beast,* without *-e,* as well as in the expected form *beste.*

6a. Man mai longe lives weene

1

Man mai longë lives weenë
    ac him liȝet oft þe wrench;
vair weder oft went into reenë —
    veerlich maket hit his blench.
5 Þervorë, man, þu þee biþench;
    al ssel valëwi þi greenë.
Weilawei! nis king ne queenë
    þet ne ssel drink of deaþes drench.
Man, er þu vall of þi bench,
10   þi senn aquench.

2

No mai strong ne starc ne keenë
    aȝee deaþes wiþer-clench,
[ne] ȝung ne ald, ne briht and sseenë;
    al he rivet an his strenth,
15 [vor] vox and veerlich is his wrench.
No mai no man þeertoȝeenes,
    weilawei, ne þreat ne beenë,
    meedë ne list ne leeches drench.
Man, let senn and lustes stench;
20   wel do, wel þench.

3

Do bi Salomones reedë,
    man, and so þu sselt wel do;
do ál so he þee taht, and heedë
    hwet þin ending þee bringþ to —
25 ne sseltu never [eft] misdo.
Sorë þu miht þee adreedë,
    weilawei, swich weenst wel leedë
    long lif and blissen undervoo,
    þeer deaþ luteþ in þi ssoo
30   to þee vordo.

4

Man, hwi neltu þee bicnowë?
    Man, hwi neltu þee bisi?
Of velþë þu art [erst] isowë;
    wermes metë þu sselt bi.
35 Heer nafstu blissë daies þri;
    al þi lif þu drihst in wowë.
Weilawei! deaþ þee ssel þrowë
    dun, þeer þu weendest heeȝë sti;
    ín wo ssel þi welë ti,
40   in woop þi gli.

5

Werld and welë þee biswiket;
    [mid] iwis hi byeþ þi vo.
If þinë werld mid welë sliket,
    þet is vor to do þee wo.
45 Þervorë let lust overgo,
man, and eft hit [wel] þee liket.
Weilawei! hu sor*e* him wiket
    þet in o stundë, oþer two,
    wercþ him pinë evermo!
50   Ne do, man, swo!

COMMENTARY

Sources: see below.

The song is recorded in four MSS. (1) Maidstone Museum, MS A.13, f. 93ᵛ (with music); denoted M. In Carleton Brown's view (*Eng. Lyrics of the Thirteenth Century,* p. 170) the hand in which the song is written is 'not later than 1250'; but I should doubt whether the linguistic forms could be earlier than 1250. Brown also argued that the MS was compiled in the Cluniac Priory of St. Andrew at Northampton, and the text does indeed contain a few Midland linguistic forms; but for the most part the scribe seems to have been carefully following a Southern exemplar. He made a good many corrections in the course of writing, and the cancelled forms are sometimes more Southern. (2) Oxford, Bodleian Library, MS Laud Misc. 471, f. 65; denoted L. This is two separate MSS bound together; the text of the song, without music, comes in the first part. The MS is of the thirteenth century, probably the latter part; the scribe was probably a North Midlander, in view of his use of the form *ledes* 'leads' in his corrupted text of l. 29 and of *ferlik* in l. 4, but he preserves a number of South-Eastern forms. (3) London, British Library, MS Cotton Caligula A. ix, f. 246ᵛ (text without music); denoted C. This is a West Midland MS of the second half of the thirteenth century; in Mr. N. R. Ker's opinion the dating of the MS to 'a little after 1250' seems 'on the early side'. (4) Oxford, Jesus College, MS 29, f. 252ᵛ (text without music); denoted J. This is a South-west Midland MS of about the same date as Cotton.

The song is also quoted by three early homilists. (1) The first two lines are cited in the 'Kentish Sermons' in the second part of Oxford, Bodleian Library, MS Laud Misc. 471, f. 133 (in the sermon for *Dominica in Sexagesima;* cf. Hall, *Early Middle English*, p. 222, ll. 274-5). Hall dates the MS to the end of the thirteenth century, but Jordan dates the sermons 'about 1250'. This fragment is denoted K. (2) The greater part of stanza 1, in a garbled order and with l. 1 contaminated by *The Proverbs of Alfred*, ll. 108-9, is quoted in a Latin homily in London, British Library, MS Additional 11579, ff. 72ᵛ-73, which is dated to the early fourteenth century. Some corrections have been made to the English words, apparently in a different hand. This fragment is denoted B. (3) In Michel of Northgate's *Ayenbite of Inwit* (denoted A), written in St. Augustine's, Canterbury, and completed on 27 October 1342, the first stanza of the poem is quoted, with omission of l. 6 and displacement of l. 5 (London, British Library, MS Arundel 57, f. 39ᵛ; ed. Morris and Gradon, pp. 129-30).

C and J are well-known anthologies of pieces in English and Anglo-Norman, and from their contents and texts it is well established that they are not very remote copies of a common original; this is certainly true of their texts of the present song. Carleton Brown says (op. cit., p. 171) that a collation 'shows that in most cases ML agree against CJ', but the collation must have been unusually superficial even for him; the only instance he mentions is that ML preserve the original short form of the final line of each stanza, but this is an agreement in a correct reading and therefore without significance for the textual affiliations of M and L, and the same is true of almost all their agreements. But L agrees with CJ against M in well over a dozen significant readings, most of which are obvious errors: thus in l. 3 *ofte* is placed after the verb in LCJ, ll. 11-12 have been rewritten and both lines are too long in the LCJ text (l. 11 by one syllable, l. 12 by two), and in l. 38 *dun* (*adun*) has been transferred to the previous line, so that l. 37 is too long, l. 38 too short. The relationship of the four main MSS may therefore be expressed as M — L (CJ). It follows that ordinarily agreement of M with one or more of the other three MSS is conclusive of the text of the archetype. LCJ together constitute only a single witness against M, and as M undoubtedly represents a better textual tradition its readings are in doubtful cases to be given preference.

The fragments K, B, and A are too brief for their textual affiliations to be determined, but there is apparently some connection between them, as might perhaps be expected, for it must seem unlikely that three authors of works of religious instruction should independently decide to quote, in their prose, the same stanza of the same song.

The archetype of the extant MSS was itself undoubtedly corrupt. The clearest instance is in l. 39, which in the archetype obviously ended with the verb *endi* (*enden*), which fails either to scan or to rhyme. Monosyllabic words were omitted in ll. 13, 15, 25, 33, and 42, there was a wrong change from second to third personal forms in ll. 27, 29, and 30, and other errors in ll. 2, 4, 23, 38, 42, 43, and 46. Emendation of the archetypal text is essential for metre and/or sense at all these points except perhaps in ll. 23, 38, and 46, where in my view it is at least desirable. It follows that between M and the author's original

at least one copy (the archetype) must intervene; at least three between CJ and the original.

In CJ *Man mai longe lives weene* is immediately followed by another poem, *On hir is mi lif ilong* (no. 6b below), in the same general stanza-form, though with a different rhyme-pattern and metre, and of the same length (five stanzas). The juxtaposition of the two poems in CJ cannot be accidental; it must be due to a realization on the part of the compiler of the anthology that they were companion pieces, at least in form. As the stanza-form is a very unusual one for ME lyric and it cannot be coincidence that two writers should have used the same rare stanza in poems of identical length, it seems *a priori* likely that, though music is recorded only for no. 6a, no. 6b must have been intended for performance to the same tune, or some modification of it. In fact it proves possible to set the words of 6b to the tune recorded for 6a, as our settings show, with only the slightest variations, most of which consist of no more than a modification of the method of underlaying the words. This fact, taken together with the contiguity of the two pieces in CJ, may be accepted as a demonstration that they were indeed both intended for the same music. If one of them was modelled on the other, then priority must be allowed to 6a (*Man mai longe lives weene*); it is the earlier in poetic type, being a purely moralistic poem untouched by the personal devotion which is so strong in the other (though blended with moralizing), it fits the music better, with a more exact correspondence of syllables and notes, and it is the more original and technically more complex, with its regularly repeated *weilawei* at the beginning of the seventh line of each stanza. It is possible that the tune has been taken, by a pious theft, from some secular lyric, probably a love-song; and it would be easy to imagine the beginning of a Middle English lyric which combined the general sense of the opening of 6b with the metre of 6a (which is more likely to be that of the original), for example:

> Heo is al mi lives blissë
> þat i sing of in mi song.

But the assumed secular lyric might have been French or even medieval Latin; and the ultimate model for the elaborate stanza was probably Latin.

Ordinarily the metrical form of a Middle English song has to be deduced by analysis of the MS texts of all its stanzas, accompanied by close comparison with the music. In this case, as 6a and 6b are companion pieces, though differing in metre, the one must be considered with an eye to the other. The music is written in non-mensural notation but was presumably intended to be sung in a triple rhythm, and it demands a high degree of metrical regularity, both in syllable-count and in accentual rhythm. The pattern established for *Man mai longe lives weene* is in terms of syllable-count 8797888874, rhyming ababbaabbb. The rhythmical pattern is as follows:

Line	1	/x/x/x/x
	2	/x/x/x/
	3	x/x/x/x/x
	4	/x/x/x/
	5	x/x/x/x/
	6	/x/x/x/x
	7	/x/x/x/x
	8	/xx/x/x/
	9	/x/x/x/
	10	x/x/

To this pattern the author has kept very strictly. In view of the nature of the music, it has been assumed, in making my text, that whenever the reconstituted text of the archetype differs in syllable-count and/or in accentual rhythm from the norm for the line in question, emendation is necessary and legitimate; but the changes made are in fact all very slight.

The citation of the first stanza in the thirteenth-century *Kentish Sermons* and in the *Ayenbite* proves that the song was current in Kent at an early date, and the evidence of the language is that it was written there. The *a*-rhymes of stanza 3 are non-Anglian, since they rhyme OE $\bar{æ}^1$ in *reede* (l. 21) and *adreede* (l. 26) with OE $\bar{æ}^2$ in *leede* (l. 27); and if the emendation *heede* in l. 23 is correct, they must be Kentish, with ME $\bar{e}$. The loss of OE *g* in *reene* 'rain' < OE *rĕgn* (l. 3) and -*ȝeenes* < OE -*gĕgn* (l. 16) is also Saxon or Kentish. Non-WS $\bar{e}$ is required in *sseene* 'beautiful' (l. 13). Metre requires the *i*- prefix in the p.p. *isowe* (l. 33) and contracted forms of the 2 and 3 sg. pres. indic. of OE verbs of the strong and 1st weak conjugations: *went* (l. 3), *bringþ* (l. 24), *weenst* (l. 27), *drihst* (l. 36). The Southern inflexion of the present indicative plural is established by rhyme for *biswiket* (or *biswikeþ*) in l. 41. For the rest the evidence consists of spellings and forms preserved in the MSS which are inconsistent with the dialects of their scribes and must derive from the textual tradition. South-eastern *e* for OE $\breve{y}$ occurs in *senn(e)* (l. 10), *neltu* (ll. 31, 32), and *felþe* (l. 33); *ea* for OE $\bar{ea}$ in *deaþes* (ll. 8, 12); -*et* for the verbal inflexion -*eþ*; *s* for OE initial *sc* (e.g. for OE *scēne* in l. 13); *v* (in the MSS *u*) for OE initial *f*, e.g. in *þervore* (l. 5) and *valewi* (l. 6), but not *z* for initial *s*; and the infinitive *valewi* of the OE 2nd weak conjugation in l. 6. These features are in general either Southern or South-eastern; taken together they indicate an origin south of the Thames and towards the east. More specifically Kentish are *sel* 'shall' (in M, ll. 6 and 8) and *selt* 'shalt' (also in M, ll. 22, 25, 34). Finally, the *b*-rhymes in stanza 4 are most easily explicable in Kent, where the development of OE *sīgan* to thirteenth-century *sīe* (cf. Jordan, § 90) would cause it to fall together with the development of OKt *īo* to *īe* in *sīe* < *sīon* for general OE *sēon*, *bīe* < *bīon* for OE *bēon*, etc.; and the loss of -*e* from these forms, required by the metre (which must have monosyllables), is a well-established feature of Kentish. In any other dialect than Kentish these rhymes can be explained only by assuming an analogical reformation of *sīgan* as **stēon*—for which indeed there is evidence in the spellings used by M and CJ for the word in l. 38, but these may be occasioned by the rhyme-sequence itself.

Though there is no absolutely conclusive evidence, what there is all points to Kent, and my text is therefore reconstructed on a Kentish basis, chiefly by generalizing those features to which the sporadic Kentish forms in the MSS point. Thus I have generalized *v* for initial *f*, but have not introduced the *Ayenbite*'s *z* for initial *s* (though doubtless *senn* 'sin' was pronounced as [zen]). But where the forms of the MSS point to original *s* for OE initial *sc* (modern English *sh*), I have adopted the *Ayenbite*'s less ambiguous spelling *ss*, thus *sseene* instead of *seene* for *sheene* 'beautiful'. How this *ss* (or *s*) was pronounced is unknown; some think it was pronounced like modern *sh*, and it would be best in singing to treat it so. It is also disputed how the Kentish spelling *ea* in such words as *deaþ* 'death' was pronounced; one possibility is to make it a diphthong [eə], roughly the vowel-sounds of modern English (*Mal*)*aya*, another is to treat it as a mere spelling for a pure vowel [ɛː], like modern French *è* in *père*. In the present tense of verbs the ending

-*et*, which was common in southern dialects (including Kentish), has been used where the MS spellings suggest it; it may be pronounced as spelt, or the normal -*eth* ending may be substituted.

If the Maidstone MS (M) is correctly dated c. 1250, the date of composition must obviously be earlier. The second quarter of the thirteenth century would seem a suitable dating for the linguistic forms; they are not likely to have been earlier than 1220 or so. Moralistic verse dwelling on the inevitability of death and (for sinners) of damnation was popular in the late twelfth and early thirteenth centuries.

The texts of C and J were printed in parallel by Morris, *Old English Miscellany*, pp. 156-9; that of J, by Hall, *Early Middle English*, p. 29; those of M and L, by Carleton Brown, *English Lyrics of the XIIIth Century*, pp. 15-18 (all of whom use different titles). For other editions, see Hall, ii. 309.

VARIANTS

Variations of spelling are not necessarily recorded; when two or more MSS are given as having the same reading, the spelling may be that only of the first.

1 Many man wened þat he wen*en* ne þarf longe to liuene B   1 man] MLKA mon J non C   mai] may LCJKA mei M   lives] liues CJK liwes L him liues M his lyues A weene] wene MCJKA wenen L   2 ac] MLCJ and KA *om.* B   him liȝet oft] ofte him lih (*cancelled*) liþet M offte hym legeþt L ofte him legheþ K ofte him lieð C ofte him lyeþ J ofte him lyeȝeþ A him lye; (*for* lyet?) B   þe] MCJ se LK his A   wrench] LKA wreinch *after* wrenh *cancelled* M wrenh B   3 vair] fair MLB feir CJ ase uayr A   oft went] ofte him went M (⟨oftyn⟩ went (often *interlined in different hand*) B went A went offte L turneð ofte CJ   into] LCJBA to (*interlined*) M   reene] rene MLA reine CJB   4 veerlich] ferlike B and uerliche A an ferliche M and ferlik L and wunderliche J an wunderliche C   maket hit] hit makeð C maket he B turneþ he L maket M makeþ AJ   his] LCJAB is M   5 *transposed after l. 8 in* A   5 þervore] þeruore A þerfore L þarvore MCJ þarfore B   man] MLB *transposed before* þeruore A mon CJ   þu þee biþench] þu þe biþench MLCJ *om.* B þe beþench A   6 *line omitted* BA   6 ssel] sel M sal L schal CJ   valewi] valui M falewi LC falwy J   þi] LCJ þe M   7 weilawei] LC waylaway J welawey M for þere *over erasure* B þer A   nis] MLCJ is neythir *over erasure* B ne is noþer A   king ne queene] king ne quene MLJA kin ne quene C quen ne king B   8 þet] þat LCJ þat hee B   ssel] A sel M schal CJ scholen B   drink] drinke MJA drinche C drinken LB   deaþes] CA deþes LJ dethis M   drench] MLCJA drinc B   9-10 *placed before l. 7 in* B, *in order* 10, 9   9 man] LM mon CJ *om.* BA   er] MLCJA ar B   vall] ualle A falle MLCJ dun falle B   10 þi] LBA þine CJ þu M   senn] senne LB zenne A sinne M sunne CJ   a-quench] MLA quench B þu aquench CJ

11 no mai] ne mai M nis non LCJ   strong] M se strong L so strong CJ   starc] L starch M sterch C sterk J   ne] LCJ *interlined by original scribe in* M   12 aȝee] a ȝlye *altered from* a slye M þat may agein L þat may ago CJ   deaþes] LC deþes J dethis M   wiþer-clench] ML wiþer blench CJ 13 ne ȝung] ȝung LCJ þung M   ne] L and MCJ   ald] old ML olde CJ   ne] and M *om.* LCJ   briht] J brihet C brith

M brigot L and] CJ an M ne L sseene] sene L siene *altered from* sene M schene CJ 14 al] M alle CJ ac al L rivet] riueth M riueþ LCJ an] M on LJ in C his] M o LJ one C strenth] streng MLJ strench C 15 vor vox] vox M fox LCJ veerlich] ferlich MCJ ferlic L his] LCJ þe M wrench] LJ wrenh C wreinch M 16 no] ne MLCJ no man] M no mon CJ him noman L þeerto3eenes] þar to 3enes (*with* glenes gt *cancelled before* 3enes) M þar to 3eines CJ to yenes L 17 weilawei] MC welauei L waylaway J ne þreat] ne þrat3ing *replaced by* ne weping *by marginal correction* M þreting CJ weping L 18 meede] MCJ *om.* L ne] L *om.* MCJ list] liste MCJ listes L drench] LCJ dreinch M 19 man] ML mon CJ senn] sunne CJ sinne *after cancelled* lust M lust L lustes] MCJ senne L stench] ML þine CJ 20 do] ML þu do CJ wel] ML and wel þu CJ

21 Salomones] MJ salemones LC 22 man] ML mon CJ and] MCJ *om.* L so] M þanne L þenne CJ þu sselt] þu selth M þu schalt J þu schald C sal þu L 23 al so] M so L ase C as J taht] tahte C tauhte J tothte M techeþ L heede] sede ML seide CJ 24 hwet] wat M þat LCJ ending] L endinch M endinge CJ bringþ] brinch M bringeþ CJ bringet L 25 ne sseltu] ne seltu M ne sal þu L þenne ne schal þu C þenne ne schaltu J never eft] neuer CJ neuere ML 26 *line omitted in* L 26 sore] M ac sore CJ miht] mith M myht J mi3t C 27 weilawei] C weilauei L weylawey *after cancelled* wel M waylaway J swich] L suich M such J shuc C weenst] wenþ M weneth L weneð C weneþ J wel] M *om.* L to CJ 28 blissen] blisse MCJ blisce L undervoo] underuo M underfo LCJ þeer] þar M *om.* L ac CJ deaþ] deþ LCJ deth M luteþ] CJ luteth M him ledes L in] MCJ on L þi] his MLCJ ssoo] soo L scho CJ swo M 30 to þee] to him M do him L him stilliche to CJ vordo] fordo MLCJ

31 man] ML mon CJ hwi] CJ wi L fwi M neltu] M niltu L nultu CJ bicnowe] C biknowe J bicnowen L biþenchen M 32 man] ML mon CJ hwi] CJ wi L fwi M neltu] M niltu L nultu CJ bisi] bisee L bisen *altered from* bisun M biseo CJ 33 velþe] felþe ML fole fulþe C fule fulþe J art erst] art LCJ ert M isowe] MCJ comen L 34 wermes] L weirmes *altered from* wirmes M wormes C wurmes J mete] M fode LCJ sselt] selt M salt L schalt J schald C bi] be L ben *altered from* bun M beo CJ 35 heer nafstu] her nauest tu M her nauestu CJ þu ne hauest her L daies] LCJ dais *altered from* daie M þri] þre MLJ þreo C 36 al] M ac al L ac CJ lif] M lif al CJ ioie L þu drihst] þu drist M þu last CJ is turned L in] MJ ine C on L wowe] MCJ wouge L 37 ssel] sal ML schal CJ 37-38 þrowe dun] þrowen dun M dun þr . . . L adun þrowe CJ 38 þeer] þer CJ þar M hwanne L weendest] wenest MLCJ hee3e] heye M agein L he3est C heyust J sti] ste *altered from* sten M . . stie L to steo CJ 39 in] MJ ine C on L wo] M sorghe L deð C deþ J ssel] sal ML schal CJ wele] M ioie L lif CJ ti] endi CJ enden M *lacuna in* L 40 in] M on L and in J and ine C woop] wop MLCJ þi] ML al þi CJ

41 werld and] M world and CJ hwer so L wele] ML weole CJ biswiket] biswikeþ J biswikeð C biswik . . L bipecheth M 42 mid iwis] iwis MCJ man i wis L hi] hie *after cancelled* it M he L heo CJ byeþ] beþ L buth M beoð C beoþ J þi] L þin C þine MJ vo] fo L iuo M ifo CJ 43 if] MJ

M brigot L and] CJ an M ne L sseene] sene L siene *altered from* sene M schene CJ 14 al] M alle CJ ac al L rivet] riueth M riueþ LCJ an] M on LJ in C his] M o LJ one C strenth] streng MLJ strench C 15 vor vox] vox M fox LCJ veerlich]ferlich MCJ ferlic L his] LCJ þe M wrench] LJ wrenh C wreinch M 16 no] ne MLCJ no man] M no mon CJ him noman L þeerto3eenes] þar to 3enes (*with* glenes gt *cancelled before* 3enes) M þar to 3eines CJ to yenes L 17 weilawei] MC welauei L waylaway J ne þreat] ne þrat3ing *replaced by* ne weping *by marginal correction* M þreting CH weping L 18 meede] MCJ *om.* L ne] L *om.* MCJ list] liste MCJ listes L drench] LCJ dreinch M 19 man] ML mon CJ senn] sunne CJ sinne *after cancelled* lust M lust L lustes] MCJ senne L stench] ML þine CJ 20 do] ML þu do CJ wel] ML and wel þu CJ

NOTES

1-2. 'Man may expect long life, but the trick often deceives him.' The couplet is modelled on one in *The Proverbs of Alfred*, ll. 108-9:

Monymon weneþ þat he wene ne þarf,
longes lyues, ac him lyeþ þe wrench

('many a man expects what he need not expect, long life, but the trick deceives him'). The text in B has been corrupted by this.

1. *longe lives* 'long life', gen. sg. after *weene*, which in OE governed the genitive; it is a conservative feature of the language that this syntax is preserved. But whereas in *Prov. Alfr.* the gen. sg. neut. of the adj. (*longes*) is kept, it has here been replaced by a general oblique form *longe* derived from the dat. sg. (cf. the *Ayenbite*, which uses e.g. *ane* as gen. sg. masc. of the indefinite article).

2. *oft*] All MSS except B (which omits the word, probably because of the influence of *Prov. Alfr.*) agree in placing the adverb after *ac*; and this must have been the placing in the archetype. But with the words in this order, the line has only three stresses and scans x/x/xx/. In the other stanzas it is clear that the second and fourth lines (which are set to the same musical phrase and therefore must have the same rhythm) have four stresses and scan /x/x/x/, and this is certainly what the music requires. We must transpose *oft* to follow *li3et*. The author of the song has evidently followed the phrase in *Prov. Alf.* (see above), but that in its turn must have been based on a widespread proverbial expression, for *Ancrene Wisse* (Corpus MS., f. 91b/27 ff.) has:

On oðer half moni mon abit forte schriuen him aðet te nede tippe. Ah ofte him liheð þe wrench, þet he ne mei hwen he wule þe nalde þa he mahte.

This agrees with our song in including the word *ofte*, and if its placing in the prose passage reflects its normal placing in the proverb, it would explain why the scribe of the archetype shifted the word from the position which, on the evidence of the metre, the poet intended.

li3et] It is hard to know what form to use, as the MSS differ widely and are evidently using the forms of the scribes' own dialects. A's *lye3eþ* is of course authentic Kentish, but I doubt if it stood in the original; a better case could be made for *leghet* (cf. *legeþt* L, *legheþ* K)). M's *liþet* is an error for *liʒet*, and I accept this, though the scribe's cancelled *lih* may suggest that his exemplar had *lihet* (or *lihþ*). I assume a re-formed infinitive *liʒen* with vowel derived from a contracted 3 sg. pres. indic. *lihþ* with palatal mutation (cf. OKt *wrihð*, *flihð* and the *Ayenbite's wriʒþ*, *uliʒþ*, 3 sg. pres. indic. of OKt *wrīon*, *flīon*). The evidence of the MSS is that the archetype in most instances had *-et* as the inflexion of the 3 sg. pres. indic. in uncontracted forms, and I adopt this; it was common in Southern dialects.

3. *vair* 'fair'. Here all the MSS except A have initial *f*, but in comparable words there is sufficient evidence that the original had Southern *v* for OE initial *f*, and I generalize this.

oft] The MSS vary in their placing of the adverb; it seems to me better before the verb *went*, but metre is unaffected. As in l. 2, the metre requires the original monosyllabic form *oft*, against the *ofte* of the MSS.

went 'turns', contracted 3 sg. pres. indic. of *wenden* in its sense of 'turn, change'.

reene 'rain', from OE (Saxon and Kentish) *rēn* < *rĕgn*.

4. 'Suddenly it plays its trick.' The translation 'and sunshine is wondrously made' that has been published for M's reading *an ferliche maket is blench*, though one sees how it has been arrived at (Carleton Brown gives *blench* 'sunshine' in his glossary by a false identification with the Northern word *blenk* 'a sudden gleam of light'), deserves to rank with the notable howlers, like the rendering of the *Peterborough Chronicle's war sæ me tilede* (properly 'whereso one tilled', wherever there was tillage) as 'one might as well till the sea'.

veerlich 'suddenly'; OKt *ferlice* for WS *fǣrlice*. The readings of the MSS leave no doubt that the archetype read *and ferliche*. But the line must begin with a stressed syllable (see note to *oft* in l. 2 above); only in the first stanza does the fourth line begin with an unstressed syllable, even as the MSS give the text. The error here must be related to that in l. 2; evidently the scribe of the archetype, having corrupted the rhythm of l. 2 (or else received an already corrupted text), has made l. 4 conform to the false rhythm, at least at the beginning, because he knew that l. 4 had to follow the same metrical pattern as l. 2, being set to the same musical phrase. We must simply omit the *and*, as B does; but B's text is almost certainly a scribal emendation, not a preservation of the original reading.

maket hit his blench 'it plays its trick'; *his* is the neuter gen. sg. in OE and ME, as well as masculine. This may well have been the reading of the archetype, though no MSS preserves it exactly: in C *hit* is transferred to precede the verb; B and L change *hit* to *he*, probably independently, through assuming that *his* must be masculine (it is not clear what *he* was thought to refer to, for *weder* was neuter in OE and early ME); M, J, and A omit *hit*, probably independently and in order to reduce the number of syllables in the line to the normal eight. In their text, the rhythm of l. 4 exactly matches the corrupted rhythm of l. 2. If we were to assume that the archetype read *maket his blench*, we should have to assume that C, B, and L had independently emended the text by introducing a pronoun subject which the introduction of *and* at the beginning of the line had made unnecessary; and this is improbable.

5. *þu þee biþench* 'consider, take heed'.

6. *ssel* 'shall', a Kentish form. The spellings of the early MSS M and L point rather to *sel* in the original, but as explained in the

introduction above we adopt the *Ayenbite's ss* for initial *sh* (OE *sc*) because it is less ambiguous. Examples of *ss* already occur in the *Kentish Sermons*.

valewi 'fallow', 'grow yellow or pale', hence 'fade, wither'. Metre and music require the trisyllabic form given by LC, not the disyllable given by MJ. J's agreement with M is fortuitous, as its divergence from C (and L) shows.

þi greene 'thy greenness, thy youth'. The LCJ reading here seems better than M's *þe grene* 'the green'. But either makes sense.

8. *drink*] If we were to adopt the form *drinken* given by LB, the second foot of the line, as well as the first, would be a dactyl. But the norm, shown by the corresponding lines of stanzas 3-5, is a trochee as the second foot; we should therefore follow the majority of MSS, which read *drinke*, of which the final *-e* elides before *of* and is therefore omitted in our text. The rhymes of the poem show clearly that in the author's dialect *-n* had been lost from infinitives. The fact that in M its form *drinke* is set to two notes (the second being an anticipation of the note to which the following *of* is set) is without significance, for it is plain that the scribe of M did not understand elision and followed unthinkingly the written forms of the words; in ll. 9 and 10 he sets his forms *falle* and *sinne* to two notes (the second being, as with *drinke* in l. 8, an anticipation of the next note of the musical phrase), though in these two lines there cannot be the slightest doubt that the author intended elision. In the companion piece, no. 6b, the pattern is that between the second and third stresses of the eighth line of the stanza there is only a single unstressed syllable, i.e. the musical sequence required is long note – short note – long note; and this is also what is required by stanzas 3-5 of the present song. M's insertion of an additional note is unwarranted.

drench 'draught'.

9. *vall* 'fall'. The MSS have *falle*, but the *-e* of the pres. subj. sg. here elides. On initial *v* for *f* see note to *vair* in l. 3 above.

10. *senn* 'sin', a South-eastern form of OE *synn* fem. The normal ME form ends in *-e*, derived from the OE oblique cases, and all the MSS give forms with this *-e*; but here it elides.

aquench 'extinguish', 'put an end to', i.e. desist from.

11f. 'Never can the strong or the mighty or the bold prevail against Death's hostile grip, nor the young nor the old, nor the bright and beautiful.' All the adjectives are singular; and *bright* is used in its common poetic sense of 'fair, beautiful', a slightly earlier instance than the first cited by *OED*, which is from *Edi be þu* (no. 13 below).

11. *No mai*] M's reading *Ne mai* is satisfactory in sense and number of syllables, but not in rhythm, for the line must begin with a stressed syllable, whereas the negative particle *ne* is essentially unstressed. I therefore substitute the stronger negative *no* < OE *nā* 'never', which in ME could still be used directly before a verb; see *OED*, s.v. *no* adv.[1], under 1.β. The LCJ corruption *nis non . . . þat mai* was probably occasioned by the occurrence in the archetype of *no mai*, misread as *non mai*. In this usage *mai* is a principal verb, meaning 'to have power', 'to avail'.

12. *aʒee* 'against'; cf. the *Ayenbite's aye* < OKt *ongēn* with loss of final *-n*. M's *aʒlye* must be a misreading of *aʒeye* in its exemplar; similarly in l. 16 M misreads an *e* as *l* in another form

of this word when it writes *glenes* (cancelled) for *ȝeenes* (as I assume) in the exemplar. The readings of LCJ also point to *aȝe* or perhaps *age* in their common original, for L has *agein* and CJ *ago*. Carleton Brown accepts M's *aȝlye* as correct, saying that it 'preserves the rare and archaic *a-glye*' (p. 171), but there is no such word; he was presumably thinking of the word *aglyȝte* in *Pearl* l. 245, which *OED* with doubtful propriety enters under *agly*, but it does not mean 'to escape'.

13. It is essential that the third line of the stanza should begin with an unstressed syllable, for from the second syllable onwards the line is sung to a repetition of the music of the first line, i.e. the second syllable must be stressed, since it corresponds to the *first* syllable of the first line. But all four MSS begin the line with *ȝung ne* or *ȝung and* (except that M corrupts *ȝung* to *þung*), i.e. they begin with a syllable which must be stressed. The archetype must have omitted a word, and the obvious one to supply is *ne* 'nor'; in ME *ȝung ne ald* and *ne ȝung ne ald* were syntactical equivalents, but not metrical. L's *ȝung ne* is obviously right, against *ȝung and* of the other MSS; 'young' and 'old' are alternatives. But the agreement of MCJ may well mean that the archetype had *and*; if so, L's *ne* is a correct scribal emendation.

ald] In Kentish, according to the evidence of the *Ayenbite*, the singular had *ă* from unlengthened OE *ĕa*; I therefore substitute *ald* for the *old(e)* of the MSS, all of which use the Midland form developed from late OE (Anglian) *āld*.

ne (before *briht*) is an emendation; M reads *and* and the rest omit the conjunction. An unstressed word is essential, and M's *and* is unsuitable after the emended first half-line. The archetype's corruption of *ne ȝung ne ald* to *ȝung and old* must have made *ne* (which it evidently retained) seem inappropriate; M has altered it to *and*, the ancestor of LCJ omitted it.

and] The MCJ reading is here right against L's *ne; briht* and *sseene* are synonyms, not alternatives.

sseene is OE *scēne*, modern English poetical *sheen* 'beautiful'. It is clear that the archetype had the spelling *sene*, and it may have spelt *and* as *an* (an unstressed form). M after first copying *an sene* altered it to *an siene*, which he probably intended (as Carleton Brown seems to assume) as a form of the word *onsene* 'face, appearance'; but this would make no sense. The original of CJ correctly identified the words intended and normalized to *and schene*.

14. *al* may be either singular, 'everything', or more probably plural; in the latter case it is the normal ME *alle* (so spelt by CJ here), but with its *-e* elided before *he*.

rivet 'rives', 'tears to pieces', 'destroys'.

an 'on' (but here meaning 'in'), a Kentish form preserved in M. *an his strenth* 'in his strength' follows but modifies M's reading *an his streng*. This must have been that of the archetype; but the original of LCJ, taking *streng* as the word 'string', altered the text to mean 'in one string' (contextually, 'in one noose', 'in one snare'). Nevertheless I assume that the original had *strenth* (or *strenþ*), a common late OE and ME variant of OE *strengþ*, since *strenth* makes a closer assonance with the rhyme-words than does *streng*. Whichever word is adopted, it is notable that the form, though governed by a preposition, lacks *-e* and must be derived from OE *strengþ* or *streng*, not from OE *strengþu* or *strengu*, and must further show the generalization of the OE nominative, though the nouns are feminine, not of the oblique cases in *-e*.

15. 'for crafty and sudden is his twist'. The metaphor is from wrestling; so probably with *wiþer-clench* in l. 12. The word *vox* is apparently the noun *fox* used as an adjective; see *OED*, s.v. *fox* sb., sense 2(b), which cites a parallel from the *Ormulum*. I supply *vor* 'for'. The line as given in the MSS is a syllable too short and begins with a stressed syllable; the archetype must have omitted an unstressed word at the beginning of the line. I assume that *vor* dropped out before *vox* by homoearchy.

16–18. 'Never can any man prevail against that, alas, nor [can] threat or entreaty, bribery or cunning, or a physician's potion.'

16. *No mai*] The MSS have *ne mai*, but this line, like l. 11 above, must begin with a stressed word; and considerations of style require the two lines to be parallel. I therefore again substitute the stressed *no* 'never' for *ne*. The examples cited by *OED*, s.v. *no* adv.[1], 1.β, show that ME did not avoid using the adverb *no* and the adjective *no* in the same phrase, as the emended text (*No mai no man*) uses them here.

-toȝeenes] The rhyme is imperfect, but the original cannot have had *to-ȝene*, as Carleton Brown suggests, for such a form did not exist; the word was either *to-ȝen* or *to-ȝenes*, since the *e* was part of the added suffix *-es*.

17. *ne*] only in M, but obviously right; an unstressed syllable is needed at this point in the line.

þreat] The agreement of M as first written with CJ shows that the archetypal reading was *þreating;* the marginal alteration in M must be due to collation with a MS which had L's reading *weping*, which is inferior in sense. But *þreating* (or *weping*) is a syllable too many if we accept M's preceding *ne;* and if we do not, we must stress *þreating* on the second to make it fit metre and music. It seems much better to assume that the archetype had substituted *þreating* for the simplex *þreat*.

18. *meede* 'reward, bribery', from OE *mēd* fem. The form with *-e*, which is normal in ME, is derived from the OE oblique cases.

ne] As this line begins with a dactyl, we must have *ne* before *list*, though MCJ agree in omitting it. L has *ne*, but it is very unlikely that this is a preservation of the archetypal reading; it is probably to be associated with L's omission of *mede*.

list 'artifice, cunning', from OE *list* fem. The normal ME form was *liste*, derived from the OE oblique cases, and MCJ here read *liste* (for which L substitutes the East Midland plural *listes*). But the metre requires a monosyllable. OE feminines did not invariably generalize the oblique form in ME: in this poem we have *strenth* or *streng* in l. 14 (see the note above), established by rhyme as well as metre, *ending* in l. 24, and *world* in l. 43, all derived from the OE nominative. I assume that the poet's dialect allowed him choice between forms with and without *-e*, which he exercised in accordance with the requirements of metre; in this line he has *meede* from the oblique cases but *list* from the nominative. If we read *liste* there is a metrical irregularity requiring modification of the music. See also note to *drink* in l. 8.

19. *let* 'abandon, leave'. The vowel was originally long (WS *lǣtan*, OKt *lētan*) but was often shortened owing to weak stress, and I assume shortening here.

20. *þench* 'think' < OE *þencan*.

21. *Salomones reede* 'Solomon's advice'. The reference is to Ecclesiasticus vii. 40, *In omnibus operibus tuis memorare novis-*

sima tua, et in aeternum non peccabis. The same text is attributed to Solomon in *Ancrene Wisse* (Corpus MS, f. 31b/25).

23. *al so,* written as two words in M, is OE *eall swa* 'exactly as', and the adverb *al* bears the first metrical stress of the line. It is perhaps possible, in view of the stressing, that the author intended *al* to mean 'everything': 'do everything as he taught thee'. But the other MSS treat *al so* as a unit and substitute synonyms meaning 'as' (*ase* C, *as* J, *so* L).

taht 'taught'; the full form of the p.t. sg. is *tahte* (as in C), but the *-e* elides before *and.*

heede] The MSS leave no doubt that the archetype read *sede* 'said', but this makes difficult sense and syntax, for we should have to translate ll. 23–24 as 'Do exactly as he taught thee, and he said what thy end brings thee to', which does not fit well with l. 25, 'never again shalt thou sin'. Sense and syntax require a word meaning 'remember' or 'consider' to correspond to *memorare* in the Biblical text cited (see note to l. 21), and this is provided by the emendation of *sede* to *hede* 'heed' (which in our spelling-system becomes *heede*), for the meaning is then 'Do exactly as he taught thee, and take heed what thy end brings thee to — never again shalt thou sin'. The imperatives are used with conditional force: 'If thou do . . . and if thou take heed . . . thou shalt never again sin'.

There is however the difficulty that the imper. sg. of the verb *he(e)den* 'heed' < OE *hēdan* should be endingless, whereas the rhyming and metre require a form ending in *-e*. It is probably a sufficient explanation that the imper. sg. of the 'regular' verb derived from the OE 2nd weak conjugation (to the pattern of which the conjugation of *heed* eventually conformed) always ended in *-e*; the imper. sg. of *heed* has probably been remodelled as *heede* after such words as *looke* 'look'. One should doubtless also make some allowance for the influence of the pres. t. subj. sg., which was *heede,* especially when the imperative has conditional force. The ME noun *he(e)de* 'heed', derived from the verb, regularly has *-e* from its first appearance (so in the Kentish *Ayenbite*), which would seem to imply that the verbal stem was taken as *he(e)de,* not as *he(e)d*; and it is the verbal stem which is used in the imper. sg. As the emendation to *he(e)de* gives so exactly what sense and syntax require, the difficulty of the accidence is not a decisive objection.

25. ML, which are in agreement except in details of spelling, must represent the reading of the archetype, but it is a syllable short unless we read *nevere* as trisyllabic, and even so the line has only three natural stresses where four are needed. It was doubtless to cure this fault, and to tighten up the connection in sense, that the original of CJ added *þenne* at the beginning of the line; but this scribal emendation cannot be original, and in any case the line must begin with an unstressed syllable. I supply *eft* after *never.* It seems possible that in the exemplar of the archetype *never* was spelt *nefre,* probably with the *-re* expressed by the conventional abbreviation, and that *eft* dropped out after *nef'* by a form of homeoteleuton.

26–8. 'Sorely thou mayest fear for thyself, alas, such as [i.e. thou who] expectest to lead well a long life and to enjoy pleasures.'

The MSS all have *wenþ* (*weneð,* &c.) for *weenst* in l. 27, *his* for *þi* in l. 29, and *him* for *þee* in l. 30, i.e. from l. 27 onwards the archetype had the forms of the 3rd person singular. But this leaves l. 26, in which MCJ have *þu miht* 'thou mayest', entirely isolated and with little or no meaning in the context — which is

probably why the line was omitted in L. I assume that from l. 26 onwards was intended to be a single sentence meaning that such a person as expects to have a long and pleasant life may well fear for himself; and the only question is then whether it was originally in the 2nd or 3rd person. The former is consistent with the style of the poem; moreover the archetype is unlikely to have got the beginning of the sentence wrong. What I think put the scribe of the archetype off the track was the use in l. 27 of *swich* to mean 'such as' (for which see *OED,* s.v. *such* dem. adj., sense 6(b)); he did not recognize this rare use and took the word in its ordinary demonstrative sense, i.e. to mean 'such a one', and therefore changed all the subsequent forms to the 3rd person.

28. *blissen*] *blisse* MSS, but two syllables are needed for metre and the final *-e* of *blisse* should elide before *undervoo,* since any sense-pause comes after *lif.* I assume that the original used the Southern (and Kentish) plural *blissen* to prevent elision, and that the archetype substituted *blisse,* the ordinary plural form (but commonly, in ME, indistinguishable from the singular).

29–30. 'where Death lurks in thy shoe to destroy thee'. Carleton Brown cites the parallel, 'Deth is hud, mon, in þy gloue' from one of the friar William Herebert's poems (Brown, *Religious Lyrics of the XIVth Century,* no. 23, l. 31) which I should think is influenced by the present song. Herebert's use of the 2nd person is some support for the emendation adopted here.

29. *þeer* 'there' (but in this instance used as a relative, 'where'), from OKt *þēr,* WS *þōer.* I assume a long vowel (Kentish *ẹ̄,* which we spell *ee*) when the word is used in isolation or is stressed (as in *þeertoȝeenes* in l. 16), but not when it is unstressed, as in *þervore.*

luteþ 'lurks' < OE *lūtaþ.*

ssoo 'shoe'. The archetype must have had the spelling *so* (or perhaps *soo,* as in L), for this alone will account for M's corruption *swo* 'so'. The original of CJ correctly interpreted the form and normalized it to *scho.*

30. *to þee vordo*] M's reading *to him fordo* must represent the archetype; L's *do him fordo* in essentials supports M and shows that the 'split infinitive' (which the scansion requires) stood in their common original. CJ, in lengthening the line, remove this feature of the syntax. On the emendation of *him* to *þee* see above.

31. *neltu* 'wilt thou'; M preserves the Kentish form.

þee bicnowe 'recognize thyself', i.e. acknowledge your own nature, confess your vices.

32. *þee bisi* 'consider thyself'. *Bisi* is a Kentish form of *bisee,* from OKt *bisīon* for general OE *bisēon*; similarly *bi* < OKt *bīon* (l. 34), *þri* < OKt *þrīo* (l. 35), *fi* < OKt *fīon* (l. 39), and *gli* < OKt *glīo* (l. 40). For the particular reason for restoring these Kentish forms, against the MSS, see the discussion of the original dialect in the general comment on the text, above. M's original spelling *bisun* at this point, and his *bun* in l. 34, involve the Southern and Western use of *u* for the rounded vowel [ø:] derived from OE *ēo,* for which CJ have the more usual thirteenth-century West Midland *eo.*

33. *velþe* 'filth'; both M and L preserve South-eastern *ĕ* < OE *y̆.*

erst 'first'. I supply the word; the line as given in the MSS is a syllable short, and the sense is improved by the addition, since the point is that man first begins in 'filth' and ends as 'worm's food'. The ideas are conventional. The omission of *erst* would be more easily explicable if the exemplar of the archetype had used the spelling *ert* (as in M) for *art*; but the latter is the Kentish form.

34. *wermes* 'worm's', the South-eastern form of OE *wrm*, preserved by L. M originally wrote *wirmes*, the East Midland form, but then wrote *e* over *i*; it is not clear whether the final result is to be read *weirmes*, or the *e* is to be taken as a substitute for the *i*, but in either event it seems likely that M's exemplar had *e*.

mete 'food', the original general sense of the word. This is M's reading, where LCJ have *fode*; M is more likely to represent the original.

35. *nafstu* 'thou hast not'. The disyllabic form is required by the metre.
daies þri 'for three days', i.e. even for three whole days.

36. *drihst* 'endurest, spendest'. M has *drist*, but this is probably an East Midland form based on the ME infinitive *drien*, and is unlikely to have been Kentish. I assume a form from OKt *drihst* developed by palatal mutation from OKt *driohst*: either *dricst* or *drihst* is possible.
wowe 'woe' < the OE variant *wāwa* (see *OED*, s.v. *wowe*). But L's *wouge* shows that the scribe misinterpreted it as a form from OE *wōh* 'evil'.

37–8. M's *þrowen dun* certainly preserves the word-order intended, though Carleton Brown, as unprepared as the scribe of the original of LCJ for the run-on line, emends the one MS that gives the correct text. Run-on sense is in fact reasonably common in ME verse; *Havelok* has examples exactly the same as this, and ll. 27–8 above are a partial parallel.

38. *weendest*] The MSS read *wenest*, but (i) in Kentish the 2 sg. pres. indic. of this verb should be contracted, as in the *Ayenbite* (cf. l. 27 above, though this is an emendation for the 3 sg.), whereas the metre here requires two syllables; (ii) the past tense seems to me to give better sense.
heeʒe 'high' adv., < late OE (Kt) *hēge*. The CJ reading *heʒest* 'highest' is attractive, but if it is original we must assume that M and a precursor of L had independently cut down *heʒest sti(e)* to *heʒe sti(e)*. M has *heye ste*. L itself has corruptly *agein*, but this is evidently a substitute for *aʒe*, in turn a misreading of *heʒe*, so that indirectly L supports M.
sti 'ascend' < OE *stīgan*; metre requires the infinitive without *to*, as in M. In L there is a lacuna owing to damage to the leaf, but it evidently agreed with CJ in inserting *to*. The forms *ste* M and *steo* CJ represent a reformation of the infinitive on the model of contract verbs such as *wrēon*, i.e. they are as if from an OE *stēon*; but in this text the reformation may have been directly occasioned by the rhyme-sequence.

39. *ti* is from OKt *tīon* for normal ME *tee* from OE *tēon*, and is here used in what *OED* describes as 'the most usual sense in ME', namely 'proceed', 'go': 'thy prosperity shall pass into misery'. The archetype plainly had here the reading *endi*, which neither scans nor rhymes.

40. *woop* 'weeping'; *gli*, Kentish form of *glee*, 'merriment'.

41. *biswiket* 'deceive', a Southern present tense plural, established by rhyme with the 3 sg. verbs of the following lines.

42. The agreement of MCJ shows that the archetype had

iwis, hi be(o)þ þin ivo

which is a line of the right number of syllables. But as the rhythm required for this line by the metrical pattern, and imposed by the music, is /x/x/x/, the archetype's line involves the stressing on *iwis* on its prefix, which seems impossible; and it is also suspicious, though not impossible, that the second and third metrical stresses fall on the pronouns and leave the verb unstressed. L avoids the difficulty by reading *Man, iwis* at the beginning of the line and *fo* for *ivo* at the end. But though its line scans perfectly, it must be due to intelligent scribal emendation, in view of the MCJ agreement. I do not accept L's emendation because it involves the use of the vocative *man* three times in the one stanza, which seems excessive; but I follow the direction in which L points. For *iwis* I substitute the synonymous adverbial phrase *mid iwisse*, of which the *-e* here elides before *hi*; William of Shoreham attests the currency of *mid iwisse* in Kentish. With L, I substitute *vo* for *ivo*; the *Ayenbite* has *uo(n)* six times beside more frequent *yuo(n)*.
hi 'they'. But the archetype may have had *hie*, the form finally written by the scribe of M.
byeþ 'are'. I substitute a Kentish form for those given by the MSS (which all, however, agree that the inflexion was *-þ*).
þi in the emended line is unstressed and therefore uninflected; cf. the *Ayenbite*, which uses *þi* as the uninflected form before consonants.
vo 'foes', with loss of *-n* from the plural (*y*)*uon* used by the *Ayenbite*, which is developed from OE *gefān* sb. pl. The loss of *-n*, like that of the *i-* prefix, is probably under the influence of the adjective *fo* < OE *fā(h)*; it is proved here by rhyme.

43. The MS readings (*if þi werld* M, *ʒef þe world* CJ; lacuna in L) throw the first stress of the line on to the conjunction *if* (*ʒef*). But this line, to fit the music, must begin with an unstressed syllable, and the most economical emendation is to alter M's *if þi werld* to *if þinë werld*, in which *þine* is the OE nom. sg. fem. of the possessive, used before the feminine noun *werld*. Kentish was a very conservative dialect which retained grammatical gender into the fourteenth century, and the *Ayenbite* shows a tendency to use inflected *mine* and *þine* before feminines (though the instances are accusatives); a century earlier, at the time of composition of this song, there is no difficulty in assuming the continued use of the old inflected nom. sg. fem. when the pronoun was stressed, as it must be here.
sliket 'flatters'; see *OED*, s.v. *slick* vb., which under sense 2(a) records an instance of the absolute use of the verb, in similar sense, from Gower. The MSS agree that the archetype read *þe sliket* 'flatters thee', but metre and music require the omission of the pronoun; presumably the scribe of the archetype did not understand the absolute use and wished to make the verb transitive. But the emendation means that *OED*'s only instance of the verb used transitively in the sense 'flatter' (sense 2(b)) disappears.
The sentence means 'If thy world flatters with prosperity, that is in order to do thee harm'.

45–6. 'Therefore, let desire pass by, man, and afterwards things will be very pleasing for thee'. The present tense *liket* is here used with future reference. The poet is adapting a proverb which also occurs in the Jesus MS of the *Poema Morale*, l. 15 (an interpolated line), in *The Proverbs of Hendyng*, st. 8, l. 7 (ed. G. Schleich, *Anglia* li (1927), p. 252), and twice in the

Ancrene Riwle (Ancrene Wisse); see the note by Hall, ii. 312. For the first of the *A.W.* instances the Pepys MS. (ed. Påhlsson, p. 49) has 'Lete lust ouergo & eft it wil þe lyke, as þe versifiour seiþ', but which 'versifier' the redactor had in mind there is no means of telling.

46. M's text here is *man, and eft it sal þe liken,* which has the right number of syllables and rhythm but does not rhyme exactly; LCJ read (with variations of spelling) *man, and eft hit þe liket,* which rhymes exactly but is defective in number of syllables and in rhythm. The form of the proverb in the Jesus MS of *Poema Morale* (*. . . and eft hit þe likeþ*) agrees with LCJ; M's reading is exactly paralleled in *The Proverbs of Hendyng* (*. . . and eft hit shal þe liken*) and rather less exactly in *Ancrene Wisse* (*. . . ant hit te wule likin,* Corpus MS 32b/14; *. . . ant hit te wule eft likin,* 64b/24–25); but cf. the Pepys MS., which shows independent knowledge of the source. My text follows LCJ for the rhyme but supplies the necessary extra syllable by inserting *wel* where M has *sal.* It assumes that the transmission of the text has been influenced by the various forms of the proverb that were current; that the common original of LCJ omitted *wel,* and that in M's line of descent *wel* was first misread as *wol* (cf. *wule* (*wil*) in *A.W.*), which was then replaced by *sal* 'shall', as in *Prov. Hendyng* (with the consequential change of the rhyme-word from *liket* to *liken*).

47. *wiket* 'serves', a verb formed on ME *wike* 'office, function'; not in *OED.* The meaning of the sentence is 'What a grievous service he does himself who in one hour, or two, earns himself torment for evermore.' Carleton Brown's derivation of *wiket* from OE *wīcan* 'yield, fail', which with its derivatives *gewican* and *onwican* is rare and recorded chiefly in early texts, is improbable.

48. *o* 'one', an analogical form of *oon, on* 'one' modelled on unstressed *a* beside *an* indefinite article and used, like *a,* before consonants. I accept L's form here; the word is metrically unstressed and a monosyllable is required. C's *on* would also do; MJ's inflected *one* is unmetrical.
stunde 'hour'; OE *stund* fem., but here the normal ME form *stunde,* derived from the OE oblique cases, is required, and is given by the MSS. The *-e* does not elide before the *o* of *oþer* because a sense-pause intervenes.

49. *wercþ* 'works'. I substitute this South-eastern form < OE *wȳrcþ* for those of the MSS. L's *a winnet,* though corrupt, may show that a precursor had East Midland *wircþ.*
pine 'torment'. Elision of the *-e* fails at the mid-line pause; cf. *stunde* in the previous line. One could alternatively emend to *pinen* 'torments' (cf. *blissen* in l. 28), but it is unnecessary.

50. The text given is M's. The common original of LCJ appears to have read *man, ne do þu swo,* from which L omitted *man* to produce an attractive line of the right length, and to which CJ added *nowt* before *swo* to produce their characteristically lengthened version of the last line of the stanza. There is little to choose between M and L; but CJ support M in saying that the word *man* originally occurred in the line, and it must go where M puts it.

6b. On hir is mi lif ilong

1

On hir is mi lif ilong
   of wam ich willë singë
and herȝen hirë þeramong
   þat gan us bootë bringë
5   of hellë pinë þat is strong
and brout us blis þat is so long
   al þuruh hir childíngë.
Ich biddë hirë, on my song,
   he ȝeve us good endíngë
10   þau we do wrong.

2

Al þis world hit shal ago
   wið serwë and wið sorë,
and al þis blis we shul forgo,
   nofþink it us so sorë.
15   Þis worldë nis but ur ifo,
   þarfor ich þenchë hennë go
   and do bi godes lorë.
Þis worldes blis nis wurð a slo.
   Ich biddë, God, þin orë
20   nu evermo.

3

Too long habbe ich sot ibee,
   wel sore i me adredë;
iluved ich habbë game and glee
   and eiht and fairë wedë.
25   Al þat is dwolë, wel i see,
   þarfor ich willë sennë flee
   and letë mi sothédë.
Ich biddë hirë me bisee
   and helpë me and redë
30   þat is so free.

4

Þu art hele and lif and liht
   and helpest al mankennë;
þu havest us ful wel idiht —
   þu ȝeve us wele and wennë.
35   Þu broutest dai and Evë niht;
he broutë wou, þu broutest riht,
   þu álmes, and he sennë.
Þu do us merci, levdi briht,
   wen we shul wenden hennë,
40   so wel þu miht.

5

Gelt ich habbë, weilawi!
Senfúl ich am and wrecchë.
Awrec þee on me nu, levdí,
er deþ me hennë fecchë —
45   to nimë wrech ich am redí —
and let me live and amendi,
þat feendes me ne drecchë.
For minë senn ich am sorí;
of þis lif ich ne recchë.
50   Levdí, merci!

COMMENTARY

Sources: see below.

This religious song, which I assume, for reasons stated in the commentary to the previous piece (no. 6a, *Man mai longe lives weene*), to have been intended for singing to the same music, is recorded, without music, in four MSS. (1) London, British Library, MS Cotton Caligula A. ix, f. 246ᵛ (denoted C), and (2) Oxford, Jesus College, MS 29, f. 253ᵛ (denoted J). On these two MSS see the introductory notes to no. 6a above. In them the present piece, no. 6b, immediately follows no. 6a. The Jesus MS, owing to the loss of the leaf which originally followed f. 253, lacks stanza 3 (which in CJ is written as stanza 4) except for its first line, and the whole of stanza 5. (3) Cambridge, Trinity College, MS 323, ff. 81ᵛ–82 (denoted T). This is a thirteenth-century MS and was written by a North-east Midland scribe, for it has examples of *i* for unstressed *e* (thus *lernin, sulin, helpit*, &c.), *sunnin* as the plural of 'sin', and *wissin* (equivalent to East Midland *wissen*) for OE *wissian*. But it was undoubtedly a copy of a West Midland exemplar, for it also has distinctively West Midland spellings, e.g. *gon* 'gan', *wunne* for OE *wўnn* 'joy', &c. In the result there is a curious mixture of West Midland and East Midland features, even within the one word: thus *gomin* 'game', *sunnin* 'sins'. (4) London, British Library, MS Royal 2 F. viii, f. 1ᵛ (on a fly-leaf), in a hand of the late thirteenth century; denoted R. This is a poor and ill-spelt text, probably written by a North-west Midland scribe (cf. *amovnge* l. 3, the use of *ng* for *nk* in *nof þinget* l. 13, *þenge* l. 16, and the corrupt *givvs*, probably for *giv(e) vs*, in l. 9); but there are other forms more characteristic of the SW Midlands, and beside these a good many Eastern forms. This text also has had a complex history.

C and J are as usual descended from a common original. R often agrees with them against T, and in a number of these cases (e.g. ll. 6, 11, and 38–39) T seems to be right, i.e. CJR agree in error. It follows that CJR must have a common ancestor not shared by T, and the affiliations may be expressed as (CJ)R — T. Ordinarily the agreement of T with one or more of the others must be conclusive of the reading of the archetype. CJR constitute only a single witness against T; but as T's line of descent does not seem to have been, in detail, a good one, in doubtful cases more weight is to be allowed to the evidence of CJR.

The archetype, to judge especially from T and R, had some oddities of spelling, especially in regard to the letter *h*, which it seems to have added initially, or omitted both initially and elsewhere, somewhat arbitrarily; it was probably written by an Anglo-Norman scribe. C and J regularize the spelling on a Western basis pretty successfully. Textually the archetype was good, but not perfect; it cannot have been the author's original. In l. 20 all four MSS read *nu and*, which makes the line too long; and in l. 33 they all have *us havest* where *havest us* is required. In both cases the error is one which could arise independently in the two branches of the stemma, but it probably descends from the archetype. Error in the archetype must be assumed in ll. 1 (*is al* for required *is*), 21 (*ich habbe* for *habbe ich*), and 41 (*agult* for *gelt*), for these three lines as given in the MSS have eight syllables scanning as four iambs, whereas the corresponding lines of stanzas 2 and 4 (ll. 11 and 31) have seven syllables scanning as a four-stress catalectic trochaic line; and if the assumption that this song was meant for the same music as no. 6a is correct, it is the shorter trochaic lines of stanzas 2 and 4 (which fit the music) which have the right rhythm, and the longer iambic lines of stanzas 1, 3, and 5 which are wrong. All are easily emended. Elsewhere the archetype would seem to have recorded correctly the words, though not necessarily the forms, of the original. The archetype of this piece was seemingly nearer to its original than that of 6a above, and though this may mean no more than that its scribe was a more careful copyist, it is probably a further indication that 6b was written later than 6a, so that less time had elapsed between the date of composition and the writing of the extant MSS.

Though the stanzas of 6b are the same in general structure as those of 6a and fit the music recorded for the latter, they are rhymed differently and there are considerable metrical differences. In no. 6a seven of the ten lines of the stanza are trochaic, or at least begin with stressed syllables; only the third, fifth, and tenth lines are iambic. In the present poem every line except the first is iambic; it is indeed this prevalence of iambic rhythm which must have caused the corruption in the archetype of the first lines of stanzas 1, 3, and 5 (see above), the lines being re-cast to make them iambic. The altered rhythm means that the words are fitted to the music in a different way; and as part of this re-fitting, three of the lines are shortened by a syllable. The first line is reduced from eight syllables to seven, and the third from nine to eight; each loses its final unstressed syllable, which in effect is transferred to the beginning of the following line. The other line which is shortened is the seventh, reduced from eight syllables to seven and from four stresses to three. The relationship of words to notes is consequently much changed, and it is not until the end of the ninth line that 6b reaches the same point in the music as 6a; only the last line of the stanza coincides exactly in the two songs. It is evident that whether or not the author of 6b knew 6a, his variations from its metre were deliberate contrivances, part of the process of writing words to fit a tune. But the more complex stanza of 6a fits the music better.

The metrical pattern of the present song is then, in syllable-count, 7787887874, rhyming ababaababa; except for the first line of the stanza, the eight-syllabled lines carry the *a*-rhymes, which are masculine, and the seven-syllabled lines carry the *b*-rhymes, which are feminine. The longer lines have four stresses, arranged x/x/x/x/; the shorter lines have three, arranged x/x/x/x, except in the first line of the stanza, which runs /x/x/x/ with four stresses. The short final line is, as in no. 6a, two iambs and rhymes on *a* with the eight-syllabled lines. The end of the stanza is less clearly marked than in 6a, where the last three lines rhyme together. As the music requires, the rhythmical pattern is strictly maintained. There are, it is true, points·in the verses where the natural stressing of a word or a phrase would lead to the substitution of a trochee for an iamb (e.g. l. 42, which begins with *senful* 'sinful', or l. 36, where the sense really requires rhetorical stress on the contrasted pronouns *he* 'she' and *þu* 'thou'); but the music precludes metrical variation, and the author must have intended that, at least in singing, the normal iambic rhythm would be maintained (as is possible — in the case of *senful* by shifting the stress to the suffix). A good deal of artificial suffix-stressing is in fact called for, especially in the final stanza, which is metrically the least successful.

The order of the stanzas varies in T, R, and CJ. As Carleton Brown points out, the variation concerns the placing of the stanza beginning *þu art hele,* which is fourth in T, third in R, and second in CJ; the other stanzas have the same relative order in all four MSS. I take T, the independent MS, to have the right order, for in it the two stanzas directly addressing Mary in the second person singular come together at the end of the song. I assume that in the common original of CJR the stanza *þu art hele* was moved from fourth to third place in order to bring together, as fourth and fifth, those beginning *Too long habbe ich* and *Gelt ich habbe,* which have a superficial appearance of belonging together. But in this order, preserved in R, the stanza *þu art hele*, which is obviously addressed to Mary, is made to follow immediately ll. 19–20, which properly run:

> Ich bidde, God, þin ore
> nu evermo

so that there is a sudden and unannounced switch from addressing God to addressing Mary. To avoid this R re-wrote l. 19, substituting *leuedy* for *ich bidde, God*; but the original of CJ has shifted the stanza *þu art hele* still further, to second place, so that this stanza addressing Mary comes after the first, which speaks of her in the third person and in l. 8 says 'Ich bidde hire, on my song'. But only T's order is really satisfactory.

The text has passed through a Western copy (or copies) before reaching the extant MSS, for Western forms occur not only in the West Midland MSS C, J, and R, but also in T, written by a North Midland scribe. But the original dialect seems to have been that of the South-east Midlands. The rhyme at l. 21 establishes non-Northern loss of -*n* in the p.p. *ibee*, and the *þ*-rhymes in stanza 3 are non-Anglian (see note to l. 27). Those in stanza 4 establish Eastern *ĕ* < OE *ĕo* in *henne* < OE *heonane,* and South-eastern *ĕ* < OE *ȳ* in -*kenne, wenne,* and *senne* < OE -*cynne, wynne,* and *synne*; only in the South-east would these rhymes be good. But in l. 14 T and even the West Midland J and R attest that the archetype had *ĭ* < OE *ȳ* in *nofþink* < OE *ne ofþynce*; the author's dialect may therefore

have varied between *ĕ* and *ĭ* for OE *ȳ*. At l. 46 rhyme requires the form *amendi* 'amend', whence it follows that in the original dialect the OE second weak conjugation retained its separate identity; this implies a Southern (or West Midland) location. But in l. 46 even the West Midland C agrees with T in giving *live(n),* which implies *live* for OE *lifian* in the archetype (though the original may have had *libbe* < *libban*). Metre requires the prefix *i-* in the p.ps. *ibee* (l. 2) and *iluved* (l. 23). The present indicative plural does not occur; *do* (l. 10) and *drecche* (l. 47) are subjunctives. The MS spellings, especially of T and R, suggest that the archetype's forms showed loss of OE *h* after OE *ō* (*brout-* < OE *brōht-,* ll. 6, 35–6; *wou* < OE *wōh,* l.36) and in *þau* 'though' (l. 10), and *w-* for *wh-* (OE *hw-*) in *wam* 'whom' (l. 2) and *wen* 'when' (l. 39); these are Southern or South-eastern features. But the archetype does not seem to have had *v* for initial *f*. The nominative sg. fem. of the 3rd personal pronoun appears to have been *he* in the archetype. There are no words from ON, though the form of the interjection *weilawi* (l. 41) is doubtless influenced by Norse **wei*; the MSS use native forms of the word 'though' in l. 10. The only words from French are *amendi* (l. 46) and *merci* (l. 50), perhaps because the author was consciously aiming at a popular audience. The evidence, though slight, suggests an origin in the extreme South-east Midlands.

The date of composition, in view of the dating of C and J and the fact that their exemplar must itself have been at least two removes from the original, must be before 1275 and probably before 1250. This is consistent with the state of the language, and especially with the fewness of adopted words in an area especially open to French influence.

VARIANTS

Spelling variants are not necessarily recorded.

1 on] CJT in R   hir] hire CJRT   is] is al CJRT   2 wam] R vam T hwam CJ   ich] CJ ic RT   wille] JT wolle R wule C   singe] CJR singen T   3 herȝen] heryen JR herien CT   þeramong] CJT þar amoung R   þat] R þad T heo CJ   gan] R gon CJT   bringe] CJR bringen T   6 and] ant RT heo CJ   brout] R brut T brohte C brouhte J   blis] blisse CJRT   so] T *om.* CJR   7 þuruh] þureh J þurut T þurht C þur R   hir] hire CJRT   childinge] clyldynge R childinke T childinge C childþinge J   8 ich bidde] CJ ic bidde R we biddit T   on] JR one C in T   mi] CJR ure T   song] CJT songe R   9 he] T heo CJ þat R ȝeve us] J ȝeoue us C yef us T gyvvs R   good] god CJRT   endinge] CJR hendinke T   10 þau] T þauh J þah C þey R do] R don CJT   wrong] CJT wronge R

11 þis] CRT þes J   hit] hid T *om.* CJR   shal] schal CJ shaal R sal T   ago] CJ agoo R agon T   12 *lacking in* J   12 wið] C wid T wyth R   serwe] serue T seorhe C sorevve   wið] C wid T wyt R   13 blis] blisse RT lif CJ   we shul] we svvlle R we schule C schulleþ J ic mot T   forgo] CJ vorgoo R forgon T   14 nofþink it] nof þingit T nof þinget hit R ne of þinche it J ne of þunche hit C   us] CJ hvs R me T   15 *and* 18 *interchanged in* R   15 þis] CJT þes R   worlde] world CJRT   but] bute JT bote R butent C   ur ifo] ure ifo CJR ure fo T   16 þarfor] T þarfore CJ þarvore T   ich] CJ ic RT   þenche] CJ þenge R wille T   henne] RT hirne C hire J   go] goo R gon T atgo CJ   17 do bi] CJR lernin T   godes] CJR godis T   18 þis] CJT þes R   worldes] RT liues CJ   blis] T

blisse C blysse JR   wurð] C wurþ J wrd T wrt R   a slo]
CRT al so J   19 ich bidde god] CJ i bidde god T leuedy
R   ore] CJ hore T horee R   nu] nu and
CJRT   evermo] euer mo J eueremo C heuer more T hevre
more R

21 too] to CJRT   long] longe CJRT   habbe ich] ich
habbe CJ ic abbe RT   sot] CRT soth J   ibee] ybee R
iben T ibeo CJ   22-30 *lacking in* J (*leaf lost*)   22 wel] CR
ful T   sore] CR sorre T   i] y RT ich C   adrede] CT
ofdrede R   23 iluved] iluued C yloued R ylouid T   ich
habbe] C ic abbe RT   game] gamen R gomen C gomin
T   and] CT an R   glee] gle RT gleo C   24 and eiht
and] heyte and R and heuir T and prude and C   faire] fayre
RT feire C   wede] C ywede R wedin T   25 þat] C þad T
hyt R   dwole] dvole R dweole C nout T   wel] CR ful wel
T   i] C ic RT   see] seo CT hit nv see R   26 þarfor]
þarfore C þar vor R þerfore T   ich wille] yg wlle R ich þenche
C we sulin T   senne] sunne C ur sunnis T hem R   flee] R
flen T fleo C   27 lete] R alle C *om.* T   mi] my R mine C
ure T   sothede] RT sot dede C   28 ich bidde] C hy bidde
R we biddit T   me bisee] to me biseo C us to seo T þet yss so
free R   29 and helpe me] C helpen hus R þad con wissin
T   and rede] CR and redin T   30 þat is so free] þat is so
fre T þat is so freo C wel hit may be R

31 þu art] C þv eart J þov ert R heo is T   liht] CJ liȝt R licte
T   32 and] CJT þov R   helpest] CJ helpe .. R helpit
T   mankenne] mancvnne R monkunne CJ moncunene
T   33 þu] CJR ho T   havest us] us hauest CJ hvs hauest
R us hauet T   idiht] J idiȝt C ydyyt R idiit T   34 þu ȝeve]
þu ȝeue CJR ho yaf T   wele] T weole CJR   wenne] wnne
R wunne CJT   35 broutest] brovtest R brutis us T
brouhtest J brohtest C   niht] nyht J nyhyt R nith T niȝt
C   36 he] JR heo CT   broute] brovte R brout T brouhte
J broȝte C   wou] T woht C wowe R wo J   broutest] brov-
test R brouhtest J Broȝtest C brout T   riht] ryht J ryhyt R
riȝt C rid T   37 almes] almesse CJT helmes R   he] R heo
CJT   senne] sunne CJRT   þu do] T bisih CJ bysy
R   us merci] T to me CJR   levdi] leuedi JR lauedi
CT   briht] bryht J brytd R brit T briȝt C   39 wen] wene T
hwenne CJ wan R   we] T ich CJ hy R   shul] sulin T shal
R schal CJ   wenden] R wende CJ *om.* T   henne] RT
heonne CJ   40 so] CJR ful T   miht] C myht J mytd R mit T

41-50 *lacking in* J (*leaf lost*)   41 gelt] agult CRT   ich] C
ic T ig R   habbe] CR haue T   weilawi] weilawei C
weylawey R waylaway T   42 senful] sunful CT svnvvl
R   ich] C ic T ig R   and] R an C a T   wrecche] C
wreche T wreg. R   43 awrec þee on me nu] awrec þe nu on
me C bysy to me R þu do me merci T   levdi] leuedi C suete
leuedy R lauedi brit T   44 *and* 47 *interchanged in* R   44
er] C here R ar T   deþ] C deed R det T   henne] T honne
C hvnne R   fecche] C veȝge (*or* vezge) R wecche T   45
to nime] to nyme R do nim þe C yif me þi T   wrech] wreche
C bote R loue T   ich] C ic T ig R   46 and let] R oþer let C
let T   live] liue T liuen C libbe R   47 þat] C þad T þe
R   feendes] fendes T no fend R no feond C   drecche] C
dregche R letten T   48 for] CR of T   senn] svnne R
sunnes C sunnin T   ich] C ic T ig R   49 of] CT þat
R   þis lif] my lif T liues R þis world C   ich] C ic T y
R   recche] CT regche R   50 levdi] leuedi CR lauedi
T   CR *add* Amen *at end*

NOTES

1. If the line is to fit the music of 6a and conform to the metrical pattern of ll. 11 and 31 (which seem to preserve the
intended rhythm of the stanza; see introduction above), the
preposition *on* must be stressed and the pronoun *hir*
unstressed; the rhythm is trochaic. The scribe of the archetype,
evidently expecting iambic rhythm as in the other lines of the
stanza (and perhaps because he was not prepared for the stressing of the preposition) inserted *al* after *is*, converting the line
into an eight-syllabled iambic line. To this pattern he also
adapted ll. 21 and 41; but fortunately the original rhythm is
preserved in ll. 11 and 31, doubtless because they were not
easy to change — indeed, there is no way of making either of
them begin with an iamb.
ilong means 'dependent'.

2. *wam* 'whom', a comparatively early use as a simple relative;
but the word is found thus, governed by a preposition, from the
late twelfth century.

3. *herȝen* 'praise', from OE *hergan, herian*. The word was
originally disyllabic, since the OE *g* (*i*) represented the Gmc.
consonant [j], and disyllabic pronunciations undoubtedly survived in ME; the word scans here as two syllables. JR have the
spelling *heryen*, which is probably intended to show a disyllabic
pronunciation but is ambiguous, since *y* in ME spelling can
stand for vowel as well as consonant; I subsitute ȝ, a specifically
consonantal letter (but in the 'performing' text the spelling
reverts to *her-yen*). *OED* does not record *herȝen* as a ME spelling variant, but it has *heryhen*, in which *yh* is a consonantal
digraph representing [j] and therefore equivalent to ȝ. CT use
here the spelling *herien*, which wrongly suggests three syllables.
þeramong, 'in the course of the song'.

4. *gan . . . bringe* 'brought'; *boote* 'remedy, deliverance'.

5. *of helle pine* 'from the torment of hell'. *Helle* is the old gen.
sg., used to form a virtual compound.

6. *brout* 'brought'; the normal ME *brouchte* or *brouȝte*, but the
final *-e* is here elided, and the forms of the MSS, in this and
comparable words, show that loss of OE *h* after back vowels
was a feature of the spelling of the archetype.
blis] *blisse* MSS, but the scansion shows that in the author's
dialect the monosyllabic form, from the OE nom. sg. *bliss,* was
used, not the disyllabic *blisse* from the oblique forms.
so long 'so enduring'. This is T's reading; CJR omit *so*. But if
blis is a monosyllable (as it must be in l. 13 below), the line is a
syllable short without *so*. Probably the original of CJR omitted
so to compensate for the change of *blis* to *blisse*. T's line in any
case seems to me to run better.

7. *þuruh* 'through', 'by means of'. A disyllabic form
(developed from OE *þurh* by the intrusion of a glide-vowel
between *r* and *h*) is required by scansion; J has *þureh*, but the
archetype is more likely to have had *þuruh*, in view of T's *þurut*.
hir] The MSS have the full form *hire*, but the monosyllabic *hir*,
developed originally under weak stress but used here in
stressed position, is what is needed.
childinge 'child-bearing' is stressed on the suffix, as often.

8-9. 'I pray to her, in my song, that she give us a good end.'
ȝeve is present tense subj. sg., with its *-e* elided. The spelling is
J's, which here preserves an East Midland form (< OE *gefe*),

where C's *ʒeoue* has West Midland *eo* (developed in the infinitive *geofan* < *gefan* and then generalized in the present stem).

10. *þau* 'though'. This is T's form and is likely to be that of the archetype; it shows loss of *h* from ME *þauh* (as in J) < *þah* (as C), an unstressed development of OE *þēah*.

11. *ago* is an infinitive, 'pass'.

12. *serwe* 'sorrow'. The rarer form with East Midland *e* (West Midland *eo*, as in C) as the stem-vowel is likely to be original. For an explanation, see Jordan, § 36, Anm. 3.
sore 'pain, grief', from the OE noun *sār*. The *-e* is the dative inflexion.

13. *shul* is plural of *shal*. The full form was *shule(n)* < OE *scŭlon*, and it is variants of this which CJR give. But the metre requires a monosyllable, and there are two possibilities at this date: (1) the reduced form *shul*, developed under weak stress and then generalized; (2) the singular *shal*, used as a plural. The latter is less likely in a non-Northern text before 1300. T substitutes *ic mot* 'I must', but the plural of the other MSS is more suitable.

13-14. 'and we must forgo all this happiness, however grievously it may displease us (to do so)'. More literally, l. 14 means 'even if it does not displease us so grievously'. For this type of construction, see *OED*, s.v. *never*, 4 (*never so*), e.g. *ne beo þe song neuer so murie* 'however merry the song may be' (*O. & N.*, l. 345). The addition of *never* strengthens the construction but does not change its essential nature; there is probably an ellipsis of 'as in fact it is', thus 'even if the song be by no means so merry [as in fact it is]'.
nofþink it is for *ne ofþinke it*, with elision of both the unstressed *e*'s, and *ofþinke* is present tense subj. sg. of *ofþinken* < OE *ofþyncan* 'displease'.

15. For the scansion of the line, we must either substitute a disyllabic form for the *world* of the MSS, or read disyllabic *buten*. C has *butent* but JRT agree on *bute* (*bote*), of which the *-e* will elide before *ur*. It seems better to replace *world* by a disyllable, since this brings the metrical stress on to *nis* and leaves *but* unstressed, which seems more natural. The choice is then (having regard to the spelling of the MSS) between *woreld* and *worlde*. If we assume that the author's full form of the word was *worlde* (derived from the oblique cases of an OE feminine), then his use of a monosyllable in l. 11 above can be explained by elision before *hit*; whereas if we choose *woreld* here, his use of *world* in l. 11 will be a mere inconsistency.
ur] The MSS have the full form *ure*, but the *-e* elides.
ifo 'foe' < OE *gefā*. This is the CJR reading; T's *ure fo* is equally possible and metrically equivalent.

16-17. 'Therefore I think to go hence and act according to God's doctrine.'

18. *worldes*] so RT; a re-formed genitive singular with *-es* from the strong masculine declension, as in Orm.
slo 'sloe', taken as an example of something valueless.

19. 'I beg, O God, for thy mercy.'

20. It is clear from the MSS that the archetype read *Nu and evermo*, but this is a syllable too many; and it is inconceivable that the author would have contravened the most obvious structural feature of the stanza-form, especially when to do so would have involved a difficult and displeasing variation of the music. We could reduce the line to four syllables by sub-

stituting the contracted form *er* (modern *e'er*) for *ever* (cf. *ermor* 'evermore' in Robbins, *Secular Lyrics,* no. 60, l. 2), but the rhythm of the line would still be wrong; the first syllable, set to a short and unaccented note, must be unstressed, the second, set to a long and accented note, must be stressed, and it would be highly artificial to throw the stress on to *and*. The alternative is to omit *and,* as in our text. The scribe of the archetype obviously thought the sense intended was 'now and in the future' and that the phrase qualified *ore*, i.e. that the poet was praying that God's mercy might be shown him now and in the future. But as emended the two adverbs qualify the verb *bidde,* and this really gives better sense in the context; the poet, having seen the error of his former way of life, now prays constantly for God's mercy. For the sense 'constantly, continually' see *OED*, s.v. *evermore*, sense 2. If the RT agreement means that the archetype read *evermore*, then CJ's *evermo* is a correct emendation made by their common original; the last two lines of the stanza, in this poem, should not rhyme together.

21. The first metrical stress falls on *too*. The inversion of the order of subject and verb, *habbe ich* (which causes elision of the *-e* of *habbe*), is common in a sentence which begins with an adverbial phrase. But the scribe of the archetype, by reading *ich habbe,* prevented the elision and turned the line into four iambs with the first stress on *long,* i.e. he made it follow the same pattern as his text of l. 1, whereas the music requires the pattern shown by ll. 11 and 31.
long] The MSS have *longe,* the full form with the adverbial suffix *-e,* but it elides.
sot 'a fool'. The word is found in late OE and is adopted from medieval Latin *sottus;* see Onions, *Oxf. Dict. Eng. Etym.,* s.v.

22. *i me adrede* 'I fear for myself'.
It is not clear from the MSS what was the author's form of the pronoun 'I'. Normally the MSS give the full form, variously spelt *ich, ic,* or *ig.* So regularly before a vowel (*ich am*) or *h* (*ich habbe*) and in *ich wille.* Before other consonants *ich* etc. remains the norm, but the reduced form *i* (or *y*) occurs sporadically in one MS or another (six times in all), and it is possible that this represents the author's practice. Nevertheless I give *ich* except here, where RT agree on *y*, and in l. 25, where C gives *i*, much against the scribe's normal practice.

23-24. 'I have loved sport and pleasure and wealth and fine garments.'

23. *iluved*] Such a form was normally trisyllabic in ME, but the metre here requires only two syllables; and as the line must start with an unstressed syllable we must keep the prefix *i-.* Though loss of *e* from the p.p. suffix *-ed* did not become common until much later, it is generally accepted by philologists that the process of loss was syncope in phrasal groups (cf. Luick, § 475), and such a phrase as *iluved ich habbe* presents very favourable conditions for the syncope. In particular *luved ich* is a unit with the stress-pattern /x\, and loss of the middle (weakest-stressed) syllable in words with this stress-pattern is attested from early ME (cf. Luick, § 456.2). The conventional spelling used by the scribes often failed to show syncope even in independent words; syncope that occurred only in phrases, i.e. in connected speech, was not shown until the fourteenth century, and then only rarely. But it must have been earlier and more common than the written forms reveal.

24. *eiht* 'property', 'wealth', < OE *ǣht*. The reading is based on R's. C's *prude* 'pride' gives good sense but cannot possibly

account for the readings of the other two MSS which give this line. If we assume that the archetype had the spelling *heite* (for normal *eihte, eiȝte*), this would directly account for R's *heyte;* and it is conceivable that *heite* might be misread as *heu'e*, i.e. as an abbreviation for *heuere*, whence T's *heuir*. It is at least apparent that a relationship exists between R's *heite* and T's *heuir* which makes it impossible to regard C's *prude* as the archetypal reading. It must be a deliberate substitution, in C or its exemplar, for a form which the scribe who made the substitution did not understand.

25. *dwole* 'error, delusion'. The form given is based on R's *dvole*, representing OE *dwola;* as the form with *o* seems to have been rare in ME, it is unlikely to have been introduced by the scribe. C's *dweole* represents OE *dweola; the Eastern equivalent was *dwele*. In R's spelling, *o* is unlikely to be a West Midland spelling for the vowel [ø] < OE *ĕo*.

26. R's corrupt *hem* is perhaps some reason for supposing that the archetype had the South-eastern form *senne* here. In any case the rhymes in the next stanza require *senne*.

27. 'and abandon my folly' (*or* 'my follies'). The suffix *-hede* < OE *hǣdu was feminine, and could therefore be unchanged in the plural in early ME; that the word could be used in the plural is shown by *Cursor Mundi's* phrase *all yur sotthedis* (cited by *OED*, s.v. *sothead*). But as *mi* must be uninflected, though metrically stressed, it is rather more likely that a singular is intended.

C has *sot dede* 'foolish deeds', but its text for the line has been re-written (with *alle* for R's *lete*, which is much more likely to be original). It is a difficulty in C's text that *sot* is uninflected; if it is the adjective *sot* (as taken by *OED*) it ought to add *-e* in the plural. We could assume a compound *sot-dede*, but there is no parallel. If *sothede* is accepted, then OE *ǣ²* in this word is rhyming with OE *ǣ¹* in the rest of the rhyme-words; this is non-Anglian rhyming.

28-30. 'I pray to her who is so generous to give heed to me and to help and advise me.'

28. *me bisee* is an emendation based on C's *to me biseo*, which gives good sense but is a syllable too many, unless *hire* is treated as a monosyllable; but in l. 8, in the same phrase *ich bidde hire*, it is two syllables, and T's altered text treats it as two here. C has substituted the intransitive use of the verb (see *OED*, s.v. *besee*, sense 1(b)) for the transitive (sense 3(b) in *OED*). Both in C and in the emended text, the simple infinitive is used after *bidde*. R re-writes the text here; *þat ys so free* is brought up from l. 30 so as to follow immediately on *hire* (which it qualifies), and the pointless *wel hit may be* is substituted in l. 30. T is also re-written, though less drastically.

31. *hele* 'salvation'.

33. The agreement of the MSS shows that the archetype read *þu us hauest*, which makes the first two feet of the line trochees; the scribe of the archetype, consciously or unconsciously, has made the rhythm of l. 33 parallel to that of l. 31. But the musical setting cannot accommodate a variation of metrical rhythm; we must emend to *þu havest us* to restore the normal iambic rhythm.
us . . . idiht 'made dispositions for us'.

34. *ȝeve* 'gave', 2 sg. past indic. from OE *gǣfe* (WS *gēafe*), with elision of the inflexion *-e*.
wele and wenne 'well-being and joy'.

36. *he broute wou* 'she brought evil'. *Wou* is ME *wouh* (*wouȝ*) < OE *wōh*. That the spelling *wou*, without *h* (as in T), was that of the archetype is shown by R's corrupt *wowe* < OE *wāwa* 'woe' and J's *wo* < OE *wā* 'woe'.

37. *almes* 'alms, charity'. Reduced (here perhaps by elision) to two syllables from OE *ælmesse*, but the scansion requires the normal OE and ME stressing on the first syllable; the second metrical stress of the line falls on *and*.

38. There is here a straight conflict between T's reading *þu do us merci*, adopted in the text, and that of CJR, *Bisih to me*. T's text is adopted because it scans as it stands; if the CJR variant were adopted, we should have to insert *þu* before *levdi briht* to supply the unstressed syllable necessary at that point in the line.
levdi] Here and in ll. 43 and 50 metre requires the disyllabic form of the word, though the scribes write forms (*leuedi, lauedi*) that at least in superficial appearance are trisyllabic.

39. *wenden henne* 'go hence', i.e. die.

40. *so wel þu miht* 'as thou well canst'.

41. *gelt* 'sinned', a South-eastern form of the verb entered by *OED* as *guilt*, q.v.; *OED* cites, under sense 1, from the *Poema Morale*, l. 27, *Al to lome ich habbe igult*. The MSS read *agult* here, which makes the line four iambs; cf. the notes to ll. 1 and 21 above.
weilawi] This form, for *weilawei* etc. in the MSS, is plainly required for rhyme. *OED* does not record *weilawi*, but it does record a twelfth-century *wilawei*; and if *wi* can be substituted for *wei* in the first syllable, it obviously can be in the last. Such interjections are liable to arbitrary alteration.

42. *senful* 'sinful'. Again I substitute *e* for the *u* of the MSS.
wrecche 'wretched', from OE *wrecca*, used as an adjective.

43. I follow C's text of this line, which is obviously superior and makes good though not simple sense; it means 'Avenge thyself on me now, lady', i.e. impose retributive punishment on me in *this* life. But I vary from C's word-order, which puts *nu* before *on me*; the effect is that a heavy stress is thrown on *me*, which I do not think can have been intended. The sense requires the main emphasis to be on *nu*, and this is achieved by bringing it to the end of the phrase, before the sense-pause. The pronoun *me* is better unstressed, as it is in the emended text.

T and R, presumably because they did not understand the true text, both revert, with slight changes, to their texts of l. 38. But as their texts are different, it must be coincidence that they both looked to the same line for a substitute for the one that they did not understand; the occurrence of the word *levdi* must have been the link. Their substitutes for C's text are trite.

44. 'before Death fetches me hence'.

45. The text of the first half of the line is a conflation of R and C. T merely re-writes something which its scribe did not understand; so do R and C, but less unrecognizably. The reconstituted text means 'I am ready to accept punishment'; *wrech* is from OE *wrǣc* fem., 'retributive punishment' (normal ME *wreche*, but the *-e* here elides), and the sense continues that of l. 43. C has obviously mistaken *wreche* 'punishment' for *wrecche* 'wretch' (the word that occurs in l. 42); hence the alteration of the text to *do nim þe wreche* 'Do take the wretch'. But C nevertheless keeps the spelling *wreche* appropriate to

the 'punishment' word, in contrast to its *wrecche* in l. 42. R keeps *to nyme* 'to accept', but substitutes the commonplace (and in the context inappropriate) *bote* 'help, deliverance' for *wreche*, thus reversing the intended meaning.

46-47. 'And let me live and reform, so that fiends may not afflict me.'

46. *and let* is R's reading; T omits *and*, but an unstressed word is needed at the beginning of the line. C's *oþer* 'or' is a substitution forced on the scribe by his change of the previous line; after 'do take the wretch' he could not continue with 'and let me live'.
amendi] This intransitive use in the sense 'to reform oneself' is earlier than any cited by *OED*, s.v. amend, sense 1(c).

47. *feendes* is from T; the alternative *no fe(o)nd* of RC is virtually equivalent, but *feendes* fits the music slightly better.

48. *mine senn* 'my sins'; the normal ME plural is *mine senne*,

but the *-e* is here elided . R has *svnne*, presumably meant as a plural; the other two MSS have unambiguous re-formed plurals (*sunnes* C, *sunnin* T). All three MSS have Western *u* for the vowel, but I substitute South-eastern *ĕ* < OE *ў*.

49. 'I do not care for this (worldly) life.' The inconsistency with l. 46 is only superficial.
þis lif is a conflation of the readings of C and T. Though R is obviously corrupt, it supports T that some form of the word *lif* stood in the archetype; but C's *þis* is preferable to T's *my*, which involves an irreconcilable inconsistency with l. 46. C's *þis world* avoids any clash with l. 46, but can hardly stand against the (partial) agreement of T and R.

50. I do not think the *Amen* of CR is original; it was probably added in the common original of CJR because the song ends with a prayer. None of the MSS give an *Amen* for the companion piece (no. 6a), and T lacks it here.

7. Worldes blis ne last no throwe

1

Worldes blis ne last no þrowë;
    it went and wit awey anon.
Þe langer þat ich hit iknowë,
    þe lass ich findë pris þaron;
5   for al it is imeind mid carë,
mid serwen and mid evel farë,
and attë lastë povre and barë
    it lat man, wan it ginth agon.
Al þe blis þis heer and þarë
10   bilucth at endë weep and mon.

2

Al þe blis of þissë livë
    þu shált, man, enden inë weep —
of hus and hom, of child and wivë.
    [A,] sali man, nim þarof keep!
15   For þu shalt al bileven heerë
þet eiʒtë warof lord þu weerë;
wan þú list, man, upon þe beerë
    and slapst þat swithë dreeri slep,
shaltu have with þee no feerë
20   but þinë werkes on a hep.

3

Al shal gon þat man heer oweþ;
    al hit shal wenden into naut.
Þe man þat heer no good ne soweþ,
    wan othrë repe he wurth bikaut.
25   Þinc, man, forþi, wilstu hast miʒtë,
þat þu þi geltes heer ariʒtë
and werchë good bi dai and niʒtë
    ar þan þu be of livë laut.
Þú nost wannë Crist ur driʒtë
30   þee oskeþ þat he hath bitaut.

4

Man, wi sestu þout and hertë
    o worldes blis þat nout ne last?
Wi þolstu þat þee softë smerte
    for þing þat is unstedëfast?
35   Þu lickest huni of þorn, iwis,
þat sest þi luvë o worldes blis,
for ful of bitternessë it is.
    Ful sorë þu miʒt been ofgast
þat heer despendest eiʒt amis,
40   þarþurw been into hellë cast.

5

Þinc, man, warto Crist þee woutë,
    and do wey preed and felth and mood.
Þinc wu deerë he þee aboutë
    o roodë mid his sweetë blood.
45   Himselven he ʒaf for þee in pris
to beien þee blis, ʒif þu be wis;
biþinc þee þannë, and up aris
    of senn, and gin to werchë good
þarwils timë to werchen is,
50   for siker elles þu art wood.

6

Al day þu miʒt understondë,
    and ti miróur bifor þee seen,
wat is to doon and wat to wondë
    and wat to holden and to fleen;
55   for al day þu sicst mid þin eië
wu þis world went and wu men deië.
Þat witë wel, þat þu shalt dreië
    as oþrë dede, and eek ded been;
þar ne helpþ nowiʒt to leië —
60   ne may no man be deþ aʒeen.

7

Shal no good been unforȝoldë
ne no quedhéd ne wurth unbout;
wannë þu list, man, under moldë,
þu shalt haven as tu hast wrout.
65   Biþinc wel forþi, ich þee reedë,
and clansë þee of ech misdeedë,
þat he þee help at tinë needë
þat so deerë hath þee about,
and to heven-blissë leede
70   þat ever last and failleþ nout.

COMMENTARY

Sources: London, British Library, MS Arundel 248, f. 154 (A); Oxford, Bodleian Library, MS Rawlinson G. 18, ff. 105^v-106 (R); Oxford, Bodleian Library, MS Digby 86, ff. 163^v-164 (D).

Of the three MSS, A represents a distinct textual tradition, as is shown by its detailed readings and its omission of the sixth stanza. R and D obviously have a common ancestor; they both give stanzas 2 and 3 in a wrongly reversed order, and have many detailed agreements in error; but each of them has treated its exemplar with some freedom, as is shown by their variations, occasionally extreme, from one another. As against A, RD constitute only a single witness when they agree; and Napier was undoubtedly right in his view that A was closest to the original. But A is by no means perfect, and the readings of R and/or D are often preferable. My text is an eclectic one, but chiefly follows A; its spellings and forms are mostly taken as a basis, but I vary freely from them, when it seems desirable, for the sake of consistency or to indicate better the pronunciation and scansion.

Both A and R give the music, with some variations in detail. It is of the type which requires syllabic but not rhythmical uniformity, stanza by stanza. The syllabic scheme is 8898999888, and it is clear, from collation of the MSS, that the author kept to his pattern with great fidelity; any apparent variation from it is undoubtedly due to scribal error. Although it was not musically necessary, the author was also very successful in preserving in the later stanzas the rhythmical patterns established line by line in the first, but there are some variations. In ll. 35-37, 39, 45-47, and 49 he uses monosyllabic rhyme-words where the normal pattern has disyllabic, and the unstressed syllable is transferred to an earlier position in the line; and there are other variations from the normal rhythm of that line of the stanza in ll. 43, 53, 63-64, and 68. In total, the rhythm varies from the norms established by the first stanza in only 13 of the 60 lines of the following stanzas, and even so only slightly, in spite of the fact that syllabic regularity was alone essential. There are no variations in stanzas 2 and 3.

Carleton Brown, *Eng. Lyrics of the XIIIth Century.*, p. 201, draws attention to some parallels in the text to the *Poema Morale*, a late twelfth-century work, probably from Essex; and the linguistic features required by metre and rhyme, or shown by spellings (chiefly in A) which may descend from the archetype, strongly suggest that the song was written in the South-east Midlands, probably in the London area. One may point briefly to (1) the contracted Southern forms of the 3 sg. pres. indic.; (2) the inconsistent rhyming of OE $\bar{æ}^1$ on both OE $\bar{e}$ (which is Kentish or Anglian) and OE $\bar{e}a$ (Saxon, but not originally Essex); (3) the rhyming of both $\bar{æ}^1$ and $\bar{æ}^2$ on OE $\bar{e}$, on the face of it a Kentish feature; (4) shortening of $\bar{æ}^2$ to $\breve{a}$ in *last* (l. 32) and *ofgast* (l. 38), which is non-Kentish; (5) Saxon and Kentish $\bar{e}$ < OE $\breve{e}g$ in *aȝeen* (l. 60); (6) sporadic Essex spellings in A; (7) spellings with *e* for OE *y*, chiefly in A (but A also has isolated *u* and *i* spellings); (8) non-Kentish *w* < *ȝ* in *oweþ* (l. 21); (9) *e*-spellings for OE $\bar{e}o$ in all MSS, except sporadically in R. Other features are commented on in the notes. The mixture of features looks like that to be expected in a London text.

The Digby MS is to be dated between 1272 and 1282, and comes from Worcestershire (see Carleton Brown, op. cit., pp. xxviii-xxxii, and B. D. H. Miller, *Annuale Medievale*, iv (1963), 23–57); it may, Brown suggests, 'have been compiled in a house of friars'. The Rawlinson MS belongs to the second half of the thirteenth century; Napier dated it about 1265. On Arundel 248, which is later though it gives the best text, see the introductory notes to no. 12 below. As R and D are separated from the author's text by at least their common ancestor, and as the latter, in view of the corrupted state of its text, is unlikely to be a direct copy of the original, the date of composition must be set back some way from the date of the MSS. In poetic type (almost purely moralistic, and untouched by the newer style of personal and devotional religious poetry) the song is characteristic of the late twelfth century and the first half of the thirteenth; taking into account the style of the music, and the fact that OE *g* has become *w* in *þrowe* < OE *þráge* 'time' (l. 1) and in *oweþ* in l. 21 (as the rhymes show), it was probably written about the end of the first half of the thirteenth century.

For details of earlier editions of the texts of the three MSS see Carleton Brown, op. cit., p. 201. He himself prints A and R, with occasional citation, in his notes, of variants from D. There has been no previous critical text.

VARIANTS

2 it] A hit RD (*and so throughout*)   went and wit] A wit and wend R wint and went D   3 langer] A lengur R lengore D   iknowe] RD knowe A   4 þaron] A þeron RD (*and similarly throughout*)   5 mid] A wid R wiþ D   6 mid] R with AD   serwen] A serewen D sorewe R   mid] A wid R wiþ D   evel] euel D iuel A uuel R   7 atte] A at þe RD   8 lat] A let RD   man] A mon RD (*and so throughout*)   wan] A wen RD (*and so normally*)   ginth agon] A ginneþ agon D ginnet gon R   9 þis] AR þat is

D   þare] hare A   þere RD   10 bilucth] bilocth A
bilouketh RD   at] AR an D   weep] wep A wop RD

11 þisse] RD hese A   12 ine] A in RD   weep] wep AR
woep D   13 of child] AD ant child R   14 A] *supplied*;
om. ARD   sali] A seli RD   nim] A tak RD   keep]
kep AR koep (!) D   15 for] RD *om.* A   al] AR; D *trans-
poses after* for   16 þet eiȝte] þe eykte R þeite A eiȝtte
D   lord þu] A louerd þ(o)u RD   17 man] mon RD *om.*
A   þe] A *om.* RD   18 slapst] A slepest RD   15 at] A
þene D a R   swithe] suithe A swyþe R longe D   dreeri]
dreri AD druye R   19 shaltu] ne salt tu A ne shaltu R ne
schalt þou D   have] haue A haben R hauen D   20 a] A
an RD.

21 man heer] man hier A her mon RD   oweþ] D houet A
howet R   22 al] RD and al A   wenden into] D wenden
to R bicome to A   naut] A nout R nowt D   23 þe man] þe
mon RD þe A   soweþ] D sowet AR   24 othre] A oþer
RD   repe] repen AR repeþ D   wurth] wrth A worth
RD   bikaut] A bicaut D bikakt R   25 þinc] A þenc R
þenk D   wilstu] A wil þu R þe wile þou D   hast] auest A
hauest RD   miȝte] mithe A mykte R miȝtte D   26 þat
þu] AR *om.* D   geltes] gultes D gultus R gulte A   heer]
hier A here R her D   ariȝte] arithe A arikte R to riȝtte
D   27 werche] A wrche R do D   niȝte] nithe A nikte R
bi niȝtte D   28 þan] A þen R *om.* D   live] liue A lisse R
þis lif D   ilaut] ilakt R jlawt D laut A   29 þu] AR for þou
D   wanne] R wene D wan A   ur] ure R oure D hure
A   driȝte] drithe A drikte R Driȝtte D   30 oskeþ] hosket
A asket R acseþ D   he] RD þe A   hath] hauet R haueþ D
þauet A   bitaut] A bitakt R bitawt D.

31 sestu] A seestu R sest þou D   þout] A loue RD   32 o]
A on RD   worldes] RD werldes A   33 þolstu] A þolestu
R þolest þou D   þat þee] þat þe A þat te R þin D   softe] A
so ofte R herte D   smerte] RD ismerte A   34 þing] A
loue RD   unstedefast] AR onnstudefast D   35 lickest]
AD likest R   36 sest] D seist A seest R   luve] loue ARD
worldes] RD werldos A   37 *line omitted by* A; *text from*
RD   bitternesse] D bitternis R   38 ful] AD *om.*
R   miȝt] D mith A mikt R   39 þat] AR for after þat þou
D   heer despendest] hier despendest A despendes here R
spenest þer D   eiȝt] heite A heikte R *om.* D   40 þar þurw
been] werþurh ben R to ben þar þurew A leste þou be
D   cast] A jcast D itakt R

41 þinc] A þenc R þenk D   warto] A warof R werof
D   wroute] AD wroukte R   42 wey] RD way A
preed] prede A prude RD   and] A of RD   felth] felthe
A fulthe R herte D   and] AD *om.* R   mood] mud A mod
RD   43 þinc] A þenc RD   wu] A wou RD   aboute]
abowte D boute A bokte R   44 mid] A mit R wiþ D   his]
RD is A   blood] blud A blod RD   45 himselven] imself
A himself R *om.* D   he] AR ȝe D   gaf] AR ȝaf D   for]
AR *om.* D   in] R ine A his bodi in D   46 beyen] bein A
buge R bugen D   be] AR art D   47 biþinc] A biþenc
RD   þanne] þan A mon RD   up] AR oup D   48
senn] senne A slovþe R slewþe D   and gin] and agin A an
gin R and bigin D   to werchen] D werchen A to worche
R   49 þarwils] A wil R þe wile D   werchen] AD worchen
R   50 siker] A *om.* RD   þu art] AR ich telle þe
D   wood] wud A witles ant wod RD

51–60 *stanza omitted by* A; *text from* RD   51 þu] R þou
D   miȝt] D mikt R   understonde] R understonden
D   52 ti] R þi D   bifor] R biforen D   53 doon] don
RD   and wat] an R wat is D   wonde] wonden R shonden
D   54 and] ant R and wat D   55 þu] R þou D   sicst]
sigst R sist D   mid] wid R wiþ D   eie] egven R eien
D   56 wu] wou R hou D   went] R wend D   wu] wou
R ou D   deie] deiegt R deien D   57 þat wite] R For wite
þe D   dreie] dreigen R deien D   58 as .... been] ase þe
dede and eke ded ben D det al so an oþer det R   59 þer ...
nowiȝt] ne helput nout þer non R ne halt þer no mon D   to]
R for to D   leie] ligen R hahen D   60 may] R mai
D   be] ben D bu R   deþ] D det R   aȝeen] aȝein D
ageyn R

61 shal no good been] scal no gud ben A ne wort no god þer R
nis þer no goed D   unforȝolde] vnforȝolde D unforiolden
altered from unfoþiolden A unforgulde R   62 no quedhed]
no qued A non uuel R non euel D   ne wurth] ne wrth A ne
worth R nis þer D   unbout] A unboukt R vnboust D   63
wanne] R wan A mon wen D   þu] AR þou D   man] A
mon R *om.* D   molde] RD molden A   64 þu] AR þou
D   haven] hauen RD auen A   as] AR so D   tu] AR
þou D   hast] auest A hauest RD   wrout] AD wrokt
R   65 biþinc] A biþenc þe R þenk D   wel] AR mon
D   forþi] AR þerfore D   ich þee] I þe D us ics A hic
R   66 þee] þe RD *om.* A   ech] ecs A þine RD   he]
AD Crist R   tine] A þine RD   68 deere] dere AD dure
R   hath] hauet A haued R haueþ D   about] D bout A
iboukt R   69 and] D an A ant R   heven] euene A
heuene RD   leede] lede AR þe lede D   70 last] A lest
RD   failleþ] faillet A failet R ne faileþ D

NOTES

1. *worldes*] All three MSS here agree on the form with *o*, which
I generalize, though elsewhere A substitutes his normal form
werld.
ne last no þrowë 'does not last for a moment'. *Last* is a contracted Southern form of the 3 sg. pres. indic., answering to an
uncontracted *lasteth.*

2. *it*] RD regularly have *hit*, A regularly *it*; but A often drops
the initial *h* of other pronouns, e.g. *is* for *his, im* for *him.* I
compromise by using *it* when the word is metrically unstressed,
hit when it is metrically stressed.
went and wit 'goes and departs', again Southern contracted
forms. RD read *wit and went*, reversing the order; as there is
nothing to choose between the readings, I prefer A as being
generally more reliable.

3. *langer*] so A, apparently an Essex form with *ă* for OE *ĕ* by *i*-
mutation before a nasal; but the form might be influenced by
the positive *lange* (though one would expect *longe*).
iknowe] RD's form with the prefix *i-* (< OE *gecnāwan*) is
required by the metre, against A's *knowe*; the retention of the
prefix is on the face of it a Southernism.

4. *lass* 'less'; *pris* 'value'.
þaron] A regularly has *þar* 'there', *war* 'where'. These might be
Essex forms with *ā* for OE *ǣ*, but could equally well be due to
unstressed developments.

5. *imeind* 'mingled'.
mid] The forms of the MSS vary inconsistently between *mid,
wid,* and *wiþ*, but suggest that the original had *mid.*

6. *serwen* 'sorrows'; A's form is supported by D.

evel] The MS forms *uuel* R, *euel* D, and *iuel* A show all three ME dialectal developments of OE $\bar{y}$. I choose D's form as being most consistent with the apparent South-eastern origin of the poem, but it may be due to the D scribe, whose use of the spelling may be a personal preference. A's *iuel* runs counter to his normal use of *e*-spellings for OE $\bar{y}$ and may therefore be derived from his exemplar.

7. *atte* is a contraction of *at the*.

povre 'poor'; the final -*e* elides before the vowel of *and*.

8. *lat* 'leaves', a contracted 3 sg. pres. indic.; in vowel the form is also Southern, with ME $\breve{a} <$ late OE $\breve{æ}$ by shortening of $\bar{æ}^1$, where Kentish and Anglian dialects had $\breve{e}$.

wan 'when'; *ginth agon* 'begins to depart'. A's form of the latter phrase is the only one which fits the metre.

9. *þis* is a running-together of *þe is* meaning 'that is, which is'; it is required by the metre, and is correctly preserved by both A and R. It is a remarkable feature of the poem that here and in l. 33 unusual elisions were carefully shown by the spelling; and it is a tribute to A's accuracy that in both places it preserves the abnormal spellings.

þare 'there' (OE *þara*).

10. *bilucth*] A's spelling *bilocth* is ambiguous, but I assume that its *o* stands for *ŭ* by shortening of OE $\bar{u}$ in *bilūcan* (cf. *bilouketh* RD). The meaning is 'encloses, encompasses' — in the context, virtually 'amounts to'.

weep 'weeping'; A's form, against *wop* RD, is supported by the rhyme in the next stanza.

mon 'lamentation' (modern English *moan*).

11ff. The second stanza is displaced in RD to follow the third; that A's order is correct seems to be shown by the echo in l. 11 of the phrase *al þe blis* used in l. 9. Carleton Brown *English Lyrics of the XIIIth Century*, pp. xxv–xxvi, says that this change in the order of the stanzas, and the 'insertion of an additional stanza', in R and D, 'are not variations due to scribal transmission', by which he means that they are due to oral transmission; but this, like most of his judgements on textual matters, is due to a very superficial consideration. The detailed agreements of the MSS in minor features of spelling (cf. the notes to ll. 6 and 9 above) and some of their corruptions (especially R's in l. 58, which is due to misunderstanding of a South-eastern form *dede* 'did' preserved in its exemplar) show that the transmission of the text was by a purely written tradition. It is perfectly possible to transpose and omit stanzas even when one is copying from a written exemplar.

11. *þisse*] dative sg. (originally masculine and neuter) of *this* (OE *þissum*). A has *hese* for *þese*, a new dative formed from the nom. *þes*; *OED* lists *þese* as a feminine dative, but there is no reason in its method of formation why it should be only feminine, and in A it is used with an originally neuter noun. A's unusual form may well be derived from the archetype, but I have preferred RD's normal form *þisse*, in part because *þese* would inevitably look like a plural to most modern readers. *live* is dative sg. of *lif* 'life'.

12. *shalt* bears the metrical stress.

ine (two syllables) is an extended form of the preposition *in*, found both in South-eastern and in West Midland texts. Though given only by A, it is essential for the metre.

13. In syntax the line is parallel to *of þisse live* in l. 11, i.e. it depends on *blis*: 'all the pleasures . . . of house and home, of child and wife'. *Wive* is dative sg. of *wif* 'wife'.

14. The line as given in the MSS is a syllable short. The possibilities of emendation seem limited to two. (1) To substitute for *þarof* the extended form *þaroffĕ*, but this leaves the rhythm of the line irregular. (2) To insert an unstressed monosyllable at the beginning of the line, and so regularize both syllable-count and rhythm. The obvious alternatives are the pronoun *þu* and the interjections *a(h)* and *o(h)*, and we choose *a* as being the likeliest to be omitted (especially as it could be mistaken for the indefinite article, which a scribe might deliberately omit because he judged it to be wrongly used). As the MSS agree, any emendation here presupposes error in their archetype or independent but identical error in both branches of the textual tradition. For the line as emended (but not for the form of the interjection), cf. Carleton Brown, *Eng. Lyrics of the XIIIth Cent.*, no. 82, l. 34:

> ah, feyre leuedis, be onwar!

sali 'miserable', an Essex form for the normal ME *seli* < OE *sǣlig*; though only A gives this form and it is inconsistent with the forms of comparable words in the text (including words in rhyme), it may survive from the archetype and be an indication of the locality of origin, and we retain it for its interest. In syntactical function the word is a weak adjective used with a vocative, and the hypothetical early ME form would be **salie (*selie)*; but the -*e* has been lost in accordance with the principle that unstressed *e* is dropped after $\bar{\imath}$ if the stem-syllable is long.

nim 'take'; RD in fact have *tak*, but A's older word is more likely to be original.

15. *bileven* 'leave, abandon'.

heere (two syllables) is an extended form of *heer* 'here' required by metre and rhyme. The spelling in the MSS is *here*.

16. *þet*] AR have the definite article *þe*, which in A is run on to the following word, since it begins with a vowel. But this is just what should not happen; the metre requires the article to be separate, and in ME, when elision was not desired, it was common to employ the full form *þet* before a vowel. I assume that this was what the author intended, and emend accordingly. It may even be that the word was intended to have demonstrative force: 'that wealth, those possessions', not simply 'the wealth'.

weere (*were* MSS) has Anglian or Kentish $\bar{e} < \bar{æ}^1$, as the rhyme with *heere* and *feere* shows; similarly *beere* 'bier' in l. 17.

17. *list* 'liest'.

18. *slapst* 'sleepest', possibly another Essex form with $\bar{a} <$ OE $\bar{æ}$; but the vowel might be Southern $\breve{a} < \breve{æ}$ by shortening of $\bar{æ}$.

slep] Here the noun 'sleep' has Southern ME $\bar{e} <$ OE $\bar{æ}^1$, shown by the rhyme with OE $\bar{e}a$ in *hep* 'heap'. The variant developments of OE $\bar{æ}^1$ shown by the rhymes in this stanza are most easily explicable in the mixed language of London.

19. *shaltu* 'shalt thou'. All the MSS insert *ne* at the beginning of the line, but there is no room for it in the metre; the line must have only eight syllables, and none of the others can be omitted. I assume independent error in A and the exemplar of RD; to use the negative particle *ne* before the verb in a negative sentence, even though it contained another negative word,

was so normal in ME syntax that scribes were apt to introduce
it when the author had not himself used it.

feere 'companion' (OE *gefēra*).

20. *a*] RD have *an* and may well represent the original, since to
use *an* before *h* was the earlier ME idiom; but in such details I
follow A when there is little or nothing to choose.

21. *heer*] A has the spelling *hier* (also in ll. 23, 26, and 39),
which is found in certain South-eastern (particularly Kentish)
texts and may well descend from the archetype; but I think it
better to normalize, as the significance of the spelling is
doubtful.

oweþ 'owns, possesses'. The frequent concurrence of A and R
in giving *-et* as the inflexion of the 3 sg. pres. indic. (as they do
here) may well mean that it was a feature of the archetype; but
I normalize, as D does. The significance of the form *-et* of the
inflexion is doubtful, but its persistence from late OE
throughout ME suggests that it was a genuine phonetic variant,
not a mere spelling; it occurs especially in Southern and South
Midland texts.

22. I adopt D's form of the line, which alone scans correctly.

naut 'naught'. A and D regularly omit *ȝ* (*gh*) from such words
(cf. *bikaut* 'becaught' l. 24, *wroute* 'wrought' l. 41, etc.), and it is
likely that this was a feature of the archetype.

24. *othre* is plural of *oþer* (*other*), equivalent (here) to modern
others. It is A's reading; RD have the uninflected *oþer*.

repe] an emendation of *repen* in AR; the form without *-n* is
needed to permit elision of the *-e* before *h*. Otherwise the line
would be a syllable too long unless we omitted *he*; but the pronoun is idiomatic and all three MSS have it.

wurth 'will be' (literally 'becomes'); *bikaut* 'ensnared'.

25. *þinc*] so A, regularly; RD equally regularly have *þenc* or
þenk. Theirs is the original form of the verb, but I follow A as
the MS which is generally closest to the archetype.

forþi 'therefore'; here stressed on the second, but on the first in
l. 65.

wilstu] a contraction of *wils þu* 'whilst thou'. The stress is on the
pronoun.

hast] Here and elsewhere the metre requires the contracted
forms *hast* and *hath* (developed from *havest* and *haveth*), but
the scribes (including A) invariably give the full forms. This is
frequently the case in these songs; the contracted forms must
have been in much more common use than one would judge
from the written texts.

26. *geltes*] All three MSS (in A's case against the scribe's usual
practice) give here the South-western spelling *u* for OE *ȳ*, and
it must seem probable that the archetype had *gultes;* but I
substitute *geltes* (used in other poems in A) for the sake of
consistency. The word is the modern *guilts* in the sense 'sins'.

ariȝte 'set right'. A, in accordance with his usual practice, has
the spelling *arithe*, and similarly with all comparable words;
but the rhymes show that in the poet's speech *ȝ* (*gh*) was not
silent after *i*, and I normalize the spelling by adopting D's use
of *-iȝt*. R has the idiosyncratic *-ikt*.

28. *ar þan* 'before'; *þan* in origin is the dative sg. of *that*.

29. *þu* bears the metrical stress; *nost*, a contraction of OE *ne
wast*, means 'knowest not'.

wanne 'when'; the disyllabic form shown by RD is required by
metre, against A's *wan*.

driȝte 'lord' (OE *drihten*, with loss of *-n*).

30. *oskeþ*] *hosket* A; a form of 'ask' with retained long vowel
from OE *āscian*. It is probably South-eastern; cf. Kentish *oxy*
< *ācsian*.

hath] A's spelling *þauet* might be interpreted as a contraction
of *þe* 'thee' (dat. sg.) and *hauet,* meaning 'hath to thee', which
would make good sense ('will ask thee for what he has
entrusted to thee'). But it is characteristic of A that it freely
confuses and interchanges the letters *þ* and *h*; in this poem it
has *hare* for *þare* (l. 9), *hese* for *þese* (l. 11), *þe* for *he* (l. 24, and
perhaps in l. 23), *þar* for *har* (= *ar*, l. 28). In this line A reads *þe
þauet* where RD have *he hauet* (*haueþ*), and it seems best to
assume that in both words *þ* is merely a mistake for *h*. In that
case we must understand 'to thee' in the subordinate clause,
from the pronoun at the beginning of the line.

It looks, from the readings of the MSS, as if the archetype
itself did not show the monosyllabic form of the verb that the
metre requires; perhaps readers and singers were expected to
know that *hath* (or *haþ*) could be substituted where *haueþ* or
hauet was written.

bitaut 'entrusted', a spelling of *bitauȝt* p.p. of *bitechen*
'beteach'.

31. *sestu*] for *setstu* 'settest thou'. The spellings of the MSS,
here and in l. 36, show that *setst* had been reduced to *sest* by loss
of the first *t* and that the reduced form stood in the archetype.
But the spellings with *ei* and *ee* in individual MSS show confusion with the verbs *see* and *sey* 'say'.

þout 'thought'. I prefer A's reading; RD's *loue* 'love' shows the
link between them.

33. *þolstu* 'sufferest thou, dost thou endure', from *þolen* 'to
suffer' (OE *þolian*).

softe] a contraction of *so ofte*, required by the metre and correctly preserved in A.

smerte] so RD; *ismerte* A. If we admitted A's form to the text,
the metre would be unaffected, for the preceding *-e* would
elide. Similarly in l. 40, where A has *cast* but RD have forms
with the *i-* prefix; again metre is unaffected. In l. 3 the metre
proves that the author used a form with the prefix, and it is
possible that he did in ll. 33 and 40; but I do not think we
should assume so when the metre does not require it and the
evidence of the MSS is contradictory. There is moreover no
evidence that the prefix was ever used with the verb *smerten*.

Smerte is the past tense subjunctive of the verb 'smart' used
impersonally, meaning 'to cause pain (to)'. The line means
'Why do you permit that pain should so often afflict you?' i.e.
that you should suffer anguish.

34. *unstedefast* 'transitory'.

35. *lickest* 'dost lick'; R's *likest* is perhaps due to confusion with
the verb *like*.

36. *luve*] The final *-e* is not elided, though the next word begins
with a vowel, because of the mid-line caesura.

37. *bitternesse*] A unfortunately omits this line, and we are
therefore dependent on R and D; R has *bitternis* and D *bitternesse*. But four syllables are needed. D's form will do, providing that we assume failure of elision, though there is no
sense-pause before *it* and we cannot, of course, adduce the
mid-line caesura as an explanation. The extent to which elision
fails in ME verse does not seem to have been carefully considered. Luick, whose distinction of the various cases of loss of
final *-e* is much more precise than that of earlier writers, says

that loss in hiatus before a following vowel or the *h* of weak-stressed words (i.e. loss by elision) is 'almost without exception' in Orm and likewise in later poets (*Hist. Gram.*, § 452); but his statement goes much too far, though it is true enough of Orm. Failure of elision, otherwise than before a sense-pause or at mid-line, undoubtedly occurs; thus *Havelok* has a number of instances in which there is no elision before the final stress of the line (e.g. *Wiltu don mi willë al*, l. 528; and similarly ll. 743, 884, 1145, 1165, 1725, 2235, 2397, 2408). The position is rather that though elision was normal, because it reflected ordinary connected speech, it was not obligatory. Here it seems best to accept D's text. I do not think that we should gain anything by retaining *hit*, the spelling of both R and D; the pronoun is unstressed, and the failure of elision is not made more likely by the use of the full ME spelling.

An alternative solution would be to read, against the MSS, the plural *bitternesses,* which occurs several times in *Ancrene Wisse* (early thirteenth century); there would then be no question of elision. One of the *Ancrene Wisse* instances (Corpus MS., f. 99b/26–7) is miscopied *bitternesse* in the Cleopatra MS. (f. 173/5).

38. *miȝt* 'mayest' (present tense); *ofgast* 'terrified'.

39. *heer despendest*] A's text scans best. The other two show how scribes spoilt metre by changes in word-order.

40. *parþurw been*] My text accepts R's word-order, but replaces its *werþurh* 'wherethrough' by *parþurw* 'therethrough, thereby' on the model of A's *parþurew.* Either 'whereby' or 'thereby' is grammatically possible, but the latter is more usual ME idiom, and A is generally the best text, though it changes the wording and word-order and spoils the metre at this point. *been* is the simple infinitive: 'thereby to be cast into hell'. On *cast* see the note to l. 33 above.

41. *wroute* 'wrought', 'created'.

42. *do wey* 'put away, set aside'.
preed 'pride'. A's spelling *prede* has ME *ẹ̄* (spelt *ee* in my text) from OE *ȳ.*
felth 'filth', i.e. probably sexual lust; A's spelling shows *ĕ* from OE *ў.*
mood 'anger, wrath'. Three of the Seven Deadly Sins are here mentioned.

43. *wu* 'how' (< OE *hwū beside *hū*); *aboute* 'abought', p.t. of *aby, abuy* 'to pay for, to redeem'.

45. *himselven*] This trisyllabic form (from the OE dative sg. *him selfum*) is required by metre; *(h)imself* in A and R must show independent substitution of the alternative form.
ȝaf 'gave', the native form with initial *ȝ (y)*. A has *gaf,* the form with *g* derived from Norse, but this is certainly due to the East Anglian scribe; it would hardly occur in a thirteenth-century text from the London area, for in London the native form was normal until much later. R's apparent support of A is illusory, for R does not use the letter *ȝ* and replaces it by *g* (or by *k*) wherever it occurs; thus he spells *dreien* (or *dreiȝen,* as it must have been in his exemplar) as *dreigen* in l. 57. In the same way his *ageyn* in l. 60 is misleading; it means the same as D's *aȝein* and does not really show the form with [g], which is due to Norse influence.

46. *beien* 'buy' (*bein* A, but two syllables are needed); a South-eastern form based on the 3 sg. pres. indic. *beyeþ* < OE *bygeþ.*

47. *þanne*] *þan* A, but the disyllabic form is needed; elision fails at the caesura.

48. *senn* 'sin' (*senne* A), another South-eastern form. The RD reading 'sloth' (*slovþe* R, *slewþe* D) has much to commend it, especially as we have had three others of the Deadly Sins in l. 42. There is a straight choice between the RD and the A readings. I follow A as the most reliable MS; there is some case to be made for its more general sense.
and gin] Metre and sense require this reading, though no MS exactly gives it. R's *an gin* is probably meant as the two parts of the word *angin,* as Carleton Brown takes it; A and D keep *and* but substitute for the simple *gin* two different forms with prefixes (*agin* A, *bigin* D). The three MSS are independently altering *and gin.* The meaning is of course 'and begin'.

49. *þarwils* 'therewhiles', i.e. 'whilst'. A clearly preserves the original word. In the thirteenth and early fourteenth centuries *therewhile(s)* is recorded only in the East and South-east of England (see *OED*).

50. Only A's form of the line scans; RD omit *siker* and insert *witles ant* after *art,* but this makes one syllable too many.
siker 'surely, certainly'; *elles* 'otherwise'; *wood* 'mad'.

51ff. A lacks this stanza. Carleton Brown *op. cit.,* pp. xxv-xxvi, speaks of the 'insertion' of an 'additional' stanza in RD, but I can see nothing to justify this view; the stanza conforms in metre, style, and thought to the rest of the poem. It is much more likely that A has left it out, whether by inadvertence or to shorten an over-long poem. For the text we are dependent on R and D, neither of which is an accurate copy, and emendation is necessary at several points.

51. *miȝt* 'mayest', as before. *Al day* is rather 'every day', 'always'.

52. Literally 'and see thy mirror before thee'. The idea is that a man can see his own fate reflected in those of others.

53. *to doon* 'to be done'.
and wat] a blend, for smoothness of metre, of the readings of R and D.
to wonde 'to be avoided' (< OE *wandian*). D's *shonden,* a rare verb meaning 'to harm, injure' from the noun *shond* 'shame', is nonsense in the context.

55. *sicst* 'seest', from OE *sihst*; mis-spelt *sigst* in R (probably for *siȝst*). D's *sist* is a new form.
eie 'eyes' (*eien* D, *egven* R). Here and in all the rhyme-words the MSS have *-en,* but the signs are that in the author's language final *-n* had been lost except (i) in monosyllables, (ii) before a vowel or *h* beginning the next word. Cf. in particular *driȝte* (l. 29), where the loss is proved by rhyme. The scribes tend to restore *-n,* but inconsistently.

56. *went* 'goes', a contracted 3 sg. pres. indic., equivalent to Midland *wendeth.*
deie 'die', a word of Norse origin which at this date would not occur in a Southern dialect.

57. *þat wite wel* 'know that well', 'recognize clearly'. I accept R's text, which scans.
dreie 'suffer' (*dreigen* R; D repeats *deien* 'die' from the previous line).

58. '(thou shalt suffer) as others did, and also be dead'. Textually this is a desperate place. Both MSS make sense of a sort,

but neither scans and R does not rhyme. My text is primarily based on D, but accepts R's evidence that some form of *oþer* occurred in the common exemplar of R and D; I assume that D has corrupted *oþre* 'others' to *þe* 'the' because the scribe misunderstood *dede,* a South-eastern form of *did,* as the adjective 'dead'. R on the other hand has evidently taken *dede* as a spelling of *deþ* 'does' (which occurs, spelt *det,* at the end of his line) and has largely re-written the line on this assumption to make it mean '(suffer) death as an other does'.

59. 'There it does not help at all to lie' (i.e. tell lies).
þar] Neither MS has the adverb at the beginning, though they do not agree exactly on its placing; but the metrical scheme requires a stressed syllable at the beginning of this line.
helpþ] metre requires the contracted form, which is suggested by D's corrupt *halt.*
nowiȝt] *nout* R, but the full form is needed for scansion. It presumably means 'not at all', though it could mean 'no creature'; D evidently so took it, for he substitutes *no mon.*

60. 'No man can oppose Death.'
aȝeen 'against'; both scribes gives the normal form with *ei,* but the Saxon form, with ME *ē* (here spelt *ee*) < OE *ē* < *ĕg,* is needed for the rhyme with *been* 'be'.

61. *unforȝolde* 'unrequited'. A has *unforiolden,* with retention of the full *-en* ending of the strong past participle, and for the rhyme-word in l. 52 has correspondingly *molden,* which is perfectly possible (< OE *moldan,* dat. sg.). But the forms without *-n* of RD are more consistent with those used elsewhere. The scribe of A in other places adds *-n* to words in which it was certainly not original; cf. no. 15, l. 4 (MS *greten,* spoiling the rhyme), l. 8 (MS *bicomen,* spoiling metre and rhyme and necessitating an improper form *loven* instead of *love* for the rhyme-word in the line before), l. 41 (MS *biloken,* spoiling metre), and l. 50 (MS *ibunden,* spoiling rhyme).

62. *quedhed*] The RD reading *uuel* (*euel*) 'evil' gives the right number of syllables but a very bumpy rhythm (unless the *ne*

'nor' at the beginning of the line is stressed, which seems impossible); and it is hard to believe that A, the best MS, would substitute the rare word *qued* for the common synonym *evel* if the latter had stood in the archetype. But *qued* will not scan; we must have a word of two syllables. I therefore adopt the derivative *quedhed,* found in differing forms in two early fourteenth-century Kentish writers, William of Shoreham and Michel of Northgate (see *OED,* s.v. *qued*). I assume that A has substituted the simplex *qued,* of the same meaning, either deliberately or by error (homeoteleuton), and that the exemplar of RD translated the rare South-eastern derivative by the ordinary English word *evel* 'evil'. ME poets often, though artificially, put the metrical stress on the suffix *-head* (or *-hood*); it is in favour of the emendation that if *quedhed* is so stressed, the scansion of the line conforms to the norm for the second line of a stanza.

61–62. The sense follows Innocent III's *De contemptu mundi,* lib. iii, c. 15: 'Ipse est iudex iustus . . . qui nullum malum praeterit impunitum, nullum bonum irremuneratum'.

63. *list* 'liest'; *molde* 'mould, earth'.

64. *tu* is a form of *þu* 'thou', with assimilation of *þ* to *t* after *s.*
hast] the contracted form (or alternatively perhaps *hafst*) is required by metre, though it is not shown by the MSS.

65. *reede* 'advise'. In this sequence of rhymes, OE *ǣ¹* (in *misdeede,* and probably in *reede*) and OE *ǣ²* (in *leede*) rhyme with OE *ē* (in *neede*). The obvious explanation is the influence of Kentish, in which alone both *ǣ¹* and *ǣ²* regularly became *ē*; but raising of *ǣ²* to *ē* in Anglian (before a dental?) might also account for ME *ē* in *leede.*

66. *clanse* 'cleanse'; the vowel is *ă.*

67. *tine* 'thine', with assimilation of *þ* to *t* after *t.*

68. The final *-e* of *deere* 'dearly' is not elided because the word stands before the mid-line caesura.

70. *last* 'lasteth', another contracted 3 sg. pres. indic.

8. Fuweles in the frith

Fuwëles in þe frith,
    þe fishes in þe flood—
    and I mon waxë wood.
4   Much sorw I walkë with
    for best of bon and blood.

COMMENTARY

Source: Oxford, Bodleian Library, MS Douce 139, f. 5

This apparently artless little song is playing on the conventions of the medieval love-lyric. It is spring, when the birds in the woodland and even the fishes in the stream mate and are happy; but the poet is suffering the pangs of unrequited love.

The MS has been dated 'c. 1270', and the song was probably composed towards the end of the first half of the thirteenth century, perhaps in East Anglia (see note to l. 3 below).

NOTES

1. *Fuweles* 'birds' (three syllables; *foweles* MS); *frith* 'woodland'.

2. *fishes*] *fisses* MS, with the predominantly South-eastern (especially but not only Kentish) spelling *ss* for OE *sc,* modern English *sh.* Whether the *ss* spelling indicated any difference from the normal pronunciation is debatable; it seems better to normalize in this text.

3. *mon* 'shall' < ON *mon*. The occurrence of this word shows clearly that the poem must have been written within the area of the old Danelaw, i.e. in East Anglia or the East Midlands or the North. If the spelling *ss* in MS *fisses* is original and not due merely to a scribe, East Anglia would seem the likeliest; but the evidence is very slight.

waxe 'grow, become'; *wood* (*wod* MS, and similarly the rhyme-words) means 'mad', here mad with love.

4. *Much*] *Mulch* MS, apparently a confused spelling which blends the full form *muchel* and the reduced form *much*. The metre shows that a monosyllable is intended, i.e. the fully-reduced *much*, not *muchë*.

sorw] so MS. The full form was *sorwe*, but the -*e* is elided before the following vowel. The *w* should be run on to the next word.

walke 'toss and turn', 'roll about' (in his bed, when he should be sleeping); this is the original sense of the verb, though it is comparatively rare in ME.

5. *best*] *beste* MS, with the normal -*e* of a superlative; but here it elides before *of*, and so we omit it.

best of bon and blood is a conventional phrase of ME poetry, meaning in effect 'the best of human-kind', the most beautiful of living beings, and specifically the best of woman-kind.

9. Perspice, Christicola / [Resurrexit Dominus]
Sumer is icumen in / Sing, cuccu, nu

1

[*Resurrexit Dominus.*
Dominus Resurrexit.]
Perspice, Christicola —
 quæ dignacio!
Cælicus agricola,
 pro vitis vicio,
5 filio

non parcéns exposuit
 mortís exicio;
qui captivos semivivos
 a supplicio
10 vitæ donat

ét secúm coronat
 in cæli solio.

2

Sing, cuccú, nu! Sing, cuccú!
Sing, cuccú! Sing, cuccú, nu!
15 Sumer is icumen in —
 lhudë sing, cuccú!
Groweþ sed and bloweþ med
 and springþ þe wudë nu.
 Sing, cuccú!

20 Awë bleteþ after lomb,
 lhouþ áfter calvë cu;
bulluc sterteþ, buckë verteþ —
 murʒë sing, cuccú!
 Cúccu, cúccu!

25 Wel þu singest, cúccu;
 ne swik þu naver nu.

COMMENTARY

Source: London, British Library, MS Harley 978, f. 11ᵛ.

In the MS, the well-known English words are written above the Latin, and this has been taken to mean that the secular English song was written first, and that the Latin was a pious *contrafactum* made later. But the order in which a scribe copies words is not necessarily the same as the order in which they were composed; and the scribe's arrangement may in fact be due to a simple practical consideration. Anyone who has to copy out parallel texts in Latin and English, or for that matter in French and English, will rapidly discover that almost invariably the English words require more space than the Latin or the French. A scribe who writes his Latin or French text first, and arranges the spacing of his musical notes to fit the Latin or French words, will inevitably find, when he comes to write in his parallel English text, that there is not enough room for it;

examples, among the texts here edited, are the Guildhall MS of no. 4 (French above English), and the Arundel MS of no. 15 (Latin above English), in both of which the scribes found it impossible to keep the English text aligned with the French or Latin text and with the music. The sensible thing is to write the English text first, aligning the notes with it, in the assurance that there will then be ample room for the Latin text; this is what the scribe of MS Harley 978 chose to do, with the consequence that he has produced an exceptionally tidy and clear lay-out.

It has also been asserted that the Latin text does not fit the music, but this is nonsense, as our setting shows; in syllable-count the two versions exactly correspond, and the chief difficulty in fitting words to music concerns the English text (see note to l. 25). With more reason it has been remarked that the accentual rhythms of the Latin diverge from those of the English, which would be a fault in words written for music which has itself a strongly marked metrical rhythm; but this is true only if it is assumed that the Latin words were intended by their medieval author to be invariably pronounced with the correct Classical stressing — by no means a safe assumption (see further the notes to ll. 6, 7 and 11). It is important also to recognize the variation of stressing of the word *cuccu* in the English text, on which the fitting of the words to the notes, and the matching of the English and Latin words, depends. In view of the origins of the music (which are learned, not popular), it seems to us that the Latin and English versions were probably written by the same man (doubtless the composer of the music), and even that the Latin may have been written first; and this view may gain some support from an analysis of the stanzaic structure.

In terms of syllable-count both the Latin and the English verses run 75763 76854 66. The structure is rather clearer in the English version; it subdivides into two groups of five lines, followed by a two-line conclusion. The rhyme-pattern of the Latin is less regular and more sophisticated (it uses throughout two-syllable and three-syllable rhymes, whereas the English uses predominantly monosyllabic rhymes), but it is best to analyse its structure similarly, as two groups of five lines followed by a two-line conclusion. If we use x to denote an unrhymed line, and (cc) etc. to denote a line with internal rhyme, the rhyming pattern of the two poems is then:

Latin　　ababb　　xb(cc)bd db
English　xe(ff)ee　xe(gg)ee ee

In the English, the first line of each of the five-line groups is unrhymed, and the third line of each has internal rhyme. These two features also occur in the second five-line group of the Latin; but if differs in not rhyming the fifth line with the second and fourth (owing to the different method used in the Latin to tie in the two-line conclusion with the rhyme-scheme of the rest). An argument for the priority of the English might perhaps be founded on the greater regularity of its rhyme-pattern; on the other hand it might be argued that the rhyme-pattern in the English is a blend of that of the second Latin five-line group (which is chiefly followed) and that of the first (which is followed at the end, in making the fifth line rhyme with the fourth). But the best way of regarding the case is to take the Latin and English words as constituting, metrically, a single composition, in which the rhyme-pattern shifts from that of the first five-line group in the Latin to that of the English, with the second Latin five-line group as an intermediate stage. The two-line conclusion of the Latin is so interwoven into the rhyme-pattern of the preceding group of lines that it virtually forms part of it; but the two-line conclusion of the English stands apart as a separate couplet, two lines of equal length rhyming together (though on the same vowel as runs throughout the English verses) and forming a conclusion to the whole work. Nevertheless the metrical rhythms of the final couplet are more suited to the rhyme-scheme of the Latin than of the English, for the second-last line ends in an unstressed syllable, the last in a stressed; and this would suggest that the metre was originally devised for the Latin and then reproduced, with a deliberately altered rhyme-scheme, in the English. This view of the Latin and English metrical and rhyming structure, as a continuous development leading up to the final English couplet, seems to us to correspond to the musical effect when the Latin and English texts are sung continuously as a single musical composition.

In the MS the *pes* of the English section is given at the end, with precise directions for its method of singing. We print it in italics before the English verses. As was normal, a fitted text is not given for the Latin. But if, instead of vocalizing for the *rondellus* of the Latin section, it is desired to have words to sing, as in the English, then an appropriate phrase, consistent with the possible origins of the musical notes on which the *rondellus* is built, would be *Resurrexit dominus,* which fits the music, has the same rhythm as the words of the English *pes,* and can like them be reversed in order (*dominus resurrexit*) for the second part of the *pes.* The difference in apparent theme between the religious Latin and the secular English song is not absolute; the one is for Easter, in celebration of Christ's death, harrowing of hell, and resurrection, the other proclaims the renewal of life in the spring, of which the cuckoo is harbinger.

In sharp contrast to the other early pieces printed in this volume, and to most of the later ones, the English words are given in the MS in the forms presupposed by the music and the metre (note especially the contrast between *groweþ* and *bloweþ* in l. 17 and the contracted *lhouþ* 'loweth' in l. 21, which is exactly what is required). This remarkable and unusual precision of the text must mean that it was directly copied from the composer's autograph, with unwonted respect for his forms. Nevertheless there are a few slight blemishes, which I have ventured to correct. In l. 23 the scribe used the ambiguous spelling *murie,* which would ordinarily be taken as indicating a trisyllabic form where a disyllabic is certainly required; I substitute the unambiguous *murȝe* with the consonantal letter ȝ (which in the 'performing' text, by modernization, becomes *murye*). In l. 25 the scribe seems to have copied the words in the wrong order (see the note below) and incidentally to have produced a verbal form *singes* which is irregular for his dialect. In l.19 I normalize his spelling *wde* to *wude,* and in the Latin I replace the letter *e,* when it stands for the open vowel developed in medieval Latin from the Classical diphthong *ae,* by *æ.* Otherwise I give the texts in the spellings of the MS, except for distinguishing between *v* and *u.* I add accents to indicate stress.

The forms of the English text are those of a Southern dialect, doubtless that used in Reading Abbey, where the MS was written. The MS is thought to have been completed about or a little after 1240, and the song was probably composed in Reading Abbey about this date. The English linguistic forms can hardly be much later.

NOTES

6-7. These two lines, and the corresponding lines in the English (ll. 20-21), are treated in the musical setting as a single phrasal unit with regularly alternating stressed and unstressed syllables; and it follows that metrical stresses must fall on the second syllables of *parcens* and *mortis.* Similarly *secum* in l. 11 is stressed on the second. These shifted stressings were characteristic of the medieval French pronunciation of Latin, and must also have influenced the contemporary English pronunciation (assuming, as is probable, that the author of the words of this song was a native speaker of English). In ll. 6 and 11, but not in l. 7, the disyllable which is stressed on the second is preceded by a monosyllable. See further the Introduction to the Texts, above, p. 47 ff., and especially pp 49-50 and the footnote there referring to Norberg, *Introduction,* pp. 25-27. To an English poet the use of these shifted stressings in Latin verse might seem a licence comparable with the artificial shift of the stress to such suffixes as *-hood* and *-ness* in English words.

11. The music shows that the rhythm of the line is /x/x/x (see note to l. 25 below); the first stress therefore falls on *et*, the second on the *-cum* of *secum*, though the latter in Classical Latin was stressed on the first syllable.

13-14. These lines are the *pes* of the English version, written at the end in the MS. The poet takes advantage, here and elsewhere, of the naturally level stress of the imitative bird-name *cuccu* to give it metrical stress sometimes on the first syllable (which has doubtless always been the English stressing of *cuckoo* used as a noun) and sometimes on the second (as in French *coucou*). The stressing intended is partly to be determined by the rhythm of the music and of the corresponding Latin line. Normally the word is stressed on the second (as in French); but the English stressing is used in ll. 24 and 25.

Line 13 gives the form of the *pes* to be used by the singer of one of the two parts; he has a musical rest at the end of the whole line, before repeating it. Line 14 gives the form to be used by the singer of the other part (the instruction being that the two shall start singing the *pes* simultaneously); he sings the shorter phrase of the *pes* first and has a rest at mid-line.

15. *is icumen* 'has come'; *icumen* is the past participle.

16. *lhude* 'loudly'. The *lh* spelling represents a voiceless *l* (like the Welsh *ll*) developed from the OE initial group *hl* and retained in conservative Southern dialects in ME. Singers who try to produce *h* followed by *l* will almost certainly get the right sound.

17. *sed* and *med* are from OE *sǣd* and *mǣd*, with *ǣ*[1], which in a Southern dialect gives ME *ę̄* (the open vowel); similarly *bleteþ* in l. 20, from OE *blǣtan*.

18. *wude*] *wde* MS. The letter *w* was newly introduced at this time (in place of the native consonantal letter known as *wynn*), and there was still uncertainty about its use; in particular, as it was in origin a 'double *u*', as its traditional English name still proclaims, it was often thought unnecessary to write yet a third *u* after it in such a word as this.

20. *awe* 'ewe'. The form is a Southern variant of ME *owe* developed, by stress-shift to the second element of the diphthong, from OE *eowu*.
lomb] The vowel is ME *ǭ* (the long open vowel) from late OE *ā* by lengthening before *mb*.

21. *lhouþ* 'loweth', from OE *hlōwan* (cf. note to l. 16). The contracted monosyllabic form shown by the scribe's spelling is required by the music and the metre. The word is unstressed, and the first metrical stress of the line falls on the first syllable of *after*; cf. the note to ll. 6-7 above.

22. *sterteþ* 'starts, leaps, capers'; *verteþ* 'breaks wind'. Initial *v* for *f* is a mark of Southern and West Midland dialects.

23. *murʒe*] *murie* MS. The metre and music show that a disyllabic form is required, i.e. a form developed from OE *myrge* not *myrige*; we substitute *murʒe* as a less ambiguous spelling. The vowel represented by the spelling *u* is [y] (like the *u* in modern French *mur*), the OE sound preserved in Southern and West Midland dialects, but re-spelt in a French way.

25. The musical notation in the MS, as altered by a later hand, distinguishes clearly between long and short notes, and the former regularly correspond to stressed syllables (as is natural, in view of the strong rhythm of the music). The altered notation here shows that the first, third, and fifth syllables are to be sung to long notes, the second, fourth, and sixth to short notes; and though this is not original it is certainly in accord with the composer's intention, as far as the musical accentuation is concerned. The metrical pattern required by the music is therefore /x/x/x. Texts of the *Cuckoo Song* regularly keep the MS reading *Wel singes þu, cuccu*, which readers are doubtless accustomed to scan x/x/x/ to match the following line; but this runs plainly counter to the music, which cannot be altered. If the MS text is kept, in singing the stress must be taken off the first syllable of *singes* and put on the second — a stressing as impossible in OE and ME as it is in modern English. Though the scribe's text is generally very accurate, we are driven to conclude that he has here copied the right words in the wrong order, and that the text should be *Wel þu singest, cuccu*. He has probably followed (though unconsciously) the normal rule of OE and ME word-order that in a sentence beginning with an adverb the verb precedes its subject. But this rule was by no means absolute: thus *OED*, under *well* adv., cites several early instances of sentences beginning with *well*+pronoun subject+verb (e.g., under sense 5, *wel he com bi him* from the *Lambeth Homilies, c.* 1175); cf. also Carleton Brown, *English Lyrics of the XIIIth Century*, p. 25, l. 37, [W]*el þou wost*.

The scribe's form *singes* is an impossible one for his dialect; at this date the 2 sg. pres. indic. ended in *-es* only in Northern dialects, and in the Midlands and South the ending was *-est*. His spelling *singes þu* is a compromise between the contracted form *singestu* and the full form *singest þu*. If we transpose the order of words, so that the metrical rhythm may coincide with that of the music, we must read *þu singest*.

As *wel* is metrically stressed, it was very likely pronounced with a long vowel, for which the appropriate spelling in our system would be *weel*; the *Ormulum*, a little earlier, distinguishes metrically unstressed *well* (with short vowel) from stressed *wel* (with long vowel). But as the length of the vowel is not certain, we leave the scribe's spelling *wel* in the text.

26. *swik* 'cease'; *naver* 'never', a Southern form. The musical notation (as altered) shows that in this line the first, third, and fifth syllables are to be sung to short notes, the second, fourth, and sixth to long notes; its musical and metrical rhythm is therefore different from the preceding line. Both have six syllables, but l. 26 is iambic, l. 25 is trochaic; and similarly the corresponding Latin lines.

III. CRUCIFIXION LAMENTS OF THE THIRTEENTH CENTURY

10. (i) Stabat juxta Christi crucem
(ii) [Stood the moder under roode]

1

Stabat juxta Christi crucem,
stabat videns vitæ ducem
    vitæ valefacere.
Stabat mater, nec jam mater,
5   et quid sit eventus ater
    novo novit funere.

2

Stabat virgo spectans crucem
et utramque pati lucem,
    sed plus suam doluit.
10   Ista stabat, hic pendebat,
et, quæ foris hic ferebat,
    intus hæc sustinuit.

3

Intus cruci conclavatur,
intus suo jugulatur
15   mater agni gladio;
intus martyr consecratur,
intus tota concrematur
    amoris incendio.

4

Modo manus, modo latus,
20   modo ferro pes foratus
    oculis resumitur;
modo caput spinis sutum
cujus orbis totus nutum
    et sentit et sequitur.

. . . . . . stood ho þeerë neeh.

5

25   Os verendum litum sputis
et flagellis rupta cutis
    et tot rivi sanguinis;
probra, risus, et quæ restant
orbitati tela præstant
30   et dolori virginis.

5

Þat leefli leer wiþ spadel schent,
þat fairë fel wiþ scurges rent —
    þe blood out stremed overal.
Skarn, upbraid, and schames speechë,
al hit was to sorwes eechë —
    i wa þu was biluken al.

6

Tempus, nacta trux natura,
nunc reposcit sua jura;
    nunc dolores acuit.
Nunc extorquet cum usura
35   gemitus quos paritura
    natura detinuit.

6

In þat blisful barnes birdë
wrang wes wroht to wimmenë wirdë,
    ac kindë craved nou þe riht.
Þennë þu looh, ac nou þu weep;
þi wa wes waken þat tennë sleep —
    childing-pines has tee nou piht.

7

Nunc, nunc parit, nunc scit vere
  quam maternum sit dolere,
    quam amarum parere;
40   nunc se dolor orbitati
  dilatus in partu nati
    præsentat in funere.

8

Nunc fit mater, sed mæroris,
servat tamen hic pudoris
45   virginalis gratiam;
nam pudicos gestus foris
non deflorat vis doloris
    intus urens anxiam.

9

Triduanus ergo fletus
50   læta demum est deletus
    surgentis victoria;
  læta lucet spes dolenti,
  nato namque resurgenti
    conresurgunt gaudia.

10

55   Christi novus hic natalis
  formam partus virginalis
    clauso servat tumulo;
  hinc processit, hinc surrexit,
  hinc et inde Christus exit
60   intacto signaculo.

11

Eja mater, eja læta!
Fletus tui nox expleta
    lucescit in gaudium.
Nostræ quoque lætum mane
65   nocti plus quam triduanæ
    tuum redde filium.
      Amen.

7

Nou þu moostes, lavëdi, lerë
wimmenë wa þat barnes berë,
  þa bitter and ta balë þrawes;
for in his ded þe wa þu ʒuldë
in childing þat tu þolë schuldë
  þurh modres kindëlikë lawes.

8

Ah, lavdi, þah þu wanges wetë,
þah þee wer wa at unimeetë,
  þi lates weeren lastëles;
þi weep ne wemmedë noht þin hew
þat madë þi leer ful louk and lew —
  swa sari wimman never nes.

9

Al þi karë wes overcumen,
þe þriddë dai þi joië cumen,
  ded and devel driven doun,
hwennë þi sunë uprisen wes
to þinë welë and urë pes —
  blis he broht in ilk a toun.

10

Þi luvë-sunes uprisíng
wes selli lik to his birdíng;
  bitweenë twa is litel schad.
For swa glem glidis þurh þe glas
of þinë bodi born he was,
  and þurh þe halë þurh he glad.

11

Mildë moder, maiden a,
of al þi karë coom þu þa
  hwennë þi sunë risen wes.
Lavdi, bring us out of wa,
of sinnë, of sorwë, of sich alswa,
  to blissë þat is endëles.
    Amen.

COMMENTARY

Sources: English Text: Oxford, Bodleian Library, MS Tanner 169*, p. 175; Latin Text: Paris, Bibliothèque de l'Arsenal, MS 135, ff. 282ᵛ-283ᵛ (see further below).

The Latin text on which this and the next two pieces is based is shown to have been current in England not only by the use made of it by three English poets, but also by its occurrence in MSS of English provenance. The Latin text above is based on that given (with music) in Paris, Arsenal, MS 135, a missal originating in Canterbury; but I have collated the text with Cambridge, St. John's College, MS 111, f. 106ᵛ (which also gives the music and an incomplete text of no. 11 below, but is inaccurate both in the Latin and English words and also, it seems, in the music) and with the edited text given by G. M.

Dreves in *Analecta Hymnica Medii Aevi*, viii. 55-56. Dreves knew the Arsenal MS but at some points he rejects its readings where they seem to me superior. I have followed the Arsenal text except where Dreves's seemed better; I have been guided to some degree by the readings of the St. John's MS and by the translations of the English versions. A list of variants is given below.

The Latin text is a 'regular' sequence, i.e. one in which, under the influence of hymn-form, the same metrical pattern is preserved through every stanza; but a regular sequence differed from a hymn in its music, for in a hymn each stanza was sung to a repetition of the same melody, whereas in a sequence the tune differed from stanza to stanza. The music was such that what was required of the verse-writer was syllabic and not rhythmical regularity, and it is obvious that the Latin text follows without variation the syllabic pattern 887887. But its author seems also to have intended regularity of accentual rhythm, though at the cost of some departures from the stressings of Classical Latin. In l. 24 the stressing of *sentit* on the second illustrates Norberg's rule that a disyllable may be so stressed if it follows a monosyllable. What is more striking is the number of times that trisyllables which should properly be stressed on the second (penult) are in fact stressed on the first and third: *so amoris* l. 18, *natura* l. 36, *dilatus* l. 41, *præsentat* l. 42, *surgentis* l. 51, *intacto* l. 60, and *lucescit* l. 63. Such stressings arose from the medieval French tendency to shift the stress to the last syllable, with the consequence that a secondary stress was also thrown on to the first. Their frequency in this poem may suggest that it was of French authorship, but an English author would be possible, for there is evidence that, under French influence, such stressings were also current in the English pronunciation of Latin. Allowing for them, the Latin poem preserves complete regularity of metre.

The author of the English poem, by contrast, seems to revert somewhat to the earlier, 'irregular', sequence-form. He quite freely allows himself to add an extra (unstressed) syllable to the normal pattern, so that lines that are eight syllables in the norm become nine, and those that are seven in the norm become eight. In ll. 39 and 42 he even adds an unstressed syllable to both the beginning and the end of the line, so that what should normally be a seven-syllable line in fact has nine. But analysis of his text shows that he never allowed himself to forget the basic requirement of sequence-writing, imposed by the fact that the second half-stanza was intended to be sung to an exact repetition of the melody to which the first half-stanza had been sung: the second half-stanza had to mirror the first, i.e. (in this case) the first and fourth lines had to have exactly the same number of syllables, and similarly with the second and fifth, the third and sixth. He allowed his rhythms to vary, unlike the Latin poet, because the type of music did not demand rhythmical regularity; but with the probable exception of l. 65 (see note below), the syllable-count of the lines of the second half-stanza was intended exactly to repeat whatever had been that of the first. But the copyist was not so meticulous. As far as the words are concerned, his text was a very accurate one (only one or two slight changes seem called for); but he was not nearly so careful to use the forms of the words which the metre required, and as a result the intended balance of the half-stanzas was often upset. Yet he has been scrupulous in fitting the music to the words. If, owing to his use of a longer form of a word or to his (not infrequent) failure to realize that a final -*e* before a vowel was to be elided, a line had too many syllables, he adapted the music to the lengthened line, usually by repetition of notes; if a line had too few syllables, a rarer case, he set two notes to a single syllable or, as we assume, omitted a note that had been repeated. His adaptations are revealed, in most cases, by comparison with the music of the corresponding line in the other half-stanza. A little knowledge of or attention to metre, and a greater discrimination in the choice of word-forms, would have made this careful adaptation unnecessary. But there is this to be said for the scribe, that in so adapting the music to the words he was carrying out the intentions of the original musician; for the latter does not mechanically repeat the tune of the first half-stanza in the second, but so skilfully adapts the musical setting to the rhythm and sense of the words as to suggest that the one man both made the English translation and adapted the music.

The MS of the English text is believed to have been written at St. Werburgh's Abbey, Chester, but it is plain from many of the spellings and forms which the West Midland scribe failed to alter that the original was written in a Northern dialect, as Napier (who first printed the English poem) pointed out. I restore Northern spellings throughout my text. It was Napier's view that the language could hardly be later than the middle of the thirteenth century, and this seems to me a well-founded judgement. The metre shows that there has been no phonetic loss of final -*e*; it is regularly preserved except (i) where it is elided before a vowel or *h*, (ii) where special factors caused early phonetic loss in all ME dialects, (iii) when by grammatical simplification an inflexional form with -*e* is replaced by an endingless form; such grammatical simplification was earlier in the North than elsewhere. As phonetic loss of -*e* proceeded rapidly in Northern dialects in the later thirteenth century, this text, in which -*e* is so well preserved, can hardly be later than 1250. But on the other hand the development of a diphthong *au* in *þrawes* and *lawes* (see note to l. 39) is against a date much before 1250. The poem must have been written about the middle of the century, not very much earlier than the date of the MS.

Unfortunately the text of the English sequence is defective; the first four stanzas and their music (except for part of the last line of the fourth) must have been written on the verso of a preceding leaf which has been lost. In order to facilitate comparison with the following two pieces, I number the first full surviving line as 25 (since it corresponds to l. 25 of the Latin original); in Carleton Brown *English Lyrics of the Thirteenth Century*, no. 4, this first full line of the English text is numbered as l. 1. Carleton Brown gives the spellings of the MS, which I modify freely.

The author of *Stond wel, moder* (no. 11 below) probably knew this piece and was in part consciously modifying it. From the way his poem begins one may perhaps guess that the present one began something like

> Stood þe moder under roode
> and biheeld wiþ sari moode
>   hir sonë deyen on þe tree

(or perhaps, in view of the Latin, *þe lard of lif upon þe tree*). We take this purely conjectural first line as our title for the English poem.

VARIANTS (Latin text)

In the following list of variants, A stands for the Paris Arsenal MS, J for the St. John's College MS, and D for Dreves's edited text. For Dreves's authorities, and a very selective citation of variants from them, see *Anal. Hymn.* viii. 56.

2 videns] AD nitens (*after* ducem) J, *but* uidens *is written above the line over* ducem   vitæ] JD mundi A   3 vitæ] *erased in* J   4 mater (*first*)] JD uirgo A   nec jam] JD nec non A   5 et] AD *abbreviation properly used for enclitic* que J (*and so elsewhere*)   6 novit] AD uenit J   8 pati] AD spectans J   11 ista] JD Iua A   quæ] A quo J quod D   14 suo] AJ sui D   16 consecratur] AD conclauatur J   20 pes foratus] JD perforatus A   22 sutum] AJ tutum D   23-4 cujus . . . sequitur] AD modo corpus sic erutum modo quod sit tenditur J   25 litum] AD lutum J   26 flagellis] AD flagello *corrected to* flagellis J   rupta cutis] AD rupto tutis J   27 tot] AD sit J   32 reposcit] A exposcit

D   36 natura] A naturæ D   40 nunc] D et A   43 fit]
D scit A   sed] D vim A   mæroris] A doloris D   44
hic] D hec A   53 nato] A leto D   54 gaudia] A omnia
D   63 lucescit] D lucessit A

The text of J ends at the end of l. 27, at the foot of the page of the MS; presumably it was completed on the recto of a following leaf which has been lost.

In l. 22, the AJ reading *sutum*, literally 'sewn', is evidently used to mean 'pricked' (as by a needle); it seems better than the reading *tutum* 'guarded' which Dreves adopts.

In l. 43, A's reading *Nunc scit mater vim mæroris* (misreported by Dreves) owes *scit* to l. 37 and *vim* to anticipation of l. 47. But *mæroris* is evidently right, for it makes an alliteration with *mater*; moreover the variant *doloris*, adopted by Dreves, is plainly an anticipation of the rhyme-word in l. 47. In the next line (l. 44), Dreves's *hic* is obviously right; it refers back to *mæror* (or *dolor*) in the previous line. A's *hec* (i.e. *hæc*), which refers back to *mater*, was forced on the scribe by his changes in l. 43.

In l. 53, A's *nato* is supported by the alliteration and by *sune* in l. 52 of the English text. Dreves adopts the variant *leto*, which he takes as being for *a leto* 'from death'; it is possible, but far from certain, that this variant may have been responsible for the rendering given by the author of no. 12 below in his l. 50 (*þo he ros fram deth to live*).

NOTES (English text)

24. '. . . she stood there near'. The line lacks three syllables at the beginning; they would have stood, with the rest of the first four stanzas, on the lost page of the MS.
ho] so MS, but the Northern original is much more likely to have had *scho*.
þeere neeh] *þere neh* MS, but in each word the vowel would have been ME *ę̄* (which I spell *ee*) < Anglian *ē* in a Northern dialect.

25. *leefli* 'lovely' (OE *lēoflic*). The MS has *leueli*, but the original disyllabic form is certainly required by the metre.
leer 'countenance' (OE *hlēor*).
spadel schent 'defiled with spittle'. The MS has *spald ischent*, but it is most unlikely that a Northern author at this date would use a past participle with the *i-* prefix, nor is there any other suggestion in the text that he did; the form of the p.p. must be due to the West Midland scribe. But if we reduce *ischent* to *schent*, we must substitute a disyllabic form of *spald*. The latter (recorded by *OED* under *spold*) is a rare metathesized form of OE *spatl, spadl, spaðl* (for which see *OED*, s.v. *spattel*). *OED* does not record a ME *spadel*, but only *spatel*; but the OE *spādl* of the Lindisfarne gloss would give a ME *spādel* in a Northern dialect, and I therefore give this form, though of course the recorded *spatel* would fit the metre equally well.

26. *fel* 'skin'.

27. *overal* 'everywhere'.

28. *skarn* 'scorn', derived from OF *escarn*. The MS has *skoarn*, with the early WMidl. *oa* spelling for ME *ǭ*. The *o* forms of this word are difficult to explain (see *OED*); it looks very much as though the vowel in this early adoption was identified with OE *ā* and so became *ǭ* in the South and Midlands, but remained *a* in early texts. If so, it would also be *a* in the North (though later Northern writers have the *o* form).
schames speeche] *schome speche* MS. *Schome* has WMidl. *o* for Gmc. *ă* before a nasal; *a* would be more likely in a Northern

text. The word appears to be used as an adjective, but there is no parallel for this; it is more probably a genitive, and in the North one would expect the ending to be *-es*. Cf. in particular the phrase *shames death* 'death of shame' used chiefly in Northern texts (*OED*, s.v. *shame* sb., 3(d)). The *-s* of the ending may have dropped off either because of the following *s* of *speeche* (possibly by genuine phonetic simplification, possibly by scribal error) or because the WMidl. scribe has substituted an older inflexional form (< OE *sceame* gen. sg. of *sceamu*).

29. *sorwes*] *sorhes* MS, a WMidl. spelling for more normal ME *sorȝes*. But the rhyme at ll. 39 and 42 shows that the voiced back spirant ȝ must have already become *w* in the author's dialect, and I therefore substitute the later form *sorwes*.
eeche (*eche* MS) 'increase', a noun: 'it was all to the increase of (your) sorrow'.

30. 'You were completely enclosed in misery'.
wa 'woe', a Northern form with retention unchanged of OE *ā*. The MS has *woa*, which is not (as Carleton Brown supposed) a scribal blending of Northern *wa* and Midland *wo*, but a WMidl. spelling with *oa* as a symbol for ME *ǭ*, parallel to *ea* as a symbol for ME *ę̄*. The scribe also uses the simple *o* (thus *wo* in l. 44). But in l. 35 the MS itself retains the Northern spelling *wa*, and so elsewhere in comparable words. I regularize *a* throughout in all such words.
þu] the scribe uses both *u* and *ou* as spellings for OE *ū*; the former is the older and may alone have been used in the original, but I mostly follow the scribe's spellings. The pronoun *þu* 'thou', which is always metrically unstressed in the poem and may have had a shortened vowel, he spells *þu* except for *þou* in l. 62, where I substitute *þu*.
was] the use of this form as 2 sg. past indic. is a Northern feature; normally in ME the form is *were*.
biluken 'shut in, enclosed'.

31. *barnes* 'child's', not in ME a specifically Northern word. The MS has *bearnes* from the normal OE form *bearn*, with lengthening of *ea* before *rn*; but in the North one would expect *barn*, either from Northumbrian *barn* (without breaking) or from *bĕarn* with failure of lengthening, and the MS itself has *barnes* at l. 38.
birde 'birth'. The MS has *buirde*, a WMidl. spelling with *ui* for [y:] from OE *y* lengthened before *rd*; but for the rhyme-word *wirde* in l. 32 the MS itself retains the Northern form.

32. *wrang*] *wrong* MS, again a Midland or WMidl. form.
wes] The rhymes of the poem establish both *wes* and *was* for 'was'. In non-rhyming position I use *wes* when it is metrically unstressed, *was* when stressed; there is some support for this distinction in the MS, perhaps fortuitously, for it has *was* in l. 29, *wes* in ll. 32 and 35 (but *was* in l. 49).
wimmene 'women's' gen. pl. (*wommone* MS).
The line means literally 'wrong was done to women's destiny'. The idea, a very common one, was that the painless birth of Christ was an offence against the natural fate of women to suffer pain in childbirth, and that it had to be paid for in the end by the pains Mary suffered in watching his crucifixion.

33. 'But Nature now demanded its due.' The MS has *kuinde*, another WMidl. spelling.

34. *looh* 'laughed' (< OE *hlōh*); *loch* MS. The MS uses both *ch* and *h* as spellings for OE *h* after vowels (i.e. for modern *gh*); as

h is the normal WMidl. spelling, it is possible that *ch* was that of the original. But I reject *ch* as likely to mislead a modern reader (since it suggests the sound of *ch* in *much*) and normalize *h*. In such words as *looh, neeh, wroht, riht* it is equivalent to the later *gh* and should be pronounced as a spirant.

weep 'wept' (OE *wēop*, p.t. of *wēpan*). The line means 'then you laughed, but now (i.e. on this later occasion) you wept'. The MS has *wep þu* for *þu weep*, an obvious error.

35. *tenne* 'then', with assimilation of *þ* to *t* after *s*.
sleep 'slept' (OE *slēp*, p.t. of *slǽpan, slēpan*).

36. 'The pains of childbirth have now pierced you.'
childing-pines has] *childing pine haues* MS. The scribe sets *haues* as two syllables, but to a repeated note; comparison with l. 33, an eight-syllable line, and its music shows that the contracted monosyllable *has* is required and that the repeated note should be deleted. But in a Northern dialect of this date *has* (or the MS *haues*) can be either sg. or pl.; and a plural sense 'childbirth pains' seems to me preferable to a singular 'childbirth pain'. The plural of *pine* in a Northern dialect would certainly be *pines*. I assume that the scribe has substituted the sg. *pine* for the pl. because he mistook *haues* for a sg. verb — unless indeed he meant *pine* as a plural, a reduction of *pinen*; but the final *-n* was normally kept in the nom. pl. of nouns of this type in the WMidl.

It may be observed that the suspicion arises three times that the MS has omitted a final *-s*, in every case in a word which in the WMidl. did not belong to the *-es* declension (the 'strong' masculine): *pine(s)* here, *schames* (*schome* MS) in l. 28 above, and *sunes* (*sone* MS) in l. 55. In none of these cases is emendation absolutely necessary, providing we assume (here and in l. 55) that elision of final *-e* has failed at the caesura; but in each case emendation seems to me a marked improvement.

tee (*te* MS), a form of *þe(e)* 'thee' with assimilation of *þ* to *t* after *s*.

37. *moostes* (so MS) 'wert obliged (to)'; Northern 2 sg. past indic. of *moot* 'may', 'must'.
lavedi (*lauedi* MS): metre here requires the three-syllable form, a ME modification of *lavdi* < OE *hlǽfdige*, and the word is set to three distinct notes in the music. But in ll. 43 and 64, though the scribe writes *lauedi* and *leuedi*, two syllables only are called for; to fit his wrong three-syllable forms to the music the scribe is obliged to repeat a note.
lere here obviously means 'learn', as often in ME, though it is from OE *lǽran* 'teach'.

38. *bere*] pres. tense pl. The rhyme with *lere* infin. (OE *lǽran*) proves (i) that the poet could if he wished use the Midland plural inflexion *-e(n)* as well as the Northern *-es*; (ii) unless the rhyme is inexact, which is unlikely in this case, the lengthening of *ĕ* in an open syllable to identity with ME *ē* < OE *ǣ*.

39. *þa* 'those', and similarly *ta* later in the line; the latter has *t* from *þ* after a preceding *d*. The Northern forms are kept in the MS.
bale] here used as an adjective meaning 'deadly, dire' parallel to *bitter*, though it is properly a noun. The adjectival use is derived from the common use of the noun as the first element of a compound, e.g. *bale-stour* 'fatal struggle, death-throe', OE *bealo-sorg* 'dirus ægritudo'.
þrawes] *þrehes* MS, obviously an error for *þrahes*, since the rhyme-word in l. 42 is spelt *lahes*. *þrahes* and *lahes* are

WMidl. spellings with *h* for normal ME *ȝ*, and therefore imply *þraȝes, laȝes*. The sense shows that the former is the pl. of the modern *throe* 'pang', of which it is indeed the earliest example. The ME forms of this word are (except in this instance) *prowe*, Northern *þrawe*, and the most probable etymology (though not given by *OED*) is that it is the same word as ME *prowe*, Northern *þrawe* 'time', from OE *þrāg*; the spelling with *h* in our MS really requires an OE word with *g* as the etymon. The sense-development must then be the same as that of *stound*, which passes from 'time, a period of time' to 'a hard time, a period of affliction' and thence to 'affliction, pang, pain' (cf. *OED*, s.v. *stound*, senses 1 and 2). It follows that here OE *āg* in *þrāg* is rhyming with OE *ǎg* in late OE *lǎgu* 'law', but this would be an exact rhyme only when both had become the diphthong *au*, which in turn depends on the development of *w* < ME *ȝ* < OE *g*. OE *þrāg* has become Northern ME *þrāȝe* and thence *þrāwe*, and finally [þrauə] (without further change of spelling); late OE *lǎgu* has become ME *lǎȝe* and thence *lǎwe*, and finally [lauə]. I assume this development, though admittedly the poet elsewhere has inexact rhymes of short vowels with long (see note to l. 43 below), and therefore adopt the spellings *þrawes* and *lawes* appropriate to the stage of development implied by the rhyme.

40–42. 'For at his death you repaid the pain which you ought to have suffered in giving birth, according to the natural laws of motherhood.'

40. *ded* 'death', a form probably due to confusion of the adjective *dead* and the noun; it is chiefly but not entirely Northern. *ȝulde* (so MS) is 2 sg. past indic. of *ȝeelden* 'yield' in the sense 'pay, repay, render'. Here the old form of the 2 sg. of the past indicative of a strong verb is kept; contrast the instances discussed in the note to l. 62 below.

41. *schulde* (so MS), a Northern form of the 2 sg. of the past indic. of *shall*, for normal ME *schuldes(t), scholdest* (cf. *OED*, s.v. *shall*, A. Inflectional Forms, 8). The form *schulde* of the 1 and 3 sg. is used also for the 2 sg.; cf. the note to l. 62 below.

42. *þurh*] *þurd* MS, and similarly *þurt* in ll. 58 and 60. Napier compared the eleventh-century and ME spelling *þurþ*, but this is not in fact the same, though it may be related. I normalize the forms, whose significance is doubtful.
kindelike] *kuindeliche* MS. I substitute the Northern form of the suffix.
lawes] *lahes* MS. See note to l. 39 above.

43. *lavdi*] *lauedi* MS. See note to l. 37 above.
þah . . . wete 'though you wet (your) cheeks', i.e. wept; the idiom is Northern (cf. *OED*, s.v. *wang*[1]).
þah] in a Northern text *þoh* would be more likely, but at this early date *þah* is still possible, and I retain the MS form.
wanges] *wonges* MS, a Midland or WMidl. form.
wete] The sequence of tenses shows that this is past subj., from OE (Anglian) *wētte*, but the spelling and the rhyme show that *tt* has been reduced to *t*; cf. *scho wongys wete* (past t.) in Wyntoun's *Chronicle* (quoted by *OED* s.v. *wang*). Early simplification of double consonants is a Northern feature. But the vowel must have been shortened, and the rhyme is therefore an inexact one between *ĕ* in *wete* and ME *ē* in *unimeete* < OE (Anglian) *ungemēte*. Cf. the inexact rhymes between *lasteles* (with ME *ē* in the suffix) and *nes* in this stanza, and between *wes* and *pes* 'peace' in the next.

44. *þah þee wer wa*] An impersonal idiom, literally 'though misery were to thee', i.e. although you suffered misery. The MS has *were*, but set to a single note (correctly); under weak stress the final *-e* has been lost and the form reduced to a monosyllable. It is 3 sg. past subj.
at unimeete 'to an immoderate degree'.

45. 'Your looks were unblemished.' *Lates* (*loates* MS) is from ON *lát*; *lasteles* is formed on *last* 'blemish' from ON *lǫstr*.

46–7. 'Your weeping, which made your countenance very pale (?) and wan, did not disfigure your appearance.' The sense is hardly self-consistent and is certainly not an exact rendering of the Latin; I take it that the idea is that her beauty was not permanently disfigured, where the Latin says that there was no external sign of her inward suffering.

46. *hew*] *heau* MS, but wrongly; *eau* is a WMidl. spelling appropriate to words with OE *-ēaw*, but *hew* is from OE *hīw*, *hēow*. The sporadic use of *ea* in the MS seems to be due solely to the scribe.

47. *louk*] Apparently, as Carleton Brown took it, a form of the adjective *luke* (preserved in *lukewarm*), the etymology of which is unclear; but if it is from an OE **hlēowc* (perhaps the stem of a verb **hlēowcian*, but hardly **hlīewcian*, as *OED* assumes), this could give in ME both *lewk* (*leuk*) and *lowk* (*louk*), and thus explain the variant forms. *Luke* (from *lewk*) has the sense 'feeble' as a development of 'tepid'; but here it would have to mean 'unhealthy, pale'.
lew is from rare OE *-lǣwe*, *-lēwe* 'blemished, weak', but here apparently 'wan', a sense recorded in the early seventeenth century by Cotgrave.

49. *al*] *ah* MS, but I see no point in the use here of the interjection and assume misreading of the exemplar, probably because of l. 43 above.
kare] If the word were taken as a monosyllable, with silent *-e*, the line would be a regular eight-syllable trochaic line, in conformity with the Latin, and it would be unnecessary, in the corresponding line of the second half-stanza (l. 52), to insert *up-* and to assume failure of elision at mid-line (see the note below). But *kare* (< OE *cearu*) should be two syllables in early ME, and there is no sign of loss of *-e* from such words in this text; in l. 62 *kare* certainly scans as two syllables. Moreover failure of elision at mid-line must be assumed in l. 53 if it is to have nine syllables and match l. 50, whose text and scansion seem to be beyond doubt. I therefore assume that the present l. 49 is to be accepted as having nine syllables (as the scribe also assumed), and that l. 52, which as the scribe writes it has only seven, is to be emended to conform.

49–51. 'Your sorrow was completely overcome, the third day your joy (was) come, death and the devil (were) driven down.'

49. *ded* 'death', as before.

52. *hwenne*] *þwen* MS. Napier compared *þwarle knot* in *Sir Gawain and the Green Knight* for modern Lancs. *wharl-knot*, but this change is from *þw* to *hw* (*wh*), not *vice versa*. The scribe's *þ* is probably a mere error; *þ* and *h* were not infrequently confused.
The line in the MS is two syllables short (see note to l. 49 above) and is identical with the scribe's form of l. 63, which seems suspicious; the author is unlikely to have written two identical lines for different points of the stanza, and it is easy for one of two similar lines to corrupt the other. In l. 63 the

scribe's text is almost what is required; to make it match l. 66 in syllable-count all that is needed is the substitution of *hwenne* for his *hwen* (cf. his own *þenne* and *tenne* in ll. 34–35). If therefore ll. 52 and 63 were not originally identical, it must be l. 52 that has been corrupted by l. 63; and l. 52 is two syllables short of the corresponding line of the first half-stanza. One can be supplied, as in l. 63, by the substitution of *hwenne*, the other by replacing MS *rise* by either *arisen* or *uprisen* (with the full *-en* of the p.p., usual in the North). I choose *uprisen* because (a) it is common in Northern texts (cf. *OED*, s.v. *uprise* sb. and vb. and *uprisen*), whereas *arise* is rare; (b). *uprising* occurs in l. 55 below; (c) *uprisen*, with its stronger prefix, seems to require a stronger caesural pause before it and so to make more natural the failure of the *-e* of *sune* to elide (which must be assumed if there is to be a gain of a syllable). Cf. the failure of elision at mid-line in the next line.

53. *þine*] dat. sg. (< OE *þinum*); so MS.
wele 'well-being' (OE *wela*). On the failure of elision see note to l. 49.

54. *broht*] *brocte* MS, perhaps a miscopying of *brochte*; but I normalize and omit the *-e*, which is elided.
ilk a] *icha* MS, but I substitute the Northern form; it means literally 'every single'.

55 ff. This stanza plays on the traditional idea that just as Christ was born without effect on the intact virginity of his mother, so he escaped from the tomb without trace and without damage to it.

55. *luve-sunes* 'beloved son's' (literally 'love-son's'). The MS has *luue sone*, in which *sone* must be meant as gen. sg. (< OE *suna* gen. sg. of *sunu*); but in a Northern dialect of this date one would expect *sunes*. The WMidl. scribe has presumably substituted the more archaic grammatical form of his dialect.
uprising 'resurrection'. The MS has *uprisinge*, and similarly in the next line *birdinge*, but if the *-e* is pronounced it makes these two lines one syllable longer than the corresponding lines in the second half-stanza, which is contrary to the requirements of sequence-form. The suffix in OE was *-ing* (*-ung*), but was a feminine, and in ME *-e* was added, as normally in feminines, because of the analogy of the oblique cases. In this dialect either the *-e* has never been added, or it has been dropped again by early phonetic loss after a secondarily stressed syllable. In both lines the poet inverts the natural stress and places his metrical stress on the suffix; this was very common in ME verse with words that ended in a suffix that bore secondary stress in normal speech.

56. *selli* 'strangely, remarkably'; *birding* 'birth'.

57. 'Between (the) two there is little difference.' *Schad* (MS *schead*) is the OE neuter noun *(ge)sc(e)ad* 'division, distinction, difference'. For *is* the MS has *his*, perhaps merely an instance of otiose initial *h*, which is common in ME; but the scribe may have thought that *his litel* meant 'his littleness'.

58–60. 'For he was born of your body as a ray of light passes through glass, and he glided through the intact tomb.'

58. *glem*] *gleam* MS, a correct WMidl. spelling (OE *glǣm*).
glidis] so MS, with the distinctively Northern *-is* inflexion of the 3 sg. pres. indic.

59. *þine*] *þi* MS, but the metre requires another syllable. Cf. l. 53 above, and the note.

60. *þurh* (first) 'through' (*þurt* MS).
hale 'whole, unbroken, intact' (*hoale* MS).
þurh (second) 'tomb' (*þurch* MS). The normal ME form is *þruh* (*þruȝ, þrugh,* etc.) from OE *þrūh,* but forms with the *r* transposed to follow the vowel are genuine (see *OED,* s.v. *through* sb.[1], under β forms) and occur *inter alia* in Northern texts; and as this example is earlier than any cited by *OED* I do not like to normalize it. In this word the *u* was long ([uː] as in modern *boot*), in *þurh* 'through' it was short ([u] as in modern *put*).
glad 'glided' (< OE *glād,* past tense of *glīdan*). The MS substitutes the WMidl. form *gload*; this, with its substitution of *schead* in l. 57, completely spoils the rhyme.

61. *a* 'always', a Northern form from OE *ā* (*oa* MS).

62. *coom* (*com* MS) 'came' (< OE *cōm*). In OE, and normally in ME, the 2 sg. past indic. of strong verbs ended with the inflexion *-e,* i.e. in this case it would be *cōme, coome*; but in this Northern text the endingless forms of the 1 and 3 sg. past indic. are used also for the 2 sg. (cf. *was* for normal ME *were* in l. 30, *looh* for *looȝe* or *lowe* and *weep* for *weepe* in l. 34).
þa 'then' (*þoa* MS).

63. *hwenne*] *hwen* MS, but metre and music require an extra syllable.
risen] *rise* MS, but a Northern dialect would have the full *-en* ending of a strong past participle.

64. *lavdi*] *leuedi* MS, but the line must have only seven syllables to match l. 61, whose musical setting shows that it was written by the poet as a short line.

65. If the line is to be metrically regular, the final *e*'s of *sinne* and *sorwe* (*sorhe* MS) must be elided before the following *of,* though this would involve elision over a marked sense-pause. It is possible that this may have been what the poet intended, though if so there would here be a conflict between the poet's intention and that of the musician, who otherwise work in such harmony that we have suggested above that they may have been one and the same man. For in the MS both *sinne* and *sorwe* are set as two syllables, and in addition the scribe puts a dividing line after the two words, corresponding to the sense-pause. As he does this only here, he seems to be deliberately emphasizing that in this case there are to be pauses in singing and that elision is not to occur; the intention is evidently to protract the line and to stress the meaning. There seems no reason to doubt that the scribe is correctly representing the musician's intention. It may also have been the poet's, for deliberately extended lines are sometimes found in Latin sequences; thus in Adam of St. Victor's Easter sequence, *Zyma vetus expurgetur* (conveniently accessible in *The Oxford Book of Medieval Latin Verse,* ed. Raby, no. 164), ll. 16–17 are extended lines which vary from the normal metre and are not matched by the corresponding lines (ll. 22–23) of the answering half-stanza. Adam seems, it is true, to be following the pattern of ll. 13–14 of the earlier sequence *Laudes crucis attollamus* (op. cit., no. 147), which have the same metre and are irregular in the same way; but the examples show that for special purposes there might be breaches of the symmetry of the sequence-form.

On the reasons for replacing MS *sorhe* by *sorwe* see note to l. 29 above.
sich 'sighing, grief'. As the scribe uses *ch* as a spelling for the spirant developed from OE *h* (i.e., in the same phonetic value as the later *gh*), it is possible that his *sich* may represent the later noun *sigh*; but it is not very likely, as *sigh* sb. and verb are not recorded until *Cursor Mundi* (c. 1300). It is more likely that *sich* is a form (with elision of *-e* before *alswa*) of the rare early ME noun *siche,* derived from the ME verb *sichen* 'to sigh', a new infinitive formed on the stem of *sicheþ* < OE *sīceð,* 3 sg. pres. indic. of *sīcan*. It is further possible that the Northern original had the commoner ME noun *sik(e)* derived from the verb *siken,* the direct representative of the OE infinitive *sīcan*.
alswa 'also'; the MS has *al swoa,* but keeps the Northern form *wa* for the rhyme-word in l. 64.

66. *is*] *his* MS.

11. Stond wel, moder, under roode

1

'Stond wel, moder, under roodë,
bihold þi child wiþ gladë moodë;
    bliþë moder miȝtu be.'
'Sun, hu mai i bliþë stondë?
5 I see þi feet, i see þin hondë
    nailed to þe hardë tree.'

2

'Moder, do wey þi weepíngë;
i þole þis ded for mannes þingë —
    for ownë giltë þoli non.'
10 'Sun, i feel þe dedë-stundë;
    þe swerd is at min hertë grundë
    þat me bihiȝtë Simeon.'

3

'Moder, reu upon þi beren!
Þu wash awey þo bloodi teren
15   þat do me wersë þan mi ded.'
'Sun, hu miȝt i teres wernë?
I see þo bloodi floodes ernë
    ut of þin hertë to mi feet.'

4

'Moder, nu i mai þee seyë,
20 beter is þat ich onë deyë
    þan al mankín to hellë go.'
'Sun, i see þi bodi swungen,
þi brest, þin hond, þi foot þurȝ-stungen;
    no selli [nis] þou me be wo.'

5

25 'Moder, if i dar þee tellë,
if i ne dey, þu gost to hellë;
i þole þis ded for þinë sakë.' 45
'Sunë, þu beest me so mindë;
ne wit me nouȝt, it is mi kindë
30 þat i for þee þis sorwë makë.'

6

'Moder, merci; let me deyë
for Adam ut of hellë beyë 50
and mankín þat is forloren.'
'Sunë, wat sal me to redë?
35 Þi pinë pineð me to dedë;
let me deyë þee biforen.'

7

'Moder, nu tarst þu miȝt lerë 55
wat pinë þole þat childrë berë,
wat sorwë have þat child forgon.'
40 'Sun, i wot, i kan þee tellë —
buten it be þe pine of hellë,
morë sorwë ne wot i non.' 60

8

'Moder, reu of moder karë,
nu þu wost of moder farë,
þou þu be clenë maiden-man.'
'Sunë, help at allë needë
allë þo þat to me greedë,
maiden and wif and fool wimmán.'

9

'Moder, mai i no leng dwellë,
þe time is cum i fare to hellë;
þe þriddë day i rise upon.'
'Sun, i willë wiþ þee fundë.
I dey, iwis, of þinë wundë;
so reuful ded was never non.'

10

Wan he ros, þan fel þi sorwë;
þi blissë sprong þe þriddë morwë —
wel bliþë moder wer þu þo.
Moder, for þat ilkë blissë,
biseech ur god ur sinnes lissë;
þu be ur sheeld ayen ur fo.

11

Blissed be þu, queen of hevnë;
bring us ut of hellë levnë
þurȝ þi deerë sunes miȝt.
Moder, for þat hiȝë bloodë
65 þat he shad upon þe roodë
led us into heven-liȝt.
Amen.

COMMENTARY

Sources: London, British Library, MS Royal 12 E. i, ff. 193–194ᵛ; London, British Library, MS Harley 2253, f. 79ʳ⁻ᵛ; Oxford, Bodleian Library, MS Digby 86, f. 127ʳ⁻ᵛ; Cambridge, St. John's College, MS 111, f. 106ᵛ; Dublin, Trinity College, MS 301, f. 194; London, British Library, MS Royal 8 F. ii, flyleaf.

The text of this well-known English sequence is given, in whole or in part, in six MSS. (1) MS Royal 12 E.i (denoted R) gives a complete text, with music (but not for all stanzas); it is of the early fourteenth century, and gives the text in East Midland forms. (2) MS Harley 2253 (denoted H) gives a complete text, without music. It is a Herefordshire MS, and the most recent dating is to the fourth decade of the fourteenth century. (3) MS Digby 86 (denoted D) lacks the last two stanzas and gives no music. It is a West Midland MS (probably from Worcestershire), dated between 1272 and 1282. (4) MS St. John's College Cambridge 111 (denoted J) gives the Latin text of *Stabat juxta Christi crucem* (no. 10(i) above) fitted to the music and, beneath it but not properly aligned with the Latin words and the music, the English text of *Stond wel, moder,* both

texts are given as far as l. 27. As the surviving text is on the verso of a leaf, it is probable that the rest was on the recto of a following leaf which has since been lost. The English text is in the forms of a South-eastern dialect, almost certainly that of Kent, though a Northern or North Midland copy must lie behind the extant MS (see note to l. 23 below). M. R. James, in his *Catalogue of the MSS of St. John's College, Cambridge,* dated the MS 'early thirteenth century', but this seems to refer only to the main part of the MS; the last three folios (105ᵛ-107) contain various short items in different hands, for which he gives separate datings. Item 5 (the Latin and English sequences) he dates simply 'thirteenth century'. It is probably of the late thirteenth century; the English sequence is unlikely to have been written before 1250 (see below), the J text is separated from the archetype by at least four intervening copies, and the linguistic forms of the MS appear to be those of the late thirteenth century or even of the early fourteenth. (5) MS Trinity College Dublin 301 (denoted T) gives a complete text without music. It is of the early fourteenth century, and combines obvious Northernisms with Midland forms; some, and probably all, of its Northernisms must derive from the common ancestor which it shares with J. (6) MS Royal 8 F.ii (denoted F) contains in its fly-leaves extracts from a Latin sermon in which the first stanza of *Stond wel, moder* is accurately quoted (naturally without music). Carleton Brown assigns the date 'about 1300'.

The text of R represents a distinct tradition from that of the other MSS, which have shared errors. Within the latter group, H stands somewhat apart from DJT, and there is a special link between J and T as far as J goes; though their final dialectal colouring is very different, both derive from a Northern intermediary, T perhaps directly, J through at least one intervening copy. The affiliations may be expressed as R — H[D(JT)]. Ordinarily agreement of R with one or more of HDJT must be conclusive of the archetypal text. But the archetype was itself a copy and not fully accurate; cf. the notes to ll. 15 and 24 below, amongst others. At certain points H, D, and T vary so markedly from the text given by R (supported sometimes by other MSS) that it is clear that there has been deliberate re-writing, in most cases confined either to H or D but in a couple of instances shared with T; this re-writing has taken place at various stages in the descent of the HDJT group. Nevertheless I judge that the text was transmitted in writing rather than orally; the variations seem those characteristic of a written tradition (except where there is this deliberate revision), and some of the textual errors seem plainly due to the misreading of copy. R gives the most reliable text; the next most useful is H, despite its comparatively late date. T has some strange corruptions and confusions, but is nevertheless very useful, especially in confirming R's text against H's in the last two stanzas, where only these three MSS are running.

The English poet of *Stond wel, moder* may have been influenced, in his adoption of the form of a dialogue between Christ and Mary, by the Latin dialogues between Mary and St. Anselm or between Mary and St. Bernard to which Carleton Brown refers (*English Lyrics of the XIIIth Century*, p. 204), but his direct model was the eleven-stanza Latin sequence *Stabat juxta Christi crucem* (no. 10(i) above). The obvious demonstration is that the music of the English sequence is an adaptation of that of the Latin; indeed the J scribe tries to fit the Latin and English words to the same musical notation. It is a natural consequence that *Stond wel, moder*, like the more direct English rendering *Jesu Cristes milde moder* (no. 12 below), has the same number of stanzas as the Latin; so presumably had the earlier Northern rendering (no. 10(ii) above) in its complete state. In *Stond wel, moder* the adoption of dialogue form causes wide divergences of sense and material between English and Latin, but there are also correspondences: e.g. stanzas 7 and 8 of the English deal with the same subject-matter as stanzas 6 and 7 of the Latin, and stanzas 9 and 10 of the English correspond to stanzas 9 and 11 of the Latin. It seems likely that the author of *Stond wel, moder* knew the Northern rendering. There is also some link, though it may be indirect, with the Arundel version (no. 12), since both have a reference to Simeon not found in the Latin; but it may have been independently introduced, for it is fairly conventional. It seems possible that the author of *Stond wel, moder* may have known *Planctus ante nescia* (addendum to no. 4 above); he would have found in it a model for the dramatic expression of Mary's grief, and he could have taken details from it — the reference to Simeon (ll. 47–50 of the *Planctus*) and Mary's desire to die with Christ (l. 52 of *Stond wel, moder*, ll. 69–72 of the *Planctus*). If not by *Planctus ante nescia* itself, he must at least have been influenced by similar writings.

The Latin *Stabat juxta Christi crucem* is a regular sequence in trochaic metre with a stanza-pattern (in terms of syllable-count) 887887. This basic pattern is reproduced in the final stanza of *Stond wel, moder*, but in it alone. Elsewhere the English poet, like the author of the Northern version, allowed himself to modify the verse-line by adding a syllable at various points. He never does this in the first line of each half-stanza, which always asserts the basic rhythm and is a four-stress trochaic line, in agreement with the Latin. But he varies the second and third lines of each half-stanza at will. Stanza 1 has the pattern 897897, with an added unstressed syllable at the beginning of the second line of each half-stanza. Stanza 8 runs 888888, with an added syllable at the beginning of the third and sixth lines. Stanzas 2–7 and 9–10 add a syllable (in principle unstressed) at the beginning of the second and third lines of each half-stanza and so have the pattern 898898, which in terms of frequency of occurrence is the norm for the English poem. These variations in the number of syllables of course require modifications of the musical setting, by repetition of notes. But the poet, despite his variations, seems not to have lost sight of the basic requirements of the sequence, that the two halves of each stanza should balance each other; apparent cases of imbalance, in individual MSS, are to be attributed to miscopying by the scribes and must be set right by the editor. The scribes themselves seem occasionally to have recognized this; see, for example, the note to l. 26 below.

For this style of music rhythmical regularity was not essential, though the Latin poet in fact provided it. The English poet also preserves a high degree of metrical regularity, when allowance is made for the effects of the addition of syllables at the beginning and ending of lines (in particular, the conversion of the second and third lines of each half-stanza, in his most frequent variant of the stanza-form, into iambic lines). But occasionally he inverts the stress in the first foot of what would normally be, in his metre, an iambic line: so in ll. 20, 41, and 48, and possibly (depending on how one stresses the words) in ll. 18 and 45. In l. 42 the first two feet are trochaic, the last two iambic. The stressing of *weepinge* (l. 7) and *wimman* (l. 48) on the second syllable, at the line-end, is the common artificial inversion of stress *metri causa*; but the similar stressing of *mankin* on the second in ll. 21 and 33, in each case in mid-line, is probably natural, since this word and the synonymous *mankind* seem to have varied in stressing in ME.

The original dialect of *Stond wel, moder*, as attested chiefly by its rhymes, was that of the East Midlands. That it was not Northern is shown by the development of OE *ā* to *ǭ*, proved by the rhyming at ll. 9 and 54; and it was not Western or SW, for OE *ēo* in *erne* < *eornan* (l. 17) rhymes with *ě* in *werne* < *wernan*. It was not a Saxon dialect, for *greede* < OE *grǣdan* (probably with *ǣ¹*) in l. 47 rhymes with *neede* < OE *nēd*; nor was it Kentish, for OE *ǣ¹* in *rede* < *rǣd* (l. 34) rhymes with OE *ēa* in *dede* 'death'. This rhyming of OE *ǣ¹* on both ME *ē̜* and ME *ȩ̄* rules out Essex and suggests a border or mixed dialect open to both Saxon and Anglian influence. At ll. 15, 18 the assonance *ded* 'death' — *feet* ignores the distinction between ME *ē̜* and ME *ȩ̄*; such rhyming is generally Northern and Eastern. In l. 32 *beye* 'buy', with South-eastern *ě* < OE *ȳ*, is established by rhyme and retained even in the Western manuscripts D and H; but elsewhere the MS spellings (except in the probably Kentish MS J) suggest that the archetype had *i* for OE *y*. If so, the poet wrote in an East Midland dialect in which South-eastern variants occurred sporadically and could be used for convenience of rhyming. At l. 13 metre and rhyme require the disyllabic form *beren* for MS *bern* < OE *bearn* 'child' (with ME *ẹ̄* from late OE *ēa* by lengthening); this form shows the development of a glide *e* between *r* and *n*, a process which seems to be specially common in Eastern texts (Jordan, § 146 Anm. 2). The East Midland present tense indicative plural inflexion *-e(n)* is established by rhyme in ll. 38, 39, and 47. The spellings of the MSS are primarily due to their own scribes, but it may be remarked that R's use of *s* and *ss* for OE *sc* (modern English *sh*), which is generally an Eastern and South-eastern spelling, is confirmed by D in one instance (*sal* 'shall' in l. 34). As for vocabulary, the Norse-derived *deye* is used several times and is plainly original. R's *þou* 'though' must have been the form used in the archetype, in view of D's error in l. 45; it is a reduction of *þouȝ* < ON *þŏh*, which in the thirteenth century is Eastern and Northern. So, as a general rule, is the form *ded* 'death', which occurs repeatedly and is confirmed by rhyme. The form *tarst* 'at first' is otherwise found only in *Havelok*, probably a text from South Lincolnshire (or western Norfolk); see further the note to l. 37. The extension of the weak plural inflexion *-en* to the noun *teren* in l. 14, for the sake of rhyme (against normal *teres* in l. 16), is a warning against a location too far to the North; but the Norfolk *Genesis and Exodus* similarly uses *meten* 'cibos' (for normal *metes*) for the sake of rhyme (cf. Hall's extract in *Early Middle English*, ll. 133 and 309). Other resemblances of detail between the forms of the poem and those found in texts from Norfolk or South Lincolnshire are pointed out in the notes. We can probably think of *Stond wel, moder* as having been written within an area bounded on the north by a line drawn from King's Lynn through Bourne, and on the south by one from Ely to Huntingdon. If the Latin sequence was one that was current especially in Benedictine houses, there were a number in this area; Peterborough would suit well.

For the date of composition a *terminus ante quem* is provided by the dating of the Digby MS to 1272–82. The language shows a number of conservative features. Originally feminine nouns have plurals in *-e* (or less probably *-en*) in ll. 5 and 53, as rhyme shows, and the MSS preserve traditional feminine genitive singulars in *moder* (ll. 43, 44) and *helle* (l. 62). Except in words commonly weakly stressed (e.g. *wer* 'were', *ur* 'our'), final *-e* is in general well preserved. The metre requires the dative (or 'prepositional case') ending *-e* in nouns (thus *þinge* l. 8, *gilte* l. 9, *grunde* l. 11, *bloode* l. 64), adjectives (*glade* l. 2), and stressed possessives (*þine* ll. 27 and 53). But if we credit the readings of R, which in several instances are confirmed by other MSS, the present tense of the verb, indicative and subjunctive, was becoming uninflected by the loss of *-e*; uninflected monosyllabic forms are required by the metre for the first person singular in *þole* ll. 8 and 27, *feel* l. 10, *dey* l. 26, *fare* l. 50, and for the third person plural in *þole* l. 38 (cf. *have* l. 39, but in this verb weak stress gave rise to common reduced forms). This incipient loss of final *-e* is unlikely in an East Midland dialect before 1250, and the same is true of the lengthening of OE *ĕ* in the open syllable of *bere*, shown by the rhyme at ll. 37–38. On the other hand we must allow for the fact that D is separated by at least two intervening copies from the archetype, and that the archetype was itself already corrupt and was not the author's original. If the Northern English version (no. 10(ii) above) was written about 1250 and if the author of *Stond wel, moder* knew it, as I suppose, then the composition of the latter might be dated about 1260, which

would allow time for several stages of copying before D was written. It is likely to be earlier than the Arundel version (no. 12 below), which probably belongs to the last quarter of the century.

VARIANTS

Variations of spelling are not ordinarily recorded. When two or more MSS are cited as having the same reading, the spelling given is that of the MS first cited; the other(s) may or may not agree.

1 stond] RHDF stand JT   2 bihold] D biheld R biholt HF bihalt JT   child] RHDJF sonne T   glade] RHDTF glede J   3 bliþe moder] RHJTF moder bliþe D   miȝt tu] F mittu R miȝt þou DH mai þu JT   be] RHDT ben F bie J   4 sun] svne RJ sone DHT son F   hu] JT quu R hou DHF   mai] JRDTF schulde H   i] T y H hi F ich D *om.* RJ   stonde] HDJF stonden R stande T   5 þi] JTF þin RH þine D   i see] (h)i se RHTF and DJ   þin] RH þine DJT þi F   honde] HDF honden RJ handle T   6 nailed] JRHF I-nayled DT   þe] RHDT þo J þat F   tree] tre RHDTF trie J

7 moder do wey] RHDT do wai moder J   8 þole] RHJT þolie D   þis ded] RJT deþ HD   mannes] R manis T monnes D man J mon H   þinge] thinge R kynde HT kuinde D kende J   9 owne] owen R mine DJ my HT   gilte] R gilt T gult H gelte J gultes D   þoli] RJ þole y H ne þoli T ne þolie I D   10 feel] fele RHDJT   þe dede-] RHT dede J þe deþes D   stunde] RT stounde HD wunde J   11 þe] RHJT þat D   12 bihiȝte] byhytte R byheyte D bihet JTH

13 reu ... beren] do wei þine teres D   reu] RT rewen J þou rewe H   upon] RT of J al of H   beren] bern RHT barne J   14 þu] RHDJ *om.* T   wash] wasse R wosshe H wip D wipe T vipe J   þo] R þe HDT þi J   teren] R tern HT teres DJ   15 þat don] it don R it do T hit doþ H hy doþ D þei do J   werse] RJT worse HD   þan] RJT þen H þene D   ded] RHJT deþ D   16 miȝt i] mitti R miȝtte ich D may y H mai JT   werne] HDT wernen RJ   17 þo] R þe HT þine D þi J   bloodi] blodi RHDT blod J   floodes] flodes RT stremes H woundes D on flod J   erne] HJT herne D hernen R   18 ut of] huth of R from HD fro JT   þin] RHDT þi J   to] RHDT on to J   mi] JTH min R þi H   feet] fet RH fot DJT

19 nu] RHDJ min T   seye] HD seyn R sai JT   20 ich] HD ic RJ ik T   one deye] RDHT hauen deit J   21 þan] RJT þen HD   al] RHT alle D *om.* J   mankin] T mankyn R monkun D mankenne J monkunde H   22 see] se RHDT si J   swungen] swngen R Iswonge D ysungun T suingen J byswngen H   23 þi] RT þine D *om.* HJ   brest] RJ fet T honde D *om.* H   þin] R þine D þine D þi T and J *om.* H   hond] R hend J heued T fet HD   þi] RDT ond HJ   foot] fot R fet J bodi D brest T honde H   þurȝ-stungen] þur-stungen R þurtet sting J thuret stungen T þourh out stongen H Istounge D   24 no selli nis] no selli RJ no sellik T no wonder H hit is no wonder D   þou] RT þey D þah H þat J   be] RHDT is J   wo] RHDJ wa T

25 if] RHT wel J now H   i] JT y RH ich D   dar þee] dar þe RT þe dourste H mai þe J shal þe H   telle] HDJT tellen R   26 if i ne dey] if i ne deye T yif y ne deye R ȝef y ne deȝe H if ich ne deye D bot i deie J   gost] RHDJ gos T   27 þole] RHT þolie DJ   þis ded] R hys ded T ded H deþ D det

J þine] RHJT monnes D 28 beest me] best me R me
bihest D me art T art H so] RD suo T meke and
H minde] RHT milde D 29 ne wit me nou3t] ne wyt
me naht H with me nout R wite ye me noth T Icomen hit is
D it is mi] RH it is of T of monnes D kinde] RT kynde
H kuinde D 30 i] T y RH ich D for þee] for þe RHT
sike and D þis sorwe] þis sorewe H sorghe T serewe D
sorye R

Stanza 6 is displaced in H *and follows stanza 2* 31 let]
RHD lat T deye] HDT deyen R 32 for] RHT and
D ut of] RHD fro T beye] HD beyn R bringe T 33
mankin] monkun D al mankin R for mankin T his kun
H forloren] RT forlore HD 34 wat] RDT what
H sal] RDT shal H to rede] RH tho rede T þe stounde
D 35 þi] RT þine D my H pine] RT pinen D peyne
H pineð me] pined me R pyneþ me H bringys me T me
bringeþ D to dede] RHT to þe grounde D 36 let] RD
lat HT deye] TH deyn R dey D biforen] RT bifore HD

37–38 *For this couplet* T *reads* [M]oder mine, thor thu stan-
dest,/ of þe pine nu thu fondest. 37–39 *For these lines* D
reads Swete moder, nou þou fondest/ of mi pine, þer þou ston-
dest;/ wiþ-houte mi pine nere no mon. 37 nu tarst] nutarst
R nou H mi3t] mith R miht wel H lere] leren
RH 38 wat] R whet H pine] R sorewe H þole]
þolen R haueþ H childre] R children H bere] beren
RH 39 wat] R watht T whet H sorwe] R sorewe H
wimman T have] hauen R hit is H tholes T þat child
forgon] R þat chil for-gas T wiþ childe gon H 40 sun] sune
RDT sorewe H i wot] TRD ywis H kan] R con H mai
DT telle] HDT tellen R 41 buten hit] bute it R bote hit
HD bot tetht T 42 more sorwe] RT more serewe H of more
pine D ne] RH *om.* DT

43 reu of moder kare] RHT of moder þus I fare D 44 nu]
RDT for nou H of moder] RHT wimmanes D fare]
RH ware T kare D 45 þou þu be] RT þou þou be H þou art
D man] m.. R (*leaf torn*) mon H on D an T 46 help at
alle] H hepl at alne T help alle at R þou helpest alle D 47
me] RHT þe D greede] grede H greden R greten T wille
grede D 48 maiden] HT m..den R may D and wif] D
wyf RHT and] RDT ant H fool] fol RHT fowel
D wimman] wyman RT wymmon HD

49 mai i] may y H y may RT I ne may D leng] long T lengore HD *lacuna in* R dwelle] HDT duellen R 50 cum]
come H cumen RT comen D fare] R shal H go DT 51
For this line D *substitutes* I þolie þis for þine sake (*cf. l.*
27) þridde day] H þride doi T *lacuna in* R upon] RH
opp T 52 i wile] y wyle R ik wile T y wil H Iwis I wille
D wiþ þee] wiþ þe HT withe R *om.* D funde] T founde
D funden R founden H 53 dey iwis] deye ywis HT deye
almest D *lacuna in* R of þine wunde] of þine wnden R of
þine wndes T for þine wounden H I falle to grounde D 54
reuful] R reuli T serwful D soreweful H ded] RHT deþ
D was] RT nes HD non] HD naan T *lacuna in* R

55 wan] T when H *lacuna in* R þan] R þo HT þi] R hy T
hire H sorwe] R sorewe H soreche T 56 þi] thi T þe R
hire H sprong] H sproing T spr ... R þe þridde] H i the
þrdde T *lacuna in* R morwe] morewe H morghen T *lacuna
in* R 57 wel] wen R *om.* HT wer] R were H wor
T þu] R þou H þtho T 58 moder] [M]oder T mod .. R
leuedy H for þat ilke] HT *lacuna in* R blisse] H ded T

lacuna in R 59 biseech] bisech RH eke T ur god] vre
god RT þi sone H ur sinnes] vre sinnes RT of sunnes
H lisse] H lesse RT 60 ur] ure TRH sheeld] sheld
H seld T chel R ayen] R a3eyn H again T ur] ure TRH

61 blissed] blisced R blessed H [I]blessed T queen] quen
RT ful H hevne] heuene RT blysse H 62 bring . . .
helle] R thu sild us fro helle T let vs neuer heuene H levne]
leuene R deuene T misse H 63 þur3] þurth R þurþg T þourh
H deere] dere RT suete H mi3t] mith R myht H micht
T 64 moder] R louerd HT hi3e] hithe R ilke
HT bloode] blode R blod HT 65 he shad] he sadde R
þou sheddest H þu bledes T upon] vpon R on H hone
T roode] rode RT rod H 66 led] R þou bryng H thu do
T into] RH in tho T heven-li3t] heuene lith R heuene
lyht H heuene riche T

NOTES

3. *mi3tu* 'mayest thou'; *mi3t* is 2 sg. pres. indic.
be] the rhyme with *tree* establishes that the infinitive has lost its
final -*n*; similarly *seye* l. 19, *telle* ll. 25 and 40, *dwelle* l. 49, *lisse*
l. 59. I therefore generalize the form without -*n*. The scribes,
and particularly the scribe of R, show a marked tendency to
add -*n* where it cannot have been original.

4. *Sun* 'son'. The full form is *sune* (*sone*), but we omit the final
-*e* when it is elided. The spellings of the MSS, as is usual, do not
show the elision (though at this point F has *son*).
hu 'how'. R's *quu* is a spelling-variant of the form *hwu*, i.e. it
involves the use of *qu* as a spelling for OE *hw*. This use of *qu* is
found in Norfolk texts, and sporadically in the Laud MS of
Havelok; the latter has *qui* 'why' (l. 1650) and *hwou* 'how' (l.
2992). R also has *w* for OE *hw* in *wat* 'what'; this spelling is also
found in Norfolk texts and in *Havelok* (*wat* l. 453 etc., *wan* l.
220, *weþer* l. 292).
mai i 'can I'. The omission of *i* in R and J must be independent,
and due to the fact that the previous word ended in -*i*.
stonde 'stand'. Only R adds -*n*; see note to l. 3 above.

5. *honde* 'hands'. The noun is an OE feminine, and this is the
earliest ME form of the plural, directly developed from OE
handa. But RJ give the later form *honden*, with added -*n*.

6. *nailed*] Metre always requires the form of the p.p. without
the prefix *i*-. This is an indication, at this date, that the poem
does not come from the South Midlands.

7. *do wey* 'put away', 'desist from'. The spellings of the MSS
(except of the Kentish J) keep ME *ei* < OE *ēg* distinct from ME
ai, as one would expect in a thirteenth-century text.

8. *þole þis ded* 'suffer this death'. JT support R in reading *þis*
here. But for metre the phrase must be only three syllables; it
follows that the final -*e* of *þole* must be silent. The West Midland scribes of D and H, for whom the -*e* was necessarily pronounced, omitted *þis* to compensate. That *ded* and not *deþ* was
the author's form is shown by the consensus of the MSS at the
various points where the word occurs and by the assonance at l.
15 (since a *d* — *t* assonance is more likely than a *þ* — *t* assonance).
þinge 'sake'. Only R keeps this reading, which is shown to be
correct by the rhyme and the superior sense. The -*e* is the
inflexion of the dative singular.

9. *owne* '(my) own'. For this use of *own* without preceding

possessive see *OED*, s.v. *own* adj., sense 2. This is again the reading of R alone; but I substitute the form *owne* (dat. sg.) for the scribe's *owen* because of the evidence that the dative inflexion was well preserved in the author's language, except in unstressed words and when elision occurs. Either form is metrically satisfactory.

gilte 'guilt'. I accept R's form with ĭ for OE ȳ because the evidence of the spellings is that the archetype had *i* for *y* except in the one case (*beye* l. 32) where South-eastern ĕ is needed for rhyme; thus H, though a West Midland MS, retains *i* spellings in a couple of instances. But if one were to assume that the author's dialect was perfectly consistent in this respect, one would have to generalize *e*-forms on the evidence of the rhyme.

þoli 'suffer I'; the pronoun is run on to the verb as an enclitic, as the spellings of R, J, and T show.

10. *feel*] All MSS have the normal ME spelling *fele*, but the metre shows that either the verb must be intended as a monosyllable or *þe* should be omitted. J does omit *þe*, obviously because in the Kentish dialect of its scribe *fele* could not be pronounced as a monosyllable and the scribe noticed that the line was too long; but DHT agree with R in reading *þe*, and it must have been present in the archetype.

þe dede-stunde is probably singular (with -*e* from the oblique cases of the originally feminine noun *stund*), meaning 'the hour of death' or 'the pain of the hour of death' (cf. *OED*, s.v. *stound* sb.[1], sense 2(a)). It could be plural, meaning 'the pangs of death', but the sense 'pang' (*OED*, sense 2(b)) is not recorded until somewhat later and is chiefly Northern. *Dede* with added -*e* is a composition-form of *ded* 'death'. For the whole compound cf. ON *dauða-stund* 'hour of death'.

11. *min herte grunde* 'the bottom of my heart'. *Herte* is historically a gen. sg. < OE *heortan*; but the phrase is virtually a compound.

12. *bihiȝte* 'promised'. The metre requires a trisyllabic form of the past tense, and *bihiȝte* is the normal ME spelling corresponding to R's *byhytte*. The reference to Simeon is not in the Latin sequence.

13. *reu* 'have pity'; *beren* 'child'. RHT have *bern* < OE *bēarn*, with ēa by lengthening of earlier ĕa before *rn*; but metre and rhyme require the disyllabic form *beren*. This is developed from *bern* by the intrusion of a glide *e* between *r* and *n*; cf. the form *barin* cited by *OED* from *The Proverbs of Alfred*. The latter, and J's *barne*, have ME ă < OE unlengthened ĕa. For the rhyme here, compare *boren* 'born' rhyming with *koren* 'corn' in *Havelok* ll. 1878-9, and similarly *coren* with *boren* and *biforen* in *Gen. & Exod.* (Hall's extract, ll. 213-14, 269-70).

14. R's *wasse* 'wash', with *ss* for *sh*, may represent the spelling of the archetype, but I normalize here.
Only R has *þo* 'those', but it is clearly better in sense. The form *teren* for normal *teres* 'tears' (as in l. 16, where all MSS agree) is used by the poet for the sake of rhyme.

15. *þat do me werse* 'which afflict me worse'. There is a textual difficulty here. R's *it don* must represent the archetype; it is supported on the other side of the stemma by T's *it do* and by H's *hit doþ* (in which *doþ* is evidently a plural); D's *hy doþ* and J's *þei do* are scribal modifications, in which the plural verb is maintained and the pronoun is altered to the plural. But though *it* could be used in ME with indefinite or even with

plural reference, this usage seems to have been restricted to cases in which it was followed by a plural form of the verb *to be* (see Mustanoja, *Middle English Syntax*, pp. 132-3, and cf. German *es sind*, French *ce sont*); there seem to be no parallels for the extension of the usage to other verbs. One must conclude that the archetype was corrupt at this point (cf. l. 24 below), and that emendation is needed. But the scribal emendations are unsatisfactory; they do not explain the corruption of the archetype. I assume that the author wrote *þat do(n)* and that the abbreviation *þᵗ* for *þat* was misread as *yt* 'it'. I prefer JT's *do* to R's *don*; *be* l. 3 shows loss of -*n* in a monosyllable, *forgon* in l. 39 shows its retention, but in mid-line before *m* the form without -*n* is perhaps a little more likely. (An alternative emendation would be *it be(n)*, using the ME idiom referred to above; but it would be less easy to explain how the archetype of the extant MSS corrupted *be(n)* into *do(n)*.)
ded 'death', as before.

16. *miȝt i* 'could I'; *miȝt* is here past tense, for the full form *miȝte* (of which the -*e* is elided). We should perhaps read *miȝti* with enclitic *i*, in view of R's *mitti*, but this would be an ambiguous spelling. H and JT substitute the present tense *may* (*mai*), probably independently.
werne 'refuse', 'refrain from'.

17. Again only R has *þo* 'those', though it is clearly right.
erne 'run'.

18. *Ut of*, following R's *huth of*, is required by metre; the *from* (*fro*) of DHJT reduces the line to seven syllables, which, though it agrees with the Latin metre, fails to balance l. 15 above, which has eight syllables in all MSS (or perhaps nine in D).

20. *one* 'alone' < OE *āna*, weak form of *ān* 'one'. J's *ic hauen* at this point looks like a misdivision and misreading of a Northern text *ich ane* (read as *ic haue*); see note to l. 23 below.

21. *mankin* < OE *mancynn* 'the human race' is stressed on the second. See note to l. 9 above on the treatment of OE ȳ.
go is 3 sg. pres. subj., where modern English would use the conditional 'should go'.

22. *swungen* 'beaten'. R has the spelling *swngen*, which occurs also in the Laud MS of *Havelok*, l. 226. The metre of l. 50 shows that OE *cumen* p.p. has lost its final -*n* and been reduced to *cume*, which in that line, by elision of the -*e*, becomes a monosyllable. Loss of -*n* in the strong p.p. is a non-Northern feature. Similarly -*n* is lost in the infinitive (see note to l. 3) and in the present tense plural (e.g. in *greede*, l. 47). It is possible that the form without -*n* ought to be generalized in the strong p.p., but here -*en* is given not only by R (which tends to add -*n*) but also by HJT, and for the rhyme-word *stungen* HT as well as R have -*en*. The author's dialect may well have varied.

23. 'Thy breast, thy hand, thy foot pierced through.' The reading given is R's; its singulars *hond* 'hand' and *foot* (spelt *fot* in R) agree with ll. 19-20 of the Latin (*Modo manus, modo latus, / modo ferro pes foratus*). DHJT here vary sharply from each other, but it is clear that their common ancestor had substituted the plurals *honde* and *fet* for the singulars, for the sake of sense. But *honde* for *hond* increased the number of syllables by one; and it looks as though *þurhut* 'throughout' had also been substituted for *þurh*, for H has *þourh out*, J *þurtet*, and T *þuret*. The result was an overlong and unmetrical line which provoked re-writing; H's is the most successful version (*fet and*

honde þourh out stongen), for it produces a regular eight-syllable line, at the expense of omitting *brest* (corresponding to the Latin *latus*).

J's text is very interesting, for it includes the monosyllabic mutation-plural *hend* 'hands', which is derived from ON and is characteristic of Northern ME texts; it cannot be due to the South-eastern scribe of the extant MS J. T's *heued* is evidently a corruption of this *hend*, which must have been introduced into the text by their common ancestor, and it follows that the latter must have been by a Northern scribe. Cf. the note to l. 20 above, which explains a corruption in J as a misreading of a Northern form *ane*; but there T correctly substitutes the Midland *one*. J's *þei* in l. 15 is another form which cannot be due to its South-eastern scribe, and must be due to a Northern or East Midland copyist; but this is an innovation introduced into the text after J's line of descent had diverged from T's. J's textual tradition is evidently complex.

24. *no selli nis* 'it is no wonder'. The concurrence of RHJT shows that the archetype read *no selli þou me be wo*, an exclamatory sentence ('no wonder if I am wretched'), but this is one syllable too few and gives only three natural stresses in the line. D adds *hit is* at the beginning of the line, which gives four stresses but is a syllable too many. The solution must be to add *is* or *nis* after *selli*, and the negative verb *nis* is the more idiomatic. At this point the archetype itself was plainly corrupt, i.e. it was not the author's autograph but a copy.

For *selli* both H and D read *wonder*. This may indicate some cross-link between the two, of which there are other signs, though D usually goes with J and T; but they may independently have substituted the synonymous and metrically equivalent word.

þou 'though' is here the reading of R and T; D and H have forms descended from the native *þēah* (*þēh*). But in l. 45 the evidence is clear that *þou* was the form of the archetype. The Laud MS of *Havelok* has the same spelling (l. 124 etc.).

me be wo 'I am wretched' (literally 'woe be to me', an impersonal idiom).

26. *if i ne dey*] The MSS have the spelling *deye* (*deʒe*), and the concurrence of RHJT shows that this was the archetypal reading. But it seems to make the line, exceptionally, one of ten syllables whereas l. 29, the corresponding line of the second half-stanza, had only nine syllables in the archetype. The solution is that here again the inflexion *-e* of a present tense form of a verb has been lost, and in our text we omit the *-e*. Two of the scribes, in whose dialects *-e* was still regularly maintained, recognized the metrical imbalance and attempted to cure it by emendation. J substituted *bot i deie* in l. 26, thus saving a syllable; it is a neat modification but cannot be original. D on the other hand re-wrote l. 29 as *Icomen hit is of monnes kuinde*, thus expanding it to ten syllables so as to balance l. 26 as he scanned the latter.

27. *þole þis ded*] so R, supported in effect by T, whose *hys* is an obvious error for *thys*. Cf. l. 8 above, and the note there.

28. *beest* 'art'. In OE *bist* meant 'will be' or was used in gnomes and maxims ('consuetudinal use') and was not a synonym of *eart*, but in ME the distinction was lost in East Midland dialects. The MSS other than R alter the form: H and T substitute *art*, D has the corrupt *bihest* 'promise', which suggests that the West Midland scribe did not even recognize the spelling *best* which presumably stood in his exemplar.

minde 'mindful, considerate'. That the archetype had the spelling with *i* (for OE *y*) is shown by the agreement of H and T with R, and by D's corrupt *milde*.

29. *ne wit me nouʒt* 'do not blame me'. Again the readings of the MSS show that the archetype had *i* for OE *y* in *kinde*.

30. Unless there has been independent error, the agreement of R with TD in omitting *þis* before *sorwe* must show that the word was lacking in the archetype. If so, H's insertion of *þis* would be a scribal emendation for the sake of metre and would not necessarily be the original reading. Some monosyllable is certainly required; an alternative possibility would be a form of *such*. But it is better to accept H's *þis*, especially as it might have descended from the archetype.

R's error *sorye* for *sorwe* 'sorrow' may perhaps show that its exemplar had at this point the spelling *sorʒe* (cf. T's *sorghe*). But it might equally be due to the use, in R's exemplar, of the old letter *wynn* instead of *w*; the Laud MS of *Havelok* has instances of *wynn*, and also errors due to confusion between *y* and *wynn*.

32. *for . . . beye* 'in order to buy', i.e. to redeem. *Beye* is a South-eastern form, with *ĕ* for OE *ȳ* in the stem *byg-*; but such *e*-forms are found, beside *i*, in Norfolk, Huntingdonshire, and Cambridgeshire (cf. Jordan, § 40).

33. *forloren* 'lost, ruined'. T supports R in giving the form *forloren* (and *biforen* in l. 36); but see note to l. 22.

34. *wat sal me to rede* 'what shal [be] to me as advice?', 'what am I to do?'.

The spelling *wat* is given at this point by RDT and is presumably that of the archetype; cf. note to l. 4 above. The three MSS also agree in the spelling *sal* for *shall*, which I therefore retain. In the fourteenth century *sal* is a Northern form, but in the thirteenth is found in the Norfolk texts *The Bestiary* and *Genesis and Exodus* (whereas later Norfolk texts have *xal*); *sal* also occurs in the Laud MS of *Havelok* (l. 628).

35. 'Thy torment tortures me to death.'

ME *pine* is from OE *pín* fem. < Latin *poena*; the *-e* is derived from the oblique cases and is normal in ME. The word scans as a disyllable in this poem except when elision occurs (l. 41). R's spelling *pined* for the verb suggests that its exemplar had at this point the spelling *pineð*, which I adopt; the letter *ð* was going out of use in the later thirteenth century and was often miscopied as *d*. The *-e* of *dede* 'death', as that of the rhyme-word *rede*, is the dative inflexion.

37-39. T's text of these lines is radically altered, though it preserves the gist of the original text; D re-writes further, plainly on the basis of T's text, as if to give something to correspond to ll. 11-18 of the Latin text. But the original text, as given by R and H, corresponds to stanzas 6 and 7 of the Latin, and particularly to stanza 7 of the Northern English version (no. 10 above); the same rhyme-words *lere* and *bere* are used in ll. 37-38 of the two English versions, which, if it is a coincidence, is a remarkable one.

37. *nu tarst* 'now for the first time'; cf. *þo tarst* 'then for the first time' in *Havelok* l. 2688, a very striking resemblance, for the form *tarst* is not elsewhere recorded. It is a reduction of *at arst* 'at first' < OE *æt ærest* (cf. *OED*, s.v. *erst*), with aphesis of the unstressed vowel of the preposition (treated as if a prefix). Carleton Brown read R's form as *mitarst*, but no such word is

known and the scribe certainly did not write it; he wrote very clearly *nutarst,* with the *n* and *u* distinguished and a slight space between them. (His *i,* in the neighbourhood of minims, usually has an accent-mark over it; there is none here.) H has *nou* but omits *tarst,* probably because it was a local word unknown in the West Midlands; to make up for the lost syllable he inserts *wel* before *lere.* The re-writing in the common ancestor of T and D may have been provoked by the occurrence of this unusual word.

38. 'What pain they suffer who bear children.'
The fact that both T and D re-write ll. 37-38 means that in l. 38 there are only two witnesses to the original text, R and H; in l. 39 D is still aberrant, and T gets back to the original text only in the second half of the line. Unfortunately in ll. 38-39 R and H, though agreeing in the gist of what they say, differ radically in the details of the wording; one or other has been unfaithful to its exemplar, and there can be little doubt that the innovator is the later MS H, for R's text is superior in sense and style and is supported by T in the second half of l. 39. The motive for H's alterations was probably that its scribe found difficulty in scanning the transmitted text; and it is true that the easiest way of producing a text that is regular in metre is to conflate the texts of R and H. But this is unsound method, and I follow R. The difficulty is that R's text of the first half of l. 38 (*wat pine þolen*) has a syllable too many as it stands; either we must read *wat pin þolen,* treating *pin* as a monosyllable (despite l. 35), or we must read *wat pine þole* and treat *þole* as a monosyllable. The latter gives more regular rhythm and is consistent with the uninflected present tense forms of ll. 8, 10, 26 and 27. It involves of course a contrast between the monosyllabic *þole* in mid-line and the inflected *berë* (required by metre and rhyme) at the line-end; but ME verse often treats words differently in mid-line and at the line-end.

39. 'What sorrow they have who lose a child.'
This again is R's text, supported in the second half-line by T; it involves the comparatively rare use of *forgon* to mean 'to go without, to lose' (*OED,* s.v. *forgo,* sense 7(b)). H's sense ('what sorrow it is to go with child') is by contrast conventional in phrasing and of dubious truth. But in R's text we must assume, for scansion, (i) that the *-e* of *sorwe* is not elided before *h,* (ii) that *have* is a monosyllable. The latter presents no difficulty, for the word was commonly reduced under weak stress; we can read, instead of R's *hauen,* either *han* or *have* (with silent *e*); I choose the latter as nearer to R's spelling.

40-42. 'Son, I know, I can assure you — unless it be the torment of hell, I do not know any greater sorrow.'

40. The RDT agreement in reading *i wot* must mean that this was the reading of the archetype; H's *ywis* 'certainly' is superficially attractive but in fact gives weaker sense.

41. *buten*] Though RHD agree on the form without *-n,* the metre requires a disyllable, and the full form *buten,* which makes elision impossible, is therefore preferable.

43-44. 'Mother, have pity on a mother's troubles, now that you know about a mother's condition.'
moder is historically genitive singular.

44. *nu* is a conjunction, 'now that', not an adverb.

45. *þou þu*] so RT, supported by H (*þou þou*); the latter, apparently but not truly repetitive (since it means 'though thou'),

explains why D omits one or other word, presumably the conjunction. The readings here presuppose *þou* as the form of 'though' in the archetype.
clene 'clean', i.e. pure, unblemished.
maiden-man is an *ad hoc* formation, involving *man* in its general sense of 'human being'; it means 'a virgin human' and is in explicit contrast with its rhyme-word *wimman < wíf-man.*

46. *at alle neede* 'in every necessity'. The reading is H's, supported by T, and is clearly right; R's *alle at nede* is irregular in scansion and inferior in sense. D somehow corrupts *help at* into *helpest* and inserts *þou* before it.

47. 'all those who cry to me.' It is possible but unlikely that the rhyme depends on OE *nēad* for normal *nēd*; it is rather on Anglian **grēdan* for WS *grǽdan.*

48. Only D reads *and* before *wif.* We must therefore assume either that RHT have independently omitted the word or that D's reading is a scribal emendation. The latter seems more likely. Nevertheless it appears to be a correct emendation; *and* is required if l. 48 is to balance l. 45 in syllable-count and in rhythm.
fool (fol MSS) 'foolish', doubtless in the sense 'morally loose'.

49. *mai i*] H's word-order, with the pronoun after the verb, is required for metre; R and the common ancestor of DT must have independently substituted the conventional word-order.
leng] The traditional comparative adverb, meaning 'longer', is required by metre, against the later *lengore* of DH. T's *long* is an obvious corruption of *leng.* There is a lacuna in R, here and elsewhere in the remaining stanzas, owing to the tearing of the leaf.

50. *fare*] The MSS differ here. H's *shal* is very idiomatic, but R is the best witness and is most likely to represent the archetype. But again a monosyllable is needed for scansion, and the inflexion *-e* must have become silent. It was doubtless because *-e* was still normally pronounced in Midland dialects that H and the ancestor of DT have independently substituted monosyllables (*shal* H, *go* DT); if either of these had stood in the archetype there would have been no occasion for scribal alteration.

52. *funde* 'hasten, go'. The vowel was probably long (as in ME *hus,* later *hous*), owing to OE lengthening before *nd*; DH use the spelling *founde(n),* in which *ou* is an indication of a long vowel. So with the rhyme-word *wunde* in the next line.

53. *dey* 'die'; here the inflexional *-e* is elided before the following vowel.
iwis 'in truth, certainly, indeed'.
wunde 'wounds', historically a feminine plural. R has *wnden* and H *wounden,* and the archetype may well have had *wunden,* since the rhyme-word, an infinitive, may have been *funden* (RH give *-en* for it, but TD *-e*). But the positive evidence is that in the author's dialect the infinitive had lost *-n,* and I therefore substitute the earlier plural *wunde* for the *wunden* to which the scribal forms point. Cf. *honde* in l. 5, where the same problem arises.

54. 'There was never any death so pitiable.' T supports R in reading *was* against the negative verb *nes* given by DH.

55f. D omits the last two stanzas, probably because they desert the dialogue form; but they are certainly original, being given by MSS on opposite sides of the stemma (including T, which is related to D). It is in these two stanzas that Mr. R. H. Robbins's discovery of T is especially useful, for previously one had to rely on two MSS only, R and H, which differ a good deal; and though in fact T's evidence has not caused any changes in a text which we had formed without its aid, its confirmation of this text at various points is very welcome.

55. *Wan* 'when'; so T. This would also have been R's form, though in fact there is a lacuna in R here owing to the tearing of the leaf; cf. *þan* later in the line in R. The same form *wan* occurs in *Havelok,* l. 220.

þi] so R; T's *hy* is an error for *thy.* Here and in the next line H substitutes the 3rd person *hire,* but that this is not original is in any case shown by H's own *þou,* agreeing with R's *þu,* in l. 57.

56. *þi*] *thi* T. R has *þe,* but H's *hire* shows that there was originally a possessive at this point, and *þi* is in any case better sense.

57. *wel*] An obvious emendation for R's *wen.* An unstressed monosyllable is required here. HT omit the word, perhaps because the corruption to *wen* had already occurred in the archetype; *wen* 'when' does not make sense, and an obvious way of correcting the sense, though not the metre, would be simply to omit it.

wer] so R, rightly (unless we accept T's Norse-derived *wor,* which is equally suitable metrically); a monosyllable is required. Both *wer* and *wor* are unstressed forms, with loss of *-e,* of *were* and *wore* respectively. But H has *were,* the regular ME 2 sg. past indicative.

þo 'then'.

58. *Moder*] T supports R against H's *Leuedy.* The Latin text has *mater* in l. 61, where the Northern English version has *moder*; but the latter has *lav(e)di* several times elsewhere, which may account for H's reading.

for . . . blisse 'for the sake of that same bliss.' From H, partly supported by T; lacuna in R.

59. 'Beseech our God to remit our sins.' This is R's text, except for the substitution of monosyllabic *ur* for the scribe's *vre*; T's agrees at the significant points. H's text means 'beseech thy son for remission of sins', but the RT construction, with accusative and infinitive after *biseech,* is the more natural.

lisse] so H. This, the normal form, is required by the rhyme with *blisse.* But R and T agree on *lesse,* which is a recorded variant of *lisse* with *ĕ* by lowering of *ĭ,* though in this instance there may be confusion with the verb *lesse* 'lessen'. R and T may have substituted *lesse* for *lisse* independently; if not, there must have been an error in the archetype which H has corrected. As H is in any case re-writing the line, it looks very much as though the scribe has hit on the correct word almost by accident.

60. Again monosyllabic *ur* is required by metre, against the MSS.

sheeld] R's spelling *chel* is at least in part (the omission of *s* at the beginning) due to carelessness; but the lack of *d* at the end may show actual loss in speech (cf. T's *chil* 'child' in l. 39). Omission of a final consonant is common in the Laud MS of

Havelok, which has *shel* 'shield' at l. 489 and other similar cases (*hel* 'held', *gol* 'gold').

ayen 'against'. I adopt R's spelling, which shows loss of *g* from OE *ongeagn* (or *ongegn*). This loss, though characteristically Saxon, is also found in East Midland dialects; cf. Orm's *onnȝæn* and *ayen* in *Havelok,* l. 489 etc. In view of Orm's form, I assume that the vowel is ME *ę̄.*

61. *Blissed*] I accept R's spelling (but with *ss* for his *sc*), against H's normal *blessed* (supported by T). The form with *ĭ* (by raising of *ĕ*) was a common variant from the thirteenth century onwards; it occurs in *Havelok,* l. 2873 (an instance which should be referred to OE *blessian* rather than *blissian,* as in Sisam's glossary). This variant of *bless* with *ĭ* assisted, and was itself assisted by, the confusion of the two verbs *bliss < blissian* 'make happy' and *bless < blessian* 'hallow, sanctify, etc.', which was primarily due to semantic contact.

hevne] *heuene* RT, but a disyllable is required, either *heven* or *hevne.* I choose the latter because I take dative *-e* to have been well preserved in the author's dialect. Similarly with the rhyme-word *levne* in the next line.

62. *helle levne* 'the lightning (i.e. the flames) of hell'. *Helle* is historically a feminine genitive singular.

63. *miȝt*] *mith* R, and similarly R has *lith* for *liȝt* 'light' in l. 66. This is a familiar type of East Midland spelling, and is common in the Laud MS of *Havelok.*

64. *Moder*] so R. The two lines of descent of the MSS diverge here, for HT have *louerd,* with consequential *þou sheddest* H, *þu bledes* T in place of *he shad* in the next line. R seems certainly to be right, for the final prayer should be addressed to Mary, as in the Latin sequence; but it is possible that the original had at this point not *moder* but *levdi,* for the Northern English version has *lavdi.*

hiȝe 'high, noble', a re-formed weak adjective based on the strong adjective *hiȝ.* R's spelling *hithe,* which uses *th* not for OE *ht* (as in the instances discussed in the note to l. 63) but for OE *h,* is probably confused; but it may be a miscopying of *hiche,* with the common early ME use of *ch* for the voiceless spirant. The scribe may indeed have intended *hiche*; the third letter is not much different from the *c* of his *blisced* in l. 61. Here again R seems to preserve the correct text, against the other line of descent, for HT have the commonplace *ilke* 'same' in place of *hiȝe.*

65. *shad* 'shed'. R has *sadde,* with *s* for *sh* (cf. notes to ll. 14 and 34), but we normalize to avoid confusion. The full form of the p.t. sg. was *shadde,* but here there is elision and we omit the *-de.*

66. *led* 'lead', with long vowel (ME *ę̄*). This is R's reading; H has *þou bryng* and T has *thu do.* Probably their common ancestor had H's reading; certainly it introduced the pronoun, but this is unmetrical. As R is right in not giving the pronoun, it is probably right also in the verb.

heven-] A disyllable is required, where all three MSS have *heuene*; the ordinary composition-form (< OE *heofon*) must be substituted.

12. Jesu Cristes milde moder

1

Jesu Cristes mildë moder
stood, biheeld hir son o roodë
    þat he was ipined an;
þe sonë heeng, þe moder stood
5 and biheeld hirë childes blood,
    wu it of his wundes ran.

2

Þo he starf þat is king of lif,
dreerier never nas no wif
    þan þu weerë, levdi, þo;
10 þe briȝtë day went into niȝt
þo Jesu Crist, þin hertë liȝt,
    was iqueint with pine and wo.

3

Þi lif drei ful hardë stundes
þo þu sei his bloodi wundes
15   and his lich o roodë doon.
Hisë wundes sor and smertë
stungen þurw and þurw þin hertë,
    as tee hiȝtë Simeon.

4

Nu his hed with blood bisprunken,
20 nu his side with spere istungen
    þu biheeldë, levdi free;
nu his hondes sprad o roodë,
nu his feet iwash with bloodë
    and inaillet to þe tree.

5

25 Nu his lich with scurges beten
and his blood so wide utleten
    maden þee þin hertë sor.
Warso þu gun cast thin eien
pinë strong þu sei him dreien —
30   miȝtë no man þolë mor.

6

Nu is timë þat þu ȝeeldë
keendë þat þu him withheeldë
    þo þi child was of þee born;
35 nu he oskeþ with goulíngë
þat þu him in þi childíngë
    al withheeldë þar biforn.

7

Nu þu fondest, moder mildë,
wat wif drieth with hir childë,
40   þei þu clenë maiden be.
Nu þee is ȝolden hard and deer
þe pinë warof [þo] þu weer
    in þi childing quit and free.

8

Soon, after the niȝt of sorwë,
45 sprong þe liȝt of edi morwë
    in þin hertë, sweetë may;
þi sorwen wen[den] al to blis
þo þi sonë, al mid iwis,
    ros upon þe þriddë day.

9

Wella! wat þu weerë blithë
50 þo he ros fram deth to livë!
    Þurw þe holë ston he glod;
also he was of þee boren —
bothen after and biforen
    hol bilof þi maidenhod.

10

Newë blissë he us broutë
55 þat mankén so deerë boutë
    ánd for us ȝaf his deer lif.
Glad and blithë þu us makë
for þi sweetë sones sakë,
    edi maiden, blisful wif.

11

Queen of heven, for þi blissë
liȝt al urë sorinissë;
    wend ur ill al into good.
Bring us, moder, to þi sonë;
65 mak us evrë with him wunë
    þat us boutë with his blood.
        Amen.

COMMENTARY

Source: London, British Library, MS Arundel 248, ff. 154ᵛ-155.

This poem is another rendering of the Latin sequence *Stabat*

juxta Christi crucem, of which the text is given above (no. 10(i)). The English author evidently made it his aim to write a 'regular' sequence that should exactly follow the metrical pattern of the Latin, as far as the syllable-count 887887 was concerned; for even in the MS text there are only six lines (ll. 15,

18, 25, 30, 48 and 63) which, when allowance has been made for elision, loss of final -e, or obvious variant forms, do not conform to this syllabic pattern, and of these only two are 'paired' lines, i.e. the corresponding lines of the two half-stanzas. In the other four cases the irregularities are not matched in the other half-stanza and must be due to scribal error, since they offend against the basic requirement of sequence-form. Thus in 66 lines there are only two whose irregularity, in number of syllables, might, since it is 'paired', be due to the author; and it is easy to reduce both of these to regularity. It seems clear that the author intended complete regularity of syllable-count, and that the apparent irregularities are due to scribal error; and editing must proceed on this assumption. The author allowed himself some variety of rhythm, but here again it seems to me that he has not been served well by the copyists, and that several of the rougher lines are due to faulty transmission of the text.

Final -e is normally well preserved, in grammatically or etymologically justified cases, but there are a number of instances in which metre or rhyme shows that it has been lost where it would normally be pronounced in ME (e.g. ll. 20, 30, 40, 41, 46 and 57). This would ordinarily be taken, in an early poem, as a Northern feature. Yet the i- prefix is used, and established by metre, in ll. 3 and 12. This is the same situation as in no. 15(ii) below (*Gabriel fram heven-king*), recorded in the same Arundel MS, and in general the dialect of the two pieces seems identical. Both are translations from Latin originals, and both exhibit great skill in reproducing exactly the metrical form of their originals (at the cost of treating final -e as something that can be dropped when it is convenient to do so); the conclusion that they are by the same author seems inevitable.

We can get closer to the place of origin of the two poems because of the use, in l. 34 of this piece, of the word *goulinge* 'usury'. It is a rare derivative of *gavel* 'tribute, interest', and *OED* has only two instances, in the form *gavelinge,* from two Kentish texts of the early fourteenth century; ours is to be added, and is earlier. But more particularly in its actual form *goulinge* it is derived from *goul(e),* a development of *govel* < OE *gofol,* which is a variant of the normal ME *gavel* < OE *gafol.* In OE *gofol* is found only in *The Battle of Maldon,* a poem probably written in Essex; in ME *govel* occurs only in East Anglian texts; and *goule* (*gowle*) itself occurs in *Vices and Virtues* (Essex) and the *Promptorium Parvulorum* (Norfolk). The use of the word, in this form, therefore makes it probable that the present poem, and no. 15(ii) also, were written either in East Anglia or Essex; and the early (though only partial) loss of -e would seem to make East Anglia more likely than Essex, and Norfolk more likely than Suffolk. In ll. 40-41 OE $\bar{æ}^1$ in *weer* 'were' rhymes with ME $\bar{e}$ < OE *ēo* in *deer* 'dear'; on the other hand *utleten* in l. 26 (which has OE $\bar{æ}^1$ if it descends directly from OE -*lǣten,* though it may represent earlier ME -*lēten,* as in Orm) rhymes with *beten* (with ME $\bar{e}$ < OE *ēa*). Such variation in the rhyming of OE $\bar{æ}^1$ is found in the Norfolk texts *The Bestiary* and *Genesis and Exodus.*

To judge from its language and style, this version of the sequence is of later date than nos. 10(ii) and 11; and from parallels of phrasing it would seem that its author knew both of them.

MS Arundel 248 gives the words and music of four English religious songs (nos. 7, 12, 14 and 15(ii) in this book), along with various French and Latin religious songs (of which one, a Latin and French song to our Lady, was 'after the song *Aaliz*', presumably a secular love-song). The MS was written, not by a single hand, towards the end of the thirteenth century. Its contents are extremely miscellaneous, but are almost all religious or theological or things that might be useful to a preacher; it is a collection made by and for clerics. According to the British Museum catalogue, the MS had been given to H. Savil Jr. by Thomas Foxcroft of 'Christall', which is the modern Chrishall (formerly *Cristhall,* etc.) in the extreme North-west of Essex, just south of the southern border of Cambridgeshire. The spellings of its English texts, especially the use of *e* for OE $\bar{y}$ and $\bar{y}$ and of *u* (a very distinctive feature) for OE $\bar{o}$, especially in certain words, are consistent with an origin in this general neighbourhood; the former occurred, north of the Thames, in Essex, Suffolk, and to some extent in Norfolk and Cambridgeshire (see Jordan, § 40), the latter in Suffolk and Norfolk (cf. Jordan, § 54 Anm.). To judge from its contents, the MS is one which might have belonged to a Franciscan house, of which the nearest to Chrishall, within the area suggested by the spellings of the MS, were in Cambridge and Bury St. Edmunds. But the four English songs are almost certainly of diverse origin. The present piece, and no. 15(ii), were probably composed, as remarked above, in East Anglia, i.e. in the same general area as that in which the MS itself was written (though the texts given in the MS are certainly copies, and not very accurate in their representation of the original linguistic forms). No. 7 above seems to come from the South-east Midlands, probably the London area; so does no. 14 below, though it is likely to have, at least ultimately, a different source from no. 7, since it is not included, as no. 7 is, in the Digby and Rawlinson MSS. The occurrence of the four songs together in the Arundel MS does not, therefore, mean that they are all by the same author; they are a collection made by the compiler(s) of the MS. A curious orthographic feature of the English texts is a constant misuse of the letter *þ*, mostly for *h*; this suggests a scribe who was unused to the traditional English letters. The letter *h* itself is often misused; it is omitted from words which should have it, both stressed and unstressed, and conversely initial *h* is often wrongly used in words, again both stressed and unstressed, which should lack it. For *ch* (e.g. in *ich, swich*) the scribe uses *cs* or *chs* (*ics, ichs,* etc.). Such aberrations are usually, and with good reason, taken to be signs of an Anglo-Norman scribe, unfamiliar with correct English pronunciation and spelling. They are corrected in my texts.

NOTES

1. *moder*] The rhyme with *roode* is imperfect, as the *r* was pronounced in ME. But it shows that the author still used the original long vowel in *moder,* which in the system of spelling which we normally use would therefore be better spelt, in this instance, *mooder.*

2. *stood*] *stud* MS, and so elsewhere; similarly *blud* for *blood* (1. 5), *bludi* (l. 14), *gud* for *good* (l. 63). As in other poems, we normalize these characteristic spellings of the Arundel scribe. *biheeld*] *biheld* MS, but the vowel was originally long and probably still was; the same applies to *heeng* (*heng* MS) in l. 4.

3. *ipined* 'tortured'; metre confirms that the author used the form with the prefix *i*- (so MS). *an*] *on* MS, but the rhyme requires the variant *an.* Cf. *fram* 'from' in no. 15, l. 1. These forms may either show the survival of WGmc *ă* or be newly developed under weak stress.

4. *sone*] The metre shows that here the final *-e* is not elided before *h*.

5. *hire*] Metre here requires the disyllabic form; contrast *hir* in l. 2 (where the MS wrongly has *hire*).

6. *wu* 'how'.
his] *hise* MS. In ME *his* was given a plural form *hise* when used to qualify a plural noun, and the scribe uses it in several such cases (here and in ll. 14 and 23, but not in l. 22); but except in l. 16 the metre shows that the author used the older uninflected form.

7. *þo* 'when' (here); but in l. 11 it means 'then'. Other examples of the sense 'when' are in ll. 14, 33 and 50.
starf 'died', past t. sg. of *sterven* (the modern *starve*).
is king] *king is* MS. Though it may be argued against the change that it assumes that the scribe has altered a normal to an inverted word-order, it is more likely that a ME poet would bring two unstressed syllables together at mid-line than in the last foot; and the music gives prominence to the third-last syllable in the line, which seems more appropriate for *king* than for *is*. The scribe seems also to have changed the word-order, to the detriment of metre, in the following line.

8. *dreerier* 'sadder, more sorrowful'.
never nas] *nas neuerre* MS. The line as given in the MS has the right number of syllables (if *never* is taken as disyllabic), but has only three natural stresses; and even if both *nas* and *never* are stressed, there are clashing stresses at mid-line, which the poet seems to avoid. Transposition of the words solves the difficulty.
no] originally omitted by the scribe, and then interlined; this may suggest that he was distracted at this point, and explain the transpositions of word-order assumed in this line and the preceding.
wif 'woman', the older sense of the word.

9. *levdi*] *leuedi* MS, but as usual the disyllabic form is required.

10. *briȝte*] *brithe* MS, and similarly *nith* 'night' (ll. 10, 43), *lith* 'light' (ll. 11, 44), *mithte* 'might' (l. 30); but I normalize.
went 'turned, changed'.

11. *þin*] *hin* MS, a reversal of the usual error in this MS of writing *þ* for *h*.
herte 'heart's', an older genitive sg. < OE *heortan*.

12. *iqueint* (so MS), 'quenched'; again the *i-* prefix is required by metre.

13. *þi lif* 'thy person', 'thy being'; cf. *OED*, s.v. *life*, 6(a), but this is an earlier instance than any *OED* cites, and more obviously concrete.
drei 'suffered, endured'.
stundes 'pangs', a sense developed from 'times of hardship', and that in turn from the basic sense 'times', in such contexts as the present.

14. *sei* (*seye* MS) 'saw'. The 2 sg. indic. of the past tense was properly *seyë* < OE *sēge*; here there is elision before *h*.

15. *lich*] *bodi* MS. Both here and in l. 25 the MS reading *bodi* disturbs the metre and gives the line a syllable too many as compared with the corresponding line of the other half-stanza; and there is a consequential discrepancy with the musical setting. The author must have used the older word *lich*, for which

a scribe has substituted the more up-to-date synonym.
doon (*don* MS) 'done' in the sense 'placed'.

16. *hise*] here the disyllabic plural form used by the scribe is needed for metre.

17. *stungen* 'pierced'.
þurw . . . þurw] *þureu . . . þurw* MS, but the same monosyllabic form is required in each case. The spelling *þurw* for 'through' is characteristic of this scribe.

18. Cf. no. 11, l. 12, 'þat me bihȝte Simeon'. The parallel is the more striking because there is no reference to Simeon in the Latin sequence (cf. no. 10(i) above).
tee (*te* MS) 'thee', with *þ* assimilated to *t* after *s*.
hiȝte] *bihichte* MS, in the same sense 'promised'. But the line is too long by a syllable; we must either substitute the simplex *hiȝte* or the alternative past tense form *bihiȝt* (without *-e*). The latter keeps closer to the wording of no. 11, l. 12, but the former gives more regular metre, parallel to l. 15 above (as emended), and I choose it for this reason.

19. *hed*] *heued* MS, but the monosyllable is certainly required.
bisprunken 'besprinkled', strong p.p. of *besprinken*. See *OED*, s.v. *sprink* vb., which is more accurate than the entry under *besprink*; this example is earlier than any cited for either word.

20. *side* < OE *sīde* should have a pronounced final *-e* in ME, but it is here dropped, though no elision is possible; the line is parallel with l. 23 and must have only eight syllables.

21. *biheelde* (*bihelde* MS); the inflexion *-e* of the 2 sg. past indic. eg. of a strong verb is here retained.
levdi] *leuedi* MS.

23. *iwash*] *washen* MS. We change the form of the p.p. for the sake of metrical regularity. The musical setting is somewhat in favour of a word stressed on the second syllable, for in what is normally the lower of the two parts the note to which the second syllable is set is higher and therefore more prominent. The Arundel scribe has a distinct tendency to add *-n* to words from which it was, in ME, often lost; his exemplar may have had here *iwashe* (but with unpronounced *-e*). The author of this piece frequently uses the *i-* prefix of p.ps. (cf. *istungen* in l. 20), and there are several instances in the poem of the loss of *-e* (see the introductory note above); the Southern and South Midland p.p. *iwashe* could therefore be reduced to *iwash* in the author's speech. The Norfolk *Bestiary* has the strong p.p. *towrong* 'twisted awry' in l. 42 (rhyming with *unstrong*), which shows that complete loss of the suffix *-en* is possible in the area to which we assign this song.

24. *and*] *an* MS, the unstressed form of *and*; but the word here bears metrical stress.

25. *lich*] *bodi* MS; see note to l. 15 above.
beten] here OE *ēa* in *bēaten* rhymes with OE *ǣ¹* in *lǣten*, a 'Saxon' type of rhyme; but Cambridgeshire, Norfolk, and Suffolk appear to have belonged to the area in which the 'Saxon' development of OE *ǣ¹* was found (Jordan, § 49).

26. *so wide utleten* 'so widely diffused'.

27. 'made thy heart sore within thee'. *þee* (*þe* MS) is dative in function. It is interlined in the MS, and *wel* has been deleted after *herte*; evidently the scribe had omitted the pronoun and supplied another word to make up the required number of syllables but fortunately decided to return to the text of his

copy. If he had not done so, emendation would have been difficult, and any editor attempting it would have run the risk of being accused of treating the MS with undue freedom. The instance shows how easily a scribe could spoil metre, leaving no other clear sign of miscopying.

28. *gun cast*] *castest* MS. The line as written by the scribe has the right number of syllables but only three natural stresses; to put a metrical stress on *þu* immediately before the stressed syllable of its verb *castest* would be very artificial and produce clashing stresses at mid-line where there is plainly no pause in sense. Moreover the fourth syllable in the line is set to a doubled (lengthened?) note in the lower part, which would seem inappropriate for the inflexional ending *-est*. I assume that the scribe has substituted the simple past tense *castest* for one formed with the auxiliary *gan* (equivalent to the later *did*). *Gan* itself is the form of the 1 and 3 sg., though it might be extended to the 2 sg. in a text of this date; but the proper form of the 2 sg. was *gunne*, which under weak stress, as an auxiliary, would be liable to early reduction to *gun*. Two somewhat earlier East Anglian texts, the *Bestiary* and *Genesis and Exodus*, though they seem to have no examples of the 2 sg. indic., preserve the historical distinction between *gan* and *can* 1 and 3 sg. indic. and *gun(n)e(n)* and *cun(n)e(ṅ)* for the pl. indic. and the subjunctive; presumably they would have had *gun(n)e* and *cun(n)e* for the 2 sg. indic. But a monosyllable is needed here, and I therefore read *gun*, though *gan* would be possible. At this date *didst cast* would be unlikely; but *Havelok* l. 707 has an instance of *dede it tere* in a context where the meaning 'tarred it' is more likely than 'had it tarred'. The occurrence of the neologism *didst cast* would give the scribe a good reason for substituting *castest*; but *gun cast* is more probable in ME.
eien pl. 'eyes'. The Arundel scribe has something of a habit of adding *-n* where his copy cannot have had it; but I let his forms stand where there is no special reason to doubt them.

29. *sei*] see note to l. 14 above. Carleton Brown reads the MS here as *soie*, but in any case this would merely be an error for *seie*.

30. *miȝte*] *ne mithte* MS. Verbs in negative sentences were in ME so often preceded by the particle *ne*, even when there were other negative words in the sentence, that scribes show a distinct tendency to add it where it was not intended by the author. Its insertion here makes the line a syllable too long, in comparison with l. 27.
þole] *þolie* MS. Only two syllables are required. Short-stemmed verbs of the OE *-ian* conjugation preserve *-ien* beside *-en* in the *Bestiary*, and the scribe's form is not necessarily false to the original dialect. But forms like *þolie(n)* were properly trisyllabic, and though they might have been reduced to two syllables by a change of the *i* to the consonant *y*, it is much simpler to substitute the variant *þole*.
mor] so MS. As the word is from the OE comparative adjective *māre* (though here used as an adverb, in place of *mā*), it should properly end in *-e* in ME; here again historical *-e* has been lost.

31. *ȝeelde*] *ȝielde* MS (cf. *ȝiolden* MS for *ȝolden* in l. 40). The *i* apparently represents a vocalic glide after the palatal consonant. The word is 2 sg. pres. subj.; 'now is the time for you to yield'.

32. *keende* 'Nature', a South-eastern form of *kind*; MS *kende*.
withheelde] *withelde* MS, here and in l. 36. The MS form probably divides *wit-helde*, since *wit* is a common spelling of *with*; I normalize.
oskeþ 'asks' (*hoschet* MS). Cf. no. 7, l. 30, and note.

34. *goulinge* 'usury, interest'. Here and in the next line the verbal noun adds *-e* to the OE feminine suffix *-ing*; contrast *childing* in l. 42. The suffix naturally has secondary stress, but in rhyming position there was often an artificial inversion of the stress, as here, so that it shifted from the stem to the suffix.

35. *þat* 'what'.

36. *þar biforn* 'there before', 'on that previous occasion'.

37. *fondest* 'dost experience'.

38. *wif dreieth*] *wyman drith* MS. The MS text has the right number of syllables, but (a) it requires us to put a metrical stress on *with* immediately after a stressed monosyllabic verb, (b) it has clashing stresses at mid-line, (c) I doubt whether in the author's dialect the contracted 3 sg. *drith* would have occurred for *dreieth*. The emended text assumes that, just as the scribe substituted *bodi* for the older *lich*, so here he has substituted *wyman* for *wif* in its older sense of 'woman' (established in l. 8, where rhyme forbids substitution); and that to accommodate the added syllable he further altered *dreieth* to *drith*.
The sense is 'what a woman suffers'.

40. *þee is*] *þes* MS (the *s* interlined above, as an afterthought). The MS form is a contraction of *þe is* 'thee is', and gives the line the right number of syllables, assuming that *deere* at the end (*dere* MS) has its original disyllabic pronunciation. But if l. 41 is emended as I think it should be, it follows that in the present line *deer* (monosyllable) must replace *deere* (disyllable); and as a further consequence *þee is* must replace the scribe's contracted *þes* to restore the full number of syllables.

41. *þo*] om. MS. The line as written by the scribe has the right number of syllables, if his *were* at the end is taken as a disyllable, but has only three natural stresses; we can hardly stress both syllables of *warof* to make up a fourth. A stressed syllable is needed between *warof* and *þu*, and I assume that *þo* 'then' has dropped out before *þu*. But as the line should only have eight syllables, it follows that *were* should be a monosyllable, and I substitute *weer*, since the rhyme with 'dear' requires ME *ē* in 'were' — here the Anglian development of OE *ǣ*[1], in contrast to the rhyme at ll. 25–26 above. Loss of final *-e* in 'were' is common owing to weak-stressed forms, but in *deer* < OE *dēore* it is a case of early loss of *-e* in a word which in ME should retain it. Contrast the adverb *deere* in l. 56 below.
weer < OE (Anglian) *wēre* is 2 sg. past indic., equivalent to the later *wert* or *wast*. Cf. *weere*, with retained *-e*, in l. 49.

42. *in þi*] *ine ti* MS.
childing] *chiltuing* MS, a confused spelling.
quit] *quite* MS; the *-e* is perhaps a French feminine inflexion, but is wrongly used here.

43. *Soon*] *Sone* MS. The scribe intended two syllables, for he repeated the musical note; but l. 46 has only a single syllable and a single note to correspond. We must I think take it that the author intended elision of the *-e* of *soone* before the vowel of *after*, in spite of the sense-pause, and that the scansion is //xx/x/x.
sorwe] *sorwen* MS. The scribe's form is a plural, but though 'night of sorrows' is not impossible sense, 'night of sorrow' is

more likely (cf. *fletus tui nox* in l. 62 of no. 10(i)), and I suspect that here the Arundel scribe has been indulging his propensity to add *-n*. He probably began by replacing *morwe* in the next line by the full form *morwen* and in consequence made *sorwe* into *sorwen*; but he was doubtless influenced by *sorwen* in l. 46, where the plural seems to me to be correct.

44. *sprong* 'sprang, arose'.
edi 'blessed'.
morwe] *morwen* MS; cf. note to l. 43. The *-n* is not needed to prevent elision before the following word *in*, in view of the line-division.

45. *may* 'woman, maiden'. Cf. Orm's *maʒʒ*, presupposing OE *mǽg* (so Luick, § 384 Anm. 5; Holthausen, *Altengl. Etym. Wb.*), not OE *mǽg(e)* 'kinswoman', as often assumed (cf. *OED*, s.v. *may* sb.[1]). The rhyme here is on OE *ǽg* in *dǽg > day*.

46. *wenden*] *wen* MS. The scribe has omitted *den* by homeoteleuton in the sequence *(sor)wen wenden*. Carleton Brown reads *wen[de]*, but *wenden* is better, to prevent elision before *al*; and the plural form of the verb, which both the textual and the metrical reasons support, confirms that *sorwen* 'sorrows', which is good sense, is correct, as against the singular *sorwe* 'sorrow'.
al 'entirely', an adverb.
blis] *blisse* MS, but *blis* is already used after a preposition in the *Bestiary*, and in the next line we must read *iwis* for MS *iwisse*.

47. *sone*] elision fails because of the caesura.
al mid iwis 'altogether with certainty', 'with complete certainty'. In this idiom the adjective *iwis* is used as a noun.
iwis] *iwisse* MS, an undoubted variant, but the line must have only eight syllables to match l. 44 above.

48. *ros*] *aros* MS, which makes a syllable too many.
pridde 'third'; *tridde* MS.

49. *Wella*, an interjection (OE *wel-lā*); the MS has *welle*, a recorded but more ambiguous form.
wat þu weere blithe 'how happy you were'.

50. *he ros*] *þaros* MS, a mis-spelling of *haros*, which in its turn is intended as a contraction of *he aros* 'he arose'; but in view of the undoubted substitution of *aros* for original *ros* in l. 48 it is better to read the straightforward *he ros*.
live, dat. sg. of *lif* 'life'.

51. 'He glided through the complete (i.e. unbroken, intact) stone.' Cf. no. 10(ii), l. 60 above; neither is a close translation of the Latin.
þurw] *þur* MS.
he] *þe* MS, and similarly in ll. 52 and 55.

52. *also* 'likewise, in the same manner'.

54. *hol bilof* 'intact remained'.

55. *blisse*] here two syllables, without elision before *h*, in part because of the mid-line caesura.
broute 'brought', the characteristic spelling of this MS, with omission of *ʒ* (*gh*) after *ou*.

56. *manken*] *mankin* MS. but for consistency I substitute the South-eastern form with *e*, used elsewhere in the MS.
deere boute 'dearly bought'; the original could equally well have had *deer aboute* 'dearly paid for'.

57. *ʒaf* 'gave', the native form with *ʒ*, not the Scandinavian form with *g* that might well be expected in the dialect of this author. The MS has *þaf*, with *þ* in this instance misused for *ʒ*.
deer] *dere* MS, but the form with loss of final *-e* is essential if the line is to have only seven syllables and match l. 60 below. Cf. l. 40 and note above.

61. *blisse*] here again two syllables are required; compare l. 55 and contrast l. 46. The author is plainly taking advantage of current variants.

62. *liʒt*] *lithe* MS. In the spelling-system used by the scribe, *lithe* could equally well be a spelling of the verb *liʒt* 'light', i.e. make light, lighten, assuage, or of the verb *lithe* (from the adjective *lithe*), which also means 'assuage'. It is a toss-up, but the dictionary evidence suggests that *liʒt* 'light' was more common and more often used with words like *sorinisse*.
sorinisse] *sorinesse* MS, but the rhyme requires the form in which the *e* of the suffix had become *i*.

63. The MS reads *and went hur yuel al in to gud*, which *inter alia* is two syllables too many. One can be saved by the omission of *and* at the beginning; the scribe did not understand the construction, with parallel clauses not connected by a conjunction, and has added *and*. Similarly at the beginning of l. 65 a word has been erased; apparently there too he had added *and* but thought better of it. The other syllable can be cut by (i) replacing the native *yuel* 'evil' by its synonym *ill* derived from Norse; (ii) omitting *al*; (iii) omitting *in*. I choose the first alternative because there is no obvious reason why the scribe should have inserted either *al* or *in*, whereas he has thrice elsewhere substituted one synonym for another; and the substitution of *yuel* for *ill* has parallels in other texts. The noun *ill* in the sense 'evil' might well be expected in an East Anglian text.

64. *wune* 'dwell' (*wone* MS).

65. *with his*] *wit þis* MS.

IV. SONGS OF THE LATER THIRTEENTH AND EARLY FOURTEENTH CENTURIES

13. Edi be thu, heven-queene

1

Edi be þu, heven-queenë,
   folkes froovre and engles blis,
maid unwemmed, moder cleenë,
   swich in world non oþer nis.
5 On þee hit is wel eþ-seenë
   of allë wimmen þu hast þe pris.
Mi sweetë levdi, heer mi beenë
   and rew of me ȝif þi will is.

2

Þu astiȝë so dai-rewë
10   deleð from þe derkë niȝt.
Of þee sprong a leeme newë;
   al þis world [hit] ha ð iliȝt.
Nis no maid of þinë hewë —
   so fair, so scheenë, so rudi, so briȝt;
15 [mi] levdi sweet, of me þu rewë
   and havë merci of þi kniȝt.

3

Sprungë blostm of onë rootë,
   þoli gost þee rest upon;
þat was for mankínnes bootë
20   and her soul aleesë for on.
Levdi mildë, soft and swootë,
   ich crië merci, ich am þi mon,
to hondë boþen and to footë
   on allë wisë þat ich kon.

4

25 Erþ art tu to goodë seedë,
   on þee liȝtë þeven-dew;
of þee sprong þet edi bleedë —
   þoli gost hit on þee sew.
Bring us ut of kar, of dreedë
30   þat Evë bitterlich us brew;
þu schalt us into hevnë leedë —
   wel sweet is [us] þet ilkë dew.

5

Moder ful of þewes heendë,
   maidë dreiȝ and wel itauȝt,
35 ich am in þi luvë-beendë
   and to þee is al mi drauȝt.
Þu me schild, ȝe from þe feendë,
   as þu art free and wilt and mauȝt,
[and] help me to mi lives eendë
40   and makë wið þi sunë sauȝt.

COMMENTARY

Source: Oxford, Corpus Christi College, MS 59, f. 113ᵛ.

This song, printed by Carleton Brown, *English Lyrics of the XIIIth Century,* as no. 60, is accompanied in the MS by two other English lyrics, which he prints as nos. 59 and 61. The MS, as he has shown (cf. op. cit., p. 212), comes from Llanthony Priory in Gloucestershire, an Augustinian house, and it was his view that these lyrics 'in all probability were not copied from another MS but were composed by the possessor of the book who, as I surmise, was chaplain at Llanthony and master of a grammar school' (op. cit., p. xxvii).

There is no difficulty in accepting this view of no. 59, a hymn to God the Father, which is a free translation of a Latin hymn which immediately precedes it in the MS and is known from no other source. The English rendering was originally drafted in the MS in plummet and was subsequently inked in in somewhat different spellings; and from the palaeographical details (op. cit., p. 213) it appears that the English rendering must have been made after 1265. As the two other English poems come much later in the MS, the same dating must *a fortiori* apply to them, or rather to the date when they were written in the MS. But there is this qualification to be made to Carleton Brown's view of no. 59: the man who composed it was certainly not a native of Gloucestershire and was probably not the man who wrote the ink text, for in ll. 21–24 the rhymes require the East Midland or Northern form *hille* < OE *hyll* where the scribe has the SW Midland spelling *hulle,* and the same sequence establishes the adjective *ille* < ON *illr,* which at this date was certainly an Eastern and Northern word (cf. also *lest* 'vice' in l. 14). In l. 12 *neor þe* seems a false Westernizing of *ner þe* 'near thee', in which case its rhyme-words were also originally written with *e.* The plummet spellings show Eastern or Northern *nede* where the ink text has *neode,* and several times have *a* for OE *ā* (e.g. *lauerd* 'lord'), at this date either a Northern or an archaic spelling. It looks as though the author came from the NE Midlands, the ink scribe from the SW Midlands.

The third of the English pieces (no. 61 in Carleton Brown) is a short poem to the Virgin written in superficially the same stanza-form as *Edi be þu* and in the same spellings; there are some resemblances in phrasing, and it has the air of an inferior imitation. In it, too, there are signs that the SW Midland spellings do not properly represent the dialectal forms of the author; *gleo* (l. 21) is rhymed with *cherite* and *me*, and words from Norse occur in l. 5 (*calle*, at this date predominantly Eastern and Northern, though it occurs in *Ste. Marherete*) and l. 12 (*sauchte*). These stanzas could hardly be sung to the tune of *Edi be þu*, for their metre is too rough and could not be reduced to sufficient regularity by credible emendation. Both no. 59 and no. 61 were written by a poet accustomed to count stresses rather than syllables and indifferent to the order of stressed and unstressed syllables, i.e. they are in the normal versification of ME 'literary' lyrics as distinct from songs. No. 61 may well have been written by the same man as no. 59, though there is little positive evidence for the supposition.

But Carleton Brown's thesis can hardly be applied to *Edi be þu* (his no. 60), the only one of these poems to be accompanied in the MS by music. It is true that in the margins of the MS there are written certain textual variants, evidently intended as replacements of the words first written in the text, which have the appearance of an author's revisions (and improvements) of his own work; but these begin only with the sixth stanza, and affect it and the seventh. *Edi be þu*, as given in the MS, in fact falls into two distinct parts. The first five stanzas make up a song of reasonable length, complete in itself, which concludes, in stanza 5, with a prayer to Mary (partly anticipated in stanza 4) for protection against the Devil, for aid, and for intercession with her Son — the conventional ending for such a poem. The verses are a religious love-poem in which, in characteristic medieval fashion, the ideas and language of a medieval love-lyric are applied to the worship of Mary; she is a high lady of incomparable beauty, and the poet is her 'man' and her 'knight' who begs for her 'pity' and 'mercy' and who is bound to her by the fetters of love. He writes in the first person and his final prayer is for himself.

In the last three stanzas, which go on after an obvious conclusion has been reached, this personal quality is entirely lacking; the words 'I' and 'my' are not used at all. The sixth stanza continues the theme of Mary as the ideal mistress and keeps so close to the original rhyme-pattern and metre that it can be regularized by only slight emendations; if it were not for the marginal corrections alluded to above, it would be easy to regard it as a verse of the original song that had got displaced (it could fit in well enough after stanza 3, which begins with an allusion to the tree of Jesse, picked up in stanza 6 by a reference to Mary's descent from David). But it is rather an addition, elaborating the ideas of the earlier stanzas; cf. the first half of l. 43, which repeats that of l. 13. The seventh and eighth stanzas completely lose sight of the 'love-poem' convention and are explicitly doctrinal; the eighth ends with a perfunctory repetition of the prayer for protection in stanza 5. The first five stanzas appear to be a SW Midland copy of a poem written in the SE Midlands (see below); but the other three seem really to have been written in the SW Midlands. In stanza 6 there is a rhyme-sequence *kunne* 'kin' — *sunne* 'sun' — *kunne* 'can' (2 sg. pres. indic.) — *wunne* 'joy' (< OE *wynn*) which, though not a perfect rhyme in any ME dialect, is at least an eye-rhyme in SW Midland spellings; and in l. 63 there is used the word *bolde* 'dwelling' which in ME literary use is predominantly West

Midland and South-western (Trevisa). In stanza 7 there is what seems to be a significant parallel to a passage in the West Midland *Ancrene Wisse (Ancrene Riwle)*. But the most serious difference is that stanzas 7 and 8 depart from the original rhyme-scheme in a way that is really incompatible with the musical setting. In the first five stanzas (and the sixth) the even-numbered lines end with 'masculine' rhymes, i.e. with a stressed syllable; but in the last two stanzas they end with 'feminine' rhymes (i.e. words ending, in this case, with -e), and the lines are therefore increased in length by an unstressed syllable which (except perhaps that at the end of l. 54) cannot possibly be elided. For this additional syllable the composer did not and could not provide; the music is written on the assumption that these lines will end in a metrically stressed syllable, and the musical phrase correspondingly ends in a long and musically stressed note. If stanzas 7 and 8 are to be sung to the music, this long note has to be split, which is very unsatisfactory, especially as the final note of the whole song has to be so treated. Moreover at other points the metre of stanzas 7 and 8 diverges so radically from the norm that it can only be made to conform to the rhythmical pattern of the music by drastic emendation. These two stanzas, like Carleton Brown's nos. 59 and 61, have been written according to the metrical conventions of ME 'literary' verse, not of a song.

For these reasons I reject the final three stanzas of the MS text as an addition to the original song made by someone who did not appreciate the metrical requirements imposed by the musical setting. But he was probably not the same man as wrote nos. 59 and 61 in Carleton Brown's collection, in view of the linguistic differences (especially the SW rhyme-sequence and the SW word *bolde*). If in Llanthony Priory there was one brother who could write verse, there may well have been two (or even three); indeed two hands appear in the Latin verses of the MS (see Brown, op. cit., pp. 212–13). The three rejected stanzas are printed as an appendix to these notes; the rest of this discussion is confined to the first five stanzas, taken as constituting the original song. In view of the medieval fondness for such symbolism, it is perhaps not fanciful to point out that the number five had special associations with the cult of Mary (cf. *The Ancrene Riwle*, trans. Salu, pp. 17–18).

From the state of its text one might be tempted to deduce that the song was originally written down from memory, for though its gist is well preserved its details obviously are not. The clear and strong rhythm of the music as transcribed is not matched by the irregular metre of the text as the scribe gives it. Words are given in forms not intended by the poet, or in the wrong order; little words that do not much affect the sense are omitted or added; in several places the syntactical construction is altered. These are common signs of memorial transmission, but in the circumstances the variations from metrical regularity are probably due to conscious revision (for the worse) by the versifier(s) of Llanthony. That the irregular metre is the fault of those who transmitted or copied the text, and not of the original author, is shown by the ease with which the metrical scheme can be deduced from the extant words and from the music, and in most places by the obviousness of the emendations which restore regularity. In such a case as this, where there is only the one MS, which gives a text not credible in detail, an editor must have recourse to conjectural emendation, as slight as is necessary to recover metrical regularity and fit the words to the music.

At many points of the stanza the strongly-patterned music

will not accommodate any variation from the metrical norm. But towards the end of the even-numbered lines of each stanza it will tolerate either one or two unstressed syllables before the final stress of the line. In the twenty lines involved, the text even as given in the MS clearly has only a single unstressed syllable (when allowance is made for normal elisions) in sixteen instances. In two an additional syllable is produced by the scribe's use of the forms *hauest* (l. 6) and *haueð* (l. 12), where regularity can easily be restored by substituting the contracted forms *hast* and *ha ð* 'hath'. The two remaining cases are l. 14, where the MS text is *so rudi swo bricht,* and l. 20, where it is *alesen for on.* Both of these could be regularized by the substitution of synonyms (*red* for *rudi, free* for *alesen*), but it does not seem to be among the faults of the scribe to replace one word by another (as distinct from the use of the wrong forms of words). I have therefore decided, though not without hesitation, that although the author normally preserved metrical regularity at this point in the even-numbered lines where the music would allow a variation, in these two cases he did permit himself a slight departure from his normal scheme and that it is better not to emend.

At another point, in the sixth line of the stanza, there can be no doubt that he allowed a variation. Here the second stress of the line is followed by two unstressed syllables in stanzas 1–3, by only one in stanzas 4 and 5; and in stanza 4 (l. 30) no emendation is possible. The poet has evidently varied his scheme for the last two stanzas. Again the music will fit either form of the line, for in the corresponding bar there are three notes which can be sung separately when there are three syllables (one stressed and two unstressed), but of which the first two can be sung together to the stressed syllable when there is only one unstressed.

This song provides an instance, rare among our texts, of an author and a composer who were apparently distinct men and not working in complete accord. The matter concerns the elision of final *-e.* Elision normally occurs before a vowel or the *h* of an unstressed word, but may fail if the words are separated by a pause; and most ME poets treated the end of a verse-line as constituting a pause so marked that a final *-e* at the end of a line is never elided, even if the next line begins with a vowel. The rhymes of the song show quite clearly that the poet worked on this normal assumption. But the composer as plainly did not; for him the unit was not the verse-line, but the couplet, and each successive couplet is set to a continuous musical phrase. A final *-e* at the end of the odd-numbered lines (which is where it in fact occurs) was therefore, for the composer, in mid-phrase and liable to be elided if it was followed by a vowel at the beginning of the next verse-line. Now in stanza 1 it so happens that the sixth and eighth lines begin with a vowel; the composer elided the *-e* at the end of the fifth and seventh lines, and set the last word of each of these lines as if it were a monosyllable. But as the elision was not designed by the poet and the conditions for it had arisen by mere chance, it does not follow that similar elisions will necessarily be possible in later stanzas. By luck elision is possible, in stanzas 2–5, in five of the eight instances at the end of the fifth and seventh lines; in the three where it is not, the singer must split the note to accommodate the syllable for which the composer did not allow. What the composer has done is to set the first stanza as he scanned it, without observing that the poet had intended it differently and that subsequent verses could not regularly be scanned in the same way. In the 'literary' text above the final *-e* at the end of

these lines is marked as pronounced, since this was the intention of the poet; but in the 'performing' text we follow the intention of the composer and omit it whenever elision is possible.

The stanza-form that has been assumed in editing the text is, in terms of syllable-count, 87878998, and the accentual rhythm is as follows:

/x/x/x/x
/x/x/x/
/x/x/x/x
/x/x/x/
/x/x/x/x
x/x/xx/x/
x/x/x/x/x
x/x/x/x/

Emendation *metri causa* has been directed to the restoration of this pattern whenever the MS text diverges from it, with the exception of the acknowledged variations already discussed.

An editor aiming to restore the text of a ME poem must also make assumptions about the author's dialect. Superficially the forms used in the song are those of a SW Midland dialect, in all probability that of Gloucestershire (cf. the spellings with *eo* for OE *ēo* and *ēo, u* for OE *ў,* sporadic *e* for OE *ǽ, em* 'am', *ert* 'art'), but they are not consistently used and in some cases are plainly not original. We must go behind them to discover the dialect of the author. The use of the Norse words *boþen* (l. 23) and *sauʒt* (l. 40) rule out Southern dialects, though not those of the West and SW Midlands; so probably, at this date, that of *upon* (l. 18), a word which seems to have been formed on ON models. The 2 sg. pres. indic. *mauʒt* 'mayest' (l. 38) is Anglian, not Kentish or WS. The development of OE *ēo to ē* proved by the rhyming of *feende* (l. 37) < OE *feond* with words with late OE *ē* < *ě* before *nd* is East Midland (or Northern), and is utterly at variance with the SW Midland scribe's spelling with *eo.* OE *ǣ²* in *cleene* (l. 3) rhymes with OE *ē*; the same sound in *leede* 'lead' vb. (l. 31) rhymes with OE *ǣ¹* in *seede* and *dreede* 'dread' and with the word *bleede* 'blossom, fruit', which varies between *ē* and *ǣ¹.* Such rhymes of *ǣ²* could be Kentish, or due to the Anglian raising attributed (though doubtfully) to the influence of a following dental. OE *ǣ² + w* in *(dai)rewe* < OE *rǣw* (l. 9) rhymes with OE *ēow;* only in Kent can the former sound have become ME *ęu.* OE *ēaw* in *dew* (ll. 26, 32) and in *brew* p.t. (l. 30) rhymes with OE *ēow* in *sew* 'sowed' (l. 28). This rhyme-sequence presents a difficulty. If we were to follow Luick § 378, we could explain it as showing a change of ME *ęu* to *ęu;* but this paragraph in Luick is mistaken in its general theory (that the changes of *ęi* and *ǭu* to *ęi* and *ǭu* were associated with the assumption of open quality by *ě* and *ǒ,* which in fact was an independent and earlier change), and especially in its assumption that ME *ęu* could become *ęu,* which is asserted merely for the sake of logical consistency and against the evidence. No ME dialect should by natural development have identified OE *ēaw* and *ēow.* One might postulate for *sow* a new analogical p.t. as if from OE **sēaw,* in view of the known contact, in verbs whose past stem ended (or came to end) in *-w,* between the OE 2nd and 7th strong conjugations; but this would be to divorce the explanation of the rhymes in stanza 4 from those in stanza 2. The likeliest explanation is that in a dialect bordering on Kent (in particular in London) there would be variation between *ęu* and *ęu* in words with OE *ǣw,* and that this might by analogy lead to the occasional substitution of the commoner diphthong *ęu* for the rarer *ēu* in words with OE *ēaw*, though these should only have *ēu*. The forms of *mon* 'man' (l. 22) and *kon* 'can' (l. 24), rhyming with *upon* and *on* 'one', show OE *ŏ* before a nasal, which in ME is predominantly but not exclusively West Midland; such forms in the thirteenth century sometimes occur in poets apparently writing in the London area, and may well have been a literary convention, since they provided easy rhymes for the awkward but common preposition *on*. The p.ps. *ilịʒt* (l. 12) and *itauʒt* (l. 34) have the Southern or South Midland *i-* prefix.

It is evident that the rhyming scheme, with its requirement of four rhymes on each of two syllables in every stanza, has put the poet's technique under some strain and that he has been driven to doubtful expedients, but it is hard to think of any place in England where such a medley of dialectal features could be found in a few stanzas other than London; and I conclude that the dialect is a literary amalgam, essentially East Midland but modified and indeed confused by features from other dialects known in London but imperfectly understood by the poet. I therefore remove from the text Western features, other than the one (*ŏ* for *ă* before *n*) which is confirmed by rhyme.

The MS text and spellings are given by Carleton Brown, op. cit., no. 60. In the notes below I record all alterations of the text, but not necessarily alterations merely of spelling. For the three rejected stanzas see the end of the notes.

NOTES

1. *Edi* 'blessed'.

be] *beo* MS. I reject everywhere the scribe's SW Midland *eo* spelling, which he himself does not use with complete consistency (cf. his *heuene* in this line) and which does not represent correctly the author's pronunciation.

heven-] *heuene* MS, a trisyllabic form representing the OE gen. pl. *heofena*; but the metre requires two syllables, and the author obviously intended a normal compound noun (OE *heofon-cwēn*).

2. *froovre* 'consolation' (MS *froure*), a generalization of the oblique stem *frōfre* of OE *frōfor* fem. For the retention of the long vowel (ME *ō*, which we spell *oo*) in this word cf. *Ormulum*, l. 9650. The final *-e* is here elided, as in *Ormulum*, l. 8786.

and] The MS always uses the ampersand. I assume East Midland *and*, not West Midland *ond*.

engles 'angels', probably to be taken as gen. pl., not sg.

3. The MS reads *moder unwemmed & maiden clene*, which is two syllables too many. Omission of & gets rid of one. If we transpose *maiden* and *moder,* and assume for *maiden* the form *maide* (with loss of *-n*) which the MS itself has in ll. 13 and 34, then the final *-e* will elide before *unwemmed*. But elision is possible only if the words are transposed; it seems a clear case of words copied in the wrong order, in a context in which the sense is not really affected. In ME monosyllabic *maid* occurred only as a result of elision in dialects which preserved final *-e,* as this author's does.

5. *wel eþ-seene* 'very evident'. The MS has *wel eþ sene,* as if *eþ* were an independent adverb, doubtless because in the West Midlands the historical adverb *eþe* was replaced by *eþ,* deduced from such compounds as *eþ-sene* 'easily visible, manifest'. But the poet must have intended the compound. In OE compounds

in *eaŏ-* (*ēaŏfynde, ēaŏgesēne*) were stressed on the prefix, but in ME on the stem, as metre and alliteration show; in particular the *Poema Morale* (Jesus Coll. MS), l. 340, has *þat is wel eþ-sene* at the line-end, rhyming with *þene wey so schene*. So stressed, the MS text fits the metre and the music, which it would hardly do if *eþ* were an independent adverb; moreover Eastern texts seem to have kept the historical form *eþe* for the adverb.

6. *hast*] *hauest* MS. The music will allow of two syllables, but the monosyllabic form is metrically more regular at this point (but cf. l. 14 below).

þe] *þet* MS, but it is not apparent why the demonstrative should be used here; neither 'that prize' nor 'that praise' seems to have much point. It is much more likely that the poet intended the ME phrase *to haven* (or *beren*) *the pris* 'to have the preeminence, to surpass' (cf. *OED,* s.v. *price* sb., 11).

7. *levdi*] *leuedi* MS, but as usual metre requires the earlier disyllabic form.

beene 'request'.

8. *rew* 'rue', 'have pity'.

will] *wille* MS, the normal ME form, but the *-e* elides and is therefore omitted, as regularly in such cases.

9. *astiʒe*] *asteʒe* MS. The original form of the 2 sg. past indic. of this verb (meaning 'arose') was *astiʒe* < OE *astḗge*; the MS form is a new analogical one, due apparently to contact in form with the verb *liʒen* 'tell lies'. As the re-modelling had taken place in the West Midlands, it seems possible that the MS form is due merely to the scribe, and I restore the historical form.

9–10. *so dai-rewe deleŏ* 'as dawn divides' (i.e. separates itself). The MS reading is *so þe daiʒ-rewe þe deleŏ* 'like the dawn which separates itself', a reading which radically offends against the metre and cannot fit the music; moreover it is weaker in style. The copyist was evidently not prepared for the run-on sense.

10. *niʒt*] *nicht* MS. The scribe commonly but not regularly uses *ch* to represent the front and back voiceless spirants (OE *h*), but it seems better to generalize the more usual spelling with *ʒ,* which he also uses (and in the 'performing' text to use *gh*).

11. *sprong* 'sprang'. The word has ME *ǭ* < late OE *ā* by lengthening of *ă* before *ng.*

leeme 'ray, sun-beam' (*leome* MS).

12. *al þis world hit*] *þat al þis world* MS. The MS text will scan and fit the music only if we put heavy stresses on 'that' and 'this' and make 'all' and 'world' metrically unstressed, which seems excessively artificial. By reading *al þis woreld* and assuming an unexpressed relative we could keep l. 12 in the same subordinate syntactical relationship to l. 11 as it has in the MS text; but omission of the relative does not seem to be established before the later fourteenth century, and though disyllabic *woreld* still occurs in South-eastern texts in the early thirteenth century the poet certainly treats *world* as a monosyllable in l. 4. The reading adopted in the text seems the best solution; it assumes that the copyist, to tighten up the syntax, has changed a coordinate clause to a subordinate one.

13. *maid*] *maide* MS, but the *-e* elides before *of*. The reduction of *maiden* to *maide* by loss of *-n* took place in the first instance before consonants, but later *maide* was generalized and could also be used before vowels, where the *-e* will elide; the MS text is evidence of this generalization.

þine] The metre requires the -e to be pronounced. This is the dat. sg. (or 'post-prepositional') form of the possessive pronoun, used here where the metrical stress falls on the first syllable and the sense ('there is no maiden of *your* complexion') justifies some emphasis on the pronoun. Elsewhere in the poem possessives are unemphatic in sense and metrically unstressed, and uninflected forms are used even after prepositions; in l. 35 the scribe writes *þine* but metre requires *þi*. Here in l. 13 elision of -e fails before an *h* which begins a stressed word (though the article *þe* elides before *holi* in ll. 18 and 28 and before *heven-* in l. 26).

14. *rudi*] The use of the word introduces a metrical variation (see above). We could regularize either by reading *so rudi-briʒt* (but though colour-compounds of this sort are found in OE, *ruddy-bright* itself is not recorded until the eighteenth century) or by substituting *red* for *ruddy*, since *red* was still quite often used in this sort of context in reference to the complexion. But it seems best to retain the MS reading and accept the metrical variation, since it is not inconsistent with the music.

15. *mi levdi sweet*] *swete leuedi* MS. The line must begin with an unstressed word, and *mi* is supplied on the model of l. 7. But this gives the line a syllable too many; and by transposing *swete* to follow the noun its final -e can be elided before *of*. The reversal of word-order, as compared with l. 7, is paralleled in *of me þu rewe* (l. 15) against *and rew of me* (l. 8); the poet is practising a rhetorical inversion which the scribe has failed to appreciate.

17. 'Blossom sprung from a single root', a reference to the tree of Jesse. The *o* of *blostm* (*blostme* MS, but the -e is elided) was originally long but by this time short.

18. *þoli* 'the holy', with the article run on to the adjective by elision of its *e*, as was common. The scribe writes *þe holi*.
rest p.t. 'rested' (*reste* MS, but the -e is elided).

19. *þat was*] *þet wes* MS, possibly unstressed forms (though the demonstrative is metrically stressed), but probably West Midland forms with *e* for OE *ĕ*. I normalize, here and elsewhere.
mankinnes] *monkunnes* MS, a West Midland form, which I alter to that of the East Midlands. It is true that *mon* 'man' is established by rhyme in this very stanza, but I assume that it and *kon* 'can' are used for convenience of rhyming and may not represent the forms natural to the poet.

20. 'and in order to free their souls in exchange for one', i.e. for Christ. *Soul* (assumed to be for *soule*, but with -e elided) is probably singular, literally 'their soul'; this was the common ME idiom (since each has one soul).

The MS reading is *& heore soule to alesen for on* and presents a series of difficulties. (1) The line must begin with a stressed syllable. Whatever solution is adopted, it seems essential to replace *heore* by the unstressed monosyllabic form *her*. (2) Metre and music show that there should be only one unstressed syllable between the second and third stresses of the line. As the scribe gives the word-order, it would be necessary to have a monosyllabic form *soul* in place of his *soule*. But *soule* is the usual ME form, derived from OE *sāwle*, oblique singular of the feminine noun *sāwol*. OED provides no evidence of a singular *soul* (*saul*) except for dialects in which -e was beginning to be lost generally, though Luick § 453. 1, assumes *sawl* and *soul* as direct ME developments of the OE nominative *sāwol*. In our text the normal ME *soule* could be reduced to *soul* only by

elision, since there is no sign of the general loss of -e. (3) In the scribe's text, the preposition *to* is another metrically otiose syllable. It could be elided before the following vowel, thus *taleese* where *to alesen* is written, as was not uncommon; but if *to* is kept, even thus reduced, it will prevent the elision of the -e of *soule*.

There seem to be four possible solutions, as follows (an elided -e being here shown by italicization):

    (i) and her soul taleesë for on
    (ii) and taleese her soulë for on
    (iii) to aleese her soulë for on
    (iv) and her soule aleesë for on

Of these, (i) involves following the rather dubious assumptions of Luick's § 453.1. It is true that early ME *soul* might be alternatively explained as a back-formation from the plural forms *soule(n)*, *soules* or as an analogical form beside normal *soule* on the model of *bliss* (from the OE nominative) beside *blisse* (from the OE oblique singular), &c., but the evidence of *OED*'s list of forms is against the assumption of an early ME *soul*. Alternatives (ii) and (iii) both involve a change of word-order, and (iii) also involves the omission of *and* at the beginning of the line. The last version involves the omission of *to* and the assumption that the infinitive *aleese* in l. 20 and the noun *boote* in l. 19 are both governed by the preposition *for* in l. 19. In ME it is not very common for *for* alone (as distinct from *for to*) to govern an infinitive, but the idiom is well-established; cf. in particular the *Poema Morale*, Lambeth MS, l. 180, *Ne brekeþ neure drihte helle gate for lesen hi of bende.*

The choice seems to lie between (ii) and (iv). Hesitantly, I choose the latter, because it seems a little more likely that a scribe should insert *to* before an infinitive that appeared to lack a governing preposition than that he should alter the word-order so as to bring an object from position after the infinitve to position before it. In other words, if (iv) were the original text it would be more likely to provoke change than if (ii) were.

For MS *alesen* I read *aleese*, assuming loss of -n. In all four alternatives given above, we could reduce the line to complete metrical regularity by replacing *for on* by *anon* 'immediately', since the preceding -e would then elide; but this changes the meaning, and as the music permits an extra syllable at this point of the line it is better to retain *for on*.

22. *crie*] *crie þe* MS. The expression *to cry merci* 'to entreat pardon' can be used with or without a personal pronoun as indirect object; cf. *OED*, *cry* vb., 1. The music will allow of only one unstressed syllable at this point, and as the -e of *crie* must in this text be pronounced (it is the inflexion of the 1 sg. pres. indic.), the pronoun *þe* 'thee' must be omitted.
am] Here the scribe himself uses *am*, which I generalize.

23. *to honde boþen*] *boþe to honde* MS. In the word-order of the MS, the -e of *honde* should elide before *and*, which would make the line a syllable short; and in any case this line should begin with an unstressed syllable to fit the music. Transposition cures the second fault, and the substitution of the common variant *boþen* for *boþe* prevents elision. For post-position of *boþe(n)* see *OED*, s.v. *both*, B. adverb, 2; presumably the scribe did not like this order.
For *boþen* as an adverbial form see our no. 12, l. 53; Carleton Brown, *English Lyrics of the XIIIth Century*, no. 15, l. 20 and no. 20, l. 9; and *Havelok*, ll. 173 and 958.

25. *Erþ art tu*] *þu ert eorþe* MS. In the word-order of the MS the final *-e* of *eorþe* cannot be elided; and though the music could allow the extra syllable, it is unlikely that a variation would occur so early in the stanza. No other stanza has one at this point. By inverting the word-order we make it possible to elide the *-e* before *art*. Note the inverted word-order in the two lines following.

The MS has Western spellings; *ert* is especially a SW Midland form, apparently an alteration of *art* on the model of *em* < *eom* beside *am*. I substitute Eastern forms, and use the assimilated form *tu* of *þu* after (in my text) the *t* of *art*.

þeven-dew 'the heaven-dew', the dew of heaven. The MS has *þe heouene*, but the article must be elided. For *dew* the MS has *deuȝ*, and similarly with the rhyme-words (MS *seuȝ*, *breuȝ*, *deuȝ*). These are falsely archaic spellings, since none of the words had OE *g*; in some words later thirteenth-century *w* was from earlier *ȝ* < OE *g*, but not in these. There is no point in keeping these false and misleading spellings.

27. *þet*] *þeo* MS. The scribe has used the nom. sg. fem. of the definite article, since OE *blēd, blǣd* 'blossom, fruit' was fem. I doubt whether this very conservative preservation of grammatical gender can have been a feature of the original, especially as the poet elides the article before *h* and was likely to do so before a vowel. Commonly, to prevent elision, *þat* or *þet* (originally the nom. neuter) was used before a vowel, and I assume this here; as the word is metrically unstressed, though it has some demonstrative force, I prefer the unstressed form *þet*.

28. *þoli* 'the holy' (*þe holi* MS). Cf. 1. 18 above.

hit] *hire* MS, a clear case of the preservation of grammatical gender (cf. note to l. 27). But as I doubt whether it is original and indeed think it must be due to the SW Midland scribe, I substitute *hit*.

sew 'sowed', a strong past tense < OE *sēow*. On the rhyme, which on the face of it is inexact, see the introductory discussion of the author's dialect (above).

29. *Bring*] *þu bring* MS, but this makes the line a syllable too long, and it must begin with a stress.

kar 'care'. The MS has *kare*, but the *-e* elides in spite of the sense-pause that must divide it from the following *of*. The expressions *of kar(e)* and *of dreede* must be intended to be parallel: 'save us from the trouble, the fear . . .'.

30. *brew* 'brewed', < OE *brēaw* p.t. sg. of *brēowan*, a strong verb of class 2.

31. *hevne*] *heouene* MS, but only two syllables are possible, and as the poet's language preserved dative forms (cf. *pine* l. 13, *feende* l. 37) *hevne* is preferable to uninflected *heven*.

32. *is us* 'is to us'. The MS omits *us*, but as the *-e* of its *swete* must elide before *is* the line as it gives it is a syllable short. The addition also improves the sense. The omission is due to homeoteleuton.

þet] *þe* MS, but elision must be prevented; cf. note to l. 27. *Ilke* means 'same'.

33. *þewes heende* 'gracious virtues'. The diphthong of *þew*, as of *dew* and *brew* in the previous stanza, is properly ME *ęu* < OE *ēaw*, which in the normalized spelling-system used in these texts we should ordinarily spell *eaw*; but the anomalous rhymes in stanza 4 leave it uncertain how the poet in fact pronounced these words.

34. *dreiȝ* 'patient'.

35. *am*] *em* MS, possibly unstressed form, since the word is metrically unstressed, but more probably a Westernism.

þi] *þine* MS, the inflected dat. sg. form; but here the metre leaves no doubt that the uninflected *þi* is required.

luve-beende 'bonds of love'. The MS has *loue-bende*, but in this text it seems justifiable to replace the unphonetic *o* by *u*, since the scribe himself uses the spelling *sune* for 'son' in l. 57.

36. *drauȝt* 'attraction, inclination'.

37. *ȝe* 'yea', 'indeed'. Carleton Brown prints *schildȝe* as one word, and similarly *Iherdȝe* in his no. 59, l. 9; but *schildȝe* and *Iherdȝe* are impossible forms for *schild* imper. sg. 'shield' and *iherd* or *ihered* p.p. 'praised'. Miss Sisam has pointed out to me that in both cases *ȝe* is properly a separate word, the adverb *yea*, for which see *OED*, s.v.

38. *as*] *ase* MS, but the monosyllable is required.

art] *ert* MS.

free 'liberal, generous'.

mauȝt 'mayest'; 2 sg. pres. indic. of *may* (not past tense).

39. *and help*] *help* MS, but this line must begin with an unstressed syllable. Probably an ampersand has been omitted in copying.

lives 'life's', the historical form of the gen. sg.

40. *make*] *make me* MS. The music is transcribed as three notes, so that the extra syllable could be fitted in, but it is very unlikely that the poet intended a variation here; the pronoun is meant to be understood from the previous line, the scribe has made it explicit.

sauȝt 'reconciled'.

APPENDIX

The text of the three rejected stanzas, as spelt in the MS, is given below in the left-hand column. On the right is given a rewritten text, regularized in metre (except for the ineradicable fault of the feminine rhymes in the even-numbered lines), which was prepared for performance and can be sung to the music, provided that the long notes at the end of the even lines are split to allow for the additional syllable. In view of the probability that these added stanzas were composed at Llanthony and that the MS text is as its author intended, the regularized version is not presented as a reconstruction of what the author wrote, but as what he might perhaps have written if he had understood the requirements of the music more fully than he evidently did.

6

Þu ert icumen of heʒe kunne,
   of dauid þe riche king;
nis non maiden under sunne
   þe mei beo þin euening,
45 ne þat swo derne louiʒe kunne,
   ne non swo treowe of alle þing.
Þi loue us brouchte eche wunne;
   ihered ibeo þu, swete þing.

Þu art cum of heʒë kunnë,
   of David þe richë king;
nis no maiden under sunnë
   þat mai be þin evening,
þat so dernë luvë kunnë,
   ne non so trew of allë þing.
Þi luvë brouʒt us eechë wunnë;
   ihered be þu, sweetë þing.

7

Seolcudliche ure louerd hit diʒte
50   þat þu, maide wiðute were,
þat al þis world bicluppe ne miʒte
   þu sscholdest of þin boseme bere.
Þe ne stiʒte ne þe ne priʒte
   in side, in lende, ne elleswhere;
55 þat wes wið ful muchel riʒte,
   for þu bere þine helere.

Selcuðlich ur Lord hit diʒtë
   þat tu, maidë butë werë,
þat tis world bifon ne miʒtë
   scholdest of þi boosmë berë.
Þee ne stiʒtë, þee ne priʒtë,
   in sidе, in leendë, ne elleswherë;
and þat was wið ful muchel riʒtë,
   for þat tu beerë þin helerë.

8

Þo godes sune aliʒte wolde
   on eorþe al for ure sake,
herre teʒen he him nolde
60   þene þat maide to beon his make.
Betere ne miʒte he, þeiʒ he wolde.
   ne swetture þing on eorþe take.
Leuedi, bring us to þine bolde,
   & sschild us from helle wrake.

Þanne God aliʒtë woldë
   on erþ al for urë sakë,
herrë teʒen him he noldë
   þan þat maidë, to his makë.
Bet ne miʒt he, þeiʒ he woldë,
   ne swettrë þing on erþë takë.
Mi levdi, bring us to þi boldë
   and schild tu us from hellë wrakë.

44. *evening* 'equal' (who can compare with you).

45. 'who can love so intimately'.

46. *treowe*] so marginal correction; in text *swete*.

47. *þi loue us brouchte*] so marginal correction; in text *þu bring us in to*. But the substituted text involves failure of elision at mid-line.
eche 'eternal'.

48. *ihered* 'praised'.

49. *Seolcudliche* 'strangely'; so margin, as correction of *swetelic* 'sweetly' in text.
diʒte 'ordained'.

50. *were* 'husband'.

51-52. 'that thou shouldst bear from thy bosom him whom this world could not encompass'. Cf. *Ancrene Wisse* (Corpus MS, f. 19b/16-18): te lauerd þet al þe world ne mahte *bifon* bitunde him inwið hire meidnes wombe.

53. 'Neither stitch nor pang afflicted thee'.

54. *lende* 'loin'.

56. *helere* 'healer' (and in religious contexts 'Saviour').

57. The line as written in the MS offends radically against the metrical scheme and cannot possibly be fitted to the music, for it has an added syllable at the beginning of the stanza, where the tune cannot be adapted. Only severe re-writing can get rid of the fault — though it may be remarked that to replace 'God's son' (who was also Mary's son) by 'God' reduces a little the incongruity of His choosing her to be his 'mate'.

59. *teʒen* 'tie, unite' (in marriage); not 'thane', as Carleton Brown absurdly glosses it. *Herre* is 'higher', i.e. of higher birth. 'He did not wish to unite himself more highly than (to) that maid, to be his mate'. In the reconstructed text, *to his make* means 'as his mate'.

61. If *betere* is adjective, parallel to *swetture* in the next line, the sense is 'Even if he had wished, he could not take on earth a better or a sweeter thing'. But if it is adverb (as *bet* is in the reconstructed text), then the sense is 'He could not (do) better if he had wished, nor take a sweeter thing on earth'.

63. *bolde* 'dwelling', a word common in place-names except in the South of England, but rare in ME literary use and found chiefly in West Midland texts and in Trevisa, who was from Cornwall.

64. *helle wrake* 'the vengeance of hell'.

14. The milde Lomb, isprad o roode

1-2

Þe mildë Lomb, isprad o roodë,
heng bi-urnen al o bloodë
for ur geltë, for ur goodë —
    for he ne geltë nevrë nout.
5   Feaw of his him warn bileved;
dred hem had him al bireved
wan he seyen herë heved
    to so schanful deth ibrout.

3-4

His moder, þat him stood bisiden,
10 ne let no ter on other biden
wan hoe sei hir child bitiden
    swich pine, and deien geltëles.
Saint Johán, þat was him deerë,
on other halve him stood eek feerë
15 and biheld with murnë cheerë
    his maister þat him loved and ches.

5-6

Sore and hard he was iswungen,
feet and handes þurw istungen;
ac mest of all his othrë wunden
20   him ded his modres serwë wo.
In al his pine, in al his wrakë
þat he drei for mannes sakë,
he sei his moder serwë make;
    wel reufullich he spac hir to.

7-8

25 He seidë, 'Wiman lou! me heerë,
þi child, þat þu to mannë beerë.
Withuten sor and weep þu weerë
    þo ich was of þee iborn;
ac nu þu must þi pinë dreien
30 wan þu sicst me with þin eien
pinë þole o rood, and deien
    to helen man þat was forlorn.'

9-10

Saint Johán þe vangelistë
hir understood þurw hes of Cristë;
35 fair he kept hir, and biwistë,
    and served hir fram hand to foot.
Reuful is þe menëgingë
of þís deth and tis départíngë;
þarín is blis meind with weepíngë,
40   for þárþurw us kam allë boot.

11-12

He þat starf in urë keendë
leve us so been þarof meendë
þat he give us atten eendë
    þat he hath us to ibout.
45 Milsful moder, maiden cleenë,
mak on us þi milcë seenë
and bring us þurw þi sweetë beenë
    to þe blis þat failleth nout.

COMMENTARY

Source: London, British Library, MS Arundel 248, f. 154.

Though this piece is described by Carleton Brown (*English Lyrics of the XIIIth Century,* p. 200) as a sequence, perhaps because the stanzas subdivide into half-stanzas, it is in fact written hymn-fashion, with one metrical pattern repeated through every stanza; and it is so set by the musician, with a single melody to which each half-stanza (for the composer took the half-stanza as his unit) was to be repeatedly sung. The basic metrical scheme (most nearly exemplified in the final stanza) is trochaic, 88878887; but the poet freely allows himself to introduce an additional unstressed syllable at the beginning of the line, i.e. to turn the line into an iambic measure, and he does so in such a way as to destroy the symmetry not only of the two halves of each stanza (which in a sequence should exactly balance each other) but also of the successive stanzas, no two of which have exactly the same form of the basic metrical pattern. Yet the verbal text does not seem to be corrupt, except in the forms of some of the words and, as I think, at ll. 10 and 46; many of the metrical variations cannot possibly be removed by emendation and almost all even of those which

might be so removed seem to be due to the author. The metre would in a ME poem (as distinct from a song) be regarded as perfectly acceptable and indeed firmly shaped, and in this instance I see no reason to interfere with it. But the variation of the metre of course involves a complication for the musical setting. Though the lay-out in the MS hardly suggests it, we must assume that when a line begins with a stressed syllable (i.e. in a metrically 'normal' trochaic line), this first stressed syllable should be sung to two notes; and when an additional (unstressed) syllable is introduced at the beginning, it should normally be sung to the first of the two notes. But in the case of the second line of the half-stanza the extra syllable has to be accommodated at a later point in the musical phrase.

On the Arundel MS, in which this piece comes, see the introductory notes to no. 12 above. Like no. 7 above, the present song seems to come from the South-east Midlands, probably the London area; but it may have a different ultimate source from no. 7, since it is not included, as the latter is, in the Digby and Rawlinson MSS. Linguistic features established by rhyme are as follows. (1) The Midland and Southern change of OE *ā* to ME *ǭ* (l. 20; but the rhyme with *to* preposition is inaccurate). (2) The East Midland and Northern change of OE

$ēo$ to $ē$ (ll. 13, 29). (3) OE $ǣ^1$ rhyming with OE $ē$ (ll. 26-7, 45), which is non-Southern (except for Kent) and originally non-Essex. (4) OE $ǣ^2$ rhyming with OE $ēa$ (ll. 5-7), which is non-Kentish and originally non-Essex. (5) The South-eastern change of OE y to e (ll. 41-42). (6) The full *-en* inflexion preserved in strong p.ps., in combination with the *i-* prefix; the combination suggests the South Midlands. (7) The *-en* inflexion in nouns (*bisiden* l. 9, *wunden* l. 19, *eien* l. 30), which is generally Southern or South and West Midland. (8) The Norse-derived *deien* 'die' (l. 31). It is in the South-east Midlands that all these features could be found.

The text as given in the MS (except for the correction of the Arundel scribe's characteristic error of writing *þ* for *h*) is printed by Carleton Brown, *English Lyrics of the XIIIth Century*, no. 45 (pp. 77-78). In my text the spellings are modified.

NOTES

1. *isprad o roode* 'spread on the Cross'.

2. *heng* 'hung'. The vowel varied in length; in such cases I normally assume in my spelling the short vowel. Similarly with *biheld* in l. 15.
bi-urnen (*bihornen* MS), p.p. of *bi-irnen* 'berun, run about or over'; the sense here is 'covered completely with blood' (*o bloode*, literally 'of blood').
bloode is dat. sg., and perserves the inflexion *-e*; similarly *gelte* 'guilt' sb. and *goode* 'good' in l. 3. But in l. 1 *roode*, being from an OE feminine, might have *-e* even in the nominative. The preservation of the dative inflexion is a conservative feature, and shows that this song is either of earlier date or was written by an author who spoke a more conservative (probably more southerly) dialect than nos. 12 and 15(ii), preserved in the same MS.

3. *ur* 'our'; the MS has *hure* in both cases, but the metre requires the unstressed monosyllabic form.
gelte 'guilt', a South-eastern form with $ĕ$ for OE $ȳ$. Such spellings occur in the other songs of the Arundel MS; in this case the South-eastern development is confirmed by the rhymes in ll. 41-43.

4. *he*] *þe* MS, and so repeatedly.
gelte p.t., 'sinned' (*OED*, s.v. *guilt* vb.).
nout, a form of *nought* (i.e., in this instance, of *not*). In the Arundel MS the spirant represented in OE by *h* (in ME by *ȝ*, *gh*, etc.) is regularly omitted between the diphthong *ou* and *t*; cf. *ibrout* in l. 8. The natural interpretation is that it had become silent in this position, though some scholars doubt this. Words that should end in OE *-ht*, ME *-ȝt*, usually rhyme together, as here.

5. *feaw* 'few'; so spelt in MS, indicating the ME diphthong $ęu$ < OE $ēaw$.
warn 'were'. The spelling may show Essex $ā$ < OE $ǣ^1$, but is more likely to depend on early shortening under weak stress, thus $wǣron > wǎron > warn$. But the form is neither Anglian nor Kentish.
bileved 'left'. The line means 'few of his people were left to him'.

6-8. 'Fear had deprived him of them all, when they saw (*he seyen*) their head [i.e. their leader] brought to so shameful a death.'
he is the native form of the nom. pl. of the 3rd personal pro-

noun, from OE *hīe*, *hēo*; *þei* 'they' is from ON. As one might have expected the latter in the Arundel scribe's own dialect, *he* here may have stood in his exemplar.
seyen 'saw' represents OE (Anglian) *sēgun*; contrast *warn* in l. 5 above.
schanful is from OE *scandful* 'shameful'. The MS has *s⟨c⟩anful*, with *c* interlined, perhaps by a different hand; perhaps the exemplar had *sanful*, with the generally South-eastern use of *s* for OE *sc* (modern English *sh*).

9. *His*] *þis* MS.
þat] *þar* MS, meaning 'there'. The MS reading could be retained if we were to translate *ne let* in the next line as 'and did not let', but this is against ME idiom, which normally uses *ne* 'nor' only after a negative in the first part of the sentence. Emendation seems preferable.
stood] *stud* MS. The Arundel scribe often uses *u* as a spelling for OE $ō$ (modern English *oo*), especially in this word. He probably used a dialectal (East Anglian) pronunciation with the vowel [y:] (as in modern Scottish *guid* 'good'). But he is by no means consistent in the use of this spelling with *u* and there is nothing to suggest that the authors of the poems used the dialectal pronunciation; I therefore normalize the spelling by substituting *oo* except in *must* in l. 29 (on which see the note below).

10. 'let no tear wait for another', i.e. wept incessantly.
on other biden] *other vnbiden* MS, in which *vn-* is a spelling of (or rather a copyist's error for) the adverbial prefix *on-* (OE *onbīdan* 'wait for'). But more regular metre is obtained by detaching *on* from the verb and placing it before *other* as a preposition; and *to bide on* is a known idiom.

11. *wan* 'when' (as in l. 7 above); initial *wh-* (OE *hw-*) is often *w-* in this MS.
hoe (*þoe* MS) is one of the many forms of the nom. sg. feminine pronoun of the 3rd person, developed from OE *hēo* (*hīe*). It is probably a variant on the more common spelling *heo*, originally representing a pronunciation [hø:], but by this date in the East Midlands [hø:] would have become [he:]. It may be that there was an attempt to keep *heo* in order to make a purely graphic distinction from the masculine pronoun *he*, and that, when *heo* no longer had a distinct phonetic significance, the order of the vowel-letters was arbitrarily reversed.
sei 'saw'.
bitiden 'befall'. The line means 'when she saw such torment befall her child'.

12. *swich* 'such'; MS *swics*.
and deien gelteles 'and (saw him) die without guilt'. The vowel of the suffix *-les* is long (ME $ē$ < OE $ēa$), as the rhyme shows.

13. *Johan* is stressed on the second, as often in ME; so also in l. 33.

14. 'also stood as a companion to him on the other side'.

15. *with murne cheere* 'with sorrowful countenance'. For the rare adjective *mourn* see *OED*.

16. *loved* (*louede* MS) here scans as a monosyllable. In this instance the process of reduction is that the medial *e* has been syncopated, to give *lovde*, and then the final *-e* is elided before the following vowel.
ches 'chose'. The vowel is long (ME $ē$ < OE $ēa$ in *cēas*).

17. *iswungen* 'beaten'. In this word and in *istungen* in the next

line the vowel was originally short (OE *ŭ*), but was subject to lengthening before *ng*. Modern English pronunciation shows that the short vowel often remained or else was restored by a later re-shortening, but Orm shows by his spellings that he had ME *ū* in both these words. Here they assonate with *wunden* 'wounds', in which also the *u* was originally short but in which ME *ū* was normal (as modern English [u:] shows). The probability is that the assonance depends on the long vowel, ME *ū* (pronounced like modern English *oo*) in all three words.

18. *þurw* 'through'. This is the usual spelling in the Arundel MS, and is evidently a development of earlier *þurʒ*. It is normally a monosyllable, as here.
istungen 'pierced'. On the vowel, see note to l. 17 above.

19. *mest* 'most' (OE *mǣst*). The MS has *mes*, a mere error.
all] *alle* MS, the full plural form; but the *-e* is elided before the following *h* of unstressed *his*, which the MS spells *is* (it commonly but not regularly omits *h* from the unstressed forms of the pronouns).
wunden 'wounds'. The OE plural was *wunda* > ME *wunde*, and it is possible that the *-n* has been added by the Arundel scribe, who shows a distinct tendency to do this; if so, we should have to omit *-n* not only from this word, but from *iswungen* and *istungen* in the two preceding lines. But Southern and Western dialects of ME often re-formed plurals in *-e* as plurals in *-en*, and the forms of the MS probably are those of the original.

20. *ded* 'did' (*dede* MS), another South-eastern form. The line means 'his mother's sorrow caused him misery'.
serwe] *sorwe* MS, but in l. 23 the MS has *serwen*. It is very unlikely that the author would have varied his form, with no advantage gained, in the space of three lines. As the form with *e* is much rarer, it is less likely to have been substituted by a scribe; I therefore assume that it descends from the original in l. 23, and alter *sorwe* to *serwe* in l. 20. Other poems in the Arundel MS show both forms; in no. 12 the scribe uses *sorwe*, undoubtedly correctly (it is required by rhyme in l. 43), in no. 7, l. 6, he has *serwen* (confirmed by the Digby MS). As no. 7 seems to come from the same general area as the present song, its use of *serwen* is some confirmation of the assumption that *serwe* was the original form here. Cf. also *serwe* in no. 6b, l. 12, another song from the South-east Midlands.

21. *wrake* 'suffering'.

22. *drei* 'endured', from OE *drēah*. This form, like *sei* 'saw' (ll. 11, 23) < OE *sĕah*, shows loss of the spirant (OE *h*) after a diphthong ending in *i*.

23. *serwe*] *serwen* MS, apparently a plural formed by adding *-n* to earlier *serwe*, *sorwe* < OE *sorga* fem. pl. But here there can be little doubt that the Arundel scribe has added the *n*, wrongly, for the ME phrase was 'to make sorrow' (*serwe* or *sorwe maken*), not 'to make sorrows'; see *OED*, s.v. *sorrow* sb., 4. In this same line he has wrongly added *n* to the infinitive *make* (*maken* MS), as the rhyme with *wrake* and *sake* shows.

24. *reufullich* (*reufuliche* MS) normally means 'sorrowfully', but 'pityingly, compassionately' is possible and would seem better here.

25-26. 'He said, "Behold, woman! hear me, thy child, whom you bore as a man"', i.e. to whom you gave birth in human form.

27. *sor and weep* 'pain and weeping'.

28. *þo* 'then'.
ich] *ics* MS, the same spelling-convention as in *swics* for *swich* in l. 12 above.

29. *must*] so MS. This may be merely another example of the Arundel scribe's use of *u* for ME *ọ̄* < OE *ō*. But in this case it is possible that the spelling shows shortening of the vowel to *ŭ*, as in the modern form of the word, and I therefore retain the scribe's form instead of normalizing it to *moost*.
dreien 'endure'. For the common conception that Mary, having suffered no pains at Christ's birth, must in compensation suffer them at his death, see no. 10(i) above and its English translations (nos. 10(ii), 11, and 12).

30. *sicst* 'seest', < OE *sihst* with the change of the spirant to a stop before a following spirant.

31. *pine þole* 'suffer torment'.
rood] *rode* MS, but the *-e* elides.

32. *helen* 'heal', and thence 'save, redeem'. The *n* may well have been added by the scribe.
forlorn 'lost, damned'.

33. *Saint*] *seint* MS, but contrast the scribe's *saint* in l. 13 above.
vangeliste 'evangelist'. This aphetic form was used after the definite article, the *e-* being absorbed by the article. The MS has *wangeliste*; this spelling with *w* was common in ME but was apparently unphonetic, and I normalize it.

34. *understood* (*understud* MS) 'supported, maintained'.
hes 'command' (OE *hǣs* fem.). The MS has *hese*, but the *-e* in any case will elide.
Criste] The rhymes show that the vowel is short, which was the quantity naturally developed in ME from the OE form of the name (since vowels were shortened before *st*). The pronunciation with ME *ī*, the long vowel, was also current in ME; it is normally explained from Romance influence, but this may have been assisted by the survival of a long vowel in the oblique forms (*Cri-stes*, *Cri-ste*), in which the syllable-division, by taking *st* into the next syllable, would act against the shortening of the vowel. Here, however, the *ī* developed in the nominative is used in the dative.

35. *biwiste* 'looked after, cared for'.

36. *served*] *serwed* MS. This spelling is possibly an example of the South-eastern (and later especially Cockney) change of *v* to *w*, but it is perhaps a little too early for this explanation; it may be merely a confused spelling, similar to the use of *w* for v in *evangelist* (cf. note to l. 33).
fram 'from', a characteristic form of this MS.
hand] *and* MS, and similarly *andes* 'hands' l. 18, *alue* 'halve' l. 14, *arde* 'hard' l. 17. These are characteristic mis-spellings of the Arundel scribe.

37. 'Pitiable is the remembrance'.
meneginge (< OE *mynegung*, with altered form of the suffix), meaning 'memory', is another South-eastern form with *ĕ* < *ў̆*. Both *g*'s are pronounced as in *get*.

38. *tis* 'this'; the initial *þ* is assimilated to *t* after the preceding *d*.
departinge 'separation', i.e. of Christ and Mary. The stresses fall on the first and third syllables.

39. *meind* 'mingled'.

weepinge takes metrical stress on the second syllable, an artificial inversion of the natural stress.

40. *þarþurw* 'therethrough, by this means'.

alle boot 'all deliverance (from sin)'. The disyllabic form *alle*, originally plural, was used in later ME directly before a noun, even when singular, whereas *al*, the old singular form, was used before an unstressed pronoun or article.

41. *starf* 'died', p.t. sg. of *sterven*.

in ure keende 'in our nature', i.e. in our humanity. In *keende* (*kende* MS) and in *meende* (*mende* MS) the vowel was originally short (OE ў) but was subject to lengthening in OE itself (to ӯ), and it is probable that it was long for the poet. It has had the South-eastern development of OE ӯ to late OE ē, whence ME ẹ̄, which we spell *ee*.

42-44 '. . . grant us to be so mindful thereof that he may give us, at the end, what he bought for us then' (i.e. at the crucifixion); may he grant that we shall so keep his death in mind that we may deserve to be given, finally, what he gained for us by his death.

42. *meende* (*mende* MS) 'mindful', < OE *mynde*. On the vowel, see the note to *keende* in l. 41.

43. *give* (*giue* MS)] The scribe uses the form derived from Scandinavian *gifa*, not the native form (with initial ʒ or y) from OE *gefan*. But there is no guarantee that his form is the author's.

atten 'at the' < OE *ætþæm*. The -*n* is a relic of the -*m* of the OE dative of the definite article, preserved as a fossil before a word beginning with a vowel.

eende (*ende* MS). As this word has original *e*, the rhyme proves the South-eastern development of OE *y* to *e*. In *ende* the *e* was originally short, and the modern English pronunciation proves that this short vowel was often preserved (or restored by renewed shortening) in ME. But it was subject to OE lengthening before *nd*, and was often long in ME; in that case it was ME ẹ̄ < OE ē, which we spell *ee*. The rhyme is more likely to be on the long vowel than the short, though the latter is possible.

44. *hath*] The MS reads *hauet*, but to regularize the metre we must either substitute the monosyllabic form *hath* or omit *to* later in the line. I choose the former alternative; a scribe is more likely to have substituted *hauet* for *hath* than to have inserted a word, and *to*, though not essential, adds to the sense. *to*] so MS, for *þo* 'then, at that time', with assimilation of *þ* to *t* after *s*.

45. *milsful* 'merciful'.

46. The MS reads *mak þi milce up on hus sene*, which scans satisfactorily. But the correct ME form of the imperative singular of the verb 'to make' was *make* (with pronounced -*e*) < OE *măca*, and monosyllabic *mak* (written by the scribe and required by the metre of the line as he gives it) should not occur in a dialect in which final -*e* was regularly preserved, as it evidently was in this author's, except as a result of elision. The rearrangement of the word-order in our text is to permit of elision; the omission of *up*, which is unnecessary for sense, is a consequence. There is, I think, some gain in style also, by bringing *on us* to a more prominent position in the line and removing *þi milce* further from *milsful* in the preceding line. The emendation assumes that the word-order was altered by a scribe in whose language (i) final -*e* was often lost, so that *mak* could occur where no elision was possible, and (ii) *upon*, which originally seems to have been modelled on ON (see *OED*), was in common use as a variant to the simple *on*. Both these conditions would apply in East Anglia, where the Arundel MS was probably written. Cf. l. 10 above for another instance where the scribe seems to have altered the word-order.

milce 'mercy, favour', from the oblique singular of OE *milts* fem. In this word the *c* was originally pronounced *ts*, but by the date of this song it had probably become merely *s* (though the spelling *milsful* used in the previous line is not entirely conclusive, since reduction of *ts* to *s* would be more likely before a suffix beginning with a consonant).

seene (*sene* MS) is an adjective meaning 'apparent, evident', not the p.p. of the verb *see*.

47. *beene* (*bene* MS) 'prayer, intercession'.

48. *failleth*] *faillet* MS. The -*et* ending was common in ME spelling, in Southern dialects especially, and is regularly used in the Arundel MS in uncontracted forms of the 3 sg. pres. indic.; but I normalize it in the songs of this MS.

15.   (i)   Angelus ad virginem
           (ii)   Gabriel fram heven-king

1

Angelus ad virginem
   subintrans in conclave,
virginis formidinem
   demulcens, inquit 'Ave!
5   Ave regina virginum!
Cælí terræque dominum
   concipies
   et paries
     intacta
10   salutem hominum,
   tu, porta cæli facta,
medela criminum.'

1

Gabriel, fram heven-king
   sent to þe maidë sweetë,
broutë hir blisfúl tidíng
   and fair he gan hir greetë:
'Heil be þu, ful of grace ariʒt!
For Godes son, þis heven-liʒt,
   for mannes lov*e*
   wil man bicom*e*
     and takë
fles of þee, maidë briʒt,
   mankén free for to makë
of sen and devles miʒt.'

2

'Quomodo conciperem
    quæ virum non cognovi?
15 Qualiter infringerem
    quod firma mente vovi?'
'Spiritus sancti gracia
perficiet hæc omnia.
    Ne timeas
20   sed gaudeas
        secura,
quod castimonia
    manebit in te pura
deí potencia.'

3

25 Ad hæc, virgo nobilis,
    respondens, inquit ei,
'Servula sum humilis
    omnipotentis dei;
tibi, cælesti nuncio,
30 tantí secreti conscio,
    consentiens
    et cupiens
        videre
factúm quod audio,
35   parata sum parere
deí consilio.'

4

Angelus disparuit
    et statim puellaris
uterus intumuit
40   vi partus salutaris.
Quí, circumdatus utero
novém mensíum numero,
    hinc exiit
    et iniit
45   conflictum,
affigens humero
    crucém qua dedit ictum
hostí mortifero.

5

Eya, mater domini,
50   quæ pacem reddidisti
angelis et homini
    cum Christum genuisti,
tuum exora filium
ut se nobís propicium
55   exhibeat
    èt deleat
        peccata,
præstáns auxilium,
    vitá fruí beata,
60 post hoc exilium.

2

Mildëlich him gan andswere
    þe mildë maidë þannë:
'Wichëwisë sold ich bere
    [a] child withutë mannë?'
Þangel [hir] seid, 'Ne dred tee nout;
þurw þoligast sal been iwrout
    þis ilchë þing
    warof tidíng
        ich bringë;
al mánken wurth ibout
    þurw þinë sweet childíngë
and ut of pine ibrout.'

3

Wan þe maiden understood
    and þangels wordes herdë,
mildëlich with mildë mood
    to þangel hie andswerdë:
'Urë lords þewë maid iwis
ich am, þat heer aboven is.
    Anentis me
    fulfurthed be
        þi sawë
þat ich, sith his wil is,
    [a] maid, withutë lawë,
of moder have þe blis.'

4

Þangel went awei mid þan
    al ut of hirë siȝtë;
hirë womb arisë gan
    þurw þoligastes miȝtë.
In hir wes Crist bilok anon,
sooth God, sooth man in fles and bon,
    and of hir fles
    iborë wes
        at timë.
Warþurw us kam good won;
    he bout us ut of pinë
and let him for us slon.

5

Maiden-moder makëles,
    of milcë ful ibundë,
bid for us him þat tee ches,
    at wam þu gracë fundë,
þat he forgive us sen and wrake
and clene of evri gelt us make
    and heven-blis,
    wan ur time is
        to stervë,
us give, for þinë sake,
    him so heer for to servë
þat he us to him take.

COMMENTARY

Sources: English text: London, British Library, MS Arundel 248, f. 154; Latin text: see below.

The Latin religious song *Angelus ad virginem* appears to have been very popular in the later Middle Ages, especially perhaps in England; it is mentioned by Chaucer in *The Miller's Tale* as one of the accomplishments of Nicholas, the 'hende' undergraduate of Oxford:

> And al above ther lay a gay sautrie
> on which he made a-nyghtes melodie
> so swetely that all the chambre rong;
> and *Angelus ad virginem* he song;
> and after that he song the Kinges Noote,

which may not have been so pious. The text of *Angelus ad virginem* is given in four extant MSS of British provenance, of which the first three have different settings of the music. (1) MS Arundel 248, which gives both the original Latin and the English version; denoted A. (2) London, British Library, Cotton Fragments XXIX (denoted C), which gives the Latin text; badly damaged by fire, so that the words are not always legible. (3) Cambridge, University Library, MS Additional 710, ff. 127-130ᵛ (the 'Dublin Troper', denoted D), which gives the Latin text and three versions of the music. (4) Cambridge, University Library, MS Gg. i. 32, f. 5ᵛ (denoted G); complete Latin text, without music. Of these, A belongs to the end of the thirteenth century, C to the late thirteenth or early fourteenth century, D to the mid-fourteenth century, and G to the fifteenth century. We have collated their texts with (5) that printed by Dreves, *Analecta Hymnica* viii, no. 51 (p. 49), from a Cluniac Missal printed in Paris in 1550 (denoted P). The text given by Dreves and Blume, *Ein Jahrtausend Lateinischer Hymnendichtung,* ii. 242-3, is a mere revision of that in *Anal. Hymn.,* with a few changes of spelling and punctuation. A MS of the end of the thirteenth century, from the Benedictine monastery of St. Arnoul, which was in the Municipal Library of Metz (MS Metz 535), was unfortunately destroyed, with many others, in the war of 1939-45.

Most variants in the Latin texts are confined to a single MS, and serve only to show that none of the extant MSS is derived from another. P does not share errors with any of the British MSS, and would therefore seem to represent an independent tradition, as must in any case be probable. The fifteenth-century G gives an obviously contaminated text; it shares significant errors with D (at ll. 50 and 52) and with C (*peperisti* for *genuisti,* properly in l. 52), and rather less significant errors with A (at ll. 47 and 48). But there is also no consistent relation between the three early MSS ACD. AD agree in an apparent error in l. 41, AC seem to have agreed (though C's text is now damaged) in the error *soli* at l. 48, and CD agree in an error (which might, however, be independent) at l. 46. It looks as though all the extant British MSS ultimately derive from texts made in a single centre where there were several copies of the song and collation of one with another, producing contaminated texts, was possible. In the circumstances recension in the strict sense cannot be used; but the agreement of P, since it is apparently quite independent, with one or more of the British MSS must ordinarily be conclusive. When P differs from the British MSS the latter, being much earlier, are to be preferred.

Angelus ad virginem may have been written after 1246, when the Council of Béziers prescribed the devotion of the Angelic Salutation (Hefele-Leclercq, *Histoire des Conciles,* v. 1734-59), and was obviously earlier than the English translation, which must date from the late thirteenth century. The dates of the MSS in any case make the third quarter of the thirteenth century the probable period of composition. Dreves and Blume, *Jahrtausend,* ii. 243, express the opinion that the Latin song perhaps originated from Cluny Abbey or from the Parisian priory of St. Martin des Champs, but their reason for this guess is merely that they had found their text in the Cluniac Missal printed in Paris in 1550 and that this contains an appendix of sequences for St. Martin, whereas earlier editions of the Cluniac Missal had not contained *Angelus ad virginem.* But they themselves point out that a text also occurs in a late thirteenth-century MS of English provenance in the British Library (presumably they refer to A); and this, the other early MSS of British provenance, and the Metz MS, really destroy the basis of their argument. It is indeed possible that the song was written in France; the frequency with which the stress is shifted to the second syllable of disyllables may be evidence of this, and the fact that the British MSS seem to have a common original of which P is independent would be consistent with the song's having been introduced into England from France. Its inclusion in the 1550 Cluniac Missal does not seem a very good reason for supposing that it was of Cluniac origin; but there was a Cluniac house at Thetford, well within the area in which the English version is likely to have been composed and in which the Arundel MS was written (see the commentary on no. 12 above).

In the Arundel MS the complete Latin text is written out first, under the musical stave, on five lines (one for each stanza), but only the words of the first stanza are really correctly laid under the musical notes; the words of the later stanzas are kept roughly parallel line by line. The English words, which follow below the Latin on five more lines of text, required much more space, and in consequence are not correctly aligned with the Latin or with the music (or indeed with themselves). The Latin text is not especially accurate and contains a sprinkling of errors apparently peculiar to this MS. The English text is also undoubtedly a copy; the words are mostly correctly given, though there are several minor errors, but the linguistic forms are certainly not those intended by the author and there are a good many of the spelling errors characteristic of the Arundel scribe.

The song, though regarded by Dreves and Blume as a sequence (which accounts for their way of numbering the stanzas, as 1a, 1b, etc. for 1, 2, etc.), is in fact a song to be sung 'hymn-fashion', i.e. each stanza is sung to a repetition of the same melody. It is therefore a technical requirement that the succeeding stanzas should follow a regular pattern, certainly of syllable-count and also of metrical rhythm. The regularity of syllable-count is obvious in the Latin; the pattern is 777788443676. The rhythmical structure is as follows:

Line	1	/x/x/x/	7	x/x/
	2	x/x/x/x	8	x/x/
	3	/x/x/x/	9	x/x
	4	x/x/x/x	10	x/x/x/
	5	/xx/x/x/	11	x/x/x/x
	6	x/x/x/x/	12	x/x/x/

In the sixth line, the rhythm is to be deduced rather from the English text and from the music, for in three of the five stanzas the Latin text begins with a disyllable which would, in Classical

Latin, be stressed on the first syllable. But it is clear, from other lines, that the author of the Latin text allowed himself great freedom in the stressing of disyllables, which he sometimes stressed on the first syllable (as in Classical Latin), sometimes on the second (as was especially common in the medieval French pronunciation of Latin); examples of disyllables stressed on the second are *cæli* (1. 6), *dei* (ll. 24 and 36), *tanti* (1. 30), *factum* (1. 34), *novem* (1. 42), *crucem* (1. 47), *hosti* (1. 48), *nobis* (1. 54), *præstans* (1. 58), *vita* and *frui* (1. 59). A more striking aberration from Classical stressing is *mensium* (1. 42) stressed on the second, but even for this there are parallels in medieval Latin lyric (see note to 1. 42 below).

The conformity of the English text to the metrical pattern has been concealed by the Arundel scribe, who used linguistic forms (presumably those which he regarded as correct) which altered the number of syllables in the words and/or the incidence of the metrical stresses. But by substituting other forms known to have been current we can bring the English lines into conformity with the metrical scheme; and in such a case it is to be assumed that the forms which produce regularity of metre were those intended by the original author. Only in three places is emendation (as distinct from substitution of variant forms) required, and the emendations are slight; in two cases the change consists only in the insertion of the indefinite article in circumstances in which its use was optional in ME. The English author observed the rhythmical pattern with less recourse to stress-variants than the Latin author had done. In l. 11 he stresses *manken* 'the human race' on the second syllable (as in modern English *mankind*), in l. 22 on the first (as in OE *manncynn*); the word varied in stress in ME. In l. 3 the metrical stress is put on the suffix in *blisful* and *tiding*; but this artificial inversion of the natural stress was very common in ME verse. The preposition is given metrical stress in the phrases *sent to* (1. 2), *fles of* (1. 10), and *free for* (1. 11), and the possessive pronoun must be stressed in *his wil* (1. 34) and *ur time* (1. 56) — in both cases in conformity with the sense — and also in *ure lords* (1. 29), though here it would be truer to say that *lords* is subordinated to the following noun. For the rest the stressings are natural. But in order to adhere to the syllable-count the English poet has allowed himself often to drop a final *-e* which in ME would normally be expected in the word concerned. Apart from cases explicable by elision (including elision, which the poet may have allowed, at the line-end if the next line begins with a vowel or *h*) and from weak-stressed forms, *-e* is lacking from *tiding* (ll. 3 and 20), in contrast to *childinge* in l. 23), *son* (1. 6), *love* (1. 7), *andswere* (1. 13), *seid* (1. 17), *sweet* (1. 23, in contrast to *sweete* in l. 2), *mildelich* (1. 27), *maid* (1. 35), *give* (1. 58), and *take* (1. 60). Non-final *e* is lost in *lords* for *lordes* gen. sg. (see note to 1. 29, below).

It is clear that the author spoke a relatively advanced dialect in which final *-e* was already being lost before the end of the thirteenth century. But it was not a Northern dialect. The indications are that it was East Anglian, probably that of Norfolk, especially if, as I have suggested, *Gabriel fram heven-king* was by the same author as no. 12 above (see the introductory note to the latter). It is consistent with such an origin that the vocabulary contains a number of words of Norse derivation: *heil* (1. 5), *won* 'hope' (1. 46), *slon* 'slay' (1. 48), *take* (ll. 9 and 60), *(for)give* (ll. 53 and 58), in addition to *lawe* (1. 35) and *tiding* (ll. 3 and 20), which occur in late OE and are of general currency in ME. See also the note to *ibunde* (1. 50).

In the English text given above, the words are in the forms required by the metre, and the scribe's spellings, which are often aberrant, are modified and regularized, sometimes without notice. F. J. Furnivall, *The Harleian MS 7334 of Chaucer's Canterbury Tales* (Chaucer Soc., Series I, 73; 1885), pp. 695-6, gives a careful transcription of the forms of the MS (and of the Latin text as given by the Arundel MS), with a facsimile of the MS facing p. 695. The English text is also given by Carleton Brown, *English Lyrics of the XIIIth Cent.*, pp. 75-76.

Another English version of *Angelus ad virginem* was made, some time after 1426, by the blind Shropshire poet John Audelay; see *The Poems of John Audelay*, ed. E. K. Whiting, EETS o.s. 184 (1931), pp. 159-60, no. 21. In the MS (Bodleian Douce 302) the words are given without music, but three stanzas have been set to the tune by John Stevens, *Music and Poetry in the Early Tudor Court* (1961), pp. 40-41. But it seems to us unlikely that Audelay really meant his version to go to the music, which it fits badly, even allowing for the fact that the scribe's forms may not be those intended by the author. Thus, to take a single example, the third line of the stanza has seven syllables and trochaic rhythm, in agreement with the Latin and the requirements of the tune, only in stanzas 3 and 5; it cannot be reduced to less than eight syllables in stanzas 1 and 4 or to less than nine in stanza 2, and in all three stanzas the rhythm is iambic, directly counter to the music. The same sort of thing applies throughout. It must have been a mere 'literary' translation, like those of the friar William Herebert a century earlier.

VARIANTS (Latin text)

The readings of the Paris text of 1550 (P) are given as printed by Dreves in *Anal. Hymn.* viii, p. 49. In appropriate cases I substitute, in my text of the Latin, *æ* for the *e* of the MSS.

4 inquit] ACDG inquit ei P   11 porta cæli] ACDG coeli porta P   14 quæ] ACGP quem D   15 infringerem] ACGP confringerem D   quod] ACGD quæ P   27 servula] CDGP ancilla A   sum] ADGP sis C   28 dei] ADGP om. C   29 cælesti] ADGP celestis C   30 conscio] ACGP concio D   40 salutaris] ACDG virginalis P   41 qui] DGP quo A cum C   circumdatus] CGP circumdatur AD   43 hinc] CDGP post A   45 conflictum] ACGP afflictum D   46 affigens] AGP affligens CD   47 qua] D quo P qui AG *illegible in* C   48 hosti] DP soli AG . . li C   mortifero] ACDP tantummodo G   50 pacem reddidisti] ACP Christum peperisti (*from l. 52*) G Christum credidisti D   51 angelis] ACDG angelo P   et] ACDP om. G   homini] ACDP hominibus G   52 cum] ACP dum G que D   Christum genuisti] AP Christum peperisti C pacem reddidisti (*from l. 50*) DG   54 se nobis] ACG sit nobis D nobis se P   57 peccata] ACDG reata P

NOTES

A few notes on the Latin text are interspersed with those on the English; they are distinguished by the addition of the letter L to the line-reference, thus 41L. References without this addition are to the English text.

1. *heven*] *evene* MS. The scribe inconsistently omits *h* from words which should have it, and adds it to others which should not (thus *hut* for *ut*, l. 24). His spellings are normalized in our text. The combinative form *heven-*, without final *e*, is required by the metre.

2. *maide*] so MS here, though everywhere else *maiden*. As the scribe has a very marked tendency to add *-n* where the author obviously did not intend it, I assume that *maide* comes from his exemplar; and I regularize this form *maide* (or its reduced form *maid*) except in l. 25, where the metre shows that there was no elision before a vowel, and in l. 49 in the compound *maiden-moder*.

3. *broute hir* 'brought her'; as usual in the Arundel MS, OE *h* (modern English *gh*) is omitted after *ou*.

The MS originally read *brout þire*, but an *e* is interlined and marked for insertion after the *t*, perhaps not by the original scribe. This text repeatedly has *þire* for *hire*, as a particular instance of the scribe's misuse of the letter *þ*. Here metre requires the monosyllabic form *hir*. But at this one point Carleton Brown retains *þire* and glosses it 'this'; *þire* was, however, a specifically Northern form which is highly unlikely to have occurred in this text, and in any case is always plural, meaning 'these'. We substitute *hir* for *þire*, but otherwise retain the MS text (as corrected). This involves assuming (a) that the final *-e* of *broute* is not elided before the *h* of *hir* (cf. no. 12 above, l. 4, *þe sonë heeng*); (b) that *tiding* is, at least in origin, a plural, representing early ME *tidinge* < late OE **tidunga* nom. pl. fem., but with loss of *-e*. *OED* records *tiding* as a plural form for the thirteenth and fourteenth centuries. Cases in ME in which *tiding* is used without preceding article or demonstrative (e.g. *Havelok* l. 1926) may really be old plurals, and are certainly parallel to the use here; in sense, and probably in history, they are comparable to the modern use of *news* as a singular. *Blisful* may likewise be a plural adj., with loss of *-e*. The sense is therefore 'he brought her happy news'.

4. *fair*] *faire* MS, but the adverbial suffix *-e* is elided.
gan . . . greete 'greeted'.
hir] *hire* MS, but the monosyllable is again required by the metre.

5. *heil be*] The metrical stress is on *heil*, as the fifth line of the stanza begins with a trochee.
ariȝt] *arith* MS, and similarly *lith* 'light', *brith* 'bright', *mith* 'might' for the rhyme-words in this stanza. This use of *-th* for OE *-ht* is characteristic of the Arundel MS and is very common in Eastern texts, but we normalize.
The sense of *ariȝt* is probably 'straightaway, immediately'.

7. *love*] *louen* MS, an obvious case of false addition of *-n*; the scribe was probably looking ahead, and had already decided in his mind that he was going to write *bicomen* at the end of the next line, and therefore wrote *louen* here to keep the assonating words parallel. In fact the metre requires a monosyllable, i.e. the *-e* has been lost from ME *love* < OE *lufu*.

At the beginning of the line, the word *so* has been inserted before *for* by the same hand as corrected *brout* to *broute* in l. 3, but here the addition is certainly wrong; it looks as though an unsuccessful attempt has been made to erase it again.

8. *bicome*] *bicomen* MS, the full form of the p.p., but the metre requires two syllables only; we must therefore substitute the form without *-n*. The remaining *-e* of the strong p.p. inflexion is then also lost, in this case perhaps by elision, since the next line begins with a vowel.

9. *take*] *taken* MS, and similarly *maken* MS in l. 11; but the evidence is so strong that in the author's dialect *-n* had normally been lost from disyllables and that the scribe is responsible for adding *-n* that we substitute forms without it.

10. *fles* 'flesh' (so MS); this is a common ME form, thought to have been developed in derivatives such as *fleslich* < OE *flǣsclīc* and thence transferred to the simplex. The rhyme in ll. 43–4 shows that the *-s* was really pronounced as [s] and was not a mere spelling for *-sh*.
maide] *maiden* MS, but see note to l. 2 above. As the phrase is a vocative, the weak adj. *briȝte* (with *-e*) might be expected in a ME dialect which regularly preserved final *-e*, but metre and rhyme here require uninflected *briȝt*.

11. *manken*] *maken* MS, by omission of the abbreviation-mark for *n* which should stand over the *a*; in l. 22 *manken* is properly written. The meaning is 'mankind' < OE *manncynn*, and the scribe's spelling shows South-eastern *ĕ*, which we retain.

12. *sen* 'sin'; *senne* MS, but the *-e* is elided. Again *ĕ* < OE *ў*.

13. *him*] *im* MS.
gan andswere 'answered'. The MS has *andsweren*, but the metre requires two syllables only; not only has the *-n* been lost, but also the *-e*, though here no elision is possible.

15. *wichewise* (so MS), 'in what way', 'by what means'.
sold 'should'; so MS, and similarly *sal* 'shall' in l. 18. Such forms are later Northern, but in the thirteenth century occur in the Norfolk texts *Genesis and Exodus* and *The Bestiary*.
ich 'I'; *ichs* MS, and so also in l. 21, but *ics* in ll. 30 and 34.
bere] *beren* MS, but again metre shows that *-en* has been lost. In theory the *-en* might be carried on to serve as the unstressed syllable at the beginning of the next verse-line (see next note), but I doubt whether the author employed this technique; and normal rhyming practice required a monosyllable *ber* to rhyme with *andswer* in l. 13. We use, in the text, a silent *e* to indicate the length of the vowel.

16. *a child*] *child* MS, using the noun without indefinite article, as was good ME idiom. But the line as given by the scribe is a syllable short, and the missing syllable is at the beginning, for the fourth line of the stanza begins with an iamb. Evidently the poet intended the alternative idiom, using the indefinite article. In ME pronunciation *berë child* (with pronounced *-e*) and *ber a child* must have been indistinguishable, and it is possible therefore that the scribe's error had a phonetic basis; but cf. l. 35 below, where omission of the indefinite article is non-phonetic.
withute] *with huten* MS, but I assume once more that the scribe has added the *-n*; similarly in l. 35 below.
withute manne 'without a husband' is an example of the ME idiom in which no indefinite article is used. In *manne* metre and rhyme require *-e* to be pronounced; it is the dative inflexion (early ME *manne* dat. sg., in place of OE mutated *menn*). It is characteristic of these East Midland dialects of c. 1300 that they retain obsolescent inflexions while beginning to show the general phonetic loss of *-e*.

17. *Þangel hir seid*] The MS has *þangle seide*, which has the right number of syllables but the wrong metrical rhythm, for though the first foot must be a trochee, the second must be an iamb. The first step in reconstruction is to replace the scribe's *seide* (the full ME p.t. form) by *seid*; monosyllabic *seyd* is common in Robert Mannyng of Brunne's *Handlyng Synne* (e.g. ll. 5627, 5655), a South Lincolnshire text dated 1303. But I do not think we can read *þangele seid*; OF *angele* scans as two syllables, the first *e* being silent, and though a trisyllabic ME *angele* would be easy to explain, it is not likely that *-e* would be

kept at the end of a trisyllabic word in the author's dialect. Moreover the word 'angel' scans as two syllables elsewhere (ll. 26, 28, 37). Finally the music requires, as the third syllable of the line, one that is fairly strong though metrically unstressed, for it is set to two notes. I therefore assume that the scribe has omitted the word *hir*. For his *þangle* I substitute *þangel*; it seems to me that in a dialect in which *-e* was being lost, the author's spoken form was much more likely to have been *angel* than *angle* (the latter a form from OF). The MS spelling *seide* may show confusion of ME *ai* and *ei*, but is more likely to be the new analogical p.t. formed on the infinitive *sey* than a direct descendent of OE *sægde*.

ne dred tee nout 'do not fear for thyself'; *tee* (*te* MS) is a form of *þe(e)* 'thee', with *þ* assimilated to *t* after the preceding *d*. On the loss of OE *h* (modern English *gh*) after *ou* see note to l. 3 above, and cf. the rhyme-words in this stanza.

18. *þurw* 'through', the characteristic spelling of this MS for normal ME *þurʒ* < OE *þurh*. The word regularly scans as a monosyllable.

þoligast 'the Holy Ghost', with elision of the vowel of the definite article, as often in ME. In the last syllable there has been shortening of the vowel (OE *ā* > late OE *ǎ*); OE *hālig gāst* has been treated as a compound, with reduced stress on the final syllable. The form is not a Northernism.

iwrout (so MS), 'wrought', 'performed'. The prefix *i-* is required by metre, here and in l. 22 below (unless *ibout* were an error for *about*, i.e. *abouʒt* p.p. of *aby* 'pay for, redeem'); in l. 24 *brout* could be substituted for *ibrout* if the *-e* of *pine* were pronounced, but there is no need to do so. The *i-* prefix, though generally Southern and South Midland in ME, is also found in the East Midlands; and it occurs in the Norfolk *Bestiary*.

19. *ilche* 'same', 'very'.

20. *tiding* (so MS), 'news'; stressed on the second, as in l. 3.

22. *wurth* 'will be' < OE *weorþ* (WS *wierþ*), contracted 3 sg. pres. indic. of *weorþan* 'become'. The MS has *wrth*, but the omitted vowel must be *u*; *Genesis and Exodus* has *wurð*.

ibout is modern English 'bought' in the sense 'redeemed'; cf. no. 12, l. 56.

23. *þurw*] *þur* MS, but I restore its usual form (cf. note to l. 18).

þine sweet] *þi swete* MS, but this, though the right number of syllables, is the wrong rhythm. For *þi* we must substitute the inflected dative form *þine*, as in the MS itself in l. 58, and for *swete* the monosyllable *sweet*, with loss of *-e* (OE *swēte*); contrast l. 2 above, but compare *deer* (*dere* MS) < *dēore* in no. 12 above, ll. 40 and 57.

childinge 'child-bearing', with metrical stress on the suffix. The rhyme and the metre require the form with *-e*, added in ME to the OE feminine suffix *-ung* (*-ing*), and here retained; contrast *tiding* in ll. 3 and 20.

24. *ibrout* 'brought'; the same form occurs in no. 12, l. 8, where the metre requires the *i-* prefix.

25. *understood*] *understud* MS, and similarly *mud* MS for *mood* in l. 27. These characteristic spellings of the Arundel scribe, with *u* for OE *ō*, may represent a pronunciation with [y:], as in Scottish *guid* or *gude* for *good*. As they occur in all four poems that the scribe copied, though these are of diverse origin, the spellings are evidently due to the scribe himself and not to his exemplars, and he does not use them consistently; in l. 42 the

MS has both *suth* and *sooth*. We normalize the spelling, using *oo* for ME *ǭ* < OE *ō*.

26. *þangels*] *þangeles* MS, but if the author's dialect is more likely to have had *angel* as the nominative (see note to l. 17), it is likely to have had *angels* rather than *angles* for the genitive. The *e* of the definite article is elided, as the scribe's spelling shows.

28. *þangel*] *þangle* MS.

hie (so MS) 'she', one of the many ME spellings of the feminine personal pronoun. How it was pronounced is doubtful (possibly [hje:], with the *i* pronounced as the modern consonant *y*); singers may if they wish substitute *she*, which was already in use in the part of the country that the song comes from.

29. The MS reads *hur lordes þeumaiden iwis*, a striking example of how a scribe can copy the right words and yet completely falsify the rhythm by choosing the wrong forms. The fifth line of the stanza must begin with a trochee; *hur* must therefore be replaced by *urë* 'our', the full ME form < OE *ūre* (contrast l. 56, where the scribe writes *hure* but *ur* is required). But as this adds a syllable, and as the third syllable of the line should be metrically unstressed but fairly heavy (cf. note to l. 17), *lordes* has to be replaced by the contracted *lords*. The scribe's *þeumaiden* has the right number of syllables but the wrong rhythm, for /x/ is needed, not //x; he has written a compound (not recorded by *OED*), as if from OE **þeow-mægden*, where what is needed is *þewe maid*, in which *þewe* is the weak adjective (OE *þēowa*, fem. *þēowe*) used after a possessive (or alternatively the OE feminine noun *þēowe* 'bond-woman' used as the first element of a compound). On the replacement of *maiden* by *maide* (of which the *-e* here elides) see note to l. 2 above. The sense in either case is 'bond-maiden'.

Loss of non-final *e*, as in *lords* for *lordes*, is treated by the text-books as a fifteenth-century development in words which previously were of two syllables, but though this is generally true of Southern (including London) English it is certainly not true of more northerly dialects. Robert Mannyng's scansion often depends on reduction to *-s* where the scribe writes *-ys* or *-es*; thus in *Handlyng Synne* (1303), l. 9153:

> Goddys mércy déd hyt fró hem wére

where we must read *Gods* for *Goddys*. Cf. also l. 9064:

> And seyd, 'On Goddes halve, y yow forbede',

where again the metre requires *Gods*, probably unstressed.

30. *þat . . . is* 'who is above', i.e. in heaven above; the relative clause qualifies 'our Lord' in the previous line, not *ich* 'I'.

31–33. 'Let thy saying concerning me be fulfilled.'

31. *anentis* 'concerning, as regards', a form of *anent* with the adverbial and prepositional suffix *-es* added; but here the latter is spelt *-is*, originally a Northern and North Midland development, but also found early in South Lincolnshire (Robert Mannyng).

32. *fulfurthed* 'performed'. The word occurs only here in this form, but elsewhere as *fulforthien* &c. (see *MED*, s.v.). It is formed from the adverb *full* used as a prefix (cf. OE *fulfremman* 'perform') and the OE verb *forðian* 'further, perform', but with the vowel of the stem influenced by *furðor* 'further' (unless the scribe's *u* once again represents ME *ǭ* < OE *ō* by lengthening before *rð*). Carleton Brown's derivation

from OE *fyrþr(i)an* is impossible. The use of the prefix may owe something to ON (cf. ON *fullgøra* 'fulfil').

33. *þi sawe* 'thy saying', i.e. what you have said.

34. *sith*] *sithen* MS, but the reduced monosyllabic form is required. *OED*, s.v. *sith*, does not record the monosyllabic form used as a conjunction in the sense 'seeing that' until Wycliffe, though the form with *e* (*zeþþe, seþþe*) is earlier; but this is an accident of record, for the full form *siþþen* is found in this sense from the late twelfth century. Here the final *-n* has been dropped, and the *-e* then elides.

35. *a maid*] *maiden* MS. The MS reading is the correct number of syllables but the wrong rhythm, for the line must begin with an iamb. On the scribe's tendency to add *-n* and in particular to substitute *maiden* for *maide* see note to l. 2 above; but here we must assume that the *-e* of *maide* has been lost also, though no elision is possible. Insertion of the indefinite article, as in l. 16 above, restores the correct scansion.
withute lawe 'contrary to natural law'; *lawe* is here an abbreviation of the expression *cundeliche laȝe* 'natural law' or *lawe of kynde* 'law of nature'.

36. *have* is present tense subjunctive where we should use the conditional: 'that I . . . should have the happiness of a mother', i.e. of motherhood. Carleton Brown's punctuation makes *of moder* depend on *lawe,* but this is obviously wrong.

37. *Þangel*] *Þangle* MS.
mid þan 'with that', 'thereupon'; cf. *OED*, s.v. *with*, sense 16(b), where *wiþ þan* is cited from *Genesis and Exodus*.

38. *siȝte*] *sithte* MS, where *sithe* would be more in accord with the scribe's usual system (cf. his *mithe* for *miȝte* in l. 40).

39. *arise gan* 'began to swell up'. The scribe himself here writes *arise* without *-n*.

40. *þoligastes*] cf. l. 18 above, and note.

41–48L. The intended sense is taken to be: 'And he, having been enclosed in the womb for the space of nine months, issued from it and entered the conflict, taking on his shoulder the cross, with which he dealt a blow to the deadly enemy.'
   The readings of the MSS vary confusingly, but in l. 41 the agreement of P with DG establishes *qui*, and that of P with CG establishes *circumdatus*. At the other point of difficulty, in l. 47, D's *qua* makes easily explicable grammar and sense, since *crux* is regularly feminine in medieval Latin; P's *quo*, if meant as the adverbial conjunction ('whereby') and not as the relative pronoun, would give the same sense, but it is doubtful whether it could be correctly used in such a sentence and it is more likely to be an error for *qua*; AG's *qui*, possibly intended to mean 'he who', does not fit the run of the sentence if *qui* is correct in l. 41. We therefore accept *qua*, though it is given only by D.

41L. The first metrical stress of the line falls on *Qui*.

41. Similarly in the English text the first metrical stress is on the preposition *in*, not the pronoun *hir*.
hir] *hire* MS, but the reduced (unstressed) form is required.
wes] *was* MS, but see note to l. 44 below.
bilok 'enclosed', strong p.p. of *biluken* < OE *bilūcan*. The MS has *biloken,* the full form of the p.p., but this makes a syllable too many; the reduced form without *-n* is required, and its *-e* then elides before *anon.*

42L. For the stressing of *mensium* on the penult, contrary to Classical usage, cf. the well-known lyric *Dum Dianæ vitrea* from the *Carmina Burana* (conveniently available in *The Oxford Book of Medieval Latin Verse*, ed. Raby, pp. 322–4), ll. 16–17, a couplet which scans as two trochaic tetrameters catalectic:

> roris soporiferi
> mortalium generi.

42. *sooth* 'true'.
fles] *fleas* MS, and so in the next line, in contrast to *fles* in l. 10. In early ME spelling, *ea* represented the long vowel $\bar{e}$, which is to be expected in ME *flesh* < OE *flǣsc* (with $\bar{æ}^2$). But if the special form *fles* is derived from *fleslich* < OE *flǣsclīc*, shortening of the vowel to $\breve{e}$ is to be expected, and it is on $\breve{e}$ that the rhyme in ll. 43–44 depends. The scribe's *ea* is therefore misleading, though it may represent his own pronunciation of the vowel.

43. *hir*] so MS, rightly; the metre requires the unstressed monosyllabic form.

44. *ibore*] *iboren* MS, which of course scans equally well; but the evidence is overwhelming that the author's dialect had lost *-n* except in monosyllables and before vowels.
wes] *was* MS, but the rhyme requires the common variant *wes*. This was in origin an unstressed form, except in Kent and the West Midlands; but unstressed forms were often generalized and used in stressed position, as here.

46. 'Whereby good hope came to us.'

47. *bout* 'bought', i.e. redeemed; *pine* 'torment'.

48L. The agreement of DP must establish *hosti mortifero* 'the deadly enemy' as original. The alternative reading of ACG, *soli mortifero*, would mean 'the only agent of death', but involves taking *mortifer* as a noun, whereas it is normally an adjective (as in DP). It is not easy to see how either *hosti* or *soli* could be corrupted into the other.

48. 'and allowed himself to be slain for us'. The infinitive *slon* (with *-n* retained in a monosyllable, as the rhyme with *won* shows) is from ON *slá* (against normal OE *slēan*). Strictly it is the object of *let* and itself governs *him* ('he allowed the slaying of himself'), but the syntax is usually more loosely explained by saying that the infinitive is used 'in passive sense'.

49. 'Peerless virgin-mother'. *Maiden-moder* is plainly intended as a compound, though the words are not hyphenated by Furnivall and are separated by a comma by Carleton Brown. I assume that in such a special formation, the full form *maiden* (as written by the scribe) is likely to have been used.

50. *milce* (*milche* MS) 'compassion, mercy'.
ful ibunde 'fully endowed'. In the author's dialect there has evidently been blending of early ME *bun* (later *boun*) < ON *búinn* p.p. of *búa* 'dwell' (for which see *OED*, s.v. *bound* ppl. adj.[1]) and ME *ibunde* < OE *gebunden* p.p. of *bindan* 'bind'. The form here is from the latter, but the sense from the former, which in ON, used adjectivally, can mean 'endowed (with)': cf. *at flestum íþróttum vel búinn* 'well endowed with very many accomplishments'. So here the sense is 'fully endowed with compassion'.

51L. *angelis et homini* 'to the angels and to mankind'. This is the reading of the three early MSS ACD, and seems right; the use of *homo* in the singular to mean 'mankind' was very common. But the combination of plural and singular invites change; G has *angelis hominibus*, to the ruin of rhyme, and P has *angelo et homini*, which is probably only a more sensible emendation than G's. Note that P's reading brings vowels into hiatus without elision, which the ACD reading avoids, and that everywhere else in the poem the word *angelus* occurs in the singular (since it refers to Gabriel), so that P may unthinkingly have substituted the singular here.

51. 'pray for us to him who chose thee'. *Bid* is imperative sg. of *bidden* < OE *biddan* 'pray', and *ches* is < OE *cēas*, 3 sg. past indic. of *cēosan* 'choose'. For *tee* 'thee' the MS has *þe*, but cf. l. 17 above, where the MS itself shows assimilation of *þ* to *t* (in that case after *d*, here after *t*).

52L. The agreement of P with A must show that *genuisti* is the original text; it follows that C and G must have a common ancestor which substituted *peperisti* (displaced in G to l. 50).

52. *wam* 'whom'; *funde* 'foundest', 2 sg. past indic. of 'find' (OE *findan*), conjugated with a strong past tense.

53. *Forgive* here, and *give* in l. 58, owe their form to East Scandinavian *gifa*, in contrast to the native form *(for)yeve* < OE *(for)gefan*.
sen 'sin' (*senne* MS, but the *-e* elides), with *ĕ* < OE *ÿ*; *wrake* 'hostile action', and here apparently 'evil-doing'.

54L. P's word-order *nobis se* enables *nobis* to be correctly stressed on the first syllable, whereas *se nobis* the ACG reading (corrupted in D), makes the metrical stress fall on the second syllable. But in a text in which disyllables are so often stressed on the second, the reading of the early MSS may well be original, especially as the preceding word is a monosyllable; P's word-order is probably an emendation.

54. *gelt* 'guilt'; so MS, with South-eastern *ĕ* < OE *ÿ*.

55. *heven-*] *eune* MS.

56. *wan* 'when'. For *ur* 'our' the MS has *hure,* but though the word is metrically stressed the monosyllabic form is required.

57L. For *peccata,* the reading of ADG and apparently (as far as it can be made out) of C, P has *reata,* which gives a trisyllabic rhyme with *beata* in l. 59. But (i) the other four stanzas have only disyllabic rhymes at this point; (ii) *reata* is irregular grammar, for it implies a singular *reatum,* second declension neuter, in place of the normal *reatus,* fourth declension masculine. The reading of the early MSS is to be preferred. But it is easy to see how the false Latin form *reata* given by P could have arisen; it could, for example, have been wrongly deduced from the final stanza of the Nativity hymn *Cælum, gaude, terra, plaude* by Peter the Venerable, Abbot of Cluny (d. 1155), which begins:

Ora, mater, Deum natum
nostrum solvat ut reatum.

57. *sterve* 'die'; *steruen* MS, and similarly *seruen* for *serve* in l. 59, but the *-n* is likely to have been added by the scribe.

58. The *-e* of *give,* which is 3 sg. pres. subjunctive parallel to *forgive* in l. 53, has been dropped, though no elision is possible. The syntax of the English is confused here, for *give* has a dual function: 'may he give us the bliss of heaven when it is our time to die, [and may he grant us], for thy sake, so to serve him here that he may take us to himself.' In effect *give* has two alternative objects, *heven-blis* and the infinitive *for to serve,* and has to be translated twice, as 'give' and 'grant'. As the stanza consists of a single complex sentence, it is perhaps not surprising that the author has lost grip of it a little; and he may have been influenced by the loosely-used infinitive in l. 59 of the Latin.

59L. *frui* is an infinitive expressing purpose: 'for the enjoyment of the blessed life', 'in order that we may enjoy the blessed life'.

16a. Brid one breere

1

Brid onë breerë,   [briht] brid onë [trewë],
Kynd is com*e,* of Lovë   lovë to cravë:
'Bliðful bird, on me,   [on me] þu rewë;
or greið, leef, greið þu me,   [þu me] my gravë.'

2

5 Ich am so bliþë   so briht brid onë breerë
whan I see þat hendë,   [hendest] in hallë.
He is whit of lim,   [of lim and leerë];
he is fayr, and flur,   [and flur] of allë.

3

Mihtë ich hirë,   [hir] at willë havë,
10 stedëfast of lovë,   lovëli, trewë
(of mi sorw he may,   [he may] me savë),
joy and bliss wer er,   [wer er] me newë.

COMMENTARY

Source: Cambridge, King's College, Muniment Roll 2 W. 32.

This love-song is recorded in the unlikeliest of places, on the back of an official copy of a papal bull which formed part of the muniments of the priory of St. James by Exeter. This was a Cluniac house, affiliated to St. Martin des Champs of Paris, and founded a little before 1142. The bull, dated 1199, deals entirely with the affairs of the priory, and the copy was probably made contemporaneously in the mother-house in Paris and sent to St. James's to be kept as part of its archives. The priory was suppressed some time after 1428 and in 1444 its lands were granted to King's College, Cambridge; its deeds, including the copy of the bull, came with the lands, and are still preserved among the muniments of King's. The existence of the song was reported by John Saltmarsh, 'Two Medieval Love-Songs set to Music', *The Antiquaries Journal*, xv (1935), 1-12; he gives a facsimile of the MS, a transcription of the words (correct except in one detail), an edited text and a commentary; text and commentary are of little value, and no account is taken of the music, which shows that the word-text is gravely defective but which itself has errors.

The song was obviously written on the back of the copy of the bull long after 1199. Saltmarsh dates the hand to the fourteenth century (he appears to think it is about 1325), but is of opinion that the language of the song is that of the thirteenth century. This is undoubtedly a correct judgement (for one thing, the scribe was evidently copying a text which used the letter ð, which he copies as *d*), though I should think it unlikely that the song was composed before about 1275, for the personification of l. 2 seems to be influenced by *Le Roman de la Rose*.

The words of the song have undoubtedly been miscopied. An essential feature of the poet's technique (to which Miss Sisam drew my attention, though she is not responsible for my application of the principle) is that usually a word or words at the end of the first half-line is repeated in the second. This feature the scribe's text preserves in ll. 2 and 10, where the repetition was essential to sense as well as to metre; but elsewhere, where the repetition served only a metrical purpose, he has omitted it. In l. 1 he gives a repetition which cannot have been exactly as intended. The result of his omissions is that after l. 2 the words of stanza 1 (which alone are laid under the musical notes) get out of proper alignment with the music; the true alignment had to be restored after the word-text had been edited (except for final details). This editing in its turn depended on the determination of the metrical pattern, which must be essentially the same for all three stanzas, since the music is mensural and has a strongly marked rhythm. The metrical pattern for the first line of the stanza was the most difficult to determine, for l. 1 proved to have an error (see the detailed note on this line below), and the difference in rhythm between l. 1 as the scribe gave it and his text of ll. 5 and 9 made it uncertain whether the latter were correctly copied and if so how they were intended to scan. But there seems to be only one way of emending l. 1 so as to bring metrical and musical rhythm into harmony, and this gives a metrical rhythm to which l. 9 can easily be made to conform and of which l. 5 is a simple modification. The rhythm of the second line is given by the scribe's correct texts of ll. 2 and 10. That for the third line is given by his text of l. 3, once one realizes the principle of repetition and sees that *on me* should have been repeated. That for the fourth line is given most clearly by the scribe's text of l. 12, providing that the necessary repetition of *wer er* (written 'wer*e* Eer*e*' by the scribe) is made good. The rhythmical pattern thus established is as follows:

Line	1	/xx/x	/x/x/x
	2	/x/x/x	/xx/x
	3	/x/x/	x/x/x
	4	/x/x/	x/x/x

Line 2 is made up of the same half-line units as line 1 but in reverse order, and line 4 repeats line 3; the first pair make up a symmetrical, the second a repeated pattern. That this was the intended basic metrical scheme is shown by the fact that a text made to conform exactly to it proved to fit the music and indeed to help the emendation of the musical text. But further consideration of the scribe's word-text suggested that the author himself had permitted a metrical variation at two points: in l. 4 he introduced an extrametrical unstressed syllable at the beginning of the line, and similarly in l. 5 he introduced an extrametrical unstressed syllable at the beginning of the second half of the line. In each case the preceding bar (bar 13 in the case of l. 4, bar 2 in the case of l. 5) contains a 'spare' unstressed note, so that the additional unstressed syllable can be shifted back to the last note of the preceding bar. In effect the point of beginning the verse-line (or half-line) is altered, in relation to the music, in these two places. This would seem not to be a normal technique in music of this type and at this date; but the scribe's word-text (which apart from the minor metrical irregularity is perfectly satisfactory, and which cannot be emended convincingly) indicates that the author did employ it. It would be the easier to explain if he were writing words for a pre-existing tune, so that he knew that there was a note to spare at the end of the preceding bar at these two points and that in consequence his additional unstressed syllable could be accommodated without difficulty.

As for the rhyme-scheme, the scribe's text shows stanza 3 rhyming abab. In stanza 2 he uses the same half-line for l. 7b as is used for l. 10b in stanza 3. It seems obvious that the author would not have repeated a half-line in this way; the words *loveli, trewe* are plainly right for l. 10b, since they show there the usual repetition and make a rhyme, and are as plainly wrong for l. 7b, where they fail to make good the mid-line repetition and are incorrect in rhythm. They must be replaced, and if the reconstruction proposed in the note to l. 7 is valid, then stanza 2 also has the rhyme-pattern abab. In stanza 1 the scribe's text rhymes the second and fourth lines, but not the first and third; and as this is a breach of the pattern of the other two stanzas, emendation seems to be justified. An obvious one is available, which makes stanza 1 also rhyme abab. It may be added that this emendation makes the rhyme-sounds of stanza 1 the same as those of stanza 3, but in the reverse order, so that the full rhyme-pattern is ababcdcdbaba, which is so symmetrical as to suggest that the reconstruction of the rhyme-scheme is indeed correct.

The verse of the song is strongly influenced by the Middle English alliterative tradition. Except in the first line of the stanza, the first half of each line has three stresses, the second two; this was a common pattern in the ME long alliterative line. In the song the alliteration of metrically stressed syllables is obvious, but it is decorative rather than functional; some lines (e.g. l. 5) are, judged by the tradition of pure alliterative verse, much over-alliterated, others (ll. 3, 9, 10 and 12) have no alliteration linking the two half-lines other than that necessarily provided by the repetitions at mid-line. But the debt to alliterative verse is so clear that I print the song in long lines with a mid-line space to mark the caesura.

The song must obviously have been copied on to the back of the duplicate of the bull in the Priory of St. James by Exeter, but there is no sign in its language that it was copied by a Southwestern scribe. He must have been a native of Norfolk, or alternatively have been following mechanically the spelling of a Norfolk exemplar, for the text shows two features which appear to occur together only in Norfolk. These are (i) the use of *qu* for OE *hw* in *quan* for *whan* 'when' (l. 6) and *quit* for *whit* 'white' (l. 7), and (ii) the spelling *yhe* used for the pronoun 'she', which is a variant on *ʒhe* and *ghe,* both of which are found in Norfolk texts. But it is unlikely that the song was composed in Norfolk; final *-e* is far too well preserved for a Norfolk text of the last quarter of the thirteenth century (it is never lost by phonetic process, except by elision), and the fact that in l. 11 the *-e* of *sorwe* 'sorrow' elides before the pronoun 'she' suggests that the author's form was *he* (or some other form beginning with *h*) where the scribe writes *yhe.* If the reconstruction of l. 7b is correct, in stanza 2 *leere* < OE *hlēore* dat. sg. is rhymed with *breere* < OE (Anglian) *brēre* dat. sg.; this means that the poem was written in the East, where OE *ēo* had become ME *ē,* and within the area in which Anglian *ē* for WS *ǣ¹* was current. The use of the Norse-derived verb *greiðen* 'prepare' points to the Danelaw area, though by the later fourteenth century the word was current in London English (Chaucer uses it). The evidence is that the poem was written in the East Midlands, towards the south of the area.

Miss Sisam has drawn my attention to a carol-burden which must be related in some way to the present song. Gonville and Caius College, Cambridge, MS 383 gives the text of a carol (printed as no. 455 in R. L. Greene, *The Early English Carol*) which was evidently meant to go to the tune of an earlier carol; and to indicate this tune the scribe writes, before his own burden, that of the earlier carol in the form *bryd on brer y tell yt to none oþer y ne dar,* and again after his own stanza 1 he wrote and deleted *brid on þe brere etc.* If the two burdens, earlier and later, indeed went to the same tune, they both need some editing of their linguistic forms to produce identity of rhythm. The burden of the early carol must have run:

Brid on þe [*or* onë] brer, y tellë hyt
    to nón oþer, y ne dar.

That of the later carol (Greene's no. 455) must properly have run:

Wer it undo that is ydo
    I woldë be war, be war.

Unfortunately there is no other record of the earlier carol. The Caius MS is dated to the early fifteenth century, but there is no means of knowing how much older the early carol may have been; it may have been as old as the thirteenth century, for the carol-form was already well-established in England before 1300. As the carol was a more popular form, and our song is sophisticated both metrically and musically, the odds are that the song-writer was drawing his material from the carol and not *vice versa.* The carol-burden makes the situation a little more explicit; someone (probably, as in the song, a man) is telling a secret (again probably, as in the song, a love-secret) to a 'bird on a briar' because he dare tell it to no one else (a detail not in the song).

As the text has had to be rather heavily edited, the words as written by the scribe are given here. They are written across the page as if prose; the first stanza is written under the musical notes (but after l. 2 the words are not correctly laid under the notes), and stanzas 2 and 3 then follow. The beginning of stanza 2 follows the end of stanza 1 in the same line, but the difference is marked by a change in the style of the writing and by the cessation of the musical notation. The beginning of stanza 3 is marked by a paragraph-mark and a large capital.

bryd one brere brid brid one brere kynd is come of loue loue to craue blid ful biryd on me þu rewe or greyd lef *greid* þu me my graue Hic am so bliþe so bryhit brid on brerre quan I se þat hende in halle yhe is quit of lime loue li trewe yhe is fayr and flur of alle ¶ Mikte hic hire at wille hauen stedefast of loue loue li trewe of mi sorwe yhe may me sauen Ioye and blisse were Eere me Newe

For *bryhit* (l. 5) Saltmarsh reads *bryʒit,* but the fourth letter is *h.* The *E* of *Eere* in the last line is hardly distinguishable from the *w* of the preceding *were,* but in my view Saltmarsh is certainly right in reading *Eere*; metre and sense require it, and not a repetition of *were* (as read by Robbins, *Secular Lyrics of the XIVth and XVth Centuries,* p. 147, footnote).

NOTES

1-4. The sense is 'Bird on a briar, bird on a tree, Nature has come to beg for love from Love: "Gracious lady, have pity on me; or prepare, beloved, prepare for me my grave".' The transition to an imaginary speech in ll. 3-4 is somewhat abrupt, but is prepared for in l. 2; the lover, having told the 'bird on briar' that 'Nature' has come to make a plea to 'Love', then rehearses the terms of 'Nature's' speech. In reality, this is the lover's plea to his mistress, an elaboration on the conventional 'Grant me your love, or I shall die.'

1. The scribe's text:

Bryd one brere brid brid one brere

looks right, except at the end where it fails to rhyme; in particular it shows a repetition at mid-line of the sort which it is necessary to assume was characteristic of the poem. But the metrical rhythm of the scribe's line can only be /xx/x/ /xx/x, with clashing metrical stresses at mid-line on either side of the caesura; *brid* must have full metrical stress both at the end of l. 1a and at the beginning of l. 1b, and no other way of scanning the line, as the scribe gives it, is conceivable. But in his text of the music, the first of the two mid-line *brid*'s falls on the first note of bar 3, the second on the second note of the same bar; this does not seem a valid way of setting two syllables which have equal metrical stress and are separated by the mid-line caesura. The solution seems to be to emend the scribe's *brid brid* to *briht brid* on the model of the phrase in l. 5; both words then belong in the second half-line, after the caesura, and as the adjective *briht* takes stronger stress than *brid* (since it precedes) the metrical rhythm is brought into conformity with that of the musical setting.

Brid originally meant 'young bird, chick', but here has its modern sense (recorded from early in the thirteenth century) though not its modern form; the metathesis of *r* which turned *brid* into our *bird* did not occur, except in the North, until about 1400.

one] At both points in this line the scribe treats *one* 'on' as a disyllable, and certainly metre and music require two syllables. The word is an extended form of the ordinary preposition *on,* made by the addition of the adverbial suffix *-e* (cf. *OED,* s.v. *one, onne*). It was originally an adverb, but came to be used also as a simple preposition, i.e. it was used as a mere variant of *on;* cf. *OED,* loc. cit., and also the *Ayenbite*'s *ane* beside *an* 'on'. But in l. 3 the poet uses the ordinary preposition; he is taking advantage of linguistic variants for metrical convenience.

In the carol burden recorded in Gonville and Caius MS 383 (see the introductory notes above), the scribe writes *Brid on þe brere* as well as *bryd on brere,* and obviously it would satisfy the metrical and musical requirements of the present song if one were to read *on þe* in place of *one* in l. 1. But (i) the more general sense 'bird on briar' is probably better than the more precise 'bird on the briar'; (ii) the King's roll is much earlier than the Caius MS and is more likely to give the original form; (iii) the Caius MS itself varies between *on þe* and *on.* By the fifteenth century, when it was written, the extended form *onë* would have lost its final *-e* and been reduced to a monosyllable; and as the carol-burden evidently was intended to begin with a dactyl (as is shown by the later burden written to fit its music) *on þe* may well have been a substitute for original *onë* in order to restore the two syllables that the music of the carol must have required.

breere is modern English *briar* < OE (Anglian) *brēr*; the *-e* is the dat. sg. inflexion.

trewe is from OE *trēowe,* dat. sg. of *trēo* 'tree'. The MS here again has *brere,* but this means that there is no rhyme with l. 3 and that the second half of l. 1 is a mere repetition of the first, whereas in every other line of the song the second half-line shows variation as well as repetition. I take the song to have been deliberately patterned throughout, and therefore reject a reading which breaks both the stylistic and the rhyming patterns. There is no necessary inconsistency between 'briar' and 'tree'; the poet may have had a thorn-bush in mind.

2. *Kynd* (Nature) and *Love* (the goddess of love, Venus) are allegorical figures, of the type common in medieval love-allegory; this is a sophisticated feature of the diction and thought of the song. But by Nature the speaker evidently means himself, a man driven by natural desires; and he appears to identify his beloved with the goddess of Love, in view of the terms of his plea in ll. 3-4.

3. *bliðful* is a formation on OE *bliðe* and would therefore originally have been *bliðeful,* but the *e* has been lost by the early ME process of syncope in trisyllabic words with the stress-pattern /x\ (cf. Luick, § 456.2). OE *bliðe* meant 'kind' as well as 'happy'; in *blitheful* the sense 'kind' is recorded from c. 1300, that of 'happy' not until the sixteenth century (see *OED*). This may be an accident of record, but the sense 'kind, gracious' is what is appropriate here.

bird is the ME poetical word *bird(e)* 'lady, maiden,' the Eastern and Northern variant of Western *burde* < OE **byrde* 'embroideress'. The MS reads *biryd,* which has not unnaturally been taken as a mis-spelling of *brid* 'bird'. But in ll. 1 and 5, where the word intended is certainly 'bird', the scribe uses the correct early ME spelling *brid* (or *bryd*); only here does he use a different form. His *biryd* is better regarded as a spelling of *birde* 'maiden', for the *-e* of the full form will elide here before *on,* and the scribe's *y* can well be explained as the common early ME glide-vowel developed between *r* and a following consonant, which is found in Eastern texts. The gain to sense of taking *biryd* as a spelling of *bird(e)* 'lady' is obvious; otherwise we are faced with the absurdity of a bird being asked to have pity on a man or to prepare for him his grave.

In the late thirteenth century, in the South and Midlands, there was no possibility of confusion between *brid* 'bird' and the word for 'lady, maiden', even in East Midland dialects where the latter had the form *bird(e)*; for the metathesis that changed *brid* into the modern *bird* (and affected similarly other words) did not begin to operate until about 1400. A century

earlier, the distinction between *brid* 'bird' and *bird(e)* 'maiden' would have been as clear-cut and absolute as those in modern English between *grid* and *gird, grit* and *girt, slid* and *sild, slit* and *silt.* An audience would not confuse the two words, nor could a poet play on either of them in a double sense. Later, when they were confused in form, such a word-play would be possible; but it would be anachronistic to look for it in this poem.

It has been suggested that Eastern and Northern *bird(e)* 'maiden' might itself, by metathesis, have become *brid.* This is possible but unlikely, for its phonetic structure does not conform to that of words in which metathesis of post-vocalic *r* to pre-vocalic position normally occurred (cf. Jordan § 165 and better Luick § 714.1, and add to their examples *thrill* < *thirl*). Apparent examples of *brid* for *bird(e)* are to be otherwise explained. In the Harley lyric *Blow, Northern Wind,* l. 16, the scribe writes *brid* where the word for 'maiden' might have been expected; but he cannot himself have thought that this was the word meant or he would have used his Western spelling *burde,* as in ll. 5, 10, and 35. But he was copying a more Northerly original, as is shown by the occurrence in l. 63 of the form *slo* 'slay' (from ONb or ON *slá*), and he has probably retained unchanged a Northern spelling *brid* 'bride'. For it is known that there was confusion in use between *brid(e)* 'bride' < OE *brȳd* and the poetical *bird(e)* 'lady' < OE **byrde* (cf. N. Davis's glossary to Bennett and Smithers, *Early Middle English Verse and Prose,* with reference to this example), and the alliteration in the Harley lyric (*brid so breme*) strongly suggests that the word intended by the poet was *bride,* at least in form. Similarly in the Harley lyric *Weping haveþ myn wonges wet,* l. 40, the scribe writes *þis briddes breme.* But he is again copying a non-Western original (Eastern, within the area of Norse influence, but far enough South to permit the use in rhyme of the contracted 3 sg. pres. indic.), and his original evidently again had the word *brides* 'brides', used with the poetical sense of 'ladies'; his spelling with *dd* is due simply to misidentification of the word intended. These examples certainly show that a West Midland scribe, 'translating' non-Western originals, might confuse with the general ME word *brid* 'bird' the Eastern and Northern *brid(e)* 'bride' when it was used in a special poetical sense (due to confusion with *birde* 'lady') which made its identification difficult. But within any Midland or Southern dialect the position is as stated in the previous paragraph, that until c. 1400 the words *brid* 'bird' and *bird(e), burde* 'lady' were distinct in form.

on me] The repetition at the beginning of the second half-line is essential if the words are to fit the music. See the general introduction above for the assumption that such repetition was a regular part of the author's plan. But in none of the three stanzas does the scribe's text show a repetition in either the third or the fourth line.

rewe 'have pity'. In form the word is pres. subj. sg. (OE *hrēowe*); the OE imperative sg. was *hrēow* > ME *rew,* without *-e.* But in the next line *greið* is imperative. Perhaps a fine distinction of sense is intended; *rewe* expresses a wish or prayer ('may you have pity'), *greið* is more peremptory ('or else you will have to prepare for me my grave').

4. The scribe's text of the line has metrical rhythm but is too short; *þu me,* the last two syllables of the first half-line, should be repeated at the beginning of the second. But then, though the second half-line has the right number of syllables and the proper rhythm, the first half-line has a syllable more than normal, the unstressed *or* at the beginning of the line. It is obvi-

ously needed for sense and cannot be omitted. One could omit the first *greið* and read:

> Or, leef, greið þu me, þu me my grave,

a line in which it would be possible to give greater emphasis to the *or* than to the following vocative *leef* 'beloved' and so produce the right metrical rhythm. But this is rather forced. Moreover the repetition of *greið* in the scribe's text is effective, and the first half-line, as he gives it, looks right; if this were not a song no one would think of emending his text—the *or* would be accepted as an extrametrical unstressed syllable, or anacrusis, at the beginning of the line. The same situation recurs at the beginning of the second half of l. 5. In each case the preceding bar contains three notes, of which only the first is stressed (since the tune is in triple rhythm); and depending on whether the two unstressed notes are ligatured or taken separately, the music can accommodate either one unstressed syllable or two between the last metrical stress of the third line and the first stress of the fourth (or, in the other instance, between the last stress of the first half-line of a stanza and the first stress of the second half-line). The evidence of the scribe's text is that the author took advantage of this detail of the musical setting. It does not seem justifiable to alter for the worse the transmitted word-text merely to avoid the conclusion that the author was aware of the technical possibility of varying the fit of words to music.

5. 'I am as happy as a bright bird on a briar.' Here *blíþe* obviously has its normal meaning of 'happy'. Compare Robbins, *Secular Lyrics of the XIVth and XVth Centuries*, no. 204, l. 4:

> Then was I glade as bryde on brer.

Robbins op. cit. p. 147 punctuates the scribe's text as:

> Hic am so bliþe, so bryhit, brid on brere,

which would give the meaning 'I am so happy, so bright, bird on briar'. But as the caesura in the first line of the stanza comes after the fifth syllable, the two units of sense must be *ich am so blíþe* and *so briht brid one breere*, i.e. there is a *so . . . so* correlation ('as happy as'); and this is confirmed by the rhythm of the second half-line. For if *brid* were an independent vocative, it would have to bear metrical stress; but the basic rhythm for the second half-line is /x/x/x (which the music requires) and *brid* must therefore be metrically subordinate to *briht* and form a unit of sense with it. Taken as Robbins takes it, the sentence-stress would be hopelessly at odds with the musical rhythm.

The second half-line is, however, abnormal in that it begins with an extrametrical unstressed syllable *so* which has no counterpart in the first lines of stanzas 1 and 3. This could simply be omitted, but only at the cost of completely changing the meaning ('I am so happy, bright bird on briar') and of removing the only element of repetition at the beginning of the second half-line. If the line as given by the scribe could not be fitted to the music it would have to be emended; but in fact the *so* at the beginning of the second half-line can be fitted to the last note of the preceding bar (i.e. it can be treated musically as if it belonged to the end of the first half-line). Cf. the note to l. 4 above.

briht] The scribe's *bryhit* is probably an Anglo-Norman spelling; the word was always a monosyllable.

one] Here the scribe has the normal form *on*, but both the metrical rhythm and the music require the disyllabic form *onë*, as in l. 1.

6. *þat hende* 'that gracious person'.

The failure of the scribe to show the mid-line repetition is unfortunate. If we were to assume the normal pattern of exact repetition, we should read for the second half-line *hende in halle*; but it would then be necessary to assume failure of elision, for the half-line to be metrically regular should have five syllables, with the pattern /xx/x. It is true that in l. 9 the scribe's text, if correct, shows a similar failure of elision; but failure of elision before a following vowel was unusual, except at mid-line or when a sense-pause intervened, and one is reluctant to assume it twice in so short a poem, especially when it is after all only a deduction that exact repetition of *hende* was intended. By reading *hendest* and assuming repetition with variation (as in *love, loveli* in l. 10) one avoids the metrical difficulty, with perhaps some slight gain in sense ('when I see that gracious person, [who is] the most gracious in hall'). Both *hende in halle* and *hendest in halle* were in use as alliterative tags.

7. *He* 'she', from OE *heo*. The scribe writes *yhe*, a different phonetic development from the OE variant *hie*; but the author's form of the pronoun would seem to have been one of those beginning with *h-*, and *he* is the nearest to the form written by the scribe. In spite of its obvious ambiguity, it was not uncommon in early ME and survived in later ME. The form *hi*, which in later ME was more widespread, would be equally suitable metrically.

lim] The scribe writes *lime*, the dat. sg. form appropriate after the preposition *of*. But metre and music require a monosyllable (cf. ll. 3 and 11). We must assume that the nom.-acc. form *lim* of the OE neuter noun has, by syncretism, been substituted for the dative; the process was very common, and is almost invariable in the *Ormulum*, an East Midland text of earlier date. For the second half-line the scribe's text gives *loveli, trewe*, identical with 1.10b. This is plainly wrong, since (i) the author would not have repeated an identical half-line in so short a poem, (ii) the scribe's text lacks the repetition of a word or words from the first half-line, (iii) the corresponding half-lines in stanzas 1 and 3 can only be reconstructed in such a way as to make them begin with an unstressed syllable followed by a stressed, which fits the music, whereas the scribe's text makes this half-line begin with a stressed syllable followed by an unstressed, which runs counter to the musical rhythm. He must simply have anticipated 1.10b. Reconstruction of the original is not very difficult. It must have begun with a repetition of the phrase *of lim*, and the remaining three syllables must have the rhythm x/x; the first of them was almost certainly *and*. The phrase was probably alliterative. There seem two obvious alternatives: *of lim and lende* 'of limb and loin', which does not give satisfactory sense here, and *of lim and leere* 'of limb and face', which gives good sense; the lady has fair-skinned arms and face. It must be a confirmation of this reconstruction that *leere* makes a good rhyme, in an Eastern dialect within the Anglian area, with *breere* in 1.5.

For the use of *leer* 'face, countenance' in such contexts in alliterative prose and verse cf. *OED*, s.v. *leer* sb.[1], sense 2. The form here, with *-e*, is the old dative singular, which contrasts with the use of the accusative *lim* in the first half-line; in the reconstructed second half-line, dative *lime* would itself become *lim* by elision before *and*. The author is using grammatical variants to suit his metrical convenience; it was a common practice.

8. *he* 'she' (*yhe* MS), as before.

The sense of the line is 'She is fair, and the flower, the flower of all'. The first half-line is not complete sense in itself; the line does not mean 'she is fair and a flower, and the flower of all'. For similar lines, in which the first half-line is incomplete in sense, cf. ll. 3, 4, 9, 11 and 12, in contrast to ll. 1, 2, 5 and 10, in which the sense moves on in the second half-line and the verbal repetition is in form, not in sense. In ME the word *flur* does not seem to have been applied to persons without some qualifying addition: *flur of parradis (parays), flour of chevalrye, flur of alle,* and similarly *hore blostme* 'the flower of them' (*Ureisun of ure Lefdi,* l. 22).

9. The text is as the scribe gives it, except for the spelling and the repetition at the beginning of the second half-line, which he omits. But it involves the assumption that elision fails in the phrase *mihte ich* (since the metrical pattern requires that this should constitute a dactyl), though it is in precisely this sort of phrase that elision is shown not only by scansion, but also by spellings (cf. Luick, § 452). For comment on the general question of failure of elision before a vowel or the *h* of a normally weak-stressed word, see the general Introduction (pp. 43-4 above) and note to no. 7, l. 37. To prove failure of elision in instances like the present is normally very difficult, for most ME verse is tolerant of metrical variation, so that it is hard to say what rhythm the author intended; moreover it is only in exceptional cases that we can be confident that the transmitted text is what the author wrote. But in *Havelok* l. 1035, where the MS reads:

> Wore he yung, wore he hold,

it seems more likely that this is meant as an eight-syllable line scanning /xx//xx/ than as a six-syllable line scanning /x//x/, though the latter pattern does occur in the poem (e.g. ll. 2184-5); and in Chaucer's *Hous of Fame,* l. 314:

> Non other auctour alegge I,

the scansion must be x/x/xx/x/, with failure of elision of the *-e* of *allege,* since the verb must be stressed on the second (as it is elsewhere in Chaucer, four times in all). Although in our song there are various ways in which the scribe's text might be emended, it seems better to accept it as an example of a similar failure of elision before the pronoun *ich (I).*

hire at the end of the first half-line retains its *-e* before the caesura, but the repetition at the beginning of the second half-line loses the *-e* by elision before *at.*

wille] so MS, the more common ME form derived from OE *willa* weak masc.; here the *-e* does not elide before stressed *have.*

10. The adjectives of course qualify *hire* in the previous line. In the second half-line, the repetition with variation is very neat.

11. 'She can cure me of my sorrow.' For *save* 'cure' see *OED,* sense 7, but its earliest instance is from Langland. Perhaps the use here is only a special contextual application of the general sense 'to deliver or rescue from . . . hurt' (*OED,* sense 1 (a)).

The line is a parenthesis, interrupting the main sentence, as its shift to present tense shows; it is l. 12 which completes the sense of ll. 9-10. The rhyme-scheme shows that the lines are copied in the correct order.

sorw] *sorwe* MS, the normal ME form derived from OE *sorge,* the inflected oblique singular of *sorg.* But the metre requires a monosyllable, so that elision of *-e* must be assumed, and it follows that the author's form of the pronoun 'she' must have been one beginning with *h,* though the scribe writes *yhe;* cf. note to l. 7 above.

12. *joy*] *Ioye* MS, the form from OF *joie,* but the *-e* elides.

bliss] Metre requires the monosyllabic form from the OE nom. sg., where the scribe writes the more common ME disyllabic *blisse* from the OE oblique cases. Cf. no. 6b, l. 6, and note.

wer] *were* MS, the *-e* being expressed by a flourish over the *r* which the scribe may have added without much deliberation. ME *were* was often reduced to a monosyllable under weak stress; but in any case the *-e* would here elide.

er is the modern *e'er,* the monosyllabic contracted form of *ever,* which is recorded from early in the thirteenth century. The scribe writes *Eere,* the final *-e* being again expressed by a flourish over the *r;* if he had any reason for it, it was probably that the full form was commonly written *euere* in ME. But a monosyllable is certainly required, and the evidence is that the contracted form was always a monosyllable. The scribe's *Ee* is to express the length of the vowel, without regard to its quality; but as we restrict *ee* to the representation of the close vowel, ME *ẹ̄,* whereas this word had the open vowel, ME *ę̄,* we are obliged by our system to alter the spelling to *er,* which in any case is more characteristic of thirteenth-century orthography.

The two words *wer er* must be repeated in the second half-line.

16b. (i) Maid in the moor lay

1

Maid in the moor lay, [maiden] in the moor lay,
sevenyht[es] fullë, seveniht[es] fullë.
Maiden in the moor lay, [maiden] in the moor lay,
sevenihtes fullë — [*fullë,*] ant a day.

2

5   Wel was hirë met*e*. [Wel,] wat was hirë met*e*?
Þe primërolë, ant the — þe primërolë, ant the —
Wel was hirë met*e*. [Wel,] wat was hirë met*e*?
The primërolë, ant the — [*the sweetë*] violet.

3

10

[Wel was hirë drynk.] Wel, wat was hirë drynk?
[Þe coldë water of the — þe coldë water of the —
Wel was hirë drynk. Wel, wat was hirë drynk?]
Þe coldë water of [þe] — [*the freshë*] wellë-sprink.

4

15

Wel was hirë bour. [Wel,] wat was hirë bour?
[Þe redë rosë, ant the — the redë rosë, ant the —
Wel was hirë bour. Wel, wat was hirë bour?]
Þe redë rosë, ant the — [*the whitë*] lili-flour.

16b. (ii) Peperit virgo (Richard de Ledrede)

1

Peperit virgo, virgo regia,
mater orphanorum, mater orphanorum.
Peperit virgo, virgo regia,
mater orphanorum, plena gracia.

2

5

Præbuit honorem vox angelica
regi angelorum, regi angelorum.
Præbuit honorem vox angelica,
regi angelorum cantando gloria.

3

10

Puero feruntur tria munera
obsequio magorum, obsequio magorum.
Puero feruntur tria munera
obsequio magorum cum stella prævia.

4

15

Tribuat salutem virgo cælica,
sola spes lapsorum, sola spes lapsorum.
Tribuat salutem virgo cælica,
sola spes lapsorum in hac miseria.

5

20

Angelo docente natí magnalia,
vigilia pastorum, vigilia pastorum —
angelo docente natí magnalia,
vigilia pastorum, laus ét læticia.

6

Virgo, prece pia per tua munera,
regina supernorum, regina supernorum —
virgo, prece pia per tua munera,
regina supernorum, duc nós ad supera.

COMMENTARY

Sources: English text: Oxford, Bodleian Library, MS Rawlinson D. 913, flyleaf; Latin text: Red Book of Ossory, f. 71.

In the Rawlinson MS the English lines are written as prose, and the phrasal repetitions are not shown for stanzas 3 and 4 (nor, according to the view here taken, completely in stanzas 1 and 2); see the text as printed by K. Sisam, *Fourteenth Century Verse and Prose*, p. 167. It was Sisam who supplied *was hire drynk* (the last word in the MS spelling *dryng*) in l. 9 and *þe* in l. 12. His text is followed, but with the repetitions more nearly completed, by Robbins, *Secular Lyrics of the XIVth and XVth Centuries*, pp. 12-13. The text given above is further emended; see the rest of this introduction, and the notes on the text below.

The Red Book of Ossory is an official record-book of the diocese which was started by Richard de Ledrede (Leatherhead), an English Franciscan who was appointed Bishop of Ossory in 1316. In order that his clergy might not sing *cantilene teatrales, turpes, et seculares* and so corrupt ears and mouths dedicated to God, the Bishop wrote pious Latin songs in their place, to be sung to convenient tunes; the words of these songs, sixty in number, are recorded in the Red Book, with some indications of the secular tunes to which they were to go. Thus *Peperit virgo*, according to a marginal note in the MS, went to

the tune of [*M*]ayde y[*n*] *the moore* [*l*]ay, as was first pointed out by R. L. Greene, ' "The Maid of the Moor" in the *Red Book of Ossory*', *Speculum*, xxvii (1952), 504-6. I follow the Latin text given by Greene, but with one change. For the Red Book has, in my view, an error in its setting-out of stanza 1, the only stanza for which it gives the repetitions in full; it repeats the phrase *mater orphanorum* (corresponding to *sevenihtes fullë* in the English text) not only in what I print as l. 2, where the repetition is correct and is confirmed by the Rawlinson MS, but also in l. 4, so that the latter, according to the Red Book, would run:

mater orphanorum, mater orphanorum, plena gracia.

But this is opposed to the evidence of the Rawlinson MS, which sets out in full both stanzas 1 and 2; it shows repetition of the whole phrase in the second line of the stanza, but no repetition in the fourth. Greene (op. cit., p. 506, and also in reporting the Latin and English texts to Bukofzer for *The New Oxford History of Music*, iii, 119) assumed that the Red Book was right and the Rawlinson MS was wrong. But this, while appearing to produce a symmetrical stanza, in fact produces an asymmetrical one. A much more probable result is achieved if one follows the lay-out of the Rawlinson MS not only for the English, but also for the Latin (as is done above); one then gets for the Latin a stanza (except in stanza 1) of four lines each with six stresses (or of eight short lines, each with three stresses). If the arrangement of the Red Book is followed, there is excessive repetition, and the run of sense in the second half of the stanza (which is continuous in our arrangement) is interrupted.

The details of the establishment of the English text are discussed in the notes below; in general it may be said that the Rawlinson MS is reliable except (i) in the forms or spellings used for a few words, (ii) in its failure to show all the necessary repetitions. With the one exception discussed above, the Red Book's text of the Latin is to be accepted. Nevertheless it shows a number of variations of metre, as follows:

(1) In the first half of ll. 1 and 3, a stressed syllable is lacking as compared with the corresponding lines of later stanzas in both the English and the Latin texts. In l. 1, Ledrede was following exactly the model provided by his seemingly correct text, *Mayde yn the moore lay,* of the corresponding English phrase; but in preserving the same text and rhythm in l. 3 he was probably diverging from the original (see the notes to ll. 1 and 3 below).

(2) At the beginning of the second half of the first and third lines of stanzas 5 and 6 he inserts an extra unstressed syllable. (In stanza 5, it may be noted, the stress must fall on the second syllable of *nati,* though elsewhere disyllables are correctly stressed on the first.)

(3) At the end of the first and third lines in stanzas 1, 2, and 4 he fails to provide an unstressed syllable between the last stress of the first (or third) line and the first stress of the second (or fourth), though the English text always has such a syllable (in stanza 1, at the end of the first and third lines; in the rest, at the beginning of the second and fourth).

(4) Except in stanza 1, he inserts an extra unstressed syllable at the beginning of the second half of the fourth line. It seems possible that in the English text known to him this half-line was different in its metrical form from that shown in all stanzas by the Rawlinson MS, and he may at this point have been carefully following the variations of the English text that he knew. What this text may have been is suggested by the words printed in italics and within square brackets in the English text given above; these words are lacking in the Rawlinson version. See further the notes to ll. 4, 8, 12 and 16 of the English text, on pp. 192-3 below.

(5) The remaining metrical variation in the Latin certainly has a model in the English, as given by the Rawlinson MS itself. This is the extra syllable at the beginning of the second half of the second line in stanzas 3, 5, and 6 of the Latin, which follow the model of stanzas 2-4 of the English (whereas this half-line in the Latin stanzas 1, 2, and 4 follows its counterpart in stanza 1 of the English).

It is impossible to tell whether the variations in stanzas 5 and 6 of the Latin (in particular variation (2) above) had models in lost stanzas of the English text. As far as we can judge from the surviving evidence, only variation (3) is unlikely to have had any parallel in the English song, as it was known to Ledrede; otherwise the Latin probably follows closely, but not exactly, the metre of the English text as he received it. He shows skill in his reproduction of the English repetitions (or some of them), and if anything he improves on the English rhyme-scheme. The Latin text rhymes together the first, third, and fourth lines of the stanza (as the English does), using always the same rhyme-vowel *-a* (where the English has changing rhymes), and in every stanza the second line ends in *-orum,* just as in the English the second line ends in unstressed *-e* (in stanza 1 *fullë,*

in stanzas 2-4 *the*). It is not a perfect *contrafactum,* but it is a clever one.

The English text of the Rawlinson MS was written by a Southern scribe; it uses the spelling *st* for OE *ht* in *seuenist(es),* an originally Anglo-Norman spelling found chiefly in Southern texts, and still more significantly the form *chelde* 'cold' from late WS *cēald.* But the rhyming of *drynk* (spelt *dryng* in the MS, a 'reverse' spelling, i.e. one the opposite of phonetic) with *sprink* (spelt *spring* in the MS, the traditional spelling) shows the change of *ng* in *spring* to *nk,* a phonetic development which in stressed syllables is characteristic of the North-west Midlands; and the rhyming of *mete* 'food' (OE *mĕte,* two syllables) with *violet* (which seems never to be recorded with final *-e* in English while *-e* was still pronounced) in stanza 2 clearly shows loss of *-e* in the former word, a change which would not be found in the late thirteenth or early fourteenth century in a southern or South Midland dialect. The song must have been written in the North-west Midlands, and I therefore replace the Southern form *chelde,* in my text, by the Midland form *colde.* In view of the date of Richard de Ledrede's occupancy of the see of Ossory, from 1316 to somewhat after the middle of the century (when he was nearly 100 years old), *Peperit virgo* must have been written by 1350 at latest; a more realistic dating would be between 1316 and 1330. *Maid in the moor lay* must be earlier still, perhaps a good deal earlier, to allow knowledge of the song to reach Ireland; the probability is that it was written in the thirteenth century. Loss of final *-e,* which its text shows in *mete,* began in the North in the thirteenth century and was far advanced by 1300 in Northern and North Midland dialects, as it was also in the Anglo-Irish dialect of the Kildare poems; a song written in the North-west Midlands at any date after 1250 might well show sporadic loss of *-e.* But it should be added that though this explanation (a North-west Midland text copied by a Southern scribe) is how a philologist would normally interpret the linguistic evidence of the Rawlinson text, it is now known that medieval Anglo-Irish characteristically blended the features of various English dialects; *Maid in the moor lay* may itself be Anglo-Irish, which would be consistent both with its currency among the clergy of Ossory and with the inclusion in the same MS of the fragmentary carol known as 'The Irish Dancer'. Though the language of *Maid in the moor lay* looks later than that of *Brid one breere,* this may be merely because it was written in a less conservative dialect.

The point of the comparison is that when the textual editor of these songs was working on *Brid one breere,* it occurred to him that its use of repetition, length of line, and length of stanza (all of which are distinctive in ME verse) were remarkably similar to, though not identical with, those of *Maid in the moor lay* (and of *Peperit virgo*); and he wondered whether *Maid in the moor lay* might have been written to go to the same tune. And indeed it proves to fit the tune recorded for *Brid one breere* very well — on balance perhaps rather better. There are various points of difference, which may for convenience be discussed with reference to the bars of our modern transcription of the music. (In what follows I use the abbreviations B for *Brid one breere,* M for *Maid in the moor lay,* and P for *Peperit virgo,* and I take my examples chiefly from the first stanzas of each.)

(1) In bar 1, all three texts have three syllables in stanza 1, corresponding to the three notes of music. But in later stanzas M and P have four syllables, so that the music has to be adapted by splitting the first minim (in the modern transcription) into

two crotchets, making bar 1 (thus adapted) the same as bar 3, whereas in B in all stanzas there is a variation between the two bars. (2) In bar 6, which has four notes, B has only two syllables, so that three of the notes have to go to the stressed syllable. M has four in stanza 1 (-*nihtes fullë*), and so has P in stanzas 1, 2, and 4 (*orphanorum,* etc.), so that in this, the standard metrical form, there is one syllable for each note. But in stanzas 2-4 of M there is an additional unstressed syllable at the end (unless there is an 'overlap' of parts; see below), and similarly in stanzas 3, 5, and 6 of P; to accommodate this extra syllable the final note of the bar has to be split in these stanzas. (3) In bar 7, which has five notes, B has five syllables (*Lovë, lovë to*), M and P have four (*sevënihtes, mater orpha-*). In B there is an exact correspondence of syllables and notes, but its text is rather rushed — in particular, the stressed syllable of the second *love* has to go to a single short note. (4) In bar 12, with six notes, B has only two syllables (*me þu*), of which the first has to carry four notes. M and P each have four syllables (*maiden in the, virgo regi-*), of which the first two each carry two notes, the second two each a single note. (5) In bar 16, B has two syllables (*me thu*) for the two notes. So has M in the Rawlinson text, in all stanzas; but in the text as emended to conform with P there are three syllables (thus *ant the — þe* in stanza 2) except in stanza 1 (*fulle*). P has two syllables in stanza 1, three in stanzas 2-6. For P and for the emended text of M it is necessary to split the last note of the bar, except in stanza 1. B and the unemended text of M here fit better than P and the emended text of M. (6) The same situation as in bar 12 recurs in bar 17, which has the same six notes. B has only two syllables (*me my*), P has four (*plena graci-*). In M the Rawlinson MS gives only two syllables (*ant a* in stanza 1), which agrees with B; the emended text has four (*fullë, ant a*) to agree with P. (7) In bar 18, the final bar, M and P have a single syllable (*day, -a*), which enables the song to end with a single long note (a dotted minim in the modern transcription); B has two syllables, a 'feminine' ending to the verse-line (*gravë*), which in the MS are set to two notes (a minim and a crochet in the transcription). As between B and M, the balance of advantage seems to be slightly with M, which has a nearer agreement between the number of syllables and the number of notes; and it seems possible that, though the tune is actually recorded for B, it may originally have been meant for M. At least the words of M fit the tune, though in a somewhat different way; the situation is similar to that of no. 6b above, which fits the tune recorded for no. 6a (though in this case there is the difference that the two sets of words are recorded in juxtaposition in the Cotton-Jesus anthology).

That *Brid one breere* and *Maid in the moor lay* can be fitted to the same tune is not a coincidence explicable by their use of a commonplace stanza-form; their rhythms are not identical, but both are distinctive and without parallel. In the whole recorded corpus of ME lyric I do not know of another poem whose metrical rhythms and stanza-form would allow it to be fitted to this music, though I have looked through all the pieces printed in Carleton Brown's and Robbins's collections.

Interpretations of *Maid in the moor lay* have differed widely. It has, for example, been taken as a religious allegory; but as Greene very reasonably points out, it evidently did not seem to be a religious poem to the Bishop of Ossory. It does not necessarily follow that he thought it a *cantilena turpis;* this expression is used in a general account of his motives in writing his pious *contrafacta,* and in individual cases he may have had no particular objection to the words of a song except that they

were secular — indeed he may have had no objection at all, and may merely have wished to steal the tune. On the face of it, *Maid in the moor lay* is innocent enough; but it may have been less innocent than it seems. The key to it must surely be in the first stanza, marked off from the rest by its narrative form; it is a concise exposition of the situation envisaged in the song. It tells us that a girl has slept 'in the moor' for a week and a day; and the season of the year is indicated by the flowers mentioned in stanzas 2 and 4 — though to be sure those of stanza 2 are spring flowers, and those of stanza 4 summer flowers. But if we ask why a girl should go off and sleep out on the moor, an obvious answer is to visit a lover — either a shepherd whose work took him out on the moors in summer (cf. the situation in no. 21 below, though there the girl invites her shepherd-lover to visit her) or less probably an outlaw. A song dealing, however discreetly, with such a situation might seem to the bishop capable of putting wrong ideas into the heads of his clergy. And it is by no means certain that we have the full text of the English song. The strip of parchment that is bound in as a fly-leaf of the Rawlinson MS gives mere fragments of a number of songs, such as 'The Irish Dancer' (no. XV(D) in Sisam's *Fourteenth Century Verse and Prose,* the burden and first verse of a carol) and the quatrain:

> Al nist by þe rosë, rosë,
>   al nist bi the ros*e* i lay;
> darf ich noust þe rosë stel*e*
>   and ȝet ich bar þe flour away.

It would be uncharacteristic of the MS if it gave the full text of *Maid in the moor lay.* It gives four stanzas (two in abbreviated form), but the Bishop's *contrafactum* has six; and though there is obviously no reason why a *contrefactum* should be exactly the same length as its original, the pieces in our collection show that there was some tendency to make *contrafacta* match their originals in the number of stanzas. Moreover the technical problem which the Bishop had set himself was a difficult one, and it would not be expected that he should write more stanzas than he felt were required of him to match the length of his original. It is also to be remembered that his stanzas 5 and 6 show a metrical variation not found in any of the four surviving English stanzas. It seems likely enough that the English song properly had a couple more stanzas than the Rawlinson MS gives. Now in stanzas 2–4 it has told us of the girl's food, her drink, and her 'bower' (bed-chamber); it would be a logical progression to go on to the pleasures of the bed-chamber in a fifth stanza. Any lost stanzas may have been more objectionable to a bishop than those which survive.

It has been suggested to me that the technique of stanzas 2–4 of *Maid in the moor lay* is reminiscent of a type of traditional song in which a word is led up to and then held back, generally by a deliberate breaking-off or interruption; and when the word that was held back is finally supplied, it is different from what was expected. Commonly the word suggested is vulgar or salacious, the word actually used is harmless. A medieval example of the type is the piece printed as no. 30, with the title 'Silver White', by Robbins, *Secular Lyrics of the XIVth and XVth Centuries,* pp. 26–27; it is from Cambridge, University Library, MS Additional 5943, f. 170ᵛ. But if the author of *Maid in the moor lay* had this technique in mind, he has used it either very innocently or with great sophistication; for there is no salacious suggestion, and the word that is held back and finally supplied is always the obvious and expected word.

Perhaps he was teasing his audience by using a suggestive technique innocently; or it may be that his is a sophisticated version of a popular poem that was much more outspoken or used the technique in its ordinary suggestive way, so that he was in effect teasing his audience by their recollection of the popular song which his had replaced. But this is very speculative. It is more likely that his technique aimed at a gradual approach to a climax which, as suggested above, may have come in a lost fifth or sixth stanza, and that the treatment was deliberately delicate. However delicate it may have been, a song dealing with young love on the moors would not have appealed to Richard de Ledrede, a harsh and rigorous man, 'the scourge of heretics' and obviously a strict moralist.

Regardless of the tune for which it may have been written, the literary form of *Maid in the moor lay* suggests two possible modes of performance. (1) It may have been meant for a single singer, who in stanzas 2–4 pretended to hold a dialogue with himself and even to interrupt himself (though it would not be easy, I think, to find analogues for this conception in ME literature). If so, then in stanzas 2–4 there is an additional syllable at mid-line in the second line of the stanza, requiring the splitting of the final note of bar 6 if *Maid in the moor lay* is set to the tune of *Brid one breere;* but stanzas 3, 5, and 6 of *Peperit virgo* also show an additional syllable at this point. (2) It may have been meant for two voices, who would presumably sing stanza 1 in unison and then conduct the dialogue of stanzas 2–4 by singing in alternation the two halves of each line (singer A taking the first half, and singer B the second, of each line, though they might join in unison for the last line, or perhaps the last half-line, of each stanza). In this case there could be an overlap of the parts in the second lines of stanzas 2–4, for it is a remarkable technical feature of these lines that the last word before and the first word after the mid-line caesura is always the same, the definite article *the.* If the second singer interrupted the first in this line, coming in with *the* while the first was singing his *the,* then the two singers could sing together the last note of bar 6, each to the same word; and by this 'over-lap' the additional syllable in the second line would in effect be eliminated, and with it the necessity for splitting the final note of the bar. But in the 'performing text' below (p. 269) we give a setting for a single voice, which makes possible easier comparison with the setting of *Peperit virgo.*

Notes on the text of *Maid in the moor lay* follow. For obvious reasons, the text has been established without any reference to the music recorded for *Brid one breere.* It is based on comparison of the readings of the Rawlinson MS with the text of *Peperit virgo* as given by the Red Book of Ossory; for as the Latin is explicitly recorded as a *contrafactum* of the English song, the metrical patterns of the two must be reconcilable, and those of the Latin may legitimately be taken as a guide to (though not necessarily conclusive of) the original text of the English.

NOTES

1. *Maid*] Red Book [M]ayde, Rawlinson MS *maiden.* The rhythm is different, for the -*e* of the Red Book's form will elide before *in,* giving the pattern /xx/x. Though this differs from the pattern of the corresponding half-line in later stanzas, it is to be accepted, since it agrees with that of the opening words *Peperit virgo* in the *contrafactum* (and also with the opening of *Brid one breere*). The Rawlinson form *maiden* is that required in the

second half-line, as reconstructed; the scribe appears to have been confused between the two half-lines.

For the second half-line (of which the English is unfortunately not given in the Red Book) the Rawlinson MS has simply *in the mor lay,* which gives a half-line of two stresses, /x/x. But this is too short; in every stanza the Latin has a half-line of five syllables, /x/x/, and in stanzas 2–4 of the English text, if *hire* is disyllabic, the second half of the first line also has three stresses. It seems clear that the Rawlinson MS should have repeated *maiden* at the beginning of the second half-line, as *virgo* is repeated in the Latin; but to prevent elision the form required is the full *maiden,* which gives a half-line of three stresses scanning /x/x/x.

At the end of the line, the metrically unstressed word *lay* is in effect transferred from the beginning of the second line, which is where the unstressed syllable comes in stanzas 2–4. The Latin text similarly has an unstressed syllable at the beginning of the second line in stanzas 3, 5, and 6; but in stanzas 1, 2, and 4 it omits the unstressed syllable altogether.

2. *sevenyhtes*] In both places in l. 2 the Rawlinson MS reads *seuenyst (seuenist),* the old uninflected plural (OE *seofon niht*); but in l. 4 it has *seuenistes,* the regularized plural made by extension of the strong masculine ending -*es.* The latter must have been the form intended by the author; the Latin is quite explicit that each half of l. 2 should consist of six or seven syllables with three stresses, and stanzas 2–4 of the English all have seven syllables. Presumably the more conservative uninflected form was substituted by the Southern scribe of the MS; but fortunately he has not been consistent. I replace the scribe's *st* spelling by the more normal *ht.*

3. *Maiden*] So Rawlinson MS at the beginning of the line. Though this gives, for the first half-line, a rhythm /x/x/x which differs from that adopted for the first half of l. 1 (whereas the Latin repeats l. 1 exactly), it is probable that the Rawlinson scribe is right here; his is the normal rhythm, as established by the later stanzas of both the English and the Latin texts. Compare *Brid one breere,* in which the rhythm of the third line differs from that of the first in every stanza. It would be possible to emend the Latin into conformity with the normal rhythm (thus *peperit [et] virgo*), but it seems more likely that Ledrede has repeated l. 1 without change than that his scribe has corrupted the text.

At the beginning of the second half-line the Rawlinson scribe again omits to repeat *maiden;* cf. the note to l. 1 above.

4. The second half-line in the Rawlinson MS has only three syllables, *ant a day,* and similarly in stanzas 2–4. The lines as given in the MS are complete in sense and effective in rhythm, and there is no reason to suppose that they are corrupt. But the Latin text has five syllables scanning /x/x/ in stanza 1, and six syllables scanning x/x/x/ in stanzas 2–6. The discrepancy between the two texts might be due merely to a different method of fitting syllables to notes, but Richard de Ledrede seems intent to imitate closely the English text as it came to him, not merely to write new words to fit, in however changed a way, the same tune; it is improbable that he would have used a half-line of five or six syllables if the English text known to him had only three. It seems likely, therefore, that he knew a different version of the English song, in which the phrase used to complete the sense in the final half-line of each stanza was longer than in the Rawlinson version. How the phrase may have been

lengthened is suggested by the words printed in italics, within square brackets, in our text of the English song. In this stanza I assume a mere repetition of the adverb *fulle* at the beginning of the final half-line. It is possible, indeed, that the occurrence of *fulle* in this position suggested Ledrede's use of *plena*. See further the notes to ll. 8, 12, and 16 below.

The provision of this hypothetical expanded text does not mean that I think it superior. Even if this, or something like it, was the version known to Ledrede, the Rawlinson text seems to me neater and more economical in its way of completing the sense, and more likely to be original. Though the Rawlinson scribe shows some tendency to omit repetitions, in stanzas 2–4 it cannot be a mere repetition that is involved.

In the MS text, and also in the emended version, elision of the final -*e* of *fulle* fails before *ant*.

5. *hire*] so MS. The word must have its full disyllabic form if the line is to begin with two trochaic feet, which is the pattern of the corresponding Latin line; so in ll. 9 and 13 below.
mete] At the line-end, the word must be a monosyllable, by loss of final -*e* from OE *mēte*. This is shown (*a*) by the rhyme with *violet* (so written by the scribe), which itself must end with a stressed syllable (since every stanza, in both texts, has a 'masculine' ending); (*b*) by comparison with the corresponding words in stanzas 3 and 4, *drynk* (OE *drinc,* strong masc.) and *bour* (OE *būr,* strong nt.), which are necessarily monosyllables. Similarly at the middle of the line *mete* must also be taken as a monosyllable; again it corresponds to *drynk* and *bour* in stanzas 3 and 4.

It follows that in the line as given by the Rawlinson scribe, an unstressed monosyllable must have been omitted between *mete* and *wa* , for stanza 1 of the English and all stanzas of the Latin show that we should not have clashing stresses at mid-line in the first and third lines of the stanza. The parallel of l. 1 suggests that the omitted word may have been identical with the first word of the line, i.e. that it was *wel.* There are two indications in the scribe's own text that this was so. Here in l. 5 he writes, at the beginning of the line, *welle wat* for *welle was* (Sisam's emendation); his error would be explicable if *welle wat* had indeed occurred in the second half-line. The second is the scribe's text of l. 9, which reads

Welle wat was hire dryng

and is most probably explained by the error of homeoarchy — his eye has jumped from *welle was* at the beginning of the line to *welle wat* at mid-line, and the first half-line has gone. To explain the two errors merely from the resemblance between *was* and *wat* would be less likely.

For the use of *well* as an independent preliminary word to introduce a statement or question see *OED,* s.v. *well* adv., sense 23, and Bosworth-Toller, s.v. *wel,* II. The idiom sounds modern, but was already old when the song was written; King Alfred uses it, before an imperative.
wel] MS *welle,* regularly. The spelling is without etymological justification and is surprising in a fourteenth-century Southern scribe; it is possible, in view of the way in which the word is used (as I assume in my emended text) in the second half of this and other lines, that he was influenced by the form of the ME interjection *welle* from OE *wel lā* (cf. *OED,* s.v. *wella*).
wat] so MS, regularly; the spelling is probably due to the Southern scribe, since the change of *wh-* to *w-* in early ME is usually a Southern feature. But the North-west Midland

Gawain-poet alliterates *wh-* with *w-,* and spellings with *w-* for *wh-* occur in *Pearl.*

6. *primerole* 'primrose'. The -*e* does not elide before *ant,* though it is not at mid-line; but a slight sense-pause is possible, which I mark with a comma. That the word scans as four syllables, without elision, here and in l. 8, is shown by comparison with the corresponding phrase *coldë water* in ll. 10 and 12, and with the Latin.

8. In the second half of the line the Rawlinson text again gives only three syllables, the word *violet,* so that the line reads:

The primerole ant the violet.

But corresponding to *violet* the Latin text has *cantando gloria,* scanning x/x/x/, so that again it seems that the English text known to Richard de Ledrede must have differed from that of the Rawlinson MS. It must have had three syllables, scanning x/x, before *violet,* and I conjecture that the half-line read *the sweete violet* (since *sweete* is an adjective recorded as used with *violet* in ME). But I put this forward only as a possible reconstruction of the text known to Ledrede, not as a correction of an error in the Rawlinson MS, whose text seems to me preferable.

9. *drynk*] *dryng* MS, a reverse spelling; the word was always pronounced as in modern English. On the scribe's form of the line see note to l. 5 above.

10–11. The Rawlinson scribe does not write out these lines. They are to be assumed (with Sisam and Robbins, but with variations in detail) from the text which the scribe does give for l. 12. Similarly with ll. 14-15 below.

12. *colde*] The weak adjective, with inflexional -*e,* used after the definite article. The scribe writes *chelde,* the Southern form from late WS *cēalde.*
þe at the end of the first half-line is not now legible in the MS, though traces remain; it was supplied by Sisam.
For the second half-line the Rawlinson MS reads *welle-spring* (where the rhyme requires *welle-sprink* with unvoicing of *ng* to *nk,* a characteristically North-west Midland development). But again it seems likely that the text known to Richard de Ledrede had a longer phrase, with a rhythm matching his *cum stella praevia;* it may have read either *the freshë wellë-sprink* or *the cleerë wellë-sprink* (since both adjectives are found used with *spring* or with *well* in ME). In this text the native word *freshe* seems to me more likely than the French-derived *cleere.* Again I prefer the Rawlinson version.

16. *rose*] The -*e* is not elided; cf. *primerole* in ll. 6 and 8.
ant the] *ante* MS, showing assimilation (*ant þe* > *ant te* > *ante*). I restore the fuller forms which the scribe uses elsewhere.
Again in the second half-line, which in the Rawlinson text is simply *lilie-flour,* the text known to Richard de Ledrede may have been longer, with a rhythm corresponding to his *in hac miseria* x/x/x/. An obvious choice is *the whitë lili-flour*; but the Rawlinson version is better.
lili-] *lilie* MS, the traditional form from OE *lilie* weak fem., but the metre certainly requires two syllables; the -*e* has been lost in pronunciation, perhaps but not necessarily because *lili-flour* is here a compound. Cf. the loss in *mete* in ll. 5 and 7.

17. Worldes blisse, have good day / [Benedicamus Domino]

1

Worldes blissë, havě good day;
nou fram min hertë wend away!
Him for to loven min hert is went
þat þurʒ his sidë sperë rent
[and] shed his hertë blood for me,
nayled to þe hardë tree.
Þat sweetë bodi was yteend,
with naylės þree ypreend.

2

Ha Jesú! þin holi heved
with sharpë þornes was byweved;
þi feyrë neb was al bispet,
with spotě and blood meynd al bywet.
Fro þe crunë to þe to
þi body was ful of pině and wo
and wan and red.

3

Ha Jeśu! þi smartë ded
be my sheeld, and me ared
fram devles lorë.
Ha, sweet Jesú, þin orë!
For þině pines sorë
tech riʒt min hertë lovë þee
hwas hertë blood was shed for me.

[*Tenor:* Benedicamus Domino]

COMMENTARY

Source: Cambridge, Corpus Christi College, MS 8, f. 270

The metre of this poem is deliberately varied, but not as irregular as the text given in the MS makes it appear. Among the signs of corruption, the clearest is in l.8, where the rhyme-word is moved to the beginning of the line and altered in form. As there is only the one MS, editing must necessarily be conjectural and aimed at restoring coherence between the metrical rhythm and the clear and strongly marked rhythm of the music, which is in a mensural notation. Though it seems possible that the poem may have been specially written as the words of the motet to which it is set, in l. 9 there is a divergence between the metrical rhythm clearly intended by the poet and the musical rhythm, which forces a different and less natural scansion on the line; and in l. 17 there is another, though slighter, divergence. It is therefore improbable that author and composer were the same man.

The extant copy seems to have been the work of an Essex scribe, who was responsible for the spelling *wand* for *wend* in l. 2 and probably for the regular spelling *ss* used for OE *sc* (modern English *sh*). These South-eastern features have been removed from our text, for it is probable that the original dialect was that of the East Midlands. The form *ded* 'death', established by rhyme in l. 16, is East Midland and Northern, and the Norse-derived *fro* 'from' is given by the MS in l. 13. But the *y-* prefix of the p.p. is given by the MS in l. 7 and is required by the metre both there and in l. 8; its use rules out the North and North-east Midlands. The contraction of the p.p. suffix *-ed* to *-d* in *yteend* in l. 7 (*y tend* MS) and required in the rhyme-word in l. 8 (for MS *prened*, misplaced) is against the South and South Midlands, and even in the East Midlands is in favour of a date towards the end of the thirteenth century. Lengthening of

ME *ĕ* in open syllables is shown by the rhyming of *byweved* (l. 10) and of the emended *ared* (l. 17). Final *e* is mostly preserved, but is lost from the imperative *have* in l. 1 (possibly, in this word, because of weak sentence-stress), from the p.t. *rent* in l. 4, from *sweet* in l. 19 (contrast l. 7), from the adverb *riʒt* in l. 21, and from the emended imperative *ared* in l. 17. In a thirteenth-century text such loss of *-e* is improbable in the South or South Midlands; even in the East Midlands it argues a date towards the end of the century.

NOTES

1. *blisse*] *blisce* MS.
2. *wend* 'go, depart'. The MS has the 'Essex' form *wand*, but though this variant was more widespread than Essex it is unlikely that it was an original feature of this text; in ll. 3–4 the normal forms *went* and *rent* occur, for which the Essex forms would be *want* and **rant*.

3–5. 'My heart is inclined (*went*, literally 'turned') to love him through whose side a spear tore and who shed his heart's blood for me.'

3. *is*] *his* MS.

4. *rent* 'tore'. The full ME form of the p.t. of 'rend' was *rente*, but the *-e* is here dropped; the scribe himself writes *rent*, doubtless because it is needed for the rhyme with *went* p.p. and by the music. As the following line, in its emended form, begins with a vowel, it would be possible to regard the loss of *-e* as due to elision, though this did not normally occur at the line-end; but elsewhere in the poem final *-e*'s that are normally required by grammar or etymology are lost where no possibility of elision arises.

5. The MS reads *his herte blod ssadde for me*, but though this

has the right number of syllables when both final -*e*'s are pronounced, the stresses do not correspond with the musical accents, which are clearly marked; nor is the metrical rhythm regular, though it is acceptable. Moreover, in all other cases that I know of in which *that* has a double syntactical function (used first with following *his* to make up 'whose', as in l. 4, and then re-used as the subject of a second verb, here *shed* in l. 5), the two co-ordinate relative clauses are joined by *and;* the syntax really requires the insertion of *and.* But in that case the verb *shed* must be transposed before *his,* for the music shows that the line must begin with an unstressed syllable followed by a stressed syllable. The line as emended has regular metrical rhythm and exactly fits the music.

An alternative emendation, suggested by Miss Sisam, is to replace the scribe's *ssadde* by *shed he,* so that the line would run:

his hertë blood shed he for me.

This is a very economical emendation and attractive for that reason. But as the line must have regular iambic rhythm, as the music shows, in this reconstruction *shed* is metrically unstressed and *he* is stressed, which is a little forced; moreover the last two stressed syllables in the line are *he* and *me,* which seems displeasing. As *shed* would be unstressed and set to two short and musically unstressed notes, it would be difficult for a singer to give proper force to the word. The form of the line adopted in our text runs more smoothly and makes *shed* metrically and musically stressed; and ll. 4 and 5, in our form, make a very characteristic piece of ME idiom. Admittedly the change is more radical, since it involves the insertion of *and* and the assumption that the scribe, or a predecessor, has dislocated the original word-order; but a much worse dislocation of word-order occurs in l. 8, where the rhyme-word is moved to the beginning of the line.

I replace the scribe's spelling *ssadde* by *shed.* Though the MS regularly has *ss* for *sh,* I doubt whether this was a feature of the original; it is more likely to have been introduced by the scribe. For the vowel he has *a* here and *e* in the p.p. (which he spells *ssed*) in l. 22; the author is unlikely to have varied the forms in so short a poem, and I judge that *e* is more likely to be original. For the very varied ME forms of this verb see *OED.*
herte is the old genitive singular (< OE *heortan*), preserved here and in l. 22 in the fixed phrase *herte blood,* which in ME became a virtual compound.

7. *yteend* (*y tend* MS), p.p. of the verb *teen* 'inflict suffering on, afflict, injure'. The musical setting requires the contracted form of the p.p., in place of the normal ME (*y*)*teened* (with -*ed* as a separate syllable).

8. The MS reads *prened wit nayles þre,* but *prened* is certainly the rhyme-word and must be removed to the end of the line; it follows that its form must be altered to *ypreend* to make the rhyme exact and to produce the right rhythm. The line as emended fits the music; as given in the MS it does not, for of the two notes to which MS *prened* is set, the first is unaccented, the second accented.
ypreend is p.p. of the verb *preen* 'pierce, transfix'.

9. Here and in ll. 16 and 19, the poet obviously stressed *Jesu* on the second syllable; his intended scansion for this line was /x/x/x/x, as is shown by the parallel with the next, which varies only by having an additional unstressed syllable at the beginning, thus x/x/x/x/x. But the composer has set l. 9 as if its scan-

sion were /xx/xx/x, which is possible, but only if an unnaturally heavy stress is put on *þin,* so as to make *Jesu* and *holi* metrically unstressed.
heved 'head'. The MS has *hefd,* but the earlier disyllabic form is required by both the rhyme and the music, which has two notes (accented and unaccented) to correspond to the word.

10. *sharpe*] *ssarpe* MS.
byweved 'bewoven, encircled'. The weak form of the p.p. of the verb *weave* is recorded by *OED* from the fourteenth century onwards, but must have been somewhat earlier, since it is established here by the rhyme.

11. *neb* 'face'; *bispet* 'spat upon'.

12. *spote*] *spot* MS, but I add a silent final *e* as a special warning that the vowel is long. It is a rare noun meaning 'spittle', which is recorded by *OED* from William of Shoreham (in Kent) c. 1315 and a poem called *The Castel of Love* (c. 1320) in the Vernon MS; it is also recorded in the modern dialect of Lancashire. The context in *The Castel of Love* is very similar to the present one.
meynd 'mingled'; *al bywet* 'completely wetted'. *Bywet* is p.p., not adj., and its vowel is short, as in the rhyme-word *bispet.*

13. *þe to* 'the toe'.

16. *smarte* 'painful'; *ded* 'death'.
The laying-out of the words beneath the musical notes goes wrong at this point. The interjection *ha* at the beginning of the verse-line is written below the last note of the previous line, which is followed by a rest-mark. But *ha* itself is preceded by a point, so that it is clear that the scribe knew that it began l. 16; and the point in the word-text should be taken as corresponding to the rest-mark in the music. The wrong alignment of words and music may not have been intended by the scribe, but may be a mere mechanical accident, the result of bad spacing. *Ha* belongs with the ligatured notes after the rest-mark; after that the words and notes fit each other. *Jesu* (spelt *iesu* in the MS, and so in ll. 9 and 19) is again stressed on the second syllable, which is here set to an accented note.

17. *be*] The poet must have intended the word to bear a metrical stress, since the metrical rhythm of the beginning of the line should be /x/ to match that of *Ha Jesú* in the preceding line. But the composer sets *be* as an unstressed syllable. The discrepancy is not serious, as the metrical stress on *be* can only be light.
sheeld] *sseld* MS.
me ared] an emendation for *my red* 'my counsel' in the MS. The MS text makes the line short by a syllable, and gives it only two or three stresses, depending on whether *be* at the beginning of the line is not or is stressed. Moreover *my red* 'my counsel' does not fit the context and in particular cannot be followed by *fram* 'from'. The emendation to *me ared* 'liberate me' supplies the required additional syllable and gives the line a third undoubted stress; the musical phrase correspondingly has three long and accented notes. But the scribe has fitted the music to the corrupted word-text by ligaturing the second of these long notes with the following short note, and has assigned the ligatured notes to *my.* The musical text must therefore also be emended, by breaking the ligature and giving the first of the two notes (the long and accented one) to *me,* the second to the prefix *a-* of *ared.*

The imperative singular of OE *ahreddan* 'rescue, set free'

was *ahrede,* which would become ME *arede.* In this form the first *e,* originally short, would be lengthened in the open syllable; this is required by the rhyme with *red* (OE *rēad*) and *ded* (OE *dēad*). That the lengthening had occurred in the author's dialect is shown by the rhyme of *byweved* (originally with *ĕ*) in l. 10 with *heved* (OE *hēafod*) in l. 9. But rhyme, metre, and musical setting also require us to assume that the final *-e* of this imperative *arede* had been lost. In view of other evidence of loss of *-e* in the text, this does not present a difficulty for the emendation.

18. *lore* 'teaching, counsel'.

19. This line is metrically parallel to the next, and must have the stress-pattern x/x/x/x. But this requires that the adjective 'sweet' (spelt *swete* in the MS), from OE disyllabic *swēte,* should be a monosyllable, i.e. that its *-e* should have become silent (though in l. 7 the word is still two syllables). The South-eastern scribe, for whom such adjectives in *-e* were obviously still disyllabic, took *swete* as two syllables; but this meant that the verse-line had a syllable more than there were notes in the musical phrase. He therefore in effect transferred *ha* to the previous line, writing it to the last note of a bar before a musical rest; and in this case there can be no doubt of his intention. But that he has interfered with the original setting is shown clearly by the fact that his rearrangement makes the first syllable of *swete* fall on a short unaccented note, the second on a long accented note — which is impossible, for ME *-e* was always very weakly stressed. *Ha* belongs after the rest, to the first of these notes; the second (long) note is for the monosyllabic

sweet, and the rest of the line then fits, *Jesu* again being stressed on the second syllable.

ore (*hore* MS, with falsely-added *h*) means 'mercy, grace, favour' (OE *ār*); it is an OE feminine and adds *-e* (from the oblique cases) in early ME.

21. *tech* (*thech* MS) 'teach'.

In the MS, the word *riȝt* follows *herte,* but the scribe has certainly copied the words in the wrong order; in his text, the stressed first syllable of *herte* goes to an unaccented short note at the end of a bar, the weak second syllable to a long note at the beginning of a bar. The music requires two unstressed words or syllables after *tech,* followed by regular succession of stressed and unstressed syllables; and assuming that the scribe has written the right words, we must transfer *riȝt* to follow *tech.* Words and music then fit. The meaning is 'teach properly my heart to love thee'; the scribe's order made the text mean 'teach my heart properly to love thee', which he may have thought better sense. In either order *riȝt* is an adverb, from OE *rihte,* but the scribe's spelling and the music, which provides only for a monosyllable, show that it has lost the *-e,* which was the adverbial suffix. *Love* is the simple infinitive, used after *tech.*

22. *hwas* (*ȝwas* MS) 'whose', a form with ME *ă* directly developed from the OE genitive singular *hwǣs.* It is not a Northern form with ME *ā,* the Northern equivalent of our modern *whose,* which was a newer form based on the ME nominative.

shed] *ssed* MS. See note to l. 5 above.

18. Sancta mater graciæ / Dou way, Robin

Duplum

1
Sancta mater graciæ,
   stella claritatis,
visita nos hodie,
   plena pietatis.

2
5   Veni, vena veniæ,
     mox incarceratis,
solamen angustiæ,
   fons suavitatis.

3
Recordare, mater Christi,
10   quam amare tu flevisti;
juxta crucem tu stetisti
suspirando viso tristi.

4
O Maria, flos regalis,
inter omnes nulla talis,
15   tuo nato specialis,
nostræ carnis parce malis.

5
O quam corde supplici
   locuta fuisti
Gabrielis nuncii
20   verba cum cepisti.

6
'En ancilla Domini'
   propere dixisti;
vernum vivi gaudii
   post hoc peperisti.

7
25   Gaude, digna,
tam benigna,
   cæli solio;
tuos natos,
morbo stratos,
30   redde filio.

Tenor
Dou way, Robin,
   þe child wilë weepë;
dou way, Robin.

COMMENTARY

Sources: London, British Library, MS Cotton Fragments XXIX, f. 36; Princeton, University Library, MS Garrett 119.

Though this motet cannot of course be regarded as a medieval English song, it is included here for the sake of the English words of its tenor, a charming snatch from some popular song.

The Cotton fragment is a fire-damaged leaf, in part badly discoloured, twisted and wrinkled, and cracked. It gave the full text of the words of the *duplum,* but not the words of the tenor. The greater part of the *duplum* text is still clear, but many of the words are hard to make out, and a couple are almost illegible (see the Notes below). The Princeton MS gives the Latin text of the *duplum* from l. 23 onwards (though only the feet of the letters of l. 23 remain, their upper parts having been cut away with the top of the leaf), and the English text of the tenor, written in red ink after the Latin text (with *wepe* where I normalize to *weepe* in my text above). In stanza 7 the Cotton and Princeton texts are identical; but in ll. 23–24 there are differences (see below), and Princeton is better.

The words of the Latin text are mostly a string of the conventional phrases of Marian lyrics, though the metrical technique is skilful enough; the successive pairs of stanzas have the same metrical pattern and rhyme-scheme, and the final stanza divides into two balancing halves linked by the rhyming of the third and sixth lines. In view of the English text of the tenor, the composer of the motet must have been English; but it perhaps does not follow that the Latin text of the *duplum* was also written by an Englishman. Two or three of the stressings of the Latin words would normally be taken as a sign of French origin, but it is known that, because of French influence, similar stressings were current in the medieval English pronunciation of Latin. (See further the notes to ll. 7, 18 and 20, and the discussion of medieval Latin stress on pp. 48–51 above.) In the rhymes, Classical quantities are ignored in *incarcerātīs* (l. 6) rhyming with *suavitātīs* (l. 8) and *in mălīs* (l. 16) rhyming with *regālīs, tālīs,* and *speciālīs.* This ignoring of distinctions of quantity was characteristic of the pronunciation of Latin in the later Middle Ages, in which, though the vowels were distinguished in length, it was according to native English principles and not the original Latin quantities. It may be significant that the rhymes cited ignore Classical differences of quantity in two positions characteristic of the English pronunciation of Latin, namely (*a*) in stressed penultimate open syllables, in which all vowels were made long, and (*b*) in unstressed final syllables, in which they were made short.

NOTES (Latin Text)

1. *Sancta*] Cotton has *Snt* (or perhaps *Snc*) as an abbreviation of *Sancta.* Bukofzer's suggestion (*Oxford History of Music,* iii. 112) of *Veni* was not a good guess; an adjective not an imperative is to be expected (since there is already an imperative in l. 3), it is unlikely in this poem that stanza 1 would begin with the same word as stanza 2, and the letter-forms at the beginning of stanza 1 are quite different from those at the beginning of stanza 2.

5. *vena veniæ*] These words stand at the beginning of a new line in the Cotton fragment, where the parchment is badly charred and the writing is barely distinguishable. In bright sunlight and under a strong lens I thought that it was possible to make out *uenie* as the second word and hints of *uena* as the first. In any

case, if the second is *uenie* the first must be *uena,* for *vena veniæ* 'channel of mercy' is a recurrent phrase in such contexts in Marian lyrics (cf. *Planctus ante nescia,* addendum to no. 4 above, l. 17), and the whole line *Veni vena veniæ* is the incipit of a motet in the Las Huelgas MS (Anglès, *El codex musical de Las Huelgas,* vol. iii, no. 86). Cf also the lines:

> Virgo, vena veniæ,
> mater regis gloriæ,
> visita nos hodie

in Dreves, *Anal. Hymn.,* xx, no. 244, st. 2.

6. *mox incarceratis*] hard to read but undoubted. The sense continues to the next lines; literally translated, 'come . . . soon to those imprisoned, as a solace of misery, a source of sweetness'.

7. *solamen*] Though the composer has set the word in accordance with its Classical stressing on the long penult, the metre requires it to be stressed on the first and third syllables. Such shifted stressings are essentially due to French end-stress, which brought a consequent secondary stress on to the antepenult; but they also affected the medieval English pronunciation of Latin trisyllables, though in it the main stress doubtless came in the course of time to be on the first syllable, that on the last being made secondary.

8. *suavitatis*] five syllables, i.e. the *u* and *a* of *sua-* are to be pronounced separately as if vowels in hiatus. On this 'diæresis' see Norberg, *Introduction,* pp. 30–31, who cites *suävis* as one of his examples. He remarks that such forms 'sont, comme on pouvait s'y attendre, tout à fait courantes au Moyen Age comme dans l'Antiquité'. In musical settings it is normal to treat *suavis* as three syllables.

12. *suspirando*] so Cotton. On this use of the ablative of the Latin gerund see H. P. V. Nunn, *Introduction to Ecclesiastical Latin,* p. 93 (§ 188); but the equivalent English syntactical construction is rather the earlier *a-sighing* (in which *sighing* is a verbal noun), not the present participle, as Nunn states.
viso tristi 'at the sad sight'. So Cotton, with initial *v* in *viso* and a space in *tristi* between *i* and *s.* The word *viso* was covered by the transparent paper with which the binder attached the fragment to the modern paper backing (though the covering paper has been partly pulled away) and is hard to read, but is certain.

15. *tuo nato specialis* 'special in your son', i.e. in the manner of his conception and birth.

16. *nostræ . . . malis* 'have mercy on the sins of our flesh'. So clearly Cotton (with *nostre* where I normalize, as regularly in this book, to *nostræ*). On the rhyme see above.

17. *locuta*] metrically stressed on first and third in place of the Classical stressing on the long penult. Cf. the note on *solamen,* l. 7 above; but here the composer follows the author to the extent of placing a musical stress on the third syllable.
locuta fuisti 'you spoke', in place of Classical *locuta es,* the latter being taken as a present form.

17–18. *fuisti Gabrielis nuncii*] These words are on the left of the leaf of the Cotton fragment and are hard to read, partly because of the fire damage and partly because of the binder's covering transparent paper, but the reading is certain.

20. *verba cum cepisti*] Cotton *cum verba cepisti.* If the MS text is correct, the metrical stress falls on the second syllable of *verba,*

and so also the musical stress. Such end-stressing of disyllables was a common feature of the medieval French pronunciation of Latin and affected also the English pronunciation, at least temporarily; cf. no. 15(ii) above. But here it seems better to emend by reversing the order of *cum* and *verba,* for the following reasons. (*a*) The Cotton text is not infallible; see the notes to ll. 23 and 24 below. (*b*) The transposition of the words regularizes the stressing. (*c*) It brings *verba* immediately after the genitive *Gabrielis nuncii* on which it depends. (*d*) It brings *cum* before *cepisti,* which is in accordance with the author's evident liking for alliterative groups (though in this instance it is alliteration for the eye rather than for the ear, in the medieval pronunciation of Latin). (*e*) The transposed word-order seems to fit the music better, since it makes *verba* carry the last two short notes of bar 59 (in the modern transcription) and leaves the monosyllable *cum* to take the stressed long note at the beginning of bar 60.

23. *vernum vivi gaudii* 'the spring-time of living joy'. Here the Cotton fragment reads clearly *Verum lumen lvminum,* but this does not rhyme. In the Princeton MS, which enters at this point, only the feet of the letters remain, the tops having been cut away. The last word is certainly *gaudij* and the one before is almost certainly *uiui.* The first begins with capital *V,* followed by a series of minims which probably make up *nu m.* (with a space between the *u* and *m* and a point after the *m*). Taking into account the Cotton reading *Verum,* I guess that Princeton had *Vernum,* with the *er* expressed by the usual mark of abbreviation over the *V,* as in *uericalis* and in *diuersis exercicijs*

in the following piece lower on the leaf. This reading *vernum vivi gaudii* rhymes properly, gives satisfactory sense in the context, and is less conventional than the Cotton text. The Cotton scribe has substituted a commonplace phrase for one which he either could not or did not read correctly in his exemplar; his starting-point must have been misreading *vernum* (the unexpected word) as *verum,* and the rest followed.

24. *hoc*] Cotton has *hec,* spelt in full, but Princeton has the abbreviation for *hoc* (the top cut away). The latter is better sense; Cotton's must be a misreading (*e* for *o*).

25-30. Both MSS agree exactly in details of abbreviation (with *celi* where I normalize to *cæli*).

NOTES (English text)

Dou way means 'be off, get on with you, stop it' (cf. *OED,* s.v. *do,* 53(b)), and the words are obviously addressed by a woman to an importunate or interfering husband or lover. The spelling of *way* for earlier *wey* is a clear linguistic sign that the Princeton text is unlikely to have been copied before 1280; that of *dou* for *do* is abnormal, and is perhaps due to the coalescence of the two words *do wey* into one, with consequent diphthongization of early ME *ǫ* to *ou* before *w.* The final *-e* of *wile,* though it would not seem necessary for scansion, is set to a separate note in the music; it is of course etymologically justified. If the lines used for the tenor had any continuation in the original (and the lack of rhyme suggests that they are an incomplete quotation), it may have been *and let him (me, us) sleepe.*

19. Lou, lou, lou! wer he goth!

Lou, lou, lou! wer [h]e goþ!
A lou, lou, lou! wer [h]e goþ!
For hir i les myn [h]alywater, -ter, -ter, lou!

COMMENTARY

Source: Dublin, Trinity College, MS D. 4. 9 (270), f. 37ᵛ.

This little song was discovered in a MS of Trinity College Dublin by the editor of the music of this book; it is not listed in *The Index of ME Verse* by Brown and Robbins or in its *Supplement* by Robbins and Cutler.

The MS is a collection of medieval university text-books; in particular from f. 34 to f. 113 it gives an annotated and commented text of Eberhard (Evrard) of Béthune's *Graecismus,* a celebrated grammatical text-book in verse (which, despite its title, had little to do with Greek). The original Latin verse-text is written centrally on the page, surrounded by the commentary. At various points in the book small sheets of parchment, strips much smaller than the normal leaves, have been bound in between the full leaves; their purpose was evidently to accommodate additional notes. One of these is f. 37. Its recto and the top of the verso are filled with Latin notes on rhetorical and grammatical terms, written in an academic hand of the end of the thirteenth century, which is very similar to and probably identical with the hand that writes the commentary on the main

pages. The second of the notes on the verso of this inserted strip (f. 37) begins *Articulus est punctata verborum disposi[ci]o,* and on the facing main page (f. 38), just above the level of the top of the inserted strip, there is a sentence in the commentary on the right-hand side of the page which begins identically; this doubtless explains why the strip is placed as it is.

The academic scribe used only the top quarter of the verso of the inserted strip of parchment, leaving the rest blank. Immediately below the last of his Latin notes a later scribe has ruled two five-line staves, one for the upper and one for the lower part, and has given the music and words of a two-part song. The English words are written twice, with slight variations of detail (see below), beneath the two staves. This still left rather more than a quarter of the strip blank, and immediately below the song there are scribblings, apparently mere pen-trials, in at least two and perhaps three distinct hands; these have nothing to do with the song. The latter owes its preservation to the fact that its copyist found in a university text-book a blank space of convenient size, and used it for a purpose utterly inconsistent with the nature of the book in which he was writing.

The hand in which the words of the song are written has affinities with that of MS Harley 2253, and is to be dated to the second quarter of the fourteenth century, which is consistent with the spelling-system employed. As the musical notation is to be dated in the first third of the fourteenth century, it would seem that, taking the evidence of hand-writing, spelling, and musical notation together, the song was probably copied into the MS about 1330. It may, of course, have been composed earlier, for the state of its word-text suggests that it is a copy; but though so brief a text provides little linguistic evidence, it does not seem likely that the words were written before 1300. It would probably be safe to ascribe the composition of the song to the first quarter of the fourteenth century.

In the MS the words of the song are written twice, in two long lines across the page under each musical part, as follows:

> *Upper part:* Lou lou lou wer e goz a lou lou lou wer*e* goz for hyr iles myn aly⟨w⟩at*er ter ter* lou.
> *Lower part:* Lou iii. wer e goz a lou iii wer*e* goz for hir iles myn alywat*er ter ter* lou.

In the upper part, the scribe originally wrote *hyr* with the curling mark of abbreviation, carried back over the *r*, which stands for final *e*, i.e. he wrote what was equivalent to *hyre*; but the abbreviation-mark has been erased (though it remains legible), probably by the scribe himself. There is a clear contrast with the unerased abbreviation-mark in *were* three words before. In the lower part, he wrote *hir* without final *e* or the mark of abbreviation. The monosyllabic form is preferable both metrically and linguistically (since *hir* is unstressed and the following word begins with a vowel); it must have been the realization of this that caused the upper part to be altered.

In so short a text it is not to be expected that there will be much evidence of provenance. In view of the nature of the book in which it is found, the song is likely to have been written down in a university town, which must mean either Oxford or Cambridge. The latter is more likely, in view of the scribe's use of the form *goz* 'goes' (with rounded $\bar{\varrho}$ < OE $\bar{a}$ but with the 3 sg. pres. indic. inflexion *-s*, here spelt *z*), which is specifically North or North-east Midland; his use of *w* for *wh* in *wer* 'where' and his omission of *h* in MS *alywater* 'holywater' are consistent with this, for both can be paralleled in *Havelok* (South Lincolnshire?) and in MS Arundel 248 (East Anglia). It does not follow that these are the original forms, and if my solution to the textual problem presented by ll. 1 and 2 is correct (that *e* is for *he*, the feminine pronoun meaning 'she'), it is unlikely that *goz* 'goes' was the author's form. The nearest areas to Cambridge in which *he* 'she' was used appear to have been in Essex and South-eastern Suffolk, and it is possible that the song was written thereabouts; but the evidence is extremely slight.

NOTES

1. *Lou* is an altered form of the interjection *Lo,* recorded in the thirteenth and fourteenth centuries.

1-2. *wer he goþ*] In l. 1, the MS in both parts writes *wer e goz,* which looks like three separate words but need not be, since syllables were sometimes written separately when words were being set out under notes. In l. 2, again in both parts, he writes *were goz,* with the final *e* of *were* expressed by a mark of abbreviation; this is unmistakably two words. On balance, it seems that the scribe understood *were goz* as two words, 'where goes', in which *were* was a disyllabic form (cf. Orm's *whære*), either by the addition of adverbial *-e* to OE *hwǣr* or by blending of the latter with OE *hwāra*. But in that case there would be no subject for *goz* 'goes', which seems unacceptable (unless possibly 'where goes' was a hunting-call comparable to 'gone away').

It is more likely that the scribe was confused, and that there were really three words, *wer e goz,* in which *e* was a form (with omission of *h*, as in *alywater* in l. 3) of the pronoun *he*. But it cannot be the ordinary masculine pronoun (< OE *hē*); this is ruled out by the occurrence of *hir* 'her' in l. 3, and by the obvious situation envisaged in the song — a man (apparently the holy-water clerk) watching a woman walking. What is required is evidently the feminine pronoun *he* (< OE *hēo*), meaning 'she', a form displaced in most dialects in which it should have developed because of its inconvenient ambiguity.

But if the text originally contained the feminine pronoun *he*, it cannot also have contained the form *goz* 'goes', with its *-s* inflexion of the 3 sg. pres. indic.; for the form *he* and the *-s* inflexion belonged to different dialect areas. This is doubtless why the scribe was confused; he evidently spoke a dialect in which the *-s* inflexion was used, and would not have known *he* as a feminine pronoun. The assumption that the original reading was *he* 'she' necessarily involves altering the verb to the form *goþ* which would have been used in the more southerly dialects which retained this form of the pronoun.

2. *A* is the interjection 'ah'.

3. *i les* 'I lost' (written as one word in the MS). *Les* is the strong past tense singular (OE *lēas*) of the verb *lesen* < OE *lēosan* 'lose'. The meaning here is apparently 'spilt'.

halywater (MS *alywater,* with loss of initial *h*) was treated as a compound in OE and ME; this explains the shortening of the vowel of the first syllable to *ă*, in contrast to the retention of the long vowel (OE *ā* > ME *ǭ*) in the separate adjective *holy*. The *a* of [*h*]*alywater* is therefore not a Northernism.

-ter, -ter, lou!] The words end with twofold repetition of the second syllable of *water* and a final repetition of the interjection *lou*.

20. Lullay, lullay: Als I lay on Yoolis night

Lullay, lullay, lay lay, lullay:
mi deerë moder, [sing] lullay.

1

Als I lay on ʒolis niʒt
    alone in my longing
5   me þouʒt I saw a well fair siʒt,
    a may hiar child rokkíng.

2

Þe maiden wold wiþouten song
    hir child o sleep to bring;
þe child him þouʒt sche ded him wrong
10   and bad his moder sing.

3

'Sing nou, moder,' said þe child,
    'wat schal [to] me befall
heerafter wan I cum til eld,
    for so doon modres all.

4

15   'Ich a moder, trewëly,
    þat kan hir credel keep,
is wun to lullen luvëly
    and sing hir child o sleep.

5

'Sweetë moder, fair and free,
20   be cause þat it is so,
I pray þee þat þou lullë me
    and sing sumwat þerto.'

6

'Sweetë sunë,' saidë sche,
    'weroffë schuld I sing?
25   [Ne] wist I nere yet more of þee
    but Gabriels greetíng.

7

'He grett me goodli on his knee
    and saidë, "Hail, Maríe!
[Hail,] full of grace, God is wiþ þee;
30   þou beren schalt Messíe.'

8

'I wundred michil in my þouʒt,
    for man wold I riʒt none.
"Maríe," he saidë, "dred þee nouʒt:
    let God of heven alone.

9

35   '"Þe Holi Gost schal doon al þis,"
    he said wiþouten wun,
þat I schuld beren mannis blis
    [and] Godis ownë sun.

10

'He saidë, "Þou schalt bere a king
40   in king Davitis see;"
in al Jacóbes wuniíng
    þer loverd schuld he be.

11

'He saidë þat Elizabeth,
    þat barain was bifore,
45   "a [knavë] child conceyved hath —
    to me leeve þou þe more."

12

'I answéred bleþëly,
    for (þat) his word me paid,
"Lo, Godis servant heer am I;
50   be et as þou me said."

13

'Þer, als he saidë, I þee bare
    on midëwenter niʒt
in maidenhede wiþouten kare
    be grace of God almiʒt.

14

'Þer schepperds waked in þe wold
55   [þei] herd a wunder mirþ
of angles þer, as [þeim] þei told
    þe tiding of þi birþ.

15

'Sweetë sunë, sikirly,
60   no morë kan I say,
and if I koudë, fawn wold I,
    to doon al at þi pay.'

16

Serteynly þis siʒt I say,
    þis song I herdë sing,
65   als I [me] lay þis ʒoolis day
    alone in my longing.

COMMENTARY

This carol is recorded in four MSS. (1) Edinburgh, National Library of Scotland, MS Advocates 18. 7. 21, ff. 3ᵛ-4ᵛ; thirty-seven stanzas (see below), without music. A note on f. 9ᵛ says that the MS was written in 1372 by John of Grimestone, a Franciscan friar, 'cum magna sollicitudine'; the language of his English texts is that of the North-east Midlands (cf. Greene, *The Early English Carols* (1935), p. 346; *English Carols* (1962), pp. 182-3). This MS we denote A. (2) Cambridge, University Library, MS Additional 5943, f. 169 (denoted C);

musical setting and words of stanza 1, but the burden is indicated only by the abbreviation *lolay, lolay* before the stanza and *lolay* after it. On this MS and its history see the general Introduction, pp. 22-6 above; the songs with music which it gives on ff. 161-169 are a collection made in Winchester College and copied between 1395 and 1401. (3) Cambridge, St. John's College, MS S. 54, f. 4ʳ⁻ᵛ; stanzas 1-9 and a variant form of the burden, without music. The MS is dated to the second half of the fifteenth century (Greene, *E.E.C.,* pp. 342-3; *E.C.,* p. 182); it is certainly from Norfolk, as is shown by its use of the distinctive spellings *xall,* etc. for *shall,* etc. and *qwat* for *what.* We denote it J. (4) London, British Library, MS Harley 2330, f. 120 (denoted H); stanzas 1-5, with variant form of burden, without music. The MS is dated to the fifteenth century; the carol is written in a different hand from the rest of the volume (Greene, *E.E.C.,* p. 327).

The carol is somewhat unusual both in form and content. The typical carol-form (though there are many variants) is a stanza consisting of three lines of equal length (usually of four stresses) rhyming together aaa, followed by a fourth line, often shorter, which rhymes with the burden. But this carol is written in a ballad-metre rhyming abab, and there is no rhyme-link with the burden (except, perhaps by design, in what we give as stanzas 15 and 16). It is moreover, in content, a narrative and dialogue poem; and though there are many parallels among carols, this is more characteristically a feature of the ballad. The music is reminiscent of early ballad music. It seems possible that a clerical author, for purposes of edification, has adapted a ballad-tune and ballad-metre to carol-form by the addition of a burden derived from the 'lullaby' carols, of which surviving examples are printed by Greene in *E.E.C.,* pp. 97-115.

The plan of the carol is that the Christ-child demands of his mother, who was proposing to put him to bed without singing to him, that she should sing and should tell him a bed-time story about himself, as other mothers do. She complies, though protesting that the only story she can tell about him is that of the Annunciation; she relates this and the circumstances of his birth. This material, with the author's introduction in stanzas 1-2, occupies stanzas 1-15 of the text as given in A, the Advocates' MS. But this MS then adds, in its stanzas 16-36, an intolerably long reply by Christ to his mother, foretelling the events of his life, death, and resurrection. Such predictions are found in other lullaby carols (see Greene, *loc. cit.*), but to include them in this carol seems contrary to its basic plan. Moreover, many of stanzas 16-36 are impossible to reduce to the requisite metrical scheme by credible emendation. Thus in stanzas 25 and 26 the first and third lines have feminine rhymes (i.e. they end in an unstressed syllable) which cannot be fitted to the music; indeed three of these four lines have only three stresses. Similarly in stanza 34 the second and fourth lines have feminine rhymes, with an extra unstressed syllable at the end of the line for which the music does not provide. The first lines of stanzas 16-36 are predominantly trochaic (15 trochaic, 5 iambic, including irregular lines in each case), whereas in the 16 stanzas given in our text (stanzas 1-15 and stanza 37 of the full text of A) the first lines are equally divided between trochaic and iambic. The third lines of these 16 stanzas are iambic (with four exceptions, emended in our text); in stanzas 16-36 there are 8 iambic lines (though some even of these contain a trochaic foot), 7 trochaic, and 6 which are trochaic-iambic (i.e. they begin with one or two trochees but end with

iambs). In stanzas 16-36, in the second and fourth lines (which the music requires to be iambic throughout), there are ten lines which begin with stressed syllables, most of them a syllable short of the normal count of eight syllables, for which no obvious emendation is available (as well as others which could be emended). The metre of stanzas 16-36, therefore, though superficially similar to that of our 16 stanzas, proves on analysis to be different in a way that is inconsistent with the music. These twenty-one stanzas are probably a later addition by someone who wished to make fuller and more explicit the doctrinal content, at whatever cost in prolixity—perhaps John of Grimestone himself, displaying too much solicitude. We omit them, if only for the sake of comparative brevity; but we think that the result is a gain in artistic unity. The final stanza, which deliberately repeats, with variations, the first, is thus made to follow immediately on stanza 15, in which Mary says that she can tell no more.

In view of the date (1372) of the Advocates' MS and the fact that its text is already imperfect and (as is argued above) expanded, the words of the carol are unlikely to have been written later than the mid-fourteenth century. Such a dating would suit well enough the state of its language; it might even be earlier, though there are one or two idioms not otherwise recorded until later. The original dialect was evidently that of the East Midlands, though there is little conclusive evidence. The North is ruled out by the development of OE *ā* to *ǭ* shown by the rhymes of *so* and *more* at ll. 20-22 and 44-46, and by the rhyme at ll. 43-45 which, though imperfect in the vowel, depends on the verbal form *hath* and excludes Northern *has.* This being so, the development of OE *ēo* to ME *ē,* shown by the rhymes of *free, sche, knee,* and *be* at ll. 19-21, 23-25, 27-29, and 40-42, must be Eastern. The language is too developed to be that of the South Midlands; in particular final *-e* is mostly lost, though retained in a fair number of cases, always where it is historically justified. The p.t. sg. *say* 'saw', established by rhyme in l. 63, is from the OE (Anglian) p.t. pl. *sēgun;* but the MSS agree on *sau* or *saw* in l. 5, as in the poem *Havelok* (S. Lincs.?). The form *wuniing* 'dwelling' (trisyllabic), established by metre in l. 41, depends on the infinitive *wuni(e)* < OE *wunian.* Generally the preservation of the OE second weak conjugation as a distinct form is in ME Southern or West Midland, but the infinitive in *-i(e)* remained longest in the verbs *luvi(e)* 'love' and *wuni(e)* 'dwell' and was apparently most widespread in these cases; relics of infinitive and present tense forms in *-ie(n)* are found at an earlier date in the Norfolk *Bestiary* in *luvien* and other verbs, and the Norfolk *Genesis and Exodus* has the pres. p. *wuniende.* Thus the form *wuniing* would appear possible as far North as Norfolk, but hardly further North (though it is to be remarked that John of Grimestone, a North-east Midland scribe, retains the form in copying). The fact that *-e* is to some degree preserved warns us not to look too far to the North. The spellings of A show lowering of ME *ĭ* to *ě;* they may be due only to John of Grimestone and are not certainly confirmed by rhyme, though lowering might be involved in the rhyme at ll. 11-13 (see note to l. 11, below). Such lowering is *inter alia* Northern, but is also frequently shown by the spellings of the fifteenth-century *Paston Letters* (Norfolk). On the form *said* 2 sg. past indic., which favours the North or North Midlands, see note to l. 50. The general impression is that the language is that of the East Midlands, somewhat to the North but not too far; it could well be that of Norfolk or South Lincolnshire.

The metre of the carol-stanza is basically an iambic one with a syllable-count 8686. But at the beginning of the stanza the music is such that the first line can be either a regular four-stress iambic line or, by omission of the first unstressed syllable, a four-stress trochaic catalectic line; indeed musically the latter might well be regarded as the norm. The 16 stanzas here printed are equally divided, according to the MS evidence, between the two types, and we assume that the author intended this metrical variation. Technically the music allows of the same possibility at the beginning of the third line, but here 12 of the 16 stanzas have regular iambic lines, and the other four can be emended — in stanzas 6 and 7 with some advantage (or at the lowest without disadvantage) to the idiom, in stanza 10 by a mere change of form, and in stanza 16 with indirect MS authority. I conclude that the author did not intend variation at this point, and emend accordingly.

Of the MSS, J and H have distinctive variants in common in stanzas 1-5 and are evidently closely related; even when they agree, they constitute only a single witness. J is the better of the two, but H is independent and sometimes the more correct. It is unfortunate that C gives only a single stanza, for its text of stanza 1 seems on balance the best; it represents a line of descent distinct from A's and possibly better, though it must have been written some thirty years later. A's readings are usually better than those of J and/or H, but not always; JH convict it of error, as far as they go, often enough to show that after stanza 9, when A alone is running, an editor need not follow it uncritically.

My text does not seek to reproduce exactly the spelling of A or of the other MSS; it is modified in spelling and regularized in metre. The text of A, with a couple of minor emendations, is given by Carleton Brown, *Religious Lyrics of the XIVth Century*, pp. 70-75. It is also given, with replacement of medieval letters and with five minor and obviously correct emendations (duly recorded in notes), by Greene, *E.E.C.*, pp. 103-5, who also gives on p. 106 the substantive variants (but not quite completely) of the other MSS. It should be noted that Greene's sigla differ from mine.

There is some relation between the present carol and one printed by Greene, *E.E.C.*, pp. 166-8 (no. 234) and by Carleton Brown, *Religious Lyrics of the XVth Century*, pp. 108-9 (and by others). It begins, in the text of Trinity College, Cambridge, MS 1230 (formerly O. 3. 58):

> As I lay vpon a nyth
> my þowth was on a berd so brith
> that men clepyn Marye ful of myth
> *Redemptoris mater.*

It is first recorded in fifteenth-century MSS, though it may be somewhat older, especially as the versions already differ a good deal; but the odds are that it is later than our carol and is influenced by it, as some of its textual variations (e.g. in its second line) certainly are. But it is difficult to know what weight to allow to its readings in determining the text of our carol; the author of the later carol (if it is later) did not necessarily know the true text of ours.

NOTES

1. This is essentially A's form of the first line of the burden, which is confirmed, as far as the first two words are concerned, by C's *lolay, lolay*. But at mid-line, where A has *la*, I substitute *lay lay*; the musical setting requires an extra syllable. This reading *lay lay* has some support from the forms of the burden given by J (*lullay lay lay lay*) and H (*lay lay lullay lay*).

2. *sing*] supplied; not in AJH. The second line of the burden is omitted by C. The line as given by AJH does not fit the music well, and seems a syllable short. The emendation is on the model of the burden of a carol (no. 153 in Greene, *EEC*, pp. 113-14) from the 16th-century Balliol College, Oxford, MS 354, which reads:

> 'Lulley, Jhesu, lulley, lulley.'
> 'Myn own dere moder, syng lulley.'

The addition of *sing* improves sense as well as metre.

3. *lay*] so AC; *me lay* J, *me went* H. The concurrence of AC must outweigh the evidence of the related MSS J and H, whose common original must have had J's reading *me lay*. The Balliol MS of the *Redemptoris mater* carol also has *me lay* as a variant on the *lay* of the other MSS. This would seem to be the correct form for l. 65 of the present carol, i.e. the original of JH has apparently introduced into the first stanza the form of the line appropriate to the last. Note that at the end of this line H reads *day* for *niʒt*, a reading certainly derived from the last stanza.
on ʒoolis] *on ʒole is* C, *vpon a* A, *this endyres* J, *this ender-* H. A's reading agrees with the first line of the *Redemptoris mater* carol; C's is supported by A's text of the final stanza (l. 65). It is possible that A is right and that the author intended the line in the final stanza to be more precise than that in the first, and that C's text is due to a wrong anticipation of l. 65; but C's reading is the least conventional, Christmas is obviously the appropriate time for the vision described, and it would be strange if the author held back the indication of the precise time until the end of the poem, as A makes him do. I assume that A, like J and H, has substituted a more conventional form of the line, and adopt C's reading.
niʒt] so ACJ (with variations of spelling); *day* H.

5. *me þouʒt* 'it seemed to me'. C has *my þoʒt*, a corrupted form of the idiom due in part to misunderstanding of the impersonal verb, in part to the identity of the unstressed forms of *me* and *my* in later ME pronunciation. Such alterations of impersonal constructions usually began in the North, and *my þouʒt* seems to be first recorded there. It is conceivable that C preserves what the author wrote, but A, the earliest MS, has the original form of the idiom.
well fair] so CH; *wonder* A, *semyly* J. There is little to choose, but the CH concurrence must be decisive; and theirs is the least conventional reading.
siʒt] so ACJ (with variations of spelling); *may* H, a change forced on the scribe by his alteration of the rhyme-word in l. 3.

6. *may*] so C, and H at the end of the previous line (see preceding note); *main* J, *maiden* A. Again the evidence favours C. H here has *lovely*.
hir child] so C; *child* AH, *cradyll* J. C's is the best text; the agreement between A and H is accidental, for both scribes are forced to omit *hir* by their other alterations, which are not the same.

8. *to*] so JH; *om.* A. If A's text were accepted, we should have to pronounce the *-e* of its *slepe,* but the survival of dative *-e* in this dialect is most unlikely. The JH text is much more probable; it shows the not uncommon use of the infinitive with *to* when it is separated, as here, from the auxiliary verb on which it depends.

9. *him* (before *þouȝt*)] so J; *om.* AH. The pronoun, required by metre, is reflexive, 'for his part'. Except with verbs of motion, this reflexive use was not common in ME, but *OED,* s.v. *him,* 4(b), cites instances from *Havelok* l. 286 (*him herde*) and from *Cursor Mundi* (Fairfax MS) (*him saghe, him loked*). Presumably A and H have independently omitted the pronoun because it was unusual and not required for sense. It is not likely that the scribe of J, emending *metri causa,* would introduce into the text a rare but genuine idiom.
ded 'did'; the spelling of the vowel is A's and shows lowering of ĭ to ĕ, as in similar instances elsewhere in the poem.

11. *þe*] so JH; *þat* A.
child] The rhyme depends on ĭ in *child*, probably derived from the plural. There are then two possibilities. (1) That this ĭ in *child* has been lowered to ĕ. (2) That *eld* had a by-form *ild* with ĭ; cf. the common *hild* for *held, fill* for *fell*. Such a by-form would be due to OE lengthening of ĕ to ē in *eld*, whence ME ę̄ (as in *held* < *hēold, fell* < *feoll*), followed by ME shortening, the result of which is to give ĭ. The latter seems the more likely explanation.

12. *schal*] *sal* A, and so *suld* 'should' in l. 24, etc. But these are not to be taken as the common Northern forms of these two words, in which [s] develops under weak stress; for A equally uses *s* for OE *sc* (modern English *sh*) in stressed syllables, e.g. in *sepperdis* for *schepperds* in l. 55.
schal to me] *xall of me* J, *schal me* H, *me sal* A. J's text scans, the others do not. But *of* was not the usual preposition for use with *befall,* and *to me* is much more likely to be the source of the simple dative *me* in H and A. In this instance J has probably mended the scansion of a line that was corrupted early by the substitution of the dative *me* for the phrase *to me*.

13. *til eld*] so H; *to eld* A, *to age* J. The Norse-derived preposition *til* seems likely to be the original reading here; I doubt whether the scribe of H would introduce it. I assume that the author's dialect had both *to* and *til* (cf. *Havelok*), and that *til* was deliberately used before a word beginning with a vowel to avoid hiatus. Cf. the examples cited by *OED,* s.v. *till* prep., A.1, from Robert Manning and Chaucer.
eld 'age', 'full age'.

14. *for*] so H; *om.* A. Instead of *for so doon* J has *so chuld þo,* but this, though it scans, is less good sense, and cannot stand against the partial agreement of A and H.

15. *Ich a* 'each single'. So A; *For euery* JH. The variant readings illustrate the two alternative ways of beginning the first line of the stanza. The weakness of the JH reading is that it involves repetition of the word *for,* which is metrically necessary at the beginning of l. 14 but is not necessary here.
trewely] *treuly* A, *sekyrly* JH. I accept the reading of the early MS, though modifying the form to the trisyllable that the metre requires.

16. *kan* 'knows how to'.
credel 'cradle'. This form with *e* in the first syllable is generally Northern, but is found in the Norfolk *Promptorium Parvulorum.* But its use here may be due simply to the scribe of A.

17. *wun* 'accustomed'. *OED,* s.v. *wone* adj., cites examples of the form without *y*-prefix from *Genesis and Exodus* (Norfolk), *Havelok* (S. Lincs.?), and Northern texts.
luvely 'lovingly'.

18. *and sing*] so A; *and bryngs* H, *to bryng* J. The parallel of ll. 21-22 supports A's reading.
o sleep 'asleep'.

19. *fair and free*] so A; a line-filler, but *seyd he* J, *saydþe child* H are worse. In such a context *free* means 'gentle'.

20. *be cause*] *siþen* AJH, but though this is the right number of syllables it is the wrong rhythm. The common ancestor of the three MSS must have substituted the native synonym.

21. *þee . . . þou*] so A, but JH *you . . . ye,* substituting the polite plural pronoun appropriate, in later ME use, when a child is addressing a parent.
lulle] so A; JH substitute *roke,* with variations in detail.

22. *sumwat þerto* 'something in addition'.

24. *weroffe*] so A. If its text is right, *weroffe* must be trisyllabic, with pronounced *-e*. That there was such a ME form, current in the East, is shown beyond doubt by Orm's *whæroffe* (l. 2931); cf. also *OED,* s.v. *offe.* The examples cited are all early thirteenth-century; but nearer the date of the carol there is *Havelok,* with a spelling *offe* used a number of times, and in l. 746 as the scribe writes it (not as Skeat emends it) trisyllabic *þeroffe* is required. J's text avoids trisyllabic *weroffe* by inserting *chyld* after the word, but this is tautologous, in view of *sune* in the previous line.

25. *Ne*] supplied, to give the necessary unstressed syllable at the beginning of the line. The double negative *ne . . . nere* is characteristic ME idiom. I assume that the common original of A and J omitted *ne,* probably as part of the process of expanding *nere* to *neuere* (see next note); the number of syllables was thus left the same, but the rhythm was changed. Alternatively one could read *I wistë* for AJ's *wist i.*
nere] *neuere* AJ, but substitution of the contracted form (modern *ne'er*) is required to regularize the rhythm.

26. *but* 'than'. For this use of *but* after *no more* see *OED,* sense C.5; its earliest instance is dated 1440, but *MED* cites an example from Laȝamon (early thirteenth century) and a second from the late fourteenth-century *Robert of Sicily.*

27. *grett* 'greeted'; *grette* A, but the metre shows that the *-e* has been dropped.
goodli 'courteously'; so A (spelt *godli*), but *gladly* J.

29. *Hail*] supplied to give the iambic beginning to the third line of the stanza which we assume the author intended; *om.* AJ. There is also some gain in style, for otherwise the sense must run on from l. 28 to l. 29, 'Hail, Mary, full of grace'; but run-on sense of this sort is not characteristic of the poem. The phrase 'Hayl, Mary, full of grace' (corresponding to the Latin *Ave Maria gratia plena*) is common in carols (cf. Greene, *E.E.C.,* nos. 235, 237A, 238A), and the omission here of the second *Hail* which we assume the metre requires is probably due to this fact; but in the other instances the whole phrase comes within a single line. The phrase 'Hail, full of grace' (cf. St. Luke, i. 28, *Ave gratia plena, Dominus tecum*) also occurs elsewhere, e.g. in Greene, 238B, stanza 2, 'Al heyl, full of grace'.

30. *þou beren schalt*] *beren þou salt* A, *þou xalte bere* J, but neither scans properly.

31. *michil* 'much'; so A (*gretely* J).

32. *wold* (so A) is doubtless 'would, desired', a past tense continuing the sequence of *wundred* in the previous line. But it could be the Midland present tense *wold*(*e*) 'wield' (< OE (Anglian) *waldan*) in the sense 'possess': 'I do not possess any husband'. J substitutes the present tense *know* for *wold*, but this is probably to accord with the scriptural account.

33. *dred þee nouȝt* 'do not fear for yourself'.

34. 'Do not concern yourself with the ways of God.'

36. *wiþouten wun* 'without delay', an earlier instance by far than those cited by *OED*, s.v. *wone* sb.[1], sense 4. The phrase was rare and the scribe of J obviously did not understand it, for he re-writes the line.

37. There is here a switch from direct to indirect reported speech, as was common in ME writing. Similarly in the next stanza, at l. 41, there is the same shift from direct to indirect speech; but in stanza 11, at line 45, there is an opposite change, from indirect to direct speech.

38. *and Godis owne*] *Goddys owne* J, *þe my suete* A. The latter does not scan and cannot be emended to do so. Moreover the context seems to require the antithesis between 'man's' and 'God's' which J's text offers. But the line should begin with an unstressed syllable; I therefore modify J's text by inserting *and*. For the adjective A's *suete* might be right, against J's *owne*, but it seems better to keep to J's reading if it is taken as the basis of the text; *suete* may be picked up from ll. 19 and 23 above.

From this point onwards A is the only MS running, and all emendations are necessarily conjectural. Words in square brackets are supplied for the sake of the metre.

40. *Davitis see* 'David's seat' (cf. St. Luke, i. 32, *sedem David patris eius*), i.e. properly the throne of David. But the context here, and l. 51 below (*þer . . . I þee bare*), suggest that the author took the phrase as meaning 'the dwelling-place of David' (cf. *OED*, s.v. *see* sb.[1], sense 1(c)), i.e. the city of David, Bethlehem.

41. *Jacobes*] *Jacobs* A. The line as given in the MS is a seven-syllable trochaic catalectic, such as the music technically permits, providing that the first stress is put on the preposition *in*. But we assume that the author did not intend to practise metrical variation in the third line of the stanza. Substitution of *Jacobes* for *Jacobs* (i.e. mere substitution of a variant form) permits the line to be scanned as a regular eight-syllable iambic line, with the first stress on *al*. For trisyllabic *Jacobes*, stressed on the second, see the extract from *Genesis and Exodus* given in Hall's *Early Middle English*, p. 197, ll. 2 and 5.
wuniing] On this trisyllabic form, given by A itself, see the introduction above; it is a reformation of OE *wunung* based on the stem *wuni-* of the ME infinitive *wunien* and the present participle *wuniende*. A relevant parallel is the form *wonyinge* cited by *OED* from Appendix III to *The Lay Folk's Mass Book* (EETS, 1879), which is taken from Bodleian MS Ashmole 1286, f. 223. This is undoubtedly a Midland text from within the Danelaw (cf. the pres. p. *wiþstandande*), and its forms are mostly Eastern; but there is some admixture of forms that would normally be taken as Western (e.g. the comparative suffix *-loker* and *oþur* 'other'). Its history may have been complex; but it illustrates the currency of trisyllabic *wonyinge* in the Midlands at the end of the fourteenth century.

Jacobes wuniing is 'Jacob's dwelling', the house of Jacob; cf. St. Luke, i. 32, *et regnabit in domo Jacob in aeternum*.

42. *þer* may be either the adverb 'there' or an unstressed form of the possessive 'their'.
loverd] *king* A. But this makes the line a syllable short, and is the third time the word *king* is used in the one stanza; substitution of *loverd* cures both faults. As *he* in this line is Christ, to whom Mary is telling the story, it would be more logical in indirect speech to have 'shouldst thou' instead of *schuld he*, or (if the direct speech were continued to the end of the stanza) *schal he*. It is possible that *schuld he* has been substituted for an original *þou schuldest*, so that the line may have run:

þer king þou schuldest be

but this emendation would of course leave the threefold repetition of *king* unchanged.

45. I supply *knave*; the line in the MS is two syllables short. Cf. St. Luke, i. 36, *Et ecce Elisabeth cognata tua, et ipsa concepit filium in senectute sua*.
hath marks a change to direct speech. The rhyme is inexact in the vowel; the fourteenth-century *heth* recorded by *OED* is Kentish (*Ayenbite*), and there is no possibility that this carol is a Kentish text. I do not think that A's spellings *Elizabetȝ* and *hatȝ* are phonetically significant; if they were, they would indicate spoken forms *Elizabess* and *has* (cf. the use of *tȝ* or rather *tz* for *s* in MS Cotton Nero A.x). But the spellings are in any case presumably John of Grimestone's, not the author's.

46. 'Give the more credence to me.' Elizabeth's pregnancy is cited as a proof of divine power; cf. St. Luke, i. 37.

47. *answered*] *ansuerede* A. Three syllables, stressed on the second, are what the metre requires. In OE the verb *andswarian*, being derived from the noun *andswaru*, was stressed on the first, like modern English *answer*. But in ME, when the form was affected by the verb derived from OE *swerian*, verbal stressing was often applied, i.e. the prefix was made unstressed. So here; the line is seven syllables, and the first metrical stress falls on the pronoun *I*.
blethely 'blithely', 'gladly'. Various ME forms of this adverb presuppose OE *ĭ* in the first syllable, by shortening of original *ī*. In this case A's spelling shows lowering of the *ĭ* to *ĕ*.

48. *þat*] supplied. A uses the conjunction *for*, but the older idiom *for that* is required by the metre. Alternatively one could substitute *be cause* (cf. note to l. 20 above).
paid] *paiyede* A, but metre and rhyme require a monosyllabic form. The word means 'pleased'.
et 'it', a spelling showing lowering of *ĭ* to *ĕ*.

50. *said*] *seyde* A. Properly the 2 sg. past indic. was *saidest*, but here the form of the 1 and 3 sg. is used also for the 2 sg. (perhaps aided by the analogy of the strong verbs, in which the 2 sg. ended in *-e*). The standard grammars, which treat ME inflexion very cursorily, do not say much about this development; but see Sisam, *Fourteenth Century Verse and Prose*, p. 292, who remarks that in the North, and sometimes in the North Midlands, the 2 sg. of the weak p.t. ends in *-(e)*, meaning an *-e* which may be lost. *OED* records *said*(*e*) as a 2 sg. form for the 13th and 14th centuries, but the only example cited, under A3(b), is from the Northern *Cursor Mundi*. Here we find the uninflected form used for the sake of rhyme in an East Midland text.

51. *bare* 'bore', a new p.t. sg. form derived from the plural *baren*, in which the *a* had been lengthened; the latter in its turn had been formed on the old sg. *băr*. The new form is here established by rhyme, and is probably an indication of the fourteenth-century date of the poem; but it does not help much, since such preterites are recorded from early in the century.

52. *midewenter*] midwenter A, but the four-syllabled form is needed.

53. *maidenhede* (*maydened* A) 'virginity'.

54. *almiȝt* (*almith* A) 'almighty'.

55. *þer schepperds waked* 'where shepherds kept watch'. A reads *þe sepperdis þat wakkeden*, which would still be too many syllables even if cut down, by dropping or reducing the inflexions, to *þe schepperds þat waked*. We must at least omit the relative *þat*. But the next line is also unsatisfactory, and is most easily emended by substituting *þei herd* 'they heard' for A's *herden*; and this suggests that l. 55 should be a subordinate clause. If so, it should begin with a conjunction, and the obvious change is to substitute *þer* 'where' for *þe*. The starting-point for the series of corruptions may well have been the mis-reading of *þer* as *þe*, aided perhaps by unfamiliarity with the use of *þer* as a relative adverb. Cf. the note to l. 57. *wold* 'upland country, moorland'.

56. *þei herd*] see note to l. 55. *wunder mirþ* 'wonderful merry-making'. But *mirth* can also mean 'musical entertainment', so the phrase might here mean a marvellous song.

57. *þer*] þᵗ A; emended by Carleton Brown and Greene. This is the second time in the stanza that (as we assume) A's text has corrupted *þer*; probably it was abbreviated in an antecedent copy and the abbreviation was misread.

þeim] supplied. The line is too short, and a monosyllable must have dropped out; the likeliest word to be lost before *þei* is *þeim* 'them', and it gives the required sense.

58. *þe tiding*] in time A. But this leaves *told* without an object, and though such an absolute use of the verb is known (see *OED*, s.v. *tell*, B.13), it does not seem likely here. Moreover the *-e* of *time* ought to elide before the vowel of *of*, and failure of elision does not seem likely in a poem in which *-e* is much more often dropped than kept even before consonants. The emendation normalizes the syntax and the metre and gives the required sense (cf. St. Luke, ii. 10). The MS text looks like deliberate re-writing, seeking to connect l. 58 with l. 56 ('heard marvellous rejoicing . . . at the time of thy birth'); but it leaves l. 57 in the air and is metrically unsatisfactory.

61. *fawn* (*fawen* A, but a monosyllable is needed) is a by-form of *fain*, here used as an adverb, 'gladly': 'I would gladly [do so]'.

62. 'to do everything to your satisfaction', to act entirely as you wish.

63. *say* 'saw'.

65. *me*] supplied; om. A. But see note to l. 3 above, where it is suggested that the reading of J (and less obviously of H) in l. 3 owes *me* to a reminiscence of the form that the corresponding line took in the final stanza. The insertion of *me* here gives the line the regular iambic rhythm that we assume was intended for the third line of the stanza.

The pronoun is reflexive, but can hardly be translated; for it seems clear that the fairly common ME use of a reflexive pronoun with the intransitive verbs *lie, sit,* and *rise* was due largely to confusion with the constructions appropriate to the cognate transitive verbs *lay, set,* and *rear* or *raise.*

V. SONGS IN TWO MANUSCRIPTS OF ABOUT 1400

21. Ye have so longe keepyt o

Ȝe havĕ so longë keepyt o
    [þe] scheep [up] on the green, Wilkýn,
that allë ȝower hert ys wo
    for [one] so gracius [of] hew —
5   þaȝ somë woldë ween, Wilkýn,
      how þat ȝe wexë werĕ untrew.

Ȝe may, Wilkýn, wyth rye-strawys twyn
    [ma] goodë pypis;
as ȝow longis, yn ȝowr songis
10   sayis ȝe lovĕ me best, ywis,
      and most on ȝower þowȝt.

But, that ȝe sey ȝe wol for lovĕ dey,
    arys up on þe morn
[and hast awey,] and lust to pley.
15   Thys may rymë wel, but hit
      (a lo!) acordis nouȝt.

COMMENTARY

Source: Oxford, Bodleian Library, MS Douce 381, f. 20ᵛ.

The text of this song is corrupted in the MS, as is sufficiently shown by the differences between the two versions of the first line given in the main and the tenor parts. Moreover at places the MS is almost illegible. The reconstructed text given above is therefore at some points necessarily conjectural. The spellings of the MS, or the forms presupposed by rhyme, suggest a Northern provenance; but as final -*e* is often preserved, though by no means regularly, the North Midlands seem more probable than the North itself. I alter the MS spellings, without notice in some cases, where it seems desirable to indicate pronunciation, scansion, and rhyme. The text given by R. H. Robbins, *Secular Lyrics of the XIVth and XVth Centuries*, p. xxxviii, is not fully accurate in its reporting of the MS and misinterprets the metrical form.

The music given for stanza 1 has both an *ouvert* and a *clos*, showing that it was to be repeated, but only one set of words is given to correspond. It is possible that another six-line stanza has been omitted; if so, I would guess that its last two lines were essentially the same as ll. 5–6 (i.e. that these two lines were a refrain), but that the first of the two lines, in the missing stanza, required the conjunction *þat* at its beginning. This is what the scribe actually writes, but it does not fit the sense of the stanza that he gives.

The stanzas given seem, however, to be complete in sense. Assuming that there was no other stanza, the musical setting requires the first stanza to be repeated, in whole or in part. As the scribe does not mark any intermediate point in the music as that from which the repetition is to begin, the implication of the music-text is that the whole of the first stanza is to be repeated. But this would seem pointless. From the literary point of view it would be more effective simply to repeat the last two lines; they might be sung first roguishly, and then with apprehension lest Wilkyn may indeed be untrue. Musically it is possible to repeat only these two lines, though it is contrary to the music-text as the scribe wrote it.

NOTES

1. *ȝe*] so MS, though the capital *ȝ* has been wrongly read as *I*.
keepyt] tenor part *kepyt*, main part *kepe;* the latter is an impossible form for the p.p. of this verb. The sense is 'watched over'.
o] tenor part *oo*, a common spelling of the word, which means 'always, continually'; main part omits.

2. *þe*] supplied; *om.* MS.
up] supplied; *om.* MS. Metre requires an extra syllable, and the sense is improved; Wilkin is away with the sheep, up in the hill pastures.

3. *alle*] so MS. In later ME the distinction between *al* sg. and *alle* pl. was replaced by a different distinction; *al* was used before an article, a possessive, or demonstrative, *alle* directly before a noun (in the formulation given by Macaulay, *The Works of John Gower*, ii. cxii). The real basis of the rule was evidently rhythmical, *al* being used before an unstressed monosyllable, *alle* before a stressed word; it is therefore in accordance with the rule, properly understood, that *alle* should be used here before the disyllabic *ȝower* 'your', which takes metrical stress.
wo] *sa* MS, which is nonsense, but may be due to misreading of

the Northern spelling *wa* 'woe'. In this originally impersonal construction, *wo* is used virtually as an adjective, 'woeful, wretched'. (An alternative explanation for the error might be that in an intermediate copy *sare* 'sore' had been substituted for *wa* or *wo;* omission of the abbreviation for *re* could produce *sa* from *sare*. Either explanation of the MS error assumes a Northern or North Midland exemplar in which *a* was written for Midland and Southern *o*.)

4. The line in the MS reads *for hew so gracius*. But *hew* is needed at the end for the rhyme with *untrew* in l. 6, and transposing it inevitably involves inserting *of* to give *for so gracius of hew*. But the line so changed is one syllable short of the normal eight (in this stanza); the further insertion of *one* seems obvious, and produces a line typical of ME love-poetry.

5. *þaȝ*] *þat* MS; but *þaȝ* 'though' seems necessary for sense.
wolde ween] *wolde y wene* MS. With the obsolescence of pronounced final -*e*, someone has put in *y* 'I' to supply a syllable, to the destruction of real sense; it does not seem possible, in ME idiom, for a clause beginning *how that* to depend on *wolde*. The line as emended means 'though some would think, Wilkin'.

6. *wexe*] *wex* MS, omitting the necessary -*e* (or -*en*, but -*e* is more likely to have been left off). The word is the strong p.p. of the verb *wax*, in the sense 'grown, become'.
were] so MS. The word was frequently a monosyllable even when final -*e* was generally pronounced; but here the -*e* would in any case elide before the following vowel.

7. *wyth*] *wyt* MS, a common spelling of 'with'.
rye-strawys] so MS, though it is not very clear; after *st* the scribe wrote *a* above the line (as the common abbreviation for *ra*) and it is now almost illegible.
twyn] *twyne* MS. This is the modern word *twin*, but the meaning is 'two', a Northern use at this date. Two straws were used to make a shepherd's pipe.

8. *ma*] supplied; no room for it in the MS, so it must have been simply omitted by the scribe — one of a number of omissions of little words. Some form of 'make' is required for sense, and *ma*, a contracted Northern and Midland form, is the shortest and the one most likely to have been omitted by error.
goode] only the *g* remains visible in the MS, but there is room for three more letters; the scribe may well have written *gode*, and metre requires a disyllable.
pypis] so MS, though the last two letters are faint and uncertain.

9. *as*] so MS. Linguistically the word belongs of course at the beginning of l. 9, but in a sense it goes metrically and musically at the end of l. 8, to make up for the lack of a final stressed syllable in that line as compared with l. 13 below.
as ȝow longis 'as is proper for you, as beseems you'. For *longis* the MS reads *lyst[et]h;* the first four letters are clear, but the next two are so badly rubbed as to be illegible, at least to me; the last appears to be *h*. But the parallels of ll. 7 and 12 show that internal rhyme is required in this line. If we were to read *lystis*, there would be a rhyme of the unstressed syllable of *lystis* with that of *songis*. But this is a weak rhyme; and the sense of the MS reading, 'as pleases you, as you please', is also poor in the context.

I assume that the original reading was *as ȝow longis,* which will give a perfect disyllabic rhyme with *songis* either in these North Midland forms, or in the fully Northern *langis: sangis.* In

ME there were two verbs *long*, both of which could be used impersonally. The first meant 'desire', so that the impersonal *ȝow longis* meant 'you desire'. I assume that in the transmission of the text, the original phrase *as ȝow longis* was misunderstood as 'as you desire' and replaced by the synonymous *as ȝow lysteth*. The second verb *long* meant 'to be appropriate (to)' and hence ' to befit', so that, if it were the verb intended, *as ȝow longis* would mean 'as is appropriate for you'. This is the sense that the context requires; it is proper for Wilkin to say in his songs that he loves her best. The emendation gives full rhyme and improves the sense. It is to be noted that even without the emendation, if there is to be any rhyme at all one must assume the Northern and North Midland 3 sg. pres. indic. inflexion -*is* (or -*es*), not the Midland and Southern -*eth* (-*ith*, -*yth*) used, as far as one can make out, by the scribe.

songis] *songe* MS, with room for an *s* and perhaps a trace of one; the scribe must have written *songes*, but I substitute the North Midland form *songis*, since on the whole the evidence is that in this text the ending -*es* has become -*is*.

10. *sayis*] so apparently MS, though the last letter is unclear. This is a Northern or North Midland form of the plural imperative, corresponding to Southern *sayeth*, and is appropriately used to someone who is being addressed as *ȝe*, the plural pronoun used to a single person in polite speech; the woman is using the forms of courtly language. But later ME was inconsistent in its use of the singular and plural imperative forms, and treated them as interchangeable; there is no special significance in the use of the singular imperatives *arys* etc. in the next stanza, though doubtless they are more natural and urgent. In this line, the first syllable *say*- may be regarded as belonging metrically and musically to the end of the preceding line (cf. note to l. 9 above); the second (unstressed) syllable -*is* corresponds to the unstressed *this* at the beginning of l. 15 and is sung to the same note.

ywis] *ywys* MS; here meaning 'indeed'.

11. The sense is elliptical: 'and [that I am] most in your thought'. The MS undoubtedly reads *on*, though one might expect *in*. In OE *on* was regularly used in synonymous expressions (e.g. *on þance*), but the normal ME preposition was *in*; *OED* however cites an example of *on þoht* from the *Trinity Homilies* (c. 1200). One may perhaps compare the modern *on one's mind;* OED's example comes under its sense 1(b), where it comments that in early use *thought* is often nearly equivalent to 'mind'.

12. *that* 'seeing that, since, because'.

dey] *dye* MS, but rhyme requires the variant form *dey* 'die'. For the internal rhyme, cf. l. 7 above.

13. *up on*] *uppon* MS, but sense requires the separation of the words; *up* goes with *arys*, *on* with *þe morn*.

14. *and hast awey*] supplied. Comparison with the preceding stanza and with the musical setting shows that the line should have eight syllables; the scribe has given only half a line. Comparison with ll. 7, 9 (as emended), and 12 shows that there should be internal rhyme, and this in turn suggests the reason for the omission; the omitted half-line looked like the included half-line. Hence the reconstruction; Wilkin is to haste away from his upland pasture to visit his lady. The sense of *awey* would then be 'on your way'.

lust] imperative, 'be pleased'. For this use of the verb *lust*, in the sense of the older verb *list*, see *OED*, s.v. *lust* vb., sense 3. The fact that the form used here is *lust* is perhaps an added reason for suspecting that the scribe's *lyst[et]h* in l. 9 is not original.

to] *for to* MS. Interchange of *to* and *for to*, which had become syntactically equivalent, is a frequent cause of disruption of the scansion; cf. no. 27, l. 9, where this same Douce scribe also substitutes *for to* but the other MS retains the metrically correct *to*. The opposite case occurs in no. 22, l. 5.

15. Both *Thys* and *may* are metrically unstressed; the scansion of the line is xx/x/x/.

15-16. 'This may rhyme well, but (alas!) it is not at all fitting.' The verb *accord* is used to mean 'to be in accordance with propriety' (cf. *OED*, s.v., sense 8), a sense first recorded from the later fourteenth century. It is not proper for a lady to take the initiative and invite her lover to hasten down to her to 'play'.

16. *acordis*] *acorde* MS, a mere error.

a lo] *a loo* MS, an interjection, equivalent to a modern *ah lo* (if such a combination were used). It is a modification of *we loo*, used in *Sir Gawain and the Green Knight*, perhaps by blending with *alas*. In the MS, *a loo* comes at the end, and has been ignored by previous editors though it is certainly needed to make the line the right length. But *nouȝt* in l. 16 must be intended to rhyme with *þowȝt* in l. 11, i.e. *nouȝt* is undoubtedly the last word of the poem; and it follows that the word-order of l.16 has been deranged by someone who did not understand the rhyme-scheme (cf. l. 4 above). In the second and third stanzas, the first and third lines have internal rhyme (and in the third stanza also rhyme with each other); the second and fourth do not rhyme (unless in stanza 2 there is meant to be an imperfect rhyme of *pypis* with *ywis*); and the fifth lines of the two stanzas rhyme with each other.

22. My cares comen ever anew

My cares comen ever anew;
   a, deerë God! no bootë ther nys,
for y am halden for untrew,
   wythowtyn gylt, so hav*e* y blys.

5   [For] to be trewë wunt y was
   in ony þyng þat y myȝt do,
þankyt [be] God hys gretë gras;
   now ys yt [þat] y may noȝt [þroo].

COMMENTARY

Source: Oxford, Bodleian Library, MS Douce 381, f. 22.

This song appears to have been written in the North-east Midlands. Northern features are *halden* in l. 3 (see note below) and the weak past participle *wunt* (*wonyt* MS) in l. 5 and more significantly *þankyt* in l. 7. But the North itself is ruled out by the preservation, though irregularly, of final -*e*, and by the present tense plural *comen* in l. 1 (assuming that this is original and not due to the scribe). The text of the MS is printed by Robbins, *Secular Lyrics of the XIVth and XVth Centuries,* no. 150 (p. 148).

NOTES

1. Loss of -*e* from *anew* and its rhyme-word *untrew* is shown by the musical setting, though not by the rhyme; both words originally had -*e*.

2. *deere* (*dere* MS)] The metre requires that the word should be two syllables, and it is set to two notes in the music; final -*e* in this case is retained.
boote (*bote* MS) Here the metre would be more regular if the word were a monosyllable, since *boote ther nys* is parallel to *have y blys* (*hany blys* MS) in l. 4. In the latter line, *have (han* MS) is set to two notes, and it would be possible to sing monosyllabic *boot* to the two notes that there are at this point in l. 2 in the music. But it would create difficulties for a singer; moreover in the MS the two notes of *have (han* MS) are written closer together than the two notes of *boote,* and it looks as though the scribe himself took the word as two syllables. As the two phrases are not set to a repetition of the same musical notes, a metrical variation may well have been intended.

3. *halden*] The form, which is unlikely to be due to the scribe of the Douce MS, shows ME *ā* for later OE *ā* by lengthening of Anglian *ǎ* before *ld.* Such forms are characteristically Northern, but also occur in North Midland dialects; *OED* records *halde* p.p. in Robert Mannyng of Brunne (S. Lincs.).

4. *have y*] *hany* MS (rather than *hauy,* though the letters could be so read). *Han y* seems to be a false usage (not recorded in *OED* or *MED*) of the Southern dialects of the late fourteenth and fifteenth centuries, and is evidently due to mistaken imitation of the forms of London English; in the latter *han* was an alternative to *have* in the infinitive and present tense plural, but not in the 1 sg. pres., which was only *have.* In this poem the form cannot be original, and must be due to a scribe (though not necessarily the scribe of the extant MS).

5. *For to be*] *to be* MS, but an additional syllable is needed in the first half of the line to balance l. 7, which is set to the same notes; and the line should begin with a stressed syllable, for it begins with the first note of a bar. In later ME *for to* and *to* were used interchangeably before the infinitive; cf. note to no. 21, l. 14.
trewe] Here, in contrast to l. 3 above, the final -*e* is required by the metre and is set to a separate note; for this reason it was written separately, and though it has been badly rubbed it is still perhaps faintly visible in the MS.
wunt] *wonyt* MS, a characteristically Northern form, but the contracted monosyllable *wunt* (or *wont*), which was more widespread, is needed so that *wunt y was* shall balance *gretë gras* in l. 7. The meaning is 'accustomed'.

6. *ony* 'any', a common form in the North but also found elsewhere. In the North it was due to the analogy of *mony;* in the Midlands to that of *ǭn* 'one' (cf. Luick, § 363, Anm. 6).
myȝt] *myth* MS, the common but confusing East Midland type of spelling which we normalize.

7. 'May God be thanked for His great grace.' This passive construction depends on the ME use of the verb *thank,* in the active, with a double accusative, thus *I þanke God his grete grace* 'I thank God [for] His great grace'.
For *þankyt be* the MS reads *y þankyt,* but (i) the prefix *y*- is hardly conceivable with a p.p. in the dialect of the poem, (ii) the omission of the subjunctive *be* is unidiomatic, (iii) the line should begin with a stressed syllable, since it begins on the first note of a bar. The scribe seems to have been confused by two alternative idioms, *þankyt be God hys grete grace* (which we assume to have been that intended by the author) and *y þank yt Goddys grete grace* 'I thank God's great grace for it'. He may well have meant to write the latter, but in fact he writes *þankyt* as one word and leaves *God hys* unchanged (perhaps because he took it as the periphrasis for *Goddys*).
grete is the weak adjective, with retained -*e,* used after the possessive *hys.* For the word 'grace' the scribe uses the spelling *gras,* showing the loss of the -*e*.

8. *now ys yt þat y*] The MS reads *now yt ys y,* which is perfectly idiomatic but unsatisfactory in metre; an additional syllable is needed to make the half-line balance the first half of l. 6, set to the same notes. I assume two stages of corruption: in the first *þat* (probably abbreviated *þᵗ*) was omitted after *yt;* in the second *ys* and *yt* were transposed.
þroo 'thrive, prosper', from ON *þróask.* The MS reads *do,* but

this makes a weak rhyme and poor sense (one would have to translate *noʒt do* as 'do nothing' and interpret this as 'do nothing of value, nothing pleasing'). The word *thro* (which we spell *þroo* to indicate the pronunciation) was of very limited currency in ME; *OED* cites examples only from a Northern *Metrical Homily* of c. 1325, *Cursor Mundi*, and Robert Mannyng's *Chronicle* (c. 1330; S. Lincs.). It is just the sort of word which would be liable to be replaced, because it was not understood, by a scribe from another area. For the rhyme *do – throo,* which is a perfect one, see the first of *OED*'s quotations. The sense in the recorded ME instances is 'to thrive physically, to grow' (of children); the emendation assumes the use of the word in a more general sense 'prosper' (in this instance, prosper in courtship).

23. With ryght al my hert

With ryʒt al my hert, now y yow greet
with hundert syës, my deer!
Sweet God, ʒif us gracë soon to meet
and soon to spekyn yfeer!
5   Annys, Annys, Annys, Annys, Annys!

Annys, be stedfast on allëwys
and þynk on me, my sweet Annys,
my fayr Annys, my sooþ Annys.
I love ʒowr [name, my deer Annys,
10   Annys, Annys, Annys, Annys, Annys!]

COMMENTARY

Source: Oxford, Bodleian Library, MS Douce 381, f. 22.

In the MS, which has been re-bound in modern times, the leaf (f. 22) on which this song occurs has probably been reversed at some stage; the song is now on the recto of the leaf, but must originally have been on the verso. It breaks off incomplete at the bottom of the page; the rest of the words and music, and perhaps a tenor part, must have been written on the recto of the following leaf, i.e. the complete text and music were on the two facing pages of an opening. Unfortunately the second leaf has been lost, and with it the end of the song. But the metrical scheme seems almost complete, and so does the music; we have therefore ventured to reconstruct the ending. As usual, the spellings of the MS have been altered somewhat; for the original spellings see Robbins, *Secular Lyrics of the XIVth and XVth Centuries,* no. 146 (p. 146).

The song probably comes from the East or North-east Midlands. The infinitive *spekyn* (l. 4) rules out the North; that being so, the rhyme of *deer* < OE *dēore* with *yfeer* < OE *gefēra* points to the East. The almost (but not quite) complete loss of *-e* is against the South-east Midlands. The form *hundert* 'hundred' is, from the evidence of modern dialects, West Midland and Northern, but in ME is known also in Suffolk (cf. *A Dialogue between Reason and Adversity,* ed. F. N. M. Diekstra, p. 67). The very slight evidence is in favour of the East Midlands, towards the North, but Suffolk would be possible, as final *-e* was lost early there. See also the note to l. 7.

NOTES

1. *ryʒt*] *ryth* MS. The music assumes that the first stress of this line is on *al*.

2. *hundert* 'hundred'; see above. The spelling is more likely to descend from an earlier exemplar than to be due to the Douce scribe.

syes 'sighs'. Metre and music require two syllables. This form of the noun is related to the verbal form *siʒen,* which appears to be mainly Northern.

3. *grace*] Again metre and music require two syllables. Elsewhere in the song final *-e* is silent except in *allewys,* which is treated as a virtual compound, i.e. the *e* is not strictly final. But if the final *-e* of *grace* is not to be pronounced we must emend the text to bring in an extra syllable, and there seems to be no way of doing this which is not clumsier than the transmitted text (e.g. *ʒif us grace soon for to meet* would take the metrical and musical stress off *soon,* where it clearly belongs); moreover the MS seems elsewhere to be a faithful copy of the words.

5–6. The name *Annys* is a common early form of *Agnes;* it is throughout stressed on the second syllable. For its last occurrence in l. 5 and at the beginning of l. 6 the scribe changes the spelling to *Annes,* another early form; but this is obviously his own aberration, and cannot have been intended.

6. *be*] *be now* MS, which makes the scansion of the line x/xx/xx/x/, with two anapaests where the rhyming line (l. 8) is regularly iambic. The second of these anapaests fits the music, the first does not; and *now,* which causes the trouble, is unnecessary for sense. The scribe has evidently repeated it wrongly from l. 1.
on allewys 'in every way', with the inflected *alle* used directly before a noun; in this instance it may be a fossilized survival of the old dative case of the adjective.

7. *þynk*] *dynke* MS. Certain South-eastern MSS have *d* for initial *th,* and in the later sixteenth century this is recorded as a dialectal pronunciation in East Sussex and Kent. If the scribe's spelling could be taken as surviving from the author's original, it would be in favour of the Suffolk location suggested above, against the North-east Midlands. But it seems better to normalize the spelling in our text.

8. *sooþ* 'true, faithful'.

9–10. The MS text ends at the foot of the page with *ʒowre;* the rest is supplied by conjecture (see above). But it seems obvious that l. 10, like l. 5, should consist of a fivefold repetition of the name *Annys,* and that l. 9, like ll. 7–8, should end with the name; and that leaves very little to be guessed at. In view of the constant repetition of the name, the likeliest thing of hers for him to say he loves is 'ʒowr name'.

24. I have set my hert so hy

> I hav*e* set my hert so hy,
>> me likyth no lov*e* þat lower ys;
> and all þe payn þat y may dry,
>> me þenk hyt doþ me good, ywis —
>>> me þenk yt doþ, ywis.
>
> For on that lord þat lov*e*d us all
>> so hertëly hav*e* I set my þowʒt,
> yt ys my joi*e* on hym to call,
>> for lov*e* me haþ in balus browʒt —
>>> me þenk yt haþ, ywis.

(marginal line numbers: 5 beside fifth line, 10 beside tenth line)

COMMENTARY

Source: Oxford, Bodleian Library, MS Douce 381, f. 20.

Though there is little evidence, this song was probably written in the North Midlands, and perhaps more precisely in the North-west Midlands. The form of the impersonal *me þenk* 'it seems to me' (see note to l. 4) is in favour of a location in the North or North Midlands; and so would be *haf* for *have* in l. 1, if (as is likely) this was the original form (see note below). The ending *-us* for normal plural *-es* in *balus* (l. 9) was in general a West Midland characteristic. Final *-e* is not preserved in any word, though medial *e* is kept in *hertely* (l. 7).

The song has been printed by Carleton Brown, *Religious Lyrics of the XIVth Century,* no. 129; but because he takes no notice of the musical setting he misunderstands the stanza-form and clumsily emends the refrain-line (which he gives only after the second stanza) in such a way as to ensure that it could not possibly fit the music. The scribe himself, it is true, gives the refrain-line only once (as was normal with a refrain, to save the trouble of writing it more than once); but he gives it in the form required after the first stanza (not after the second, where Brown puts it), with the right number of syllables though probably not with the right grammar, and it is for us to make a suitable variation for the second stanza without alteration of the number of syllables.

NOTES

1. *have*] The MS reads *hafe* in the main part, *haue* in the tenor part. The latter is likely to be the scribe's form, as the evidence is overwhelming that he was a Southerner; and it must be probable, therefore, that the original had *haf* or *hafe* (with unvoicing of the final consonant). This is characteristically a Northern development, but is found also in the North Midlands (Jordan, § 217). But as the parts differ, I adopt the more conventional spelling for our text.

2. *likyth*] *likyt* MS, with the common (especially Southern) *-t* ending of the 3 sg. pres. indic.

3. *payn*] *paynes* MS, but (i) the *hyt* 'it' of l. 4, though not conclusive, is in favour of a singular antecedent; (ii) the metre and setting require a monosyllable, and though a monosyllabic plural *payns* is conceivable in a Northern or North Midland dialect the plural *balus* in l. 9 is disyllabic. The balance of advantage seems to be in favour of a singular, against the MS. *dry* 'endure'; *dryue* MS but emended by Carleton Brown, correctly, for the sake of rhyme. As the word *dry* < earlier *dreye* < OE *drēogan* (of which Scottish and Northern *dree* is a variant) became old-fashioned in the South and Midlands, it was confused with *drive* (see *OED,* s.v. *drive,* sense 20). Rhyme here excludes the Northern form.

4. *me þenk* 'it seems to me'. The proper form of the impersonal expression was *me þinkeþ,* but in Northern dialects especially, owing to confusion with the personal verb *I þenke* (partly phonetic, partly semantic), mixed forms such as *me þenk,* with an uninflected verb, came into use.

4–5. *doþ*] *do* MS. There are probably two reasons for the MS reading: (i) the construction *me þenk* was taken as meaning 'I think' and was therefore expected to be followed by the accusative and infinitive, 'I think it to do . . .'; (ii) the corruption (as I assume) of *payn* to *paynes* in l. 3 has affected the form of the verb in ll. 4 and 5. Nevertheless the construction properly requires an indicative verb, which after *hyt* (*yt*) should be singular; and if we do not emend *do* to *doþ* here we get into trouble when we come to the refrain line of stanza 2 (see note to l. 10, below).

5. *ywis* 'certainly'. The word is spelt by the scribe *y wys* in l. 5, *I wys* in l. 6; he was almost certainly affected by the confusion that took *ywis* as the present tense of *I wiste* 'I knew' and so interpreted it to mean 'I know'. In fact it is a single word, an adverb, and the *y-* is a prefix (OE *gewiss*).

6. *loved*] A monosyllable, with reduction of the past tense suffix from *-ed* to *-d*. Cf. no. 6b, l. 23, and the note there, and no. 17, ll. 7–8.

7. *hertely*] Three syllables, with preservation of the medial *e*. The pronunciation is comparable to modern English *heartily*, but the latter is in fact a different formation.

9. *balus*] Two syllables, as both metre and music require. This is a spelling of the plural *bales* meaning 'torments', often (in love poetry) specifically the torments or pangs of love. Here, as elsewhere in this song, there is a deliberate ambiguity; the diction of love-lyric is applied in a religious sense. On the spelling *-us* for the plural ending *-es* see the commentary above.

10. The MS gives the refrain line only once, in the form required by the first stanza, though as I think inaccurately (*yt do* where *yt doþ* is required). But this does not fit the second stanza, and the author must have intended a variable refrain, such as is very common in later fourteenth-century lyric. The verb *haþ* in l. 9 requires *yt haþ* in the refrain-line (l. 10) of the second stanza; and this supports the assumption that in l. 4 and the refrain-line of the first stanza the form should also be a 3 sg. indic. pres., *doþ*.

25. Trew, on wam ys al my tryst

Trew, on wam ys al my tryst
    and þat y serv*e* as y best can,
þoʒ ʒe hav*e* on me unlyst,
    so hertly as y am ʒowr man —
5   a hendë hap, and þerwyth hy —
    hel þe hertë þát y [now] hav*e*;
let me nouʒt on ʒow crav*e* and cry,
    syþ ʒe mow [ʒowr] sylvë me sav*e*.

COMMENTARY

Source: Cambridge, University Library, MS Additional 5943, f. 163.

On MS Additional 5934 (formerly known as Lord Howard de Walden's MS), which gives words and music for this and the rest of the songs in this volume, see the general Introduction, pp. 22-6 above. The collection of songs with music that it gives on ff. 161ʳ–169ʳ was evidently made in Winchester College and must have been copied into this MS while its then owner, Thomas Turk, was a fellow of Winchester between 1395 and 1401. No. 30 below was obviously written in Winchester, and no. 28 is attributed by the MS to 'Edmund', who may be identified with a chapel-clerk of Winchester College; and others of the songs in the MS, which contain Southernisms in their language, may also have been written in Winchester. But the present song, which is a characteristic courtly love-lyric, was on the evidence of its language written in the South-east Midlands, doubtless in London or its neighbourhood. The forms *tryst* 'trust' (l. 1) and *unlyst* 'displeasure' (l. 3) are characteristically East Midland (or Northern), and the form *herte* 'hurt' (l. 6) is specifically South-eastern (see the note below). The state of the pronunciation of final *-e* is what might be expected in the language of London in the late fourteenth century. It is kept in *hende* in l. 5 (an emendation), in *herte* in l. 6, and in *sylve* in l. 8. Most of the cases of its loss are explicable by elision, and the forms *have* (monosyllable, as the music shows) in l. 6 and *mow* 'may' in l. 8 may be due to the generalization of reduced forms without *-e* developed under weak stress (though both words are used in stressed position). But *save* in l. 8 is an undoubted instance of loss of *-e* from a stressed word. It may not be chance that the words in which loss (otherwise than by elision) is shown are verbs.

In all the songs taken from the Cambridge MS, I modify the spelling (chiefly by the omission of otiose final *-e*) as seems expedient. Such alterations of spelling are not necessarily recorded in the notes.

NOTES

1. *trew* 'true' is a vocative, 'O faithful one' (*trewe* MS).
wam] an unstressed form of 'whom'. The use of *w* for *wh* is probably due to the copyist; the original is more likely to have had the normal *whom*.
tryst 'trust'.

2. *þat* is the relative pronoun, meaning 'whom'.

3. *unlyst* 'displeasure', a variant, not recorded by *OED*, of *unlust*. The line means 'though you feel displeasure for me', 'though you are displeased with me'.

4. 'However sincerely I am your man.' *Hertly* means 'heartily, sincerely'.
y] so originally MS, but a *t* has been added later above the line, quite wrongly, as in no. 28, l. 2.

5. The line is a parenthesis: 'a pleasing fortune, and honourable as well'.
hende hap] The MS has been read as *hete hepe*, but the first vowel of the second word is unclear and may have been meant as *a*; certainly *hape*, a recorded spelling of *hap*, makes sense, and *hepe* does not. The first word is undoubtedly *hete* and is undoubtedly nonsense; emendation is essential. I take *hete hape* to be a corruption of the alliterative tag *hende hap*; cf. the burden of the well-known lyric *Alisoun*,

An hendy hap ichabbe ihent,

though this uses the rare derivative *hendy* of *hende*. I assume, as stages of the corruption, (i) that *hende* was written as *hēde*, with the abbreviation-mark for *n* over the *e*; (ii) that this was miscopied as *hete* owing to misreading a delta-shaped *d* with almost horizontal 'ascender' as a *t*.
hy 'high'. The MS has the spelling *heʒe*, which spoils the rhyme.

6. *hel* 'heal'. So spelt in MS, correctly, for the imperative sg. of this verb did not end in *-e*, being from OE *hǣl*. But the vowel is long (ME *ē*).

herte 'hurt, wound' (*sc.* of love). *Hert*(*e*) for *hurt*(*e*) is a well-established South-eastern form, whose descendant survives in the modern dialect of Suffolk; but *OED* records it only for the verb. There is perhaps a pun on *herte* 'heart', as certainly in the song *Go hert, hert* (*hurt* MS) *with adversite*.

now] supplied; not in MS. The line as given in the MS is satisfactory in sense and metre, but is rather too short for the music, though not impossibly so. But if we emend l. 8, as I think we must, we have to add a syllable to l. 6 also, for the two are parallel lines set to the same musical phrase (with a variation at the end); and the addition makes l. 6 fit the music better. The added word *now* could be put in either before or after *y*; it is perhaps better after, for the music requires as the second-last word one that is metrically unstressed but capable of bearing a musically prominent phrase. The scansion of the line as emended is /x/x/xx/, with a metrical stress on *þat*. It should be noted that this MS gives very careless word-texts, and often omits one or more words — in extreme cases, half a line or more.

7. 'Do not cause me to beg and cry to you' (i.e. do not make it necessary for me to do so), or perhaps 'Do not leave me begging and crying to you'.

8. *syþ* 'since'. The MS has the spelling *syþþe*, but metre and music require the monosyllabic form.
mow 'may, can', the present tense plural form from late OE **mūgon*. The MS has *mowe*, but again a monosyllable is needed.

ʒowr sylve me] *me sylve* MS. The scansion requires that *sylve* should be two syllables. But even so the line as given in the MS is unsatisfactory, for it makes dubious sense and grammar: 'since you can save myself' (why *myself* and not just *me*?). The sense required is 'since you can save me yourself', and to get this we must insert *ʒowr* before *sylve*. The line would then run:

syþ ʒe mow me [ʒowr] sylvë savé.

But this will not fit the music properly, for the weak syllable -*e* of *sylve* would have to be put to a musically prominent phrase which it would not bear. We must therefore in addition transpose *me*, as in our text. The line as so emended is parallel to the emended l. 6, and both have the scansion /x/x/xx/. But in each the second-last syllable, though metrically unstressed, is an independent word capable of bearing the extra weight that the composer puts on it.

26. Danger me hath, unskylfuly

Danger me haþ, unskylfuly;
    y kan noʒt do but let hyt pass
and lyve boþe glad and myryly.
    But hit ys noʒt as hyt was,
5   and þe blame ys noʒt yn me.
    Fórsuþ, hyt ys herë wyll,
    but yf y myʒt more þan y may.

[Danger me haþ, unkyndëly,
    and makyth never sign of grace;
10 but yet my fortune, happyly,
    may be better þan hyt was,
and þe blame be noʒt in me.
    Fórsuþ, hyt ys herë wyll,
    yf but y may more þan y myʒt.]

COMMENTARY

Source: Cambridge, University Library, MS Additional 5943, f. 166; *second stanza supplied.*

The form of this song, as given in the MS, presents a problem. The music is set out as if it were a song written to the ABB formula, according to the method used for most of the songs in this collection; the closest parallel to the actual disposition of the music on the page is the French song *Plus pur lenoyr* on f. 162ᵛ. A vertical line is drawn across the musical stave at the end of l. 5, as though this were the end of the first stanza (the A part of the musical structure); what follows is the B part of the structure, intended for repetition and with a *clos* (again marked off by vertical strokes before and after it) for use with the second repetition. In the tenor part there is a vertical stroke (marking the end of the music of the first stanza) at the end of

the first line of music; under the left-hand end of the second line of music is written 'Secundus versus', meaning that this is the tenor part for the second stanza, and again a *clos* is provided, marked off by vertical strokes before and after it and with the word 'clos' written beneath it. The setting-out is exactly the same as that of the French song.

But the parallel does not extend to the words. The French song (like our no. 27, *I rede that thou*) has a first stanza of five lines, followed by a second stanza of four lines that breaks into two matching half-stanzas sung to a repetition of the same music (that of the 'secundus versus'); these two half-stanzas are written the one below the other in the MS. But the words of *Danger me hath* do not follow this pattern. Even if ll. 1-5 be taken as a 'primus versus', ll. 6-7 do not constitute a 'secundus versus' divisible into two halves; the words could only fit the musical structure if ll. 6-7 were repeated, which merely in itself would be pointless. The scribe does not indicate such a repetition, and it is at this point that even his own laying-out of this song departs from such models as *Plus pur lenoyr* and *I rede that thou* (and other pieces); for whereas in these undoubted instances of the ABB structure the music of the second stanza has two parallel sets of words written under it (the two halves of the second stanza), in *Danger me hath* there is only the one set of words (ll. 6–7), and no words at all under the *clos*.

In one other instance in this MS the scribe gives only a single stanza of a song (the carol, no. 20 above), though it is known from other evidence that it had many stanzas; and it seems likely that *Danger me hath* also had more stanzas than the one that is given. Of this there are two indications. The first is the form in which the scribe gives l. 5, which is

and þe blame be noȝt yn me.

This can only mean 'if the fault be not in me', for the use of the subjunctive *be* must mean that *and* is used in its rarer sense of 'if'. But the context obviously requires the sense 'and the fault is not in me' — so obviously that the only likely explanation of the scribe's error is that he has given in the first stanza the form of the line required by some later stanza. This in turn suggests that the form of the song was one of stanzas plus a refrain which was capable of variation; and the last two lines (the scribe's 'secundus versus'), though they are plainly not a second stanza, have the appearance of a refrain. The second indication is that these two lines are not rhymed, nor indeed is the fifth, which is surprising in so short and simple a stanza-form. This reinforces the suggestion that the song was intended to have a variable refrain, for a common technical reason for the use of a non-rhyming refrain is the intention to vary it in such a way that the line-ending will be affected. And if we inspect the last two lines with this possibility in mind, it is evident that the last line could be completely altered in sense by an alteration of word-order. As the scribe gives it,

but yf y myȝt more þan y may,

it means 'unless I could do more than I can' and implies that the lover's situation is hopeless, because he is being asked to do more than is possible. If however it is altered to read:

yf but y may more þan y myȝt

the meaning is changed to 'if only I can do more than I could', which would be a suitable concluding line — there is hope for him yet, if only he can do in the future better than he has managed to do in the past. It would be pointless to provide a final line capable of variation in this way unless it was intended that the song should consist of two contrasting stanzas (or perhaps more than two — but two seems the likeliest number). My reconstruction is based on this assumption. Each stanza consists of a quatrain plus the variable refrain (counting the fifth line as part of the refrain, though it could be regarded as the cue for the refrain, like the last line of a carol-stanza). In the first stanza, the lover proceeds from defiant insouciance to a wry admission that things are not what they were and an assertion that it is not his fault — it is how she intends things to be, unless he could do more than he finds possible. The counterpart is that he should in the second stanza proceed from the apparent hopelessness of the present situation to a realization that things may be better in the future, if the fault be not in himself — indeed, she intends that it shall be so, if only he can

do in the future more than he could in the past. The stanza supplied has been written to carry out this pattern, and makes use of the scribe's form of the fifth line (wrongly given in the first stanza) and the varied form of the last line; and on the assumption that the second stanza would have closely matched the form of the first (which would account for the scribe's error in giving the wrong form of the fifth line in the first stanza) it uses the same rhyme-sounds and makes the fourth line end with the same two words.

The question remains of what notice is to be taken of the scribe's way of setting out the music. There seem to be two alternatives. (1) To treat the *clos* provided both in the main and in the tenor part as being intended for use only at the end of the second stanza. This involves treating the scribe's indication of music that follows the ABB pattern as a mere error. (2) To accept his distinction of two 'verses' as being to this extent valid, that it is based on a distinction between the main part of the stanza (the quatrain and the cue-line that announces the refrain) and the refrain itself, and to accept also the indication that the music to which the refrain is set was to be repeated — in other words, to sing the last two lines of each stanza (the refrain-lines) twice, using the *clos* for the repetition at the end of each stanza. To do this would be to accept that the scribe was right about the musical structure, that it was indeed ABB, even though the words provided did not follow this pattern in the same way as in the other songs in the MS. The song would then, as reconstructed, follow what might be called a 'double ABB' pattern (ABB ABB), with the qualification that in this case the B part of the words was merely repeated, whereas in other cases we have rather B^1 and B^2 — different words following the same metre and capable of being sung to a repetition of the same music, except for the *clos*. We adopt the second alternative in our setting on p. 281. For a quite different solution of the problem, see the note on p. 223 below.

The stanza given by the scribe, unlike most of the pieces in this Cambridge MS, contains no Southernisms; it is written in the literary language of London. As final *-e* is lost except in the possessive *here* 'her' (l. 6), it must have been written late in the fourteenth century by a man whose language was much more advanced in this respect than that of Chaucer and Gower and who was presumably of a younger generation.

NOTES

1. *Danger* originally meant 'dominion, power', and was a technical term of medieval love-poetry, signifying a mistress's power over her lover, or 'servant'. *Unskylfuly* means 'unreasonably, beyond reason'. The line therefore means 'I am in a lady's power, beyond reason'.

2. *kan*] *ne kan* MS, but the metre shows that the poet did not use the negative particle before the verb. The sense is 'I can do nothing but let it pass'. For *but* the MS has *bote*, here and in l. 7.

4. *But*] *Buȝt* MS (previously read as *Suȝt*, which is meaningless). There is no reason for the insertion of the ȝ; probably the scribe did not pronounce it in such words as *noȝt* and *myȝt* and put it in unthinkingly before a final *t*. The sense is 'but things are not as they were'; in OE and ME *hit* 'it' is often used to mean 'things in general'.

5. *ys*] *be* MS. See the commentary above. It is improbable, in a fourteenth-century poem, that this line is intended to rhyme with *unskylfuly* in l. 1 and *myryly* in l. 3; ME *ę̄*, when

shortened, became ĭ, and there is no reasonable doubt that the unstressed spoken form of *me* was *mŭ* (hence, in part, the confusion between *meself* and *myself*), but in rhyming position this weak form of *me* would not be expected. It is more likely that the fifth line of the stanza, like the sixth and seventh, was left unrhymed.

6. *Forsuþ*] *ffor suþþe* MS, i.e. *forsooth* 'indeed, in truth'. The vowel of the second syllable was shortened to *ŭ* from the fourteenth century onwards.
here 'her'. The disyllabic form is required by the musical set-

ting. For *wyll* the MS has *wylle,* but in this case a monosyllable is needed.

7. 'unless I could do more than I can'.

9. For the assumed rhyme *grace:was* cf. no. 22 above, ll. 5-7, and Robbins, *Secular Lyrics of the XIVth and XVth Centuries,* no. 28, ll. 12-14. It is in fact common from the fourteenth to the sixteenth century, and depends on the use of *ă* in *grace.*

10. *happyly* in the reconstructed text is used in the sense 'by chance, with luck'.

27. I rede that thou be joly and glad

I rede þat þou be joly and glad
          and ever more, and þou aspy
ho be to angry oþer to sad,
          put hym out of þy company;
5   and so þou miȝt be myry and glad.

For by my trouþ, an angry man,
          and hym ouȝt lyky amys,
he wol do al þat ere he can
          to make men anger as hys.

COMMENTARY

Source: Cambridge, University Library, MS Additional 5943, f. 161; Oxford, Bodleian Library, Douce 381, f. 22ᵛ.

This is the only one of the late fourteenth-century songs to be given by both the Cambridge MS (denoted C in the notes below) and the Bodleian MS (denoted B). The linguistic forms are in general those of the literary language of the time, but there are two clear signs of Southern influence: B's infinitive *lyky* in l. 7, which the metre requires, and C's spelling *bue* for *be* (< OE *bēon*) in l. 5. The song is characteristic of the Winchester College collection and may well have been written there; there is a particular link of sense with ll. 7-8 of the following song.

NOTES

1-2. These lines are badly rubbed in B and l. 1 is illegible.

1. *þou*] *þu* C, a characteristic spelling of this MS, and so in ll. 2 and 5, where B has *þᵘ,* the usual abbreviation for *þou.* I adopt *þou* as the normal spelling at this date.

2. *and* (second instance in line)] & B, *om.* C. The word (here meaning 'if') is essential to both metre and sense.

3. *ho be* 'anyone who is'. Assuming that the MSS are right in reading *hym* in l. 4 and that *ho be* is therefore singular, the verb *be* must be subjunctive. (1) There is a tendency for clauses of indirect speech (here an indirect question) to have the verb in the subjunctive if they depend on a conditional clause whose own verb is in the subjunctive, as *aspy* is here. (2) Clauses introduced by general relative pronouns tend to have the verb in the subjunctive because they involve an element of uncertainty of meaning, 'anyone who may chance to be' (cf. Mus-

tanoja, *Middle English Syntax,* Part I, pp. 461-2). The latter is probably a sufficient explanation.
angry] so B as I read it; *wronge* C, but a disyllable is needed.

4. *hym*] so both MSS. Emendation to *hem* 'them' would enable *ho be* in the previous line to be taken as 'any who are', with *be* the normal East Midland indicative plural, but it seems better to follow the MSS and to accept that *be* is 3 sg. pres. subj. (see note to l. 3).

5. *miȝt*] *mist* C, with the common (originally Anglo-Norman) spelling *-st* for *-ȝt;* it is found mostly in Southern MSS, as in this case. We regularize the spelling. The form *miȝt,* which survived into the fifteenth century, is the old 2 sg. pres. indic. of *may,* i.e. it means 'mayest', and its use is probably another sign of the Southern origin of the song, for Southern dialects were conservative. It must be preferred to B's reading *schalt,* for no scribe of *c.* 1400 would substitute the obsolescent form *miȝt* if his exemplar had the straightforward word *schalt.*
be] so B; *bue* C, a Southern spelling with *ue* for the sound [ø:] < OE *ēo,* which was preserved in Southern (and West Midland) dialects.

6. *trouþ*] *trouþe* B, *truþe* C, variant forms of the same word. Both scribes add *-e,* but the metre shows that it is silent.

7. *and* again means 'if': 'if anything please him badly', 'if anything displease him'.
ouȝt lyky] *lyky ouȝt* B, *like out* C. Metre requires the transposition of the word-order. Evidently there was already an error in the common original from which the two MSS descend. Metre also requires two syllables for the verb, and we must therefore accept B's *lyky;* C's *like* will not do, for (i) there is no sign in this song of the retention of pronounced *-e,* (ii) in any case elision would occur in this line. *Lyky* is a Southern form of the verb

like 'please' (< OE *lician*), and *ouȝt* (*out* C, with omission of ȝ) is a form of *aught* 'anything'.

8. *he* (first)] so B; *ho* C, by misreading of *e* as *o*, a common error.

ere is the modern *e'er* 'ever'. B reads *euer*, C omits the word; a monosyllable is needed here for the metre, and there is a good deal of evidence that where the full form *euer* was written, the contracted *er* (*ere*) was often used in pronunciation.

9. The sense of the line is 'to cause men anger like his'.

to] so C; *for to* B.

anger] so B as I read it, though it has been read as *angri*. C has *angeri* and continues his line accordingly.

hys] so B as I read it, but it is rubbed and unclear; *he ys* C. Metre and rhyme both clearly demand *hys*, and it follows that *anger* must be right earlier in the line.

28. Thys Yool, thys Yool (Edmund)

Thys ȝool, thys ȝool,
þe bestë red þat y kan
ys for to be a myry man,
and levë kar*e*, and put out stryf;
5   þus þynk y to led*e* my lyf
      thys ȝool, thys ȝool.

And wam y may fynd angrí,
y wol lev*e* hys company
      thys ȝool.

10   Thys ȝool askyth þat ech a man
shal mak*e* þe myrþë þat he kan,
and so wol y, with ryȝt good cheer,
to bygynnyng of þis new ȝeer.

Thys ȝool ȝev*e* y my lady bryȝt
15   my hert and lov*e* and al my myȝt,
'and pray [y] ȝow to be ȝowr man
and ȝow servy ryȝt as y kan
      þys ȝool.'

COMMENTARY

Source: Cambridge, University Library, MS Additional 5943, f. 162.

In the MS there is written, below the main part of this song, the note *quod Edmund* 'said Edmund', an attribution of authorship, and the records of Winchester College give Edmund as the name of a clerk of the chapel in 1396-7 (see the general Introduction, p. 26 above). The song was obviously written for the Yuletide feast, probably rather for New Year's Day than for Christmas (cf. l. 13, and the reference to New Year's gifts in ll. 14-15). Its shift into the terms of courtly love-lyric in the third stanza is uncharacteristic of the songs that seem to have been specially written for the Winchester collection, but this stanza cannot be a later addition; it is required for the musical form, stanzas 2 and 3 being sung to a repetition of the same music. The whole song is more elaborate than others in the collection, but it has links of sense with the preceding piece.

The song is written in the standard forms of the literary language, with one Southernism (*servy* in l. 17, but this may not be original; see the note below). Final *-e* is preserved in *beste* (the 'weak' adjective) in l. 2, in *leve* infin. in l. 4, and in *myrþe* in l. 11, but is lost (otherwise than by elision) in *kare* 'care' in l. 4, *lede* in l. 5, and *make* in l. 11. The apparent difference from no.

27, in which pronounced *-e* does not occur, is probably fortuitous; the pieces are too short for the occurrence or non-occurrence of pronounced *-e* to be significant.

NOTES

1. *ȝool*] *ȝol* MS, and so throughout; but the word has ME *ǭ*, which we spell *oo*.

2. The metre could be made more regular, to match that of l. 3, by inserting *which* before *þat*, but the setting is for the text as transmitted.

red (so MS) is the word *rede* 'advice', 'counsel' (OE *rǣd*); the vowel is long (ME *ē̜*).

y] so MS originally, but a *t* has been inserted above it to make the abbreviation for *that*, unnecessarily and wrongly.

5. The first metrical stress is on *þus*, the second on *y*.

7. The first metrical stress is on *And*, the second on *y*. At the end of the line, there is artificial stress on the suffix of *angri*. *wam* is 'whom', an unstressed form common in this MS.

8. *company* is stressed on both the first and the last syllable.

10. *askyth*] *askyt* MS.
ech a] *eche* MS. Metre and setting require two syllables, but the

word 'each', though often spelt with final -*e* (as in the MS), was properly a monosyllable (< OE *ǣlc*). What is needed is the ME idiom *ech a man* 'each single man'.

12. *ryȝt*] *ryt* MS, a spelling of *right* indicating that the spirant represented by *ȝ* (*gh*) had become silent in the scribe's speech; similarly *bryt* in l. 14. But in l. 15 the MS has *myȝt*, and in l. 17 it has *ryth* 'right'. Despite the inconsistency in spelling, the rhyming indicates that for the author Edmund the spirant was still pronounced, and we normalize all the words.

cheer] *chere* MS, and similarly *ȝere* for the rhyme-word in l. 13. The rhyme is apparently on Midland *ȝeer* (with ME *ę̄*) < OE (Anglian)) *gēr* (though the same form would occur in Kentish). In a Southern dialect (other than Kentish) one would expect that *ȝer* would have ME *ę̄* < OE (West Saxon) *gēar*. Probably the rhyme is on ME *ę̄*, but see the note to no. 29, l. 4, where the same problem arises.

13. *new*] *newe* MS, set to two notes as if a disyllable, as it originally was. But the metre requires a monosyllable; cf. l. 17, where the phrase *as y kan* corresponds to *þis new ȝeer* in l. 13.

14. *ȝeve y*] *y ȝeue* MS, but the parallel of *askyth* in l. 10 (which

goes to the same music) suggests that the stressed syllable should precede the unstressed. English word-order originally required that in a sentence beginning with an adverb or adverbial phrase the verb should precede the subject; Edmund has followed this older rule, the scribe (as often) has imposed the newer word-order of prose.

16. The poet breaks into direct speech to his lady.
pray y] Again there is inversion of the word-order. The MS omits the pronoun *y* 'I' after the word ending in *y*, but both sense and metre require it.

17. *servy*] *seruy* MS. This is a form (at this date generally Southern) of the infinitive of *serve*. Metre requires two syllables, but the Midland *servë* would do as well if the -*e* were pronounced; cf. *levë* in l. 4, which had no variant form in -*y* because it belonged to a different conjugation.
The MS has the word-order *and servy ȝow*, scanning x/x/, but the parallel with l. 13 (set to the same music) requires *and ȝow servy*, scanning /x/x, to balance *to bygynnyng*; and the musical phrasing demands this stress-pattern.
ryȝt] *ryth* MS, but see note to l. 12 above.

29. Wel wer hym that wyst

Wel wer hym þat wyst
to wam he myȝtë tryst,
    but þat ys on a wyr*e*.
For oft men but hold cheer;
5   and trystly frendis fur an neer
    þai walkyth in þe myr*e*.

Wold God þat allë such
a mark had, lyt*e* or much,
    þat al men myȝt yknow
10   how her hert stent, and mouȝt
as ryȝt as norþ and sowþ
    to þylkë hy, but slow.

COMMENTARY

Source: Cambridge, University Library, MS Additional 5943, f. 162ᵛ.

This song is again written in the forms of the standard literary language, intermingled with Southernisms. Obvious examples of the latter are the present tense plural *walkyth* (*walkytt* MS) in l. 6, *yknow* 'recognize' in l. 9, and *stent* 'stands' in l. 10; *fur* 'far' in l. 5 is probably also dialectal. On the rhyme between *cheer* and *neer* in ll. 4-5 see the note below.

The style of the song is clumsy and its meaning is not clear in detail, and matters are not helped by the obvious unreliability of the text given by the MS.

NOTES

1. 'It would be well for him who knew'.

2. *wam* 'whom', as in the preceding pieces.
myȝte] *myȝt* MS, but two syllables are required for the metre. The poet makes sporadic and irregular use of final -*e* as a met-

rical convenience, but in every case with historical justification. Compare the preceding song.
tryst] *tryste* MS, but here a monosyllable is needed; the MS itself has *wyst* as the spelling of the rhyme-word. For the most part I omit otiose final -*e*. *Tryst* is a form of *trust*, characteristic of the literary language of the East Midlands.

3. 'but that hangs on a thread.' The reference of 'that' is vague, but presumably it means 'knowing whom to trust'. For the use of 'wire' to mean something insubstantial and undependable, a mere thread, cf. Chaucer, *Troilus and Criseyde*, iii. 1636:

    For worldly joie halt nought but by a wir.

For *on* the MS reads *in*, but if this is retained I do not see what acceptable sense can be given to the line.

4. *but hold cheer* 'only put on a show', 'only assume an appearance of friendliness'.
As *cheer* (< OF *chere*) had ME *ę̄*, the rhyme here seems to depend on *ę̄* in *neer*, which in turn presupposes OE (Anglian or Kentish) *nēr*; if so, this is a rhyme based on Midland or Kentish

pronunciation. In a Southern dialect other than Kentish one would expect that 'near' would have ME *ẹ̄* derived from OE (Saxon) *nēar,* and the rhyme here might possibly be on ME *ẹ̄;* for in late ME there was a process of lowering ME *ẹ̄* to ME *ę̄* before *r* which could produce *ę̄* in *cheer.* But I assume that the rhyme is on *ę̄* and therefore spell both words with *ee.* The MS spellings are *chere* and *ner.* Cf. the note to no. 28, l. 12.

5. *trystly*] *OED* records *tristly* and its variant *trustly* only as adverbs, but here *trystly* must be an adjective meaning 'trustful'. It may be simply a scribal error for *tristy,* but it is not necessary to assume this; *-ly* is an adjectival as well as an adverbial suffix.

fur 'far' is a form deduced from the comparative *further.* The line is hypermetrical, with four stresses instead of the normal three; but as the first stanza is set to music which is not repeated, this sort of metrical variation is permissible.

6. *þai*] *þ* MS. The emendation is necessary for sense. Perhaps the scribe did not recognize the ME grammatical trick of resuming a noun-subject by a logically unnecessary personal pronoun. His work in any case is very careless.

walkyth is a Southern present tense indic. plural. The MS has *walkytt,* in which the *-ytt* is presumably a variant on *-yt, -it;* this *-t* ending for normal *-th* occurs elsewhere in the MS, and is itself generally a Southern feature.

myre] *myste* MS. The scribe appears to have got confused about the rhyme-scheme. It is very unlikely that the third and sixth lines would have the same rhyme-sounds as the first and second in a stanza apparently designed to have the pattern aabccb; and in any case it is not easy to think of a word ending in *-ist* that would fit l. 3, whereas *myre* is an obvious substitute for *myste* in l. 6. The sense is that trustful friends, deceived by hypocrites, walk into the mire.

7. *wold* 'would'; *wol* MS, an obvious error.

alle such (*alle suche* MS), 'all who pretend friendliness'. The author's jumps of sense leave a lot to the reader.

8. *a mark had*] *had a marke* MS. The transposition is required for regularity of metre; this phrase must have the same rhythm as *as ryȝt as* in l. 11, which is set to the same notes. The scribe has substituted normal prose word-order for the inverted order used by the poet.

lyte or much 'small or large'. For *or* the MS has *oþer,* but the monosyllabic form is required; for *much* the MS has *moche.*

9. *yknow* 'recognize', < OE *gecnāwan.* By the late fourteenth century the word seems to be Southern.

10. *her hert* 'their heart', the usual ME idiom; each has one heart. The following verb, *stent,* is likewise singular, and is distinctively Southern; it is the contracted 3 sg. pres. indic.,

with *i*-mutation of the stem-vowel, of *stonden* 'to stand'.

stent, and mouȝt] *and moȝt stent* MS, which is ungrammatical and meaningless, and does not rhyme. Transposition is essential.

mouȝt (*moȝt* MS) is from OE *mŭhte,* a variant of *mihte* 'might', p.t. of *may;* here *myȝt* is used in l. 9, *mouȝt* in l. 10 for the sake of assonance. Despite the scribe's spelling, it is plain that the vowel (originally *ŭ*) has been lengthened to ME *ū,* for which the appropriate spelling at this date is *ou,* and it is probable, though not certain, that the spirant represented by *ȝ* has been lost (cf. Dobson, *Eng. Pron. 1500-1700,* ii. § 177). The assonance is between [mu:(x)t] for *mouȝt* and [su:þ] for *sowþ.* One could make an eye-rhyme by adopting the recorded spelling *mowth* in place of the scribe's *moȝt,* and *sowth* in place of his *sowþe,* and it is possible that the author intended this; but the rhyme would not really be improved, for such spellings as *mowth* were unphonetic.

The meaning of *myȝt* in l. 9 and *mouȝt* in l. 10 is 'could' rather than 'might'.

11. 'as directly as north and south', like one following a compass bearing.

12. *to þilke hy* 'hasten to the same', again extremely vague in reference (cf. *þat* in l. 3, *such* in l. 7). Perhaps the meaning is 'hasten to those who are marked out as trustworthy'.

but slow] *but sowe* MS, but it is hard to see what sense can be given to this. *OED,* s.v. *sow* sb.[2], records a noun of obscure origin meaning 'drain', so that the phrase in the MS might be taken, perhaps, as meaning 'without ditch' (or even 'without falling into a ditch', with reference to l. 6), but this is forced; and in modern dialects the word is pronounced [sau], which will not make a good rhyme with *yknow.* In a poem entitled *The Festivals of the Church,* evidently written in the North-east Midlands in the later fourteenth century and preserved in B.L. MS Royal 18 A.x (printed by Morris as an appendix to his *Legends of the Holy Rood,* EETS, 1871), there occur the lines:

> Whasshe þi sowle white as snowe,
> and in þat bed þis barn schal þe bynde;
> in a cote, withoute slow,
> oure lady lolled þi leve frende.

(Morris, op. cit., p. 214, ll. 135-8.) *OED,* s.v. *slow* sb., says that in this passage the sense of *withoute slow* is 'not clear, perhaps "without delay" '. It is hard to see what other sense is possible; it is a tag of the type of *withouten* (or *but*) *abode, withouten frist, withouten* (or *but*) *hone, let, delay,* etc. *Slow* is obviously a noun, and must be from earlier ME **slowe* 'slowness' beside *slowth* (cf. *trewe* < OE *trēow* fem. 'faith' beside *trewth*). In our song *but slow,* in the same sense 'without delay', will fit the context and make a good rhyme with *yknow;* and as the scribe's text of the song is obviously unreliable I make the emendation.

30. Me lykyth ever the lenger the bet

Me lykyþ ever þe lenger þe bet
     by Wynchestyr, þat joly cyté.
Þe toun ys good and wel yset,
     þe folk ys cumly on to see.

5   Þe ayr ys good, boþe yn and out.
     Þe cyte stont bineþ an hyllë,
þe ryvers rennyth al about.
     Þe toun ys rulyd uppë skyllë.

COMMENTARY

Source: Cambridge, University Library, MS Additional 5943, f. 164ᵛ.

This pedestrian little song was obviously written by a resident in Winchester, but not necessarily by a native; indeed it might seem rather to express the feelings of one who had come to live in the city and found that he liked it. Like other songs in this collection, its language contains Southernisms — the plural *rennyth* (*rennyt* MS) in l. 7 and the contracted 3 sg. pres. indic. *stont* in l. 6.

NOTES

1. *Me lykyþ* properly means 'pleases me', and *Wynchestyr* would originally have been the subject of the verb. But here the syntax is altered, and *me lykyþ . . . by* is used as if it meant 'I am pleased . . . by'.
ever þe lenger þe bet means 'always the longer the better', 'continually better as more time passes'; it is a common ME idiom.

2. *Wynchestyr*] *Wyngestyr* MS, a spelling which appears to show voicing of [tʃ] to [dʒ].
cyte 'city', and so in l. 6. The MS at both places has the spelling *syte,* which I alter to avoid the suggestion of modern English 'site'. In l. 2, at the end of the line, the word retains its French stressing on the second syllable; but in l. 6, in mid-line, it has English stressing on the first.

3. *toun*] *ton* MS, here and in l. 8. For *good* the MS has *god* here but *go⟨o⟩d* in l. 5.

4. *cumly*] *comely* MS; I alter the spelling to make the disyllabic pronunciation more explicit.

see] *sue* MS, a Southern spelling (cf. the note to no. 27, l. 5, on the word *be*). But the rhyme here rules out the Southern vowel-sound [ø:] which this spelling originally represented.

5. *ayr*] *ayer* MS, but a monosyllable is required.

6. *stont* 'stands'; so clearly MS, though it has been read as *stent.* Of the two forms, *stent* (used in no. 29, l. 10) is an unaltered survival of the OE (West Saxon) contracted and mutated 3 sg. present indic., *stont* is a partly regularized ME form, with the vowel taken from the infinitive *stonden.* Both are specifically Southern.
bineþ 'beneath'. The MS has *under,* but the metre and still more clearly the music require a word stressed on the second syllable.
hylle] so MS, set under the music as two syllables, and similarly *skylle* in l. 8. Both words were originally monosyllables and ordinarily remained so, but disyllabic forms with *-e* occur in ME. The music is better suited by disyllabic forms, and thus confirms the scribe's way of treating the words. Whether the author of the words intended disyllables is another matter; all the other lines end in stressed syllables.

7. *ryvers*] *ryuerys* MS, but the metre requires two syllables only.
rennyth] *rennyt* MS. Cf. the note to no. 29, l. 6, on *walkyth.*

8. *rulyd* 'governed'; *ruelyd* MS.
uppe] *apon* MS, but the metre and still more clearly the music require a word stressed on the first syllable, whereas *upon* was always stressed on the second. I therefore substitute the synonymous thirteenth- to fifteenth-century *uppe* < OE *uppan* (for which see *OED,* s.v. *up* prep.[1]) in its sense 'according to'.
skylle 'reason'. On the disyllabic form, see note to *hylle* in l. 6 above.

31. Pater noster, most of myght

Pater noster, most of myȝt,
     þat al þys word [at erst] hast wrout,
help me, synful wrechyd wyȝt,
     for synnë þat I perysch nowt.

5   *Pater noster,* have pety on me
and help me [from] synn [away] to flee,
     [now] and ever to wurch þy wyll.
Pater noster, yblessyd þu be,
for þyne [own deer] son þat deyd on tree;
10   help me, wrecchë, þat y ne spyll.

COMMENTARY

Source: Cambridge, University Library, MS Additional 5943, f. 167ᵛ.

The three remaining English songs of the Cambridge MS Additional 5943 are all religious, and their common authorship is evident from their close conformity to a single pattern. Whether the same author wrote nos. 27, 29 and 30 is more doubtful, but all these pieces resemble each other in language, employing a mixture of the standard East Midland literary language and some Southernisms, and retaining final -e occasionally for metrical convenience, though it is mostly lost. If the secular and religious pieces are by the same author, then in view of the link between no. 27 and no. 28 they may all be by Edmund the chapel-clerk, though in fact the MS attributes only no. 28 to him — perhaps because its final stanza called for attribution to a particular person.

In this song there are no distinctively Southern forms; though *wurch* 'work' and *yblessyd* (with y- prefix) might be more likely in a Southern writer, they could be used by a Londoner.

The text is printed by Carleton Brown, *Religious Lyrics of the XVth Century,* no. 54 (p. 84); but in view of the history of the MS the song must have been written in the late fourteenth century.

All three of the religious songs have especially unreliable texts in the MS, words and phrases being omitted to the detriment of sense and metre and the fit of words to notes. This may mean that the exemplar from which the scribe of the Cambridge MS worked had been made by a more careless copyist than the exemplar from which the secular songs were taken. But if, as I suppose, this copy of the collection was made from sheet-music used by choristers, the sheets giving the secular songs might well have been written by a different copyist from those giving the religious songs. The texts of the secular songs are also unreliable, though less seriously so. Even if all the songs from no. 27 onwards were written in Winchester College, it is obvious that Turk's copy cannot have been made from the originals.

NOTES

1. *most of my3t* 'greatest in power'.

2. *word*] *worde* MS, a common form of *world.*
at erst] supplied; *om.* MS. The line as given in the MS is too short, both metrically and for the music; the latter fact the scribe himself recognized, for he wrote the word 'wrought' twice, once at the point to which the omission brought it, and again under the musical phrase where he realized it belonged. Two additional syllables are needed, and *at erst* 'in the beginning' fits the sense; the recurrence of -*st* in *erst* and *hast* may have caused the omission.
wrout 'wrought'. The scribe's spellings are *wrot* where he first wrote it and *wrote* at the repetition; they appear to show (i) that he did not pronounce 3 (*gh*) in such words, and (ii) that the ME diphthong *ou* had become identical with long *ǭ* in his speech. But he may well have been confused; he probably misunderstood the form *word* earlier in the line, and was thinking of writing words and not of creating worlds. We should at least correct *wrot*(*e*) to *wrout* (cf. the spelling *nowt* for the rhyme-word in l. 4), and it is possible that we should go further and normalize the spelling of both words, thus *wrou3t* and *now3t.*

4. *perysch*] *perycsche* MS, a confused spelling (silently corrected to *perysche* by Carleton Brown). For the pronoun the scribe appears to have written the 'long *i*', though his letter could be read as an abnormal form of *y.*
nowt is the adverb *nought* 'by no means', of which *not* is a reduced form.

6. The MS reads *and helpe me synne for to flee,* but the line is much too short for the musical setting, and it cannot be extended merely by assuming that the final -*e*'s were pronounced, (i) because the imperative *help* ought not to have a pronounced final -*e*, (ii) because in the music there is a rest after the fifth syllable, presupposing a marked mid-line caesura, which would split the word *syn-në* into two if, against linguistic propriety, we made *hel-pë* two syllables. In l. 9 this musical rest must obviously precede the relative pronoun *þat*; it cannot come between the pronoun and its verb. The second half of l. 9 must therefore be *þat deyd on tree,* with the rhythm x/x/, and the second half of l. 6 (set to the same music) must have the same rhythm. Hence my reconstruction *away to flee,* which assumes (i) that a copyist has omitted *away,* (ii) that *for to* has been substituted for *to* (cf. note to no. 21, l. 14). But if the second half-line is made into *away to flee,* then *from* is needed for sense before *synn*; and this insertion also makes the syllables of the first half-line match the musical setting.

7. *now*] supplied; *om.* MS. The first half of the line must have four syllables with the rhythm /x/x; cf. l. 10, set to the same music.
wurch 'work', 'perform'. The MS has *worch,* but the vowel was pronounced as short *ŭ.*

8. *yblessyd*] so MS, as correctly read by Carleton Brown; certainly not *th blassyd,* as it was read by an earlier editor.
þu] *mote þu* MS. A copyist has introduced *mote* 'may' to make explicit the optative force of *be,* but his version is a syllable too long. One could read *yblest moot þu be,* reducing *yblessyd* to two syllables; but this would not be so good a rhythmical parallel to *have pety on me* in l. 5 and would fit the music less well.
þu 'thou' is a characteristic spelling of the scribe of this MS, whether the word is stressed or unstressed. In no. 27, which also exists in the Douce MS, the scribe of the latter writes *þᵘ,* the abbreviation for *þou*; but here, where there is no one to contradict him, I accept the Cambridge scribe's *þu.*

9. *for*] *ffor* MS, and similarly in no. 33, l. 7.
þyne own deer] *þyne* MS (*e* imperfect; read as *þyn* by Carleton Brown). It is inconceivable that in this author's speech the disyllabic dative form *þinë* < OE *þīnum* should be preserved; but the music and the parallel with l. 6 (which goes to the same musical phrase and is written above l. 9 in the MS) show that more syllables than one are needed at this point. A word beginning with a vowel must have been omitted after *þyne,* for at this date *þyne* would not be used before a consonant. The obvious alternatives are *own* and *only.* But the former by itself would still leave the first half of the line too short for the musical setting; and though *only* would be metrically long enough, its second syllable is rather too weak for the musical phrase to which it would have to be sung. A second, independent, word seems to be needed by the music, and so we choose *own deer* 'own dear'.
son] *sone* MS, but a monosyllable is required. Then as now the *o* was a spelling-substitute for *ŭ.*

10. *wrecche*] so MS, and not *wreeche* as printed by Carleton Brown (probably a printer's error). The first *e* is expressed by a curl over the *r*, whereas in l. 3 *wrechyd* is written *wchyd* with a superscript *e* above the *c* (a conventional abbreviation for *re*). The metre requires two syllables, and it seems therefore that here the final *-e* of *wrecche* (< OE *wrecca*) is preserved.

Alternatively one could emend to *wrecchyd*, but in the songs of this MS final *-e* is occasionally kept.

spyll] *spylle* MS, and similarly *wylle* for *wyll* in l. 7; but both lines should end with a stressed syllable. Loss of *-e* is the norm in these songs, despite the scribe's spellings.

32. 'Ave Maria' I say

'*Ave Maria*' I say to þat blessyd mayd
  þat moder ys wythowt [any] mannys mone;
þe same word sooþli þe angel Gabríel sayd
  to Mary moder and may alone in one.

5   *Ave Maria!* y have [thee] in mynd;
      werso y wend, in wel or in wo,
   wel me defend, [both bifore and bihynd,]
     þat y ne stend for no maner fo.

COMMENTARY

Source: Cambridge, University Library, MS Additional 5943, f. 168.

On the religious songs of the Cambridge MS see the commentary to the previous piece. In this song the word *mone* in l. 2 is probably Southern by this date; after 1300 *OED* records it only from William of Shoreham, a Kentish writer, and from John of Trevisa, a Cornishman. The arbitary form *stend* in l. 8 is only conceivable in the South.

The complicated metrical patterns of this little piece, with its dactyllic and anapaestic feet, have at several points been too much for the scribe. They also caused rhythmic difficulties for the musical setting, the stressings of which vary in l. 1 from those which I assume the poet intended. The scribe's laying out of the words beneath the notes is so unreliable that it is of little help.

NOTES

1. The intended metrical stressing I take to be /xx/xx/xx/x/.

2. *wythowt*] *wyt owt* MS.

any] supplied; *om.* MS. The parallel line (l. 4) shows that the metrical pattern is a line of five stresses, thus x/x/xx/x/x/. It follows that l. 2 as given in the MS is two syllables short, and also that *wythowt* must count as two unstressed syllables. What is needed therefore is a word of two syllables beginning with a stress, either before or after *mannys*; and *any* seems an obvious choice, especially as its omission before *mannys* is easy to account for.

mone 'sexual intercourse' (OE *(ge)māna*). Trevisa in the same context uses the phrase *wiþ oute mannys mone* to translate *non humano semine* (see *OED*, s.v. *mone*).

3. The scansion of the line is x/x/xx/xx/x/, which varies from that of l. 1 only at the beginning. This scansion assumes that the poet put the stress on the second syllable of *Gabriel*, which is how the musician set the word. In quantitative Latin verse both *Gabrĭhel* and *Gabrīhel* are found (Norberg, *Introduction*, p. 19); the latter of these would be stressed on the second syl-

lable. In ME verse the name is almost always stressed on the first and third syllables or on the first alone (in which case there sometimes occur the reduced forms *Gabrell, Gabryll, Gabrol*), but here stressing on the second seems clearly established. So, possibly or probably, in l. 2 of no. 92 in Carleton Brown's *Religious Lyrics of the XIVth Century*, and in l. 57 of no. 6 and l.5 of no. 71 of his *Religious Lyrics of the XVth Century*; the last of these three instances seems to me the likeliest. There are other instances in which the assumption that the name has its normal stressing involves a metrical inversion which, though acceptable, would be avoided if the stress were on the second syllable.

sooþli] *soþli* MS.
Gabriel] so MS; *r* expressed by writing *i* above *e*.

4. *moder*] *modur* MS, but the variant spelling seems to have been adopted because the scribe was altering what he had first written, I think *madin*.

may means 'maid', but is a distinct word (< OE *mæg*).

in] *no* MS, which is nonsense. The meaning is 'mother and maiden in one, alone', i.e. Mary alone is both mother and maiden.

5. *thee*] supplied; *om.* MS. The music requires an extra syllable, and the sense is also improved.

6. *werso*] *wereso* MS, but only two syllables are needed. The word is 'whereso', wheresoever, with the use of *w* for *wh* which is characteristic of this MS.

7. The second half-line has been entirely omitted, probably by homeoteleuton, since it must (like the first half-line) have ended with *-nd* because of the rhyme with l. 5. The obvious candidate is *both bifore and bihynd*, a common ME antithetical tag which both alliterates and rhymes and is of the same type as *in wel or in wo* in the previous line. It could hardly be more banal, but it is not too banal for this quatrain.

8. *stend*] *stende* MS. This form, not recorded in *OED*, is apparently an arbitrary alteration, for the sake of the internal rhyme with *wend* and *defend* in ll. 6 and 7, of *stent*, the South-eastern

form of the word *stint* 'halt, discontinue'. There has perhaps been confusion or blending with *stond* 'stand', of which the 3 sg. pres. indic. was *stent* in Southern dialects (including Kent, where *stent* was also the dialectal form of the word *stint*). An alternative explanation is that *stend* is meant as a form of the verb 'stand', in the sense 'remain motionless' and (in the context) 'fail to advance'; the variation in the 3 sg. pres. indic.

between *stent* (as in no. 29, l. 10) and *stont* (as in no. 30, l. 6) might seem to justify *stend* beside *stond* in the infinitive. But it is more likely that there has been confusion between *stond* and the *stent* form of *stint*, for the sense is more easily explicable from the latter.

no maner fo 'foes of no sort', a common ME idiom; but *fo* is a singular, as in the alternative construction *no manner of foe*.

33. Credo in Deum that ys

Credo in Deum þat ys
    withowt begynnyng and end,
þat mad*e* heven and erþ
    and al þat ys þeryn.
5   Joyful, we schold evermo*r*e
    [owr Lord God havyn] in mynd,
for he ys [war and] wys;
    [he] bryng us to parfyt blys.

All owr lyf ys meynd wyth wo
10   werso-ever þat we go,
    wyl we beeþ in þys leed;
but in God alon*e*, ywys,
    þer nys no ful parfyt blys,
        hoso tak ry3t good heed.

COMMENTARY

Source: Cambridge, University Library, MS Additional 5943, f. 168ᵛ.

On the religious songs of the Cambridge MS see the introductory note to no. 31 above. A clear Southernism in the language of this song is the plural inflexion *-þ* in *beeþ* (l. 11); the MS also uses the Southern spelling *uy* for the vowel of this word (see the note below).

The first stanza is unrhymed, unless an imperfect rhyme was intended in ll. 7–8 between *wys* 'wise' and *blys* 'bliss', and the scribe has left so many words out that all one can do is to fudge up the metrical rhythm in such a way that the words will fit the notes. Words in square brackets are supplied.

NOTES

1. *ys*] *y* MS.
2. *without*] *wtowt* MS.

4. *þeryn*] so MS; previously read as *hyn*, but the first letter is *y* (for *þ*) with the abbreviation-mark for *er* above it.

5. *Joyful*] so MS as I read it; previously read as *scyful*, which is arrant nonsense.
schold] *scolde* MS; previously read as *stolde*.

6. For the phrase *have in mind* cf. no. 32, l. 5. But the reconstruction of the first part of the line is necessarily entirely conjectural.

7. *ys war and wys*] *y wys* MS, with an abnormal curving stroke over the first *y*. Though the scribe wrongly writes *y* for *ys* in l. 1 of this song, it looks as though he thought that what was required here was the adverb *ywys* 'certainly', commonly written as if it were two words (cf. l. 12 below, where *ywys*

rhymes with *blys*). Perhaps he thought that the sense here should be 'for he indeed bring[s] us to perfect bliss'. But he writes *bryng*, not *bryngeþ* (*bryngyt*, &c.). One could reconstruct the text as:

    for he [may wel,] ywys,
    bryng us to parfyt blys.

But it would be contrary to the evident plan of the first stanza to rhyme ll. 7 and 8 together; more importantly, this reconstruction would leave l.8 lacking an unstressed syllable at the beginning which the music, and the partial metrical parallel with l. 4, both require. It seems more likely that the scribe has been confused by ll. 12-13 than that the same rhyme *ywys : blys* was used twice in so short a poem. In the reconstruction adopted, *war and wys* means 'prudent and wise'; it was a common alliterative tag.

8. *he bryng* 'may he bring'. For the insertion of *he* see the preceding note.
parfyt 'perfect', a form derived from OF in which the vowel of the second syllable was probably long (ME ī). The MS has here the spelling *parfyth*, and in l. 13 *parfy3t* (with the conventional abbreviation for *per-* or *par-*). The endings *-yth* and *-y3t* are variant spellings used in this MS for such words as *right* spelt *ryth* or *ry3t*; their use in the word *parfit* 'perfect' is due to 'inverted' or 'reverse' spelling and shows that the spirant represented by *3* (*gh*) had become silent, in the scribe's speech, in such words as *right*.
blys] The scribe writes the word twice, first at the point in the music to which his omissions in the previous lines had brought it, and then at (or at least near) the proper place, at the end of the music of the first stanza (which is clearly marked in the musical notation).

9. *All*] *al le* MS, clearly divided and set to different notes; the scribe obviously thought the word was two syllables, but he was certainly wrong. (i) The metrical scheme requires a monosyllable, so that the rhythm of l. 9 may match that of l. 12, set to the same notes. (ii) Even when final *-e* was regularly pronounced (as it was not by this author), it would normally elide before *owr*. (iii) Though in the later fourteenth century *allë* could be used with singular nouns, it was not so used when an unstressed article or pronoun came between the adjective and the noun, as *owr* does here. Both grammar and metre require uninflected *all*.

meynd] *megnid* MS, quite clearly. The scribe was evidently hesitating between *meynd* (which the metre requires) and *mengid,* alternative forms of the p.p. of *meng* 'mingle'.

10. *werso-ever*] *wer so hever* MS.

11. *wyl* (so MS) 'while'.

beeþ] *buyþ* MS. The *-þ* is the present tense plural inflexion in Southern dialects. The *uy* is a Southern spelling for the vowel developed from OE *ēo,* but the evidence is that the author did not use this pronunciation (cf. the notes to no. 27, l. 5, and no. 30, l. 4); in this very line *leed* (spelt *led* by the scribe himself),

which has OE *ēo,* rhymes with *heed* < OE *hēdan.* As the rhyming is on the East Midland development of OE *ēo* to ME *ē,* I normalize the spelling to *ee.*

leed] *led* MS (and not *bed,* as previously read, which is nonsense). This is the word entered by *OED* as *lede* < OE *lēode* (German *leute*), meaning 'people', 'nation', and hence 'land'; here *in þis leed* means 'on this earth'.

The scansion of this line, and of l. 14, is /x/ /x/, with clashing stresses at mid-line, and this is evidently not due to corruption but as the author intended; for the composer deals with the situation by interposing a rest between the clashing stresses.

12. *but* 'except' (*Bot* MS).

13. *nys* 'is not'.

parfyt] see note to l. 8 above.

14. *hoso* 'whoso', but here used, as often in ME, to mean 'if anyone' and therefore followed by the subjunctive verb *take.*

tak] so MS, showing loss of final *-e* (in this instance the singular of the present subjunctive). But the vowel is long (ME *ā*), not short *ă*.

heed] *hed* MS.

Additional Note on Song No. 26

The word-text of *Danger me hath, unskylfuly*, as given by the scribe, is incomplete. The reconstruction proposed above (pp. 212-4) assumes that he gives only the first stanza of a two-stanza song with variable refrain. A more conservative reconstruction would be as a song of the AB^1B^2 type frequent in the Winchester collection. This would conform to the scribe's way of setting out the music of this and other pieces in the MS; it would also obviate the necessity of assuming that the last two lines of each stanza (the 'refrain lines') of the suggested two-stanza version were meant to be sung twice, a device which would be unusual in the music of the time. If the song followed the AB^1B^2 pattern, the scribe's first five lines must be the A section and his last two the B^1 section, and he has omitted the words of the B^2 section. If so, it consisted of two lines only, identical in syllable-count and rhythm with the scribe's last two lines (since the B^2 section goes to the same music, except for the *clos*, as the B^1 section) and almost certainly rhyming with them (since this is normal in AB^1B^2 songs). Probably also, if two lines have been omitted, there was something about their word-text to provoke omission, e.g. the second may have resembled the last line actually written by the scribe so closely that it either invited purely accidental 'eye-skip' or confused his mind. Finally of course the two omitted lines would have completed the sense of the song in an acceptable way. The version that follows is based on these assumptions.

Danger me haþ, unskylfuly;
  y kan noȝt do but let hyt pass
and lyv*e* boþe glad and myryly.
  But hit ys noȝt as hyt was
and þe blam*e* ys noȝt yn me.

Fórsuþ, hyt ys herë wyll,
  but yf y myȝt more þan y may.
[Yet y may her anger styll,
  yf but mor*e* þan y myȝt y may.]

The last four lines would mean: 'Indeed, it is *her* will, unless I could [do] more than I can. Yet I may appease her anger, if only I can [do] more than I could.' This is no worse sense than in other songs in this MS. The first of the supplied lines is mere guess-work, but in Chaucer the commonest rhyme for the noun *wille* is *stille* and both he and Gower use the verb *stille* 'quieten, appease, etc.' The second deliberately uses the words of the scribe's final line, but in different order and sense; the rhyme-word is unchanged, but in medieval verse identical rhymes were allowed.

This reconstruction can easily be fitted to the music-text as set out on p. 281. The first seven lines are the same as in stanza 1 of the suggested two-stanza version (bars 1-29); the two added lines go to the repeat of bars 22-7 plus the *clos* (bars 30-31). No further word-text is assumed in this version, which is set out in full on p. 291.

MUSIC

Edited by
F. Ll. **HARRISON**

MUSIC

Note on the Transcriptions

In the cases of some of the pieces that follow, the original notation may allow of interpretation in one of two ways: as mensural (i.e. with definite note-lengths of fixed proportional value), or as non-mensural (i.e. with approximately and flexibly equal note-lengths, as in plainsong). In the past, many editors, following the example of Friedrich Gennrich in his transcription of *troubadour* and *trouvère* songs, have almost invariably transcribed in mensural notation (according to the 'rhythmic modes') songs whose original notation is susceptible of either interpretation. In an important recent study of some of these melodies and their relation to the poems, Hendrik van de Werf's *The chansons of the troubadours and trouvères* (Utrecht, 1972), the writer has provided 'justification for rejecting the usual unproven and ineffective theory that all chansons of the troubadours and trouvères were meant to be performed in some form of fixed and regular meter', and has found 'an abundance of reasons for assuming that the vast majority of the chansons were performed in what may be called a *free rhythm* largely dictated by the flow and the meaning of the text' (p. 44). The present editor's belief that this is also true of many monophonic (and some polyphonic) songs in other repertories has been confirmed by the experience of editing these songs in collaboration with their text-editor.

Even where a non-mensural interpretation has been adopted, the method of transcription has varied with various editors. For the transcription of items whose notation is interpreted here as non-mensural (these are nos. 1-3, 4, 7, 8, 10-12 and 14), the following procedures have been adopted:

1. All notes are notated as quavers, whatever may be the note-shape in the original.

2. The quavers are grouped, by bracing, in such a way that the first note of each brace has a stressed syllable in the text.

3. A separate quaver at the beginning of a text-line is unstressed; a separate quaver at the end of a verse-line is stressed.

4. The sign x above a note shows that its syllable is unstressed.

5. The sign / above a note shows that its syllable is stressed. Exceptionally in no. 8, on account of differences in note-lengths between the two parts, only those syllables are to be stressed which have a stroke above their note(s).

6. A slur, in the pieces mentioned, is used to indicate that the notes under the slur are ligatured in the original notation. It does not have its modern use of showing a number of notes to be sung to one syllable. No. 8 is again an exception, for the reason given.

7. Consequently, a syllable under the first of a number of notes should be continued until the next syllable occurs, however the notes concerned may be grouped by slurs.

8. A comma above the staff in nos. 1-3 indicates a half-line, where a slight break may be made, without necessarily taking a breath.

It is clearly of the utmost importance to the performance of these songs that singers bring to their performance an understanding of their poetic as well as musical background, structure and meaning, along with the intention to project these factors in an auditory presentation that is as meaningful as possible.

The words underlaid beneath the music are exactly as established by the literary editor, except that in no. 13 *(Edi be thu, heven-queene)*, for the reason given on p. 168 above, the final *e* of certain words is treated as unsounded, though it is marked as sounded in the literary text. Also, for practical reasons of legibility and spacing, the editors have modified slightly the accentuation marks and the punctuation used in the literary texts, replacing dashes, for example, with other punctuation.

The following songs have been recorded on Argo record ZRG 5443: nos 1, 5, 8, 9, 11, 13 and 15 (ii) (first version).

1. SAINTE MARIE VIERGENE

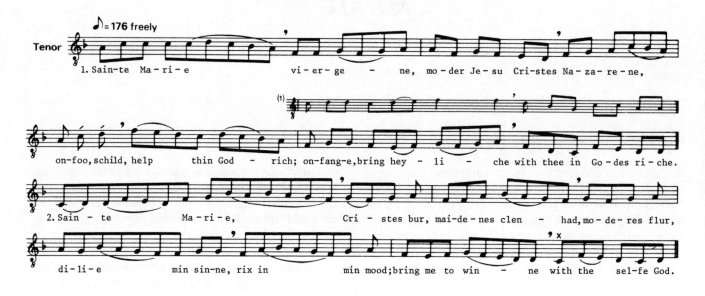

2. CRIST AND SAINTE MARIE[2]

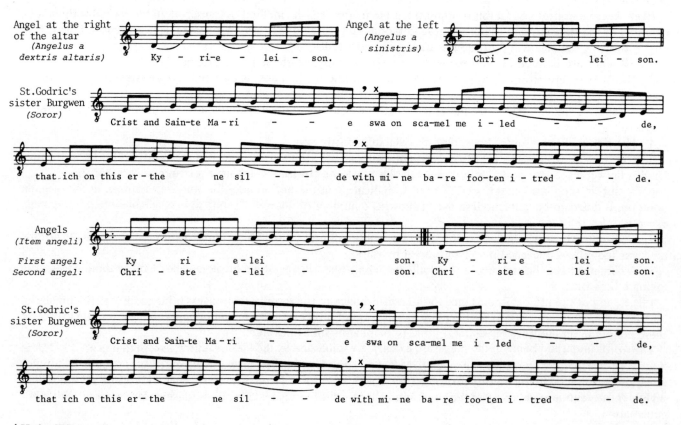

[1] Harley MS.

[2] This song may be sung by female voices an octave higher throughout.

3. SAINTE NICHOLAS, GODES DRUTH

Tenor or Baritone

Sain-te Ni - cho - las, Go - des druth, tym - bre us fai-e — re scoo-ne hus.

At thi bur-the, at thi ba-re, Sain-te Ni - cho-las, bring us wel tha-re.

4. (i) EYNS NE SOY KE PLEYNTE FU
4. (ii) AR NE KUTH ICH SORGHE NON

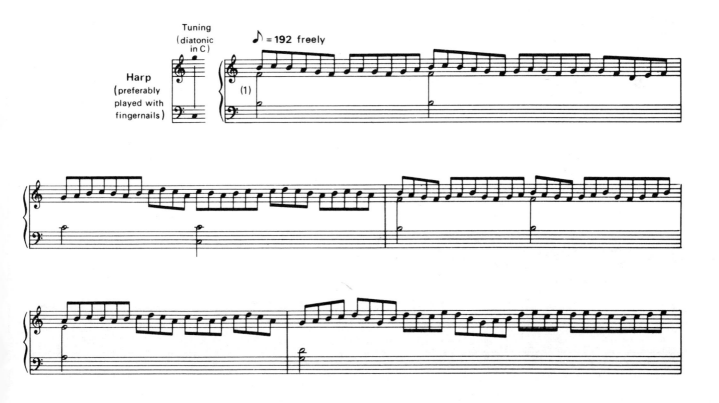

---

[1] Minims in the harp part should be allowed to sound through the quavers written above them.

230

Tenor

♪ = 150 freely (throughout)

(1)
(1a) *English.* Ar ne kuth ich sor-ghe non, nu ich moot i - ma-ne mi mon;
French. Eyns ne soy ke pleyn-te fu, o - re, pleyn dan - gus-se, tres - su;

Harp

♪ = 192 freely (in interludes)

kar-ful, wel sor ich si - che.
trop ai mal e con-trey-re.

---

[1] The texts are alternatives (both are in the MS); the harp interludes are the same for both.

(2b) *English.* Ich and mi-ne fee-ren su-me (God wot ich ne ly-ghe noht)

for o-thre han mis - nu - me been in thys pri-sun i-broht. (2b) *French.* Jo e mi au-tre cum-pai-gnun

(Deus en set la ve-ri-te) tut pur au-tri mes - pri-sun su-mes a hun-te li - vre.

234

238

4. *ADDENDUM:* PLANCTUS ANTE NESCIA
(Godefroy of St. Victor)

♪ = 150 freely

E / R / M

1a. Plan-ctus an - te ne-sci - a, plan-ctu las-sor an - xi - a, cru-ci-or do - lo - re;
b. or - bat or - bem ra-di - o, me Ju-dae-a fi - li - o, gau-di-o, dul - co - re.

2a. Fí-li, dul-cor u - ni-ce, sin-gu - la-re gau - di-um, ma-trem flen-tem re-spi-ce con-fe-rens so - la - ti-um.
b. Pectus, men-tem, lu - mi-na torquent tu-a vul - ne-ra; quæ ma - ter, quæ fe - mi - na tam fe-lix, tam mi - se-ra!

3a. Flos flo-rum, dux mo-rum, ve - ni-æ ve-na, quam gra-vis in cla-vis est ti-bi poe - na!
b. Proh do - lor! Hinc co-lor ef - fu-git o-ris; hinc ru-it, hinc flu-it un - da cru-o - ris.

4a. O quam se-ro de - di-tus, quam ci-to me de - se-ris! O quam di - gne ge - ni-tus, quam ab-je-cte mo - re-ris!
4b. O quis a-mor cor-po-ris ti-bi fe-cit spo - li-a! O quam dul-cis pi - gno-ris quam a-ma - ra præ - mi-a!

E = Évreux MSS; R = Rouen MS; M = Paris MS. See page 296.

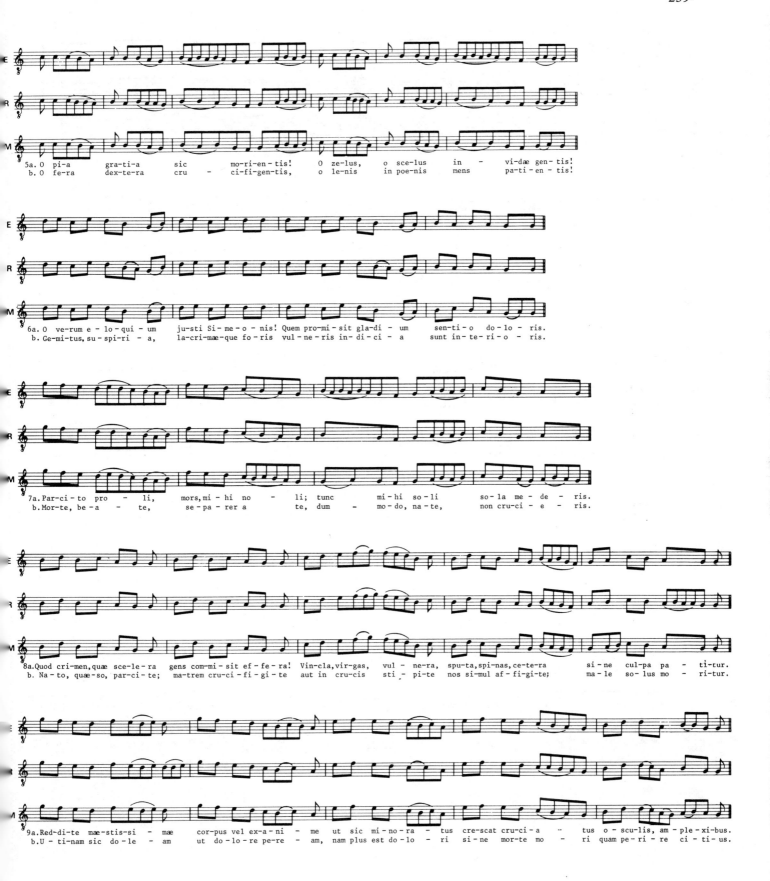

5a. O pi-a gra-ti-a sic mo-ri-en-tis! O ze-lus, o sce-lus in - vi-dæ gen - tis!
b. O fe-ra dex-te-ra cru - ci-fi-gen-tis, o le-nis in poe-nis mens pa-ti - en - tis!

6a. O ve-rum e - lo-qui - um ju-sti Si-me-o - nis! Quem pro-mi-sit gla-di - um sen-ti-o do-lo - ris.
b. Ge-mi-tus, su-spi-ri - a, la-cri-mæ-que fo-ris vul-ne-ris in-di-ci - a sunt in-te-ri-o - ris.

7a. Par-ci-to pro - li, mors, mi-hi no - li; tunc mi-hi so-li so-la me - de-ris.
b. Mor-te, be-a - te, se-pa-rer a te, dum - mo-do, na-te, non cru-ci - e - ris.

8a. Quod cri-men, quæ sce-le-ra gens com-mi-sit ef - fe-ra! Vin-cla, vir-gas, vul - ne-ra, spu-ta, spi-nas, ce-te-ra si - ne cul-pa pa - ti-tur.
b. Na-to, quæ-so, par-ci-te; ma-trem cru-ci-fi-gi-te aut in cru-cis sti - pi-te nos si-mul af-fi-gi-te; ma-le so-lus mo - ri-tur.

9a. Red-di-te mæ-stis-si - mæ cor-pus vel ex-a-ni - me ut sic mi-no-ra - tus cre-scat cru-ci-a - tus o-scu-lis, am-ple-xi-bus.
b. U - ti-nam sic do-le - am ut do-lo-re pe-re - am, nam plus est do-lo - ri si-ne mor-te mo - ri quam pe-ri-re ci - ti-us.

10a.Quid stu-pes,gens mi - se-ra, ter-ram se mo - ve - re, ob-scu-ra-ri si-de-ra, lan-gui-dos lu - ge - re?
 b. So - lem pri-vas lu - mi-ne, quo-mo-do lu - ce - ret? ae-grum me-di - ca-mi-ne, un-de con - va - le - ret?

11a.Ho - mi - ci-dam li - be-ras, Je-sum das sup-pli-ci - o; ma-le pa - cem to - le-ras, ve-ni-et se - di - ti - o.
 b.Fa - mis,cae-dis,pe - sti-um sci-es do-cta pon-de - re Je-sum ti - bi mor - tu-um Bar-ra-bam-que vi - ve - re.

12a.Gens cae - ca,gens fle-bi-lis, a - ge poe-ni-ten - ti-am, dum ti-bi fle-xi - bi-lis Je-sus est ad ve-ni-am.
 b.Quos fe - ci-sti, fon-ti-um pro-sint ti-bi flu - mi-na, si-tim se-dant o - mni - um, cun-cta la - vant cri-mi-na.

13a.Fle-te,Si - on fi - li-ae, tan-tae gra-tae gra-ti-ae (ju-ve-nis an-gu - sti-ae si-bi sunt de-li-ci-ae), pro ve-stris of - fen - sis.
 b.In am-ple-xus ru - i-te, dum pen-det in sti-pi-te, mu-tu-is am-ple - xi-bus; se pa-rat a-man-ti-bus brac-chi-is pro-ten - sis.

14. In hoc so-lo gau - de - o, quod pro vo-bis do - le - o. Vi-cem,quae-so, red-di-te: ma-tris dam - pnum plan - gi - te.

241

5. MIRI IT IS WHILE SUMER ILAST

6a. MAN MAI LONGE LIVES WEENE

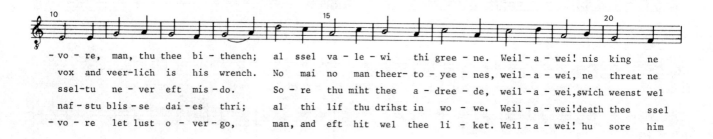

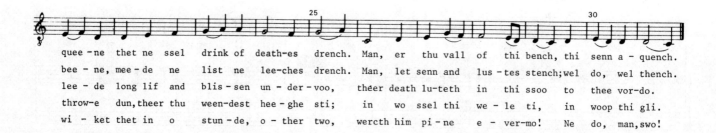

6b. ON HIR IS MI LIF ILONG[1]

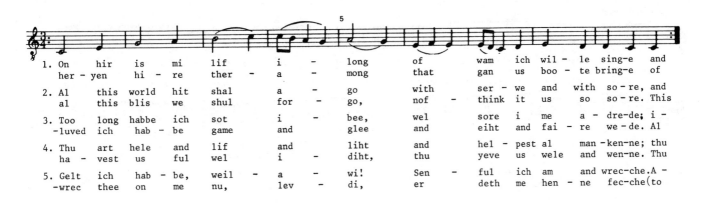

1. On hir is mi lif i - long of wam ich wil - le sing-e and
   her - yen hi - re ther - a - mong that gan us boo - te bring-e of
2. Al this world hit shal a - go with ser - we and with so - re, and
   al this blis we shul for - go, nof - think it us so so - re. This
3. Too long habbe ich sot i - bee, wel sore i me a - dre-de; i -
   -luved ich hab - be game and glee and eiht and fai - re we - de. Al
4. Thu art hele and lif and liht and hel - pest al man - ken-ne; thu
   ha - vest us ful wel i - diht, thu yeve us wele and wen-ne. Thu
5. Gelt ich hab - be, weil - a - wi! Sen - ful ich am and wrec-che. A -
   -wrec thee on me nu, lev - di, er deth me hen - ne fec-che (to

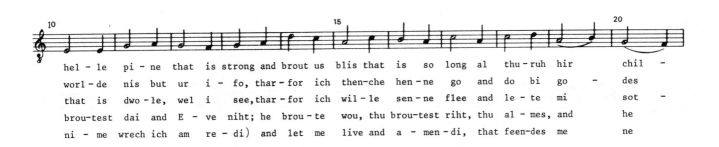

hel - le pi - ne that is strong and brout us blis that is so long al thu-ruh hir chil -
worl - de nis but ur i - fo, thar - for ich then-che hen - ne go and do bi go - des
that is dwo - le, wel i see, thar - for ich wil - le sen - ne flee and le - te mi sot -
brou-test dai and E - ve niht; he brou - te wou, thu brou-test riht, thu al - mes, and he
ni - me wrech ich am re - di) and let me live and a - men-di, that feen-des me ne

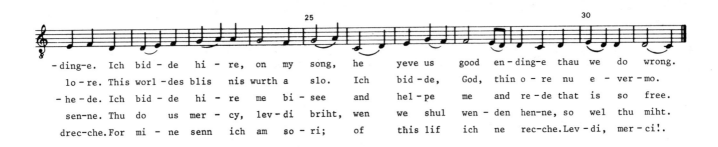

-ding-e. Ich bid - de hi - re, on my song, he yeve us good en - ding-e thau we do wrong.
lo - re. This worl - des blis nis wurth a slo. Ich bid - de, God, thin o - re nu e - ver - mo.
- he-de. Ich bid - de hi - re me bi - see and hel - pe me and re - de that is so free.
sen-ne. Thu do us mer - cy, lev-di briht, wen we shul wen - den hen-ne, so wel thu miht.
drec-che. For mi - ne senn ich am so - ri; of this lif ich ne rec-che. Lev - di, mer - ci!.

---

[1] The words of this song have been matched to the tune of no. 6a by the editors.

7. WORLDES BLIS NE LAST NO THROWE

♩ = **184** freely

1. Worl-des   blis ne last no   throw-e;   it went and   wit a - wey a - non.
2. Al the   blis of this-se   li - ve   thu shalt, man, en - den   in - e   weep:
3. Al shal   gon that man heer   ow - eth;   al hit shal wen-den   in - to   naut.

The lan-ger that ich hit   i - know-e,   the lass ich fin-de   pris thar - on;
of hus and hom, of child   and   wi - ve.   A, sa - li   man, nim   thar-of   keep!
The man that heer no good   ne   sow-eth,   wan o - thre repe, he   wurth bi - kaut.

for al   it   is   i-meind mid   ca - re,   mid ser - wen and mid   e - vel   fa - re,
For thu   shalt   al   bi - le - ven   hee-re   thet eigh-te war-of   lord thu   wee-re;
Thinc, man,   for - thi,   wils-tu hast   migh-te,   that thu thi gel-tes   heer a - righ-te

and at - te   la - ste povre and   ba - re   it lat man, wan it ginth   a - gon.
wan thu list, man, u - pon the   bee-re   and slapst that swi-the dree - ri   slep,
and wer - che good bi dai and   nigh-te   ar than thu be of li - ve   laut.

Al the blis this heer and   tha-re   bi - lucth   at en - de   weep and   mon.
shal-tu have with thee no   fee-re   but thi - ne wer-kes   on a   hep.
Thu nost wan - ne Crist ur drigh-te   thee o - sketh that he   hath bi - taut.

4. Man, wi   se-stu thout and   her - te   o worl-des blis that   nout ne   last?

Wi thol-stu that thee sof - te   smer-te   for thing   that is un - ste-de - fast?

Thu lic - kest hu - ni of thorn, i-wis,   that sest thi lu - ve   o worl - des blis,

for ful of bit-ter-nes-se   it is.   Ful so - re   thu might been   of - gast

that heer de - spen-dest eight a - mis,   thar-thurw been in-to   hel-le   cast.

8. FUWELES IN THE FRITH

9. PERSPICE, CHRISTICOLA / [RESURREXIT DOMINUS]
SUMER IS ICUMEN IN / SING CUCCU, NU[2]

[1] A stressed note or group is indicated by a stroke; notes or groups without a stroke are unstressed.

[2] See note on page 250 for ways of performance.

[3] The Latin text is supplied; these parts may be vocalized on the syllable *o*.

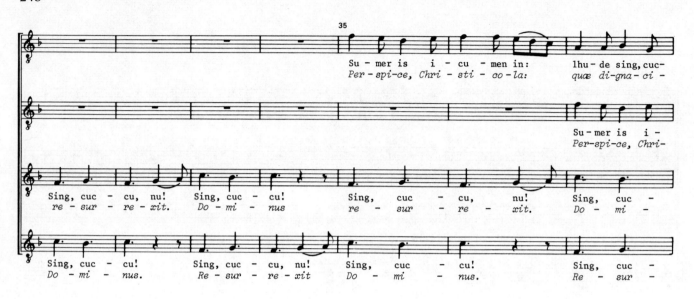

This transcription may be used for performance in any of the following ways:
1. In four parts to the Latin text, continuing without pause to performance in six parts to the English text. The singers of the two lowest parts should change text at bar 31.
2. In the same way with the English text before the Latin, the singers of the two lowest parts changing at bar 31.
3. In four parts to either text, ending by observing the bracketed pause in bar 30.
4. In six parts to either text, beginning with bar 31.

10. (i) STABAT JUXTA CHRISTI CRUCEM

5a. Os ve-ren-dum li-tum spu-tis et fla-gel-lis ru-pta cu-tis et tot ri-vi san-gui-nis;

Arsenal MS

5b. pro-bra, ri-sus, et quae re-stant or-bi-ta-ti te-la præ-stant et do-lo-ri vir-gi-nis.

6a. Tem-pus, na-cta trux na-tu-ra, nunc re-po-scit su-a ju-ra; nunc do-lo-res a-cu-it.

6b. Nunc ex-tor-quet cum u-su-ra ge-mi-tus quos pa-ri-tu-ra na-tu-ra de-ti-nu-it.

7a. Nunc, nunc pa-rit, nunc scit ve-re quam ma-ter-num sit do-le-re, quam a-ma-rum pa-re-re;

7b. nunc se do-lor or-bi-ta-ti di-la-tus in par-tu na-ti præ-sen-tat in fu-ne-re.

8a. Nunc fit ma-ter, sed mæ-ro-ris, ser-vat ta-men hic pu-do-ris vir-gi-na-lis gra-ti-am;

8b. nam pu-di-cos ge-stus fo-ris non de-flo-rat vis do-lo-ris in-tus u-rens an-xi-am.

9a. Tri-du-a-nus er-go fle-tus læ-ta de-mum est de-le-tus sur-gen-tis vi-cto-ri-a;

9b. læ-ta lu-cet spes do-len-ti, na-to nam-que re-sur-gen-ti con-re-sur-gent gau-di-a.

10a. Chri-sti no-vus hic na-ta-lis for-mam par-tus vir-gi-na-lis clau-so ser-vat tu-mu-lo;

10b. hinc pro-ces-sit, hinc sur-re-xit, hinc et in-de Chri-stus e-xit in-ta-cto si-gna-cu-lo.

11a. E-ja ma-ter, e-ja læ-ta! Fle-tus tu-i nox ex-ple-ta lu-ce-scit in gau-di-um.

11b. No-stræ quo-que læ-tum ma-ne no-cti plus quam tri-du-a-næ tu-um red-de fi-li-um.

A - - men.

10. (ii) [STOOD THE MODER UNDER ROODE]

stood ho thee-re neeh.

♪=184 freely

5a. That leef-li leer with spa - del schent, that fai-re fel with scur-ges rent: the blood out stre-med o - ver-al.

5b. Skarn, up-braid, and scha - mes spee - che, al hit was to sor-wes ee-che: i wa thu was bi - lu-ken al.

6a. In that blis - ful bar-nes bir-de wrang wes wroht to wim-me - ne wir-de, ac kin-de cra - ved nou the riht.

6b. Then-ne thu looh, ac nou thu weep; thi wa wes wa-ken that ten-ne sleep: chil-ding-pi - nes has tee nou piht.

7a. Nou thu moo-stes, la-ve-di, le - re wim-me-ne wa that bar-nes be - - re, tha bit-ter and ta ba-le thraw-es;

7b. for in his ded the wa thu yul-de in chil-ding that tu tho-le schul - de thurh mod-res kin-de-li-ke law-es.

8a. Ah, lav-di, thah thu wang-es we - te, thah thee wer wa at u - ni-mee-te, thi la-tes wee-ren la-ste-les;

8b. thi weep ne wem-me - de noht thin hew that ma-de thi leer ful louk and lew; swa sa-ri wim-man ne - ver nes.

9a. Al thi ka-re wes o - ver-cu-men, the thrid-de dai thi joi-e cu - men, ded and de - vel dri-ven doun,

9b. hwen-ne thi su-ne up-ri-sen wes to thi-ne we - le and u - re pes; blis he broht in ilk a toun.

10a. Thi lu-ve-su-nes up-ri - sing wes sel - li lik to his bir-ding; bi-twee-ne twa is li-tel shad.

10b. For swa glem gli-dis thurh the glas of thi-ne bo-di born he was, and thurh the ha-le thurh he glad.

11a. Mil-de mo-der, mai-den a, of al thi ka-re coom thu tha hwen-ne thi su-ne ri-sen wes.

11b. Lav-di, bring us out of wa, of sin-ne, of sor-we, of sich al-swa, to blis-se that is en - de-les.

A - men.

11. STOND WEL, MODER, UNDER ROODE

♪ = 184 freely

1a. 'Stond wel, mo-der, un-der roo-de, bi-hold thi child with gla-de moo-de; bli-the mo-der migh-tu be.'

1b. 'Sun, hu mai i bli-the ston-de? I see thi feet, i see thin hon-de nai-led to the har-de tree.'

2a. 'Mo-der, do wey thi wee - ping - e; i thole this ded for man-nes thing-e; for ow-ne gil-te tho-li non.'

2b. 'Sun, i feel the de - de - stun - de; the swerd is at min her-te grun-de that me bi-high-te Si-me - on.'

3a. 'Mo-der, reu up - on thi be - ren! Thu wash a - wey tho bloo-di te - ren that do me wer - se than mi ded.'

3b. 'Sun, hu might i te-res wer - ne? I see tho bloo-di floo-des er - ne ut of thin her - te to mi feet.'

4a. 'Mo-der, nu i mai thee sey-e, be - ter is that ich o - ne dey - e than al man-kin to hel-le go.'

4b. 'Sun, i see thi bo-di swung-en, thi brest, thin hond, thi foot thurgh-stung - en; no sel-li nis thou me be wo.'

5a. 'Mo-der, if i dar thee tel - le, if i ne'dey, thu gost to hel-le; i thole this ded for thi-ne sa-ke.'

5b. 'Su-ne, thu beest me so min - de; ne wit me nought, it is mi kin-de that i for thee this sor-we ma-ke.'

6a. 'Mo-der, mer-ci; let me dey-e for A-dam ut of hel-le bey-e and man-kin that is for-lo-ren.'

6b. 'Su-ne, wat sal me to re-de? Thi pi-ne pi-neth me to de-de; let me dey-e thee bi-fo-ren.'

7a. 'Mo-der, nu tarst thu might le-re wat pi-ne thole that chil-dre be - re, wat sor-we have that child for-gon.'

7b. 'Sun, i wot, i kan thee tel-le: bu-ten it be the pine of hel - le, mo-re sor-we ne wot i non.'

8a. 'Mo-der, reu of mo-der ka-re, nu thu wost of mo - der fa - re, thou thu be cle-ne mai-den-man.'

8b. 'Su-ne, help at al-le nee-de al-le tho that to me gree-de, mai-den and wif and fool wim-man.'

9a. 'Mo-der, mai i no leng dwel-le, the time is cum i fare to hel-le; the thrid-de day i rise up-on.'

9b. 'Sun, i wil-le with thee fun-de. I dey, i-wis, of thi-ne wun-de; so reu-ful ded was ne-ver non.'

10a. Wan he ros, than fel thi sor-we; thi blis-se sprong the thrid-de mor - we; wel bli-the mo-der wer thu tho.

10b. Mo-der, for that il-ke blis-se, bi-seech ur god ur sin-nes lis - se; thu be ur sheeld a-yen ur fo.

11a. Blis-sed be thu, queen of hev-ne; bring us ut of hel-le lev - ne thurgh thi dee - re su - nes might.

11b. Mo-der, for that high-e bloo-de that he shad up - on the roo - de led us in-to he - ven - light.

A - men.

12. JESU CRISTES MILDE MODER

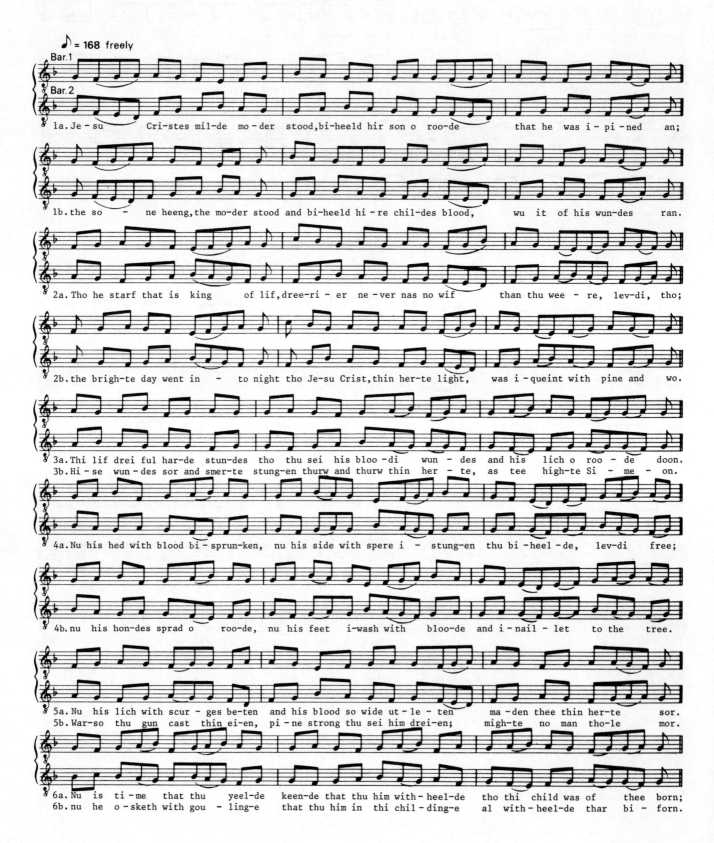

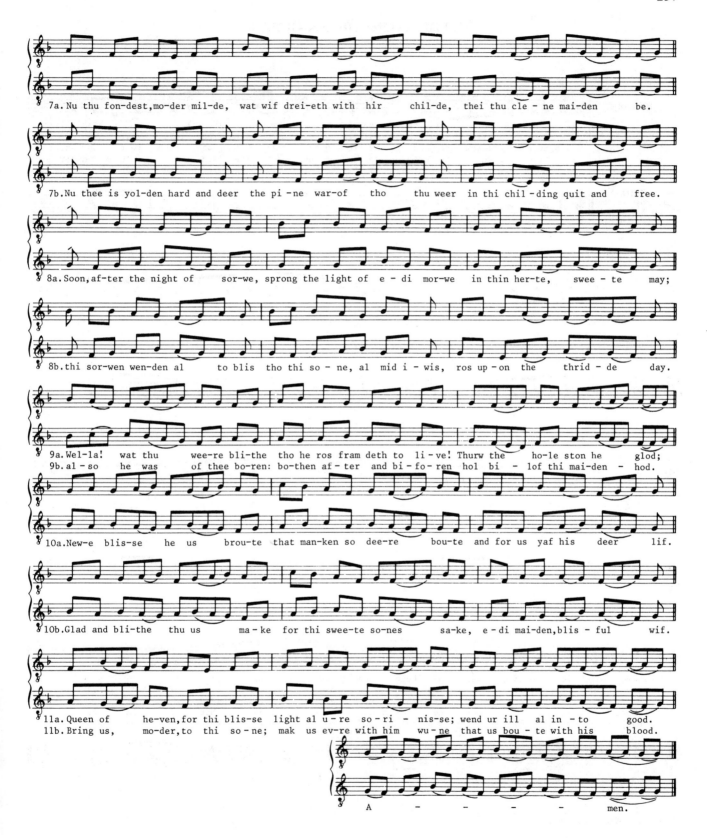

7a. Nu thu fon-dest, mo-der mil-de, wat wif drei-eth with hir chil-de, thei thu cle - ne mai-den be.

7b. Nu thee is yol-den hard and deer the pi-ne war-of tho thu weer in thi chil-ding quit and free.

8a. Soon, af-ter the night of sor-we, sprong the light of e - di mor-we in thin her-te, swee - te may;

8b. thi sor-wen wen-den al to blis tho thi so - ne, al mid i - wis, ros up - on the thrid - de day.

9a. Wel-la! wat thu wee-re bli-the tho he ros fram deth to li - ve! Thurw the ho-le ston he glod;

9b. al - so he was of thee bo-ren: bo-then af - ter and bi - fo - ren hol bi - lof thi mai-den - hod.

10a. New-e blis-se he us brou-te that man-ken so dee-re bou-te and for us yaf his deer lif.

10b. Glad and bli-the thu us ma - ke for thi swee-te so-nes sa-ke, e - di mai-den, blis - ful wif.

11a. Queen of he-ven, for thi blis-se light al u - re so - ri - nis-se; wend ur ill al in - to good.

11b. Bring us, mo-der, to thi so - ne; mak us ev-re with him wu - ne that us bou - te with his blood.

A - - - - men.

258

13. EDI BE THU, HEVEN–QUEENE

14. THE MILDE LOMB, ISPRAD O ROODE

1. The mil-de Lomb, i - sprad o roo - - de, heng bi-ur-nen al o bloo - de
for ur gel-te, for ur goo - de, for he ne gel-te nev-re nout.

2. Feaw of his him warn bi-le - - ved; dred hem had him al bi - re - ved
wan he se-yen he - re he - ved to so schan-ful deth i - brout.

3. His mo-der, that him stood bi-si - - den, ne let no ter on o - ther bi - den
wan hoe sei hir child bi - ti - den swich pine, and dei-en gel-te - les.

4. Saint Jo - han, that was him dee - - re, on o - ther halve him stood eek fee - re
and bi - held with mur - ne chee - re his mai-ster that him loved and ches.

5. Sore and hard he was i - swung - - en, feet and han-des thurw i - stung-en;
ac mest of all his oth - re wun - den him ded his mod-res ser-we wo.

6. In al his pine, in al his wra - - ke that he drei for man-nes sa - ke,
he sei his mo-der ser - we ma - ke; wel reu-ful-lich he spac hir to.

260

7. He sei-de, "Wi - man lou! me hee - - re, thi child, that thu to man - ne bee - re.

With-u - ten sor and weep thu wee - re tho ich was of thee i - born;

8. ac nu thu must thi pi-ne drei - - en wan thu sicst me with thin ei - en

pi - ne thole o rood, and dei - en to he-len man that was for - lorn."

9. Saint Jo - han the van-ge-li - ste hir un-der-stood thurw hes of Cri - ste;

fair he kept hir, and bi - wi - ste, and ser-ved hir fram hand to foot.

10. Reu - ful is the me-ne-ging - e of this deth and tis de - part-ing-e;

thar-in is blis meind with wee - ping - e, for thar-thurw us kam al-le boot.

11. He that starf in u - re keen - de leve us so been thar-of meen - de

that he give us at - ten een - de that he hath us to i - bout.

12. Mils-ful mo - der, mai-den clee - ne, mak on us thi mil-ce see - ne

and bring us thurw thi swee - te bee - ne to the blis that fail-leth nout.

15. (i) ANGELUS AD VIRGINEM

♩. = 80

1. An - ge - lus ad vir - gi - nem sub - in - trans in con - cla - ve, vir - gi - nis for -
2. "Quo - mo - do con - ci - pe - rem quæ vi - rum non co - gno - vi? Qua - li - ter in -
3. Ad hæc, vir - go no - bi - lis, re - spon - dens, in - quit e - i, "Ser - vu - la sum
4. An - ge - lus dis - pa - ru - it et sta - tim pu - el - la - ris u - te - rus in -
5. E - ya, ma - ter do - mi - ni, quæ pa - cem red - di - di - sti an - ge - lis et

- mi - di - nem de - mul - cens, in - quit "A - ve! A - ve re - gi - na vir - gi -
-frin - ge - rem quod fir - ma men - te vo - vi?" "Spi - ri - tus san - cti gra - ci -
hu - mi - lis o - mni - po - ten - tis de - i; ti - bi, cæ - le - sti nun - ci -
- tu - mu - it vi par - tus sa - lu - ta - ris. Qui, cir - cum - da - tus u - te -
ho - mi - ni cum Chri - stum ge - nu - i - sti, tu - um ex - o - ra fi - li -

- num! Cæ - li ter - ræ - que do - mi - num con - ci - pi - es et pa - ri - es in - ta - cta sa -
- a per - fi - ci - et hæc o - mni - a. Ne ti - me - as sed gau - de - as se - cu - ra, quod
- o, tan - ti se - cre - ti con - sci - o, con - sen - ti - ens et cu - pi - ens vi - de - re fa -
- ro no - vem men - si - um nu - me - ro, hinc ex - i - it et in - i - it con - fli - ctum, af -
- um ut se no - bis pro - pi - ci - um ex = hi - be - at et de - le - at pec - ca - ta, præ -

- lu - tem ho - mi - num, tu, por - ta cæ - li fa - cta, me - de - la cri - mi - num."
ca - sti - mo - ni - a ma - ne - bit in te pu - ra de - i po - ten - ci - a."
-ctum quod au - di - o, pa - ra - ta sum pa - re - re de - i con - si - li - o."
-fi - gens hu - me - ro cru - cem qua de - dit i - ctum ho - sti mor - ti - fe - ro.
-stans au - xi - li - um, vi - ta fru - i be - a - ta, post hoc ex - i - li - um.

15. (ii) GABRIEL FRAM HEVEN-KING[1]
(First version)

♩. = 80

Tenor

1. Ga - bri-el, fram he - ven-king sent to the mai - de
2. Mil - de-lich him gan and-swere the mil - de mai - de
3. Wan the mai - den un - der-stood and th'an - gels wor - des
4. Th'an - gel went a - wei mid than al ut of hi - re
5. Mai - den-mo - der ma - ke - les, of mil - ce ful i -

Psaltery
(or other
suitable
plucked string
instrument)

[1] The Latin text, *Angelus ad virginem,* can be sung to any of the five versions of *Gabriel fram heven-king.*

15. (ii) GABRIEL FRAM HEVEN-KING
(Second version)

15. (ii) GABRIEL FRAM HEVEN-KING
(Third version)

15. (ii) GABRIEL FRAM HEVEN-KING
(Fourth version)

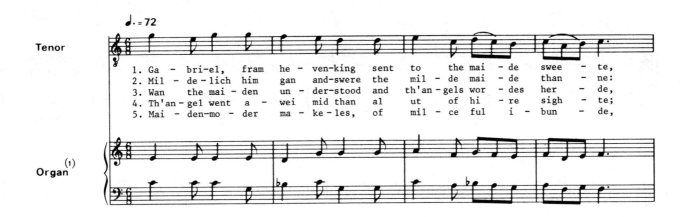

1. Ga - bri-el, fram he - ven-king sent to the mai - de swee - te,
2. Mil - de-lich him gan and-swere the mil - de mai - de than - ne:
3. Wan the mai - den un - der-stood and th'an-gels wor - des her - de,
4. Th'an - gel went a - wei mid than al ut of hi - re sigh - te;
5. Mai - den-mo - der ma - ke-les, of mil - ce ful i - bun - de,

brou - te hir blis - ful ti - ding and fair he gan hir gree - te:
"Wi - che-wi - se sold ich bere a child wi-thu - te man - ne?"
mil - de-lich with mil - de mood to th'an-gel hie and - swer - de:
hi - re womb a - ri - se gan thurw th'o - li - ga - stes migh - te.
bid for us him that te - ches, at wam thu gra - ce fun - de,

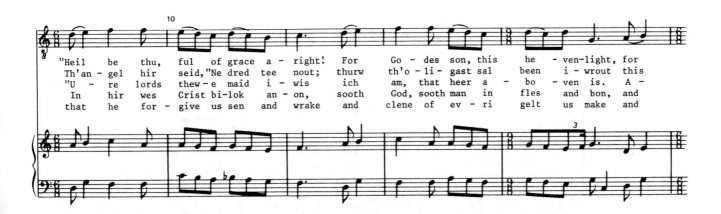

"Heil be thu, ful of grace a - right! For Go - des son, this he - ven-light, for
Th'an - gel hir seid,"Ne dred tee nout; thurw th'o - li - gast sal been i - wrout this
"U - re lords thew - e maid i - wis ich am, that heer a - bo - ven is. A -
In hir wes Crist bi-lok an - on, sooth God, sooth man in fles and bon, and
that he for - give us sen and wrake and clene of ev - ri gelt us make and

¹ Or Contralto and Baritone.

² Small notes to be used only in vocal performance.

man - nes love wil man bi - come and ta - ke fles of thee, mai - de
il - che thing war - of ti - ding ich bring - e; al man - ken wurth i -
- nen - tis me ful - fur - thed be thi saw - e that ich, sith his wil
of hir fles i - bo - re wes at ti - me. War - thurw us kam good
he - ven - blis, wan ur time is to ster - ve, us give, for thi - ne

bright, man - ken free for to ma - ke of sen and dev - les might."
- bout thurw thi - ne sweet chil - ding - e and ut of pine i - brout."
is, a maid, wi - thu - te law - e, of mo - der have the blis."
won; he bout us ut of pi - ne and let him for us slon.
sake, him so heer for to ser - ve that he us to him take.

15. (ii) GABRIEL FRAM HEVEN-KING
(Fifth version)

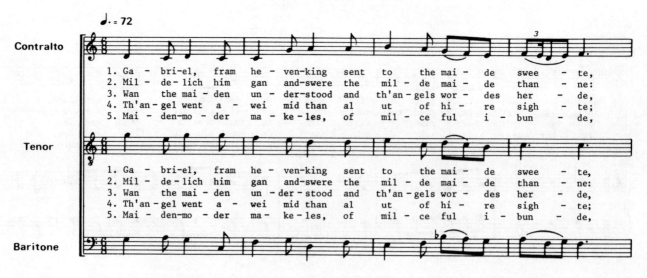

Contralto

1. Ga - bri-el, fram he - ven-king sent to the mai - de swee - te,
2. Mil - de-lich him gan and-swere the mil - de mai - de than - ne:
3. Wan the mai - den un - der-stood and th'an - gels wor - des her - de,
4. Th'an - gel went a - wei mid than al ut of hi - re sigh - te;
5. Mai - den-mo - der ma - ke-les, of mil - ce ful i - bun - de,

Tenor

1. Ga - bri-el, fram he - ven-king sent to the mai - de swee - te,
2. Mil - de-lich him gan and-swere the mil - de mai - de than - ne:
3. Wan the mai - den un - der-stood and th'an - gels wor - des her - de,
4. Th'an - gel went a - wei mid than al ut of hi - re sigh - te;
5. Mai - den-mo - der ma - ke-les, of mil - ce ful i - bun - de,

Baritone

brout - te hir blis - ful ti - ding and fair he gan hir gree - te: "Heil be thu,
"Wi - che-wi - se sold ich bere a child wi-thu - te man - ne?" Th'an - gel hir
mil - de-lich with mil - de mood to th'an-gel hie and - swer - de: "U - re lords
bid for us him that te ches, at wam thu gra - ce fun - de, that he for -

ful of grace a - right! For Go - des son, this he - ven-light, for man - nes love wil
seid,"Ne dred tee nout; thurw, th'o - li - gast sal been i - wrout this il - che thing war -
thew-e maid i - wis ich am, that heer a - bo - ven is. - nen - tis me ful -
Crist bi-lok an - on, sooth God, sooth man in fles and bo' of hir fles i -
-give us sen and wrake and clene of ev - ri gelt us make he - ven-blis, wan

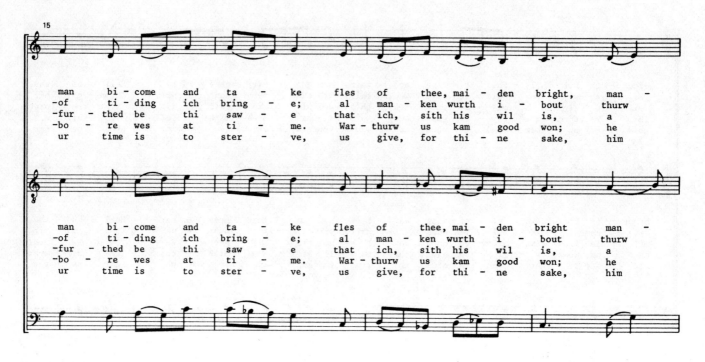

man   bi - come and   ta -   ke   fles of   thee, mai - den bright, man -
-of   ti - ding ich   bring -   e;   al   man - ken wurth i - bout thurw
-fur - thed be   thi   saw   -   e   that ich,   sith his wil is,   a
-bo - re   wes   at   ti   -   me. War - thurw us kam   good won;   he
ur   time is   to   ster -   ve, us   give, for thi - ne   sake, him

man   bi - come and   ta -   ke   fles of   thee, mai - den bright man -
-of   ti - ding ich   bring -   e;   al   man - ken wurth i - bout thurw
-fur - thed be   thi   saw   -   e   that ich,   sith his wil is,   a
-bo - re   wes   at   ti   -   me. War - thurw us kam   good won;   he
ur   time is   to   ster -   ve, us   give, for thi - ne   sake, him

-ken   free for   to   ma   -   ke   of   sen   and dev - les   might."
thi -   ne   sweet chil -   ding -   e   and   ut   of   pine i - brout."
maid,   wi - thu - te   law -   e,   of   mo - der have the   blis."
bout   us   ut   of   pi   -   ne   and   let   him for   us   slon.
so   heer for   to   ser -   ve   that he   us   to   him   take.

-ken   free for   to   ma   -   ke   of   sen   and dev - les   might."
thi -   ne   sweet chil -   ding -   e   and   ut   of   pine i - brout."
maid,   wi - thu - te   law -   e,   of   mo - der have the   blis."
bout   us   ut   of   pi   -   ne   and   let   him for   us   slon.
so   heer for   to   ser -   ve   that he   us   to   him   take.

16a. BRID ONE BREERE

1. Brid o-ne bree-re, briht brid o-ne trew-e, Kynd is come, of
2. Ich am so bli-the so briht brid o-ne bree-re whan I see that
3. Mih-te ich hi-re, hir at wil-le ha-ve, ste-de-fast of

Lo-ve lo-ve to cra-ve: "Blith-ful bird, on me, on me thu
hen-de, hen-dest in hal-le. He is whit of lim, of lim and
lo-ve, lo-ve-li, trew-e (of mi sorw he may, he may me

rew - e; or greith, leef, greith thu me, thu me my gra - ve."
lee - re; he is fayr, and flur, and flur of al - le.
sa - ve), joy and bliss wer er, wer er me new - e.

16b. (i) MAID IN THE MOOR LAY[1]

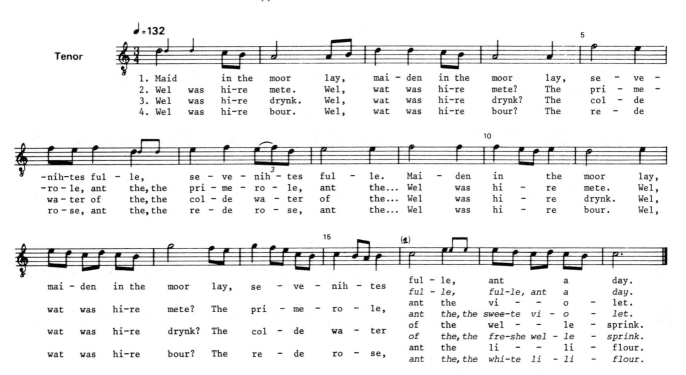

1. Maid in the moor lay, mai - den in the moor lay, se - ve -
2. Wel was hi-re mete. Wel, wat was hi-re mete? The pri - me -
3. Wel was hi-re drynk. Wel, wat was hi-re drynk? The col - de
4. Wel was hi-re bour. Wel, wat was hi-re bour? The re - de

-nih-tes ful - le, se - ve - nih-tes ful - le. Mai - den in the moor lay,
-ro-le, ant the,the pri - me - ro - le, ant the... Wel was hi - re mete. Wel,
wa-ter of the,the col - de wa - ter of the... Wel was hi - re drynk. Wel,
ro-se, ant the,the re - de ro - se, ant the... Wel was hi - re bour. Wel,

mai - den in the moor lay, se - ve - nih - tes *ful - le, ant a day.*
ful - le, ful-le, ant a day.
wat was hi-re mete? The pri - me - ro - le, ant the vi - - o - let.
ant the, the swee-te vi - o - let.
wat was hi-re drynk? The col - de wa - ter of the wel - - le - sprink.
of the, the fre-she wel - le - sprink.
wat was hi-re bour? The re - de ro - se, ant the li - - li - flour.
ant the, the whi-te li - li - flour.

[1] The words of this song have been matched to the tune of no. 16a by the editors.

[2] Of the alternative word-texts given for the last three bars, the first, printed in roman, is that of the Rawlinson manuscript; the second, printed in italics, is a hypothetical text, emended to agree with the rhythms of *Peperit virgo*.

16b. (ii) PEPERIT VIRGO
(Richard de Ledrede)

17. WORLDES BLISSE, HAVE GOOD DAY / [BENEDICAMUS DOMINIO]

18. SANCTA MATER GRACIAE / DOU WAY, ROBIN

Tenor: San - cta ma - ter gra - ci - æ, stel - la cla - ri - ta - tis,

(1) Baritone (or suitable instrument): Dou way, Ro - bin, the child wi - le wee - pe; dou way, Ro -

vi - si - ta nos ho - di - e, ple - na pi - e - ta - tis. Ve - ni,

- bin.

ve - na ve - ni - æ, mox in - car - ce - ra - tis, so - la - men an - gu - sti - æ, fons su -

- a - vi - ta - tis. Re - cor - da - re, ma - ter Chri - sti, quam a - ma - re

tu fle - vi - sti; jux - ta cru - cem tu ste - ti - sti su - spi - ran - do vi - so tri -

- sti. O, O, O Ma - ri - a, flos re -

274

19. LOU, LOU, LOU! WER HE GOTH!

Mezzo-soprano or high Countertenor: Lou, lou, lou! wer he goth! A lou, lou, lou! wer he

Baritone: Lou, lou, lou! wer he goth! A lou, lou, lou! wer he

goth! For hir i les myn ha - ly - wa - ter,

goth! For hir i les myn ha - ly - wa - ter.

- ter, - ter, lou! [oo]

- ter, - ter, lou! [oo]

20. LULLAY, LULLAY : ALS I LAY ON YOOLIS NIGHT

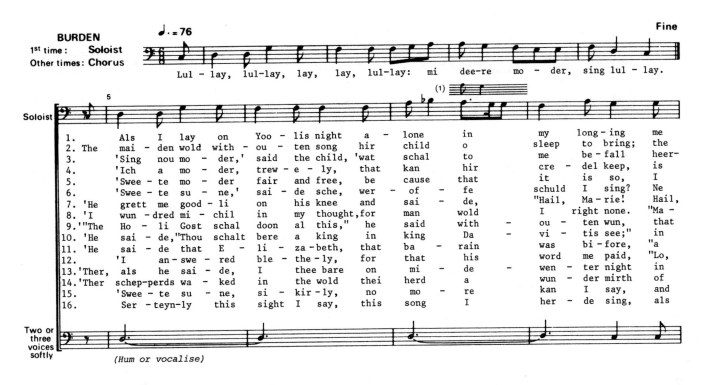

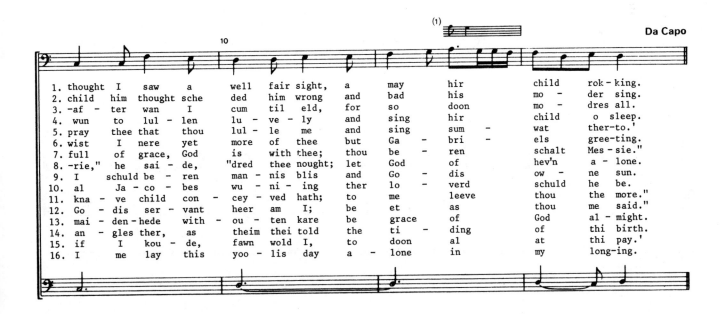

¹ The alternative forms are suggested by the editor, to be used if desired.

21. YE HAVE SO LONGE KEEPYT O

♩. = 104

Tenor
Ye have so long-e kee-pyt o the scheep up on the

Viola

green, Wil-kyn, that al - le yow-er hert ys wo for one so gra-ci-

-us of hew, thagh so-me wol-de ween, Wil - kyn, how that ye

we-xe were un-trew, thagh we-xe were un-trew. Ye may, Wil-
But, that ye

- kyn, wyth rye-straw-ys twyn ma goo-de py-pis; as yow long - is, yn yowr
sey ye wol for love dey, a-rys up on the morn and hast a-wey, and

song-is say - is ye love me best, y-wis, and most on yow - er thowght.
lust to pley. Thys may ry - me well, but hit (a lo!) a-cor - dis nought.

---

[1] The point from which the repeat is to be made is not shown in the MS. A repeat of the last two lines of the stanza, though unusual, is suggested by the editors.

22. MY CARES COMEN EVER ANEW

278

23. WITH RYGHT AL MY HERT

24. I HAVE SET MY HERT SO HY

Tenor / Viola

I have set my hert so hy, me li- kyth no love that low - er
on that lord that loved us all so her - te - ly have I set my

ys; and all the payn that y may dry,
thowght, yt ys my joie on hym to call,

me thenk hyt doth me good, y - wis,
for love me hath in ba - lus browght;

me thenk yt doth, y - wis. For
me thenk yt hath, y - wis.

280

25. TREW, ON WAM YS AL MY TRYST

26. DANGER ME HATH, UNSKYLFULY

1. Dan - ger me hath, un - skyl - fu - ly; y kan noght do but let hyt
2. Dan - ger me hath, un - kyn - de - ly, and ma - kyth ne - ver sign of

pass and lyve bothe glad and my - ry - ly. But hit ys noght as
grace; but yet my for - tune, hap - py - ly, may be bet - ter than

hyt was, and the blame ys noght yn me. For - suth,
hyt was, and the blame be noght yn me. For - suth,

hyt ys he - re wyll, but yf y myght more than y may. more than y may.
hyt ys he - re wyll, yf but y may more than y myght. more than y myght.

[1] The second stanza is supplied, and may be omitted if desired. For an alternative reconstruction see page 291.

27. I REDE THAT THOU BE JOLY AND GLAD

28. THYS YOOL, THYS YOOL
(Edmund)

[1] This part is indicated 'quod Edmund'.

283

284

29. WEL WER HYM THAT WYST

30. ME LYKYTH EVER THE LENGER THE BET

31. PATER NOSTER, MOST OF MYGHT

Pa - - ter no - - ster, most of myght, that al

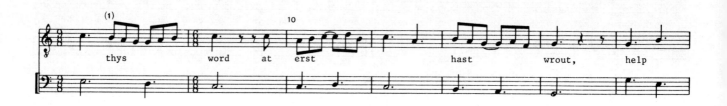

thys word at erst hast wrout, help

me, syn - ful

wre - chyd wyght, for syn - - ne that I pe -

[1] In performance the rhythm of bar 8, with a repeated note on the same syllable, and that of bar 10, with a tied note, should be clearly distinguished here and elsewhere, as they are in the original notation.

- rysch nowt. Pa – ter no – – ster,
Pa – ter no – – ster,

have pe – ty on me and help me from
y – bles-syd thu be, and for thyne own deer

synn a – way to flee, now and e – – ver to
son that deyd on tree; help me, wrec – – che, that

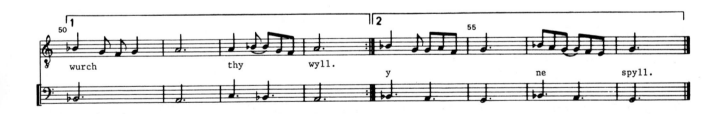

wurch thy wyll.
y ne spyll.

32. 'AVE MARIA' I SAY

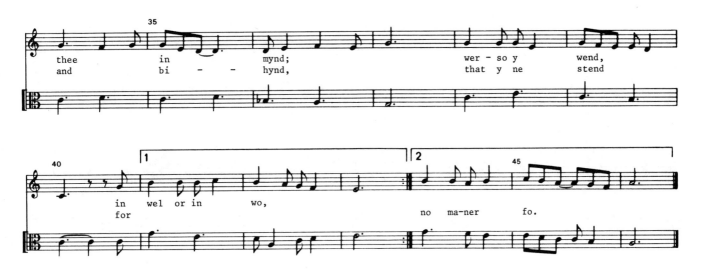

thee in mynd;
and bi - - hynd,
wer - so y wend,
that y ne stend

in wel or in wo,
for
no ma-ner fo.

33. CREDO IN DEUM THAT YS

♩. = 92

Treble

Viola or Organ

Cre - do in De - - um that ys with - owt be - gyn -

- nyng and end, that made he - - ven and erth and

al that ys the - - ryn. Joy-ful, we schold e - ver - more

290

26. DANGER ME HATH, UNSKYLFULY
(Alternative Reconstruction)

Tenor
Viola

Dan - ger me hath, un - skyl - fu - ly; y kan noght do but let hyt

pass and lyve bothe glad and my - ry - ly. But hit ys noght as

hyt was, and the blame ys noght yn me. For - suth,
Yet y

hyt ys he - re wyll, but yf y myght more than y may.
may her ang - er styll, yf but more than y myght y may.

MUSICAL COMMENTARY

F. Ll. HARRISON

MUSICAL COMMENTARY

I. RELIGIOUS SONGS BY SAINT GODRIC

1. Sainte Marie viergene
2. Crist and Sainte Marie
3. Sainte Nicholas, Godes druth

Sources: 1, 2 and 3: London, British Library, MS Royal 5 F. vii, f. 85, in the order 2, 1, 3. No. 1 is headed 'Cantus beati Godrici de sancta Maria' and no. 3 is headed 'Cantus eiusdem de sancto Nicholao'. Facsimile as frontispiece to G. Saintsbury, *A History of English Prosody,* ii, London, 1906. 1 (first verse only): London, British Library, MS Harley 322, f. 74v; Cambridge, University Library, MS Mm. iv. 28, f. 149.

The sources which give both music and words of the songs reputed to have been revealed to or composed by St. Godric (d. 1170) are dated quite close to his lifetime. The two, Harley 322 and the Cambridge manuscript, in which *Sainte Marie viergene* is inserted into Reginald of Durham's story of St. Godric's life, have been dated late twelfth century and *c.* 1200 respectively. The leaf with all three songs in the Royal manuscript, which also contains an account of the saint's life, was written at the beginning of the thirteenth century. The version of the fourth line of the first verse of *Sainte Marie viergene* in the Harley manuscript, which seems to be the earliest of the surviving sources, varies noticeably from and lies a fifth higher than this line in the other two manuscripts. It also has *g afg a* on 'virgine' (as the word is written in these sources) where the other two manuscripts have *f gfg a*. In this version the tune rises a second time to its highest note *f'* and ends on its opening note *a* through a falling third cadence, making it a perfectly consistent tune in the fourth mode (*e*-mode with the plagal *ambitus*) transposed up a fourth. In the Cambridge and Royal manuscripts this line of the tune begins on *f* and falls to the lowest note *c* of the tune immediately before the stepwise cadence *fedd*. While this makes the tune end in the first mode (*d*-mode with the normal *ambitus*), the idiom of the first three lines is not normal for this mode, nor is the range of the third line, which goes to *f'* (*e'* is the rarely used extreme note of plainsong tunes in the first mode).

The second verse, which survives only in the Royal manuscript, has a low tessitura and a small range, and its second and third lines are repetitive and devoid of climax. It is, however, an orthodox first mode tune in its beginning and ending and in its general idiom. The hypothesis suggests itself that the version of the Harley manuscript represents an earlier stage of the song when it had one verse only, whose music, whether revealed or composed, was coherent and complete in itself. The composition of a second verse to a different tune (making a form which fits no usual category of song), in a distinctly different range and a different mode, may have been the occasion for changing the range and mode of the last line of the first verse to agree with the added verse. The first verse's transposed position of the fourth mode, though admitted in the medieval Tonale, was rare in plainsong. Its use suggests that Godric, who in his 'saintly' period was a hermit and not a literate cleric, may have been responsible for the first verse in the Harley manuscript's version of the song. The more orthodox and formal character of the second verse suggests that it may have been the work of one whose normal musical vocabulary was that of an institutional cleric.

The tunes to which the angels sing their *Kyrieleison* and *Christe eleison* invocations in no. 2 may be actual plainsong tunes, since they use common formulae of the first mode. Burgwen's song can be interpreted as also being in the first mode with *b* flat, but in the plagal *ambitus* and transposed up a fifth to end on *a*. That Burgwen's music is written in the octave below *c'* does not mean that it must be sung at that pitch. Plainsong was freely transposed in performance, and chants for nuns were constantly written in their chantbooks at the same pitch as for men.

J. B. Trend, in his discussion of St. Godric's songs (*Music and Letters,* ix, 1928, p. 111), transcribed single notes as quavers and ligatures (joined notes) as grouped quavers. Gustave Reese, in his transcription of *Crist and Sainte Marie* in *Music in the Middle Ages* (New York, 1940, p. 241), accommodated Burgwen's song to three-four time (representing the 'modal' musical rhythm used in the late twelfth and early thirteenth centuries). However, he gave the angels' music in plainsong notation, presumably to be performed non-mensurally in notes of approximately equal length, regardless of the varying note-forms, in which it is nowadays generally thought medieval plainsong was sung. The editors of the *Historical Anthology of Music,* in their transcription of *Sainte Marie viergene* (vol. i, Cambridge, Mass., 1954, no. 23a), represented the longs of the Royal manuscript (they did not use the other sources) as crotchets, its breves as quavers and its ligatures as grouped quavers. Since they expressed in their commentary a preference for 'a free rhythmic rendition over one in modal rhythm' in this song and in *Worldes blis ne last no throwe* (no. 7, below) they apparently did not intend the modern note-forms they used to have their usual relative values. While these editors' preference for a non-mensural interpretation of these songs is sound, it seems preferable that transcriptions for present-day use should convey that all the notes in songs of this kind are roughly, and very flexibly, equal in length, whatever their shape in the original notation. It seems desirable too in a modern edition that its notation should as far as possible take account of the significant rhythmic characteristics of the words and of their effect on the musical rhythm.

Since observance of their poem's system of caesuras and stresses is an essential part of a valid performance of these songs, the quavers of the transcriptions are grouped in such a way that the stressed syllables normally fall on the first quaver of a group, the mid-line caesura is indicated by a comma and the end of a verse-line by a bar-line, and ligatured notes in the manuscript are shown by slurs. A single quaver at the beginning of a line is unstressed, at the end of a line it is stressed. Godric's use in one instance of two stressed syllables in succession, and in several instances of more than one unstressed syllable to constitute a 'dip' at the beginning of a half-line, necessitates the use in these cases of the usual signs / for a stressed syllable and x for an unstressed. It is suggested that the singer should observe the caesura without, however, necessarily taking a breath.

NOTES

1. Sainte Marie viergene
1st verse: The *f* on the second syllable of 'viergene' is supplied; the notes on that word in the Harley MS are *g afg a*. The *g* on the third syllable of 'onfange', and the corresponding *d* in the Harley MS version is supplied.
2nd verse: the penultimate and antepenultimate notes *d* and *c* are ligatured.

2. Crist and Sainte Marie
The tune to which the angels sing their first *Kyrieleison* and *Christe eleison* after Burgwen's first singing of her song is written once only in the MS. It is preceded by the words 'Item angeli' and the text below it is written *Kyriel. Christel.* I interpret this in the way shown in the transcription. The music of the angels' next *Kyrieleison* and *Christe eleison,* which is also indicated 'Item angeli', is written in an abbreviated form as the first seven notes of their original tune over the abbreviation *Kyriel,* followed immediately by the original tune complete over the abbreviation *Christel.* I take this to mean that each angel sings the complete tune again.

3. Sainte Nicholas, Godes druth
The seventh note, a repeated *d'*, is omitted. The slurred group *cb* on the second syllable of 'faire' corresponds to a plicated note *c* in the MS. The *f* for the second syllable of 'burthe' is supplied.

II. SONGS OF THE EARLIER THIRTEENTH CENTURY

4.(i) Eyns ne soy ke pleynte fu
(ii) Ar ne kuth ich sorghe non

Source: London, Guildhall, Records Office, *Liber de antiquis Legibus,* ff.160ᵛ – 161ᵛ; facsimile in C. Page, 'A Catalogue and Bibliography of English Song from its beginnings to *c.*1300', *R.M.A. Research Chronicle,* 13 (1976), p. 83.

Addendum: Planctus ante nescia

Sources (music): Paris, Bibliothèque Mazarine, MS 1002, ff. 235–7; Rouen, Bibliothèque Municipale, MS A506 (formerly 666), ff. 94ᵛ–96ᵛ; Évreux, Bibliothèque Municipale, MS 1.2, ff.3ᵛ–4ᵛ; Évreux, Bibliothèque Municipale, MS 39, ff. 1ᵛ–2.

This song was printed with its music by Friedrich Gennrich in an article entitled 'Internationale mittelalterliche Melodien' (*Zeitschrift für Musikwissenschaft,* xi, 1928–29, pp. 346–7). In

his book *Grundriss einer Formenlehre des mittelalterlichen Liedes* (Halle, 1932, p. 143) Gennrich printed the words and music of a *Planctus Mariae Virginis,* with a text beginning *Planctus ante nescia,* by Godefroy of St. Victor (*fl.* 1170–90), sub-prior of the Abbey which also had as a member the sequence-writer Adam of St. Victor (d. 1177 or 1192, the latter according to Jean de Toulouse, seventeenth-century author of the Annals of St. Victor).

The first printed transcription of Godefroy's *planctus* was published in 1896 by Dom Joseph Pothier in the *Revue du chant grégorien* (vol. v, pp. 17–19). This life-time student of Gregorian chant, who in 1859 had entered the Benedictine Abbey of Solesmes, centre of plainsong research and revival, found himself unable to accept the plain evidence of its four manuscripts. Although certainly acquainted with plainsong tunes in *g*-mode, and with the sequence *Lauda Sion Salvatorem* (whose first stanza ends with the notes *a b a g f g g*), he could not believe that the close proximity of *b* natural and *f* natural in some tune-formulae and cadences in Godefroy's *planctus* was intended. He therefore printed it four notes higher, ending on *c'* with *b* natural, and commented:

> Quant au chant lui-même . . . plus d'une difficulté, et même, disons-le, des impossibilités pratiques. Au lieu de finir en *ut* comme nous le donnons plus haut, il est écrit de manière à se terminer en *sol*; ce qui oblige à dièser le *fa* . . . . le notateur . . se trompait, et allait probablement contre l'idée musicale de l'auteur, à moins que celui-ci, lui aussi victime de l'esprit de système, n'eût pas en lui-même sur ce point sa liberté d'allure et d'inspiration. Ceux de nos lecteurs qui voudraient malgré cela s'en tenir rigoureusement à ce qui est noté dans les manuscrits, n'auront, en se servant de notre notation, qu'à chanter tout le morceau avec bémol continu, s'ils peuvent y réussir.

It seems clear that the tritone relation which so troubled Dom Pothier (whose early musical training was as a cellist at the Paris Conservatoire) was characteristic of some of the most prevalent tune-formulae in sequences, *planctus* and *lais.* Even to the present day, however, some editors of medieval music still show themselves victims (to paraphrase Dom Pothier) of the spirit of the post-sixteenth-century Western tonal system by adding editorial flats and/or sharps to medieval tunes, so negating one of their essential characteristics.

Pierre Aubry thought that the tunes of the French *lais* he edited were sung in measured notes in triple rhythm (*Lais et descorts,* p. xxiv), though he printed them only in a diplomatic copy and gave no transcriptions into modern notation. Friedrich Gennrich transcribed both *Ar ne kuth ich sorghe non* and one of the Évreux versions of Godefroy's *Planctus* in triple measured rhythm. The original of *Ar ne kuth ich sorghe non* is written in plainsong notation, probably of the second quarter of the thirteenth century. Both the historical background of the *lais* and their method of matching tunes to texts make a measured-note interpretation of the music inappropriate and unlikely, and in fact a mensural interpretation of the rhythm of this song is ruled out by the differing stress-patterns of its texts. While the half-stanzas of the *Planctus* agree both in syllable-counts and stress-patterns, this is not true of either the French or English text, the corresponding lines of whose half-stanzas occasionally disagree in syllable-count and rather more often disagree in stress-pattern. The scribe was able to allow for these differences by writing each half-stanza separately (half-stanzas of sequences and Latin *lais* were commonly written separately, though this was not strictly necessary in the case of poems with agreeing half-stanzas). The stress-patterns of the first line of each half of stanza 2, for example, show these differences in the French and English texts:

	Stress-pattern
2a (French) Jesu Crist, veirs deu, veirs hum	/x/x/x/
(English) Jesu Crist, sooth God, sooth man	/x/x/x/
2b (French) Jo e mi autre cumpaignun	/xx/x/x/
(English) Ich and mine feeren sume	/x/x/x/x

It is impossible that the three different stress-patterns involved in these lines, which are all sung to the same tune, should be sung in an identical measured rhythm. The separate transcriptions here of items 4(i) and 4(ii), with French and English texts, and of three musical versions of Godefroy of St. Victor's *Planctus,* take account of the significant rhythmic characteristics of their words on the same principles as do the transcriptions of St. Godric's songs (nos. 1–3).

Most of the notes in the Guildhall manuscript are written as longs. Apart from these, there are some diamond-shaped notes, both separately and in a group in which two such notes follow an oblique long with stem to the left. There are some plicated notes with two downward stems, and there are groups of two, three and four notes ligatured in the normal ways. Plicated notes occur in the following places: in stanza 1 on 'kuth', 'moot', the first syllable of 'tholich' and 'for'; in stanza 3 on the first syllable of 'boote', the second syllable of 'bringe', on 'yef' and on 'in'; in stanza 4 on the first syllable of 'worldes'; in stanza 5 on 'us' in the third line and on the first syllable of 'wusit'. Each plicated note has been transcribed as two notes, one at its pitch and one a step lower. Tied notes in the transcription, as on the second syllable of 'sorghe' in the first line of the first stanza, represent two longs set closely together in the manuscript. Most staves in the manuscript have four lines, a few have five; the changes to five lines are shown in the notes.

An optional prelude and accompaniment for diatonic harp, preferably plucked with the finger-nails, written within the playing range *c* to *g″*, has been added. The prelude has a quasi-improvised upper part in free rhythm over the tune of the first line, in a style similar to that of some of the sacred vocal polyphony associated with St. Martial de Limoges in the first half of the twelfth century. The accompaniment has a structural outline in fourths, fifths and octaves, and an upper part which complements the voice's tunes somewhat in 'gymel' fashion, in which two voices occupying the same pitch-range interweave with constant crossing and recrossing (see, e.g., no. 12). The notes written as semibreves should be allowed to continue sounding until the succeeding semibreve.

NOTES

(References are by half-stanza and line of half-stanza; where the stanza-number does not include a or b the note applies to both half-stanzas)

Ar ne kuth ich sorghe non (c³, e.g., means c-clef on third line) 1a,1 clef c⁴/1b, 1 clef c⁴, five lines/2a,1 four lines/2a,4 clef c⁴/2b,1 clef c³/2b,4 clef c⁴; MS has *g* three times on 'livere'/3a,3 *g* and *f* are separate longs/3b,1 clef c³/3b,6 MS has *g* twice after *f*/4a,1 clef g⁴/4a,3 clef c⁴ on five lines before ¹*f*/4b,1 clef c³/4b,2

clef c³ on four lines/5b,1 MS has third *g* erased at end/5b,4 no further music after *a*

Planctus ante nescia

In both of the Évreux MSS there are two lines of text below each line of music; consequently, there are no variants between half-stanzas. In the Rouen and Mazarine Library MSS the music is written separately for each half-stanza, and some variants occur. As in *Ar ne kuth ich sorghe non*, plicated notes have been transcribed as two notes, one at its pitch and one a step lower.

E (MS 39):12,4 last note *c* on 'ad' is erased. *E* (MS 1,2): 4,4 no flat. *R*:2b,2 notes on first syllable of 'vulnera' are *abaa*/2b,4 notes on second syllable of 'felix' are *aab*/12b,1 notes are *d de c de f ede d*/12b,2 notes on first syllable of 'tibi' are *ed*/13b,2 notes are *agdcbag*/13b,4 notes on fourth syllable of 'amantibus' are *bagf*.

M: 3b,6 notes are *bab g f ga g*/4b,1 *d* only on first syllable of 'corporis'/12b,3 notes are *gagafac*

5. Miri it is while sumer ilast

Source: Oxford, Bodleian Library, MS Rawlinson G. 22, f. 1ᵛ; facsimile in John, J. F. R. and C. Stainer, *Early Bodleian Music,* i, London, 1901, pl. iii.

This item survives on a single flyleaf, now rather battered, which is bound in at the beginning of a manuscript written about 1200 A.D. which contains psalms, canticles, a litany and other sacred items, all in Latin. E. W. B. Nicholson pointed out (in the Catalogue of Manuscripts of the Bodleian Library) that there is a prayer for 'our bishop and abbat' in the main manuscript, that this could not refer to a Gilbertine house, which had no abbots, and that St. Botulph comes first of four English saints in the litany. He therefore connected the main manuscript with the Benedictine Abbey of Thorney in Cambridgeshire, adding that 'in any case it may be taken as almost certain that the volume is East Midland'. There is no certainty that this is also true of the flyleaf with music, though it may be. Nicholson's date of *c.* 1225 for this leaf seems right for the musical notation, which is in the manner of the early thirteenth century.

The fly-leaf has portions of two songs with secular French texts, both of which are stanzaic, that is, their music is written once with one stanza of text below it, followed by the text of other stanzas to be sung to the same music. These are followed by the music, with text below, of *Miri it is*. If there were further stanzas of this, as seems probable, they would have been written on a following leaf.

It seems certain that this cannot be merely an isolated leaf of song-jottings, but must be a leaf from a book which contained French songs in the *trouvère* manner and perhaps other songs than *Miri it is* of the same type with English words. The contents of this leaf appear to have been written by one hand, and its size and layout are very similar to those of some surviving thirteenth-century French *chansonniers* containing troubadour and *trouvère* songs (for information about facsimiles see G. Reese, *Music in the Middle Ages,* New York, 1940, p. 206, n. 32; the early part of the *Chansonnier de Saint-Germain,* which was edited by P. Meyer and G. Raynaud in 1892 for the *Société des anciens textes français,* is about the same date as the leaf with *Miri it is*). The initial letter of each poem in French *chansonniers* was usually enlarged and often decorated. Space was left for this in the layout of *Miri it is* and of the preceding French song, but the spaces were not filled in. Thus there is a strong possibility that this page is a unique survival from a *chansonnier* with songs in both vernaculars. There seems to be no other direct evidence for the existence of collections of this kind.

The notation of *Miri it is,* and of the French songs on the leaf, is of the overtly unmeasured type which is most often interpreted, in the context of secular songs, in patterns based on the rhythmic modes (see Reese, op. cit., pp. 206–11). Though there are cases in which this would be inappropriate, a regularly stressed rhythm seems suitable both to the strongly metrical structure of the text and to its prevailingly syllabic relation to the music. The notation is therefore interpreted here in the iambic pattern of the first rhythmic mode, though the shape of the two-note ligatures has suggested for them transcription in the trochaic rhythm of the second mode.

An obvious characteristic of the tune is its descent in each phrase from a relatively high note to a relatively low one. Plainsong tunes, virtually without exception, rise from a relatively low note in their range to a relatively high one and then descend. Another feature of the tune which is seldom found in plainsong tunes, though it may be observed in some hymns, is its repetition of phrases in agreement with the poetic structure:

Bars of Music	Phrase-unit	Lines of Stanza	Number of Syllables
1–6	A	1–2	8, 5
7–12	A	3–4	7, 4
13–16	B	5	7
17-20	B	6	7
21-23	C	7	6

An optional prelude-postlude for viola (representing the large medieval fiddle) and harp has been added here. This and the added accompaniment for harp underline the aptness of the tune for accompaniment by a shifting drone, a feature common to a number of surviving medieval tunes, and one which also underlies a good many oral-tradition tunes from musically conservative regions such as Highland Scotland and Spain.

NOTES

The note-values are reduced to one-sixteenth of the original (long=crotchet). The tune begins in the MS with *e'* four times; for text reasons one of these is omitted. The rests in bars 20, 26, 30 and 34 are editorial, and the last note is missing from the MS. The note *b* in bar 35 is unclear and might be *c'*.

6a. Man mai longe lives weene

Source: Maidstone Museum, MS A. 13, f. 93ᵛ; facsimile in C. Page, 'A Catalogue and Bibliography of English Songs from its beginnings to *c.* 1300', *R.M.A. Research Chronicle*, 13 (1976), p. 82.

The music of this song is written in non-mensural notation of the first half of the thirteenth century on a staff of four very lightly ruled lines. The text scribe, who may or may not also have written down the music, did not leave enough space for the music above and between the lines of the first stanza, which

alone has the music. Though as a result the highest and lowest notes of the tune run into the letters above or below, they can nevertheless be distinguished from them, and the pitches of the notes are otherwise clear, with one or two exceptions. Each of the first two words of the text of the first stanza has a double note above it, though both are one-syllable words. Thereafter there are single notes, one double note and a very few ligatures of two, three and (once) four notes. The scribe's use (in bars 13 and 25 of the transcription) of a curiously ungainly note-form, apparently for two ligatured notes of which the second is higher than the first, reinforces one's impression of an inexperienced or unaccustomed writer of music. Apart from the first note *c'* he did not write any music over lines 3 and 4 of the stanza, and it is assumed that he intended a repeat of the music of the first two lines.

The metre of the poem and the mainly syllabic character of the setting are both suited by triple rhythm, within which note-lengths are determined by the metrical position of the syllable to which they belong, though alternative readings are sometimes possible. This, and the accommodation of the music to the edited text of the poem, accounts for the rhythmical differences between this transcription and Manfred Bukofzer's, which was printed with the text of the first stanza in Gustave Reese's *Music in the Middle Ages* (p. 243).

After its repetition of the first two phrases, which together encompass a rise and fall through an octave, the tune has six phrases (the last of half length) with no element of repetition, in which it rises to the climax note *d'*, then falls through the intermediate pitch-range to the final *c*, which both begins and ends the last two phrases. Disciplined tune-architecture of this kind is characteristic both of church chant and of a good deal of *trouvère* song, and either or both of these must have influenced the composer of this music. For example, the first two bars are the same as the opening of some plainsong antiphons in the fifth mode, the best known of which is *Alma redemptoris mater*. A tune outline which includes a descending sixth (bars 25-26), though rare, is occasionally found in *trouvère* song (a similar outline is in *Mariounette douche*, quoted in my chapter 'English Church Music in the Fourteenth Century' in *The New Oxford History of Music,* iii, London, 1960, p. 86), and it also occurs in plainsong, e.g. in stanza 4 of *Stabat juxta Christi crucem* (no. 10 below) in the version of the Arsenal manuscript.

NOTES

(The references are by bar numbers.) 1 both notes are double in the MS/ 2 the repeat of *g* is omitted/ 1–9 the repeat is not written out/ 11 *g* is a double note/ 17 the *c* might be *b*, as Bukofzer read it/ 21 *e* and *f* are not ligatured/ 23 *g* and *a* are not ligatured/ 30 *e* and *d* are not ligatured.

6b. On hir is mi lif ilong

As explained in the Textual Commentary (p. 131) this poem and the music of *Man mai longe lives weene* do not occur together.

NOTES
(The notes on 6a apply also to 6b. The following are additional. The references are by bar-numbers.)

3 *b* and *c* are not ligatured/ 6 the notes are ligatured as in the corresponding bar of 6a/ 9 *d* and *c* are ligatured/ 13 *g* and *a* are ligatured/ 20 *g* and *f* are not ligatured/ 22 *d* and *c* are not ligatured/ 26 *c* and *d* are not ligatured/ 29 *d* and *c* are ligatured.

7. Worldes blis ne last no throwe

Sources: London, British Library, MS Arundel 248, f. 154; Oxford, Bodleian Library, MS Rawlinson G. 18, ff. 105^v–106; facsimile of both MSS in H. E. Wooldridge, *Early English Harmony,* i, London, 1897, pls. 34, 23 respectively; facsimile of the Rawlinson MS in John, J. F. R. and C. Stainer, *Early Bodleian Music,* i, London, 1901, pl. iv.

The music in both sources is written in a plainsong notation, once only for all the stanzas, of about the middle of the thirteenth century. The chief differences between the two versions, which agree in the main, occur in groups of two or more notes to a single syllable, where the version of the Arundel manuscript, which is transcribed here, is sometimes more ornate than that of the Oxford manuscript. The transcription of the version of the Oxford manuscript which is printed in the *Historical Anthology of Music* (ed. A. T. Davison and W. Apel, i, Cambridge, Mass., 1954, no. 23b) interprets the single notes of the original as crotchets and grouped notes as quavers joined by a brace. As in the transcription of *Sainte Marie viergene* (no. 1 in this volume) in the same publication, the editors presumably do not mean these crotchets and quavers to have their usual rhythmic relationship. J. A. Westrup, in his chapter on 'Medieval Song' in the second volume of *The New Oxford History of Music* (London, 1954, p. 251), published a transcription in mensural rhythm in three-four time of the version of the Oxford manuscript, giving only the first stanza of the poem. He commented that the tune 'is constructed from a few simple formulas with two of the lines repeated' and 'is also remarkable for its adherence to movement by step'.

One of the significant characteristics of the text of *Worldes blis ne last no throwe* is its combining regular syllable-count with occasionally irregular stress. Departures from the stress-pattern established in the first three stanzas occur in thirteen of the succeeding forty lines of the poem. The transcription assumes that the song is sung in plainsong rhythm, in which each note has approximately equal length. The quaver is used for this basic note-value, and stressed syllables, lines of the poem and ligatures in the manuscript are shown in the same way as in nos. 1–3 (see p. 295–6).

NOTES

(References are to lines of the first stanza; *A* signifies the Arundel manuscript, *R* the Rawlinson manuscript.)
1 the four-note group on 'no' is unclear in *A* and might be *bag; R* has *bag* at this point/ 2 *R* has *ga* on the first syllable of 'anon'/ 3 after the first four notes *R* reads *bag a bag a gf;* the four notes on 'hit i-' are one group in *A*/ 4 *R* has *a* for *aba* on 'lass' and *ga* for *gfga* on 'thar-'/ 5 on the first five syllables *R* has *b b cdc d cb*/ 6 instead of the first three notes *abc* in *A* there are four notes *bbbc* in *R*/ 7 *A* has double notes on the first syllable of 'laste' and the first syllable of 'bare'; *R* has *a* twice for 'povre'/ 8 after the first five notes *R* has *b a gfg a*/ 9 in *R* this line reads *b c b b ag a b ag a gf*/ 10 in *R* this line reads *g a a gf g fed f gabag fg.*

8. Fuweles in the frith

Source: Oxford, Bodleian Library, MS Douce 139, f. 5; facsimile in H. E. Wooldridge, *Early English Harmony,* i, London, 1897, pl. 7.

It is possible to interpret the plainsong-style notation of this song in measured rhythm related to the rhythmic modes, and this has been done by the editors of *Early Bodleian Music* (vol. ii, London, 1901, p. 10) and, with differences of detail, by Harold Gleason in his *Examples of Music before 1400* (New York, 1942, p. 47). However, while the poem has three stresses in each line it is not metrically regular, and while the music is based on common tune-formulae it is rarely syllabic, but has groups of two to five notes on a syllable. The song seems therefore best suited to performance in approximately equal-note rhythm, with attention to the shifting stresses of the text. As in other songs in this kind of rhythm, the transcription given here has the quaver as the basic note-length and uses slurs to show ligatures in the original notation. The accommodations of note-values which are necessary in this song between the two voices involve the occasional use of crotchet and dotted crotchet, here used with their usual rhythmic relationship to the quaver. Since their use makes less apparent the placing of the stresses, stressed groups and notes have been indicated throughout by a stroke. Groups and notes without a stroke are unstressed. In the original manuscript a short vertical line is used to mark off the notes on a word or group of words, though not systematically nor always in the same places in both voices. Lines of this kind were regularly used in manuscripts of plainsong written by or for Franciscans.

When a thirteenth-century composition for two or more voices was based on plainsong, as in settings of ritual items like Graduals and Alleluias and in motets, the plainsong tune was invariably in the lowest voice. Similarly, a composer writing an original composition would usually begin by writing the lowest voice. It is therefore *a priori* probable that this is true of *Fuweles in the frith,* as of *Jesu Cristes milde moder* (no. 12). The upper voice of *Fuweles in the frith* moves within the narrow range of a sixth, and has not the appearance of having been made of current tune-formulae. The lower voice has a range of an octave, and uses tune-phrases of the same type as those of *Jesu Cristes milde moder* and *Worldes blis ne last no throwe* (no. 7). The music of the first line, for example, is virtually identical with the lower voice of the first line of *Jesu Cristes milde moder.* The technique of adding a second voice above a composed, adapted or derived voice was known as 'descant' (Latin, *discantus*). Gustave Reese (*Music in the Middle Ages,* New York, 1940, p. 389) described the technique of *Fuweles in the frith* as 'gymel' and this has been followed by some later writers. The two voices of *Fuweles in the frith* have distinct ranges (*d* to *d'* and *d'* to *b'* flat respectively) and different clefs, and do not cross. Their technique is therefore descant.

Taking these characteristics into account, it seems probable that the music of this song was composed by someone acquainted with the procedure of using common tune-formulae, and also with the style of plainsong and with the current way of writing descant.

NOTES

Upper voice: the *b* flat signature is supplied; it affects one note only and may be disregarded at will/line 1, the first three notes

are ligatured/ line 2, the five notes on the second 'the' are ligatured three and two.
Lower voice: line 1, the first three notes are ligatured/ line 2,
the two notes on 'in' are not ligatured; the MS has a second *g*
after the dotted crotchet *g*/line 4, the *g* on the second syllable of
'walke' is double.

9. Perspice, Christicola / *Tenor:* [Resurrexit Dominus]
Sumer is icumen in / *Tenor:* Sing cuccu, nu

Source: London, British Library, MS Harley 978, f. 11ᵛ. This
page is reproduced in colour as the frontispiece of vol. vii of
Grove's Dictionary of Music and Musicians (London, 1954)
and on the sleeve of the record 'Medieval English Lyrics'
(ARGO ZRG 5443).

The manuscript's instructions for the performance of the *rota*
are:

> Hanc rotam cantare possunt quatuor socii; a paucioribus
> autem quam a tribus vel saltem duobus non debet dici,
> praeter eos qui dicunt pedem. Canitur autem sic: tacentibus
> ceteris unus inchoat cum hiis qui tenent pedem, et cum ven-
> erit ad primam notam post crucem inchoat alius, et sic de
> ceteris. Singuli vero repausent ad pausationes scriptas, et
> non alibi, spatio unus longae notae.

This may be translated:

> This canon may be sung by four companions, but should not
> be sung by fewer than three, or two at the least, in addition to
> the two who sing the *pes.* It is sung thus: one singer begins
> with those who maintain the *pes,* the others being silent, and
> when he comes to the first note after the cross-sign (+)
> another begins, and so with the other singers. Each one shall
> be silent at the written rests, and not elsewhere, for the time
> of one long note.

There is also a separate instruction for each singer of the *pes*:

> Hoc repetit unus quotiens opus est, faciens pausationem in
> fine, i.e., one singer repeats this as often as needed, making a
> rest at the end (this refers to the rest of the value of a long,
> represented in the transcription by the rests in the fourth
> bar).
> Hoc dicit alius, pausans in medio et non in fine, sed
> immediate repetens principium, i.e., the other sings this,
> making a rest in the middle (represented in the transcription
> by the rests in the second bar) and not at the end, but
> immediately repeating the beginning.

The transcription provides a choice of the following ways
of performance:

1. In four parts, the minimum prescribed in the manuscript,
to the Latin text, continuing without pause to performance
in six parts to the English text, the two texts thus running
straight through as disposed in the text section. The singers
of the *pes* should change texts at bar 31, if not vocalizing.
2. In the same way but with the English text before the Latin,
the singers of the *pes* changing at bar 31.
3. In four parts to either text, ending by observing the bracketed pauses in bar 30.
4. In six parts to either text, beginning at bar 31.

The singing of the *rondellus* alone in bars 1–4, 31–34 and
65–68 is not required by the original instructions, but may help
to clarify the design of the piece in performance.

NOTES

The Latin text *Resurrexit Dominus* for the *rondellus* is added
and optional; there is a red cross in the *rota* before the *a* on the
first syllable of 'lhude'; the *b* on the second syllable of 'cuccu' in
the *rota* at bar 25 in the leading part is a square note without
stem.

III. CRUCIFIXION LAMENTS OF THE THIRTEENTH
CENTURY
10. (i) Stabat juxta Christi crucem
(ii) [Stood the moder under roode]
11. Stond well, moder, under roode
12. Jesu Cristes milde moder

(Three English versions, and the Latin, of the sequence *Stabat
juxta Christi crucem, stabat videns vitae ducem*)

Sources:
10 (i) Paris, Bibliothèque de l'Arsenal, MS 135, ff. 282ᵛ–283ᵛ.
10 (ii). Oxford, Bodleian Library, MS Tanner 169*, p. 175;
fascimile in John, J. F. R. and C. Stainer, *Early Bodleian
Music,* i, London, 1901, plate v; diplomatic copy in ibid., ii, p.
8.
11. London, British Library, MS Royal 12 E. i, ff. 193–194ᵛ
(with music for stanzas 1–6); Cambridge, St. John's College,
MS 111, f. 106ᵛ (stanzas 1–4 and half of stanza 5); facsimile in
C. Page, 'A Catalogue and Bibliography of English Song from
its beginnings to *c.* 1300', *R.M.A. Research Chronicle,* 13
(1976), p. 82.
12. London, British Library, MS Arundel 248, ff. 154ᵛ–155;
facsimile in H. E. Wooldridge, *Early English Harmony,*
London, 1897, pls. 35–36.

The Tanner manuscript in the Bodleian lacks all but the last
four words of the text and music of the first four stanzas of
Stood the moder under roode, but the music of the surviving
stanzas corresponds to that of the Latin sequence in the
Arsenal manuscript. The Royal manuscript in the British Library has music for stanzas 1 to 6 of *Stond wel, moder, under
roode* (though its words are complete) and the St. John's College, Cambridge, manuscript has music for stanzas 1 to 5 (with
both Latin and English texts), and again the music of both
corresponds to that of the Arsenal sequence for these verses.
While the first four stanzas of *Stood the moder under roode*
cannot be reconstructed for lack of text (though we know what
the music would have been, apart from differences of detail), it
has been possible to complete *Stond wel, moder, under roode* by
adapting the music for stanzas 6 to 11 from the Latin sequence
in the Arsenal manuscript. The scribe of the St. John's College
manuscript wrote down the Latin text directly under its music,
placing the syllables correctly, and wrote below it the English
version, whose syllable-count often differs from that of the
Latin. Since the scribe made no attempt to reconcile these
differences, his version of the music is not valid as a setting of
the English text. It is printed above the Arsenal manuscript's
version of the music of the Latin text, in order to show their
differences.

In spite of the norm of metrical and musical correspondence between each half of a poetic stanza, the composer-adapter, whether of a Latin or English version, did not always copy exactly the tune of the first half-stanza, but at times made changes which were clearly intentional. Those which result from the inheritance of a corrupted text or from the scribe's failure to scan his text correctly have been emended, and the musical changes are shown in the Notes below. But musical differences which are clearly not in either category, such as those between the two halves of stanza 9 in *Stood the moder under roode,* have not been altered.

There is no variation between the half-stanzas of *Jesu Cristes milde moder,* whose scribe wrote both half-stanzas under the same music, which has no connection with that of the Latin sequence. Its composer seems to have worked with simple tune-formulae within a limited range of pitch, putting his two parts together in the manner later called 'gymel'. In a number of places he wrote parallel unisons, which have not been changed in the transcription.

Performance by two equal voices which are contrasted in timbre seems the most obvious possibility. An alternative might be performance by singer and a chamber or portative organ, which seems the most appropriate instrument. It would probably be effective to sing the lower of the two parts, which has a slightly wider range and a more cumulative set of tune-formulae.

The music of *Jesu Cristes milde moder* is written in notation which has the appearance of plainsong, and would in my opinion have been sung in non-metrical rhythm, with approximately equal notes. Friedrich Gennrich, in his paper 'Internationale mittelalterliche Melodien' (*Zeitschrift für Musikwissenschaft,* xi, 1928, p. 267), printed a transcription of stanza 11 in three-four time, and this view of the musical rhythm was also taken by Gustave Reese in a transcription of the first and tenth stanzas (*Music in the Middle Ages,* New York, 1940, p. 389). However, modal rhythm, in this case the trochaic metre of the first rhythmic mode, does not give an acceptable result in this song. While the author of the text apparently intended complete regularity of syllable-count, his stresses do not work in regular trochaic feet, and his verses are therefore not singable in an unchanging musical metre. Though the normal rhythm is trochaic, lines 4, 10, 11, 40, 41 and 46 begin with an unstressed syllable and are iambic throughout. In addition, lines 5, 7, 8, and 47 turn into iambic rhythm after the first or second foot. This makes a total of ten iambic or partly iambic lines out of sixty-six in the poem. The varying stresses have been shown in the transcription by grouping the basically equal-length quavers according to the word-stress, with the stressed syllables coinciding with the first quaver in a group.

The scribe wrote a number of notes as a square note followed at the same pitch by another square note with downward stem to the right, a form which might be interpreted as plicated. In some cases this form occurs in both voices at once, in others in only one voice. Its precise meaning is unclear. Double notes occurring simultaneously are transcribed as prolongation or anticipation, and those in one voice only as normal single notes. The occurrence of all double notes is indicated in the Notes.

NOTES

10. (i) *Stabat juxta Christi crucem*
Plicated notes in both sources are transcribed as the notated pitch and the note one step below. In the Arsenal MS, in stanza 8b, line 3, *ff* on first syllable of 'anxiam' are separate, and in stanza 9b, line 2, *aa* on second syllable of 'resurgenti' are separate, the second plicated. An accidental printed above a note is editorial; a small accidental is consequent upon one indicated earlier in the MS. Both kinds should be observed in performance.

10. (ii) [*Stood the moder under roode*]
Plicated notes are treated as in the previous item, unless otherwise noted.
5a,1 the first two notes, and the fifth and sixth notes, are separate in MS/ 5b,1 fifth and sixth notes separate/ 6a, 2 *cc* on first word are separate/ 6b,3 repeated *c'* after fifth note omitted/ 8a,1 repeated *f* after second note omitted/ 8a,3 repeated *d* after first note omitted/ 9b,1 repeated *d* supplied after first note; repeated *a* supplied after seventh note/ 9b,3 repeated *g* after first note and repeated *g* after third note both omitted/ 10a,1 repeated *a* after last note omitted/ 10a,2 second note is plicated *a* with upward stem to right, transcribed as *ab*; last note is separate from previous four/ 10b,2 repeated *c'* supplied after third note/ 11a,3 repeated *c'* supplied after first note/ 11b,1 repeated *f* after first note omitted/ 11b,2 repeated *f* after second note and repeated *g* after fifth note both omitted; the scribe put a 'bar-line' after 'of sinne', after 'of sorwe' and after 'of sich', and must have intended a perceptible break for emphasis at each of these points/ 11b,3 fifth and sixth notes are separate.

11. *Stond wel, moder, under roode*
Plicated notes are treated as in *Stabat juxta Christi crucem.* 1b,1 repeat of first note omitted/ 2a,1 *b* flat is not cancelled/ 2a,2 repeat of second note omitted; *d'* on 'for' changed to *c'*/ 2b,1 repeat of first and third notes omitted/3b,1 repeat of first note omitted; *b* flats are editorial/ 3b,2 *b* flat is editorial/4b, 1 repeat of final note omitted/4b,3 repeat of first note supplied; *b* flats are editorial/ 5a,1 *b* flat is editorial/ 5a,2 the five notes on 'dey' are ligatured two and three/ 5a,3 repeat of second note omitted/ 5b,2 repeat of first note supplied/ 5b,3 repeat of first note supplied/ 6a,3 repeat of first note omitted/ 6b,3 repeat of sixth note supplied; the music ends with the penultimate note, and music for the succeeding stanzas is adapted from that of the corresponding stanzas of the Latin sequence in the Arsenal manuscript. The following notes refer to that manuscript: 7a,2 third note supplied/ 7a,3 repeat of second note supplied/ 7b,2 third note supplied/ 7b,3 repeat of second note supplied/ 8a,3 repeat of first note supplied/ 8b,3 repeat of first note supplied; tied *ff* are separate but on one syllable in MS/ 9a,2 and 3 repeat of first note supplied/9b,3 repeat of first note supplied/10a,2 and 3 repeat of first note supplied/10b,2 and 3 repeat of first note supplied.

12. *Jesu Cristes milde moder*
The voices are indicated as I and II reading downwards; since in the manuscript the music is written once for each stanza, the stanza numbers refer to the music of both half-stanzas. 1,3 I last note is double/ 2,2 II fifth note is double/ 2,3 I and II *g* for the suppressed second syllable of 'levedi' is omitted from each voice/ 2,3 II the penultimate note is double/ 3,2 I and II the penultimate double note in each voice is interpreted as a passing note/ 3,3 I repeat of fourth note *a* is omitted; penultimate note is double/ 3,3 II repeat of fourth note *f* is omitted/ 4,3 I and II the three notes on 'levdi' ('levedi' in MS) are separate/

5,1 I and II the note on the first syllable of 'scurges' is double, interpreted as anticipation/ 5,3 II the penultimate note is double/ 6,3 I the penultimate note is double/ 6,2 II the penultimate note is double/ 7,2 I the first note is double/ 7,2 I and II the fifth and sixth notes are separate/ 7,1 II the penultimate note is double/ 7,2 II fifth and seventh notes are double/ 7,3 I and II fourth and fifth notes are separate/ 9,1 II penultimate note is double/ 9,2 II penultimate note is double/ 9,3 I and II penultimate note is double in both/ 10,3 I and II the fifth and sixth notes are separate/ 11,1 II the fifth and penultimate notes are double/ 11,2 I third note is double/ 11,3 I and II repeat of the fifth note omitted; sixth and seventh notes are separate; the penultimate note is elongated/ Amen I and II the antepenultimate note is double; the two final notes are elongated.

IV. SONGS OF THE LATER THIRTEENTH AND EARLY FOURTEENTH CENTURIES

13. Edi be thu, heven-queene

Source: Oxford, Corpus Christi College, MS 59, f. 113ᵛ.

This two-part song is contained in a manuscript which Carleton Brown has shown to be from the Augustinian priory of Llanthony Maior in Gloucestershire (Carleton Brown, 'A Thirteenth-century MS from Llanthony Priory', *Speculum,* iii, 1928, p. 587). Among other things the manuscript also contains two Latin sequences with music and other English poems without music. One of the sequences, beginning *Recitemus pro haec festa,* is in honour of St. Kyneburg, to whom a chapel at Llanthony Priory was dedicated; the other sequence, which immediately follows *Edi be thu* in the manuscript and whose first line is *Orbis honor, caeli schema,* is in honour of the Virgin Mary. Both sequences would have been sung liturgically in the Mass, the St. Kyneburg sequence on her feastday and the Marian sequence probably in the Votive Mass of the Virgin. There would have been no place in the church ritual for *Edi be thu,* however, and it was probably used by the teacher in the Priory grammar-school who seems to have been the user and possibly also the compiler of the manuscript.

The first stanza of *Edi be thu* is written under the two voices, which are set down in score, i.e., one above the other; it is followed by the first two words of the second stanza under their four notes, and then by the succeeding stanzas without music. At the beginning of the first stanza the upper voice reads *f c c* (with downward plica) *a,* but at the beginning of the second stanza this voice reads *f c c b* flat. This may be taken as confirming the interpretation of *c* with downward plica as equivalent to two notes *c b.* The lower voice at the beginning of the second stanza has *g* as the fourth note, written under the *b* flat of the first voice. The lower voice at the beginning of the first stanza, however, has *a,* not followed by *g,* under the plicated *c* in the upper voice. Since this *a* would clash momentarily with the *b* flat in the upper voice the reading of the opening of the second stanza, in which the voices move in parallel thirds, has been adopted. It may be that the scribe inadvertently wrote *a* in the first stanza instead of a plicated *a.*

The musical notation is not entirely non-mensural, but neither did the scribe make consistent use of mensural note-forms. It is best suited by transcription in mensural terms, since apart from plicas there are only two cases of two-note ligatures and none of more than two notes. Mensural transcription also seems best fitted to the metrical regularity of the poem as emended. Though in some passages longs and breves can be interpreted in the usual mensural sense in triple time, a number of longs (seven in the upper voice, six in the lower, four of which coincide) must be transcribed as if they were breves, and one breve in the lower voice must be transcribed as though it were a long.

The upper voice, which is obviously the dominant one (unlike that of *Fuweles in the frith*), consists of only three tune-units, each corresponding to a line of the verse, disposed with slight variants to make the complete tune in the form ababccab. The composer gave built-in contrast to this economical material by using rising and falling fifths in a and stepwise movement in b and c. The tune's contour, especially the rising fifth immediately followed by a falling fifth in the second bar of a, suggests a secular, not a plainsong model. The lower voice has only the three notes *f g a,* and could be regarded as a slight elaboration of a shifting-drone basis on *f* and *g.* The voices are written in the same pitch-range, and in each the highest line of the staff represents *c'.* The technique of their combination is therefore gymel, as in *Jesu Cristes milde moder.* The music was probably composed by one not deeply schooled in polyphonic practice, though the scribe was obviously aware of some of the usual practices in musical notation. Since the verbal text shows signs of having perhaps been written down from memory (see p. 167), it is possible that the music also was written as remembered from performance, and it is also possible that its scribe was the *magister scholarum* of the Priory grammar-school. The music of the Latin sequences appears to have been written by the same hand, which may indicate that its writer was also a member of the priory community, as Carleton Brown suggested.

This song may be sung by two voices, as would usually be inferred from its being written in score with the text below. The alternative is suggested here of performance by voice and guitar (representing the medieval gittern), plectrum lute, or other plucked string instrument.

NOTES

There are three lines of music, each consisting of two staves which are separated by no more than the distance of a normal space. The first line has three staff-lines with *c*-clef on the highest line for the lower voice and four staff-lines with *c*-clef with *b*-flat on the third space for the upper voice. The second line has three staff-lines with *c*-clef on the highest line for the lower voice and three staff-lines with *b*-flat on the second space for the upper voice. The third line has three staff-lines with *a*-clef on the second line for the lower voice and three staff-lines with *b*-flat on the second space for the upper voice. (Perhaps the master made these unnecessary changes with a view to using the song as lesson-material in staff-notation.) The number-references here are to bars; the word-references are to the first stanza.

Upper voice: The notes on the following syllables represent a single plicated note in each case: 1 'be'/ 3 first syllable of 'folkes', 'froovre' (two *a*'s, the second plicated)/ 4 first syllable of 'engles'/ 5 second syllable of 'unwemmed'/ 7 'swich', 'world'/ 8 first syllable of 'other'; these must be separated (irregularly) in stanza 3/ 10 'wel'/ 15 'rew'/ 16 'thi'/ 2 the *g* is repeated in the MS/ 5 the *f* is repeated in the MS/ 10 the repeat of *f* is not in the MS/ 14 the repeat of *c* is not in the MS/ for a comment on the beginning of the second stanza see above, p. 302.

Lower voice: The notes on the following syllables represent a single plicated note in each case: 4 first syllable of 'engles'/ 8 first syllable of 'other'/ 10 'wel'/ 12 the two semiquavers on 'hast'/ 16 'thi'/ 1 the *g* is not in the MS for the first verse, is shown for the second verse/ 2 the first *g* is repeated in the MS/ 5 the first *a* is repeated in the MS/ 10 the repeat of *f* is not in the MS/ 11 the three *f*'s are in the MS/ 14 the repeat of the first *a* is not in the MS.

14. The milde Lomb, isprad o roode

Source: London, British Library, MS Arundel 248, f. 154; facsimile in H. E. Wooldridge, *Early English Harmony,* London, 1897, pl. 34.

This song is written in the manuscript immediately after *Angelus ad virginem / Gabriel fram heven-king* (no. 15) and on the same page. The words of the first half-stanza are written under the music, and those of the other half-stanzas in turn below the first. The scribe was obviously not concerned with placing the words clearly under their notes. The song is written in a musical notation very similar to that of no. 15 and may be by the same hand. The conjunction of the two songs brings into sharp focus the inherent rhythmic ambiguity (to us) of this kind of notation, which was sometimes also used for polyphonic music. The poems of *Angelus ad virginem / Gabriel fram heven-king* are well suited by a musical setting in mensural rhythm in triple time, and the tune survives elsewhere in polyphonic settings written unambiguously in that rhythm. The metrical character of *The milde Lomb,* however, can be made amenable to a setting with regularly accented musical measure only by suppressing notes, or adding notes not in the music as recorded. In addition, the tune has groups of from two to five notes to a syllable, which cannot be dealt with satisfactorily in a mensural rhythm.

The basic metrical scheme of the poem is 8887 for each half-stanza, all of which go to the same music. In this edition each half-stanza is numbered separately, to conform to the stanzaic musical setting. The basic metrical scheme is used in only two half-stanzas in the emended text (half-stanzas 2 and 11), and there are no less than eight other metrical patterns (8897 in 12, 9888 in 1 and 8, 9988 in 3, 9997 in 7, 9898 in 6, 8988 in 4 and 9, 8998 in 10 and 8898 in 5). Analysis of the musical notation shows that the first line can be broken down into the following nine *figurae* (i.e., single notes or groups of notes; plic = plicated; doub = of double length, shown in the notation by horizontal extension): (1) *f*; (2) *g*; (3) *a b a*; (4) *a* plic *f*; (5) *g* doub *a*; (6) *b* flat; (7) *a*; (8) *g a g g* plic; (9) *f*. This distribution of the *figurae* will accommodate the five cases of first lines which have nine syllables. To accommodate the seven cases of an eight-syllable line the first two *figurae* have been set in the transcription to one syllable. A similar break-down of the music of the other three lines shows that the second, third and fourth lines can be regarded as having respectively nine, nine and eight *figurae*. When there are eight syllables in the second line the seventh and eighth *figurae* are set to one syllable. Similarly, when the third line has eight syllables its first two *figurae*

are set to one syllable, as are the first two *figurae* in the fourth line in the five cases in which it has seven syllables.

The musical notation of this song seems to contain a relatively large proportion of *figurae* which are plicated or doubled (either by horizontal extension or by immediate repetition of the same note). There are two plicated notes and one double note in each of the first two lines, a double and a plicated note of the same pitch side by side in the third line, and two plicated notes and one double note in the fourth line. It is possible that *figurae* of this kind are attempts to suggest through relatively inflexible written symbols the scribe's recollection of subtleties of rhythm and articulation heard in performance. Many of the performance characteristics of solo vocal music before and outside the context of written 'art-music' are impossible to record adequately in written notation; and it may be that the musical scribe of *The milde Lomb* was trying to incorporate some record of practices of this kind in his notation. In the transcription given here each detail of his record has been taken into account, and the relative stresses of the text have been indicated by various groupings of the flexibly equal quavers in the same way as in some of the earlier items in this collection. A modern transcription of this kind of song, however, like its medieval original, can do little more than set out basic guide-lines for performance. It is for the individual singer to fashion his voice and the song into an effective and meaningful communication.

15. (i) Angelus ad virginem
(ii) Gabriel fram heven-king

Sources:

Version (a): Cambridge, University Library, MS Additional 710, f. 127 (tune only, with complete Latin text); facsimile in Dom Hesbert, *Le Tropaire-prosaire de Dublin,* Rouen, 1966, pl. 186.

Version (b): London, British Library, MS Arundel 248, f. 154 (tune only, with complete Latin and English texts); facsimile in H. E. Wooldridge, *Early English Harmony,* London, 1897, pl. 34.

Version (c): London, British Library, MS Cotton Fragments XXIX, f. 36ᵛ (two voices in score, with complete Latin text).

Version (d): Cambridge, University Library, MS Additional 710, f. 130ᵛ (three voices in score, without text); facsimile in Dom Hesbert, *Le Tropaire-prosaire de Dublin,* Rouen, 1966, pl. 192.

Version (e): ibid., f. 130 (three voices in score, with Latin text of the first stanza as far as the second syllable of 'paries'); facsimile in Dom Hesbert, *Le Tropaire-prosaire de Dublin,* Rouen, 1966, pl. 193.

The music of this song survives in a tune version of the late thirteenth century (in the Arundel manuscript), a two-voice setting of the late thirteenth or early fourteenth century, and a tune version and two three-voice settings all in a manuscript whose main part probably dates from the first half of the fourteenth century. This manuscript is the only one of the sources concerned whose original provenance is known. It is generally referred to as the 'Dublin Troper', and belonged in the Middle Ages to St. Patrick's Cathedral, Dublin. The chief contents are a Customary of the Use of Salisbury, sequences for various feasts including that of St. Patrick, and Marian sequences, which were probably sung in the Votive Mass of the Virgin. At the end of the manuscript in later writing are texts which include forms of installation of the archbishop, of a vicar-choral and of a minor canon of St. Patrick's. The Cotton fragment which contains the two-voice version of the song is a partly burnt, smoke-stained leaf which is one of a number of fragments saved from a fire which destroyed part of the Cotton library in 1731.

Manfred Bukofzer remarked of this song that 'the majority of manuscripts in which it is transmitted are of English origin' (*The New Oxford History of Music,* iii, London, 1960, p. 115), but he did not make it clear whether he was alluding to manuscripts containing the texts or the music, nor did he cite any others than those we are concerned with here. There appears not to be any surviving version of the music in a non-English source of the thirteenth or fourteenth century, though there was a text-version in a Metz manuscript of the late thirteenth century. A French origin for the Latin text, as suggested by Dreves and Blume, is possible, though they cited no firm evidence to support this. However, an argument for French origin might be founded on details of the scansion (on these points see p. 178).

The opening three notes of the tune correspond to the *variatio* (formulaic beginning) of a group of plainsong tunes in the seventh mode (final *g*) which at their usual pitch begin on the fifth degree of the mode with *d' b d'* (see the Sarum Tonale in *The Use of Sarum,* ed. W. H. Frere, ii, Cambridge, 1901, at p. xlviii). Though the song is also in the seventh mode it begins an octave higher than its final note, which does not happen in plainsong. The song's last cadence-phrase is its only other tune-formula usual in plainsong.

In the following discussion the music-phrases are referred to by capital letters, according to the scheme set out below.

Lines of Poem	Number of Syllables	Phrase-structure of Tune
1	7	A
2	7	B
3	7	A¹
4	7	B¹
5	8	C
6	8	C¹
7	4	D
8	4	D¹ + E
9	3	
10	6	F
11	7	D² + E¹
12	6	F

No two of the five versions of the tune agree exactly, and it would be pointless to attempt to reconstruct the original, especially since three of the versions are in the same manuscript and two of these are almost certainly by the same arranger and are written in the same hand. The notation of the monophonic version (b), like that of *The milde Lomb* (no. 14) which is written below it, has a relatively high proportion of plicated and double notes, and seems to be an attempt to record a particularly ornate manner of performing the tune. Phrases A and B are written once only in the two-voice version, and under them

the text of lines 3 and 4 is written below the text of lines 1 and 2. These phrases are repeated exactly in version (e) and with slight variation in versions (b) and (d). In phrase C version (a) is similar to versions (b) and (e) and version (c) resembles version (d), while in phrase C¹ all are basically alike. Version (d) has a form of phrase D whose repetition of the notes *c' a* makes it distinct from the related forms of the other versions. There are two forms of phrase F: in versions (a) and (b) it is based on the common cadence-formula *a g f g,* while the other versions have a *b* flat before this formula. In version (e) *f* sharp is indicated.

The two monophonic versions and the two-voice version, which are written in the manuscripts in non-mensural notation, are transcribed here in the triple measure which is explicit in the three-voice settings. The rhythm of the ligatures in the lower voice of version (c) has been interpreted in the triple measure context, taking account of the probable coincidence of notes between the two voices. Even if the validity of triple rhythm for version (b) be assumed, the rhythmic interpretation of many details in the notation must remain uncertain. The *figurae* for the first two lines of the poem, for example, ignoring the presence or absence of the downward stem to the right which in mensural notation is the distinction between a *longa* and a *brevis,* are the following: *g g* plic *e g g f e e* plic *d d e e* plic *c f e d e* ligatured *c c c.* A note followed immediately by a plicated note of the same pitch has been transcribed here as a dotted quaver followed by a semiquaver, but there is no certainty about this interpretation. The same is true of the four *figurae d d d* plic *g* for the word 'heven-light' in the first stanza, which are transcribed here as crotchet *d,* semiquavers *e d* and crotchet *g.* The transcription of the rhythm of this version is an attempt to define the kind of ornateness, and in that sense sophistication, which the scribe was probably suggesting by his complex notation.

The arranger, who may also have been the scribe, of versions (d) and (e) was acquainted with the use of points of division, and of semibreve followed by minim in the relation of major prolation, i.e., where the minim takes one-third of the rhythmic value of the perfect semibreve. There is some doubt, however, whether or not he was familiar with the practice of giving doubled value to the second of two semibreves, making it a *semibrevis altera,* before a perfect breve. Since the scribe occasionally used a semibreve following a breve, which was therefore made imperfect by position, in one voice simultaneously with two-semibreve ligature in another voice, Bukofzer (*The New Oxford History of Music,* iii, 1960, p. 116) considered that he was not familiar with the *semibrevis altera* convention, and that he intended the same rhythm by the ligature as he did by a semibreve following a breve. The other view is taken in the transcriptions here, where the rhythmic effect of doubling the second semibreve may be seen in bars 9, 11, 13 and 18 of both versions. It could be taken as confirming either view that the scribe wrote the second note of the ligature *g c* in the lowest voice in bar 13 of version (d) (which Bukofzer did not publish) in a special form, with two obliquely descending stems – perhaps to ensure that it would be sung as a *semibrevis altera.*

Discussion of the interval-theory behind the two-voice version presupposes some decisions by the transcriber about rhythm and whatever emendations or reconstructions seem needed in the not always legible fragment. A significant emendation made here is the addition of *g* in the lower voice at the beginning of bar 9. This makes the setting of phrase C equivalent to that of phrase C¹ and allies it to the interval-practice of the setting as a whole. Assuming the validity of this emendation and of the rhythmic interpretations adopted, it is clear that the arranger disposed contrary and parallel motion with a good sense of linear contrast and change. His use of successions of parallel sixths, which is relatively early in time, may imply an acquaintance with a practice possibly current in unwritten polyphony which English composers of liturgical music adopted extensively in the course of the fourteenth century.

The title of Bukofzer's doctoral thesis, which was published in Strasbourg in 1936, was *Geschichte des englischen Diskants und des Fauxbourdons nach den theoretischen Quellen*. From his reading of the relevant theoretical treatises Bukofzer came to the conclusion, among others, that descant in England was a technique in which a composer setting an already existing tune put it in the lowest voice. Subsequent research has shown that this conclusion is invalid as a general rule, and that the treatises, mostly of the late fourteenth and early fifteenth centuries, on which Bukofzer mainly relied are not prescriptions for composition but rules of elementary polyphony for singers involving improvisation at sight in two parts, not in three. Except in a few rare instances and in those where the existing tune is not put in one voice throughout, English composers of descant put the existing tune in the middle voice, as in versions (d) and (e) of *Angelus ad virginem*. Two- and three-part parallel descant, though not dealt with in the teaching treatises, was extensively written in the fourteenth century in England. Three-part descant had fifths or sixths with thirds, and occasionally with octaves (parallel octaves and fifths went out of fashion early in the fifteenth century), often in long stretches, but also in relatively short sequences, like bars 3 and 4 and several similar passages in these settings. Their composer(s) were *au fait* with these interval-practices, and also with *musica ficta* — the occasional application of sharps or flats to give a special colour of sound and/or a particular structural value to the usual intervals, as in phrase F in both settings. The simultaneous parallel fifths and sixths, producing parallel seconds, in bar 14 of version (e) have seemed to two previous editors to need emendation. Bukofzer emended the highest voice and Harold Gleason inadmissibly emended the tune (*Examples of Music before 1400*, New York, 1942, p. 52). In the transcription here the reading of the manuscript is retained.

For performance purposes the Latin text given in the manuscripts of versions (a), (c) and (e) has been replaced by the complete English text, which has been omitted from version (b) and applied to version (d). Preceding the transcriptions of the five versions the complete Latin text is given, for use with the music of any of the five transcriptions as desired. An optional instrumental accompaniment has been added to versions (a) and (b). That for version (a) is designed for a psaltery, the instrument on which Chaucer's clerk Nicholas accompanied himself singing *Angelus ad virginem*. It may be played, however, on any suitable plucked string instrument. Like the accompaniment for version (b), which is for a small diatonic harp or other plucked string instrument, it is written with octaves and fifths as the structural intervals, with thirteenth-century interval-practice in mind, and on the shifting-drone basis common to many medieval tunes. The outer voices of version (d) have been disposed in the transcription in such a

way as to facilitate their being played on an organ. At two places, in bars 6 and 16, one or both of these voices has one note fewer in the manuscript than the text requires. These have been supplied as small notes in the transcription, for use if performance by voices is desired. It is suggested that any of the five versions may be used in performance in whatever order may seem practical and musically effective. Their order here has been decided partly on those grounds.

NOTES

(References are by bar-numbers)
Version (a): 5,9 the notes on 'mai(de)', 'fair' and 'gan' represent *e'* plic in each case
Version (b): the *figurae* in phrases A and B are given above; phrase A¹ begins with *g g e* plicated upwards *g*; *figurae* in phrase C: *d* plic *f ed* ligatured *e e* plic *c de* ligatured *d d* plic *c;* in phrase C¹, following the fifth of these, they are *c* rest (apparently misplaced) *d d d* plic *g*; *figurae* in phrase D: *a* plic *c b a*; *figurae* in phrase D¹ + E: *b c ef* ligatured and plic *d d* plic *d*; *figurae* in phrase F: *g a a* plic *g gf* ligatured *g g* ligatured *g g*; *figurae* in phrase D² + E¹: *a* plic *c ba* ligatured *c def* ligatured and plic *d d* plic *d*; the penultimate *figura* in phrase F is *fg* ligatured.
Version (c): The MS gives the first nine notes of the tune, and the corresponding lower voice, for the opening of the second stanza. 9 the first note of the lower voice is supplied/ 15 the second *d* in the lower voice is *c* in the MS; the notes *c d e* in the upper voice are not visible in the MS/ 20 the flat for *b* in the lower voice is supplied.
Version (d): 8 the second note in the tune is a brevis (= dotted crotchet)/ 18 after *b* the tune was superfluous *c b a g* which is ringed in the MS.
Version (e): 22 the middle voice has *a* in the MS.

16a. Brid one breere

Source: Cambridge, King's College, Muniment Roll 2 W 32; facsimile in J. Saltmarsh, 'Two Medieval Love-songs set to Music', *The Antiquaries Journal*, xv, 1935, opposite p. 3.

The music of this song is written partly on a five-line staff — from its beginning to the end of the twelfth bar of the transcription — and partly on a four-line staff — from the thirteenth bar to the end. There is a blank four-line staff between the two staves with music. The notation is mensural and is consistent with a date shortly before or a decade or two after 1300. The scribe used longs and breves apparently in the relation of *modus perfectus*, i.e., three breves to the long, and semibreves apparently in *tempus imperfectum*, i.e., two semibreves to a breve, writing semibreves both separately and ligatured in pairs (*cum opposita proprietate*). In one instance he wrote two semibreves *c.o.p.* in ligature with a breve. While it is clear that the notation is mensural the exact rhythm intended is not always certain, either, it seems, on account of deterioration in the writing, or of scribal inaccuracy (or uncertainty), or both.

Manfred Bukofzer printed a transcription of the music with the words of the first stanza (*The New Oxford History of Music*, iii, 1960, p. 113) in which he interpreted the two semibreves and breve in ligature already referred to as a triplet of semibreves (quavers in his transcription). This could be valid in a pre-mensural context but does not seem appropriate here. He transcribed the three notes in bar 13 (of the transcription here) and also the first three notes in bar 15 as a triplet of quavers in each case, though in both the manuscript has a breve (here emended to a long in bar 13) and two semibreves. Transcribing all the semibreves as quavers does not, however, result in a transcription which is rhythmically convincing throughout, and some emendations seem necessary. These have been kept to a minimum here, consistent with taking account of the metrical structure and stress values of the edited text. This latter consideration has prompted a rhythmic modification which is not justified by the notation as transmitted, but which fits more precisely the needs of the text at that point. This is the grouping of the four notes *f e f d* in bar 7, which are equal rhythmically in the manuscript but are here transcribed as a crotchet followed by a triplet of quavers (instead of four quavers). This accommodates more comfortably the metre /x/xx of the text in this bar.

Bukofzer came to the conclusion that the scribe wrote the last six bars (in the transcription here) of the tune a third higher than they should have been. He accordingly emended the first note of bar 13 from *g'* to *e'* and wrote the following notes two degrees lower, making the song end on *a*. In the manuscript the note *g'* in question is the first note on the second staff, a four-line staff as already stated. The scribe put the *c* clef on the second of the four lines. It is conceivable that the change from a five-line to a four-line staff led him to put the clef on the second instead of the third line, as Bukofzer thought. One of the reasons for his opinion was presumably that the tune seems to be in the *a* mode if judged by its beginning. But many medieval non-plainsong tunes were made of different tune-formulae from those of plainsong, whose modal principles are therefore not relevant to them. The tune of Martin Codax's *Quantas sabedes* (*The New Oxford History of Music,* iii, p. 261), for example, begins on *a*, a note higher than its final *g*. It is not to be assumed for modal reasons, therefore, that the scribe of *Brid one breere* was mistaken in making the tune begin on *d'* and end on *c'*. The tune-material of the song consists of five units deployed in the following fashion (the bracketed numbers indicate lines of the stanza): (1) aa; (2) bb; (3) cd; (4) ed[1]. It seems certain that the repeat of d, modified only in its ending, was intended to be at the same pitch, not a third lower. Bukofzer's emendation destroys the climactic point of the tune, which occurs at the *g'* in question if no emendation be made, though this is in part an aesthetic criterion and therefore unreliable. An upward leap of a sixth within a unit, which occurs here if the *g'* be retained, is undoubtedly rare in surviving written medieval tunes. An upward sixth between units, though also rare, is less remarkable. It occurs between the fourth and fifth bars of this song. This seems an additional reason for not doubting the scribe's accuracy in bar 13.

NOTES

(References are to bar-numbers.)

The following pairs of semibreves in the MS are ligatured: 2 *ab*; 6 *fe* with the following breve; 12 all three pairs; 14 both pairs; 17 all three pairs/ 7 the MS rhythm is breve followed by four semibreves/ 8 *pace* Bukofzer, *e* on the first beat is a long, though the note-stem is short; the second *e* is supplied/ 11 *d* is a breve in MS/ 13 *g* is a breve in MS.

16b. (i) Maid in the moor lay
(ii) Peperit virgo (text by Richard de Ledrede)

The credit for the discovery that the poem *Maid in the moor lay* can be sung to the tune of *Brid one breere* belongs to the text editor, and the transcription given here is in acordance with his establishing and interpretation of the text of *Maid in the moor lay* (see pp. 190–1). The tune of *Maid in the moor lay* was also the tune for which Richard de Ledrede, Bishop of Ossory, wrote the Latin poem beginning *Peperit virgo* (see *New Oxford History of Music,* iii, pp. 118–119).

The slight modifications needed in some but not all stanzas are shown in small notes. The only other changes from the form given for *Brid one breere* which are needed in all the stanzas are the repetition of the first note (except in stanza 1) and the non-repetition of the last note.

17. Worldes blisse, have good day
Tenor: [Benedicamus Domino]

Source: Cambridge, Corpus Christi College, MS 8, f. 270.

This song has survived on the flyleaf of an early fourteenth-century manuscript. The flyleaf was cut from a double page and inserted sideways, and is a relic of a large book which contained some three hundred leaves, for its pages bear the numbers 547, 548, 557 and 558. Above *Worldes blisse* on page 547 there is the ending of a two-part song in descant style with the words 'in lyde' (then a 'barline' in the music) 'ioye and blisce bringet me to bride'. There is a transcription of this fragment in *The New Oxford History of Music,* iii, London, 1960, p. 111. The other contents of the double leaf are a French motet and some three-part *clausulae* (i.e., short wordless compositions written on an identified phrase of plainsong). The musical technique of *Worldes blisse* and its association with these items show that it was written by and for people with awareness of and competence in current methods in polyphonic music. The musical notation, which is consistent with a date of around 1300, is of the same kind as that in the later fascicles of the Montpellier manuscript, of about the same date (see the facsimile in Y. Rokseth, *Polyphonies du xiiie siècle,* i, Paris, 1935).

In musical technique *Worldes blisse* belongs to the genre motet (Latin, *motetus;* usual medieval French form, *moté*). The earliest motets, which were written in France in the first quarter of the thirteenth century, were made by supplying words to the hitherto textless upper voice or voices of a *clausula. Clausulae* were composed on the basis of a phrase of plainsong identified by the syllable or one or two words to which it belonged in the course of an item of liturgical plainsong; for example, *Manere* from the Gradual for St. John's day, or *In saeculum* from the Gradual for Easter day. The clausula convention of disposing the tenor in short units identically rhythmicized ('isorhythmic') was continued in motets when they began to be composed as such, apparently before the middle of the thirteenth century. The tune-phrase which is the tenor of *Worldes blisse* has forty notes (twenty-eight bars of the transcription) and is repeated twice, from bar 29 to bar 56 and from bar 57 to the end, each time in the same rhythm. This rhythm, in turn, consists of three repetitions of the same rhythmic pattern of ten notes, first heard in bars 1 to 7. In the analysis of an isorhythmic structure, the tune of a tenor (e.g., bars 1 to 28 of the lower voice of *Worldes blisse*) is commonly referred to as a *color*, while its unit of rhythm (which in *Worldes blisse* is seven bars long) is called a *talea* (literally, 'cutting'). The composer of *Worldes blisse* disposed the tenor in four *taleae* to one *color*, with three *colores* as the tenor of the entire composition. The tenor is written only once in the manuscript, with no indication of the two repeats.

There was more than one tenor *Domino* used in *clausulae* and motets; two of them may conveniently be seen in A. T. Davison and W. Apel, *Historical Anthology of Music*, i, Cambridge (Mass.), 1954, numbers 28 d-h, 30 and 32 c. Manfred Bukofzer was correct in pointing out that the tenor of *Worldes blisse*, which is not the same as either of the *Domino* tenors just mentioned, is actually a complete *Benedicamus Domino* tune (see his discussion and transcription of *Worldes blisse* in 'The First Motet with English Words', *Music and Letters*, xviii, 1936, pp. 225–33). However, he did not trace it to its further source, which is the music of the word *clementiam* (mostly vocalized on the second syllable) in *Qui cum audissent*, the fifth respond at Matins on the feast of St. Nicholas. The *Benedicamus Domino* tunes for a festival were originally lifted from the responds of the day in this fashion. Later the original association of a *Benedicamus* tune with its festival was loosened, and the cue indication, e.g. *clementiam*, was dropped, except in rare instances (see my *Music in Medieval Britain*, 2nd ed., London, 1963, pp. 74–76). It is unlikely that the *Benedicamus* tenor of *Worldes blisse* was associated with any particular festival in the mind of the composer. He would have known it as one of the tunes for the *Benedicamus Domino* at the end of a major office on important festivals. We know from the Customary of Lincoln cathedral of *c.* 1260, for example, that there the *clementiam* tune was used for *Benedicamus Domino* at the end of second Vespers on double feasts, and that the writer of the Customary was aware of the original respond source of each of the tunes he prescribed — the others were *in perenni* and *flos filius* (*Lincoln Cathedral Statutes*, ed. H. Bradshaw and C. Wordsworth, i, Cambridge, 1892, pp. 381, 369, 373). The composer of *Worldes blisse* may conceivably have known one or more polyphonic settings of this *Benedicamus* tune. There is one in the 'St. Andrews' manuscript, a thirteenth-century collection with largely French and some indigenous music which was used at St. Andrews Augustinian monastery in Scotland until the sixteenth century (see the facsimile in J. H. Baxter, *An Old St. Andrews Music Book*, London, 1931, ff. 7ᵛ–8).

The first thirteen notes of the tenor of *Worldes blisse* (bars 1–9) are identical with the next thirteen (bar 10 to the first note in bar 19), so that the tune has the form a a b. Repetition of this kind is common in longer vocalized sections (which in the Middle Ages were called *neumae*) of plainsong. Since its *talea*, as already noted, consists of ten notes (occupying seven bars of the transcription) the rhythmic repeat in bars 7 to 14 does not coincide with the tune repeat from bars 10 to the first note of bar 19. This is an instance *in parvo* of a technique of non-coincidence between *color* and *talea* frequently used in thirteenth- and fourteenth-century motet tenors.

Composers of French secular motets in the thirteenth century frequently quoted in an upper voice actual portions of both words and notes of *trouvère* songs, generally well-known refrains. However, an upper voice of a motet based on a plainsong tenor, as most were, rarely shared the tune-idioms of its structural voice, or if it did the resemblance would probably

have passed unnoticed, since the tenor was not usually perceptible as tune. It cannot have been coincidence that the composer of *Worldes blisse* began the upper voice with the five notes *f g' f e' c'*, identical with a phrase prominent in the plainsong (bars 5–7 of the tenor). Otherwise minor resemblances between tune formulae in the upper voice and the tenor are almost certainly unintentional.

The accepted interval-technique of thirteenth- and fourteenth-century motet writing was based on the use of a unison, octave or fifth at the beginning of each *perfectio* (of each bar of the transcription), while any interval could be used between these points. The long-standing notion that English composers were more inclined to use thirds than those of other nations is partly borne out in *Worldes blisse*, whose composer used a third at the beginning of a *perfectio* eleven times. He was quite orthodox otherwise, using only unisons, octaves and fifths at these points, and he was conservative in rarely using dissonances at other points. In a few cases the scribe's placing of notes on the staff is ambiguous. The plicated breve in bar 28 was transcribed as *c' d'* by Bukofzer, but *d' e'* seems more likely for tune reasons, though either would be acceptable on interval grounds. The apparent *d' c' e'* of the ligature of the first three notes in bar 53, which was accepted by Bukofzer though its position is doubtful in the manuscript, has been transcribed here as *e' d' e'*; the composer did not use elsewhere a fourth at the beginning of a *perfectio*. The scribe's *e'* on the first beat of bar 55 is certainly an error for *f*; a seventh would be impossible here.

NOTES

(References are to bar-numbers)
The following plicated longs are transcribed as a pair of breves in each case: 1 *f g'*; 6, *fg*; 80 *g a*. Plicated breves are transcribed as a pair of semibreves: 1 *f e'*; 17 *g a*; 18 *c' d'*; 28 *d' e'*; 62 *c' d'*. Emendations of pitch have been discussed in the last paragraph of the commentary.

18. Sancta mater graciae
   #### Tenor: Dou way, Robin

Sources: London, British Library, MS Cotton Fragments xxix, f. 36; Princeton, University Library, MS Garrett 119.

Manfred Bukofzer wrote of this item (*New Oxford History of Music*, iii, 1960, p. 112):

> This piece is the first and so far the only known motet with English words in the tenor, and, what is more, the tenor is secular and may conceivably preserve a popular refrain not otherwise known.

Bukofzer also published a transcription of the last twelve bars, based on both the sources, with the comment that the transcription, which is in duple time, was a tentative one 'because the fragment in the British Museum is hardly legible in several places, and because the English mensural notation of both fragments, though strongly suggestive of duple metre, is ambiguous. The music could be transcribed also in triple metre (third mode).'

The British Museum copy of this item is in fact complete, though the fire damage, and the repairer's use in some places of gold-beater's skin, have made it very difficult to read. Like the two-part version of *Angelus ad virginem* (no. 15 (i)), it is a survival of the fire at Ashburnham House, Westminster, in 1731 which destroyed some of the Cotton library a year after it had been installed there as a national possession. The duplum consists of eight lines of music and text, and is followed by three statements of the tenor, without text. The Princeton manuscript is one of several flyleaves formerly bound with a late fourteenth-century English copy of Walter of Lille's *Alexandreis,* which was presented with other manuscripts to the Firestone Memorial Library by Mr. Robert Garrett of Baltimore (see K. J. Levy, 'New Material on the Early Motet in England: A Report on Princeton Ms. Garrett 119', *Journal of the American Musicological Society,* iv [1951], pp. 220–39). The flyleaves have since been detached from the binding, and a few more notes and words are visible than Professor Levy could see. These do not affect his description of the leaf, which he designated as 'Fragment B':

> Fragment B (ff. 1–6, forming a single leaf, 26 cm. × *ca.* 19 cm.) was a loose leaf several centimeters broader than the page width of the present volume; the original side and lower margins are fairly well preserved, but material at the top has been cut away. Only one side (ff. 1a–6b, read together) of this fragment contains music, while the other (ff. 6a–1b) is taken up with monastic accounts dating from the fourth or fifth decade of the fourteenth century. The musical side is in an English mensural notation (using the *custos*) of the late thirteenth century.

The surviving music of this motet in the Princeton source consists of the duplum from the word 'morbo' in bar 72 to the end, followed by one statement of the tenor's music, with the underlaid text *Dou way Robin the child wile wepe dou way Robin* written in red ink. Its notation in separate notes, with a two-note ligature for 'child', provides for singing to the text, though this is a secular one. However, analogy with the use of red text in some other liturgical contexts suggests that the text may have been given here only for identification. While the evidence is contradictory, it is possible that both alternatives were contemplated — performance without the tenor text for choir use, with the tenor text elsewhere.

The duple rhythm in which Bukofzer transcribed the last twelve bars seems less suited to the complete music and text of the duplum than the triple rhythm adopted here. While there is no substantial difference in the relation of music-rhythm to text-rhythm, the use of duple rhythm occasions some crowding of the text, particularly in bar 64. The note-shapes include diamond breves (as in *Sumer is icumen in,* no. 9), and groups of three of these whose first note has a stem obliquely downwards to the left (as in *Lou, lou, lou! wer he goth,* no. 19). Both these usages are characteristic of English mensural notation of the second half of the thirteenth century. The notation of these three items may be compared with that of the duplum of *Worldes blisse, have good day* (no. 17). This is completely in accordance with Franconian practice, where breves are square and semibreves are diamond, or are paired in a ligature *cum opposita proprietate,* shown by a stem upwards to the left. The rests in the duplum of *Worldes blisse, have good day* are not fully regularized, however.

Apart from the overall question of triple or duple rhythm, transcription of the duplum of *Sancta mater graciae* must in some respects be hypothetical. The various lengths of rest in

this transcription, from the quaver in bar 15 to the bar-and-a-half in bars 5–6, all correspond to a single line, or once an apparently double line, drawn through the staff in the manuscript. While few pitches are uncertain, some note-values are decided, within certain limitations, by context — as in modal notation. However, virtually all notes which appear to be longs are transcribed as such; very occasionally a square or diamond note is transcribed as a long. Decisions on details of rhythmic interpretation must sometimes be bound up with interval-relations between the duplum and tenor.

The tenor in the British Museum manuscript is written in a succession of ligatures and single longs, which would in strict Franconian terms be interpreted in the rhythm of the third mode. The basic rhythmic pattern of this mode, expressed in terms of the transcription's reduction to one-sixteenth of the original note-values, would be a six-eight bar consisting of a dotted crotchet, a quaver and a crotchet, in that order. However, the apparent third-mode rhythm of some post-Franconian tenors, of both English and French provenance, requires interpretation in what has been termed 'alternate' third mode, that is, in a rhythm of dotted crotchet, crotchet and quaver in terms of this transcription (see E. H. Sanders, 'Duple Rhythm and Alternate Third Mode in the 13th Century', *Journal of the American Musicological Society,* xv [1962], pp. 270–90). This also applies to the tenor of *Worldes blisse, have good day,* where the manuscript's note-values are reduced to one-eighth in the transcription, giving minim, crotchet-rest, minim and crotchet for the 'alternate' third mode.

In its original context the tenor of this motet presumably had a symmetrically measured rhythm, though we cannot be certain whether this was duple or triple (or possibly optionally one or the other). This is a different situation from that in *Worldes blisse, have good day* (no. 17), where the pre-existing tenor was not symmetrically measured, and its motet-rhythm was given to it by the composer. Thirteen statements of the six-bar tune *Dou way, Robin* underlie the seven stanzas of the Latin poem of the duplum, in the following way:

Stanzas	Statements
1,2	1–3
3	4–5
4	6–8
5	9–10
6	11
7	12–13

Points of exact coincidence between stanza-ending and tenor-tune-ending occur at the end of stanzas 3 (bar 30), 4 (bar 48) and 5 (bar 60). Elsewhere the units of the duplum are so organized as to overlap the beginnings of the tenor's repetitions.

NOTES
4 shape of note(s) on third syllable of 'claritatis' is unclear/ 10 the second *g* is supplied for better text-accentuation/ 53 appears to be one note short; MS has plicated *d* for 'O'; the *b* for 'quam' is supplied/ 61 the second and third *d*'s appear to have a downward stem each/ 62 the same is true of the first two notes/ 73 notes *e' d'* in duplum not in Princeton MS/ 75 *e'* is worn or partly erased in Cotton MS/ 77 semiquavers *f' g'* represent a plicated *f'* in Princeton MS; there appears not to be a plica in Cotton MS.

19. Lou, lou, lou! wer he goth!

Source: Dublin, Trinity College, University Library, MS D. 4. 9 (270), f. 37ᵛ.

Both text and music of this two-voice song, which was discovered by this editor in December 1968, have been hitherto unnoticed. There is no other musical notation in the manuscript in which it is written, and the musical item bears no relation to the treatise in which it was inserted (see the Textual Commentary, p. 198). The discoverer was moved to look through the manuscript by the fact that its contents, as given in T. M. Abbott's catalogue of the library's manuscripts (Dublin and London, 1900), include works by Johannes de Garlandia. Musical historians have posited two writers on musical theory with this name, the earlier of whom is probably identical with the English-born author of the non-musical treatises in the Dublin manuscript.

The music is written on two five-line staves, one voice above the other. The text is written under both voices, though part-music written in this way usually had the text under the lower voice only, as in *Fuweles in the frith* (no. 8). The music scribe used note-forms which he must have meant to be interpreted in measured rhythm. In general the notation is similar to that of *Brid one breere* (no. 16a), though the notator of *Lou, lou, lou!* used a greater variety of note-forms. Among these is a *conjunctura* of three rhomboid-shaped notes descending stepwise, the first of which has a stem obliquely downwards to the left. The evidence of surviving manuscripts shows that this form was used particularly, though not exclusively, in England in the thirteenth and early fourteenth centuries. It occurs, for example, in a two-part instrumental dance in the same manuscript as *Sumer is icumen in* (facsimile in H. E. Wooldridge, *Early English Harmony,* London, 1897, pl. 18), in an *estampie* written on the back of the leaf which has *Fuweles in the frith,* and in the group of manuscripts of church music known as the 'Worcester Fragments' (see L. A. Dittmer, 'Binary rhythm, musical theory and the Worcester Fragments', *Musica Disciplina,* vii, 1953, pp. 54–56). These and other occurrences show that this *conjunctura* may be transcribed, depending on its rhythmic position and context, as two breves followed by a long, or two semibreves followed either by a long or a breve, the latter if this is immediately followed by another breve. In *Lou, lou, lou!* this *conjunctura* is used only in the upper voice, where it occurs four times and is followed either by a breve (in bars 2 and 8 of the transcription) or a long (bars 6–7 and 13–14). The final note of the upper voice, which is of doubtful shape in the manuscript, is here taken to be a long. In bars 2 and 8 the lower voice has at the same time a rising three-note ligature which means unambiguously two semibreves *cum opposita proprietate* and a breve according to the principles of notation expounded about 1260 by Franco of Cologne in his *Ars cantus mensurabilis* (ed. F. Gennrich, Darmstadt, 1957, p. 124), and subsequently widely adopted. The *conjunctura* in the upper voice in these two cases is accordingly transcribed as a pair of semibreves followed by a breve.

The *conjunctura* which appears in the sixth bar of the transcription above the word *i* in the upper voice has with it in the lower voice a descending two-note ligature *cum opposita proprietate* with the pitches *g f.* The rhythmic value of the *conjunctura* in this position must be contained within the length of two semibreves, and is here transcribed as the

modern equivalent of two minims followed by a semibreve. Three-note *conjuncturae* in continental manuscripts of the thirteenth century, whose first note was usually written as a long, also had ambivalence of this kind in their rhythmic meaning.

The scribe used three times in the upper voice — for the notes *c b c* in the sixth bar and for the notes *g f g* in both bars nine and ten — a form of ligature *cum opposita proprietate* in which the third note is written directly above the second note. According to Franco (Gennrich's edition, p. 125) and later practice this is a *ligatura perfecta* in which the third note is a long. The scribe used it here, however, to denote the rhythm semibreve-semibreve-breve. In each case it has with it in the lower voice an ascending ligature which invariably had this meaning in a mensural context. Anomalies of this kind, sometimes retained from earlier mensural practices, are characteristic of notation in England in the thirteenth and early fourteenth centuries.

Emendation is needed in the passage corresponding to the fourth bar of the transcription; the upper voice is a semibreve short, and its dots of division seem to be misplaced. Here the rhythm of the upper voice has been emended to agree with that of the lower voice. Though this scribe's notation has some anomalies and retains some pre-Franconian elements, his use of dots of division, which were a French development of the late thirteenth century, suggests a date for the writing of this item in the first third of the fourteenth century.

Some signs of erasure in the upper voice over the words *for hir i les myn* suggest that this voice originally had a different tune at this point. The erased notes appear to have been *e'* (breve) *f' e'* (semi-breves in ligature) *c'* (breve) *g' d'* (semi-breves in ligature) *e'* (long) and *f'* (breve). If the scribe wrote this originally, it made reasonably good counterpoint, except that the last two notes make parallel octaves, but it gave the upper voice a falling contour where it now has a rising one. The voices do not fit in the passage following this. Immediately after the note *a'* on the word *myn* in the upper voice there is a vertical stroke from the second line of the staff almost to the third line. The flow of both text and music at this point preclude this line's being interpreted as a rest. It is followed by an oblique ligature on *g' f'* which appears to have no stem. Assuming that the lower voice in bars 7–9, where it is clear in rhythm and in its relation to the text, is correct, both the line and the ligature in the upper voice are superfluous. It may be that the scribe wrote this line as part of an intended ligature, which he then wrote without a stem, and that he replaced both the line and the ligature by the following *conjunctura* but forgot to erase them. A vertical stroke extending across the third and fourth spaces of the upper staff after the *b'* in the twelfth bar of the transcription is interpreted as a rest of one bar, though its strict mensural meaning would be an imperfect long, equivalent to two crotchets in the transcription. This interpretation agrees with the rhythm of the last three notes in the lower voice, which are written as duplex long, long and duplex long respectively.

The interval technique of *Lou, lou, lou!* includes parallel sixths and tenths, and contrary motion inwards from an octave and outwards from a sixth and a tenth. Church music based on this technique, either for two voices or more often for the outer voices of a three-part composition, occurs in the 'Worcester' music (see, for example, nos. 87, 89 and 91 in L. A. Dittmer, *The Worcester Fragments,* Rome, 1957) and in many English sacred compositions of the fourteenth century. Though the technique was usually applied in short items with homogeneous rhythm, it was occasionally used for the outer voices of a motet whose tenor was (exceptionally) in the middle voice. Two instances of this in unpublished motets are cited in this editor's paper 'Ars nova in England: a new source' (Musica Disciplina, xxi, 1967, pp. 72 and 79). The term proto-faburden was suggested there to denote this characteristically English technique during the century or more of its use before the terms fauxbourdon and faburden appear in surviving written sources. Both terms defined a rule-of-thumb method of improvising part-music, in which a lower part was added to a cantus prius factus by singing an octave at the beginning and end of each phrase — and occasionally elsewhere at will — and otherwise parallel sixths throughout (see B. Trowell, 'Faburden and fauxbourdon', Musica Disciplina, xiii, 1959, p. 43; F. Ll. Harrison, 'Faburden in practice', ibid., xvi, 1962, p. 11). It seems certain that improvisation formulae of this kind had long existed as unwritten practices outside the sphere of church music. If this is so, Lou, lou, lou! is of special interest as an early written instance of such a formulaic polyphonic technique used in a secular song.

NOTES

Note-values have been reduced to one-eighth of the original; ligatures are indicated by slurs.

Upper voice: 4 first note is a semibreve in the MS; there are dots of division after the second and fourth notes; the rhythm has been emended to agree with that of the lower voice/ 5 g' is a dotted long in MS/ 5–7 over the words *For hir i les myn* some notes appear to have been erased — see the discussion above/ 6 second c'' is a long by Franconian principles/ 7 after a' an upward line and an oblique ligature g' f' without stem have been ignored/ 9, 10 the second g' in each bar is a long by Franconian principles/ 13 vertical line through the third and fourth spaces of the staff is transcribed as a perfect long rest/ 14 g' is no more than a black smudge of indefinite shape.

Lower voice: 3 semibreve a with upward plica-stem is interpreted as a b/ 10 ligature b c on the first half of the third beat has no stem and is not joined to the following ligature; rhythm has been emended to agree with upper voice.

20. Lullay, lullay: Als I lay on Yoolis night

Source: Cambridge, University Library, MS Additional 5943, f. 169; facsimiles (not entirely reliable) and transcriptions (unreliable) of the pages of this manuscript with music notation in S. L. M[yers], *Music, Cantilenas, Songs &c. from an early Fifteenth Century Manuscript*, London, 1906; facsimile of these pages also in *A fifteenth-century Song Book*, with introduction by Richard Rastell, Leeds, 1973.

This and nine of the following thirteen songs (nos. 25 to 33) are contained in a manuscript whose early history and ownership are dealt with on pp. 23–6. *Als I lay on Yoolis night* is the only monophonic song in this collection. Although its mensural notation is similar to that of the polyphonic songs, its rhythmic character is not the same as theirs. It has, for example, the rhythmic motif dotted minim-semiminim-minim in two places (bars 2 and 7 of the transcription) and once a dotted minim followed by three semiminims (bar 11). There are very few

rhythms involving semiminims in the other songs in this group of fourteen. They occur only in the syncopated pattern minim-semiminim-minim-semiminim in nos. 25 (bar 8) and 29 (bar 9), and as a pair of semiminims in nos. 25 (bar 10) and 32 (bar 12). Subdivision into three successive semiminims in *Als I lay on Yoolis night*, and its basic rhythmic movement of four syllables to the bar (of the transcription), as compared with two syllables to the bar in the polyphonic songs, call for a slower pace than seems appropriate to most of them. The combination of poem and tune results in one syllable only being set to three notes in the second line and to four notes in the fourth line, in each case to a distinctive rhythmic motif which seems designed to accommodate two if not three syllables. While it is possible to sing these motives in the way the scribe indicated, a plain form has been written above each motif in the transcription, and may be used if desired. An optional drone-based accompaniment to the stanzas for unison male chorus has been added. A leading-in note is supplied for the verses which begin with an unaccented syllable. In the manuscript the notes corresponding to bar 6 of the transcription are *f* five times in the rhythm of a semibreve followed by four minims, apparently to accommodate the scribe's four syllables *yol-e-is night*.

V. SONGS IN TWO MANUSCRIPTS OF ABOUT 1400

21. Ye have so longe keepyt o
22. My cares comen ever anew
23. With ryght al my hert
24. I have set my hert so hy

Source: Oxford, Bodleian Library, MS Douce 381, ff. 20ᵛ, 22, 22, 20 respectively; facsimiles in John, J. F. R. and C. Stainer, *Early Bodleian Music*, i, London, 1901 pls. xxi, xxiii, xxiii, xx respectively.

25. Trew, on wam ys al my tryst
26. Danger me hath, unskylfuly
27. I rede that thou be joly and glad
28. Thys Yool, thys Yool (Edmund)
29. Wel wer hym that wyst
30. Me lykyth ever the lenger the bet
31. Pater noster, most of myght
32. 'Ave Maria' I say
33. Credo in Deum that ys

Sources: Cambridge, University Library, MS Additional 5943, ff. 163, 166, 161, 162, 162ᵛ, 164ᵛ, 167ᵛ–168, 168–168ᵛ, and 168ᵛ–169 respectively; for facsimiles see under no. 20 above. No 27 is also in the Douce MS, source of nos. 21–24, at f. 22ᵛ; facsimile in *Early Bodleian Music*, i, pl. 24.

The musical contents of these two manuscripts are congruous in style and date, and they have one concordance (no. 27). The four leaves beginning with f. 20 in the Douce manuscript, which is a collection of leaves and fragments, also contain two songs with French texts and one with a Latin text. Their musical contents are:

f. 20 No. 24 and *Les eux overt* for two voices
20ᵛ No. 21
21 *Mon cuer* for three voices
22 Nos. 22 and 23, the latter incomplete
22ᵛ No. 27
23 *Felix namque,* incomplete

The music on f. 21 is written in black notation, i.e., with filled-in notes, and this leaf may be from a slightly later manuscript. The other items are written in white notation, i.e., with open notes. Both these ways of writing polyphonic music were used from *c.* 1400 to the early sixteenth century, when black notation went out of use.

It has been suggested that the setting of *Felix namque* is organ music (see T. Dart, 'A New Source of Early English Organ Music', *Music and Letters,* xxxv, 1954, p. 201). Unlike the other music in these leaves it is plainsong-based, being a setting of the Offertory which was used in the votive Mass of the Virgin Mary during most of the ecclesiastical year, and was often played on the organ instead of being sung. The evidence is not conclusive, however, that this setting was intended for the organ and not for two voices. Its composer used a version of the plainsong which varies from that in the Sarum Use, but agrees closely with the version in the Brigittine liturgy. This slim piece of evidence may point to Syon nunnery, which was founded by Henry V in 1414, as the place where this leaf, and perhaps some or all of the others, originated (see my *Music in Medieval Britain,* London, 1963, p. 193).

The musical contents of the Cambridge manuscript are as follows (all the items are for two voices unless otherwise shown):

f. 161 No. 27
161ᵛ nine four-line staves, empty except for two longs and a flat sign jotted down on the sixth staff from the top
162 No 28
162ᵛ No. 29
163 No. 25; also two three-voice rounds to Latin words, beginning *Si quis amat* and *Pange lingua.* The text of the latter is the first stanza of the hymn at Matins on Corpus Christi.
163ᵛ *Plus por len oyr*
164 *Je ieo hayen vos,* for three voices
164ᵛ No. 30 and a *Benedicamus Domino, Alleluia, Alleluia*
165 *Esperanse ky en mon quer*
165ᵛ *Le grant pleyser,* for three voices
166 No. 26
166ᵛ–167 *Gloria in excelsis..bone voluntatis.* The text is the verse of the first respond, *Hodie nobis celorum rex,* at Matins on Christmas Day.
167ᵛ–168 No. 31
168–168ᵛ No. 32
168ᵛ–169 No. 33, and after two blank staves No. 20
169ᵛ eight empty staves

In technique and style these songs have similarities with some polyphonic secular songs in France and Italy in the second half of the fourteenth century. The technique of writing a word-setting voice above a textless tenor, used in all the two-part songs in this group, was common in France, though less so in Italy. Some Italian composers, among them Jacopo da Bologna and Giovanni da Firenze, almost invariably wrote a

'countertenor' in the same pitch-range as the tenor. In the fourteenth century this was essentially a French technique, and the composer of no. 29 was up-to-date in being familiar with it and with its terminology. The word countertenor did not begin to appear in English usage until about 1400. The third voice of one of the songs with French text in the Douce manuscript is marked *Medius cantus de mon cur;* the term *medius cantus* was occasionally used in England in the fourteenth century (see F. Ll. Harrison, 'Ars nova in England: a new source', *Musica Disciplina,* xxi, 1967, p. 78). However, the composer of no. 29 was less up-to-date when he wrote parallel fifths between the cantus and tenor (bars 2–3) and between the cantus and countertenor (bars 14 and 16–17). The earliest surviving English prohibition of parallel fifths and octaves in two-voice writing seems to be that in Leonel Power's treatise on descant, which was written in English. The earliest surviving music by Power, who died in 1445, is in the first layer of the Old Hall Manuscript, which may be dated in the first decade of the fifteenth century (see F. Ll. Harrison, in *Die Musik in Geschichte und Gegenwart,* s.vv. 'Leonel', 'Old Hall-Manuskript').

One of the songs with French text in the Cambridge manuscript, the rondeau *Esperanse ky en mon quer,* is also in three continental sources. Of these, one was written in Italy, probably in Florence (see *Repertoire Internationale des Sources Musicales,* vol. BIV³, Munich, 1972, p. 439), one in Strasbourg (ibid., p. 256) and one probably in Melk (ibid., pp. 96-7). The two last have been dated late fourteenth or early fifteenth century, the first shortly after 1400. In the Italian source the text goes only to the word *cuer* (*quer* in the Cambridge manuscript), while the others have the first word only (written *Essperance*). The English source is thus the only one to preserve the complete text of the rondeau refrain, short as it is. This may suggest that it was derived from a French source. Since the repertories in the continental manuscripts mentioned are largely late fourteenth century, the concordances support a date of *c.* 1400 for the Cambridge manuscript. *Esperance* is written in black notation in the continental sources, while in the Cambridge source it is in white notation. It was in a discussion of the early use of white notation that Manfred Bukofzer pointed to the English concordance for *Esperance* (see his *Studies in Medieval and Renaissance Music,* New York, 1950, p. 95). The chanson has since been published, however, without reference to the version of the Cambridge manuscript (see W. Apel, ed., *French Secular Compositions of the Fourteenth Century,* III, Rome, 1972, p. 89).

These songs conform to continental practice also in their rhythm-formulae and in many of their tune-formulae. All but one (no. 27) are in the rhythm of major prolation (transcribed in our six-eight time) which was very common in French music. Italian composers also used it, though relatively less frequently, since their range of rhythmic orders was wider than that of their French contemporaries. Machaut frequently wrote in perfect time with minor prolation (equivalent to our three-four), which does not appear in these songs, and less often in imperfect time with minor prolation (transcribed in four-four time), the rhythm of no. 27. In songs in this style the tenor, and in a three-voice song the countertenor, is usually less rhythmically active than the cantus. The composer or composers of nos. 21–24, 26 and 30 used only the plainest rhythmic formulae of major prolation, without syncopations and with rare 'snaps' — the reversed form of the rhythm crotchet-quaver (in terms of the transcription). Subdivision into semiminims (our semiquavers) and the syncopated rhythm of minims and semiminims occur only in nos. 25, 29 and 32, as has been noted in the commentary on no. 20. Syncopation is almost constant in no. 27, the only song in this group in minor prolation. The typical rhythmic formulae of this Frenchified style, and particularly syncopations in which major and minor prolation (our six-eight and three-four respectively) are juxtaposed or sounded simultaneously, are most fully exploited in no. 28 and in the last three songs in the group. These three were probably devised to some extent as exercises in rhythm, a function which would be consistent with the evident pedagogical intention of their texts. The cantus parts of the last two as written lie in the range of a boy's voice.

The scribe's underlaying of the text in these songs seems careless. Some changes in underlay have been made in addition to those necessitated by text emendations. These changes are particularly numerous in nos. 31–33, where there are many more notes than syllables. Since a published facsimile is available, at least in some libraries, changes in underlay are not given in the following notes, nor have ligatures in the original notation been shown in the transcriptions, though they have been observed in the underlay as edited.

NOTES
The following abbreviations are used: C=cantus, i.e., the upper(most) part; T=tenor; Ct=countertenor; l=long; br=breve; s=semibreve(s); m=minim(s); sm=semiminim. The time-values in the original are reduced to one-quarter in the transcriptions; references to time-values and parts are to the original.

21. *Ye have so longe keepyt o*
C clef c^3 with flat on 4th space; T ind 'Tenor de I have so long kepyt oo', in clef c^5/6 MS has *sddmd*, the 2nd *d* being written over the 2nd syllable of 'grene'/11 *ed* not in MS/27 C clef change to c^2 before ^{1}*g*; T ind 'ouvert'/39-40 both parts ind 'clos'

22. *My cares comen ever anew*
C clef c^2; T clef c^5, with change to c^4 before *f* in bar 17/2 and 4 C rests are faint/11-12 C MS has *bd'* for *c'e'*/16 C rest is faint/31 T clef change to c^5 before *c*

23. *With ryght al my hert*
The viola part is supplied by the editor
C clef c^2/ 7-10 notes very unclear/15 dot after ^{2}*d*/19 dot after ^{2}*g*/37 to end no music in MS, supplied from bars 9-15

24. *I have set my hert so hy*
C clef c^2; T clef c^5, ind 'Tenor de I have set my hert so hye'/4 *br*-rest after note in both parts/9, 15 and 23 ditto/11 *br*-rest after first note in both parts/19 C *br*-rest after first note/20 T ditto/27 C ditto, *me* is not in MS; T *br*-rest after note

25. *Trew, on wam ys al my tryst*
Both parts in clef c^4, written in score/19 lower part superfluous *mg* after *b*

26. *Danger me hath, unskylfuly*
Lower part is ind 'Tenor', in clef c^4; upper part clef c^3, changing to c^2 at bar 18/ 22 lower part is ind 'secundus versus'/ 30 lower part is ind 'clos'

27. *I rede that thou be joly and glad*
C clef c^2 in Add. 5943, and in Douce 381; T in c^4 in both, ind 'Tenor' in Add. 5943/3 T Add. 5943 *d* is *br*/4 T Add. 5943 no rest/5 T no *g*, *f* is *s* followed by *s*-rest/6 C *d* is not in Douce 381; T one *b* only in both MSS/8 C *c* is two *m* in Add. 5943/9 C dot after *a* not in Add. 5943/14 T is ind 'secundus versus' in Add. 5943/16 C dot after *g* not in Add. 5943/17 C superfluous *mf* after tied *f* in Add. 5943/20 T *e* is *s* in Douce 381

28. *Thys Yool, thys Yool*
C clef c^2; T ind 'Tenor' in c^4/5-7 under T is 'quod Edmund'/23 T is ind 'secundus versus'/28 C *mgmg* for *sg*/38 T has no second ending

29. *Wel wer hym that wyst*
C clef c^2, changing to c^3 after *e'* in bar 9 and to c^2 before ^{1}*c'* in bar 15; middle part ind 'Contra Tenor', lowest part ind 'Tenor', both in clef c^4/20 Ct ind 'Secundus versus'/23 C *sc* is *mmc'* in MS/30 T ind 'clos'

30. *Me lykyth ever the lenger the bet*
C clef c^2, changing to c^1 before *a* in bar 17, to c^2 before rests in bar 24/17-18 T ind 'Secundus versus'/28 T ind 'clos'

31. *Pater noster, most of myght*
C clef c^3; lower part ind 'Tenor', in clef f^4, changing to f^3 before *c'* in bar 42, to f^4 before *f* in bar 47/12 C *g* is *smgmg*/17 T *d* is *l*/26 C *b* is *sbmb*/54-57 T not in MS

32. *'Ave Maria' I say*
C clef c^1; T clef c^3 with *b* flat/5 T flat not cancelled/7 C no flat/9 C not in MS/11 T flat of bar 7 is not cancelled/14 C *md'* after *brg'*/22 C *sc'* not in MS/41 T *e'* is *m*

33. *Credo in Deum that ys*
C clef g^2; T clef c^3, changing to c^2 before bar 6/ 11 C *b'* is *s*/12 T *a* is *s*/26-27 C *de* are *s* (black); T tied *g* is *br*

APPENDICES

1. PRONUNCIATION TABLES

E. J. DOBSON

The following tables give a summary of practical directions for pronunciation. They do not deal with points that do not arise in these songs, and the examples given for each sound are usually only a selection.

The basic table for Middle English pronunciation is Table I (Late Twelfth and Early Thirteenth Centuries); Tables II and III (respectively Late Thirteenth and Fourteenth Centuries) record only the chief differences from the pronunciation set out in Table I. Tables for Anglo-Norman and for Medieval Latin (Tables IV and V respectively) are added after those for Middle English pronunciation.

Two important general warnings are (i) that long vowels should always be pronounced pure, not diphthongized as in modern Southern English (and American and Antipodean English); (ii) that vowels before *r* and *l* at the date of these songs, except possibly the latest (and also vowels before nasals in Anglo-Norman), should not be pronounced differently from their pronunciation before other consonants.

It should be noted that in medieval spelling, both French and English, *y* was often used in place of *i* both as a simple vowel and in diphthongs, without indicating any difference in pronunciation; and similarly in diphthongs (and in the digraphs *ou* and *ow* when representing a simple vowel) *w* interchanged with *u* without indicating any difference of sound. Also *o* was often used in place of *u* when the pronunciation was that of *u*.

The stressing of English words was normally as in Modern English, and that of Latin words as in classical Latin, but there were a good many exceptions. Singers should vary the stressing as the musical rhythm requires; care has been taken, in editing the texts, to match the rhythm of the words and the music, and it may be assumed that if a syllable is set to a musically accented note, it should usually, in the opinion of the editors, be given stress.

The spellings used in this book, and especially in the performing texts, have in many respects been normalized and modernized; they are not exactly those of the manuscripts.

TABLE I: LATE TWELFTH AND EARLY THIRTEENTH CENTURIES
Songs 1–9 inclusive

SPELLING	EXAMPLES	PRONUNCIATION	PHONETIC SYMBOL
Short vowels			
a	man, art, pass, wan, what, all; schame, bare, sake	As French *a* in *patte* (or as modern Northern English *a* in *man, pass*), even before *r* and *l* and after *w* and *wh*; not as modern Southern English *a* in *man, hat*	[a]
e (*stressed*)	men, geltles, heng, erthe (*first syllable*); bere, spere, mete	Always as in Mod. Eng. *men, bed*, even before *r*	[ɛ]
e (*unstressed*)	deerĕ, maidenes	As Mod. Eng. *e* in *fairer, maiden*	[ə]
i (y)	ich, ille, ivel, birth, mirth; light, night, bright	As in Mod. Eng. *bit*, even before *r* and *gh*	[ɪ]
o	God, on, folk, wolde, for, forth, born, force; bore(n), over, thole	Always as in Mod. German *Gott* (approx. as in Mod. Eng. *God*), even before *r* and *l*	[ɔ]
u	up, sum 'some'; sumer, wurs, wurth, ful	Always as in Mod. Eng. *pull, push*, even before *r* (never as in Mod. Eng. *but, cut, curl*)	[ʊ]
u (*Southern*)	*Only in* murye (Song 9)	As in Mod. French *durer*	[y]
Long Vowels			
a	clenhad, wa; wrang; imane, hal, sali	Approx. as in Mod. Eng. *father*, but pronounced well to front of mouth	[aː]

SPELLING	EXAMPLES	PRONUNCIATION	PHONETIC SYMBOL
e (*open*)	beten 'beaten', clene 'clean', ded 'dead' (*words spelt with* ea *in Mod. Eng.*); red 'red', rede 'advise', hele 'salvation', ches 'chose'	As Mod. French *è* in *père* or *ê* in *bête,* or as Italian 'open' *e*	[ɛ:]
ee (*also* e *in some words*)	thee, free, weene, greene, deere, feere, heere; *also* e *in* me, he, she, we, the *article,* be	As Mod. German *ee* in *See* or *eh* in *Ehre,* or as Italian 'close' *e*	[e:]
i (y)	lif 'life', wif 'wife', lives, wives, wit 'blame'; birde 'birth'; child, kind, mind	As Mod. German *ie* in *Liebe* (approx. as Mod. Eng. *ee*)	[i:]
o (*open*)	go, hom 'home', mon 'moan' (*words with 'long* o' *or* oa *in Mod. Eng.*); osketh 'asks', wot 'know', slo, tho; on(e) 'one', non 'none', anon; -hod *suffix*; lore, more, sor(e); bold, old, long, song, bond, hond, lomb, womb; lord, loverd; who, whom, whos	As Italian 'open' *o* in *toro* (approx. as Mod. Eng. *au* in *laud*)	[ɔ:]
oo (*also* o *in some words*)	boot, blood, good, rood, moor; *also* o *in* moder 'mother', brother, other, povre 'poor'	As Mod. German *oo* in *Boot* or *oh* in *Sohn,* or as Italian 'close' *o*	[o:]
u	hus 'house', nu 'now', ut 'out'; grund 'ground', stund; wunde 'wounds' (*noun*), murnen 'mourn'; iswungen, stungen	As Mod. German *u* in *Mut* or *uh* in *Kuh* (approx. as Mod. Eng. *oo* in *boot*)	[u:]
Diphthongs ai (ay)	saint, maiden, fai(e)r, day, may	As Mod. Eng. *i* in *time, die*	[ai]
au (aw)	nau(gh)t, lau(gh)t, bikau(gh)t, saugh, thaugh, awe, lawes, sawe, thrawes	As Mod. Eng. *ou* (*ow*) in *thou, house, now*	[au]
ea (*Kentish*)	death(es), threat (*in* Song 6a *only*)	As Mod. German *Ehe* (approx. as Mod. Eng. *-aya* in *Malaya*)	[eə]
ei (ey) (*close*)	heyliche, eie 'eye', deie 'die', leie 'deceive', dreien 'endure', dreigh 'patient'	As Mod. Eng. *a* in *name* or *ai* (*ay*) in *wait, day*	[ei]
ei (ey) (*open*)	*Most words spelt* ei (ey), *thus* ei 'ay, ever', heil 'hail', weilawei 'alas', seyen 'say', seide, seigh 'saw', dreigh 'endured', imeind, eighte 'property', greith 'prepare'	Mod. Eng. *ĕ* as in *bet* (or French *ê*) + French *i,* pronounced quickly in succession	[ɛi]
eu (ew) (*close*)	*Most words spelt* eu (ew), *thus* hew(e) 'hue', knew, new(e), trewe 'true', rewe 'rue'; trewe 'tree' (Song 16a)	Mod. German *ee, eh* (or French *é*) + French *ou,* pronounced quickly in succession	[eu]
eau (eaw) (*open*)	feaw 'few', deaw 'dew', beauty *and some others* (*also commonly spelt* eu, ew)	Mod. Eng *ĕ* as in *bet* (or French *ê*) + French *ou,* pronounced quickly in succession	[ɛu]
oi (oy)	joie (joye)	As in Mod. Eng.	[ɔi]
ou (ow) (*close*)	groweth, bloweth 'blossoms', lhouth 'lows' (song 9), wou(gh) 'evil' (Song 6b), louk 'pale' (Song 10 (ii))	As in Mod. Eng. *lo, home, blow* (with lips rounded)	[ou]
ou (ow) (*open*)	*Most words spelt* ou (ow), *thus* owe, own, know, slouth 'sloth', slow, trouth 'troth', wowe, goulinge, though; wrou(gh)te, bou(gh)te, nou(gh)t, brou(gh)te	Mod. Eng. Eng. *au* + French *ou,* pronounced quickly in succession	[ɔu]

Consonants

As in modern English, with the following exceptions or qualifications:

r always pronounced, lightly trilled, wherever written, even after vowels, e.g. in *art, hard, for, wer, over, moder*; the preceding vowel has the same pronunciation as before other consonants.

l always pronounced, wherever written, e.g. in *half, folk, psalm*; the preceding vowel has the same pronunciation as before other consonants.

Consonants written double between vowels should be pronounced double, thus *man-nes, wil-le*, etc. Similarly *cch* in *wrecche* etc. and *gg* in *ligge* 'lie' etc. are lengthened forms of *ch* in *riche* 'rich' and *g* in *age* 'age'.

All consonants written are to be pronounced: thus *b* after *m* in *lomb*; *g* after *n* in *wrong, kinges* (i.e. as *ng* in *finger*, not as in Mod. Eng. *sing, singer*); *w* after *t* in *two* (as in *twin*); *wh* in *who, whom, whose* the same as in *which, what* (approximately as *h + w*), except when only *w* or *h* is written (e.g. *wam* 'whom' or *ho* 'who'), in which case the words should be pronounced as spelt; *lh* in *lhude* 'loudly' and *lhouth* 'lows' (Song 9) approximately as *h + l*; *wr* in *wrake, write, wrought* etc. as *w + r* (not just as *r*); *kn* (*cn*) in *know, bicnowe, knight* etc. as *k + n* (not just as *n*).

gh in *nigh, night, though, thought* etc. and *h* in *neheth* 'nighs', *briht* 'bright', *mihte* 'might', *wroht* 'wrought', *looh* 'laughed' are to be pronounced as German *ch* in *ich, Licht, ach, acht*. (This sound should perhaps also be inserted in some words normally spelt with *gh* which lack it in the manuscripts of some of the songs, e.g. *naut* 'naught', *bout* 'bout', *brout* 'brought', *wou* for *wough* 'evil'; so in Songs 6b, 7, 12, 14, and 15 (ii).)

gh in *astighe* 'rise', *heeghe* 'high', *lyghe* 'deceive', *sorghe* 'sorrow' (Song 4(ii)), *fugheles* 'birds' and *sorghe* 'sorrow' (Song 5), and *heeghe* (Song 6a) is to be pronounced as Dutch *g* in *geen* 'none', *goed* 'good'.

s is normally to be pronounced as in the same or similar words in Mod. Eng., but at the end of words (e.g. *wis* 'wise', *pris* 'price', *aris* 'arise', *as, was, his*) with the final sound of Mod. Eng. *price, rice*, not of *prize, rise*. This does not apply when an *e* follows. In Song 6a *s* at the beginning of words (e.g. *senn* 'sin') should probably be pronounced as *z*.

f at the end of words (e.g. *of, therof*) should be pronounced as in Mod. Eng. *off*, not as in Mod. Eng. *of*.

th at the beginning of words or separate elements of words (e.g. after a prefix, as in *bethink*) should always be pronounced as in Mod. Eng. *thick*, never as in Mod. Eng. *this*, except in Song 6a, in which *th* in *thervore, bithench, thi, threat*, etc. should be as in Mod. Eng. *this*; *th* in the middle of words (e.g. *dethes* 'death's', *erthe* 'earth') as in Mod. Eng. *breathes, further*; *th* at the end of words as in Mod. Eng. *oath*.

sch and *sh* are the same, pronounced like Mod. Eng. *sh*; so probably *ss* in *ssel* 'shall', *sseene* 'sheen', *ssoo* 'shoe' in Song 6a.

ch is always to be pronounced as in Mod. Eng., even in words from French (never as in Modern French).

g is to be pronounced as in Mod. Eng., 'hard' in *get, gilte, gelte* 'guilt', *meneginge* 'remembrance', etc., 'soft' in *gentil, angel*, etc. It should never be pronounced as in Modern French *gentil, rouge*.

TABLE II: LATER THIRTEENTH CENTURY

Songs 10(ii)–18 inclusive

As in Table I, except that:

(1) In words originally of two syllables, *a, e*, and *o* before a single consonant (as in *name, bare; mete* 'meat', *bere* 'bear'; *thole* 'suffer', *bore(n)* 'born' etc.) had often been lengthened and should now mostly be pronounced as 'long *a*', 'long *e*', and 'long *o*' (as defined in Table I).

(2) *gh* (*h*) is now always as German *ch* in *ich, ach*, never as Dutch *g*, in the dialects represented in the songs.

TABLE III: FOURTEENTH CENTURY

Songs 19–33 inclusive

As in Table I, with the following chief exceptions:

(1) In words originally of two syllables, *a, e*, and *o* before a single consonant (as in *name, bare; mete, bere; thole, bore(n)* etc.) had now normally been lengthened and should be pronounced as 'long *a*', 'long *e*', and 'long *o*' (as defined in Table I).

(2) The vowels of such words as *bold, old, told; song, strong; bond, hond, stond; stung, sung* were now short. So also (exceptionally) the *i* of *child* in Song 20.

(3) The use of *y* as a spelling for *i*, both short and long, is now much more frequent but has no significance for pronunciation; pronounce as *i*, short or long.

(4) 'Short *u*' was now often spelt *o* (as in *come, love*) or even *ou* (as in *double*), as in Mod. Eng., but was still always pronounced like *u* in Mod. Eng. *pull, push*, however spelt and even before *r* (never as Mod. Eng. *u* in *cut, bubble, curl*).

(5) The *o* of *who, whom, whose, womb, two* was now often pronounced as *oo* (as defined in Table I, i.e. like German *oh* in *Sohn*).

(6) 'Long *u*' in *hus, ut, hu* was normally spelt *ou* (*ow*) in the fourteenth century, as in *hous, out, how*, but was unchanged in pronunciation, i.e. it was still pronounced like Mod. German *u* in *Mut* or *uh* in *Kuh* (approx. like Mod. Eng. *oo* in *boot*).

(7) Except in such words as those discussed under (6) above, where it is a mere spelling for 'long *u*', *ou* (*ow*) was now always pronounced as 'open' *ou*, i.e. *grow, blow* 'blossom', *flow* and *owe, own, know* etc. were all pronounced with the sound defined for 'open *ou*' in Table I.

(8) 'Close' *ei* had become 'long *i*' and was mostly spelt *i* (*y*), but *ei* (*ey*) was sometimes kept in spelling, as in *eye, height;* such words are to be pronounced with the sound defined for 'long *i*' in Table I.

(9) Otherwise *ei* (*ey*) had become identical with *ai* (*ay*), and both spellings are to be pronounced with the sound defined for *ai* in Table I.

(10) 'Close' *eu* (*ew*) had changed in pronunciation, and was pronounced as a diphthong made up of Mod. French *i* + Mod. French *ou*, pronounced quickly in succession (approx. as Mod. Eng. *ee* + Mod. Eng. *oo*, pronounced quickly in succession); phonetic symbol [iu]. The same sound was mostly used for *u* (the so-called 'long *u*') in words from French, e.g. *rulyd* 'ruled' in Song 30.

(11) Consonants still as in Table I, except that:

    (a) *gh* (when written) was now always as German *ch* in *ich, ach,* never as Dutch *g.* But in *mought* 'might' (Song 29) *gh* may be silent; if so, the word should be pronounced like Mod. German *Mut.*

    (b) *s* in *as, was, his, is* should be pronounced as in these words in Mod. Eng. (i.e. as *z*).

    (c) *f* in *of* (prep.) was mostly pronounced as in this word in Mod. Eng. (i.e. as *v*).

    (d) *th* in *the, this, that, thou, thee, thy, then, than, with* etc. was pronounced as in these words in Mod. Eng.

TABLE IV: ANGLO-NORMAN
Song 4(i)

Singers should if possible consult an expert on Anglo-Norman for advice on the pronunciation of *Eyns ne soy ke pleynte fu* (Song 4(i)). The following are intended as practical directions, having regard to the date of the song (*c.* 1225).

Vowels and Diphthongs

The vowels and diphthongs should not as a rule be pronounced as in Modern French, but generally with the same values as are defined in Table I above for the English vowels and diphthongs of the same period. It would probably be better not to attempt to nasalize vowels and diphthongs before *n* and *m.* Note especially the following points:

    (1) The vowel *e* should mostly be pronounced as in corresponding words in Mod. French, but (i) *e* in *mere* 'mother' should be pronounced as Mod. French *é*, not *è* (i.e. differently from the vowel of the modern word); (ii) *e* in *plet* 'plait' and *forfet* 'forfait' should be pronounced as Mod. French *ê* in *bête;* (iii) final unstressed *e*, marked *ë* in the text as printed, should be pronounced as 'feminine *e*' or as English unstressed *e* (as defined in Table I above).

    (2) *u* when it corresponds to Mod. French *o* (as in *prisun* 'prison', *hum* 'homme', *sumes* 'sommes', *hunte* 'honte' etc.) or to Mod. French *ou* (as in *duz* 'doux', *vus* 'vous', *tut* 'tout', *pur* 'pour', *jur* 'jour', *dulcur* 'douceur', *suffrun* 'souffrons') is to be pronounced as English *u* in *push, pull* or as Mod. French *ou.* Similarly (i) *u* in the suffix *-ur* in *dulcur, dolur* 'douleur', and *seignur* 'seigneur'; (ii) *o* in *dolur, soverain, pardonez,* and *jo* 'je'; (iii) *ou* in *fous* 'fou' and in *out* 'eût'.

    (3) *u* when it corresponds to Mod. French *u* or *ui* (in *fortune, fu* 'fut', *tressu, su* 'suis') is to be pronounced as Mod. French *u* in *durer, plus, su.* Similarly in *dangusse* 'd'angoisse'.

    (4) *ui* in *trespuissant* and *uy* in *nuyt* 'nuit' is probably to be pronounced as Mod. French *u* in *pu, nu* (less probably as Mod. French *ui* in *puis, nuit*).

    (5) *o* (except in the words listed under (2)(ii) above) is to be pronounced as Italian 'open' *o.*

    (6) *ai* (*ay*) in the words *ai, maydez* 'm'aidez', *soverain, main, evain,* and *ain* is to be pronounced with the sound defined for Middle English *ai* in Table I above (i.e. it is to be as Mod. Eng. *i* in the words *I, my, nine*), not as in Mod. French.

    (7) *au* in *autre, autri,* and *maufé* is to be pronounced with the sound defined for Middle English *au* in Table I (i.e. as Mod. Eng. *ou* in *out*), not as in Mod. French.

    (8) *ei* in *mei* 'moi', *sei* 'soi', *peine, certeine* is to be pronounced as 'open' *ei* (as defined in Table I).

    (9) *eu* in *deu(s)* 'dieu' and *morteus* 'mortels' is to be pronounced as 'close' *eu* (as defined in Table I).

    (10) *oi* (*oy*) in *soy* 'sus', *assoylez, boydie, doint, joye* is to be pronounced as in Mod. Eng. *join, joy,* not as in Mod. French *pois, joie, soi.*

Consonants

All consonants written are to be pronounced, except *h* in *hum* 'homme', *l* in *dulcur,* and possibly *d* in *nad* (see below). In particular *n* in *prisun, pardun, hunte, main,* etc., *m* in *cumpaignun,* and the final consonants of such words as *trop, Deus, nus, plet, veirs, fors, tort, icels, grant* should be regularly sounded, in contrast to Mod. French usage.

r should be pronounced wherever written, with light trilling of the tongue (as in Scottish speech); the Mod. French uvular *r* should not be used.

h should be pronounced in *hunte* 'honte' but not in *hum* 'homme'.

g in *gentil* and *prenge* and *j* in *je, jo, jet, jetez, jeté,* and *joye* should be pronounced as in Mod. Eng. *gentle, engine, jet, joy,* not as in Mod. French *gentil, manger, jeter, joie.*

gn in *cumpaignun, seignur* should be pronounced as in Mod. French.

gu in *guie* 'guide' should probably be pronounced as in Mod. Eng. *guava* (i.e. as *gw*), less probably as in Mod. Eng. and French *guide.*

c in *decerte, icel(s), ceste,* and also *dulcur* 'douceur' should probably be pronounced as *ts* (as in Mod. Eng. *tse-tse*), but perhaps as *s.*

z in *maydez* 'm'aidez', *duz* 'doux', *jetez, sucurez, deliverez,* etc. should probably be pronounced as *ts,* but perhaps as *s.* Thus *maydez* should probably be approximately as Mod. Eng. *my dates,* but perhaps as *my dace.*

d in *nad* 'n'a' should probably be pronounced as English *th* in *hath*, but may have been silent.
l in *dulcur* 'douceur' was silent.

TABLE V: MEDIEVAL LATIN
Songs 4 (Addendum), 9, 10(i), 16b(ii), 18

The pronunciation of Medieval Latin in France and England, where these songs were written, was different from both the modern 'Italianate' pronunciation mostly used by English singers and the 'reformed' pronunciation of classical Latin used in modern English schools.

Stress
Mostly as in classical Latin but by no means always; follow the rhythm of the music.

Vowels and Diphthongs
Mostly as in the 'Italianate' pronunciation, but note the following:

Latin ŏ was pronounced as Italian 'open' *o*.

ō was also normally pronounced as 'open' *o*.

ĕ was pronounced as Italian 'open' *e*.

ē was pronounced as Italian 'close' *e* in earlier use (so perhaps in Song 4 (Addendum) and Songs 9 and 10(i)) but varied between 'close' and 'open', the latter often preferred, in later use (so perhaps Songs 15(i), 16b(ii), and 18).

oe was pronounced like Latin ē.

ae (*æ*) was pronounced like Latin ĕ, i.e. it was 'open' *e*.

u before a consonant belonging to the same syllable (*planctus, dulcor, dux, ullus*) was pronounced in England like Mod. Eng. *u* in *pull, push*, but in France like Mod. French *u* in *culte, succès, russe*.

u at the end of a syllable or word (*crucior, singulare, planctu*) was pronounced like French *u* in *lune, durer, du* or with the Middle English diphthong *iu* (composed as if of French *i*+French *ou* pronounced quickly in succession; phonetic symbol [iu]).

Consonants
Most consonants have their normal values, and *r* is always to be pronounced wherever written, lightly trilled. Note however the following:

c before *e, i, ae* (*æ*) in *unice, crucior, cæca, cælum*, etc. (and also before *oe*) was pronounced like *ts* (as in English *tse-tse*) until the early thirteenth century (so Song 4 (Addendum), and perhaps Songs 9 and 10(i)), thereafter as *s*, as in English *civil, crucify, celebrate* (so Songs 15(i), 16b(ii) and 18). It should not be pronounced like English *ch*, as in the Italianate pronunciation.

cc before *e* and *i* (*ecce, accipio*, etc.) was pronounced like *ks* (as if the words were written *ekse, aksipio*), as in English *accident*; not as in the Italianate pronunciation.

sc before *e, i*, and *ae* (*æ*) in *scelus, scio, nescio*, etc. was pronounced like Latin *c* before these vowels (see above), i.e. it was *ts* until the early thirteenth century (Song 4 (Addendum), and perhaps Songs 9 and 10(i)) and thereafter *s* as in Mod. Eng. *science, nescience* (Songs 15(i), 16b(ii), and 18).

t before unstressed *i*+another vowel, as in *gratia, natio, sentio, citius* was also pronounced like Latin *c* before *e, i*, and *ae* (*æ*), i.e. it was *ts* earlier and *s* later (see above). But *st* (as in *pestium*) was always pronounced as spelt.

g before *e* and *i*, as in *gens, virginem, angelus, regina*, etc. was pronounced as in Mod. Eng. *gentle, virgin, angel*.

j consonant, as in *justus, Judæa, Jesus, cujus*, was pronounced as in Mod. Eng. *just, Jacob, huger*. But the interjection *eja* was probably pronounced *eya* (as it is also spelt).

gn in *agnus, dignus, pignoris, cognovi* was pronounced, in England, as *ngn* (as if written *ang-nus, ding-nus, ping-noris, cong-novi*) but also often as spelt (as in the Mod. Eng. pronunciation of these Latin words); in France it was pronounced as in Mod. French *agneau*.

qu was pronounced as *kw* in England but as *k* in France.

v consonant, as in *versus, invidus*, was pronounced as Mod. Eng. *v*, not as *w*.

z, as in *zelus*, was pronounced as *dz* until the early thirteenth century, thereafter as Mod. Eng. *z* in *zeal*.

2. TRANSLATIONS OF TEXTS
E. J. DOBSON

1. Sainte Marie viergene

1. St. Mary the Virgin, mother of Jesus Christ the Nazarene, receive, shield, help thy Godrich; when received, bring [him] honourably with thee into God's kingdom.

2. St Mary, Christ's bed-chamber (virginal purity, flower of mothers), blot out my sin, rule in my spirit, bring me to bliss with the very God.

2. Crist and Sainte Marie

Kyrieleison, Christe eleison [Lord, have mercy; Christ, have mercy]. Christ and St. Mary thus brought me to the [altar-] table, so that I should not tread on this earth with my bare feet.

3. Sainte Nicholas, Godes druth

St. Nicholas, God's darling, graciously prepare for us beautiful dwellings. By the merits of thy birth, by the merits of thy bier, St. Nicholas, bring us safely there.

4. (i) Eyns ne soy ke pleynte fu

1. Formerly I did not know what sorrow was; now, full of anguish, I sweat it out; I have too much misfortune and harm. Undeservedly I am in prison; therefore aid me, all-powerful Jesus, sweet and gracious God.

2. Jesus Christ, true God, true man, take pity on me! Bring me from the prison into which I have been wrongly thrown. I and my other companions — God knows the truth of it — have been delivered up to shame entirely because of the misdeeds of others.

3. Lord God, who art the channel of pardon for mortals, give aid; deliver us from this punishment. Pardon and absolve, gentle Lord, if it please thee, those by whose crime we suffer such martyrdom.

4. He is foolish who places his trust in this mortal life, which so assails us and in which there is nothing but deceit. Now man is in bliss, and now he is in grief; now Fortune cures, now wounds, him whom she guides.

5. Virgin and mother of the sovereign Lord who has delivered us from the hand of the devil (who failing this would have had us all on his hook in great sorrow and torment), entreat that Lord to bring us, of his great kindness, from this sorrow in which we are, night and day, and to give us assured joy.

4. (ii) Ar ne kuth ich sorghe non

1. Formerly I knew no sorrow, now I must give voice to my grief; full of care, I sigh in great distress. Guiltless, I suffer great shame; give aid, O God, Lord of the kingdom of heaven, for the sake of thy beloved name.

2. Jesus Christ, true God, true man, Lord, have pity on me! From the prison that I am in, bring me out and make me free. I and some of my companions — God knows I do not lie — have been cast into this prison because others have done wrong.

3. Almighty, who very easily — remedy and cure of pain, King of heaven — mayest bring us out of this misery, if it is thy will forgive them, the wicked men, for whose guilt we are thrust into this evil prison.

4. Let none trust in this life — here he cannot remain; high though he ascend, Death fells him to the ground. Now man has prosperity and bliss, soon he shall lose them; worldly prosperity, for certain, lasts only for an hour.

5. Maiden who bore the King of heaven, beseech, sweet thing, thy son to have pity on us and bring us, of his great mercy, from this misery. May he bring us from this woe and teach us so to act in this life, however things may go, that we may for ever and ever have eternal bliss.

Addendum to no. 4:
Planctus ante nescia

1. Ignorant previously of weeping, I in my grief am worn out by weeping, I am tortured by sorrow; the Jewish race deprives the world of its light, me of my child, of joy, of sweetness.

2. O son, my only sweetness, my single joy, look on your weeping mother, and give solace. Your wounds torment my breast, my mind, my eyes; what mother, what woman, so happy, so miserable!

3. Flower of flowers, guide of manners, channel of pardon, how severe is your torment from the nails! Ah grief! For this reason the colour of my face flees away; for this reason there rushes, there flows, the stream of blood.

4. O so lately given, how quickly you leave me! O so honourably born, how wretchedly you die! O what love made for you the vesture of the flesh, O what bitter payment for how sweet a pledge!

5. O kindly love of the one thus dying! O hatred, O crime of the envious people! O cruel hand of the executioner, O gentle spirit, amid his torments, of the sufferer!

6. O true speech of upright Simeon! I feel the sword of sorrow which he promised. Groans, sighs, and tears outwardly are the signs of inward wounds.

7. Spare my child, Death, but not me; then you alone will cure me only. By death, my blessed son, I will be separated from you, if only you are not crucified.

8. What a crime, what evil deeds the savage people has committed! Bonds, whips, wounds, spitting, thorns, the rest he suffers without fault. Spare, I beg, my son; crucify his mother, or fix us together to the post of the cross — wrongly he dies alone.

9. Give back to a most sorrowful woman the living body or the dead, so that, thus diminished, my torment may be made greater by kisses, by embracings. Would that I might so grieve that I might die of grief, for it is more grievous to die without death [i.e. suffer a living death] than to perish quickly.

10. Why are you astonished, wretched nation, that the earth quakes, the stars are obscured, the sick lament? If you deprive the sun of light, how shall it shine? or the sick of medicine, how shall he recover strength?

11. You set free a murderer, you give Jesus up to execution; wrongly you maintain peace — there will come rebellion. When you have experienced the affliction of famine, slaughter, and pestilences, you will know Jesus to be dead to you, and Barrabas to be alive.

12. Blind nation, lamentable nation, do penance, while Jesus can be swayed to grant you pardon. The things which you have done may turn to your advantage as the rivers of the fountains, may assuage the thirst of all, may wash away all your crimes.

13. Weep for your offences, O daughters of Sion, thankful for such grace (the hardships of the young man are for him delights). Rush into his embraces while he hangs on the tree, with caresses given in exchange; he prepares himself for his lovers with outstretched arms.

14. In this alone I rejoice, that I weep for you. Grant me, I beg, a recompense: mourn a mother's loss.

5. Miri it is while sumer ilast

Merry it is while summer lasts with the song of birds; but now draws near the wind's blast and harsh weather. Alas, alas! how long this night is! And I, most unjustly, sorrow and mourn and fast.

6a. Man may longe lives weene

1. Man may expect long life, but the trick often deceives him; fair weather often turns into rain — suddenly it plays its trick. Therefore, man, take heed; all your greenness shall wither. Alas! there is neither king nor queen who shall not drink Death's draught. Man, before you fall from your seat, put an end to your sin.

2. Never can the strong or the mighty or the bold prevail against Death's hostile grip, nor the young nor the old, nor the bright and beautiful; he tears everything to pieces in his strength, for crafty and sudden is his twist. Never can any man prevail against that, alas, nor can threat or entreaty, bribery or cunning, or a physician's potion. Man, leave sin and the stink of lust; do well, think well.

3. Act in accord with Solomon's advice, man, and then you will do well; do exactly as he taught you, and take heed what your end will bring you to — never again shall you sin. Sorely you may fear for yourself, alas, you who expect to lead well a long life and to enjoy pleasures, where Death lurks in your shoe to destroy you.

4. Man, why will you not acknowledge your nature? Man, why will you not consider yourself? You are first begotten from filth; you will become the food of worms. You do not have happiness here for three days; all your life you endure in misery. Alas! Death will throw you down, where you expected to rise high; your prosperity shall give place to misery, your merriment to weeping.

5. The world and its wealth deceive you; for certain they are your foes. If your world flatters with prosperity, that is in order to do you harm. Therefore let desire pass by, man, and afterwards things will please you well. Alas! what a grievous service he does himself who in one hour, or two, earns himself torment for ever more! Man, do not so!

6b. On hir is mi lif ilong

1. On her my life depends of whom I intend to sing and in the process to praise her who brought us deliverance from the strong torment of hell and brought us such enduring bliss entirely by means of her child-bearing. I pray her, in my song, to give us a good ending, though we do wrong.

2. All this world shall pass away with sorrow and with grief, and all this bliss we must forgo, however grievously to do so may displease us. This world is nothing but our foe, therefore I intend to go hence and to act according to God's teaching. This world's bliss is not worth a bean. I beg, O God, for thy mercy, constantly now.

3. Too long have I been a fool, very grievously I fear for myself; I have loved sport and pleasure and wealth and fine garments. All that is delusion, I see well, therefore I will flee sin and abandon my folly. I pray to her who is so generous to give heed to me and to help and advise me.

4. Thou art salvation and life and light and helpest all mankind; thou hast provided very well for us — thou hast given us wealth and joy. Thou hast brought day, and Eve night; she brought evil, thou hast brought right; thou charity, and she sin. Have mercy upon us, radiant lady, when we must go hence, as thou well canst.

5. I have offended, alas! I am sinful and wretched. Avenge thyself on me now, lady, before death fetches me hence — I am ready to accept punishment — and let me live and reform myself, so that fiends may not afflict me. For my sins I am sorry; I do not care for this life. Lady, mercy!

7. Worldes blis ne last no throwe

1. Worldly bliss does not last for a moment; it goes and passes away presently. The longer that I know it, the less value I find in it; for it is all mingled with care, with sorrows and with ill-success, and at the last it leaves man poor and naked when it departs. All the bliss which is here and there amounts at the end to weeping and grief.

2. All the pleasures of this life you, man, shall bring to an end in weeping — [those] of house and home, of child and wife. Oh, miserable man, take heed of this! For you shall leave here all the property of which you were lord; when you lie, man, upon the bier and sleep that very dreadful sleep, you will have no companion with you but your piled-up deeds.

3. All shall depart that man possesses here; it shall all turn into nothing. The man who sows nothing good here will be caught when others reap. Think, man, therefore, while you have the ability, that you should atone for your sins and do good by day and night before you are snatched from life. You do not know when Christ our Lord will ask of you what he has entrusted.

4. Man, why do you set mind and heart on worldly bliss that does not last? Why do you permit that you should so often be grieved for things that are transitory? You lick honey from a

thorn, indeed, who set your love on worldly bliss, for it is full of bitterness. You may well be greatly terrified who mis-spend wealth here, thereby to be cast into hell.

5. Think, man, for what purpose Christ created you, and put away pride and filth and wrath. Think how dearly he redeemed you on the cross with his precious blood. He gave himself as a ransom for you, to buy you bliss if you are prudent; bethink yourself then and rise up from sin and begin to do good whilst there is time to act, for certainly otherwise you are mad.

6. Every day you may understand and see as if in a mirror [*more literally* see your mirror] before you what is to be done and what avoided, and what to be kept and what to flee; for every day you see with your eyes how this world departs and how men die. Know this well, that you shall suffer as others have done, and also die; in that matter it does not help at all to deceive — no man can oppose Death.

7. No good deed shall be unrequited, and no evil deed will not be paid for; when you lie, man, under the earth, you shall get what you have earned. Consider well therefore, I advise you, and cleanse yourself of each misdeed, so that He may help you in your need who has so dearly redeemed you, and may lead you to the bliss of heaven which ever endures and does not fail.

8. Fuweles in the frith

Birds in the woodland, the fishes in the stream — and I shall go mad. I toss about in great distress for the best of blood and bone.

9. Perspice, Christicola / [Ressurrexit Dominus]

[*The Lord has risen.*] Pay heed, Christian — what an honour! The heavenly husbandman, because of a blemish in the vine-branch, did not spare his son but exposed [him] to the destruction of death; and he [i.e. the son] restores from torment to life the half-living captives [of hell] and crowns [them] together with himself on the throne of heaven.

Sumer is icumen in / Sing, cuccu, nu

Sing, cuckoo, now; sing, cuckoo! Summer has come in — loudly sing, cuckoo! The seed grows and the meadow blossoms and the wood now puts forth shoots. Sing, cuckoo! The ewe bleats for the lamb, the cow lows for the calf; the bullock leaps, the buck breaks wind — merrily sing, cuckoo! Cuckoo, cuckoo! Well do you sing, cuckoo; do not ever cease now.

10. (i) Stabat juxta Christi crucem

1. She stood beside the cross of Christ, she stood watching the lord of life bid farewell to life. The mother stood, not now a mother, and has learnt from the recent funeral procession what the dire outcome will be.

2. The Virgin stood watching the cross and watching each light [i.e. the sun, and Christ, 'the light of the world'] suffer, but she mourned more for her own. She stood, he hung, and the things that he suffered openly she endured within.

3. Within, she was nailed to the cross; within, the mother of the Lamb was killed by her own sword; within, she was consecrated a martyr; within, she was wholly consumed by the flame of love.

4. Now his hand, now his side, now his foot pierced with steel is observed by her eyes; now his head pricked by thorns, whose will the whole world both observes and obeys.

5. The revered face covered with spittle, and the skin broken by whips, and such rivers of blood; insults, laughter, and the rest are the chief weapons for the bereavement and grief of the Virgin.

6. Time, harsh by inborn nature, now demands its rights; now it sharpens her sorrows. Now it extorts with usury the groans which she, when about to give birth, had withheld from Nature.

7. Now, now she gives birth, now she knows in truth how it is a mother's part to suffer, how bitter it is to give birth; now pain, deferred at the birth of her son, presents itself in grief at his death.

8. Now she is made a mother, but of sorrows, but she retains still the beauty of her virgin modesty; for the force of grief, burning her, in her distress, within, does not deface her modest outward demeanour.

9. And so the three-days-long weeping is at last cancelled by the happy victory of the risen Christ; a happy hope shines out for the mourner, for her joys rise again as her son rises again.

10. This new birth of Christ follows the pattern of the virgin birth as regards the closed tomb; from this he went forth, from this he arose, from the one and the other he issued though the seal was intact.

11. Hail, mother! Hail, happy lady! The night of thy weeping is finished and dawns into joy. Grant [us] thy son as a happy morning for our night also, which is more than three days long. Amen.

10. (ii) [Stood the moder under roode]

. . . she stood there near.

5. That lovely face defiled by spittle, that beautiful skin torn with scourges — the blood streamed out everywhere. Scorn, upbraiding, and insulting speech, it was all to the increase of thy sorrow; thou wert completely enclosed in misery.

6. In that blissful child's birth wrong was done to women's destiny, but Nature now demanded its due. Then thou didst laugh, but now thou didst weep; thy sorrow was wakened that then slept — the pains of childbirth have now pierced thee.

7. Now thou wert obliged, lady, to learn the pain of women who bear children, the bitter and the dire throes; for at his death thou didst repay the [debt of] pain which thou oughtest to have suffered in giving birth, according to the natural laws of motherhood.

8. Ah, lady, though thou didst wet thy cheeks, though thou didst suffer immoderately, thy looks were unblemished; thy weeping did not disfigure thy complexion, though it made thy countenance very pale and wan — so grieved a woman there never was.

9. All thy sorrow was overcome, the third day thy joy had come, Death and the devil were driven down, when thy son had arisen, to thy well-being and our peace — he brought happiness to every dwelling.

10. Thy beloved son's resurrection was strangely like his birth; between the two there is little difference. For he was

born of thy body as a ray of light passes through glass, and he glided through the intact tomb.

11.   Gentle mother, virgin ever, thou camest from all thy grief then, when thy son had risen. Lady, bring us out of misery, of sin, of sorrow, of sighing also, to the bliss which is endless. Amen.

11. Stond wel, moder, under roode

1.   'Stand well, mother, under the cross, behold your child with glad spirit; a happy mother may you be.' 'Son, how can I stand happily? I see your feet, I see your hands nailed to the hard tree.'

2.   'Mother, put away your weeping; I suffer this death for man's sake — for my own guilt I suffer none.' 'Son, I feel the pangs of death; the sword which Simeon promised me is at the bottom of my heart.'

3.   'Mother, have pity on your child! Wash away those bloody tears, which trouble me worse than my death.' 'Son, how could I refrain from tears? I see those streams of blood run out of your heart to my feet.'

4.   'Mother, now I can tell you, it is better that I alone die than that all mankind go to hell.' 'Son, I see your body beaten, your breast, your hand, your foot pierced through; it is no marvel if I am unhappy.'

5.   'Mother, if I dare tell you, if I do not die, you go to hell; I suffer this death for your sake.' 'Son, you are so thoughtful for me; do not blame me, it is my nature that I show this sorrow for you.'

6.   'Mother, thanks; let me die in order to buy Adam out of hell, and mankind that is lost.' 'Son, what am I to do? Your torture tortures me to death; let me die before you.'

7.   'Mother, now for the first time you can learn what pain they suffer who bear children, what sorrow they have who lose a child.' 'Son, I know, I can tell you — unless it be the pain of hell, I know no greater sorrow.'

8.   'Mother, have pity on the troubles of mothers, now that you know about a mother's condition, though you are a pure virgin-being.' 'Son, help in every need all those who cry to me, maiden and wife and foolish woman.'

9.   'Mother, I can stay no longer, the time has come that I go to hell; I rise on the third day.' 'Son, I will journey with you. I die, indeed, of your wounds; there was never any death so pitiful.'

10.   When he rose, then fell thy sorrow; thy happiness sprang up on the third morning — a happy mother indeed wert thou then. Mother, for the sake of that same happiness, beseech our God to remit our sins; be thou our shield against our foe.

11.   Blessed be thou, queen of heaven; bring us out of the flame of hell through thy precious son's power. Mother, for the sake of that noble blood that he shed upon the cross, lead us into the light of heaven. Amen.

12. Jesu Cristes milde moder

1.   Jesus Christ's gentle mother stood, beheld her son on the cross on which he was tormented; the son hung, the mother stood and beheld her child's blood, how it ran from his wounds.

2.   When he who is the king of life died, no woman was ever more sorrowful than thou, lady, wert then; the bright day

turned into night when Jesus Christ, the light of thy heart, was quenched with torment and misery.

3.   Thy being suffered very grievous pangs when thou sawest his bloody wounds and his body put upon the cross. His wounds grave and painful pierced thy heart through and through, as Simeon promised thee.

4.   Now his head besprinkled with blood, now his side pierced by the spear, thou beheldest, gracious lady; now his hands spread on the cross, now his feet drenched with blood and nailed to the tree.

5.   Now his body beaten with scourges and his blood so widely diffused made thy heart sore within thee. Wheresoever thou didst cast thy eyes, thou sawest him suffer torment — no man could suffer more.

6.   Now is the time that thou shouldst pay Nature what thou withheldest from him when thy child was born of thee; now he demands with interest what, in thy child-bearing, thou withheldest completely from him before.

7.   Now thou dost experience, gentle mother, what a woman suffers with her child, though thou art a pure virgin. Now there is meted out to thee, hard and dire, the pain from which in thy child-bearing thou wert quit and free.

8.   Soon, after the night of sorrow, there sprang up the light of blessed morning in thy heart, sweet maiden; thy sorrows turned completely into happiness when thy son, with complete certainty, rose on the third day.

9.   Lo! how happy thou wert when he rose from death to life! Through the intact stone he glided; in like manner he was born of thee — both after and before thy maidenhead remained intact.

10.   He brought to us renewed bliss who so dearly redeemed mankind and gave his precious life for us. Do thou make us glad and happy for thy sweet son's sake, blessed maiden, blissful wife.

11.   Queen of heaven, for the sake of thy bliss lighten all our sorrow; turn our evil into good. Bring us, mother, to thy son; cause us ever to dwell with him who bought us with his blood. Amen.

13. Edi be thu, heven-queene

1.   Blessed be thou, queen of heaven, people's comfort and angels' bliss, maid unblemished, mother pure, such as no other is in the world. In thee it is very evident that of all women thou hast the highest place. My sweet lady, hear my prayer and show pity on me if it is thy will.

2.   Thou didst rise up as dawn divides from the dark night. From thee sprang a new sun-beam; it has lit all this world. There is no maid of thy complexion — so fair, so beautiful, so ruddy, so bright; my lady sweet, on me show pity, and have mercy on thy knight.

3.   Blossom sprung from a single root, the Holy Ghost rested upon thee; that was for mankind's salvation, and to free their souls in exchange for one. Gentle lady, soft and sweet, I beg forgiveness, I am thy man, both hand and foot, in every way that I can be.

4.   Thou art soil for good seed, on thee the heavenly dew alighted; from thee sprang that blessed fruit — the Holy Ghost sowed it in thee. Bring us out of the misery and fear that Eve bitterly brewed for us; thou shalt lead us into heaven — very sweet to us is that same dew.

5. Mother full of gracious virtues, maiden patient and well-instructed, I am in the bonds of thy love and all my attraction is towards thee. Shield thou me, yes from the fiend, as thou art generous and art willing and able, and help me to my life's end and reconcile [me] with thy son.

14. The milde Lomb, isprad o roode

1. The gentle Lamb, spread on the cross, hung entirely drenched with blood for our guilt, for our benefit — for he never sinned at all. Few of his remained by him; fear had deprived him of all of them when they saw their leader brought to so shameful a death.

2. His mother, who stood beside him, let no tear wait for another when she saw such torment befall her son, and him die without guilt. St. John, who was dear to him, also stood keeping him company on the other side, and beheld with sorrowful countenance his master who loved and chose him.

3. Sorely and hard was he beaten, feet and hands pierced through; but above all his other wounds his mother's sorrow grieved him. In all his torment, in all his suffering which he endured for man's sake, he saw his mother lamenting; very compassionately he spoke to her.

4. He said, 'Woman, lo, hear me, your child, whom you bore in human kind. You were without pain and weeping when I was born of you; but now you must endure your pain when with your eyes you see me suffer torment on the cross, and die to save mankind, which was lost.'

5. St. John the Evangelist maintained her at Christ's command; he kept her well and looked after her, and served her hand and foot. Pitiable is the remembrance of this death and of this parting; in it bliss is mingled with weeping, for by this means all deliverance came to us.

6. He who died in our nature grant us to be so mindful therof that he may give us at the end what he has bought for us. Merciful mother, pure maiden, make thy mercy evident in us and bring us, by thy sweet intercession, to the bliss which does not fail.

15. (i) Angelus ad virginem

1. The angel, stealing into the room to the maiden, said, assuaging her fear, 'Hail! Hail, queen of maidens! Thou shalt conceive and bear, undefiled, the lord of heaven and earth, the salvation of men — thou, [who art] made the gate of heaven, the remedy for sin.'

2. 'In what way should I conceive, who have not known a man? How should I break what I have vowed with constant mind?' 'The grace of the Holy Spirit will perform all these things. Fear not but rejoice untroubled, for purity will remain in thee undefiled, by the power of God.'

3. To these words the noble maiden, replying, said to him: 'I am the humble handmaid of almighty God; to thee, heavenly messenger, who art privy to so great a secret, I give my consent, and desire to see the thing of which I hear; I am ready to submit to the will of God.'

4. The angel disappeared and at once the virgin womb swelled up by virtue of the saviour-child. And he, after being enclosed in the womb for the space of nine months, issued from it and entered the conflict, taking on his shoulder the cross, with which he gave a blow to the deadly enemy.

5. O mother of the Lord, who gavest back peace to the angels and mankind when thou didst bear Christ, pray thy son that he show himself gracious to us and that he cancel our sins, granting a refuge, for the enjoyment of felicity, after this exile.

15. (ii) Gabriel fram heven-king

1. Gabriel, sent from the king of heaven to the sweet maiden, brought her happy news and greeted her courteously: 'Hail be thou, full of grace indeed! For God's son, this light of heaven, for love of man will become man and take flesh from thee, fair maiden, to free mankind from sin and the devil's power.'

2. The gentle maiden then gently answered him: 'In what way should I bear a child without a husband?' The angel said to her, 'Fear not; this very thing of which I bring news will be done by means of the Holy Spirit; all mankind will be redeemed by means of thy sweet child-bearing and brought out of torment.'

3. When the maiden understood and heard the angel's words, she answered the angel gently, with gentle spirit: 'I am indeed the bond-maid of our Lord, who is above. Concerning me may thy saying be fulfilled, that I, since it is his will, may as a maiden, contrary to natural law, have the bliss of a mother.'

4. The angel went away with that, altogether out of her sight; her womb began to swell through the power of the Holy Spirit. In her Christ was straightway enclosed, true God and true man in flesh and bone, and was born of her flesh in due time. Whereby good hope came to us; he redeemed us from torment and let himself be slain for us.

5. Matchless maiden-mother, fully endowed with compassion, pray for us to him who chose thee, in whose sight thou didst find grace, that he forgive us sin and hostility and make us innocent of every offence, and, when it is our time to die, give us the bliss of heaven, and [grant us], for thy sake, so to serve him here that he may take us to himself.

16a. Brid one breere

1. Bird on a briar, bright bird on a tree, Nature has come to beg for love from Love: 'Gracious lady, on me, on me have pity; or prepare, beloved, prepare for me, for me my grave.'

2. I am as happy as a bright bird on a briar when I see that gracious one, most gracious in hall. She is white of limb, of limb and face; she is fair, and the flower, the flower of all.

3. If I could have her, have her at will, steadfast in love, lovely, true (from my sorrow she can, she can cure me), joy and bliss for me would be ever, be ever renewed.

16b. (i) Maid in the moor lay

1. A maid slept out on the moor, slept out on the moor for fully a week, fully a week; a maiden slept out on the moor for fully a week — [fully,] and a day.

2. Well was her food. Well, what was her food? The primrose and the — the primrose and the . . . Well was her food. Well, what was her food? The primrose and the — [the sweet] violet.

3. Well was her drink. Well, what was her drink? The cold water of the — the cold water of the . . . Well was her drink.

Well, what was her drink? The cold water of the — [*the fresh*] well-spring.

4. Well was her bedroom. Well, what was her bedroom? The red rose and the — the red rose and the . . . Well was her bedroom. Well, what was her bedroom? The red rose and the — [*the white*] lily-flower.

16b. (ii) Peperit virgo

1. A maiden gave birth, a royal maiden, the mother of orphans, the mother of orphans. A maiden gave birth, a royal maiden, the mother of orphans, full of grace.

2. The angelic voice paid honour to the king of the angels, the king of the angels. The angelic voice paid honour to the king of the angels by singing 'Glory'.

3. Three gifts are borne to the child as the homage of the Magi, the homage of the Magi. Three gifts are borne to the child as the homage of the Magi, with the star leading the way.

4. She grants salvation, the heavenly maiden, the only hope of the fallen, the only hope of the fallen. She grants salvation, the heavenly maiden, the only hope of the fallen in this misery.

5. To the angel who tells of the mighty works of her son, of the vigils of the shepherds, the vigils of the shepherds — to the angel who tells of the mighty works of her son, of the vigils of the shepherds, [let there be] glory and joy.

6. Maiden, by devout prayer relying on thy offices, O queen of heaven, O queen of heaven — maiden, by devout prayer relying on thy offices, O queen of heaven, bring us to the realms above.

17. Worldes blisse, have good day / [Benedicamus Domino]

1. Worldly bliss, good day to you; now depart from my heart! My heart is inclined to love him through whose side a spear tore and who shed his heart's blood for me, nailed to the hard tree. That sweet body was tortured, transfixed with three nails.

2. Ah, Jesu! thy holy head was encircled with sharp thorns; thy fair face was all spat upon, all wet with mingled spittle and blood. From the crown [of the head] to the toe thy body was full of pain and misery, and wan and red.

3. Ah, Jesu! may thy painful death be my shield, and liberate me from the devil's teaching. Ah, sweet Jesu, thy mercy! For the sake of thy grievous sufferings teach properly my heart to love thee, whose heart's blood was shed for me.

[*Tenor:* Let us give thanks unto the Lord.]

18. Sancta mater graciæ / Dou way, Robin

Duplum

1. Holy mother of grace, star of brightness, visit us today, full of compassion.

2. Come soon, channel of pardon, to those in prison, as a solace of misery, a source of sweetness.

3. Remember, mother of Christ, how bitterly thou didst weep; thou didst stand beside the cross sighing at the sad sight.

4. O Mary, royal flower, among all women nonesuch, in thy son unequalled, forgive the sins of our flesh.

5. O with how humble a heart thou didst speak when thou didst receive the words of Gabriel the messenger.

6. 'Behold the handmaid of the Lord' thou didst quickly say; thereafter thou didst bear the spring-time of living joy.

7. Rejoice, worthy lady, so gracious, in the throne of heaven; restore thy children, brought low by vice, to the Son.

Tenor

Stop it, Robin, the child will weep; stop it, Robin.

19. Lou, lou, lou! wer he goth!

Lo, lo, lo! where she goes! Ah lo, lo, lo! where she goes! For her I lost my holy water, -ter, -ter, lo!

20. Lullay, lullay: Als I lay on Yoolis night

Lullay, lullay, lay lay, lullay; my dear mother, sing lullay.

1. As I lay on Christmas night, alone in my desire, it seemed to me I saw a very lovely sight, a girl rocking her child.

2. The maiden wanted to put her child to sleep without singing; to the child it seemed she wronged him, and he told his mother to sing.

3. 'Sing now, mother,' said the child, 'what is to befall me in the future when I am grown up, for all mothers do that.

4. 'Every mother, truly, who knows how to watch over her cradle, is accustomed to lull lovingly and sing her child to sleep.

5. 'Sweet mother, fair and gracious, since that is so, I pray you to lull me and to sing something as well.'

6. 'Sweet son,' said she, 'of what should I sing? I never knew anything more about you than Gabriel's greeting.

7. 'He greeted me courteously on his knee and said "Hail, Mary! Hail, full of grace, God is with thee; thou shalt bear the Messiah."

8. 'I wondered greatly in my mind, for I by no means desired a husband. "Mary," he said, "do not fear; leave the God of heaven to his ways.

9. ' "The Holy Ghost is to do all this," he said without delay, that I should bear man's bliss and God's own son.

10. 'He said, "Thou shalt bear a king in king David's seat;" in all the house of Jacob he should be lord.

11. 'He said that Elizabeth, who until then had been barren, "has conceived a male child — give me the more credence."

12. 'I answered gladly, for his words pleased me, "Lo, I am here, God's servant; be it as thou hast said to me."

13. 'There, as he said, I bore you on Midwinter Night, in virginity without pain, by the grace of almighty God.

14. 'Where shepherds were watching in the uplands they heard a wondrous song of angels there, as they told them the tidings of your birth.

15. 'Sweet son, assuredly I can say no more, and if I could, I would gladly, to do everything as you wish.'

16. Certainly I saw this sight, I heard this song sung, as I lay this Christmas Day alone in my desire.

21. Ye have so longe keepyt o

You have so long been constantly tending the sheep up on the pasture, Wilkin, that your heart is filled with longing for one so pleasing of hue — though *some* would suppose, Wilkin, that you had become unfaithful.

You, Wilkin, can make good pipes with two rye-straws; as beseems you, say in your songs that you love me best, indeed, and [that I am] most in your mind.

But, since you say that you will die for love, rise up in the morning and hurry along, and take pleasure in love-play. This may rhyme well, but alas! it's not at all proper.

22. My cares comen ever anew

My cares are constantly renewed; ah, dear God, there is no remedy, for I am held unfaithful, without guilt, as I hope for salvation.

I have been accustomed to be faithful in any thing that I could do, thanks be to God's great grace; it is now that I cannot prosper.

23. With ryght al my hert

With my whole heart I now greet you, my dear, with a hundred sighs! Sweet God, give us grace to meet soon and soon to speak together! Annys, Annys, Annys, Annys, Annys!

Annys, be steadfast in all respects and think of me, my sweet Annys, my fair Annys, my true Annys. I love your [name, my dear Annys, Annys, Annys, Annys, Annys, Annys!]

24. I have set my hert so hy

I have set my heart so high, no love that is lower pleases me; and all the suffering that I can endure, it seems to me it does me good, indeed — it seems it does, indeed.

For on that lord who loved us all I have so heartily set my mind, it is my joy to call on him, for love has laid me on the rack — it seems it has, indeed.

25. Trew, on wam ys al my tryst

Faithful [lady], on whom is all my trust, and whom I serve as I best can, though you are displeased with me, however sincerely I am your man — a pleasing fortune, and honourable also — heal the hurt that I now have; do not make me beg and cry to you, since you yourself may save me.

26. Danger me hath, unskylfuly

A lady's power rules me, beyond reason; I can do nothing but let it pass and live both gladly and merrily. But things are not as they were, and the fault is not in me. Indeed, it is her will, unless I could do more than I can.

[A lady's power rules me, unkindly, and gives no sign of grace; but yet my fortune, with luck, may be better than it was, if the fault be not in me. Indeed, it is her will, if only I can do more than I could.]

[*Alternative reconstruction:* Yet I may appease her anger, if only I can do more than I could.]

27. I rede that thou be joly and glad

My advice is that you should be jolly and glad, and always, if you notice someone who may be too angry or too serious, put him out of your company; and so you may be merry and glad.

For upon my word, an angry man, if anything displeases him, will do everything that he possibly can to cause men anger like his.

28. Thy Yool, thys Yool

This Yule, this Yule, the best advice that I know of is to be a merry man, and give up care and put out strife; thus I intend to lead my life this Yule, this Yule. And whomsoever I may find angry, I will leave his company this Yule.

This Yule demands that every single man shall make such mirth as he can, and so will I, very gladly, at the beginning of this New Year.

This Yule I give my fair lady my heart and love and all my strength, 'and I pray you that I may be your man and serve you as fully as I can this Yule'.

29. Wel wer hym that wyst

Well it would be for him who knew to whom he could trust, but that hangs on a thread. For often men only put on a show, and trustful friends, far and near, walk into the mire.

Would God that all such had a mark, small or great, so that all men could recognize how their hearts stand, and could, as directly as north and south, hasten to them without delay.

30. Me lykyth ever the lenger the bet

I am pleased, always the longer the better, by Winchester, that handsome city. The town is good and well sited, the people are pleasant to look on.

The air is good, both within and without. The city stands beneath a hill, the rivers run all round it. The town is wisely governed.

31. Pater noster, most of myght

Pater noster [Our Father], greatest of power, who created all this world in the beginning, help me, a sinful wretched creature, that I may not perish because of sin.

Pater noster, have pity on me and help me to escape from sin, to do thy will now and always. *Pater noster,* blessed be thou, for the sake of thy own dear son who died on the cross; help me, wretched, that I may not be destroyed.

32. 'Ave Maria' I say

'*Ave Maria*' [Hail Mary] I say to that blessed maiden who is a mother without intercourse with any man; the same words in truth the angel Gabriel said to Mary, alone maiden and mother in one.

Ave Maria! I have thee in mind; wherever I go, in wealth or in woe, defend me well, both before and behind, that I may not halt for foes of any sort.

33. Credo in Deum that ys

Credo in Deum [I believe in God] who is without beginning and end, who made heaven and earth and all that is therein. We, joyful, should evermore have our lord God in mind, for he is prudent and wise; may he bring us to perfect bliss.

All our life is mingled with woe wheresoever we go, while we are on this earth; except in God alone, indeed, there is no full, perfect bliss, if one takes very good heed.

3. NOTES ON PERFORMANCE
F. Ll. HARRISON

The traditions and usages of European medieval music are separated from us by two revolutions in communication — printing and sound-recording — and by many changes in the taste for physical sounds and in the technical methods of their production. Translation of medieval written forms into present-day terms involves a combination of judiciously creative reconstruction and practical compromise. While arrangement and performance should as far as possible take account of historical validity, these considerations must ultimately be geared to the requirements of meaningful contemporary communication. The following comments and general observations supplement the suggestions about performance which are incorporated in the transcriptions.

VOICE–RANGES

Voice-designations are in present-day terms (tenor, mezzo-soprano, etc.) according to range and tessitura. There is evidence that the pitch of plainsong which was not being sung in alternation with an organ was largely related to the range of the particular item and was decided by its beginner. Similarly, the pitch of non-ritual singing without instruments was probably also very much a matter of convenience. Before 1400, however, there would not usually have been wide variation of pitch, since it seems that ranges corresponding to present-day bass and soprano were little used. The pitch of singing with instruments was obviously dependent on the instrument's tuning.

Present-day practice with variable-pitch instruments in Western oral traditions suggests that when the same kind of instrument was used there would have been little difference between one performer's pitch and another's or between different performances of the same song. Musicians whose routines do not include a fixed pitch-setting device seem to have little difficulty in keeping pitch-consistency. It is suggested therefore that songs with instrumental participation should not usually be transposed, and that songs without instruments should not usually be transposed by more than a relatively small interval, say a minor third either way.

TEMPO

The metronome marks given with each song are indications of editorial opinion; they should be regarded as suggestions, to be modified or not according to varying performance-factors, including acoustic conditions. However, since it seems certain that slow-tempo music was extremely rare before the fifteenth century, it is suggested that the tempo of these songs should be as brisk as is compatible with clarity of words, tune-shape and tune-detail.

VOCAL TIMBRE AND TECHNIQUE

While it would be imprudent to dogmatize about singing-timbre in medieval England, some of Charles Seeger's observations on present-day British-American oral-tradition singing are probably relevant (see pp. 73–74).

In approaching these songs, singers will probably find that if they attempt to use medieval word-pronunciation (see pp. 317–21) this will greatly help them to achieve appropriate timbre. Since the terms in which singing-timbres are conventionally described can rarely be unequivocal (sounds called, for example, 'natural' and 'open' by one performer or listener may be artificial and closed-in to the ears of another), comments like Seeger's must be complemented by some mostly negative recommendations about technique. Most present-day Western singers are trained to regard as normal the use of *vibrato* (imposed pitch-variation), of *crescendo-diminuendo* (imposed loudness-variation), of some *rubato* (imposed tempo-variation) and of some *portamento* (inserted pitch-gliding). Such characteristics of post-sixteenth-century European *bel canto* are inappropriate, however, to singing in other contexts. It is suggested that these songs should be performed without *vibrato,* and in the case of the shorter songs at a relatively constant dynamic level. Changes in dynamic level in the longer songs will be suggested from experience of the meaning of the text and the structure of the music.

INSTRUMENTS

Surviving medieval instruments are rarely available for present-day use. The making of usable replicas of medieval (as distinct from Renaissance) instrument-types has only recently begun, and little research into their techniques has yet been made. Most performances, therefore, will involve substitution. It is *not* recommended that Renaissance- or Baroque-type instruments be used. The tonal spectra of the thirteenth and fourteenth centuries were not those of the sixteenth and seventeenth; a seventeenth-century fretted viol is not a valid substitute for a fourteenth-century unfretted fiddle, nor a soft sixteenth-century many-coursed lute for a thirteenth-century plectrum-plucked gittern. Whether medieval reproductions or modern substitutes as suggested in the transcriptions are used, the suggestions given under VOCAL TIMBRE also apply to a great extent to instrumentalists. Players of bowed strings should produce a well defined sound, dynamically even and without *vibrato*; guitarists should use a plectrum or the firmest of finger-plucking; harpists should if possible use finger-nails on a small harp, and on a large one pluck the strings at the point which gives the crispest, not the lushest sound; organists should avoid reeds, and use flue-stops and light mixtures.

The use of percussion instruments would be inappropriate here, since none of the items is a dance-song. The one possible exception is no. 20, where a text may have been fitted to a pre-existing tune.